HISTORICAL DICTIONARY

The historical dictionaries present essential information on a broad range of subjects, including American and world history, art, business, cities, countries, cultures, customs, film, global conflicts, international relations, literature, music, philosophy, religion, sports, and theater. Written by experts, all contain highly informative introductory essays of the topic and detailed chronologies that, in some cases, cover vast historical time periods but still manage to heavily feature more recent events.

Brief A–Z entries describe the main people, events, politics, social issues, institutions, and policies that make the topic unique, and entries are cross-referenced for ease of browsing. Extensive bibliographies are divided into several general subject areas, providing excellent access points for students, researchers, and anyone wanting to know more. Additionally, maps, photographs, and appendixes of supplemental information aid high school and college students doing term papers or introductory research projects. In short, the historical dictionaries are the perfect starting point for anyone looking to research in these fields.

HISTORICAL DICTIONARIES OF WOMEN IN THE WORLD

Jon Woronoff, Series Editor

Historical Dictionary of Women in the Middle East and North Africa

Ghada Talhami

The Scarecrow Press, Inc.
Lanham • Toronto • Plymouth, UK
2013

Published by Scarecrow Press, Inc.
A wholly owned subsidiary of The Rowman & Littlefield Publishing Group, Inc.
4501 Forbes Boulevard, Suite 200, Lanham, Maryland 20706
http://www.scarecrowpress.com

10 Thornbury Road, Plymouth PL6 7PP, United Kingdom

British Library Cataloguing in Publication Information Available

Library of Congress Cataloging-in-Publication Data

Talhami, Ghada Hashem.
Historical dictionary of women in the Middle East and North Africa / Ghada Talhami.
p. cm. -- (Historical dictionaries of women in the world)
Includes bibliographical references.
ISBN 978-0-8108-6858-8 (cloth : alk. paper) -- ISBN 978-0-8108-7086-4 (ebook) 1. Women--Middle East--History--Dictionaries. 2. Women--Africa, North--History--Dictionaries. I. Title.
HQ1726.5.T35 2013
305.40956--dc23
2012029757

Printed in the United States of America

Contents

Editor's Foreword

Like so many other things, the glass of women's role and status in the Middle East and North Africa can look either half full or half empty. Certainly, it is half empty when compared to the role and status of women in the West, and also to women in many parts of Asia, and indeed in parts of Africa and much of Latin America. But it is certainly half full compared to where it was, say, a few decades ago, let alone a few centuries ago. Undoubted progress has been made in most places, with the notable exception of Iran. And this progress has spread into nearly every field, which is quite impressive when it comes to the right to vote if not the privilege of ruling, noteworthy in some places and some professions when it comes to employment, definitely praiseworthy in education, and almost remarkable as regards women's contribution to culture. If only one could believe that this onward and upward trajectory would continue, but it is specifically in this part of the world that progress has periodically gone into reverse, blocked by some but not all Islamic leaders, confiscated by some but not all of the assorted monarchs and dictators, and no one knows yet if the gains of the recent people's movements will play into the hands of the feminists or the Islamists.

But this *Historical Dictionary of Women in the Middle East and North Africa* is not so much about the future as it is about the present and the past. Reaching back not only centuries but millennia, it traces the path of women from ancient Egypt to modern times, marking the most important steps forward and maybe a few backward. The introduction puts this all in perspective, tracing the most important phases and aspects. Then the dictionary section provides the details, countless details on numerous women who have succeeded in one endeavor or another, some of them obviously feminists and proponents of women's advancement, but others whose interests were more limited and, indeed, some who did not consider all of this to be movement in the right direction. Along with these are entries on associations and organizations they founded or animated and some men who helped them along. Particularly useful are the entries on specific aspects such as marriage, divorce, and inheritance, or education and political activities, or Islam and other religions in one guise or another. Of course, this can just be a beginning for the study of women in the region, so, to point readers in the right direction, a copious bibliography introduces many other books and articles of interest.

This volume in the subseries Women in the World was written by Ghada Hashem Talhami. She is an academic and copious writer herself, now professor of politics emerita of Lake Forest College and formerly Susan B. Currier Chair in Women's Studies at California State University at San Luis Obispo. Her books are many, but of particular interest is *The Mobilization of Muslim Women in Egypt*. And she is also the past editor of *Arab Studies Quarterly*. Born in Amman, Jordan, and receiving some of her education in Palestine as well as Great Britain and the United States, she has a very broad view. But even more important, her studies were not limited to the contemporary period, important as that may be; earlier periods as well as can be seen from the ample references to older eras and cultures. Certainly, producing a book on such a broad and deep topic, with its countless variants, was not an easy task, but Dr. Talhami has acquitted herself extremely well.

Jon Woronoff
Series Editor

Acknowledgments

This book owes a great deal to many scholars and feminist activists whom I have known or whose work I have read over the years, even though they were not directly involved in its writing. As I began to teach and write on many aspects of Middle Eastern and Islamic history and politics, several scholars writing on women here in the United States and abroad began to uncover the significant contribution of women to these societies, past and present. It took a few years for the academic community to realize that, without the study of women, most facets of Middle Eastern and Islamic development will remain opaque. I owe a debt of gratitude to these pioneering scholars, the majority of whom were women, for opening my eyes to the social, political, economic, and ideological roles of women, even while their contributions remained mostly undeclared and unnoticed. Among these I count Mervat Hatem, whose incredible analytical feats on Egyptian women, the role of the state, and how Islam often shaped women's identity taught me a great deal. Leila Ahmed, of course, was the giant in this field, who taught us that overlooking the culpability of indigenous cultural ideologies will only obfuscate the culpability of Western influence.

Miriam Cooke taught us how to read women's texts, be they the work of early 20th-century feminists or late 20th-century Lebanese women. Maintaining a focus on women of the Levant, including those rarely studied Syrian feminist pioneers, opened up new avenues of understanding and assessment. Her devotion to her work and wonderful scholarship are only matched by another expert on Egyptian women, Margot Badran, who probably knows more about these women than many scholars of that area. Bouthaina Shaaban always impressed me with her ability to straddle the political and literary worlds and demonstrate how to read the recent history of Syrian and Islamic Lebanese women. And then there was the late Elizabeth Fernea, who quickly emerged as the expert not only on Iraqi women but on Arab and Muslim women in general. Fernea taught generations of scholars, not only feminists, the value of empathy when dealing with people of a different culture and value system. This was especially instructive for those who waded into women's history, a minefield of misconceptions, literary misreadings, and innate prejudice, without prior understandings of the context of their subjects.

My interest in women's studies has also peaked as a result of reading the work of and knowing that flaming spirit and torchbearer of Arab feminism, Nawal Saadawi, which taught me to appreciate the physical courage, ideological commitment, and sheer persistence necessary for dissipating cultural taboos of any kind, especially those pertaining to women. Finally, I would be terribly remiss if I forgot to mention Samiha Khalil and her impact on most Palestinian women, for her courage was different than that of Saadawi, although her life was equally as delineated by scorn, terror, and enormous challenges every step of the way. Umm Kahlil, as the Palestinians fondly remember her, led a life of defiance, targeting the Israelis and Arafat in equal measure. And yet, if you were to call her a feminist, she probably would have fixed you with one of her loving stares and reminded you that "woman-ness" was not about gender but about service to your community.

I am grateful to Scarecrow Press for giving me this opportunity to study women, learn about differences and similarities between one community and another, and decipher the indecipherables of women's ancient lives, myths, and legends alike. I am particularly thankful to Jon Woronoff, the editor of this series, who guided me and lent his considerable knowledge and editing skills to this volume. April Snider, also of Scarecrow Press, saw this study develop into its final shape, and I thank her for it. Without the support of Lake Forest College, which always encouraged and facilitated my research, this volume would not have seen the light of day. Special thanks go to my assistant, Margaret Hennessey, whose technical skills far outstrip mine and who faithfully oversaw the final preparation of this book from beginning to end.

Reader's Note

This book deals with women in the Middle East and North Africa, a region whose components are not always clear, and may or may not include certain countries. Sudan is included because it has a largely Arabic-speaking population and is a member of the Arab League of States. The boundaries of the Middle East here stretch to Iran and Turkey.

Some points should be kept in mind regarding the spelling of foreign names and terms. Due to the absence of a standardized form of transliteration from Arabic (which is heavily used in this work) into English, words and names have been rendered as close to the phonetic sound in the original language as possible. Only **Khomeini** and **Mecca** and **Medina** are used in the common and current journalistic usage. Thus, **al-nahdha** is preferred to the common spelling of al-nahda, **Jamal Abd al-Nasser** to Gamal Abdul Nasser, **Bourgiba** to Bourguiba, **Boutefliqa** to Bouteflika, etc.

To ease matters further, Arabic guttural sounds have been represented by a double vowel, which is now commonly used. There has been no attempt to utilize the Leiden method of transliteration, characterized by an elaborate emphasis on orthographic symbols. Thus, **Shii** is used instead of Shi'i, **Shaarawi** instead of Sha'rawi, **Baath** Party instead of Ba'th Party, etc. Occasionally, the same name may be spelled differently in different sections of this volume; for example, **Thuraya** may also appear as Thoraya, **Muhammad** may also appear as Mohammad. The reason for this discrepancy is that although an attempt has been made to be consistent about spelling in general, an author's own rendition of his or her name, usually in a bibliographic citation, has been maintained.

The name of one city was always Constantinople in English, but since the Ottoman period in the 16th century was rendered *al-Qustantiniyah* in Arabic and Turkish. Arabic sources in the 19th century sometimes rendered this as *al-Asitaneh*. In 1923, Mustafa Kemal Ataturk decreed that the capital's name should be Istanbul. This is the name used throughout this volume.

Sometimes a personal or place-name is preceded by *al-* or *el-*, the Arabic definite article "the" in English. Both are the same, reflecting variations in inflection in various Arabic dialects. Thus, names beginning with *al-* or *el-* should be sought in this dictionary under the main portion of the name.

Most translations of book titles, specific expressions, or terms from Arabic and French into English have been provided by the author.

To facilitate the rapid and efficient location of information and to make this book as useful a reference tool as possible, extensive cross-references have been provided in the dictionary section. Within individual entries, terms that have their own entries are in **boldface type** the first time they appear. Related terms not discussed in the annotation are provided as *See also* references.

Acronyms and Abbreviations

AAHR	Arab Association for Human Rights
AAWF	Aisha: Arab Women's Forum
AFTD	Association Tunisienne des Femmes Démocrates
AFU	Arab Feminist Union
AIU	Alliance Israéalite Universelle
AIWF	Arab International Women's Forum
AMIDEAST	American Mid-East Educational and Training Service
ANY	Anjumani-i Nisvan-i Yahudi (Iran)
AOHR	Arab Organization for Human Rights (Egypt)
ARAMCO	Arabian-American Oil Company
ASU	Arab Socialist Union (Egypt)
ATF	Arab Thought Forum (Beirut)
ATFG	Arab Thought Forum in Jerusalem
AUB	American University of Beirut
AUC	American University of Cairo
AUWS	Arab Union Women's Society of Palestine
AWA	Arab Women's Association (Palestine)
AWAPD	Anatolian Women's Association for Patriotic Defense (Turkey)
AWC	Arab Women's Congress (Palestine)
AWDS	Arab Women's Development Society (Kuwait)
AWEC	Arab Women's Executive Committee (Palestine)
AWSA	Arab Women's Solidarity Association
BUC	Beirut University College
CABU	Council for Arab-British Understanding
CWA	Council of Women's Affairs (Iran)
CEDAW	Convention on the Elimination of Discrimination Against Women
CHEN	Israel's Women's Army Corps

CMS	Church Missionary Society
CRÉDIF	Centre de Recherches, d'Études, de Documentation et de l'Information sur la Femme
CWA	Council on Women's Affairs (Iran)
CSCWAI	Cultural and Social Council on Women's Affairs (Iran)
CUP	Committee of Union and Progress (Turkey)
CYDD	Cagdas Yasami Desteklemi Dernegi; Contemporary Life Support Association (Turkey)
DFLP	Democratic Front for the Liberation of Palestine
DOW	Democratic Organization of Women (Iran)
DYP	True Path Party (Turkey)
ECOSOC	Economic and Social Council of the United Nations
EFU	Egyptian Feminist Union
ESCWA	United Nations Economic and Social Commission for Western Asia
FAO	Food and Agricultural Organization
FIDA	Palestine Democratic Union
FIRDOS	Fund for Integrated Rural Development of Syria
FIS	Front Islamique du Salut (Algeria)
FLN	Front de libération nationale (Algeria)
GCC	Gulf Cooperation Council
GDSPW	General Directorate on the Status and Problems of Women
GFIW	General Federation of Iraqi Women
GFSW	General Federation of Syrian Women
GIH	Global Investment House (Kuwait)
GUIW	General Union of Iraqi Women
GUPS	General Union of Palestinian Students
GUPW	General Union of Palestinian Women
HADASH	Democratic Front for Peace and Equality
HADASSAH	Women's Zionist Organization of America
HAMAS	Islamic Resistance Movement

HCIWA	High Council of Iranian Women's Associations
HISTADRUT	General Federation of Laborers in the Land of Israel
HRW	Human Rights Watch
IPFG	Iranian People's Fidaii Guerrillas
IBWA	Iranian Bureau of Women's Affairs
ICHR	International Charter of Human Rights
ICPD	International Conference on Population Development
ICWSSC	Islamic Countries' Women's Sports Solidarity Council
IDF	Israeli Defense Forces
IDWO	Iranian Democratic Women's Organization
ILO	International Labour Organization
IP	Islah Party (Yemen)
IPFG	Iranian People's Fidaii Guerillas
IWF	International Women's Forum
IWPM	Israeli Women's Peace Movement
IWSA	International Women's Union Suffrage Alliance
IWSAF	Iraqi Women's Society Against Fascism
IWSAW	Institute for Women's Studies in the Arab World
IWU	Iraqi Women's Union
JWU	Jordanian Women's Union
KRG	Kurdistan Regional Government
LDWR	League for the Defense of Women's Rights (Iraq)
LWC	Lebanese Women's Council
LWS	League of Women Students (Egypt)
MAPAI	Workers' Party of Eretz Israel (Labor Party)
MAPAM	United Workers' Party (Israel)
MATZPEN	Israeli Socialist Organization
MENA	Middle East and North Africa Region of World Bank
MIFTAH	Palestinian Initiative for the Promotion of Global Dialogue and Democracy

MOSSAD	Institute for Intelligence and Special Operations (Israel)
NAAMAT	International Movement of Zionist Women
NDA	National Democratic Alliance (Sudan)
NDP	National Democratic Party (Egypt)
NGC	National Guidance Committee (West Bank)
NGO	non-governmental organizations
NIF	National Islamic Front (Sudan)
NIF	New Israel Fund
NT	National Theatre (Egypt)
NUJBW	National Union for Jordanian Business Women
OADP	Organization for Democratic and Popular Action (Morocco)
OIC	Organization of Islamic Cooperation
OST	Socialist Workers Organization (Algeria)
PASDARAN	Revolutionary Guards (Iran)
PFLP	Popular Front for the Liberation of Palestine
PFWAC	Palestinian Federation of Women's Action Committees
PKK	Kurdistan Workers' Party
PLC	Palestine Legislative Council
PLO	Palestine Liberation Organization
PNA	Palestine National Authority
PNC	Palestine National Council
PORTA	Project of Translation from Arabic Literature
PWC	Palestine Women's Committee
PWU	Palestinian Women's Union (Gaza)
PWWC	Palestinian Women's Work Committee
RAKAH	Israeli Communist Party
RATZ	Israeli Movement for Civil Rights and Peace
RCD	Rally for Culture and Democracy (Algeria)
RMF	Rene Muawwad Foundation
SAPS	Structural Adjustment Programs

SAVAK	National Intelligence and Security Organization (Iran)
SCP	Sudanese Communist Party
SHANI	Israeli Women's Alliance Against Occupation
SHAS	National Religious Party of Israel
SSNP	Syrian Social National Party
SWU	Sudanese Women's Union
TANDI	Movement of Democratic Women (Israel)
UAE	United Arab Emirates
UAF	Union de l'Action Féminine (Morocco)
UFMF	Union Franco-Musulmane des Femmes d'Algérie
UKW	Union of Kurdish Women
UNDP	United Nations Development Programme
UNESCO	United Nations Educational, Scientific and Cultural Organization
UNFPA	United Nations Fund for Population Activities
UNFT	Union Nationale de Femmes Tunisiennes
UNRISD	United Nations Research Institute for Social Development
UNRWA	United Nations Relief and Works Agency
UPWWC	Union of Palestinian Working Women's Committees
UWCSW	Union of Women's Committees for Social Work (Palestine)
WCSS	Women's Cultural and Social Society (Kuwait)
WEF	World Economic Forum
WFRT	Women's Forum for Research and Training (Yemen)
WIDF	Women's International Democratic Federation
WIZO	Women's International Zionist Organization
WNC	Women's National Committee (Yemen)
WOI	Women's Organization of Iran
WORLD	Women's Organization for Rights, Liberties, and Development

WSIR	Women's Society of the Islamic Revolution
WWC	Women's Work Committees (West Bank)
WWCC	Wafdist Women's Central Committee (Egypt)
YAHAD	Social Democratic Israel Party
YWMA	Young Women's Muslim Association (Iraq)
YWU	Yemeni Women's Union

Chronology

2649–2150 BCE Egypt: Old Kingdom period.

2040–1640 BCE Egypt: Middle Kingdom period.

1550–332 BCE Egypt: New Kingdom period.

1458 BCE Egypt: Hatshepsut dies.

1400–1200 BCE Iran: Zoroastrianism develops as a religion.

32 BC Egypt: Alexander the Great conquers the country.

224–651 Iran: Sassanid Empire rules over the land.

267–272 Syria: Zenobia rules over Palmyra.

570 Arabia: Prophet Muhammad is born in Mecca.

622 Arabia: Muhammad leads the *hijra* (migration) to Medina, and Muslim calendar begins.

630 Arabia: Al-Uzza's temple outside of Mecca is destroyed.

ca. 630–631 Iran: Puran (or Buran) rules over the land.

632 Arabia: Muhammad dies at Medina. Fatima dies a few months after her father. Al-Khansaa dies.

639–64 Egypt: Arab armies conquer Egypt.

639–642 Egypt: The Arab Caliphate under Caliph Omar conquers Egypt.

661–750 Syria: Ummayid dynasty rules much of the Muslim world.

680 Iraq: The battle of Karbala takes place.

ca. 698 Algeria: Al-Kahina is killed in battle.

711–1492 Spain: Muslims rule over al-Andalus.

750–1258 Iraq: Abbasid dynasty rules much of the Muslim world.

786–809 Iraq: Harun al-Rashid rules over the Abbasid Empire.

801 Iraq: Rabia al-Adawiyya dies in Basra.

808 Arabia: Amat al-Aziz (Zubayda) founds an eponymous charitable foundation near Mecca.

969–970 Egypt: Al-Azhar seminary is built in Cairo by Fatimid military ruler Jawhar al-Siqilli.

969–1171 Egypt: Fatimid caliphs rule over Egypt, Syria, and Hijaz.

11th century Germany: Rabbi Gershom ben Judah outlaws polygamy and summary divorce.

1048–1138 Yemen: Arwa, Sayyida Hurra rules over the land.

1099–1187 Palestine: The crusaders establish the Latin Kingdom of Jerusalem.

1171–1250 Egypt: Ayubid dynasty rules over Egypt and Syria.

1250 Egypt: Shajar al-Durr is installed as queen.

1250–1382 Egypt: Bahri Mamluks rule over Egypt and Syria.

1382–1517 Egypt: Burji Mamluks rule over Egypt and Syria.

1520–1566 Ottoman Empire: Sultan Suleiman the Magnificent rules over the empire.

1551 Ottoman Empire: Roxelana (Hurrem Sultan) dies in Istanbul.

1785–1925 Iran: Qajar dynasty rules over the country.

19th century Ottoman Empire: Islamic charitable foundations support schools for girls and boys.

1811 Egypt: Muhammad Ali exterminates the Mamluk ruling caste.

1825 Algeria: Archbishop Charles Lavigérie is born; later launches a campaign to convert the Berbers to Christianity.

1830 France: King Charles X establishes French rule over Algeria.

1831 Egypt: Ibrahim Pasha begins his occupation of Syria.

1832 Egypt: The Egyptian School for Midwives is established in Cairo.

1837 France: Charles Fourier coins the term *féminisme*.

1838 Ottoman Empire: Government bans abortions. An internal passport system is introduced.

1841 Ottoman Empire: The Sultan issues a decree recognizing Muhammad Ali and his descendants as the governors of Egypt.

1844 Iran: The Babi movement begins.

1850s–1950s Egypt: The Arab Nahdha (renaissance) movement is in full bloom.

1851 Iran: Qurrat al-Ayn is executed. **Ottoman Empire:** The Sharia-based criminal code is revised.

1857 Ottoman Empire: A Ministry of Education is created.

1863 Iran: Bahaullah declares a new religion based on the Babi movement.

1863–1879 Egypt: Khedive Ismail rules over Egypt

1869 Ottoman Empire: A public education law is adopted.

1870 Ottoman Empire: The first girls' teachers' college is established in Istanbul.

1872 Ottoman Empire: The first government primary schools for both genders are opened.

1873–1874 Egypt: The Siyuffiyya and the Qirabiyya schools for girls are opened.

1882 Egypt: Muhammad Abduh is sent into exile, begins his residency in France, North Africa, and Syria.

1882–1956 Egypt: British occupation of Egypt.

1889 Egypt: The two girls' schools, the Siyuffiyya and Qirabiyya, are combined to create a teachers' training academy called the Saniyya School. **Palestine:** The Friends Mission School for Girls opens its doors in Ramallah.

1893 Ottoman Empire: Women are permitted to attend medical lectures at Istanbul University.

1894 Great Britain: The term "feminism" is used in the English language for the first time.

1895 Egypt: A public school system for girls is created.

1897 Ottoman Empire: Jamal al-Din Afghani dies in Istanbul.

1899 Egypt: Qassem Amin publishes his book, *The Liberation of Women.* **Lebanon:** Zaynab Fawwaz writes *Good Consequences, or Ghada the Radiant,* the first novel in the Arab World.

1905 Egypt: Muhammad Abduh dies in Alexandria.

1906 Iran: The Constitutional Revolution begins.

1907 Egypt: Nabawiya Musa is the first girl to take an admission exam for public schools. The First National Party Congress convenes in Cairo, with several women present. **Sudan:** Babikr Badri founds the first school for Muslim girls in Rafaa.

1908 Egypt: Mabarat Muhammad Ali is founded in Cairo. The National University opens. **Ottoman Empire:** The first Turkish women's club is opened in Salonika under the name "Red-White," the colors of the Young Turks. The Young Turk revolution begins and restores the 1876 Ottoman constitution.

1910 Iran: *Danish* (*Knowledge*), the first newspaper for women, is launched. **Syria:** *Al-Arus*, Syria's first women's journal, begins publication.

1912 United States: The Hadassah organization is founded in New York.

1914 Egypt: Great Britain imposes a protectorate over Egypt, severing the country's ties to the Ottoman Empire. Princess Nazli Fadhil dies.

1915 Ottoman Empire: An imperial *irade* (decree) permits Turkish women to discard the veil during office hours.

1917 Great Britain: The Balfour Declaration is issued in London, which spurs Palestinian women to create nationalist/feminist organizations. **Ottoman Empire:** Religious schools are placed under secular control. A new law is introduced granting broader rights to women. The application of the Gregorian calendar to financial transactions begins.

1918 Egypt: Saad Zaghloul seeks the permission of Egypt's High Commissioner, Sir Reginald Wingate, to lead a delegation to London to lobby for independence. **Iran:** Ten primary schools and a teachers' training college for girls are opened.

1919 Egypt: Great Britain exiles Saad Zagloul. The 1919 Revolution begins with significant participation by women. Shafiqa Muhammad Ashmawi is killed by British snipers during a demonstration in Cairo. **Iran:** *Zaban-i Zanan* (*Women's Tongue*) is published by Siddiqeh Dowlatabadi. **Syria:** Nazik al-Abid founds *Nour al-Fayhaa*, the country's first women's organization.

1920 Egypt: The Wafdist Women's Central Committee is founded. **Great Britain:** The Women's International Zionist Organization is established in London. **Iran:** The Tudeh's parent organization is founded. **Ottoman Empire:** Allied troops occupy Istanbul.

1922 Egypt: The Revolution of 1919 ends. **Syria:** Nazik al-Abid founds the Syrian Red Crescent Society.

1923 Egypt: The Egyptian Feminist Union is founded in Cairo. **Turkey:** The Treaty of Lausanne officially dissolves the Ottoman Empire. Mustafa Kemal Ataturk creates the Republic of Turkey and rapidly modernizes the state and society. The Women's People's Party is founded.

1924 Egypt: Nabawiya Musa is appointed chief inspector of women's education. **Turkey:** The Turkish government abolishes the caliphate. Members of the ruling Ottoman dynasty are forced to leave the country. The Sharia is abolished by the ruling Republican People's Party.

1925 Iran: Reza Shah begins his rule as the founder of the Pahlavi dynasty.

1926 Turkey: The Turkish Civil Code replaces the Sharia.

1927 Egypt: Saad Zaghloul dies.

1928 Bahrain: The first public primary school for girls is opened. **Egypt:** Five women are admitted as full-time students to King Fuad University in Cairo.

1929 Egypt: Women are admitted to the newly opened American University of Cairo. **Palestine:** The Arab Women's Association of Palestine is founded. Tarab Abd al-Hadi and Matiel Moghannam lead a Christian–Muslim delegation that presents the British High Commissioner with demands for the cancellation of the Balfour Declaration.

1930 Morocco: French administration issues the Berber Dahir, providing a separate judicial system for the Berber population. **Tunisia:** Tahir Haddad publishes *Our Women in the Sharia and in Society.* **Turkey:** Universities are opened to men and women.

1931 Algeria: Modernist Islamic scholar Abd al-Hamid Ben Badis establishes the Association of Algerian Ulema (clergy).

1932 Iran: The Second Congress of Eastern Women meets in Tehran.

1934 Turkey: Women are given full political rights.

1935 Turkey: The Twelfth Congress of International Women's Union convenes at Istanbul.

1936 Egypt: The Muslim Women's Association is founded in Cairo. **Iran:** Women are admitted to Tehran University.

1937–1938 Kuwait: The first two public schools for girls are opened.

1938–1964 Turkey: Sabiha Gökçen, Ataturk's adopted daughter, completes flights over the Balkan countries and around the world.

1941 Iran: Reza Shah Pahlavi is ousted and forced into exile.

1942 Great Britain: The World Zionist Organization calls for establishing a "Jewish Commonwealth" in Palestine. **Palestine:** The Ehud Party is founded.

1943 Iran: Primary education is made compulsory for boys and girls.

1945 Egypt: Aisha Abd al-Rahman publishes her autobiography, *Ala al-jisr.* The Arab Feminist Union is founded in Cairo. **Iraq:** The Iraqi Women's Union is founded in Baghdad.

1947 United States: The United Nations' General Assembly adopts Resolution 181 on November 29, calling for the partition of Palestine.

1948 Palestine: The first Arab–Jewish War results in the establishment of the State of Israel. Hind Husseini founds Dar al- Tifl al-Arabi in Jerusalem.

1949 Syria: Husni al-Zaim rules Syria from 30 March until 14 August. Women are granted the right to vote.

1951 Bahrain: The first secondary school for girls is opened. **Lebanon:** The requirement of attending Beirut College for Women prior to admission to the American University of Beirut ends.

1952 Egypt: The Free Officers succeed in overthrowing the monarchy. **Iraq:** The League for the Defense of Women's Rights is founded in Baghdad.

1953 Syria: Thuraya Hafiz runs unsuccessfully for a seat in parliament.

1954–1962 Algeria: The Union Nationale des Femmes Algériennes is founded by the Front de Libération Nationale. The Algerian revolution is launched and lasts eight years.

1954–1970 Egypt: Jamal Abd al-Nasser rules the country.

1955 Egypt: President Nasser creates the National Commission on Population Affairs. **Qatar:** The first public school for girls opens its doors.

1956 Egypt: The Muslim Brotherhood attempts to assassinate President Nasser, leading to the imprisonment of its leaders. The Egyptian Feminist Union is closed. Egyptian women are enfranchised. **Kuwait:** School girls burn their *abayas.* **Tunisia:** The National Union of Tunisian Women is founded. The Personal Status Code is adopted.

1956–1957 Algeria: The Battle of Algiers takes place, with women participating.

1957 Algeria: Djamila Bouhired is arrested in Algiers. **Egypt:** Two women are elected to the National Assembly.

1957–1958 Morocco: The first Mudawana set of laws is issued in six volumes.

1958 Iraq: Abd al-Karim Qassem overthrows the Hashemite monarchy. Naziha Jawdat Dulaymi is the first woman to be appointed minister of municipalities. **United Arab Emirates:** Sharjah establishes the first school for girls in the Trucial States (the future United Arab Emirates).

1959 Iran: The High Council of Iranian Women's Association is founded. **Iraq:** President Qassem presents a reformed personal status law. Iraqi women are enfranchised.

1961 Kuwait: The veil ceases to be required for female public employees and teachers. **Saudi Arabia:** The first public school for girls is opened.

1962 Egypt: President Nasser appoints Dr. Hikmat Abu Zeid to be the first female social affairs minister. Women are admitted to al-Azhar seminary. **Kuwait:** The constitution grants all Kuwaitis, irrespective of gender, the right to education and employment. Women are employed for the first time by the Kuwaiti Broadcasting Service and the Kuwaiti Foreign Office.

1963 Iran: Women are granted suffrage as part of Muhammad Reza Shah's White Revolution program of reform. Mehrangiz Manouchehrian is the first woman appointed to the Senate. **Kuwait:** The Arab Women's Development Society is founded.

1964 Egypt: Zaynab Ghazzali is imprisoned. **Palestine:** The Palestinian Women's Union of Gaza is founded.

1965 Kuwait: The Compulsory Education Act for boys and girls between the ages of six and fourteen is adopted. **Palestine:** The General Union of Palestinian Women is founded in Jerusalem. **Sudan:** Fatima Ibrahim is the first woman elected to parliament.

1966 Egypt: Sayyid Qutb, along with two others accused of plotting Nasser's assassination, are executed. **Kuwait:** Women are admitted to the newly founded University of Kuwait.

1967 Egypt: The Third Jurisprudence Islamic Conference convenes in Cairo. **Middle East:** The Six Day War between Israel and Egypt, Jordan and Syria takes place. **Syria:** The General Federation of Syrian Women is founded.

1968 Iran: Women's literacy corps is established. Farrokhru Parsa is appointed the first female minister of education. **Iraq:** The General Federation of Iraqi Women is founded.

1969 Israel: Golda Meir becomes the first female prime minister of Israel. **Palestine:** Yasser Arafat becomes chairman of the Palestine Liberation Organization (PLO).

1970 Sudan: Nagwa Kamal Farid is appointed the first female judge of a Sharia court.

1970–1981 Egypt: President Anwar Sadat rules.

1973 Jordan: Women are enfranchised. **Qatar:** The first female teachers' college is opened.

1974 Lebanon: The second civil war begins and continues until 1989. **Morocco:** Fatima Mernissi begins her teaching career at Muhammad V University. **Palestine:** Birzeit College becomes the first full-fledged Arab university to open its doors.

1975 Egypt: Umm Kulthum dies in Cairo. **Iran:** The Family Protection Laws are adopted. **Oman:** The first public schools for girls are opened. **United Nations:** The First United Nations Conference on Women is held in Mexico City.

1976 Palestine: Municipal elections in the West Bank and Gaza are boycotted by women. **Syria:** Najah al-Attar becomes the first female minister of culture.

1977 Great Britain: Ali Shariati dies in London. **Israel:** Miriam Ben Porat becomes a judge of the Israeli Supreme Court. **Saudi Arabia:** Princess Mishaal bint Fahd ibn Muhammad is executed.

1978 Israel: Golda Meir dies. **Palestine:** The first Women's Work Committee is founded.

1979 Egypt: Law 44 is signed by President Sadat. **Iran:** The Islamic Revolution seizes power. Celebrations of Women's Day result in huge demonstrations against the Islamic regime. Ayatollah Ruhollah Khomeini issues a directive making the veil mandatory in the workplace. Munireh Gorji is the only woman elected to the Assembly of Experts. **Jordan:** Inaam Mufti is the first woman to be named to the cabinet. **Tunisia:** The Nahdha Party is founded. **United Nations:** The General Assembly adopts the Convention on the Elimination of Discrimination against Women (CEDAW). **Yemen:** Ramziya Abbas Iryani becomes the first female career diplomat.

1980 Iran: Farrokhru Parsa is executed. **United Nations:** The Second United Nations Women's Conference is convened in Copenhagen.

1980–1988 Persian Gulf: The Iran–Iraq War takes place.

1981 Egypt: Nawal Saadawi is imprisoned by the Sadat regime. **Israel:** Violet Khouri is the first Arab woman elected mayor, in Kufur Yassif.

1981–2011 Egypt: Husni Mubarak is president.

1982 Algeria: Zhor Ounissi is appointed minister of social affairs.

1983 Kuwait: The Muslim Brotherhood forms its own women's committee. **Lebanon:** Intisar al-Wazir becomes deputy secretary-general of Fateh.

1984 Algeria: The Family Code is adopted by the government of Chadli Benjadid. **Israel:** Alice Shalvi establishes the Israel Women's Network.

1985 Egypt: Law 44 is overturned by the High Constitutional Court. Law 100 is adopted in its place. The "House of Obedience" is eliminated. **United Nations:** The third United Nations Conference on Women is held in Nairobi.

1986 Oman: Sultan Qaboos University opens, and women are admitted without a veiling requirement.

1987 Jordan: Suhayr Tal is briefly imprisoned. **Palestine:** Hamas participates in the first *Intifada.*

1989 Algeria: The Islamic Salvation Front is founded. **Iran:** Ayatollah Ruhollah Khomeini dies. **Jordan:** Layla Sharaf is the first woman appointed to the Senate. **Morocco:** Layla Abu Zeid writes *The Year of the Elephant.* **Sudan:** The Sudanese Women's Union is banned.

1990 Iran: Six Iranian chador-clad women join the march at the opening of the Asian Games in Beijing. **Saudi Arabia:** Women challenge their country's ban on driving. **Turkey:** The Women's Library and Information Center is founded in Istanbul. **United Nations:** The Cairo Declaration of Human Rights is issued. **Yemen:** The Yemeni Women's Union is established.

1991 Yemen: Waheeba Faraa becomes the first woman to join the cabinet since unification in 1991.

1992 Iran: The Islamic Countries' Women's Sports Solidarity Games are founded in Iran. *Zanan* magazine is founded in Tehran. **Kuwait:** Badriya al-Awadhi is the first woman to address parliament.

1993 Jordan: Toujan Faysal is the first woman to be elected to the lower house of parliament.

1993–1996 Turkey: Tansu Ciller becomes the first female prime minister.

1994 Egypt: The International Conference on Population and Development takes place in Cairo. **Morocco:** The first two women are elected to parliament.

1995 Egypt: The First Arab Women Writers' Book Fair opens in Cairo. **United Nations:** The United Nations Fourth Conference on Women is held in Beijing.

1996 Iran: Fourteen women are elected to the fifth Majlis, including Faezeh Rafsanjani. **Palestine:** Samiha Khalil runs against Yasser Arafat in the presidential elections. Intisar al-Wazir is the first woman appointed to the Palestine National Authority's cabinet. **Syria:** Wisal Farha is elected secretary-general of the Syrian Communist Party.

1997 Iran: President Muhammad Khatami appoints Maasumeh Ebtekar as the first female vice president of the country. Azzam Teleghani announces her candidacy for the office of president.

1997–2005 Iran: Muhammad Khatami serves as the elected president of the country.

1999 Israel: Hasniyya Jabara becomes the first Arab woman elected to the Knesset. Dorit Bennish is appointed to the Supreme Court. **Jordan:** Rima Khalaf is appointed deputy prime minister. **Kuwait:** Parliament blocks the ruler's initiative to enfranchise women. **Qatar:** Six women run unsuccessfully in municipal elections.

2000 Egypt: A new law permitting women to seek divorce unilaterally is adopted. **Turkey:** The Millennium Development Plan, making women's development a priority of the state, is adopted. **Yemen:** The Women's Forum for Research and Training is founded.

2001 Great Britain: The Arab International Women's Forum is founded. **Jordan:** A new law permitting women to seek divorce unilaterally is adopted. **Saudi Arabia:** Thoraya Obeid is appointed executive director of the United Nations Fund for Population Activities. **Syria:** Asma Akhras establishes the Fund for Integrated Rural Development of Syria (FIRDOS).

2002 Bahrain: Women are granted the right to vote. **Jordan:** Queen Rania is named to the board of the World Economic Forum Foundation. **Palestine:** Issam Abd al-Hadi is awarded the Ibn Rushd (Averros) Prize for Freedom of Thought. **Saudi Arabia:** Fire erupts in a girls' school in Mecca, causing casualties.

2003 Iraq: Huda Ammash is taken into custody by U.S. forces. Rend al-Rahim is appointed ambassador to the United States. **Jordan:** Asma Khader is appointed minister without portfolio. **Palestine:** Zahira Kamal is appointed minister of women's affairs by the Palestine National Authority.

2005 Algeria: Asia Djeber is elected to the Académie Française. **Palestine:** Issam Abd al-Hadi is nominated for the Nobel Peace Prize.

2006 Syria: Najah al-Attar is appointed the first female vice president.

2008 France: President Jacques Chirac awards Hoda Barakat the National Order of Merit.

2009 France: Andrée Chédid is awarded the Légion d'honneur. **Jordan:** Queen Rania receives the North–South Prize from the Council of Europe.

2010 Palestine: Layla Ghannam becomes the first female governor of Ramallah.

2011 Bahrain: Alaa Shehabi creates "Bahrain Watch," a website to monitor the revolution. **Egypt:** Asma Mahfouz leads demonstrations in Tahrir Square, Cairo. Bouthaina Kamel declares her candidacy for the position of president. **Syria:** Razan Zeitouneh receives the Sakharov Award for Freedom of Thought. **Yemen:** Tawakkul Karman shares the Nobel Prize for Peace with two African Women.

2012 Egypt: Parliamentary elections result in the seating of 15 women in Egypt's 680-member legislature. **Saudi Arabia:** Raja Alim receives the International Prize for Arab Fiction for her book *The Dove's Necklace.*

Introduction

The term *féminisme* was coined by Charles Fourier, an early French utopian socialist, who used it in 1837 to reiterate his earlier argument that no social progress was possible without the liberation of women. The term's English variant "feminism" began to appear in print in 1894, and the ongoing women's movement in Europe thus acquired an identifiable label. Although few people, least of all Muslim women, thought in terms of gender politics in those days, this development signified the beginning of a worldwide movement. Even today, feminism as a concept remains alien to most Middle Eastern and North African women, who view it as one more imported Western ideology. But neither Muslim women nor their Western counterparts lived in hermetically sealed worlds, and some notions eventually broke through the barrier of geographic and cultural isolation. It was not surprising to see Ottoman Turkey develop into a sieve of imported ideas for the rest of the Middle East, especially since it was in the throes of its own state-backed reforms, known as *Tanzimat*, during much of the 19th century. A writer named Ebuziyya Tevfik (1848–1913) became the first to use this term in an article, in 1899.

But even as gender consciousness was slow in developing, women in this part of the world were breaking fresh ground every day of their lives. The lack of recognition for their innovations was finally corrected almost a century later by women activists of a different generation. For example, while academics, journalists, and essayists who were focused on modernization and tracking the emergence of the first Arab "novel" as a new literary genre argued that the honor belonged to a male, a female literary expert bestowed that honor on a woman. It took someone like Bouthaina Shaaban, a Syrian writer, to argue that the first Arab novel was not *Zaynab*, which was authored in 1914 by Egypt's Muhammad Hussein Haykal. She cited at least 10 earlier novels written by women, the first being *Good Consequences, or Ghada the Radiant*, published in 1899 by Lebanese writer Zaynab Fawwaz and published by al-Maktabah al-Hindiyyeh in Cairo.

There are other surprising discoveries about the lives and works of Middle Eastern and North African women. Their domestic and maternal roles have been so entrenched that they defied scholarly attempts at redefinition for many years. We now recognize, for instance, that Middle Eastern and Muslim women were at one time warriors, as well as inciters of men in battle. Pre-Islamic history is replete with women who fought in Arabia and other parts of the Muslim world, some fighting against Muhammad and some alongside him in the early Muslim period. Their contributions during these battles were often expressed as incitement to warfare and goading male warriors with their singing or recitation of poetry. This was the role of the greatest female poet of pre-Islamic Arabia, al-Khansaa, whose lines have survived down the years as a reminder of this role. Some of the most cloistered women during the modern period have not forgotten this; Saudi Arabian women reminded the authorities recently that early Islamic women rode camels and horses in battle, demanding similar "driving" privileges today. Indeed, al-Khansaa's pre-Islamic pagan imagery glorifying the violent clashes of old was relished by later generations of Muslim readers because it represented feats of physical courage, traits valorized by Arabs before and after Islam. There was nothing feminine about al-Khansaa's elegies, especially when one reflects on what and whom she eulogized. Neither is there any doubt regarding women's capacity for military action, as illustrated by Morgan Shuster's account of the militant display of resistance by women opposed to foreign monopolies during the dying days of the Qajar dynasty in Iran. The American financial advisor to the Persian government was a witness to these events, reporting on women's daring attempt to intimidate members of the Majlis.

A second reading of Arab and Islamic history also reveals a greater incidence of powerful women who ruled directly as heads of state or became major revolutionary figures than has been commonly believed. Some, like Hatshepsut, ruled as queens of ancient Egypt; others, like the mythical Bilqis, or Queen of Sheba, and the historically documented Queen Zenobia of Palmyra, are examples of authoritative and influential Arab women. Buran (also Puran) ruled briefly in Persia during the Prophet's period, leading him to comment on her accession to power. But if women lost their authority beginning with the institutionalizing of patriarchal society at the dawn of Islam, this did not signify an utter loss of power. As early as the 11th century, an Ismaili queen allied with Egypt's Fatimid rulers reigned in Yemen. Arwa, or "a free lady" as the rest of her name read, was the shining star of the Sulayhid dynasty in Yemen. Egypt's Shajar al-Durr, who ruled for a few months in the 13th century, was not only the one leader to defeat and capture a European monarch, France's Louis IX, who led the seventh crusade, she was also a catalyst for the liquidation of the last vestiges of the Ayyubid dynasty. When Tansu Ciller became Turkey's first female prime minister in 1993, she had the memory of several role models to draw upon whenever her bid for legitimacy faltered.

Women who were merely influential but did not necessarily exercise power were obviously greater in number. To begin with, early Islam did not lack for heroines, many of whom belonged to *Aal al-Bayt*, the Prophet's line, like Aisha, Fatima, Khadija, Zaynab, and Sukayna. The sacred memory and life stories of these idealized women came down to us through the centuries, only to reemerge as political and revolutionary role models in the hands of modern ideologues like Ali Shariati, Ayatollah Ruhollah Khomeini, and others. The life story cum legend of Fatima became especially inspiring and empowering for Iranian and Lebanese Shii women. The rise of new intellectual and religious movements, such as Babism and Bahaism, did not lack women who were almost canonized by their followers. The intellectual contribution of Qurrat al-Ayn to Babism far outweighed that of her male contemporaries. It was due to her tenacity and purist ideology that the movement achieved a total break with Shii Islam. Influence also emanated from endowing charitable foundations, a role in which royal queens and consorts excelled. Some of these, like Roxelana, who endowed the Islamic institutions of Jerusalem, or Khayzuran and Zubayda, who endowed massive waterworks for the benefit of Muslim pilgrims at Mecca and Medina, immortalized their dynasties and their good works for all the ages.

At certain times, women's informal power manifested itself in the least expected places: the life story of Nourah bint Abd al-Rahman ibn Faysal al-Saud, the elder sister of King Abd al-Aziz, the founder of Saudi-Arabia, is a case in point. Not only did she wield enormous influence over the women of her family, she also instilled fear in the hearts of all men of the Saud family. She acquired the status of "first lady" in that country, although no such notion existed in Arabia at the time. The informality of her power matched the informality characterizing the entire Saudi system at the time, acquiring the semblance of normalcy.

Arab and Islamic males who qualified for the designation of "intellectuals," a term coined by Georges Clemenceau while still publisher of the journal *L'Aurore* at the time of the Dreyfus Affair toward the end of the 19th century, did not have a monopoly over the term. Even before the emergence of women's liberation movements and the attack on the veil in Egypt and the Levant, women qualified for the label by profusely producing works of fiction. Writing became a legitimate vocation for women, because it did not violate segregationist rules. In most cases, women were able to do their writing without interacting with male publishers or male fellow writers; thus, writing became compatible with veiling. Women were eventually able to have their own press and commenced to write on a variety of topics stressing their rights to education and employment outside the home, as well as demanding more rights under Sharia laws. The same compatibility of writing with segregation and veiling still operates today in countries like Saudi Arabia, where women contribute articles to the national press from the privacy of their own homes. Women's writings gradually steered away from gender-related topics and focused on poetry and fiction, as well as essays that analyzed and discussed issues of national concern. In the area of poetry writing, the 20th century proved to be an open field, allowing such talented writers as the Iraqi Nazik al-Malaika to pioneer the free verse movement. Women opened their own literary and political salons, inviting the participation of men and women. Princess Nazli Fadhil and Mai Ziyadeh operated salons that became coveted forums for the introduction of new literary and social trends as well as testing grounds for radical and unaccustomed ideas.

Yet the veil as a segregationist tool lingered, not only as a symbol of respectability and religious piety, but also as a class symbol for affluent and urban women. Christian women veiled, and Jewish women in major Muslim cities did the same whenever they left the security of the Jewish quarter. Veiling became the central theme of male feminists such as Qassem Amin, Ataturk, Reza Shah, Tahir Haddad, Habib Bourgiba, and others. Western observers, most with colonial backgrounds, latched on to this outer garment, presenting it as a symbol of Islamic backwardness and inhumanity to women. But what should be noted here is that it was only when the issue of the veil was harnessed to the national question, and only when women's liberation became a national priority, that a movement was born. It is worthy of note that another male Egyptian writer preceded Qassem Amin in attacking the veil and listing its drawbacks. This was Murqus Fahmi al-Muhami (Murqus Fahmi the Lawyer), who wrote a book in 1894 titled *The Woman in the East*, fully five years before Amin published *The Liberation of Women*. But because Fahmi was a Christian Copt, his argument lacked legitimacy. More than 100 books were published in opposition to Amin's thesis, and he himself was reluctant to force his wife's unveiling. The veil, however, made a dramatic comeback in the 1970s, several decades after Huda Shaarawi fought against veiling and its immobilizing effect on women.

The alignment of nationalism and feminism nevertheless spread beyond Egypt's borders. Feminism was nurtured by modernizing, albeit autocratic, rulers, by following policies that Mervat Hatem called "state feminism." Whether through the efforts and policies of nationalist autocrats such as Reza Shah Pahlavi, or the socialist decrees of Jamal Abd al-Nasser targeting women workers, or conscious modernizers like Mustafa Kemal Ataturk and Bourgiba, the end result was a new brand of feminism wherein the state dictated the pace of change. This category of reform was eventually rolled back as Islamic movements everywhere sought the integration of the woman's question in the formulations of a newly emerging Islamic identity. This is not to say that women's organized groups lost all autonomy, for we have seen women under the Islamic Republic of Iran carry on a steady effort to expand and redefine their rights under the Sharia. Here, the careers of Azzam Teleghani and Zahra Rahnavard are particularly instructive.

Women's ideological wars were not the result of competing belief systems and state ideologies all the time. In the 20th century, women's struggle to achieve recognition and integration in the political community as full citizens benefited greatly from their eagerness to join national revolutions such as the Algerian and Palestinian causes. Although they have yet to achieve major feminist reforms, their political acceptance and the accolades awarded such fighting heroines as Djamila Bouhired opened the gate wider for political participation. At the same time, women like the Palestinians remain loyal to the political agenda of their nationalist movement, creating their own definition of modernized gender roles. Some of the headliners on these nationalist revolutionary fronts, like Bouhired and Samiha Khalil, were reluctant feminists according to current definitions of the term. Yet both generated a flood of respect and esteem for activist women who perform the Herculean tasks of men.

Any assessment of Israeli feminism, on the other hand, will necessarily confront several issues, not the least of which is the European and Western backdrop of this society and its women. Yet even this generalization is invalidated by the case of Mizrahi women, an "Oriental" minority who always struggled to establish a footing in the predominantly East European and German transplanted culture of modern Israel. Other paradoxes emerge here that account for the complexity of this feminist case. Here we meet a few women who shattered the glass ceiling—like Golda Meir and Tzipi Livni, prime minister and foreign minister respectively, as well as Dalia Itzik, a woman of Iraqi Jewish descent who became acting president of Israel—but who are still trying to define their rights under Jewish religious law. Meir's political career, it becomes clear, resembles that of Margaret Thatcher rather than the pattern of liberation in Middle Eastern countries, in that her rise to power owes more of its momentum to the male political milieu than to organized feminist groups. Israeli women, on the whole, resemble Western feminists in another respect, namely the proclivity of their organized groups to champion pacifist and social justice causes. Israeli women's groups, particularly since the Arab defeat of 1967, have attempted to link up with Palestinian women in their efforts to resist the Israeli occupation regime over Arab lands.

Middle Eastern and North African women receive low marks from international developmental agencies for being among the least educated and represented in the formal economy. Despite major accomplishments during the last century, women, including Israelis, have yet to overcome the inequalities of religious laws. Women's major gains in this area are still limited to the reformed personal status codes of Turkey and Tunisia and limitations placed on polygamous privileges in moderately modernizing countries such as Egypt, Jordan, and Syria. *Khulu*, or a woman's right to seek divorce unilaterally upon the foregoing of dowry, is the latest and most meaningful achievement in this category. These newer interpretations of the Sharia have yet to filter down to the most conservative societies, such as those of Arab Gulf countries, where ancient, pre-Islamic customs add to the rigidity of Sharia laws. Yet one cannot deny the magnitude of changes that are constantly transforming the status of these women due to the modernizing role of the state. The most powerful agent of change in Persian Gulf countries turned out to be the state, which controls access to education and has the capacity to transform women's economic roles. Kuwaiti and Emirati women in particular have been quick to seize these new economic opportunities and are beginning to make their mark on the world of finance.

Finally, it should be remembered that some women paid and continue to pay a high price for their activism and literary creativity. Women such as Nawal Saadawi, Sahar al-Tal, Latiffa Zayyat, Zabya Khamis, Zaynab Ghazzali, Samiha Khalil, and Toujan al-Faysal have served prison terms for infringing on the rules of patriarchy and foreign occupation. Some, like Iran's former minister of education, Farrokhru Parsa, lost their lives for closely identifying with a specific ideology. These grim facts are just a reminder of how far women still have to go before achieving total gender equality and the enjoyment of full citizenship in that part of the world. But then, women who shaped the "Arab Spring," particularly in Egypt, Tunisia, and Yemen, have been the latest reminders of the rewards of perseverance and a feminist brand of nationalism. For who would have thought a few years ago that these women would shake the world and go on to become Nobel laureates and presidential candidates in 2011 and 2012?

A

ABD AL-HADI, ISSAM (1928–). Palestinian nationalist and activist who was born in Nablus, Palestine. She was educated at the American Friends Girls School in Ramallah. She came to prominence when she attended the founding meeting of the Palestine Liberation Organization (PLO) in 1964, held in Jordanian Jerusalem. A year later, she was elected president of the **General Union of Palestinian Women (GUPW)**, an official cadre of the PLO. In 1969, she and her daughter were briefly imprisoned, and later expelled, by the Israeli authorities for leading a women's sit-in and hunger strike at the Church of the Holy Sepulchre in Jerusalem. She was one of a handful of women elected to the PLO's Central Committee in 1974 and also led the Palestinian delegation to the first United Nations International Women's Conference in Mexico City. She was elected vice president of the International Democratic Women's Organization shortly after that. Upon the signing of the Oslo Peace Accords in 1993, she became an outspoken critic of the PLO's chairman, Yasser Arafat (r. 1969–2004). A strong nationalist as well as a feminist, Abd al-Hadi made headlines when she gave a new meaning to feminism in an Arab women's meeting in 1984, in Aden: she declared that since the 1920s, Palestinian women have never viewed their liberation as independent from the liberation of their homeland. She was awarded the Ibn Rushd (Averros) Prize for Freedom of Thought in 2002 and was nominated in 2005 for the Nobel Peace Prize. *See also* FEMINISM: THE TERM.

ABD AL-HADI, TARAB (1910–1976). Early Palestinian feminist, nationalist, and socialite who was born in Nablus, Palestine. She became involved in nationalist politics. Her marriage to prominent Palestinian statesman and (later) Jordanian foreign minister Awni Abd al-Hadi catapulted her to a position of leadership in feminist-nationalist circles. Her activism spanned the British Mandate period, from 1922 until 1948. In October 1929, she joined hands with Palestinian Christian feminist **Matiel Moghannam** and a Christian–Muslim delegation in presenting the British High Commissioner with demands for the cancellation of the Balfour Declaration (1917). On 15 April 1933, Abd al-Hadi delivered a rousing speech at the Church of the Holy

Sepulchre in Jerusalem, marking the Arab women's march to Christian and Muslim holy sites in protest of continued Jewish immigration to Palestine. During the 1930s, she was also active in the anti**veiling** movement. *See also* FEMINISM: THE TERM.

ABD AL-NASSER, HODA (?–). Eldest daughter of Egypt's former president Jamal Abd al-Nasser (r. 1954–1970) and his wife, **Tahiya Kazim**, who studied political science at Cairo University. Her PhD dissertation was titled "Britain and the Egyptian Nationalist Movement, 1936–1952," deliberately skirting her father's years in power. She later became the guardian of his historical legacy. Most of her teaching career has been at her alma mater, where she serves as professor of political science. She also heads the Egyptian Revolution Research Unit at *al-Ahram* newspaper. She devotes much of her time to collecting and organizing archival material in various languages pertaining to her father's tenure in office.

She completed a seven-volume publication titled *Minutes of Meetings of the Higher Central Committee of the Arab Socialist Union*, about Egypt's single hegemonic party during the 1960s. During her father's lifetime, she was viewed as his natural successor, being often referred to as the Indira Gandhi of Egypt. Despite the existence of one sister and two brothers, Hoda Abd al-Nasser was seen as closest to her father. One of her brothers, Khaled, and her sister Mona each played a political role, the first as a young man with political ambitions and the second as the wife of Ashraf Marwan, one of Egypt's recent controversial figures. But neither of the two protected Nasser's legacy as did Hoda.

ABD AL-RAHMAN, AISHA (1913–1998). Egyptian professor of Arabic language and literature who became a prominent interpreter of the Quran and a prolific essayist and journalist. Abd al-Rahman grew up in the Delta city of Dumyat (Damietta) and was privately educated by her father, who was a product of **al-Azhar**, Egypt's famed Islamic seminary. In addition to her early grounding in Arabic language and literature, a prerequisite for proficiency in Quranic studies, she received secular **education** from her mother. Abd al-Rahmnan's early literacy efforts in the form of articles for *al-Nahdha* journal preceded her admission to the Faculty of Letters at King Fuad's University (later Cairo University) in 1936 as a member of the first class of women to integrate this institution. She became a literary critic for *al-Ahram*, Egypt's oldest newspaper, writing under the pseudonym Bint al-Shati (daughter of the coast). Her doctoral dissertation was on Abu al-Alaa al-Maari (d. 1058), the blind philosopher-poet of Syria and a great figure of classical Arabic poetry. Upon her graduation in 1951, she was appointed professor of Arabic language and literature at Cairo's Ayn Shams University.

Aisha Abd al-Rahman married her professor at King Fuad University, Amin al-Khuli (d. 1966), a prominent scholar of Islamic studies who taught her the principles of literary Quranic analysis. She described her marriage, which took place in 1945, in her autobiography, *Ala al-Jisr* (*On the Bridge*), lauding his great influence over her intellectual development. Her interest in Quranic studies eventually led to endorsing traditional Islamic views such as male guardianship over women. Her writings on the lives of women in early Islam created a rift between her and secular Egyptian feminists, whom she characterized as overly Westernized. She wrote more than 60 books on various Quranic topics and issues of her day. She taught at al-Qarawiyin University in Morocco and received several honors from Saudi Arabia and from successive Egyptian governments in recognition of her contribution to the field of Islamic studies. *See also* EGYPTIAN FEMINIST UNION (EFU); QALAMAWI, SUHEIR (1911–1997); SAID, AMINAH AL- (1914–1955).

ABD AL-WAHAB, FATIMA BINT MUHAMMAD IBN. She was one of the prominent and literary descendants of the founder of **Wahhabism**, the religious school of interpretation followed by Saudi Arabia and other Persian Gulf States. Her birth date is uncertain but is usually given as around the end of the 18th century. She was one of the first women to qualify for teaching Islamic studies for both men and women. She also became a living resource on the early history of Wahhabism and the Saudi state. In 1818, she witnessed the destruction of Diriyah, the center of the first Saudi state, by the Egyptian forces of Ibrahim Pasha (d. 1848). Dubbed "lady of the two migrations," she and her nephew first fled to Oman, then to Ras al-Khayamah in today's United Arab Emirates (UAE). She returned to Riyadh upon the pacification of the Nejd region and the founding of the second Saudi state by Turki ibn Abdullah in 1825. She died in Riyadh and was interred in al-Aud cemetery. *See also* HANBAL, IMAM AHMAD IBN (780–855).

ABDUH, MUHAMMAD (1849–1905). He was a great figure of the Arab *Nahdha* (Renaissance) and one of the early male feminists who advocated the liberation of women as a necessary corollary of the broad national reform movement. He was the *mufti* of Egypt, or its highest religious authority, and as such enjoyed great credibility among all of Egypt's educated classes. He studied at **al-Azhar** seminary, Egypt's highest religious teaching institution, which he was able to reform and transform in later years. He was greatly influenced by **Jamal al-Din Afghani** (1839–1897), the founder of the pan-Islamic movement and a progressive reformer. Abduh was exiled from Egypt from 1882 until 1888 and lived in Syria, North Africa, and France. He was the editor of an influential and modernist paper while in Paris, *al-Urwa al Wuthqa* (*The Close Bond*).

Upon his return to Egypt, Muhammad Abduh continued his advocacy of Islamic modernism, claiming that in Islam, faith and reason were perfectly compatible. His views on women's rights were disseminated throughout the Muslim and Arab worlds. He argued that the low status of women was due to Egypt's exclusive reliance on one of the four jurisprudential schools of **Sharia**. He was very vocal in condemning the abuse of women, claiming that such common practices as **polygamy** were not only harmful to family unity but also based on a misreading of the Quran. He was critical of men who often resorted to violence to enforce religious observances by women. His lasting achievement was the passage of new laws that expanded the financial rights of divorced women. *See also* AMIN, QASSEM (1863–1908); FADHIL, NAZLI (?–1914); SADAT, JIHAN (1933–).

ABDUL RAZIQ, SALWA (1908–1953). She was an Iraqi poet who was recognized for her own talent but also as the mother of modernist poet **Nazik al-Malaika** (1923–2007). Abdul Raziq's pen name was Umm Nizar. She wrote poetry calling for the liberation of women in the context of Iraq's national struggle against continued British occupation even while the country was nominally independent. She taught Arabic in secondary schools, and her only book of poetry was titled *Songs of Glory*, published posthumously by her daughter. *See also* ZAHAWI, JAMIL SIDQI (1863–1936).

ABDULLAH, RANIA AL- (1970–). She is the queen of the Hashemite Kingdom of Jordan. Born to Palestinian parents in Kuwait as Rania al-Yassin, she married King Abdullah II in 1993 before his accession to the throne. She was named queen a few months after her husband's coronation in 1999. Her father was a children's doctor in one of Kuwait's hospitals who hailed originally from the Palestinian town of Toulkarem. The queen was educated in a British school in Kuwait and received a degree in business administration and computer science from the American University in Cairo (AUC). Before her marriage to the king, she worked for Citibank and Apple Computer in Amman, Jordan. Mother of four children, she devotes much of her time to improving educational conditions for Jordanian children. One of her projects, *Madrasati* (My School), was launched in 2008 as an effort to re-equip 500 schools through a public-private partnership. She was also behind the initiation of the annual Queen Rania Award for Excellence in Education. She became a member of the World Economic Forum (WEF) Foundation Board in 2002.

Queen Rania has always been interested in building bridges to other cultures and creating more awareness of Arabic and Islamic civilizations. Due to her efforts in this regard, she received the North–South Prize in 2009 from the Council of Europe. She wrote several children's stories, including *The King's Gift*, *Eternal Beauty*, and *Maha of the Mountains*.

ABID, NAZIK AL-. She was a Syrian feminist, nationalist, journalist, and institution builder. Al-Abid had a long patriotic history that dates back to the period before World War I when she wrote articles under a male pseudonym for the Damascus press. Expressing her opposition to Ottoman rule, she also called for granting women political rights. She founded the first women's organization in Syria in 1919, called *Noor al-Fayhaa* (The Light of Damascus), followed a year later by a journal with the same name. She headed a women's delegation that met the King-Crane Commission (1919) to plead for allowing Syria to achieve independence as a liberal and secular nation.

Al-Abid volunteered to serve with the Syrian Army when the French forces advanced from Beirut in 1920 to seize control of Syria, which they considered to be part of their larger Mandate system covering Syria and Lebanon. She was the only woman to parade in the streets of Damascus in full military uniform. Her photograph appeared all over the country, earning her the title "Syrian Joan of Arc." She participated in the Battle of Mayseloun, in which French forces crushed Arab resistance in Damascus, mortally wounding the Syrian commander, General Yousef al-Adhmeh. King Faysal of Syria promoted her to the rank of general in recognition of her services on the military front. In 1922, she founded the Syrian Red Crescent Society. She also participated in the Syrian Revolt (1925–1927), when she spent time with the fighters in the Ghuttah, the ring of orchards surrounding Damascus. After she was pardoned by the French authorities in Syria, she formed the Damascus Women Awakening Association and concentrated on securing women's rights. *See also* SHAABAN, BOUTHAINA (1953–); ZAIM, HUSNI (1894–1949).

ABU KHADRA, SALWA (1929–). A Palestinian feminist and nationalist who worked closely with the Palestine Liberation Organization (PLO). Abu Khadra, who was born in Jaffa, Palestine, came from a prominent family in Gaza. She received the General Certificate of Education in 1947 from Oxford University, later earning a diploma in French literature from Saint Joseph University in Beirut. In 1967, she was named to the board of the **General Union of Palestinian Women (GUPW)** and was elected to Fateh's Revolutionary Council in 1980. A few years later, she rose to membership in the PLO's Central Committee. She acceded to the positions of secretary-general of the GUPW and secretary-general to Fateh's Women's Bureau, and was also a member of the Consultative Committee of the Palestinian Constitution. She chaired the Palestinian delegation to the second United Nations International Women's Conference in Copenhagen in 1980. For many years, she supervised the education of Palestinian girls in Kuwait. *See also* ABD AL-HADI, ISSAM (1928–).

ABU KHALED, FAWZIYYA (1956–). She is a Saudi poet and professor of sociology. She was born in Riyadh and earned a PhD in sociology in the United States. In addition to her duties as a member of the teaching staff at the Girl's University College of King Saud University, she writes poetry with definite political themes and emphasis on women's capacity for attaining education and liberation. Her literary reputation was established by the publication of her poetical collection, *Until When Will They Abduct You on Your Wedding Night?* She also published two other poetry collections, *Mirage Water* (1955) and *Secret Readings in the History of Arab Silence* (1985). *See also* EDUCATION: ARAB GULF STATES.

ABU ZEID, HIKMAT (?–). She is the first woman to be appointed as a cabinet member in Egypt (1962–1965), by President Jamal Abd al-Nasser (r. 1954–1970). Born in Asyut, Upper Egypt, she became a secondary school teacher in Helwan in the 1940s. She earned a doctorate in educational psychology in 1955 from a British university, which led to an appointment as professor at Cairo's Ayn Shams University. Abu Zeid was named minister of social affairs by Nasser in 1962 when he sought to bypass the organized feminist movement of the royalist period. Her participation in his government facilitated the state's amalgamation of the privately run women's charitable organizations with the ruling party, the Arab Socialist Union (ASU). She also supervised the implementation of a battery of reforms designed to improve the economic and working conditions of female members of the peasant and petty bourgeois classes recently recruited as industrial labor. This policy, which increased women's participation in Nasser's socialist economy, came to be known as "state feminism." Abu Zeid's efforts culminated in her nomination as chair of the first Egyptian national congress, which investigated issues related to working women's industrial environment and **family planning**. The congress produced a landmark report in 1962, "Characteristics of the Path Facing the Working Women." Her commitment to Nasser's socialist and pan-Arab policies eventually resulted in an open break with President Anwar Sadat (1970–1981) over the signing of the Camp David Agreements in 1978. She led a group known as the Egyptian National Front, which called for the downfall of Sadat's government from outside of Egypt. *See also* FEMINISM: THE TERM; HUSSEIN, AZIZA (1919–); SAADAWI, NAWAL (1931–); SADAT, JIHAN (1933–).

ABU ZEID, LAYLA (1950–). Moroccan novelist and journalist whose work is widely translated into English. Her work stands out for its emphasis on the nationalist struggle of the Moroccan people against French colonialism and the transformation of Morocco's cultural identity. She writes as a witness of these changes, especially as they impact the mores of generations of women. Her most famous novel is *The Year of the Elephant: A Moroccan Woman's Journey toward Independence* (1989). She also wrote *Return to Childhood: The Memoirs of a Modern Moroccan Woman* (1999).

ADAWIYAH, RABIA AL- (ca. 717–801). She was an Iraqi mystic and poet who attained fame during the early Islamic period. Known also as Rabia al-Basri, her early life was shrouded in mystery. Several sources claim that she was born into a poor family in Basra, Iraq, where she was later abducted and sold into slavery. Her extreme asceticism and purity of heart were said to have brought about her early release from bondage. She spent the rest of her life as a poet and teacher and enjoyed a great following. She became a role model for all Sufis (mystics) by extolling God's love, claiming that the divine should be worshipped out of love, not out of fear. Her devotional poetry influenced generations of mystics, and many miracles were attributed to her. The Persian Sufi poet Farid ud-Din al-Attar (ca. 1120–ca. 1220), who wrote *The Conference of the Birds*, also wrote her biography. Her life story has inspired several biographies and motion pictures in recent years. *See also* SUFISM.

ADHAM, SORAYA (1926–). An Egyptian feminist and nationalist who is also a supporter of leftist causes. Her involvement in politics began while she was a student at Cairo University, from which she earned a degree in English literature in 1948. Later, she joined the Communist Party of Egypt, which was dedicated to ending foreign occupation and gender discrimination. The party's strategy militated against joining hands with liberal feminist institutions such as the **Egyptian Feminist Union (EFU)** and a lesser known group, the Feminist Party, led by Fatima Nimat Rashid. Instead, in the 1940s, she organized her own feminist group, the League of Women Students (LWS), which was closed down by Prime Minister Ismail Sidqi in 1946. Adham's activism and independent lifestyle led to a beating by Islamic fundamentalist youths and a short prison term. She also participated in acts of nationalist resistance against British troops stationed in the Suez Canal zone during the early 1950s and the tripartite Suez attack by Britain, France, and Israel in 1956. *See also* ZAYYAT, LATIFA (1923–1996).

ADNAN, ETEL (1925–). She is a poet, novelist, and painter of mixed Middle Eastern parentage. Born in Beirut to a Syrian father and a Greek mother from Smyrna, Turkey, she spent much of her life in France and the United States. She was enrolled at a convent school in Beirut and studied philosophy at the Sorbonne University in Paris between 1950 and 1955. Later, she attended the University of California, Berkeley, and Harvard University. She has been affiliated with Dominican College, Rafael, California, for some years, where she taught philosophy.

Adnan is multilingual; in addition to learning Arabic, Greek, and Turkish at home, she mastered English and French, which she uses in her literary work. Her poetry and essays were featured in prominent Arabic literary journals such as *Shiir* (poetry) and *Mawqif* (viewpoints), as well as *Jeune Afrique*. Her novel *Sitt Marie Rose* (*Lady Marie Rose*), which dissects anti-Palestinian, antifemale violence during the Lebanese Civil War of 1974–1989, was published in 1978 and translated into six languages. The novel was also awarded the France Pays-Arabes Award. She has published several poetry collections and essays: *Moonshots* (1966), *Five Seasons for One Death* (1971), *Jebu et l'express Beyroth Enfer* (1973), *Apocalypse Arabe* (1980), *Pablo Naruda Is a Banana Tree* (1982), *From A to Z* (1982), *Journey to Mount Tamalpais: An Essay* (1985), *The Spring Flowers Own and the Manifestations of the Voyage* (1990), *Paris, When It's Naked* (1993), *Of Cities and Women: Letters to Fawwaz* (1993), *To Write in a Foreign Language* (1996), *There: In the Light and the Darkness of the Self and the Other* (1997), *Insomnia* (2002), *Seasons* (2008), and *Master of the Eclipse* (2009). Adnan is also an abstract painter. She served at one time as the literary editor of *L'Orient le Jour*. *See also* FEMINISM: THE TERM; SHARIA.

AFGHANI, JAMAL AL-DIN (1838–1897). He was the first Islamic religious figure to call for reform and modernization in recent history. His birthplace is uncertain, but is reputed to be the village of Asadabad, near the city of Hamazan, Iran. Despite his Shii origins, he had a lasting impact on an entire generation of Sunni reformers and intellectuals throughout the Muslim world. He traveled to and lived in many countries, including Ottoman Turkey and Egypt, and was often forced to depart due to his destabilizing influence on the country's intellectuals.

Afghani was one of the first advocates of pan-Islamism, which greatly alarmed British colonial authorities. Through his writings and his intellectual activities, he was able to advocate women's rights throughout his public career. He was considered one of the major figures of the Arab Nahdha even though he was not an Arab. He was forced to leave Egypt in 1882, when the British authorities accused him of being the main inspiration behind the Egyptian nationalist uprising of Ahmad Urabi. Forced to move to Turkey, he carried on with his pan-Islamist activities, at one time maintaining an extensive correspondence with another enemy of the British, the Mahdi of the Sudan (r. 1881–1885). He always proclaimed that Muslims were capable of combining faith and reason, a message that resonated with leading Islamic modernists such as Egypt's **Muhammad Abduh**. His activities and writings were also considered an incitement to rebellion in Iran, where the Qajar rulers accused him of encouraging religious scholars to assume the guardianship of the people.

Afghani's long association with Abduh resulted in an open call for educating women and granting them full Islamic rights. He encouraged Egyptian women to attend his public lectures, a message that was heeded by a substantial number of females, who went to hear him whenever he gave talks in Cairo or Alexandria. According to a report in the Egyptian daily *Misr* (Egypt), Afghani's famous 1879 lecture at Alexandria's Zizinia Hall was sponsored by a women's association and was heavily attended by women, who sat side by side with men. During that lecture, Afghani spoke against religious fanaticism and political absolutism, calling for freedom of assembly and for educating women. The Egyptian stress on the need to integrate the question of women's liberation into the national project of reform and full independence was due in great part to Afghani's impact on Egypt's intellectual life. He died in Istanbul, where he had lived for many years as the guest of the Ottoman state. The Islamic Republic of Iran celebrated the centennial of his death in 1997. *See also* SHARIA.

AFKHAMI, MAHNAZ (1941–). She was Iranian minister of state for women's affairs under Shah Muhammad Reza Pahlavi. Born in Kerman, Iran, she was raised in a large extended family and on her father's side was descended from the Qajar dynasty, Iran's pre-Pahlavi royal family. She arrived in the United States in 1955, where she pursued graduate studies at the University of Colorado, Boulder, earning a master's degree.

By 1967, she was back in Iran, where she became a professor of English literature at Tehran University. She was among the founders of the Association of Iranian University Women and held the position of secretary-general of the Women's Organization of Iran. During the Shah's reign she was a member of Iran's High Council of Family Planning and Welfare and sat on the boards of trustees of Kerman University and Queen Farah University for Women. Afkhami has resided in the United States as a political exile since the Islamic Revolution of 1979 and continues her work as a scholar, lecturer, and activist in women's rights.

While in the United States, Afkhami became involved in several **nongovernmental organizations (NGOs)**, such as Sisterhood Is Global, Women Leaders Intercultural Forum, and Global Women's Action Network for Children. Afkhami is also a member of several organizational boards, such as the Global Fund for Women, International Museum for Women's Rights Division of Human Rights Watch (HRW), and World Movement of Democracy. She is credited with mobilizing support for the creation of the Asian and Pacific Center for Women and Development (APCWD), as well as the United Nations International Research and Training Institute for the Advancement of Women (INSTRAW). She participated in the UN Human Rights Conference in Vienna (1993) and the Fourth U.N. International Conference on Women in Beijing (1995). She has published widely on the global women's movement, women's human rights, women's leadership roles, and their rights to attain technological training and to participate in civil society.

Most of her books were published in several languages, in English under the following titles: *Women and the Law in Iran* (1993), *In the Eye of the Storm: Women in Post Revolutionary Iran* (1995), *Claiming Our Rights: A Manual for Women's Human Rights Education in Muslim Societies* (1996), *Muslim Women and the Politics of Participation* (1997), *Safe and Secure: Eliminating Violence against Women and Girls in Muslim Societies* (1998), *Leading to Choices: A Leadership Training Handbook for Women* (2001), and *Towards a Compassionate Society* (2002). Several of her books were published by Sisterhood Is Global Institute. *See also* FAMILY PLANNING IN IRAN; FEMINISM: THE TERM; PAHLAVI, ASHRAF (1919–); PAHLAVI, FARAH DIBA (1938–).

AFLATOUN, INJI (1924–1989). She was an Egyptian painter, who was also a leftist activist and feminist. Aflatoun was descended from an aristocratic Cairene family and was educated at the French Lycée in the same city. In 1945, she went to Paris as a member of Egypt's delegation to the World Congress for Women, an offshoot of the leftist Democratic Federation of Women. This event launched her career as a student political organizer, when she founded the University and Institute's Youth League. She also joined the National Executive of Workers and Students. Her interest in painting was combined with a strong desire to project and defend the rights of downtrodden Egyptian women. She held her first exhibit in 1942, which brought her to the attention of al-Sharara aka Iskra, a communist group that she later joined. In 1948, she wrote widely acclaimed books on links between the subjugation of women and colonial domination over the Egyptian state. One of these was titled *Eighty Million Women* and had a preface by Taha Hussein, Egypt's eminent philosopher and the president of Cairo University. This publication was followed in 1949 by *We the Egyptian Women*. Her persistent defense of women's rights led to a meeting with **Ceza Nabrawi**, an associate of the leading Egyptian feminist **Huda Shaarawi**, and to membership in the youth wing of the **Egyptian Feminist Union**. She also joined the Popular Committee of Women's Resistance, which carried out attacks on British military bases in the Suez Canal Zone between 1951 and 1956.

Aflatoun's efforts on behalf of women's rights were featured in the main Wafdist newspaper *al-Misri* and in the pages of *al-Masaa*. Her continued support for leftist and communist groups resulted in her imprisonment from 1959 through 1963 by the Nasserite regime. But she managed to continue painting while at al-Qanater prison, focusing mainly on the images of fellow female inmates. Her work was known for its intense colors and the highlighting of peasant women and their hardships, as well as its nationalist themes. When the UN launched its Decade for Women campaign in 1975, Aflatoun was one of the organizers of a large exhibit titled "Women Painters over Half a Century." Following the demise of all of Egypt's splinter communist parties, she joined the main opposition group, al-Tagammu (The Coalition). She died suddenly before completing her last project, the writing of her memoirs. *See also* ADHAM, SORAYA (1926–); EGYPTIAN FEMINIST UNION (EFU); ZAYYAT, LATIFA (1923–1996).

AGRICULTURE, WOMEN IN. Women's participation in agricultural work in Middle Eastern countries has rarely been recognized or seriously studied. By the 1980s, the failure of many male-run rural development projects combined with consistent efforts to produce a new awareness of this issue. The adoption of the **Convention on the Elimination of All Forms of Discrimination against Women (CEDAW)** in 1979 drew attention to the plight of Middle Eastern women in the economic sector. New policies by the World Bank, such as Structural Adjustment Programs, which demanded reforms by Third World governments prior to the allocation of massive economic assistance, continued to apply the gender-blind policies of the past. Globalized economic efforts around the world disregarded the special needs of women engaged in agriculture despite their rising representation in this form of economic activity, especially in the Middle East.

The first international agency to point to this reality was the United Nations Food and Agricultural Organization (FAO). It provided the following breakdown of women's participation in the agricultural labor force in a survey done in the early 1990s: 30.7 percent in Iraq; 33.0 percent in Jordan; 40.7 percent in Lebanon; and 52.2 percent in Syria. The report highlighted the special problems associated with women's agricultural labor, whether working on family farms or in commercialized agriculture. The FAO concluded that women remained at a disadvantage largely due to hiring practices that deny them permanent employment and deprive them of benefits. Lebanon was cited as an extreme example; 75 percent of its female agricultural labor force was made up of seasonal workers. This was also the result of excluding women from mechanized farming due to the perception of their general physical unfitness to operate farming machinery. Another problem in this part of the world was the common practice of favoring males over females in the redistribution of land due to their headship of the family. This situation was observed in Syria during the 1950s and 1960s when the state adopted land reform programs. State policies of this kind automatically led to female dependence on male family members, especially during the process of seeking state benefits such as social security.

Egypt presents another instance of disregarding women's contributions to agriculture. Fully one-sixth of the Gross Domestic Product in this country is derived from agriculture, and women's participation in this sector hovers around one-third of the total. Rapid urbanization and continued expansion of cities have reduced these numbers as more rural people are drawn to urban centers for employment. There is a stark contrast between opportunities for female participation in the work on family farms in the Delta areas of the north and in the southern part of the country. The involvement of women in secondary activities on family farms in the Delta generally exceeds that in the south. In the Delta, women supervise fowl and farm animals and take farm products to nearby market centers. In the more conservative south, it is unusual to see women as field workers or taking on marketing responsibilities. In addition, Egyptian female agricultural workers have been affected by the migration of male family members to the labor market of the Arab Persian Gulf countries. Increasingly, prosperity generated in these countries has led to male discouragement of any involvement of their women in agriculture.

Iran presents a different picture altogether; land reform programs there have led to the shrinkage, not the expansion, of the agricultural sector. The percentage of women in farm labor, according to census reports for the years 1966 to 1996, ranges from 10 to 16 percent. Most women were engaged in unpaid work on family farms and were severely underrepresented as owners of land. The situation did not improve under the Islamic republic, as is evident in the First Development Plan (1989–1993). Female ownership of land in agricultural areas continued to be limited to a few elite urban women. Even though Islamic inheritance laws do not disqualify women from land ownership, general practices discriminate against female ownership of land. The inherently conservative social system of the Islamic Republic in general favored male ownership in an effort to keep all immovable wealth in the family. Both the Shah's land reform program of 1963, which was part of a wider effort known as the White Revolution, and the Islamic Republic's more contained land redistribution program, awarded land titles to men only. In addition, most rural women seem to be oblivious to efforts by the Islamic regime to amplify women's ownership rights in recent years. *See also* SHARIA.

AICHA, LALLA (1930–). She is the daughter of King Muhammad V (r. 1957–1961) and sister of King Hassan II (r. 1961–1999) of Morocco. A pioneer of the women's movement, she utilized her education and royal status to campaign for advancing women's rights. She demonstrated her desire to end women's seclusion by delivering a speech on behalf of her father in the city of Tangier in 1947 while unveiled. She was named president of the Moroccan Red Crescent Society and continued to play a prominent role in state-sponsored activities for women. She also served as Morocco's ambassador to Great Britain (1965–1973), Greece (1969–1970), and Turkey (1970–1973). *See also* MUDAWANA, AL-.

AISHA (614–678). The third and youngest wife of Prophet Muhammad, who was also the daughter of the second caliph, Abu Baker al Siddiq (r. 632–634) and Umm Rumman. She was married at the age of nine, although the marriage was not consummated until later, and she became the Prophet's most beloved wife after his first wife **Khadija** (d. 623). Aisha was childless but grew to become a great scholar and a historian of Islam. She was also an authority on medicine and a poet in her own right. The prophet bestowed upon her the name *Umm Abdullah* (the mother of Abdullah) in reference to her nephew, Abdullah ibn al-Zubayr. By the age of 14, she was the center of a malicious gossip campaign accusing her of adultery for tarrying behind her travel caravan with a younger man. The prophet came to her defense, revealing a special Quranic chapter (24: 11–20) that established rules for leveling accusations at a free woman. His great regard for her scholarship was epitomized in his statement: "Take two-thirds of your religion from *al-humayraa*," referring to her glowing cheeks. She was a formidable memorizer and transmitter of *hadith,* or Prophetic pronouncements. She was credited with verifying and preserving 1,210 *hadiths.* She also led other women in public prayers.

Aisha's most controversial role was after her widowhood at the age of 18, when she devoted the rest of her life to the defense of the faith. In an unusual move for a woman of her exalted status, Aisha led the troops against Ali, Muhammad's cousin and son-in-law, when he made a bid for the caliphate in 656. She fought Ali in Basra, Iraq, during the Battle of the Camel, when he claimed the caliphate following the assassination of the third caliph, Uthman ibn Affan. Ali's victory at the end of this battle solidified Suni–Shii antagonism for a very long time.

Aisha's great victory was securing the burial of the Prophet in the floor of her apartment inside the Prophet's house, which doubled as the Medina Mosque. Although Shii Muslims believe her to be a controversial figure of early Islam, she is an object of veneration to Sunni Muslims, who continue to marvel at her unusual intellectual intimacy with the Prophet. Aisha, however, became the focus of modern Western detractors of Muhammad, who criticized her young age at the time of her marriage. She led a quiet life in her later years at Medina, where she was eventually buried. *See also* FATIMA (ca. 604–632); SHARIA.

AISHA: ARAB WOMEN'S FORUM (AAWF). A group of Arab women's organizations advocating the expansion of women's rights, founded in 1992. Its membership included North African and Middle Eastern **non-governmental organizations (NGOs)**. In addition to its advocacy of granting Arab women a wider array of legal rights such as formal participation in governmental and civic institutions, the forum adopted a broad social agenda. The AAWF also targets the negative impact of violence against women and their misrepresentation in the media. The forum launched programs to increase women's awareness of reproductive rights and health matters and has approved a research agenda concerning issues confronting Arab women. It has established the Women's Center in Jerusalem, which provides legal aid and counseling to women in need. The Center's website is known as *Nissa* (women).

AJAMY, MARY (1888–1965). Syrian poet, translator, and political activist who was born in Damascus. She attended English and Russian schools, becoming an accomplished linguist. She also studied nursing at the American University of Beirut (AUB), graduating in 1906. She taught school in Damascus and in Alexandria, where she practiced journalism. Most of her political activities were directed against the Ottoman occupation of Syria and Lebanon. Her nationalist activities were the result of the execution of her fiancé in Damascus in 1916, where the Ottoman governor, Jamal Pasha, suppressed Arab nationalist activities with an iron fist. She teamed up with two Lebanese feminists, Ibtihaj Qaddura and **Julia Dimashqiyyah**, to open a hospital in Damascus and an orphanage in Beirut for the benefit of families suffering the aftereffects of World War I. Ajamy remained single all her life.

Her literary magazine, *Al-Arus* (*The Bride*), founded in 1910, was the only women's journal published in Syria at the time. Most of the contributors were women who wrote under pseudonyms. She wrote under the name Layla, her mother's name. The paper lasted for 11 years.

AKHIALIYAH, LAYLA. A famous seventh-century Arab poet who was renowned for her strength of character and her good looks. She was descended from the Banu Uqayl clan of the Banu Amir tribe. She performed frequently at the palaces of the Ummayid dynasty (661–750) in Damascus, where she recited her poetry. She feuded for a long time with a famous poet, Al-Nabigha al-Judi, and professed her love to some men publicly while she was married, two unusual types of behavior in her day. *See also* KHANSAA, AL- (ca. 575–645).

AKHRAS, ASMA FAWWAZ (1975–). She is the wife of Syria's president, Bashar Assad (r. 2000–). She was born in Acton, a suburb of London, to a Syrian family that emigrated to Britain from Homs in Syria. Her father is a cardiologist, and her mother is a former Syrian diplomat. Akras graduated from Queen's College in London in 1996 with a degree in computer science and French literature. She became an investment banker, working with several Western financial institutions such as Deutsche Bank Groups and J.P. Morgan. She married Dr. Bashar al-Assad, an ophthalmologist, a short while after he succeeded his father in December 2000. As the first lady of Syria, she joined her husband on many official visits to various countries. She also maintained an interest in the protection of Syrian children. One of her most ambitious projects is the Fund for Integrated Rural Development of Syria (FIRDOS), a rural development **non-governmental organization (NGO)** that she established in 2001. *See also* SHAABAN, BOUTHAINA (1953–).

ALGERIAN FAMILY CODE (1984). This code wrote into law women's rights and obligations following the **Algerian Revolution** (1954–1962). A huge debate developed over how to reward or enfranchise women who had fought and worked for national liberation. Women who performed such roles were honored with the title of *mujahidat* (women of struggle) and included nurses, liaison officers, and fighters. Those who carried arms, such as **Djamila Bouhired**, Hassiba be Bouali, Zohra Driff, and Zulaikha Boujemaa, had even been imprisoned and tortured by French military authorities. At first, a committee that studied the women's issue produced a liberal document known as *charte nationale*. The conservative wing of the revolutionary ruling party, the National Liberation Front (FLN), managed to cast these laws into a stricter Islamic code. Despite women's participation in the revolution, only 10 women were elected to the first national assembly, which had a total membership of 194. The number of female deputies in the second parliament fell to 2 out of 138 members. When the code was aired by the national media, huge women's demonstrations took place.

A superficially revised document was finally adopted by the national assembly in June 1984, during the government of Chadli Benjedid (r. 1979–1992). The code stipulated the supremacy of the **Sharia** in matters not covered by this set of laws. The minimum age of marriage for males was raised to 21, and for females to 18. Yet these age restrictions were subject to the discretion of judges, who could easily ignore them. Traditional Islamic practices such as guardianship of the bride during religious marriage ceremonies, as well as the practice of summary **divorce**, were retained. If a woman sought to obtain a divorce, she had to prove her husband's deviance from a specific set of seven conditions, which was difficult to prove. A woman was deprived of the marital residence following a divorce. The result was that women were simply condemned to remain legal minors throughout their lives despite promises of legal equality spelled out in the constitution. While the constitution guaranteed a woman's right to choose her own spouse, the father was given the right to contest the marriage if he considered it harmful to her interests. The code also established a woman's obligation to obey her husband and his family and maintained the ban on marrying a non-Muslim husband. One Algerian feminist referred to the code as *code d'infamie.*

ALGERIAN REVOLUTION (1954–1962). Current debates among Middle Eastern feminists continue to revolve around this revolution and its significance to women. The history of French colonization of this part of the Arab-Islamic world had a great impact on the development of Algerian feminism and the adoption of a set of demands seeking gender equality in political and religious matters. Ever since King Charles X of France had acquired Algeria as a colony in 1830, Algeria had experienced massive brutality, economic deprivation, and near-total eradication of its cultural identity, even after being given the status of a *département*. When the revolution broke out, Algerian women joined the fighting as combatants who belonged to several guerrilla cells in urban centers and to units fighting in the mountains. Hardly any native women's organization existed before the revolution, so their involvement in the national struggle was unconditional, making no demands on the revolutionary male leadership. Most of the existing feminist organizations were led by French colonial women, who patronized Muslim women and sought their liberation according to the norms of European culture and social movements. Examples of these groups are the Union Franco-Musulmane des femmes d'Algeria (UFMF), which came into being in 1955, and the Association des femmes Musulmanes, which was formed in 1947. Both of these catered to elite women of both national communities. Some organizations disbanded during the revolutionary years.

According to some accounts, as many as 10,949 women participated in the revolution. Most were drawn to battle lines by male relatives without belonging to any revolutionary organizations such as the Front de Libération Nationale (FLN) and the Armée de Libération Nationales (ALN). It has been estimated that fully 20 percent of all women involved in the war came from urban centers, while 80 percent of the female participants were rural women. While the urban women belonged to French-educated middle class families, rural women were generally illiterate. Women's contributions as fighters, nurses, and couriers for the guerrillas were dramatized in the Algerian film *The Battle of Algiers*. Women as young as 14 years of age participated, but the majority were between the ages of 20 and 25. Most suffered brutal acts of torture and rape. As is typical in most guerrilla wars, women were placed mostly in inferior positions, while the higher military ranks were reserved for males. One woman in five was either killed or suffered imprisonment. The percentage of native women who occupied political positions within Algeria and in the Algerian government in exile in neighboring Tunisia never exceeded 0.5 percent.

Although many women shed their veils as a result of revolutionary activities, they never voiced any demands for reforming existing family laws. In 1957, French authorities adopted a new *Loi Cadre*, which granted Algerian women the right to vote, but this step hardly impacted their lives during their revolutionary militarized engagement. Many reasons accounted for the absence of feminist consciousness among Algerian women, the most important being their absence from the ranks of the revolutionary intellectual leadership and the hegemonic role of the FLN, which banished all rival groups from the scene. When Algeria finally achieved independence by signing the Evian Accords with the government of Charles de Gaulle (r. 1958–1969) during the Fifth French Republic in 1962, the country had weathered 132 years of white settler colonization. Immortalized by Franz Fanon (1925–1961) in his book *The Wretched of the Earth*, the Algerian revolution became a model for many anticolonial struggles throughout the Third World.

The women's issue did not emerge as a priority of the period of early independence, despite the well-publicized sacrifices of women like **Djamila Bouhired**, Djamila Boupacha, and Djamila Bouazza. Algeria's first president, Ahmad Ben Bella (r. 1962–1965), sounded a sympathetic note toward women. A hallmark of this period was a document prepared by two socialist ideologues, Mohammed Harbi and Hocine Zahouane. This *Charte d'Alger*, sometimes known as *charte nationale*, identified the most important items for the national agenda. Although liberal and progressive in tone, it was inspired by Yugoslav socialism and did not recognize gender differences, preferring instead to call all people "the masses" and to glorify the revolution's liberating impact on women. The most important grievances that were recognized were those of male veterans, not women revolutionaries. The second president of Algeria, Houari Boumedience (r. 1965–1978), moved further to the right, adopting the ideology of Islamic socialism. In an address to a female audience in celebration of International Women's Day on 8 March 1966, he emphasized the necessity of adopting **Sharia** as Algeria's family law. He also voiced his support for polygamy and other aspects of the Islamic family system rejected by most women. His period of rule led to the adoption of the **Algerian Family Code** of 1984 under president Chadli Benjedid (r. 1979–1992). As a result, Western and Third World feminists continue to argue over the wisdom of female involvement in national liberation struggles prior to obtaining official support for a feminist agenda.

ALI, FARIDA MUHAMMAD (1963–). She is an Iraqi classical singer of *maqam*, songs of specific oriental tone scales, or *maqamat*, in which each scale expresses a single mood or emotion. She was born in Karbala, Iraq, and studied with the great late lute player Munir Bashir. She is part of the Iraqi Maqam Ensemble, which performs all over the world. In 2007, she received a medal from the Algerian government during her performance at the Algeria Capital of Arab Culture Festival. She left Iraq in 1997 and moved to the Netherlands, which became her home.

ALI, PRINCESS WIJDAN (1939–). Jordanian painter and art historian who was born in Baghdad to the Hashemite royal line in that country. She married Prince Ali ibn Nayef, a cousin of King Hussein of Jordan. She founded the Royal Society of Fine Arts in 1979, which established the Jordanian National Gallery of Fine Arts in Amman, Jordan. Princess Wijdan holds a bachelor's degree from the American University of Beirut (1961) and a PhD in Islamic art history from the University of London's School of Oriental and African Studies (1993). She was the first woman to join the Jordanian foreign service, in 1962. She received training as an artist and painter from Armando Bruno and Muhanna Durra. She is best known for efforts to revive the tradition of Islamic art and her abstract paintings of Arabic calligraphy. She authored two books: *Contemporary Art from the Islamic World* (1989) and *Modern Islamic Art: Development and Continuity* (1997).

ALIA, QUEEN OF JORDAN (1948–1977). She was the third wife of King Hussein of Jordan (r. 1953–1999) and was born in Cairo, Egypt, while her father, Baha al-Din Touqan, was a diplomat serving in that country. Her mother is Hanan Hashem, and both parents are descended from well-established Palestinian families from the city of Nablus. Alia received an international education while her father served at diplomatic posts in Istanbul, London, and Rome. She received a degree in political science from the Rome Center of Chicago's Loyola University and pursued graduate studies at Hunter College, New York. She met the king while working in public relations for Royal Jordanian Airlines, which was later renamed after her. She and the king were married in 1972 after the dissolution of his second marriage, to British-born Toni Gardner. Queen Alia and the king had two children, Princess Haya (b. 1974), who later married Sheikh Rashed al-Maktoum, the ruler of Dubai, and Prince Ali (b. 1975). The royal couple adopted a third child, named Abir.

Queen Alia patronized numerous charities serving children, such as orphanages and schools for the deaf and the blind. She also raised funds for mobile medical units serving physically challenged children. One of her lasting achievements was founding a highly admired folkloric dancing group featuring the cultural heritage of Jordan. The queen perished in a mysterious helicopter crash caused by a sandstorm.

ALIM, RAJA. Saudi writer of short stories, plays, and novels who received a BA in English literature and worked in the Kindergarten Teacher Training Center in Jedda. Her prose attracted attention due to its mixing of traditional and modern themes. She is the author of several plays and short story collections, the most acclaimed of which is *The Animal River* (1974). She was awarded several international awards, the latest being the International Prize for Arab Fiction, awarded in 2011 for her book *The Dove's Necklace*.

ALIYE, FATIMA (1862–1939). She was an Ottoman novelist and a pioneer writer on women's issues. Daughter of Ahmed Cevdalt Pasha, she became a novelist and a reformer, calling for greater public educational opportunities for women. Her ideas were considered revolutionary for her times, especially as she called for abandoning the practice of marrying for purely economic advantage. She also encouraged women to seek employment outside the home. Her arguments were based on the Quran, since she always rejected Westernization. She published three books: *Reminiscences* (1892), *Famous Muslim Women* (1892), and *Polygamy* (1898). *See also* EDIP, HALIDE (1883–1964).

ALIZADEH, GHAZALEH (1946–1996). An Iranian literary critic and feminist activist who wrote novels and short stories. She was born in the city of Mashhad, Iran, but lived much of her life in Tehran and was one of the few writers who continued to focus on gender issues under the Islamic revolutionary government. Her work mirrored the style of another feminist writer, Nima Yusiji, who adopted the method of Hermann Hess in the 1920s. Both women novelists used allegorical realism in their work, resulting in surreal representation of their fictional characters. Alizadeh's most famous work was a novel titled *Khaneh Edrisi* (Persian, Edris House), which appeared in 1996. She was found dead hanging from a tree in a forest outside of Tehran, which aroused a great deal of suspicion.

ALLIANCE ISRAÉALITE UNIVERSELLE (AIU). This organization was founded to combat conversion of Jews to Christianity. The inception of this effort goes back to the conversion campaign launched in 1808 by the newly founded London Society for Promoting Christianity among the Jews. Although it did not emerge formally until decades later, the AIU employed the central precepts of France's "civilizing mission" to provide secular education as a barrier to the transmission of French social, political, and cultural ideas overseas. The Alliance's schools were at first confined to the primary level and were utilized to infuse a modern approach to Judaism into the French school curriculum. The AIU offered instruction in the French language, arithmetic, geography, history, and natural sciences in all of its private and secular schools. Boys and girls were recruited to these schools in equal numbers and received instruction at the hands of French teachers before local and modernizing instructors became available. Students were primarily from the North African and Middle Eastern Jewish minorities. If successful, indigenous students were sent to Paris, where they received further training at the École Normale Israelite Orientale and in time became the new staff in AIU's schools overseas. French authorities in North Africa encouraged the AIU to recruit native, non-Jewish students in order to promote French culture within the general population. One of the earliest efforts of the AIU was a school for indigenous Jewish girls, which opened up in the capital city of Tunis in 1882, a year after the birth of the French Protectorate over that country. Similar schools in Algeria and Morocco were also successful, enjoying the support of local rabbis and Jewish philanthropists alike. The AIU network of schools was also inspired by the *haskalah*, the movement of Jewish enlightenment in Europe.

ALONI, SHULAMIT ADLER (1928–). Israeli politician, civil rights activist, and feminist, born in Tel Aviv. Aloni joined the Palmach, the elite military group representing the Israeli Kibbutz movement of cooperative farms, which fought during the 1948 Arab–Jewish War. She received a law degree from Hebrew University in Jerusalem and joined Mapai, Israel's Labor Party, in 1959. Her long service as a member of the Knesset (Israel's parliament) began in 1965. Her strong criticism of the Israeli bureaucracy and her advocacy for civil rights led Prime Minister Levi Eshkhol (r. 1963–1969) to create the Israeli Commission for Public Complaints.

Aloni left the Labor Party in 1973 due to disagreements with Prime Minister Golda Meir (r. 1969–1974), forming her own group, the Civil Rights Movement, or Ratz. In 1974, she joined Yitzhak Rabin's cabinet as a minister without portfolio but resigned shortly thereafter in protest against the inclusion of the National Religious Party, Shas, in the cabinet. Her new party, Meretz, eventually joined Rabin's coalition cabinet, with Aloni holding the Education, Culture, and Sport Portfolio. Clashes with Shas led to her second resignation, but she remained as the minister of communications, sciences, and the arts.

After leaving the cabinet, she devoted her efforts to peace and gender issues. Her main project became the support of women who were denied marriage certificates by Israel's religious authorities because they were married outside of the country. She also led a strong campaign to end domestic violence against women. In addition, she established the Center for Peace in the Middle East in 1982, which called for reconciling with the Palestinians. She was awarded the Israel Prize in 2000, in recognition of her work on behalf of society's weakest members. *See also also* FEMINIST MOVEMENT IN ISRAEL.

ALUSI, MANAL YOUNIS (1929–). She was an Iraqi feminist and leading representative of Iraqi women during the period of Baathist rule, particularly under the presidency of Saddam Hussein (r. 1979–2003). Before rising to the position of head of the **General Union of Iraqi Women (GUIW)**, she held a number of positions, beginning with her membership in the Baath Party in 1962. After a number of years, she was chosen as a member of the Baath Professional Office. As a party insider, she was very effective in pressing for gender equality and opening professions to qualified women. *See also* DU-LAYMI, NAZIHA JAWDAT; QASSEM, ABD AL-KARIM (1914–1963).

AMARA, LAMIA ABBAS AL- (1928–). She was an Iraqi poet who popularized the free verse movement of such great poets as Abd al-Wahab al-Bayati (1926–1999) and Badr Shakir al-Sayyab (1926–1964). A member of the Sabaean syncretic sect, which predominates in southern Iraq, Baghdad, and Iran, al-Amara graduated from Baghdad's Higher Teacher's College in 1950. She taught Arabic language and literature for many years while experimenting with new poetical forms. In one of her better-known sardonic poems, "Me and My Abaya" (the black outer garment worn by Iraqi and Persian Gulf women outdoors), she describes the restrictions imposed on women who were forced to wear this cloak. Her three widely read poetry collections are *The Empty Corner*, *Iraqi Women*, and *Had the Fortune Teller Told Me*. She resides in the United States. *See also* MALAIKA, NAZIK AL-(1923–2007).

AMIN, QASSEM (1863–1908). Egyptian jurist and writer who was the first to call for gender equality throughout the Arab world. The scion of a prominent Turco–Egyptian family, he was born in Alexandria but settled with his family in Cairo, where he graduated from the Khedivial School of Law in 1881. Later, as a student at the University of Montpellier, France (1881–1885), he became aware of the discrepancy between the rights of French and Egyptian women. Upon his return to Egypt, he became chancellor of Cairo's Court of Appeals. He joined the circle of Egyptian nationalists calling for an end to British occupation of their country and for the liberation of women. Among his associates in these endeavors were **Muhammad Abduh** and **Jamal al-Din Afghani**. Both of these figures of the Arab renaissance read earlier versions of his iconic work, *Tahrir al-maraa* (*The Liberation of Women*, 1899). Portions of this book were read and criticized by progressive men and women who regularly attended the literary salon of Princess **Nazli Fadhil**.

Amin's book, which was written in Arabic and addressed to an Egyptian readership, argued that Egypt's liberation would be difficult without the liberation of women. He called for granting women more educational opportu-

nities and made a strong case against **veiling**. He also called for the elimination of **polygamy**, summary **divorce**, and arranged **marriages**. Being a
strong admirer of European liberalism and rationalism, he based his argument not on the Quran but on natural law. His other book, *al-Maraa al-
jadida* (*The New Woman*) appeared in 1900 as a sequel to his earlier work.

More than 30 books and articles came out in response to his first work,
launching a huge debate by supporters and detractors. Some claimed that
certain portions of his book were penned by Abduh. Among those who
opposed Amin's views were Mustafa Kamel (1874–1908), Egypt's pro-Islamic nationalist statesman, and **Talaat Harb** (1867–1941), the founder of
Bank Misr, who was fearful of women's competition in the workplace. But
Amin's supporters included major figures of Egyptian reform such as Saad
Zaghloul (1859–1927), leader of the 1919 Revolution, and Ahmad Lutfi al-
Sayyid (1872–1963), founder of the Egyptian University. Amin's writings
also had a great impact on the Arab educated classes and gave a great boost
to the antiveiling movement of the 1920s. Amin was among the enthusiastic
supporters of the Egyptian national university, which was opened in 1908.
By 1929, the university was opened to women after they were allowed to
attend evening lectures for a number of years. Amin became the university's
first vice president. *See also* EGYPTIAN FEMINIST UNION (EFU); SAA-
DAWI, NAWAL (1931–); SHAARAWI, HUDA (1879–1947).

AMINI, FATEMEH (1933–). Iranian educator and founder of the first
Islamic seminary for women in Iran, born in the holy city of Qom. She was
prevented from completing her **education** by her family. Amini had a reputation as a pious woman after raising her two children by herself following her
divorce in 1965. She was able to establish the first seminary for women in
Qom in 1972 with the support of the Great Ayatollah Kazem Shariatmadari.
She went on to establish three more seminaries following her first successful
endeavor, named Makteb-I Tawhid. She was also able to complete her high
school education after the Islamic Revolution of 1979, when she settled in
Tehran. There she founded another seminary in 1988, known as Fatemeh-ye
Zahra. Despite her traditional upbringing, Amini was a believer in gender
equality as an Islamic value based on the Quran, hence her interest in training
women as *mujtahids*, or interpreters of sacred texts. The Tehran seminary
that she founded eventually evolved into a social center for poor women,
with an enrollment of 250 students in 1994. *See also* KHOMEINI, AYA-
TOLLAH RUHOLLAH (ca. 1902–1989).

AMIR, DAISY AL- (1935–). An Iraqi writer of short stories who was born
in Basra, Iraq. She earned a bachelor's degree from Baghdad's Teacher's
Training college and later enrolled at Cambridge University in 1963, where

she prepared for a doctoral degree in Arabic literature under Orientalist scholar A. J. Arberry. When her father refused to pay her tuition, she returned home but stopped at Beirut, Lebanon, first. Her Lebanese stay resulted in her appointment as assistant press attaché for the Iraqi Cultural Center in Beirut. Her short stories usually dwell on the theme of female alienation and the loss of individual identity in societies that assign women fixed familial roles. Among her titles are *The Far Away Country Which We Love* (1964), *The Return of the Wave* (1969), *The Happy Arab Home* (1975), *In the Whirl-pool of Love and Hate* (1979), *Promises for Sale* (1981), and *The Waiting List: An Iraqi Woman's Tales of Alienation* (1994).

AMIRY, SUAD (1951–). A Palestinian architect and novelist who was born in Amman, Jordan, and completed her architectural studies at the American University of Beirut (AUB) in 1977. Later, she earned advanced degrees at the University of Michigan and University of Edinburgh, Scotland. A long-time resident of Ramallah, Palestine, she has devoted herself to the preservation of the traditional architectural heritage of Arab Palestine. She is a founder of Riwaq Center for Architectural Conservation, which was created in 1981 as a **non-governmental organization (NGO)** dedicated to protecting architectural work and providing employment for Arab workers. From 1991 until 1993, she was a member of the Palestinian Peace Delegation in Washington, D.C., following the Madrid Peace Conference of 1991.

Amiry is the author of several books on architecture, as well as two novels. Her works include *Palestinian Village Home*, *Throne Village Architecture*, and *Manteer: Farm Houses*. She also wrote a work of fiction that became an instant best seller, namely *Sharon and My Mother-in-Law* (2002). The novel, which has been translated into 19 languages, depicts life during the second Palestinian *intifada* (2000–2004), when Israeli Defense Forces occupied most Palestinian towns, including Ramallah. Forced to stay indoors, Amiry and her family experienced an occupation of another kind when her mother-in-law was unable to return home after a brief visit. The novel/memoir received the prestigious Italian Literary award, Viareggio. Her second novel, *Murad, Murad* (2010), describes her journey with a group of Palestinian workers who snuck across the Israeli-built separation wall looking for employment. Her other works include *Earthquake in April* (2003) and *Nothing to Lose but Your Life* (2010). Since 2006, Amiry has been serving as the vice chair of Birzeit University's board of trustees.

AMMASH, HUDA (1958–). An Iraqi scientist and Baathist activist, the daughter of former Iraqi General Salih Mahdi Ammash. She was trained as a microbiologist at the University of Missouri and the Pasteur Institute in Paris. From 1990 until 1995, she taught at Baghdad University's College of Education for Women, eventually rising to the position of dean (1995–1997). Ammash was also prominent in the Baath Party, first as the elected head of the Baghdad Baath Party branch, and later as the leader of the Baath Regional Command in 2001. She was the head of the Iraqi Society of Microbiologists. Following the American invasion of 2003, she was accused of working on the development of chemical and biological weapons and taken into custody on 5 May of the same year by U.S. military authorities. She is believed to be one of two Iraqi women who were in American military custody in 2003.

AMR, RAYHANA BINT ZEID IBN (?– 632). Rayhana was the wife of Prophet Muhammad. She was captured and later freed when her husband's Jewish tribe, Banu Qurayza, was defeated in battle in 627 in Medina. Some accounts claim that she was the Prophet's concubine. She preceded him in death by a few months.

AMROUCHE, FADHMA (1882–1967). She was a Berber singer and writer who was born in Taourith-Moussa-ou-Amar in the Algerian Kabylia region of the Atlas Mountains. She attended schools run by the Sisters of Our Lady of African Missions, which were affiliated with the order of the White Fathers. Under the direction of Algiers' Archbishop Charles Levigerie (1825–1892), the missions launched a conversion campaign targeting the Berber population on the assumption that they were Christians before the advent of Islam. Amrouche and her family converted to Christianity en masse in 1899. They later moved to Tunisia, by 1913. Amrouche was married by the missionaries to another Kabylia convert to Christianity. She and her family were mostly itinerant singers and dancers, performing traditional songs and folktales. In 1931, she wrote a book titled *Histoire de ma vie* (*History of My Life*). She is the mother of noted Berber singer and novelist **Marie Louise Amrouche**. *See also* BERBER WOMEN.

AMROUCHE, MARIE LOUISE (a.k.a. Marguerite Taos) (1913–1976). A Berber singer and novelist who was a member of a Kabylia Christianized family of singers and storytellers. Although raised in Tunisia, she often returned to the Kabilya region where her mother, **Fadhma**, was born. She later settled in France. In addition to producing and hosting programs for French national radio on life among the Kabilya Berbers, she became the first Algerian novelist to publish under her own name. Concerned with the divided loyalties of Kabilya individuals, especially those who accepted Christianity, she often wrote on the identity conflicts of people living their lives as Berbers, Tunisians, Algerians, Christians, and French in culture. She inherited her mother's interest in traditional music and produced six albums of Berber folk songs, which were warmly received in Europe and Africa. Her efforts on behalf of Berber culture were considered subversive by the Algerian government, which banned her from performing during the 1969 Pan-African Cultural Festival in Algeria. She authored four semi-autobiographical novels dealing with Berber cultural identity. *See also* BERBER WOMEN.

ANATOLIAN WOMEN'S ASSOCIATION FOR PATRIOTIC DEFENSE (AWAPD). A Turkish organization inspired by **Mustafa Kemal Ataturk** (r. 1924–1938) as he tried to mobilize the entire nation behind his independence campaign. Founded in the city of Sivas in 1879, the association organized branches throughout the country. Most members reflected the middle-class origins of Ataturk's male supporters, being the female relatives of the nation's bureaucrats, soldiers, merchants, and teachers. In 1920, some branches claimed to have a membership of about 1,090, demonstrating a determined effort to achieve liberation from the foreign occupying forces in their own country. The association organized letter-writing campaigns to the wives of the leaders of the invading armies. Members also engaged in fundraising, while some fought alongside the men on the battle front. One of these female fighters, referred to in parliamentary records as Nezahat Hanim, earned the popular sobriquet of Joan of Arc and was nominated to receive the War of Independence Medal. *See also* WOMEN IN THE TURKISH MILITARY.

ANCIENT EGYPT, WOMEN IN. Egypt's recorded history, spanning three millennia, stretches back to the conquest of Alexander the Great in 332 BCE. The role of women was constantly changing, although much of our knowledge of ancient Egyptian life is derived from the New Kingdom (1550–332 BCE). Surviving information about ancient Egyptian women relates mostly to two categories of females: the scribal elite and royal women. Female goddesses should also be considered, because in ancient Egypt the divine always merged with the human. The life stories of female goddesses, such as Isis and Hathor, the deities representing motherhood and female sexuality, respectively, tell us a great deal about the Egyptian perspective on the human existence of women. Taken together, female scribes, royal women, and goddesses provide extensive information on how women ranked during these centuries.

Royal Women: Since kings enjoyed a divine nature, the question arises: Is there any evidence of the existence of divine queenship? Only the king's mother or his principal wife enjoyed the title of "queen," whereas his daughters were merely potential queens. The status of a queen was demonstrated in her title and insignia, the latter most commonly consisting of the vulture headdress and made up from the frame of the dead bird. Originally shown as the headdress of the vulture goddess Nekhbet, it signified a queen's role as the protector of Upper Egypt, while the protector of Lower Egypt was the Cobra, worn by the goddess Wadjyt. Starting in the fifth century BCE, the vulture cap was worn by queens as their special insignia, pointing to the divine antecedents of their status as queens. By the Eighteenth Dynasty (1550–1307 BCE), Egyptian queens began to wear the double insignia of Upper and Lower Egypt. Another important piece of evidence was the *ankh* (sign of life), which was pictured carried by queens in the Fifth Kingdom (2494–2345 BCE). The *ankh* was also carried by kings and deities, but rarely by ordinary people, therefore signifying the status of a divine goddess or at least someone outside the human realm.

Royal Descent: Until recently, it was commonly believed that eligibility for the office of king passed through the female line of royal families. The only means of assuming kingship by the descendant of a deceased king or by a nonroyal contender was to marry the daughter of the previous king, who was considered the heiress queen. This meant that most of the time the incoming king had to marry his own sister or half-sister, who were both ineligible to become queens in their own right. But evidence for the existence of such a pattern of establishing legitimacy is not consistent, because certain kings such as Thutmose III, Amenhotep II, and Amenhotep III had nonroyal principal wives. The prevalence of brother–sister marriage led to the mistaken designation of such unions as royal incest. But the occurrence of this type of marriage did not bestow the rank of heiress on royal females, since some did not enter such unions and did become queens regardless. A better explanation can be found in the brother–sister marriages of deities, such as the most famous marriage of Isis to her brother Osiris. Thus, when an Egyptian king married his sister, he was following the example of the gods in order to set himself apart from his human subjects and reinforce his claim to divine kingship.

Nonroyal Wives: Egyptian kings were polygamous by the time of the New Kingdom, but the titles "principal wife" and "King's wife" were not prevalent until the Thirteenth Dynasty (1783–1640 BCE). By the Eighteenth Dynasty, the principal wives of kings were subdivided further into descendants of royal and nonroyal families. The only distinguishing mark of a principal wife from a nonroyal lineage was that she did not have the description "king's daughter" added to her name. Often these wives came from families serving the royal household such as the daughter of a nurse to Thutmose III, who ended up as a principal wife of the king. Other wives were daughters of priestly families. Some kings married daughters of foreign rulers of such places as Syria–Palestine for purely diplomatic or foreign policy advantage. Monuments mention the names Menhet, Mertit, and Menway as being the wives of kings who came from such regions. Some wives were acquired as a result of alliances with kings in Babylon, Mesopotamia. King Ramses II (r. 1279–1213 BCE) married a Hittite princess from what is now Turkey.

Marriage: None of the Egyptian sources refers to any legal or religious ceremony to sanctify marriage. The institution of marriage meant a coalition of two individuals, usually when the woman moved to reside with the man's household. The equivalent of the term "divorce" was usually used when one of the marital partners was expelled or departed out of his or her own free will. The records indicate that sometimes a third party sanctioned a marriage, such as when a head of a household gave away a captured slave in marriage to another family member. Sometimes a father gave away his daughter to another man by arranging for her to live in his house. Marriage contracts were known beginning in the seventh century BCE and down to the Ptolemaic period. These contracts were usually drawn up by the male partners and sometimes were executed long after the birth of the couple's children. The contracts served a purely economic purpose and dealt with the division of property, especially in the eventuality of a man forsaking his wife to marry another. The contracts were often drawn up to declare children as the father's heirs.

Divorce: While the concept of marriage was substantially different from what is commonly understood today, divorce was frequently practiced and did approximate the general meaning of the modern term. A man and a woman who cohabitated sometimes went their separate ways, usually as a result of the woman's infidelity or her barrenness. In addition, women were able to initiate divorce in later periods, usually in response to a man's infidelity. There was no legal or religious objection to divorce, although sometimes the dissolution of marriage was approved by the court. Remarriage was possible for both partners with no stigma attached. Polygamy was possible, but most Egyptians appear to have been monogamous due to economic limitations. Women accepted the practice of polygamy due to the low life expectancy of the times and the high probability of dying in childbirth. Members of the upper classes appear to have practiced polygamy as a status symbol, adding more wives as they rose up the bureaucratic ladder of their chosen careers. There is evidence of males having sexual relationships with female servants or socially inferior women within their households. When these relationships produced children they were not stigmatized as being illegitimate and were often featured with their parents on monuments. Yet it remains unknown whether these children inherited parts of the father's wealth or special arrangements were made to protect their interests after his death.

Adultery: Charges of adultery were usually leveled at married women, not men. Despite the absence of a legal or religious foundation for marriage, social mores dictated the faithfulness of the woman who set up a household with a man. Egyptian society looked critically at men consorting with married women, but a married woman who was caught cheating on her husband suffered serious reprisals. In some recorded cases, a man killed his adulterous wife and threw her body to the dogs, and in another a priest killed both the woman and her lover. The most common response was usually divorce, and in some marriage contracts of the late period, a woman would be threatened with the loss of financial rights.

Literacy: Although women ran the household, they were not banned from performing outside duties. Women of the upper class were involved in running sacred temples and performed funereal duties. However, bureaucracy was not open to them and was confined exclusively to males and their sons. Since a position on the bureaucratic ladder required literacy, there was no urgency to allowing women to be literate. Only boys received an education and were formally trained to be scribes. Many scenes on monuments depict male scribes at work, but a comparable scene of a female scribe is nonexistent. Women were prohibited by their lack of literacy from assuming official government positions. In some elite families, daughters were taught by literate mothers and used their skills in letter writing, but there is no surviving evidence of literary pieces penned by women.

Women's Roles outside the Family: These pertain to female servants, not to elite women. Women were employed as wet-nurses, which was a common occupation, in addition to working in milling, baking, as spinners and weavers of textiles, and in music and dancing. Other less common occupations included food preparation, the brewing of beer, manufacturing crafts, and as hired agricultural labor. A few women during the Old to Middle Kingdoms worked in administrative positions, as aides to royal women rather than as members of the official bureaucracy. Some women worked as female hairdressers in rich households. A few female physicians were known to be attached to the service of queens, but most doctors were males. Women were employed as musical performers and dancers who performed in temples and royal households. At first, most of the leaders of musical troupes appear to have been female, but this changed toward the Middle Kingdom, when men appear to have monopolized these positions of authority as well as those of individual performers. Mixed groups of men and women were later shown on monuments performing in the same troupes. Sailors on boats who frequently traveled the Nile were always men; women were not barred from the widely used means of travel but were never crew members.

Corvée or State Labor: In the highly centralized Egyptian state throughout history, every Egyptian was expected to perform free labor on public projects for a set period of time. It was believed that this form of labor continued in the afterworld. Evidence from state fields indicates men and women were liable to render this service, but whether women actually participated is not clear. Defectors who attempted to avoid this labor were punished by having their families, both male and female, incarcerated or forced to work in their place.

Land Ownership: Women were not prevented from owning land, and they often farmed it as a means of earning an income or used it as an investment. Whether women actually cultivated the land or not remains unclear, because evidence from papyrus documents refers to them simply as "citizeness." It is very clear that a certain division of labor prevailed and was only circumvented in cases of extreme economic necessity.

Inheritance: Women inherited property throughout the history of ancient Egypt. All children, irrespective of gender, shared the inheritance from their parents, with the exception of the father's office, which went to the oldest son. In most cases, property was divided without any disputes, and it was only in cases where the property was accumulated through several marriages that the writing and witnessing of a will was necessary.

Women's Burial Customs: There is very little surviving evidence of burial customs of ordinary Egyptians, but evidence for the burial of the scribal elite suggests that women were expected to enjoy the afterlife as much as men. In some instances, such as the digging of a shaft where the deceased and all of his funerary equipment were buried, the higher ranks of bureaucracy built an adjoining chapel for themselves and their families. These chapels formed the entrance to the shaft and had walls decorated with various scenes of the person's family life. Statues of the deceased were also placed there. However, women rarely owned similar chapels, one explanation being that these chapels were a privilege of scribes, and women were not part of this profession. Neither were women in most cases wealthy enough to afford such buildings. But, beginning with the Old Kingdom, women received the same funerary treatment as men and were mummified according to the latest techniques used for men. Starting from the New Kingdom, when the custom of placing a copy of the *Book of the Dead* in the tomb in order to navigate the dangers of the underworld began, women shared in this practice. The books were written differently for women, without mentioning or portraying a husband, whereas a deceased male's books depicted his wives fully.

ANJUMAN-I NISVANI YAHUDI. Initially known as Majlis-I Zanha or women's assembly, this was the oldest Persian-Jewish organization in modern Iran. The organization was founded in the early 1920s in Hamadan by Arus Khanum. It offered women classes in health care, religion, and modern housekeeping. Eventually, it joined a larger organization, known as Sazman-I Banuvan-I Yahud-I Iran (The Society of Iranian Jewish Women in Iran). Hamadan was also the location of this larger effort, attracting such organizations due to the presence of the shrine of Queen Esther nearby.

ARAB FEMINIST UNION (AFU). Founded by **Huda Shaarawi** in Cairo in 1945, this organization was the first to espouse the ideals of Arab nationalism as an integral part of the achievement of women's rights. After the founding of the **Egyptian Feminist Union (EFU)** in 1923, Shaarawi's goal was to establish links between Egyptian and international feminism. She succeeded in affiliating the EFU with the International Alliance of Women (IAW), but the relationship foundered over the refusal of the latter to support Palestinian women in their struggle against Zionism. This set the stage for the launching of an all-Arab effort to create a pan-Arab feminist organization, culminating in establishing the All-Arab Federation of Women in 1944. Created two years before the emergence of the Arab League of States, this organization became a model for what Arab unification efforts can accomplish. Shaarawi then led a delegation of Egyptian women on a tour of Syria, Lebanon, Palestine, and Transjordan (later the Hashemite Kingdom of Jordan) to create a federation of Arab feminist unions. By late 1944, the Arab Feminist Conference was convened in Cairo, and by 1945, the AFU was established. Adopting an ambitious agenda of promoting Arab nationalist causes, particularly the rights of Palestinian Arabs, the AFU also echoed the demands of the EFU of rejecting the patriarchal system and calling for reforming the Islamic personal status laws. The AFU survived the demise of the EFU, which was finally closed in 1956, but its headquarters were relocated to Beirut. *See also* NON-GOVERNMENTAL ORGANIZATIONS (NGOs).

ARAB INTERNATIONAL WOMEN'S FORUM (AIWF). This is an organization founded in London in 2001 to link together Arab women in the Middle East, Europe, and the United States. Its current membership is spread over 45 countries. The nonprofit group sponsors global conferences and programs to exchange information and provide training for women in the Arab world. The AIWF collaborates with leading Arab and international economic and political institutions and groups such as the Foreign and Commonwealth Office in Great Britain, the League of Arab States, the European Commission, the European Parliament, the World Bank, the City of London Corporation, and Dubai International Financial Center. The AIWF works for the enhancement of Arab women's leadership roles and improving their economic well-being. *See also* NON-GOVERNMENTAL ORGANIZATIONS (NGOs).

ARAB WOMEN'S ASSOCIATION OF PALESTINE (AWAP). This was founded in 1929 in Jerusalem as the first organization bringing Arab women together, following the Wailing Wall riots of the same year. The AWA emerged from the Palestinian Arab Women's Congress, which convened on

29 October 1929, with an ambitious set of goals enunciated in its bylaws. These included improving the social and economic conditions of Arab women in Palestine by providing better educational opportunities for girls and enhancing the status of women. As soon as branches were formed in several cities, the AWA followed a nationalist agenda, staging demonstrations against the British Mandate government and supporting the families of prisoners during the 1936 Arab Revolt. Following the convening of the Eastern Women's Conference in Cairo in 1938, the AWA suffered a major split, resulting in the establishment of the Arab Women's Union. The AWA survived the 1948 Arab–Israeli War, which resulted in the creation of the State of Israel, by maintaining its headquarters in Jordanian Jerusalem (East Jerusalem). Its main goal was to provide charitable assistance to the Palestinian refugees resulting from that war. See also ABD AL-HADI, ISSAM (1928–); ARAB WOMEN'S EXECUTIVE COMMITTEE (AWEC); KHALIL, SAMIHA (1923–1999); NON-GOVERNMENTAL ORGANIZATIONS (NGOs).

ARAB WOMEN'S DEVELOPMENT SOCIETY (AWDS). Founded in 1963 by Nouria al-Saadani, the AWDS is the oldest women's organization in Kuwait. Al-Sadani was a pioneering broadcast journalist who was hired by the Kuwait Broadcasting Station in 1962 and immediately plunged into women's organizational activities. When the AWDS was founded, the only other association was the Women's Cultural and Social Society (WCSS), which focused on charitable projects. The AWDS, by contrast, adopted the goal of modernizing society by improving the status of women and launched a campaign to attain political rights for women in the early 1970s. After several mobilizational women's conferences, the AWDS placed an equal rights bill before the Kuwaiti National Assembly in 1973, provoking some of the most heated debates in the history of that body. AWDS also worked with *Bidoun* women, the status-less Kuwaiti Bedouins, to integrate them into urban society. AWDS created Kuwaiti Women's Day to recognize the achievements of women. It opened the first nursery schools in the country as a service to working women. As part of its efforts to publicize its agenda, AWDS affiliated with the **Arab Feminist Union (AFU)** and organized two conferences, in 1971 and 1977. Both of these debated such issues as the personal status law of Kuwait, **polygamy**, and female suffrage. See also BAYADER AL-SALAM; NON-GOVERNMENTAL ORGANIZATIONS (NGOs); WOMEN'S CULTURAL AND SOCIAL SOCIETY—KUWAIT (WCSS).

ARAB WOMEN'S EXECUTIVE COMMITTEE (AWEC). The Executive was a coordinating committee that sought to organize the women's movement in Palestine during the British Mandate period (1920–1948). Created in Jerusalem in 1929, the committee was made up of wives and relatives of the male nationalist leadership of Arab Palestine. Its officers included **Matiel Moghannam**, Khadija Husseini, Melia Sakakini, and others. After forming the **Arab Women's Association of Palestine (AWAP)** in 1929, its members paid a highly publicized visit to the British High Commissioner and presented him with a set of demands that included the scrapping of the Balfour Declaration. Although it was expected to coordinate the activities of various branches of the Arab Women's Association, it disintegrated in the early 1930s. The Jerusalem branch of the AWAP survived as the strongest branch in Palestine. *See also* NON-GOVERNMENTAL ORGANIZATIONS (NGOs).

ARAB WOMEN'S SOLIDARITY ASSOCIATION (AWSA). This was an organization founded in Cairo in 1982, claiming that the liberation of women was inseparable from the liberation of all Arab people. Although the original membership was only 120, the AWSA presently claims an Arab membership of 3,000 women. The organization is a consultant to the United Nations Economic and Social Council (ECOSAC). The AWSA aims to form a wide network linking Arab women together and works to increase Arab women's presence in the political, economic, and cultural spheres. It also focuses on running income-producing projects benefiting women. *See also* NON-GOVERNMENTAL ORGANIZATIONS (NGOs).

ARAFAT, SABA (?–). Palestinian educator who was born in Nablus, West Bank, to Sheikh Amru Arafat, who was a learned Islamic scholar. After attending the Aishiyah Girls School in Nablus and Schmidt Girls School in Jerusalem, she matriculated in 1940 as one of two women in Palestine who earned a diploma with distinction in teaching the English language. She taught English at al-Aishiyah School from 1941 until 1948, when she was awarded a scholarship to study English at London University, graduating in 1953 with honors. She returned to the West Bank, where she taught at the Teacher's College for Girls in Ramallah (1954–1956), after which she accepted a position as a consultant for the United Nations Educational, Scientific and Cultural Organization (UNESCO) in Libya (1956–1960). She then received a master's degree in education in 1961 from Harvard University. Returning home, she was appointed as a staff member of the education department at the headquarters of the United Nations Relief and Works Agency (UNRWA) in Amman, Jordan. In 1974, she became the director of the West Bank educational programs for all of the Palestinian refugee camps throughout Jordan, which were run by UNRWA. In 1975, she was appointed a member of Bethlehem University's board of trustees. She also served as a member of the Higher Education Council's Executive Committees for all of Jordan. She resides in Amman, Jordan.

ARAZ, NEZIHE (1922–). A Turkish journalist and playwright who received great support for her activities from her family because her father was a prominent parliamentarian, serving in Turkey's second parliament until 1954. Her surrounding cultural environment was very traditional, which inspired several award-winning stories about Anatolian **Sufism**. She wrote a play titled *Afife Jale* in 1988, depicting the life of the first actress to perform on stage in Turkey. Her other stories dealt with the lives of central Anatolian women during World War I. Her *Kadin erenler* was an anthology of the life stories of female mystics throughout Islamic history. She also wrote a screenplay titled *Latife Hanim*, the name of the wife of **Mustafa Kemal Ataturk**, who was divorced only two years after her 1925 marriage to the Turkish leader.

ARWA, SAYYIDA HURRA (1048–1138). An Ismaili queen of the Sulayhid dynasty in Yemen who had a great impact on the development of that country. The rise of this dynasty was the result of the success of Fatimid rulers of Egypt (969–1171), who established the first Shii caliphate of the Ismaili sect as a rival to the Sunni Abbasid caliphate (750–1258) in Baghdad. Ismaili Shiis were known for their tolerance of other religious communities under their rule and for their encouragement of education for both men and women. From the period of al-Muizz li-Din Allah (953–975), who established Fatimid rule over Egypt and throughout this dynasty, women could avail themselves of education and formal instruction in the Ismaili religious doctrine via *majalis al-hikma* (councils of wisdom). Some of these teaching sessions were held at the great seminary built by the Fatimids in Cairo, **al-Azhar**. The Ismailis sent learned propagators of their sect to various corners of the Muslim world, Yemen being among them. By 883, the Ismaili doctrine was openly taught in Yemen, and by 906, much of that country was under their control. In 1063, an Ismaili preacher and advocate, Ali ben Muhammad al-Sulayhid, spread his control over all of that country, making it a tributary of the Fatimids in Egypt. Ali's wife, Asma, took charge of the education of her daughter-in-law, Sayyida Hurra, who was married to Ali's son, Ahmed al-Mukarram (d. 1084) in 1066. Sayyida Hurra became a political adviser to her husband. Her original name was Arwa, but she carried the title of Sayyida Hurra (noble lady). Her husband retired from ruling due to facial paralysis, an affliction he suffered as a result of a war injury.

By that time, Arwa had consolidated rule in her own hands and had her name called out immediately after that of the Fatimid caliph, al-Mustansir, in the Friday sermon at the mosque. She succeeded in relocating the capital from Sanaa to Dhu Jibla, where she built a great palace. Al-Mustansir appointed her as a great authority (*hujja*) of Ismaili teaching over all of Yemen, the first instance of bestowing such a title on a woman. She took over the reins of government in the kingdom officially in 1084, upon her husband's death. The Fatimid caliphate also appointed her as an official advocate of Ismaili doctrine over western India, leading to the rise of a new Ismaili community in Gujarat, which came to be known as the Bohra Ismailis. Later in her rule she faced a severe challenge from another Shii faction, the Zaydi Imams of Yemen. She died in 1138 after severing her relations with Cairo and supporting another religious faction. The Sulayhid dynasty suffered a great decline after her death. Today, there is a women's university named after her in Yemen.

ASHRAWI, HANAN MIKHAIL (1946–). A Palestinian professor of English and political advocate for Palestinian national goals who was born in Ramallah. She received her higher education at the American University of Beirut (AUB), earning a master's degree in 1973. She taught at Birzeit University, West Bank, where she rose to the position of department chair. In 1981, she earned a PhD in medieval and comparative literature from the University of Virginia. She became nationally prominent when she was selected as a member of the Palestinian delegation to the Madrid Peace Conference and later to the Washington Talks in 1991. During the first legislative elections of the Palestine National Authority (PNA) in 1996, she was elected as a deputy from East Jerusalem. She served from 1996 until 1998 as the minister of education in the government of the PNA, a position she later relinquished in protest against rampant corruption. She was appointed in 2001–2002 as the spokesperson of the League of Arab States on Palestinian and Arab issues.

Ashrawi remained on the faculty of Birzeit University until 1995, but in 1998 she created the Palestinian Initiative for the Promotion of Global Dialogue and Democracy (MIFTAH), a **non-governmental organization (NGO)** of which she is the secretary general. In 2003, she received the Sydney Peace Prize. She is a member of several international boards and organizations, such as the Independent International Commission on Kosovo, the American Council on Foreign Relations, World Bank Middle East and North Africa Region (MENA), United Nations Research Institute for Social Development (UNRISD), and Board of Trustees of the Carter Center, Atlanta, Georgia. She shared the United Nations Educational, Scientific and Cultural Organization's (UNESCO) Mahatma Gandhi Medal with a member of the Israeli Knesset, Zahava Gal-On, in 2005. She is a member of the Third Way, a political faction founded by PNA premier Salam Fayyad, as well as the Palestine Liberation Organization (PLO) Executive Committee since 2009. Her publications include *The Modern Palestinian Short Story, An Introduction to Practical Criticism, Contemporary Palestinian Literature under Occupation*, and *This Side of Peace: A Personal Account*.

ASHUR, RADWA (1946–). She is an Egyptian novelist, short-story writer, professor of English literature, and literary critic. She received a master's degree in English literature from Cairo University in 1972, and a PhD in African American literature from the University of Massachusetts–Amherst in 1975. Ashur holds the position of department chair of English at Cairo's Ayn Shams University and is a member of the Egyptian Higher Council of Culture, as well as the Arab Organization for Human Rights. Her literary works include *Gibran and Blake: A Comparative Study* (1978), *The Novel in West Africa* (1980), *I Saw the Palm Trees* (1989), *The Reports of Mrs. R.* (2001), and *Khadija and Sawsan* (1989). Ashur's most acclaimed work, however, is a two-volume description of the lives of Spanish Muslims after the fall of Granada in 1492. Titled *Gharnata (Granada)* (1994) and *Maryama and al-Rahil (The Exodus)* (1995), the stories provide rich historical material on the Spanish Inquisition and an imagined portrayal of what might have been cases of gender and generational conflict. The work won first prize in the First Arab Women Writers Book Fair in 1995. Her latest work, *A Slice of Europe*, appeared in 2003. Her short-story collection, *My Grandmother's Cactus*, was translated into English.

ASMAHAN (1912–1944). Also known as Amal al-Atrash, she was a renowned singer and actor in Egyptian movies. Born to a princely Druze family in Syria, she left for Egypt in 1925 in the company of her mother and two brothers to escape French attacks on their ancestral home during the Druze Rebellion. Her younger brother, Farid al-Atrash, emerged as a talented singer and composer, but her older brother Fuad disapproved of her musical career to the end of her life. Her mentor, Egyptian composer Daoud Husni, suggested that she use the stage name Asmahan at the beginning of her career in 1930. She interrupted her career to marry her cousin, Prince Hassan al-Atrash, in 1933, but the marriage ended in 1939. Her career was furthered by the superb quality of her voice and her excellent musical training. She quickly rose to be one of the leading Arab female singers of the 1930s. A second marriage, to movie director Ahmad Badr Khan in 1940, launched her movie career, and she became a rival of the renowned singer **Umm Kulthum**. In 1942, she married another movie mogul, Ahmad Salim, who was the director of the film company Studio Misr. She appeared in two musical films, *Victory of Youth* and *Love and Vengeance*. She also scored a great success with the commercial recordings of her songs. Her musical career was affected by some of her sensational and public affairs with prominent Egyptians, such as journalist Muhammad al-Tabii (1896–1976), economist and founder of Bank Misr **Talaat Harb**, and Ahmad Hasanayn, an adviser to King Farouq (r. 1936–1952). Rumored to be a British secret agent, she died as a result of a mysterious car accident on one of Alexandria's highways.

ATATURK, MUSTAFA KEMAL (1881–1938). Turkey's national hero and the founder of the Turkish modern state, born Mustafa Kemal. He was given the title "Ataturk" (Father of the Turks) by the Turkish parliament in gratitude for his military success in eliminating the threat of invasion to the homeland during World War I. He was born in Salonika (now Thesalonika, Greece) to a middle-class family. His mother, Zubeyda Hanim, was an observant Muslim, while his father, Ali Reza Bey, was an employee of the customs office. Ataturk was raised mostly by his mother due to his father's early death. As a student at a local military secondary school, he excelled in mathematics, graduating from the War Academy in 1905 with the rank of staff captain. While serving in Macedonia, he came under the influence of the Young Turks, a new nationalist and reformist movement.

He proved to be an exceptional military officer during World War I, earning accolades during the Dardanelles campaign, which culminated in the battle of Gallipoli in 1916. This stopped the Allied attempt to reach Constantinople. He also managed to take his campaign of military resistance to the Anatolian heartland, thereby refusing to accept the Treaty of Mudros of 1918 and preventing Turkey's partition. His achievement sprang from the ability to bring together various regional military organizations and mold them into a new national army. By 1920, he had created the nation's first post-Ottoman national assembly in the new capital, Ankara, which proclaimed him the country's first president. The second national assembly, which was controlled by the Republican People's Party (RPP), abolished the remaining vestiges of Ottoman rule by eliminating the caliphate. The Islamic **Sharia** from which all Ottoman laws derived was also abolished.

Ataturk's efforts to transform Turkey into a modern secular state succeeded in replacing the Islamic calendar with the Gregorian calendar and forbidding the fez headgear for males. He strongly discouraged women from wearing the **veil**, a point he reinforced publicly when his wife, Latife Hanim, appeared unveiled during their 1923 marriage ceremony (although he divorced her two years later). He popularized Western-style balls, where he used to accompany his wife to dancing events. His interest in reshaping Turkish culture led to the disbanding of the Sufi orders and the adoption of the Swiss Civil Code in 1926 in place of the Sharia. The new code of law eliminated abuses of the Islamic legal system long decried by the educated Ottoman elite. These included **polygamy**, summary **divorce**, and the inheritance system, which favored sons over daughters. To enforce his preference for a Western social system, he abolished the Arabic script and replaced it in 1928 with the Latin script. In 1934, Turkish women were enfranchised, becoming the first to enjoy political rights in the entire Muslim world. Many anecdotes illustrating his commitment to the liberation of women survive, including ordering Turkish opera composers to feature at least one female character in their work in order to instill respect for women in the national psyche. See also ANATOLIAN WOMEN'S ASSOCIATION FOR PATRIOTIC DEFENSE (AWAPD); CILLER, TANSU PENBE (1946–); WOMEN IN THE TURKISH MILITARY.

ATTAR, NAJAH (1933–). Syrian official and member of the Baath governments of Hafiz and Bashar Assad, who was born in Damascus. Her father was a leader of the Syrian uprising of 1925–1927. She completed her studies in Arabic literature at the University of Damascus in 1954 and earned a PhD from the University of Edinburgh, Scotland, in 1970. She taught school in Damascus until she was appointed director of the literature translation program at the Ministry of Culture. In 1976, she was chosen by President Hafiz Assad (r. 1969–2000) to be minister of culture in the cabinet of Prime Minister Abd al-Rahman Khlayfawi, the first woman in Syria to occupy this post. The appointment came as a surprise, because her brother, Issam al-Attar, was the exiled leader of the Syrian Muslim Brotherhood organization and was an enemy of the Baathist regime. She served briefly as a spokesperson for the Syrian government in the early 1980s when the country was confronted by the Lebanese Civil War and the Muslim Brotherhood revolt simultaneously.

During al-Attar's 24-year tenure as minister of culture, she sponsored many exhibitions, theatrical performances, and Western classical musical concerts by Syrian composer Sulhi al-Wadi. She was also credited with supporting the creation of the National Syrian Symphony Orchestra and the Syrian Opera House. She was appointed vice president of Syria in 2006, again scoring another advancement for women in that country. Not only was she the first woman to be named to this position by President Basher Assad, but she was also the only Sunni to be so elevated by the Alawite-dominated government. Her reputation as an effective official was already established due to her performance in 2002 as director of the Center for the Dialogue of Civilizations, a research institute created to dispel any intimation of complicity in the September 11, 2001, attacks on the United States. She holds two important educational positions, as a member on the board of Kalamoun University, the country's oldest private university, and as the president of the Syrian Virtual University. In recognition of her international work, Attar was awarded a medal of honor in 1983 by President François Mitterrand of France (r. 1981–1995). See also SHAABAN, BOUTHAINA (1953–).

ATTIYA, FARIDA. A Lebanese novelist, short-story writer, and translator who was born in Tripoli, Lebanon. She studied at Beirut's American School. Her works include *The Joy of Drugs for the Benefit of Botany* (1893) and *The Green Garden in Bombay's Final Days* (1899). Her historical novel, *Between Two Thrones*, published in 1912, described in careful detail the condition of the Arab provinces under Ottoman rule leading up to the Armenian massacres in Anatolia. Among her surprising findings was a letter by **Sheikh al-Azhar**, in Cairo, Salim al-Bishri, sent to Anatolia's Muslim population, in which he condemned the Armenian massacres.

AWAD, JOCELYNE (1949–). A Lebanese journalist and novelist who wrote mostly in French. She was born in Beirut, where she received a BA in literature. Her first novel was *Carre four des prophets* (1994). Her other novel, *Khamsin (Scorching Wind)*, was awarded the France-Lebanon Prize and the Prix Richelieu Senghor in 2004. She has also been the editor of *Mondanite* magazine.

AWADHI, BADRIYA AL- (1943–). She is a Kuwaiti lawyer, author, and defender of women's rights. She completed her law studies at Cairo University in 1968 and obtained a PhD in public international law from London University's College of Law in 1975. Between 1979 and 1982, al-Awadhi was the first woman to serve as the dean of the faculty of law and **Sharia** studies at the University of Kuwait. She was an adviser to the International Labour Organization (ILO) from 1983 to 1986. An outspoken publicist for women's rights, in 1992, she was the first female to address the Kuwaiti parliament on this issue. Beginning in 2003, she became the director of the Arab Regional Center for Environmental Law while running her own law practice in Kuwait City. She has an extensive writing record on matters concerning personal status law and environmental issues. She was the recipient of the Zayed International Prize for the Environment in 2004.

AYOUB, SAMIHA (1932–). Egyptian theater, movie, and television actor who is considered the Arab theater's leading lady. She was born in Cairo to a conservative family of modest means who disapproved of her interest in an acting career early in life. She first appeared on the stage at age 14 and studied at the Higher Institute of the Theatre (Maahad al-masrah al-Arabi) in the 1950s. She became director of the Modern Theatre in 1973 but spent much of her career with the National Theatre.

She traveled with the National Theatre's troupe to various parts of the world, performing at such venues as the Opéra Comique in Paris, where she played the leading female role in *Isis and Phaedra*. Her proudest moment, as she recalled in an interview, was when she performed in *The Flies (Les mouches*) with the author, Jean-Paul Sartre, and Simone de Beauvoir in the audience. She starred in many movies, such as *A Man and Two Women*, *Do Not Switch Off the Sun*, and *The Dawn of Islam*, but has not appeared in any movies since 1971. Her theater performance in classical European plays such as *The Caucasian Chalk Circle* and *The Good Person of Szechwan* by Berthold Brecht, however, did not dampen her enthusiasm for the television screen. President Nasser awarded her the State Merit Award in 1964, and she was also honored by the Kuwaiti government. She was married five times, her first husband being Egyptian movie star Muhsin Serhan.

AZHAR, AL-. The oldest seminary in the Islamic world, founded by Fatimid military leader Jawhar al-Siqilli in 969/970. The university, which was devoted originally to such Quranic studies as exegesis and jurisprudence, as well as the study of Arabic grammar, rhetoric, and science, was built shortly after the founding of Cairo (originally al-Fustat). It was named after Fatima al-Zahraa (the resplendent one), Muhammad's daughter and the saintly ancestor of the Shii Fatimid dynasty. When Egypt was restored to Sunni rule in 1171, al-Azhar suffered neglect. The Ottomans revived it as the pivotal center of Islamic learning and Arabic studies in 1517, and it emerged as the result of its revival as the main center of Arab culture in the region. Several scholars attempted to reform its curriculum in the 19th century, but only **Muhammad Abduh** finally succeeded in introducing a formal curriculum, annual exams, and modern areas of study. The greatest change introduced on this traditional institution was under president Jamal Abd al-Nasser (r. 1954–1970), who introduced the study of engineering, medicine, and modern languages in 1961. He also created special colleges for women, who were first admitted in 1962 to all of the faculties. Their numbers increased to 533 in 1965 and to 1,812 in 1969. Nasser's greatest success, however, was in securing the consent of al-Azhar's religious scholars for his state-funded **family-planning** program. Al-Azhar has turned into a center of Sunni Islam and is in the habit of issuing major *fatwas*, or religious legal opinions, on women's issues, which are received with great interest throughout the Arab world. These *fatwas*, however, are not binding. *See also* SHARIA.

AZZAM, SAMIRA (1927–1967). A Palestinian editor and fiction writer who was originally from the city of Jaffa, Palestine. She sought a literary career in Beirut, where she lived permanently as of the 1950s. She rose to the rank of editor-in-chief of a publishing company named Franklin House, which specialized in translations of American works of fiction. Azzam wrote two collections of short stories, *Time and Humanity* (1950s) and *The Feats from the Western Window* (published posthumously in 1971). She died unexpectedly as a result of a heart attack upon hearing news of the Israeli takeover of Jerusalem in June 1967. *See also* GENERAL UNION OF PALESTINIAN WOMEN (GUPW).

B

BAALBAKI, LAYLA (1936–). A Lebanese journalist, fiction writer, and administrator. Her father, Ali al-Hajj Baalbaki, was a poet who at one time was considered an ally of the French authorities in Lebanon. Born in the conservative southern region of the country, she attended St. Joseph University in Beirut and later worked as a secretary of the Lebanese parliament. Her journalistic career extended to several Lebanese papers and to the Arab press in London, where she moved in 1975 following the outbreak of the Lebanese Civil War.

Baalbaki is best known for her daring fiction, such as her first novel, *I Live* (*Ana ahya*) (1958), which was serialized in *Al-Usbuu al-Arabi*, a widely circulated journal. She continued to produce rebellious stories with daring themes despite popular outrage and negative reception of her work. Her two novels *The Dwarf Gods* (1960) and *A Spaceship of Tenderness to the Moon* (1964) were viewed as offensive to the public sensibilities and morality. All of her fiction described women's life experiences through the use of the first person singular, a novelty in Arabic literature, where female characters rarely express their feelings directly.

BADER, LIYANA (1950–). A Palestinian journalist, novelist, and political activist who was born in Jerusalem but grew up in Jericho when both cities were under Jordanian rule. She received a bachelor's degree in philosophy and psychology from Beirut's Arab University, but her studies were interrupted by the Lebanese Civil War of 1974–1989. She was actively engaged in volunteer services directed by Palestinian women's organizations in Lebanon's refugee camps. She also served as the editor of *al-Hurriya*, the official publication of the Democratic Front for the Liberation of Palestine (DFLP), an affiliate of the Palestine Liberation Organization (PLO). She followed the PLO's families as they were forced to exit Lebanon, making her residence in Amman, Damascus, and eventually Tunis. She returned to the Palestinian territories when the PLO was allowed to set up an administration first in Gaza, then in Ramallah. She was assigned a supervisory position over the

Palestine National Authority's (PNA) cinema department. She was also made editor of the major publication of the Palestinian Ministry of Culture, known as *Cultural Notebooks*.

BADRAN, REEM (1963–). A Jordanian business executive and a daughter of former Jordanian prime minister Mudhar Badran, who studied business administration and English literature in Jordan. She earned an MA in international relations and Middle East studies from a university in the United States. After serving a long term as a member of the Jordan Investment Board, where she participated in negotiating a free trade agreement with the United States, she became the chief executive officer of Kuwaiti Jordanian Holding Company in 2005. This corporation worked on developing tourism sites in the Dead Sea area and expanding phosphate mining. She also co-founded the Jordanian branch of the International Women's Forum (IWF).

BAHAI WOMEN. Bahaism is a 19th-century religious movement that broke away from Shii Islam in Iran. The Bahai faith developed out of Shiism's messianic theology in the same manner in which Christianity grew out of similar inclinations within Judaism. To signify his preparation for a new faith, Bahai founder Bahaullah took the title of Bab, or doorway. From its inception, Bahaism emphasized the equality of men and women. Gender equality extended beyond the spiritual sphere, calling for equal educational opportunities, women's eligibility for religious office, and women's absolute equality in the political realm. Women were welcomed to the top administrative positions within the Bahai structure, today constituting around one-third of the total leadership. The only administrative body from which they were barred was the universal House of Justice, which is the highest Bahai committee.

After Sayyid Ali Muhammad al-Bab declared himself in 1844 to be the Qaim, the Shii's expected messianic figure, a female follower, Fatimeh Bigum Baranghani, known as Tahirah **Qurrat al-Ayn**, emerged as one of his main followers. The Babi movement was transformed into the Bahai faith when Bahaullah took over the leadership of the movement in 1863. Tahirah became a potent and effective role model for all Bahai women as a result of her devotion and sacrifice for the new faith. She emerged as a true leader of the movement, taking a hard line and urging a complete break with Islam. Her success in inducting many women into the Babi movement, as well as her eventual death by strangulation at the hands of government agents, established her special place within the new faith.

Bahai sacred law is embodied in Bahaullah's *Kitab al-Aqdas* (*The Sacred Book*) which, not unlike the Quran, was written in Arabic, originally tolerated **polygamy** but limited it to two wives. Abdul-Baha, Bahaullah's successor, ruled in favor of monogamy, saying that the required conditions of equity could not be met by allowing multiple marriages. The Bahai Guardian who led the movement from 1921 to 1957, Shoghi Effendi, emphasized that all the laws in *Kitab al-Aqdas* were equally applicable to both genders, unless specifically stated otherwise. The Bahai holy book also made no reference to the idea of ritual uncleanliness as it applied to females, allowing women to fast and to pray during their menstrual cycles if they chose to do so. Both men and women were expected to maintain standards of chastity, and both adulterers and adulteresses were subject to the same fine. Bahaullah's original holy text, being delivered in Arabic, duplicated the Quranic method of referring to God in masculine terms, but in the later Persian version the concept of God was not gender specific.

BAKER, SALWA (1949–). An Egyptian fiction writer of short stories who was born in Cairo, her literary output began to receive great attention in the 1970s. She is considered to be an original and creative writer who often treats serious themes with comic flair. She established her literary reputation with a short-story collection titled *Zinat in the President's Funeral*, written in 1986. This was followed by additional short-story collections and novels that were translated into English by Denys Johnson-Davies, the most eminent translator from Arabic into English in the United States. Her most famous novel, which was translated into several languages and made into a movie, appeared in 1991 under the title *The Golden Chariot Does Not Rise to the Sky*.

BAKKAR, JALILAH (1952–). A Tunisian playwright and actress who is known for her artistic, social, and political criticism. She attended the École Normale Supérieur in Paris, where she studied French literature. She worked for a while with Théâtre du Sud de Gafsa in Tunisia before cofounding with her husband, Fadhel Jaibi, the first indigenous Tunisian theater, Nouveau Théâtre de Tunis, in 1975. She starred in the nascent movies of that country, including *Sacred Night*. The movie was based on Taher Ben Jelloun's (1944–) novel *Searching for Aida*, which follows the wanderings of a Palestinian woman.

BANNUNA, KHANNATHA (1940–). A Moroccan writer of short stories whose literary output consisted of short-story collections, which began to appear in the 1960s. Most of these were based on her experiences as a university student, giving voice to Moroccans in a state of crisis, particularly female intellectuals. She is interested in the Palestinian cause as a symptom of total disintegration and its impact on the minds of restless writers. Her works include *Down with Silence* (1965), *Fire and Choice* (1968), *The Picture and the Sound* (1975), and *The Storm* (1975). Her full-length novel, *Anger and the Future*, appeared in 1981.

BARAKAT, HODA (1952–). A Lebanese novelist, short-story writer, and essayist who was born in Beirut, where she received a degree in French literature from the Lebanese University in 1974. She began preparing for a PhD in 1975 while in Paris but returned to Lebanon after the outbreak of the civil war (1974–1989). She launched her journalism career shortly thereafter, working also as a translator and fiction writer. Her short-story collection *Women Visitors* appeared in 1985. She was involved in publishing a women's magazine, *Shehrezad*, and produced a novel, *The Stone of Laughter*, which appeared while the civil war raged on, earning her the Naqid Prize (The Critic's Prize). The novel, her first, was unusual because it presented a gay man as the hero. She produced another novel in 1993, *Ahl al-hawa* (*People of Love*). Her *The Tiller of Waters* won the Naguib Mahfouz medal for literature in 2000. French President Jacques Chirac awarded her the National Order of Merit in 2008. She writes mostly in Arabic and has been living in Paris since 1989, where she works for an Arab French radio station.

BARBARI, YUSRA (1923–). A Palestinian educator and social and political activist who was born in Gaza, Palestine, she completed her high school education at Schmidt Girls School in Jerusalem. She received an MA from the Faculty of Arts at Cairo University. She served as the head of the Open University for Women in the Gaza Strip and founded the Palestinian Women's Union (PWU) of Gaza in 1964. Barbari was selected as a member of the official Palestinian delegation to the United Nations General Assembly and has been a member of the Palestine National Council (PNC), the Palestinian parliament in exile, since 1964. She also headed important social welfare organizations in Gaza, such as the National Society of the Disabled. *See also* ABD AL-HADI, ISSAM (1928–); GENERAL UNION OF PALESTINIAN WOMEN (GUPW); HAMAS.

BARGHOUTI, SIHAM (1948–). A Palestinian feminist and political leader who cofounded the Palestinian Women's Work Committee (PWWC) in 1978. She was attending university in Egypt and majoring in mathematics when the War of 1967 broke out in June. This delayed her return to the West Bank until 1971, because she missed the 1967 Israeli census. Her role in founding the PWWC, which mobilized Palestinian women against the Israeli occupation regime, resulted in her being sentenced to town arrest. She was briefly jailed for noncompliance with the terms of this arrest. *See also* WOMEN'S WORK COMMITTEES (WWC).

BARON, DVORA (1887–1956). An Israeli short-story writer whose work highlighted the suffering of Jewish women brought up in a strict religious culture. She was born in Lithuania and moved to Palestine in 1911. She received her early education from her father, a rabbi, who taught Hebrew and provided religious instruction for aspiring students. Unlike most Jews of European background, who knew only Yiddish, she was able to publish short stories in Hebrew beginning at the age of 16. She became the literary editor of a major publication, but her stories focused mainly on her early life as a member of a small European community in the country. Her first volume of short stories, titled *Sippurim*, appeared in 1927 and was awarded the Bialik Prize in 1934. Another collection of short stories, published in 1943, was devoted to her life in Egypt during World War I.

BAYADER AL-SALAM. The earliest religious organization for women in Kuwait, founded in 1981 by a Syrian woman taking the title of *daiya* (religious advocate). Her name was not revealed, although it was estimated that she was around 30 years of age and had studied Islamic jurisprudence in Damascus. The main backer of this organization, the name of which translates as "Threshing Floor of Peace," was Yusef al-Rifai, a Kuwaiti merchant known for his opposition to women's equality and rights. His efforts in his capacity as a member of Kuwait's parliament in the 1970s led to the defeat of the Equal Rights Bill. His main argument against the draft law was that acceding to women's demands, such as the elimination of **polygamy**, would lead to an upsurge in adultery and diminishing **marriage** opportunities for women.

Al-Bayader was entrusted to the Syrian female preacher as a way of educating a new generation of women in traditional Islamic family values. The organization engaged in studying the Quran and impressing on its members the need to integrate Islamic practices into their daily lives. Since Kuwaiti law mandated that all civic organizations must have a written constitution or a set of bylaws and an elected board of native-born Kuwaitis, the leadership of Bayader fell to Kuwaiti members. Daughters of wealthy merchant families were among the earliest elected presidents, such as Adela al-Othman, who became the first to occupy this office. Bayader came to resemble a Sufi order, which enforced discipline on its members and a dress uniform indicative of spiritual rank. Bayader recruited mainly among high school and university students, who were required to demonstrate strength of faith before being formally inducted into the organization. Bayader was able to affiliate with several clubs and add members beyond its original size of 100 adherents.

Although it shunned politics and concentrated on Islamic self-development, al-Bayader aroused the wrath of mainstream Islamic groups and secular associates. Some of these took an interest in organizing women followers to counter the influence of Bayader, such as the Islamic Brotherhood in Kuwait, which formed its own women's committee in 1983. Bayader faced a serious challenge from female supporters of secular Arab nationalist groups, such as al-Talia (The Vanguard), which sued it for holding unauthorized public gatherings within the vicinity of government offices. Bayader paid a small fine but survived similar challenges by limiting itself to a strict religious program of collecting *zakat* (religious alms) for the benefit of needy members. *See also* SHARIA.

BAYDAS, MAYADA (1965–). A Lebanese investment banker of Palestinian origin who cofounded and directed the Development Innovations Group (DIG), which provides microfinance loans to individual women. She studied economics in Lebanon and in the United States, serving a long tenure as director of AMEEN, a Lebanese microfinance bank. By creating DIG in 2005 with an annual budget of US $7 million, she was able to expand operations into other countries such as Palestine, Iraq, and Afghanistan. She also founded a company in India specializing in extending credit to the poor.

BAYHUM, MUHAMMAD JAMIL. He was the first Muslim writer in Lebanon to call for granting women their rights. After living and traveling in many countries, he authored a book in 1921 titled *Woman in History and Legal Codes*. Although he did not address controversial issues of his time, like women's **veiling** and political rights, the book was a welcome contribution to the struggle of women in many parts of the world, including East Asia. He authored two additional books, the last being *Young Women of the East in Western Culture* (1952).

BAZ, JURJU NIQULA (1881–1959). He was an early and prolific Lebanese writer on Arab women's issues, leading others to call him "the champion of women" and "the mobile feminist encyclopedia." His magazine, *al-Hassnaa* (*Fair Lady*), called for granting women their rights, especially the right to **education**. It appeared between 1909 and 1912 and established his reputation as an authority on women's lives. He also wrote several biographies of women who were his contemporaries, such as Miriam Jahshan, May Ajami, Mary Yanni, Nazik al-Abid, and Asma Abu al-Luma. In a book titled *Laurels Wreath on Woman's Head* (1927), he wrote about outstanding women in the fields of science, religion, journalism, nursing, and philanthropy. His book *On Women* was devoted to the work of notable Arab women from Lebanon, Syria, and Egypt who figured prominently in the Arab renaissance movement or *al-nahdha*.

BEHBEHANI, SIMIN (1927–). An Iranian poet and feminist who was born to parents devoted to writing and literary activities. Her real name was Simin Khalili, and her father, Abbas Khalili, was an editor of *Eghdam* (*Action*) newspaper, while her mother, Fakhr Azami Arghoon (1898–1966), was a poet in her own right and a teacher of French. Simin wrote poetry at an early age, producing mainly verses in the traditional *ghazal* mode with emphasis on wine and love. Her poetry was also political, expressing sorrow for the human losses of the Iran–Iraq War (1980–1989) and pleading for guaranteeing liberty to all people. She was also a strong advocate of the freedom of expression and traveled and lectured widely on these topics. Iranian intellectuals have referred to her as the "lioness of Iran." She served for many years as president of the Writers' Association of Iran, and her work was translated into English by Professor Farsaneh Milani. In 2010, Iranian authorities seized her passport and denied her permission to leave Iran. She received the Freedom of Expression Prize of the Norwegian Authors' Union in 2006 and was nominated for the Nobel Prize for Literature in 1997 and 2006. Among her poetic collections are *The Broken Lute* (1951), *Footprint* (1954), *Chandelier* (1955), *Resurrection* (1971), *Paper Dress* (1992), *A Window of Freedom* (1995), *Collected Poems* (2003), *Maybe It's the Messiah* (2003), and *A Cup of Sin.*

BEHROUZI, MARYAM (?–). She was an Iranian parliamentarian who served as a legislator before and after the Islamic revolution of 1979. Her Islamic activism resulted in imprisonment during the monarchy. She sponsored and won the passage of several parliamentary bills on behalf of women, such as permitting female workers to collect retirement benefits after only 20 years of service. She also succeeded in gaining insurance benefits for women and children in the case of **divorce**. She organized a Muslim cultural and social group for women known as Zaynab's Society, which provides Islamic instruction and exegetic studies of the Quran as well as the study of Arabic. Striving for absolute neutrality in political matters, Zaynab's Society nevertheless, played an important role during the 1997 presidential campaign of conservative speaker of the Majlis Ali Akbar Nateq Nuri. Iranian analysts refer to her along with **Munireh Gorji**, who was the first female to sit in the Assembly of Experts, and **Faezeh Hashemi**, daughter of former president Ali Akbar Hashemi Rafsanjani (r. 1989–1997), as the country's important Islamic feminists. *See also* FEMINIST MOVEMENT IN IRAN.

BEINISH, DORIT (1942–). Israeli jurist who was born Dorit Werba in Tel Aviv. After obtaining a law degree from Hebrew University in Jerusalem, she served as the director of the Department of Constitutional and Administrative Law in the state attorney's office (1976–1982). In 1989, she became

Israel's state attorney, a position she held for seven years. She contributed greatly to maintaining legal restraints on the security agencies such as the army and the police. Beinish was appointed to the Israeli supreme court in 1991, where she succeeded in serving the legal rights of women and children, such as the prohibition of corporal punishment by parents.

BEJERANO, MAYA (1949–). Israeli poet and librarian who is known for her use of unusual imagery to produce precise ideas. She was born in Haifa, Israel, and studied art, literature, and music before embarking on writing poetry. Her books *Ostrich* (1978) and *Song of Birds* (1985) utilize technical images such as computers and spaceships to create vivid pictures of life's journeys and discoveries, a dominant theme in her work. Her poetry, which emphasizes all that is positive about human nature, won her several literary awards, including the Prime Minister's Prize.

BELLY DANCING. An ancient dance performed by women throughout the Middle East. Until the 19th century, this dance form was known as *raqs baladi* (local dancing), or *raqs sharqi* (Oriental dancing). By the 1900s, and due to the influx of foreign visitors and foreign troops into Egypt, Westerners began to label it "belly dancing," which they saw as a cheap form of night-club entertainment. There are definite views about the origins of this dance. Recent anthropological works, such as *Serpent of the Nile* (1989) by Wendy Buonaventura, have suggested that it dates back to the fertility and maternity rites of pharaonic Egypt. Western travelers in the Middle East described this dance as early as 1776, when Jacob Burkhardt (1818–1897) first wrote about it. Lady Mary Wortley Montagu (1689–1763) relayed her impressions of it in 1763, and French dramatist Gustave Flaubert (1821–1880) elaborated on his own personal encounters with belly dancers in 1849. Most of these accounts exaggerated the sexual nuances of the dance. Today, belly dancing is a form of folk entertainment, often performed by young women during festive occasions and family gatherings. The association of the dance with nightclubs was a phenomenon of the early 20th century, when cabarets appeared in Egypt's major cities, such as Cairo and Alexandria. *See also* CARIYOCA, TAHIYYA (1915–1999).

BEN BAZ, ABD AL-AZIZ (1912–1999). Saudi Arabian clerical scholar who served in several high positions of great influence and importance. He was born in Riyadh, Saudi Arabia's capital, and lost his eyesight by the age of 20. Despite his blindness, he became a prominent Islamic scholar and judge, rising in 1975 to the position of chair of the governmental Department of Islamic Research, Guidance and Proselytization, with the rank of minister. He attained the highest religious rank in 1993 when he was named the grand *mufti* of Saudi Arabia and head of its Council of *Ulema* (religious scholars). By sitting at the apex of the country's religious institution, he acquired great authority, entitling him to issue religious opinions, or *fatwas*, on a range of issues touching mostly on the lives of women and other political questions in his home country and throughout the Muslim world. His views were always conservative, providing a strict **Wahhabi** interpretation of Islam. His most notable *fatwa* denied that the earth was round. He consistently defended the legitimacy of the Saudi dynasty while at the same time blocking any efforts to institute Islamic reforms. *See also* SHARIA.

BEN BOUALI, HASSIBA (1938–1957). A prominent figure of the **Algerian Revolution** (1954–1962) who was born in El-Asnam (renamed Chlef) in Algeria. Her family moved to the capital, Algiers, in 1947. She was recruited to work for the revolution while still a student at the University of Algiers and began to participate in large demonstrations in 1956. As the liaison officer for Ali La Pointe, the deputy chief of the Front de Libération Nationale's (FLN) military operations in Algiers, she took part in a number of bombings and military activities for which women were highly suited. Following the Battle of Algiers in 1956–1957, which resulted from a series of bombings by the FLN, she was killed in a French attack on La Pointe's house. Algerians regard her as a leader of the female warriors who fought and contributed to the military efforts of their national struggle. The university in her hometown was later named after her. *See also* BOUHIRED, DJAMILA (1937–).

BEN PORAT, MIRIAM (1918–). An Israeli jurist and administrator who immigrated to Israel with her family in 1931 from her birthplace of Vitebsk, Russia. After finishing her law studies in 1945, she was appointed deputy state's attorney (1950–1958) and became a judge of the district court, Jerusalem (1958–1975). In November 1976, she was selected to serve as acting judge of the Israeli Supreme Court, becoming a permanent judge in 1977. She was also a law professor at Hebrew University (1964–1978). After retiring from the Supreme Court in 1988, she was appointed state controller, a position she held until her retirement from government service in 1998. She left her mark on the state controller's office, transforming it into a vigorous instrument for enforcing democratic ideals in government. In 1991, she was awarded the country's highest honor, the Israel Prize. *See also* ISRAEL, JEWISH WOMEN'S LEGAL STATUS.

BEN ZVI, RAHEL (1886–1979). An Israeli Labor Zionist activist and educator, born Rahel Yanait to a family in the Ukraine. She was active in labor socialist groups during her studies at a Russian high school and at university in that country. Before immigrating to Palestine in 1908, she had already founded the Zionist socialist party, known as Poalei Zion Party of Russia, in 1906. She became the editor of *Achdut*, the main publication of the Poalei Zion Party of Palestine. She founded the Hebrew Gymnasium, an accelerated high school, in Jerusalem, where she taught. She studied agronomy in Nancy, France (1911–1914), and in 1918, she was instrumental in the founding of Great Britain's Jewish Legion. During that same year, she married labor leader and future president of Israel, Yitzhak Ben-Zvi (r. 1952–1963). After the dissolution of Polari Zion in 1919, she organized another party, Ahdut ha-Avoda, which in 1930 became Mapai (Labor Party), Israel's long-ruling party.

Ben-Zvi's activities extended to Israel's defense system when, in 1920, she became one of several heads of the Haganah armed militia group. Her agricultural training served as the basis for developing agricultural projects employing women, such as schools and experimental farms. She represented a group known as Pioneer Women in the United States, focusing on encouraging immigration to Israel. She also worked on creating absorption centers for the new immigrants. When her husband died in office in 1963, she hoped to succeed him as Israel's first female president. Israel's prime minister, David Ben Gurion, who was the real leader of the government, chose Salman Shazar instead as Ben-Zvi's successor. Rahel Ben-Zvi's memoirs, *We Are Immigrants*, appeared in Hebrew in 1962.

BERBER WOMEN. The Berbers of North Africa are undergoing a significant cultural revival and are the most recognizable minority in that part of the world. Berber speakers constitute close to 25 percent of Algeria's population and 40 percent of Morocco's population. Beginning in the 1920s, Berber cultural associations and political parties began to emerge mainly in Algeria in the so-called Kabylia part of the country, and in Morocco and the North American and European Berber diaspora. The Berber label is generally rejected by them; they claim that they were indigenous to the land and were originally known as *imazighen*, "free men." They denounce the label of minority imposed upon them by Arab nationalist North African states. The Berber movement demands recognition of its original language, Tamazight, as another official language of Algeria and Morocco and on a par with Arabic in the media, education, and the governmental sphere. The Moroccan government finally granted their language equality with Arabic in 2011.

Berber women are generally denied leadership roles within their communities, although they are significant as cultural symbols. Opposition to the Berber cultural revival movement rests on the argument that the Arab–Berber ethnic divide was the result of French military and colonial efforts to recognize and preserve the legal codes and oral poetry of the Berber population. The French are also accused of targeting the Berber population for assimilation, viewing them as sedentary people, ruled by decentralized and democratic methods, and at the same time exhibiting very little attachment to Islam. Their women were unveiled when the French arrived, which reinforced the European view of the Berber as only superficially Islamic. The French colonial administration issued the Berber *Dhahir* (decree) in 1930, which provided a separate judicial system for the Berbers of Morocco.

At first, the reaction of Algerian and Moroccan Arab nationalists was to advocate an Arab Berber cultural identity to blunt the impact of divisive colonial policies. However, this effort gave way during the 1960s to the ideology of Arab nationalism and the call for the Arabization of all aspects of culture. The two ruling parties that emerged after independence, Algeria's Front de Libération Nationale (FLN) and Morocco's Istiqlal (Independence) Party, adopted this ideology. While Arab–Berber tensions remained submerged during the national struggle against the French in the 1950s, both of these ethnicities sought a way of reaffirming a distinct identity during the 1960s. Berber strategy in this regard sought to improve the written Berber language and develop it on a par with Arabic. The Berber Academy and the Berber Study Group were founded in Paris, and the Moroccan Association for Cultural Research and Exchange was founded in Rabat, Morocco, to develop a unified Tamazight language with its own script.

An uprising by Berber students in the Algerian Kabilya region in April 1980 led to the founding of hundreds of Berber cultural associations in North Africa and throughout the world, offering Tamazight language courses and the study of Berber history. Several Kabilya political parties began to advocate Berber linguistic rights in 1989, such as the Socialist Forces Front and the Algerian Rally for Culture and Democracy (RCD). An umbrella organization named the World Amazight Congress emerged in 1995 to formalize this movement. As a result of local mobilization efforts and pressure by international human rights groups, Algerians and Moroccans began to recognize an identity known as "Barberity" as part of the national identity. Success in introducing Tamazight into school curricula and the media led to clashes between the military and Berber youths in 1998–2001.

Women played a significant role in the Berber struggle for cultural rights, yet they were never recognized as leaders of this movement. Although the Berber movement has revived and canonized a number of historical female figures such as **al-Kahina**, Kheira, and Fathma n'Soumer, who figured prominently in Berber resistance to outside Arab, and later French, forces from the 7th to the 19th centuries, this regard for women does not extend to current generations. Recent militant Berber women such as Khalida Messaoudi and Djura Abouda, who took part in military confrontations, receive little recognition. The majority of women are only being recognized as the female relatives of the fallen martyrs of the movement. For example, a prominent figure of the Berber diaspora, Malika Matoub, is only recognized as the sister of famous militant folk singer Lonès Matoub, although she led demonstrations and staged major rallies to protest his assassination in 1998 in Algiers. She is also the author of his biography, *Matoub Lounès, mon frère* (1999). Messaoudi received some recognition when she was elected to the Algerian parliament in 1997 as a representative of the RCD Party. Despite her fame as a supporter of official recognition of the Berber culture and language, her legislative record was limited to unsuccessful efforts to reform the 1984 **Algerian Family Code**.

The Berber cultural revival led to the rise of major female artistic figures, such as Hanifa, Cherifa Quadria, and **Taos Amrouche**, who played a role in the political struggles of the Berber movement. The latter was best known for preserving and disseminating the poetry of her mother, **Fadhma Amrouche**, in a book titled *F. Amrouche, Histoire de ma vie* (1968). The Algerian government considered her work subversive enough to eliminate her from the Algerian team representing that country in the Pan African Cultural Festival of 1969. In response to the idealization of Berber maternal and village types by the musical writers of the "New Kabyle Song" genre of the 1970s and 1980s, a host of Algerian and Moroccan female singers, such as the Djurdjura Group, Malika Domrane, Nouara, Houria Aichi, and Fatima Tabaamrant, performed musical pieces critical of patriarchal Berber images and artistic forms of expression. Much of their work decried family violence against Berber women.

BISHARA, SUHA FAWAZ (1968–). A Lebanese communist and feminist figure who played a prominent role in the struggle of south Lebanon against the Israeli occupation of that part of the country. Born in the Lebanese village of Deir Mimas, she was a youthful active member of Lebanon's Communist Party. She was recruited in 1988 to assassinate Antoine Lahad, the Israeli-backed head of the Southern Lebanese Army. The attempt only succeeded in inflicting severe wounds on Lahad, who emerged with a paralyzed arm. She served a sentence at the Khiyam prison, run by the Israeli Defense Forces (IDF) in southern Lebanon. She was finally released in 1998 as a result of pressure by the international community. She spoke widely of being tortured while in prison, inspiring Randa Shahhal Sabbagh, a filmmaker, to produce a documentary about Bishara's life, *Suha: Surviving Hell*. In 2003, Bishara published her autobiography, *Resistance: My Life in Lebanon*, which she wrote while living in exile in Paris. She presented herself in this book more as a nationalist than a communist. She has been leading a quiet life in Switzerland since then, while her status as a Lebanese folk hero persists. In 2011, she and a former cell mate, journalist Cosette Elias Ibrahim, published another prison memoir, titled *I Dream of a Cell of Cherries*.

BITTARI, ZUBAIDA (1937–). An Algerian novelist who was known originally as Louise Ali Rachedi. Her only work, a biographical novel, is based on her early life as a daughter of a traditional Algerian family who married her off at age 12. Divorced by age 14, she left for France as a maid for a French family she met in Algiers. She wrote a widely popular novel called *O mes soeurs Musulmanes, pleurez (Oh, My Muslim Sisters, Weep)*. This highly tragic story detailed her difficult relationships with her husband's family contrasted with the kindness of the French family for whom she worked.

BITTON, SIMONE (1955–). An Israeli documentary film director of French Moroccan background who is also a prominent peace activist. She moved to Israel at age 12 after spending her early years in Rabat, Morocco. She always considered herself to be a member of the Mizrahi Jewish community, or oriental Jews, joining the left-wing Mizrahi Black Panthers' movement at age 16. She was also active with the leftist Matzpen Party (Israeli Socialist Organization). She studied film in Paris and was driven to use her film-producing and directing abilities in her political advocacy work after the 1982 massacres at the Palestinian refugee camps of Sabra and Shatila. Her films and articles presented Palestinian and Mizrahi Jews as twin victims of Zionist ideology. Seeking to bring Arab Jews and Palestinians together, she was successful in organizing the peace group Perspectives Judéo-Arabes, which convened the widely publicized meeting of representatives of these two groups in Toledo, Spain, in 1989. She produced and directed many movies critical of the dominant Ashkenazi European community in Israel and of Moroccan political groups, with such titles as *Citizen Bishara, Ben Baraka, The Moroccan Equation, The Bombing, Mahmoud Darwish, As the Land Is the Language, Arafat Daily, PLO, The Dialogue Desk, Daney/Sanbar, North-South Conversations, Palestine: Story of a Land, Great Voices of Arabic Music: Um Kulthum, Chouf Le Look, Life beyond Them, Between Two Wars, Mothers, Nissim and Cherie, Solange Giraud,* and *Born Tache.*

BOUHIRED, DJAMILA (1937–). She is the heroine of the **Algerian Revolution** (1954–1962), also known as the Arab Joan of Arc. She lived to attain a near-legendary reputation as the embodiment of the values of national self-sacrifice. She attended French schools and grew up believing that her native language and her national identity were unassailably French. Events during the Algerian national struggle, such as the loss of both parents and an uncle during French attacks on the Casbah, the native quarter of Algiers, helped radicalize her views. She was recruited by Said Yacef, the commander of the Front de Libération Nationale (FLN) in the Casbah area, along with other young women who could easily pass as French in order to serve as couriers and planters of plastic bombs in French cafes. The bombing campaign, which began in 1956, ended in her arrest in 1957 near Bar Simone. She was severely tortured by French military officers but refused to reveal any information about her military contacts. She had a highly public trial in Paris in 1957, which caught the attention of major French political and literary figures. The torture she endured was revealed during the trial by her lawyer, Jacques Vergès, a prominent African member of the French Communist Party. He and another French communist official, Georges Arnaud, published a pamphlet about her life, *Pour Djamila Bouhired*, which made her into a national figure with a worldwide reputation. She was initially sentenced to death, which brought about another wave of bombings by Yacef and his eventual capture in August 1957. Some leading French feminists, such as Simone de Beauvoir, also defended Djamila publicly. Due to her celebrity status and worldwide support, French President René Coty commuted her sentence to life in prison. Djamila was remanded to a prison in France but was released as soon as Algeria won its independence in 1962.

Bouhired married Vergès, her lawyer, and made an unsuccessful bid for a seat in the first Algerian National Assembly. She became an editor of a publication known as *Révolution africaine* but was forced to abandon this position in 1963 when the Algerian regime cracked down on leftist parties. This caused her to suspend her public activities for a while. She eventually divorced her husband and launched an entrepreneurial career, but continued to labor on behalf of widows and war orphans. Although the FLN government continued to honor "the revolution of the million martyrs," recognition of the many Djamilas, as she referred to her female partners in prison, remained scant. In 1981, as Algeria was debating its latest **Algerian Family Code**, Djamila wrote an open letter to President Chadli Benjedid (r. 1979–1992), titled "No to the Betrayal of the Ideas of November 1, 1954." She led large demonstrations of women protesting the latest conservative code. Today, she remains one of the most revered women in Algeria and throughout the Arab world.

BOUIH, FATINA AL- (1955–). A Moroccan writer, leftist activist, and feminist who was born in Settat Province. She attended the prestigious girls' academy of Casablanca, Lycée Chawqi, on a scholarship. She began her political career as an organizer of the national union of high school students, known as Syndicat National des Eleves, and was sent to prison as a result of leading student strikes. From 1977 until 1979, she was imprisoned in Meknes Prison, charged with conspiring against the state and membership in an illegal Marxist–Leninist organization. In 1991, she emerged as the spokesperson of the council of Moroccan women's groups, known as *al-majlis al-watani lil-tansiq* (The National Coordination Council), which came together in opposition to **al-Mudawana**, Morocco's personal status law. Bouih was also a volunteer at the first center for battered women in Morocco. Her experiences in the women's prison resulted in a book titled *A Woman Named Rachid*. The book languished for 20 years before being published in Arabic and French during the early liberal years of the reign of King Muhammad VI (r. 1999–). She ran an unsuccessful campaign for a seat on the council of the city of Casablanca in 1997 and was supported by the Organisàtion pour l'action démocratique et populaire (OADP). Her interest in the fate of prisoners after their release resulted in the founding of the Moroccan Observatory of Prisons in 1999, which helps prisoners assimilate into society. This project, with which she was assisted by her husband, was completed while she pursued a degree in sociology. She has been teaching high school Arabic since 1982.

BOURGIBA, HABIB (ca. 1901–2000). Tunisian statesman and the country's first president, who led Tunisia to independence in 1956 as the head of the Neo-Destour Party. Born in the town of Monastir, south of Tunis, he received his education at the Sadiqi College and the Lycée Carnot, two of Tunisia's prestigious educational institutions. He attained a doctorate in law and political science at the University of Paris, returning to his country in the mid-1920s. His involvement with the country's premier nationalist movement, the Destour (constitution), did not last long due to his dissatisfaction with its modest goal of political autonomy. He founded another party, the Neo-Destour, in 1934, later known as the Destourian Socialist Party. He became an advocate of liberal democracy later on and worked with three newspapers, which appeared in French: *L'Étendard tunisien*, *La Voix du tunisien*, and his own militant paper, *L'Action tunisienne*, which he founded in 1931.

Bourgiba's fame as the Arab world's most progressive leader on the women question is not consistent with his early history. During the heyday of the national struggle against French domination, he shared the views of the majority of his nationalist colleagues, who favored the veil as an appropriate attire for women. Initially, Bourgiba genuinely believed that the veil was necessary for maintaining the nation's Arab and Islamic identity. He married Mathilde Lorrain in 1927, his French lodger while he lived in Paris, and they had one son, Habib Jr., in 1927. In 1960, he married a Tunisian, Wasilah Ben Ammar, a renowned leader of women's organizations. However, once he became president, a position to which he was elected three times, earning the title "President for Life" in 1974, he began a concerted campaign to reform the **Sharia**. He undertook not the replacement of this Islamic code of laws with secular, European laws like **Mustafa Kemal Ataturk**, but rather reforming the ancient laws as a form of *ijtihad*. This meant the permissible exercise of one's faculties in order to achieve religious reforms. Bourgiba forced religious endowments to close due to rampant corruption and criticized and downgraded Islamic practices like fasting and performing the pilgrimage to Mecca. He also reduced the influence of Tunisia's foremost religious university, the ancient Zeituna seminary.

He succeeded in introducing the **Personal Status Code of Tunisia** (1956), facing minimal opposition compared to the hostility faced by Tunisia's earlier advocate of women's liberation, **Tahir Haddad**. Opposition to the code remained confined to a small group of religious jurists. Bourgiba was removed from office in 1987 by the sitting prime minister, Zein al-Abidin Ben Ali, on grounds of deteriorating mental and physical abilities. *See also* BOURGIBA, WASILAH (?–1999).

BOURGIBA, WASILAH (?–1999). The wife of **Habib Bourgiba**, former president of Tunisia, and leader of women's organizations. She was born Wasilah Ben Ammar to a prominent Tunisian family and married the Tunisian president in 1960, after he divorced his French wife, Matilde Lorrain. Wasilah Bourgiba emerged as a formidable leader of women and headed the largest umbrella organization, Union Nationale des femmes de Tunisie (UNFI) (National Union of Tunisian Women), founded in 1956. She managed to align this large block of voters with her husband's Neo-Destour Party and was frequently sent on high-profile diplomatic missions on behalf of the Tunisian government. She was divorced in 1986. *See also* PERSONAL STATUS CODE OF TUNISIA.

BURAN (r. 630–631). A Sassanian queen of ancient Iran who was also known as Puran, her rule lasted barely 17 or 19 months. Buran's name meant the girl with the rosy complexion. Her father was Emperor Khosrow II and her mother was Mariam, a daughter of Mauric, a Roman ruler. She succeeded to the throne following the assassination of her brother Ardashir and was crowned at the capital, Ctesiphon, as the 26th queen of the Sassanid dynasty. Her sister, Azarmidokht, ruled briefly after being crowned the 27th Sassanian queen. Buran's rule witnessed the beginning of the Arab invasion of Iran. Firdowsi (940–1020) author of the epic poem *Shahnameh* (*History of King*), commended Buran for improving the lives of peasants by lifting the burden of high taxes and for her just rule. One of the achievements of her brief rule was a peace treaty with Heraclius, the Roman emperor. *See also* ZOROASTRIAN WOMEN.

BUSTANI, BOUTROS (1819–1893). He was one of the major figures of the Arab renaissance, known as *al-nahdha*. Bustani produced one of the first Arabic translations of the Bible. Born in Lebanon, he was part of a movement that called for the liberalization of the rules of Arabic grammar. His journal, *al-Jinan* (*The Gardens*), espoused a modernist approach to life's major issues, the feminist cause being one of them. He wrote on the need to educate women as early as 1847, defusing the prevalent theory that women's education can result in madness or forsaking of religion. He held the view that uneducated women generated evil in society. He founded the first modern and indigenous school for boys in 1863, known as the National School, and hoped to do the same for girls. In a country dominated by Western Christian mission schools, such as Lebanon, this was an outstanding first step toward the promotion of modern Arabic education. Despite all this, Bustani actually felt that a modern school for girls would not find a hospitable environment.

BUSTANI, MYRNA (1939–). A Lebanese businesswoman and a member of the Lebanese parliament, born in Beirut. Her father, Emile Bustani, founded Middle East Airlines. She received a degree in psychology from St. Joseph's University and was thrust into an unfamiliar political role upon her father's death in 1963. She was chosen to fulfill the rest of his parliamentary term, thus becoming the first female member of the Lebanese legislature. She continued to lead the life of a socialite, becoming the manager of Hotel al-Bustan, a luxurious hotel in the town of Bayt Mirri. She spent the years of the Lebanese Civil War in France.

C

CAGDAS YASAMI DESTEKLEMI DERNEGI (CYDD). A Turkish organization called The Association to Promote Contemporary Life, which was established in Istanbul in 1989. It started out as a modernizing group, but became devoted to the promotion of secular Kemalist education and upholding the state's Westernizing ideology. It granted women from Turkey's less-developed areas scholarships to complete their university education. The organization's work expanded as a result of attempts to gain university admission for veiled women and the rise of human rights groups to protect this right, such as *Mazlum Der* (Headscarf Commission). *See also* ATATURK, MUSTAFA KEMAL (1881–1938); NON-GOVERNMENTAL ORGANIZATIONS (NGOs); VEILING IN ISLAM.

CAMILIA (1929–1950). Camilia, or lady of the camellias, was born Liliane Cohen and became an Egyptian movie actress in the late 1940s and early 1950s. Killed in an airplane crash, Camilia was rumored to be a mistress of King Farouq (r. 1936–1952) and an agent of Mossad, the Israeli intelligence service.

Born in Alexandria, with an Italian grandmother on her mother's side, her full name was Camilia Liliane Victor Cohen. She had a French father and repeatedly claimed that she was a Christian. She attended an English school in Alexandria and was introduced to show business in 1946 by Egyptian producer Ahmad Salem when she was only 17. She starred in 18 movies, the last being *The Way to Cairo* (1950). She is the subject of a movie, *Barefoot on the Bridge of Gold*. Her life and tragic death are often compared to Marilyn Monroe's.

CARIYOCA, TAHIYYA (1915–1999). An Egyptian dancer and screen and stage actress who was born in Manzala. Her original name was Badawiya Muhammad Karim Ali. Her first performance as a dancer was in the 1930s in the Cairo Casino, operated by entertainer and artistic producer **Badiaa Masabni**. Some believe that her stage name, Cariyoca, was an adaptation from a tango-type dance, the *cariyoca*, performed by Fred Astaire and Ginger Rogers in the 1933 motion picture *Flying Down to Rio*. Her life was fertile ground for gossip, particularly her rivalry with another Cairo Casino oriental dancer, **Samiya Jamal**. She acted and danced in 190 Egyptian movies and theater productions, earning the title *aalimah* (courtesan) in the theater world. She quickly rose to the position of the Arab world's uncrowned queen of the Oriental dance.

Cariyoca was also a political activist, participating in demonstrations and serving for many years as the vocal president of Egypt's actor's syndicate. When the Free Officers seized control of the country in 1952, she denounced them for not following up on their promise to restore democratic rule. This led to a short prison term in 1953 and to several prison terms in succeeding years. Before her death at the age of 84, she became a devout Muslim, exchanging her skimpy dancing outfit for the Islamic *hijab* (**veil**). She died of a heart attack, with her reputation as the queen of the Oriental dance still intact. She reputedly had gone through more than a dozen marriages during her lifetime. *See also* BELLY DANCING.

CENTRE DE RECHERCHES, D'ÉTUDES, DE DOCUMENTATION ET D'INFORMATION SUR LA FEMME (CRÉDIF). This is a Tunisian research center devoted to women's issues. It was founded in 1990 as a public agency charged with conducting research for the Tunisian government. The center became affiliated with the Tunisian Ministry of Women's, Children's and Family Affairs upon its establishment in 1992. Most of the center's work revolves around research to create databases to track the evolution of women's rights and status. It has organized international forums on women and produced many reports and publications in Arabic and French. The center also publishes a magazine titled *Info-CRÉDIF*. One of its innovative projects is the Observatory on Women's Conditions, which assesses advances made by women, especially their representation in the mass media.

CHADOR. Full-length outer cover of Persian origin, usually of black material. Worn outdoors, this garb is not mandated by Islam and is more cultural than religious in significance. While women in the countryside were free to go about without covering their full bodies, urban women, especially of the upper classes, wore the Chador to signify their station in life, which was superior to that of common folk. The Chador became unpopular during the early part of the 20th century, particularly as a result of Shah Reza Pahlavi's (r. 1924–1941) modernizing pressures. This outer cover was first abandoned by the Westernized elite women of Iran and became identifiable with traditional and poor women during the rule of Shah Muhammad Reza Pahlavi (r. 1941–1979). The Chador was eventually popularized by Iranian Islamist ideologues such as **Ali Shariati** (1933–1977). In Shariati's lectures at Tehran's Husseiniyah Ershad during the 1960s, women were urged to rethink the symbolism of their Western garments. The Chador became a badge of anti-Western identification after the Islamic Revolution of 1979 and was mandated by the Islamic regime as an obligatory form of dress for female government workers. *See also* VEILING IN ISLAM.

CHAZAN, NAOMI (1946–). An Israeli political science professor, member of the Knesset, and feminist who was born in Jerusalem to a prominent family. She lived abroad for many years when her father, Avraham Harman, was the first Israeli ambassador to the United States. She completed her bachelor's degree at Columbia University and received a PhD in African studies from Hebrew University in 1975. She held several prominent academic posts, including the directorship of Hebrew University's Truman Center for Peace Studies (1990–1992), and became professor of political science and African studies in 1994. She was elected to the Knesset in 1992 as a leading member of the leftist Meretz Party, rising to the position of deputy speaker in 1996. She has published widely on her field of study, comparative politics, as well as on women's issues and the Arab–Israeli conflict.

In 1985, Chazan was a member of the Israeli delegation to the United Nations Conference on Women. She cofounded several women's and peace organizations, such as the Israel Women's Network (1984); the Israel Women's Peace Net (1989); the Jerusalem Link/Engendering Peace Process (1996–1998), which she founded with **Hanan Ashrawi**; and the Center for Women and Politics in Israel. Her activities focused on the impact of militarism on women's rights, and she became an active member of Peace Now, the prominent Israeli peace movement. She supported the Geneva Accords of 2003, a private Israeli–Palestinian peace initiative. Another cause she supports is that of non-Orthodox Jews. She has been the president of the New Israel Fund (NIF) since 2007 and was a visiting professor of government at Harvard University. *See also* ALONI, SHULAMIT ADLER (1928–); FEMINIST MOVEMENT IN ISRAEL.

CHÉDID, ANDRÉE (1920–). A Lebanese poet, novelist, and short-story writer, born in Cairo. She received her bachelor's degree from the American University of Cairo (AUC) in 1942 and moved to Paris in 1946 with her husband, Louis Chedid. She has been living in the French capital since that time and writes mostly in French. Her first poetry collection, *On the Trails of My Fancy*, came out in English in 1943. Not unlike other Lebanese writers who write in French, such as Amin Maalouf (1949–), her work focuses on Oriental and Western themes at the same time, with the Middle East the setting of most of her novels. This was particularly true of her early novels, such as *Le sommeil délivré* (*Sleep Unbound*, 1952); *Le sixème jour* (*The Sixth*

Day, 1960), which was set in the 1947 cholera epidemic in Egypt and was made into a movie by Yousef Shahin; *L'autre* (*The Other*, 1969); and *Nefertiti et le rêve d'Akhnaton* (*Nefertiti and Akhnaton's Dream*, 1974). Her poetry uses the themes of nature and love to make a plea against rampant violence in the Middle East. Her novels emphasize women's oppression by traditional society. Among these are *The Goddess Lar* (1977), *Les nombres* (*The Numbers*, 1965), and *Le montreur* (*The Showman*, 1967). Her recent output includes poetical collections such as *Guerres* (*Wars*, 1999), *Territoires du soufflé* (*Territories of Breath*, 1999), and *Le soufflé des choses* (*The Breath of Things*, 2000). Her novel *Le message* (*The Message*) appeared in 2000. Her novels became the subject of two movies. She was given several literary awards, such as the Aigle d'Or for poetry in 1972 and the Royal Belgian Academy's Grand Prix for French Literature in 1975. In 1976, she received two awards for poetry, the Louis Lapier and the Mallarmé. She received the Prix Goncourt for poetry in 2006 and was awarded one of France's highest honors, the Legion d'honneur, in 2009.

CILLER, TANSU PENBE (1946–). Turkey's first female prime minister, who served in that position from 1993 until 1996. Born in Istanbul, she was the daughter of the governor of Bilcik Province. She earned a BA in economics from Bogazici University (Bosphorus University) in 1967, and later an MA from the University of New Hampshire and a PhD from the University of Connecticut, also in economics. After a year of teaching at Franklin and Marshall College in the United States, she taught at Bogazici University. She consulted for the Chamber of Commerce of Istanbul and for the Turkish Industry and Business Association. Her first experience with national politics was in 1990, when she served as an economic adviser to Turkish statesman Suleiman Demirel. She joined Demirel's True Path Party (DYP) and became minister of economics in the coalition cabinet of the DYP and the Social Democratic Populist Party. As prime minister in 1993, Ciller confronted tough problems like the Kurdistan Worker's Party (PKK) and its attacks in eastern Turkey. She also confronted challenges of mounting inflation and unemployment. She earned the title "the iron lady," particularly when she succeeded in forming more than one coalition government with political parties far from the center, such as Necemeddin Erbekan's Islamist Refah Party. She served as the foreign minister in Erbekan's cabinet until the military coup of 1997. She abandoned her role as a leader of the DYP after the party's defeat in the 2002 elections. Ciller was investigated by the Turkish parliament for corruption charges, of which she was later cleared. Most of these charges were related to the activities of her husband, Ozer Ucuran. She is also a member of the Council of Women World Leaders, which provides networking among current and previous women prime ministers and presidents.

COHEN, GEULAH (1925–). An Israeli politician and Knesset member who was born in Tel Aviv to an immigrant Yemeni father and a Jewish Palestinian mother of Moroccan background. She became a political activist while still in her teens. She joined Betar, a youth movement founded by the Revisionist Zionist Party of Vladimir Jabutinsky (1880–1940), and later became a member of the Irgun militia in 1942 and the Stern Gang in 1943. Both were the militant arms of the Herut Party (Land Party). She was the radio broadcaster for the Stern Gang during the 1940s, which ended her activities with the Jewish underground. She managed to flee her prison hospital in Bethlehem during the 1948 war and resumed her broadcasting career. After attending Hebrew University, she completed an MA in philosophy and Bible studies.

Cohen was elected to the Knesset in 1973, but resigned from Herut in protest against returning the Sinai Peninsula to Egypt, the result of the signing of the Camp David Accords in 1978. Her opposition to surrendering land to the Arab enemy led her to found the Tehiya (Renaissance) List in the Knesset in 1979. The List represented the Jewish settler movement Gush Emunim (Block of the Faithful). When this group failed to receive enough votes to occupy a number of seats in the Knesset in the elections of 1992, she retired from legislative politics.

Cohen dabbled in political journalism, serving on the editorial board of *Sulam* (1948–1960), a Lehi militia paper, and worked as a columnist for *Maarvi*, an Israeli daily, until 1973. Beginning in the 1970s, she became involved in activities designed to encourage the immigration of Soviet Jews to Israel and acted as the chairperson of the Knesset's Immigration and Absorption Committee. She was also known as a "territorialist" when she introduced the Jerusalem Basic Law in the Knesset in December 1980, which made it possible to declare East and West Jerusalem the capital of Israel. This step was followed a year later by her introduction of another law, annexing the Syrian Golan Heights to Israel. Her determination to enlarge Israel's territory following the June War of 1967 stopped short of extending the Israeli legal and administrative system to the West Bank and Gaza.

Cohen led a group calling for purging left-wing employees from Israel's intelligence services following the arrest of Israeli nuclear spy Mordechai Vannunu in 1986. At the same time, she was active in the campaign to win the release of Jewish American spy Jonathan Pollard from a U.S. jail. After Prime Minister Yitzhak Shamir (r. 1986–1992) appointed her deputy minister of science and technology in 1990, she reprised her earlier role of supporting Soviet immigration to Israel, campaigning for the absorption of Ethiopian Jewish immigrants. She was opposed to the Madrid Peace conference and the Oslo Peace Accords of 1993. Upon her official retirement from politics, she moved to the settlement of Kiryat Arba in the vicinity of Hebron. Her only son, Tzahi Hanegbi, was elected to the Knesset in 1992 on the Likud Party List and served in several cabinets.

Her autobiography, *Story of a Warrior*, appeared in Hebrew in 1962. An English version was published in 1966 in the United States under the title *Woman of Violence: Memoirs of a Young Terrorist, 1943–1948*. She published two additional works: *The Orange That Burned and Lit up Hearts* (1979) and *An Historic Meeting* (1986). She was awarded the Israel Prize in 2003, and in 2007 she was awarded the Yakir Yerushalayim award (Worthy Citizen of Jerusalem).

CONCUBINAGE. The past practice of maintaining a sexual relationship between a Muslim master and his female slave. Muslim law decreed that concubines, like slaves, who could be either black or white, must be of non-Islamic origin. An unequal relationship, concubinage allowed the Muslim master the freedom to end the relationship whenever he wished. The concubine enjoyed many fewer rights than a legal and free, unenslaved wife. In practice and until the early part of the 20th century, the master could have as many concubines as he could afford. He was not limited to four as in a legal **marriage**, but was expected to avoid relations with two sisters simultaneously, following the prohibition of such practice in a Muslim marriage. Neither was the master expected to pay a dowry to his concubine, because her initial purchase price usually exceeded that of a regular dowry. Common custom decreed that a man treat his concubine better than a slave, and **Sharia** law mandated that the father acknowledge the offspring of such a relationship and treat them like his legal children. Once the concubine bore a child, she would be given the title and status of *umm-i veled* (Turkish: mother of child). This changed the course of her life, because she could not be resold. Other aspects of this relationship resembled a true marriage. For instance, although a concubine did not inherit from her master, her children did. The 45-day waiting period (*uddah*) required of a legal wife upon her widowhood or **divorce** before entering into a new marital union also applied to a concubine.

A large number of concubines became readily available beginning in the initial period of the Arab conquests in the seventh century CE. Female slaves originally were acquired as a result of wars and came mostly from the Caucasus region and the Crimea, the western Ukraine region, and the Balkan countries. The influx of African slaves was a later phenomenon and saturated the markets of the Arabian Peninsula. Concubinage was practiced largely by the upper classes, and the Ottoman Empire (15th–20th centuries) experienced the greatest accumulation of female slaves. The *umm-i veled* status granted concubines the greatest amount of power during that period. The institution did not convey any stigma or loss of honor. When the Ottoman Empire disintegrated after World War I, many concubines were sent back to their original homelands. *See also* HAREM.

CONVENTION ON THE ELIMINATION OF DISCRIMINATION AGAINST WOMEN (CEDAW). This convention was adopted by the United Nations General Assembly in 1979, but did not become operative until 1981. It quickly came to be known as "The Women's Convention." It called on member states to take positive steps to alter laws and traditional practices that lead to discrimination against women. CEDAW also called for the enforcement of equality between men and women even in marital and family relationships. The convention became immediately problematic for Islamic states, which favored upholding women's traditional rights in Islam. The debate preceding the passage of the convention was characterized by a great deal of ideological acrimony, even though a large number of Muslim states had been involved in its drafting. Many of these argued that the convention was in direct conflict with the **Sharia**. When it came to the final vote, several Muslim states abstained from approving specific articles, and five states with a majority Muslim population abstained from voting on the final draft altogether.

Adoption of the convention was a slow process, but by the year 2003, at least 174 states had approved it. Of the 57 members of the Organization of Islamic Cooperation (OIC), 49 states have already adopted the convention. Six members of the League of Arab States declined. A large number of reservations were expressed by other UN member states that were not within the Islamic block. Among the most objectionable articles to the Muslim group was Article 15, which requires complete equality between men and women before the law and granting women the right to choose their own place of residence. Another objection was made against Article 16, which calls for equal treatment relating to **marriage** and family relationships, because it contradicted the Sharia. Article 9, which calls for granting women the right to pass their nationality on to their children, was also criticized. The overall argument against the convention claimed that the protection of women's human rights was used as a pretext to promote a certain discourse. The OIC called on its members to coordinate their efforts to prevent the exploitation of the human rights issue for political purposes. Muslim members voiced objections to the use of the term "equality," preferring instead such terms as "equitable" or "equivalent" rights for both genders. As a result of these debates, OIC members of the General Assembly adopted the Cairo Declaration of Human Rights in Islam in 1990, which set a different standard for Muslim states. For example, the declaration emphasizes women's equality to men in dignity but still calls for men to be responsible for the maintenance of the family.

COPTIC WOMEN. The Copts of modern Egypt are descendants of the ancient Egyptians of antiquity and make up around 10 percent of the country's population of 80 million. Although considered a minority, the Copts are generally viewed as the original people of the land. The largest segment of this group belongs to the Coptic Orthodox Church, but some are Roman Catholic and Anglican. Coptic women have long complained of being subject to patriarchal hegemony and suffering under periods of sectarian violence and persecution. It is widely agreed that Coptic women enjoy fewer rights than Muslim women despite the latters' segregated lives. The greatest gap exists in matters of **divorce**; the Coptic Orthodox Church severely restricts a woman's right to seek a divorce. Muslim women in most Arab countries can obtain a divorce without the husband's consent as a result of reforms enacted during the latter part of the 20th century. Similar reforms have yet to make their way into the Orthodox Coptic community. Yet, other facets of personal status law are the same for Coptic and Muslim women. In both communities, a woman receives half of her brother's share of an inheritance. Historically, both Coptic and Muslim women were **veiled** until the first decades of the 20th century, but Coptic women today frequently suffer harassment because of their unveiling. Within the church, patriarchal norms result in conservative practices similar to those Muslim women have come to expect from their Islamic institutions. Orthodox Church literature and sermons insist on maintaining proper codes of behavior for women, usually presenting the ideal type of womanhood as saintly virgins. Coptic women fulfill a variety of roles within the church, such as Sunday school teachers and volunteers. Some women have chosen the religious vocation of nuns, serving in numerous Egyptian convents in the Sinai Desert. *See also* ANCIENT EGYPT, WOMEN IN.

COUNCIL ON WOMEN'S AFFAIRS (CWA)—IRAN. Founded in 1992, the council was created at the behest of Iranian President Ali Akbar Hashemi Rafsanjani (r. 1989–1997) as a way of encouraging women to emulate the life of Islamic model and near-saint **Fatima.** The council was headed by **Shahla Habibi,** who acted as a special consultant to the president on women's affairs. *See also* NON-GOVERNMENTAL ORGANIZATIONS (NGOs).

CULTURAL AND SOCIAL COUNCIL ON WOMEN'S AFFAIRS— IRAN (CSCWAI). It was founded in 1987 by the High Council of the Cultural Revolution by future president Ali Akbar Hashemi Rafsanjani. Its first director was Zahra Shojai, who was charged with making recommendations for the improvement of opportunities for women in the work and educational fields and enhancing their role in political organization. *See also* NON-GOVERNMENTAL ORGANIZATIONS (NGOs).

D

DABBAGH, MARZIYEH HADIDCHI (ca. 1942–). Iranian Islamist activist and women's leader of humble origins in the city of Hamadan. Despite being married at an early age, she moved to Tehran in search of wider horizons. There she became a student of Ayatollah Saidi, who was closely allied with **Ayatollah Ruhollah Khomeini** (r. 1979–1989). She was jailed and tortured by Savak, the intelligence secret service of Shah Muhammad Reza Pahlavi, in 1963 for her Islamic activities, which left her in poor health. She sought exile in Great Britain and France, leaving her four children behind. She became a leader of public demonstrations calling for the release of prisoners from the shah's jails. Dabbagh also established a camp for training Islamist activists in Syria and received military assistance from Lebanon's Imam Musa al-Sadr (1918–1978?). In 1978, she became a bodyguard and confidant of Khomeini while he was in Paris, returning as part of his entourage when he traveled to Iran in 1979. She became a military commander during the Iran–Iraq War (1980–1988), later joining the Pasdaran, or Revolutionary Guards. She was responsible for the dismantling of several hostile organizations during the early years of the Islamic Revolution. She was a member of an official Iranian delegation to Moscow in 1988 and delivered a personal letter from Khomeini to Mikhail Gorbachev inviting him to convert to Islam. She later became the president of the Islamist Women's Society in the Iranian capital.

Dabbagh was one of four women elected to the first Iranian Majlis after the 1979 revolution. She served four terms, finally losing in the elections of 2000. In the Majlis, she supported hard-line policies on foreign relations and the economic direction of the country. Dabbagh, however, was vehemently opposed by conservative elements when she pushed her reforms on behalf of women, such as allowing them to receive their husbands' pensions, increasing the benefits of female heads of households, and allowing female students to receive scholarships for studying abroad.

DAMARI, SHOSHANA (1923–2006). An Israeli singer and prominent cultural symbol who was variously referred to as "Queen of Israeli Song," and "Voice of Israel." She emigrated to Palestine from Yemen as a child and began her singing career among the native Yemeni community. Her husband, Shlomo Bushemi, became her musical manager and opened the way for her rise to national fame, beginning with the 1948 Arab–Jewish War. She performed her nationalistic songs in several Western countries and was awarded the Israel Prize for lifetime achievement.

DANESHVAR, SIMIN (1921–). An Iranian novelist, literary translator, and university professor who is credited with writing the first literary best seller by a female author. Born to a father who was a physician, she spent her early years in the southwestern city of Shiraz. Considered the center of economic life in that region, Shiraz was also known as the birthplace of the two famous poets Hafez (1325–1390) and Saidi (1184–1291). The town was renowned for its natural beauty, which attracted domestic tourism. During World War II, Shiraz was occupied by British troops, a development that inspired Daneshvar's most famous novel, *Savushun* (*The Mourners*), published in 1969. The novel came to light after the author's return from Stanford University, where she was a Fulbright scholar in 1950. It was during that year that she married well-known short-story writer Jalal Al-i Ahmad, before accompanying him to the United States. She published a collection of short stories titled *Atash-i Khamush* (*Extinguished Fire*) in 1948 and taught art history at the University of Tehran. *Savushun*, her most widely read novel, revolves around urban and tribal life in and around Shiraz and tells the story of an idealistic man who struggles against the British occupation of his town. The novel has been described as semiautobiographical and was reprinted 13 times. It sold more than half a million copies. Daneshvar is also a noted translator of major Western literary figures such as George Bernard Shaw, Anton Chekov, and Nathanial Hawthorne. Her husband died in 1969, presumably as a result of poisoning by secret agents of Shah Muhammad Reza Pahlavi's regime.

DANISH. This was one of the oldest Iranian women's journals, which disseminated information on modern household management. *Danish*, which means "knowledge," appeared in 1910 under the direction of a female editor, Dr. Kahhal (an assumed name meaning "eye doctor"), who was also a practicing ophthalmologist. The journal was devoted to the discussion of the latest methods of child rearing, housekeeping, hygienic practices, and the management of domestic servants. Some of the ideas promoted by this journal called for the education of girls as a means of achieving equality with males. A newspaper with the same name still exists today.

DASHTI, ROLA (1965–). A Kuwaiti member of parliament who was among the first four women elected to that body in 2009. The four were personal friends and graduates of U.S. universities. Dashti faced many pressures from radical Islamist elements, who called on her to cover her hair as a precondition for participating in the work of the legislative body. She challenged them by securing a judgment in her favor from the constitutional court, which affirmed a Muslim woman's right to choose her form of dress, asserting that there were no rules barring unveiled women from parliamentary work. Dashti's father, who belongs to Kuwait's old Persian minority, was known to have married four wives and to have fathered a large number of children. Dashti's own mother was a Lebanese national from the city of Sidon. Because of this connection to Lebanon, Dashti worked for the International Red Cross as a volunteer, aiding Lebanese civilians who suffered due to the Israeli invasion of 1982.

She holds a PhD in population economics from the Johns Hopkins University and lived in the United States for 10 years. Before participating in electoral politics, she was a financial consultant for the National Bank of Kuwait and the Kuwaiti Institute for Scientific Research. In 2009, she was awarded the North–South Prize in Lisbon in recognition of her work on behalf of women's rights in Kuwait and throughout the Arab world. *See also* EDUCATION: ARAB GULF STATES.

DAYAN, YAEL (1939–). Daughter of Israeli military leader Moshe Dayan (1915–1981) and political activist and journalist who was born in Kibbutz Nahalal. She received a degree in international relations from Hebrew University. She also became active in her father's political group, the Labor Party, and was elected to the Knesset on the Labor Party list, serving from 1992 until 2003. She later became more involved with Meretz, a leftist Israeli party, in 1991. She became an activist with several peace groups, including Peace Now, the International Center for Peace, and the Council for Peace and Security. She participated in several high-profile peace meetings with Palestinian groups, particularly women. She also supported the Geneva Document, which arose out of an unofficial Israeli–Palestinian peace initiative convened in 2003 by Yossi Beilen and Yasser Abed Rabbo.

DEATH OF A PRINCESS. This Western television docudrama chronicled the 1977 execution of Saudi princess Mishaal bint Fahed bin Muhammad, which first aired in Great Britain. It detailed the tragic ending of a princess who received the death sentence for her decision to choose her husband freely. The movie resulted in a heated debate in Saudi Arabia and in the Muslim and Western worlds about the appropriateness of the punishment to the "crime." Later on, details of the incident surfaced slowly, providing a more plausible account of what had actually happened. Saudi commentators claimed that Mishaal would not have been subjected to the death sentence had not her elderly grandfather insisted on applying the maximum punishment. Her grandfather, Prince Muhammad ibn Abd al-Aziz, a brother of King Khaled ibn Abd al-Aziz, insisted on pushing through a hasty trial that did not examine the full spectrum of **Sharia** law that applied to this case.

The princess was initially married to an older relative, whom she divorced legally after a short-lived union. According to some versions of the story, the princess fell in love with and married a man much younger than her first husband who was the son of the Saudi ambassador to Lebanon. Though the **marriage** was legal, it was kept a secret and was only revealed when the young couple attempted to leave the kingdom. Arrested at the airport, the princess's husband was brought before a Sharia court, Islamic law being the only legal code applied in that country. He was beheaded as an adulterer, though the normal punishment for this offense was stoning to death. The princess was spared this punishment and was shot to death privately. The magnitude of this crime was demonstrated by the harsh sentence applied by the Saudi state to the two guilty persons, a videotape of which ended up in the possession of the British Broadcasting Service (BBC). As a result of the negative publicity generated by this case, the British ambassador to Saudi Arabia was expelled.

Death of a Princess became a sensational tool in the hands of Sharia detractors, leading many Muslims throughout the world to defend the integrity of their customs and laws. New information emerged soon afterward, revealing the real cause of this human tragedy. The Saudis claimed that the young couple did not lose their lives because they defied the will of the princess's family about the freedom to choose one's spouse, which is a woman's right according to the Sharia, but rather because they defied an important law that calls for a widow or divorced woman to wait four months (*uddah*) before becoming eligible to marry again. The waiting period is designed to determine the possibility of pregnancy from the earlier marriage and to prevent the distant chance of committing incest if a child's lineage is not absolutely clear. The movie became a classic landmark in the debate on cultural relativism.

DEMOCRATIC ORGANIZATION OF WOMEN (DOW)—IRAN. This was one of Iran's leftist women's organizations, dating back to 1944. Its Persian name was Tashkilat-e Democratik-e Zanan, and it was closely aligned with the Tudeh (Masses) Party, Iran's oldest leftist organization. It had branches all over Iran emphasizing the economic rights of women. The DOW pursued antifascist policies, echoing the main thrust of the foreign policy of the Soviet Union. The DOW and Tudeh supported Muhammad Mossadegh's (prime minister 1951–1953) efforts to nationalize the Anglo–Iranian Oil Company. Enjoying the support of many progressive male members of the Majlis, Tudeh sponsored a bill in 1944 to enfranchise women. The Majlis defeated the bill, but a similar piece of legislation was passed easily in the same year by the leftist autonomous government of Azerbaijan Province. Close alignment with Tudeh, however, did not always lead to encouraging women to join the DOW, whose appeal to a broad band of Iranian women remained limited. Always seeking inspiration from Tudeh, the DOW was never able to develop its own independent recommendations for reforming family law.

The women's issue fell further behind when Tudeh fought against any deviation from the anti-imperialist campaign of the Islamic government of Iran after 1979. The best example of this attitude was Tudeh's unwillingness to support women's anti**veiling** protests, which it saw as divisive and potentially harmful. The women's agenda was considered part of a reactionary and pro-American campaign designed to weaken the Islami-led anti-imperialist front. The Association of Iranian Communists wrote in its paper, *Haqiqat* (*Truth*), that women were leaving their responsibilities behind and exaggerating the significance of the veiling issue. The veil was not as important as democracy, it added, and did not match the urgency of Iranian independence and more pressing political issues. Women who protested the Islamic regime's enforcement of the dress code were described by one leftist writer as promoters of Western fashion. *See also* NON-GOVERNMENTAL ORGANIZATIONS (NGOs).

DEMOCRATIC WOMEN'S ASSOCIATION (DWA)—TUNISIA. An independent association that calls for eliminating discriminatory practices against women, changing patriarchal views on women, and enhancing opportunities for women's participation in political and civic organizations. Known also as Association Tunisienne des femmes démocrates (AFTD), it was founded in 1989 in the capital city of Tunis. AFTD is run by a large number of volunteers of high educational attainment who created the first Tunisian center against domestic violence on International Women's Day in 1993. The association collaborates with several governmental and nongovernmental Tunisian and international organizations. Its main goal is to increase public awareness of domestic violence and provide support and services to victims of this form of abuse. *See also* NON-GOVERNMENTAL ORGANIZATIONS (NGOs).

DIMASHQIYYAH, JULIA (1880–1954). A Lebanese writer and journalist who was born in the town of Mukhtarah near Sidon. She attended the Shwayfat Private School, where she trained to be a teacher. Her teaching career took her to Syria and Palestine, in addition to Lebanon. She also founded a philanthropic organization to assist needy women. She was best known for her magazine, *al-Maraah al-jadidah* (*The New Woman*), first published in 1921. Her publication, known for its serious articles, lasted for seven years. A Christian by birth, she married Badr Dimashqiyyah, who was a Muslim, in 1913, following a lecture she delivered calling for the opening of a sanitarium for tuberculosis patients.

DIVORCE IN ISLAM. Although permissible according to the **Sharia**, divorce was pronounced an act of last resort by Prophet Muhammad. He described it as the most reprehensible act in the eyes of Allah. The law regulating divorce attempts to safeguard rights of wives for a short period following the dissolution of **marriage**. The husband is expected to provide his wife with economic support for a three-month period. During this time, the door remains open for possible reconciliation through family mediation. A divorced woman is required to refrain from contracting another marriage for a period of four months, referred to as *uddah*, in order to determine the presence of pregnancy. Summary divorce by husbands, usually by taking an oath before witnesses, is becoming more restricted. Women have long objected to this type of divorce because of its arbitrary nature and avoidance of any previous consultation with the wife. Most Middle Eastern countries require the registration of the act of divorce in the courts for it to be considered legal and binding.

The Sharia allows granting women the right to seek a divorce if this was stipulated in the marriage contract. This right, known as *ismah*, is usually sought by high-born women who marry below their social status. Muslim women have gained the right to divorce by repudiation, known as *khulu*, in recent years as a result of the general demand to reinterpret Quranic passages in light of recent developments. The *khulu* type of divorce, similar to no-fault divorce in Western societies, requires surrendering the back dowry, or alimony, to the husband. A more common form of divorce, which has always existed, is known as *tafriq* (separation) and permits women to initiate divorce proceedings according to a set of limited conditions. These include mental illness or abandonment on the part of the husband, as well as lack of economic support. Islamic courts have worked to expand these conditions in recent years, giving women more leeway in seeking the dissolution of marriage.

Some countries deviated drastically from acceptable grounds of divorce in the past. In Turkey, the Islamic law of divorce has been replaced by Western laws, and in Tunisia, men and women were given equal rights, demanding the registration of the divorce decree in the courts. In Tunisia, one of these rights allows the divorced woman to seek single or co-guardianship of children according to additional reforms enacted in 1992. Divorce laws were also recast under the Pahlavi regime in Iran when the Family Protection Law of 1975 was adopted, assigning courts the responsibility of determining the fitness of a husband or wife to assume guardianship over children. This law was abrogated by the Islamic Republic of Iran. In 2000, however, Iran's Guardians Council, a supervisory legislative body, approved the passage of a bill expanding the rights of divorced women. *See also* ABDUH, MUHAMMAD (1849–1905); KHULU; PERSONAL STATUS CODE OF TUNISIA.

DIVORCE IN JEWISH LAW. Jewish personal status law in the State of Israel has been the exclusive domain of Orthodox Judaism since the creation of the state in 1948. This was the result of Prime Minister David Ben Gurion's grand bargain with the Jewish religious establishment to gain its support for a secular Israel. Among most sects of Judaism, divorce is not a burden on the wife, except in the case of Orthodox Judaism. Here, divorce is permissible under Jewish law, but largely as a male prerogative. A wife's ability to seek divorce is limited to a number of situations, which must be adjudicated by the courts. Grounds for divorcing a husband are limited to lack of economic support and mental or physical incompetence. In practice, males can demand a considerable amount of money as a condition for releasing the wife, or they can stipulate other difficult, but nonmonetary, conditions. If, as sometimes happens, the husband disappears without releasing a wife from the **marriage**, she is described as an *agunah*, or "anchored" to her husband. She can remain in this situation of suspension for a long time, unable to remarry. Jewish courts are not qualified to force a husband to grant divorce to his deserted wife.

The situation within most Ashkenazi European and American Jewish sects is quite different due to radical reforms that occurred in Germany in the 11th century. It was then that Rabbi Gershom ben Judah (ca. 960–1028), known as the "Light of the Diaspora," outlawed **polygamy** and summary divorce. This reform, which Jewish religious courts honored, was referred to as the "Ban of Rabbi Gershom." Severe judicial punishments were meted out to violators of the law. These developments affected mainly the Ashkenazi communities (European Jews), who by virtue of their residence within larger Christian societies inevitably veered toward monogamous marriages. In countries where separation of church and state exist, such as the United States, marriage and divorce laws are secular and apply to all religions and sects. The same development did not occur in Sephardi and Mizrahi communities (descended from Spanish ancestors and those living in Eastern countries) due to their insulation against European trends. No external incentive pushed these Oriental communities to follow suit, since the Islamic environment in which they lived condoned polygamy. Jewish communities in the Muslim world practiced polygamy as late as the 20th century, but this practice was not as widespread as in Muslim societies. Since only Orthodox marriages are recognized within Israel, where most Mizrahi and Sephardi Jews reside today, men's ability to defy injunctions against easy divorce still persist. Jewish wives are still obligated to wait for many years before being granted a divorce by their husbands. *See also* DOWRY IN JEWISH LAW.

DIXON, ZUHUR (1933–). Dixon is an Iraqi poet who highlighted the lives of traditional women. She was born in the town of Abu al-Khasib, south of Basra. She was largely self-educated, her main publications being two poetry collections, *Cities Have Another Awakening* and *A Homeland for Everything*.

DJEBER, ASIA (1936–). She is an Algerian Francophone novelist, poet, filmmaker, and defender of women's rights. She was born Fatima Zohra-Imalayon in the town of Cherchell, Algeria, into a secular Muslim family with a father who was an elementary school teacher of French. She received her early education in the city of Blida, and she later became only one of three or four native Algerians enrolled in a rigorous school with a predominantly French student body. In 1954, she attended Lycée Fenelon in Paris and later became the first Algerian woman to be admitted to the highly selective École Normale Superiéure. She also studied history at the Sorbonne University. Djeber returned to Algeria in 1955 and became a correspondent for *al-Moudjahid*, the leading publication of the Front de Libération Nationale (FLN). She interviewed prominent nationalist figures who were based in neighboring Tunisia and Morocco and continued to serve the **Algerian Revolution** in this manner until independence was achieved in 1962.

Djeber began to produce novels during the revolutionary war, beginning with *La Soif* (1957), *Les enfants du nouveau monde* (1962), *Les allouettes naives* (1967), *Femmes d'Alger dans leur appartement* (1980), *L'Amour, la fantasia* (1986), and *Ombre sultane* (1987). She also published a poetical collection, *Poèmes pour L'Algérie hereuse*. One of her unusual novels, *Loin de medine* (1994), chronicled the lives of pre-Islamic Arab heroines. Another novel appeared in English in 1999 under the title *So Vast Is the Prison*. Her own memoir, *Algerian White*, appeared in 2002, also in English. In addition, she produced highly rated movies, such as *La nouba des femmes du Mont Chenoua*, which won the Venice Bienniale Critics prize in 1979. Another film, *La Serda et les chants de l'oubli*, appeared in 1982. Her latest novel, which appeared in 2003, was titled *La Disparition de la langue francaise*. Although she writes in French, her actors use Algerian dialects in her films, bringing to life the roles of women in Algeria's nationalist struggles. The majority of her novels portray women as active participants in the Algerian Revolution, in contrast to their portrayal as moderately mobilized and autonomous actors in Franz Fanon's novels (1925–1961). In 1986, Djeber translated Egyptian feminist **Nawal Saadawi**'s (1931–) novel, *Woman at Point Zero*, into French under the title *Une voix à l'enfer* (*A Voice from Hell*).

Djeber had a distinguished teaching career at University of Rabat, Morocco, University of Algiers, Louisiana State University, and New York University. Since the outbreak of the Algerian civil war in 1979, she has been living in self-imposed exile. She is the winner of prestigious literary awards, such as the Neustadt International Prize for Literature in 1986 and the Fonlon-Nichols Prize of the African Literary Association in 1997. In 2005, she was the first North African woman to be elected to the Académie française. Djaber married an expatriate Algerian poet living in Paris, Malek Alloula. She has the additional distinction of being among the very few in Algeria who produced major literary works before and after independence. Her most famous novel, *Femmes d'Alger dans leur appartement* (*Women of Algiers in Their Apartment*), was considered too subversive in Algeria and appeared at first only in France and Italy. Its heroes are ordinary Algerian women, and it is considered to be the first consciously feminist novel published in that country. Both the FLN government and the country's Islamist opposition have criticized her for writing exclusively in French.

DORNER, DALIA (1934–). She is an Israeli jurist who became a member of the Supreme Court. She arrived in Palestine from her birthplace in Turkey in 1944 and received her early education at an immigrant absorption center. She was later admitted to the elite Riali high school in Haifa, graduating in 1951. She was active in leftist youth organizations before enrolling in the faculty of law at Hebrew University, where she graduated in 1956.

One of Dorner's longer assignments after graduation was at the Judge Advocate General Corps of the Israeli Defense Forces (IDF), where she served from 1960 until 1973 as a defender of military personnel. She was president of the Central Command District Military Court until 1979, followed by a term as an appointed judge in the Military Appeals Court. After her discharge with the rank of colonel, Dorner served from 1979 until 1984 as a member of Beersheba District Court. She then sat on the Jerusalem District Court for 10 years. At the end of this term she was appointed to the Supreme Court, from which she retired in 2004. Dorner became known for her liberal views while occupying that position; she was the first judge to render a legal opinion in support of the rights of same-sex couples while opposing gender discrimination in general. She made a legal argument against the continued hostage status of Lebanese Hizbullah leaders pending their exchange for missing Israeli soldiers. But her most conservative vote supported the right of Israel's security agencies to apply moderate pressure or torture in their investigations of those suspected of committing terrorist acts against the state.

DOWLAH, ANIS AL-. She was a a peasant Iranian woman who was a servant of Jayran, the favorite wife of Nasir al-Din Shah (r. 1848–1896), one of Persia's Qajar rulers. Upon the death of her mistress, she was taken as a wife by the shah in appreciation of her loyal service to his deceased spouse. Anis al-Dowlah became the shah's favorite wife, a status leading foreign diplomats to mistake her for Persia's official queen. She gained notoriety when she joined the faction opposing the chief minister, or Mushir al-Dowlah, Mirza Hussein Khan, for granting a sweeping concession to Baron Julius von Reuter (1816–1899), known as the Reuter concession. It is assumed by some experts on this period that her opposition to Mirza Hussein Khan was sparked by his attempt to eliminate her from a royal tour of Europe. Her campaign against the concession, however, was seen by many as a genuine reaction to the sweeping powers granted to Reuters under this agreement.

DOWLATABADI, SIDDIQEH (1881–1961). An Iranian nationalist and feminist who pioneered the **education** of women in Iran. Born to a religious family from the city of Isfahan, she was allowed to attend school dressed as a boy. Her father was a distinguished religious scholar. At the age of 14, she organized a girl's school in secret, which she was forced to close three months later. She founded one of the earliest women's organizations dedicated to education, known as Shirkat-I Khavotin-I Isfahan (Isfahan Women's Cooperative). In 1919, she established the first journal with the word *zenan* (woman) in its title, *Zaban-I Zanan* (*Women's Tongue*). This bimonthly magazine, which expressed nationalist and feminist views, shocked the deeply religious inhabitants of Isfahan. The magazine carried articles critical of the veil and called for the education of women as a way of guaranteeing their economic independence. *Zaban-I Zanan* also featured political articles dealing with parliamentary elections and criticizing the northern oil agreement with Great Britain and the 1919 Anglo–Persian Agreement. Dowlatabadi openly attacked the prime minister, Vusuq al-Dowlah, for granting excessive economic rights to Britain in that agreement. This led to a ban on her magazine and to threats on her life by traditional elements in Isfahan. After going into hiding for a while, she moved to Tehran, where she started a new *anjuman* (society) for women and published a dictionary of Iranian women. Between 1923 and 1927, she traveled abroad, touring France, Germany, and Switzerland and studying briefly at the Sorbonne. She attended the 10th congress of the International Alliance for Women's Suffrage held in Paris in 1926, where she met the president of the Alliance, Margaret Ashby. A lasting friendship developed between the two. Ashby, who was a political activist and founder of a New York magazine titled *Taking Care of Home and Children*, inspired Dowlatabadi to establish a magazine sponsored by the Iranian government.

Dowlatabadi's anti**veiling** movement eventually linked up with **Reza Shah**'s (r. 1925–1941) campaign to eliminate the veil. She founded a women's committee known as *Kanun-e banovan*, which promoted the antiveiling campaign of the shah. She was also one of the earliest Iranian women to address crowds while unveiled, delivering speeches in various settings upon her return from Europe, even in the center of the sacred city of Qom. After receiving death threats for years, she felt safer after the passage of the shah's antiveiling decree in 1936. She maintained her links to international feminists by attending the 10th congress of the Women's International League for Peace and Freedom in Geneva, Switzerland. Before she died in 1961, she insisted that no veiled women be allowed to mourn her. But her legacy and contribution to the liberation of Iranian women remain contested by both her admirers and detractors. Modern Iranian feminists who have subjected her life to a critical reading fault her for creating a **feminist movement** for the elite and promoting feminist rights along class lines. They emphasize a controversial instance during her lifetime when she arranged a **marriage** between her 70-year-old widowed father and the nine-year-old daughter of his lower-class secretary. Dowlatabadi also remains the favorite target of Iranian religious fanatics, who defaced her gravestone right after she was buried.

DOWRY IN ISLAM. The payment of dowry (Arabic: *mahr*) was known in ancient customs among the pre-Islamic Arabs and other civilizations. Islam, however, mandated that the dowry be paid to the woman and not to her father, since she was granted the right to own property and began to enjoy complete economic freedom to dispose of it in any manner she wished. The payment of a dowry is an essential component of an Islamic marriage contract. Without it, the contract could be declared invalid. The dowry is always paid by the bridegroom, even if he lacked the means to do so. In the case of an impoverished husband, the payment of a symbolic dowry is required, which usually translates into the equivalent of a quarter of one U.S. dollar. Sometimes, a certain amount is entered in the marriage document but never rendered. Symbolic dowries are also the norm in the case of the marriage of first cousins, a common and preferred form of union throughout the Muslim world. Dowries could also be in the form of immovable property, but this is rather rare, occurring only among wealthy families.

The Islamic marriage contract also stipulates the amount of a back dowry, or alimony, to be paid in the event of divorce. The back dowry (Arabic: *al-mutaakher*) is usually calculated to be much more than the amount of the initial dowry, an accepted custom since the two families always assume that the marriage will not be dissolved. The inadequacy of the back dowry due to economic changes and inflationary trends has been the topic of hot debate in recent years. Many divorced women have complained about the paucity of the amount of back dowry paid to them after so many years of conjugal life.

For instance, a movie titled *I Need a Solution (Uridu hallan)* became a sensation in Egypt during the 1970s because it focused on the story of a divorced woman facing impoverishment due to the inadequacy of her back dowry. The movie was shown on Egyptian television stations for an entire week prior to the legislative debate over Law 44, which was sponsored by **Jihan Sadat**, to drive the point home about needed reforms.

The amount of dowry has increased dramatically in recent years among the elite families of the Arab Gulf States. The dowry, thus, has been symptomatic of widening class differences, particularly in countries such as Egypt, where young men are forced to delay getting married due to this problem. In times of war or revolutions some communities, such as the Palestinians during the two *intifadas* (1987–1988, 2000–2003), have attempted to rein in this runaway trend by calling for minimizing the payment of dowries as a patriotic duty.

DOWRY IN JEWISH LAW. Under Jewish law, the wife is expected to provide a dowry to her husband at the time of **marriage**. The custom can be traced back only to the Talmudic period, reversing the earlier biblical pattern in which the groom paid a dowry, or *mohar* (Hebrew) to the bride's father. The rationalization for the bride's father giving a dowry to his daughter as a gift to her husband was due to her exclusion from inheriting from her parents upon her marriage. The groom was expected to provide his wife with gifts, while the bride brought property to the marital home consisting of land, slaves, or cattle. But the custom of *mohar* has declined in favor of the *kettubah* or the marriage contract, whereby the husband is only burdened with paying his wife a back dowry upon **divorce**, the amount depending on whether the wife was single, divorced, or widowed at the time of marriage. Dowries for orphaned or poor girls were supplied by a community fund. East European Jews maintained the dowry custom until modern times. The dowry would revert to the wife upon her divorce or her husband's demise.

Some changes in the details of the *kettubah* were introduced after the creation of the modern state of Israel. Even though matters pertaining to marriage, divorce, and inheritance remain within the domain of Jewish law, the state of Israel was able to introduce significant changes on behalf of wives. The Israeli Supreme Court provided a special reading of the 1951 Women's Equal Rights Law (No. 5711) to prevent Jewish religious law, which enables a husband to enjoy income from a wife's own investment, from applying to marriages. The court emphasized that the property of each spouse was totally independent of the capital that a wife brings into a marriage and the income from its investment.

DULAYMI, LUTFIYAH (1942–). She was an Iraqi writer who published novels, short-story collections, plays, and essays on cultural criticism. Some of her work has been translated into several languages, especially her output dealing with political, historical, and social themes relating to Arab and Iraqi women. She was born in Baghdad and worked for the Iraqi Ministry of Culture, where she honed her writing skills. She depicted the loneliness of liberated Arab women who forsake their traditional roles in society. Among her publications are novels and short-story collections such as *Who Inherited Paradise?* (1987), *A Path to the Sorrow of Men* (1969), *The Statute* (1977), *If You Were in Love* (1980), *The World of Lonely Women* (1986), *Seeds of Fire* (1988), *Hayyat's Garden* (2004), *Lighter Than Angels* (1999), and *Shahrazad and Her Narrative* (1999).

DULAYMI, NAZIHA JAWDAT. She was an Iraqi feminist and leftist leader. She became a member of the Iraqi Communist Party's Central Committee in the mid-1940s. Her organization, the League for the Defense of Women's Rights, founded in 1952, waged a successful campaign to impose harsh punishment on perpetrators of **honor crimes** and for the adoption of a new personal status law. When **Abd al-Karim Qassem** (r. 1958–1963) overturned the monarchy and created Iraq's first republican regime, he adopted most of the reforms called for by the League, such as raising the age of **marriage** for girls to 18, limiting summary **divorce**, and allowing women to inherit an equal share of the father's estate as their brothers. When this reform was adopted, it was the first such step in the Sunni world. Dulaymi also wrote a book in 1958, *A Sample from the Ordeals of the Arab Woman.* During that same year, she became the first female minister of municipalities when Qassem chose her as a member of his cabinet. The League remained her main base of power, with a membership of 42,000 in 1960. In 1963, the League was closed by the Baath regime, which toppled Qassem's government. *See also* INHERITANCE UNDER ISLAMIC LAW.

DURR, SHAJAR AL- (?–1257). Also called Shajarat al-Durr (Tree of Pearls), she was the second female ruler of a large state in the Arab world after Yemen's **Arwa, Sayyida Hurra,** who ruled in the 11th century. Shajar al-Durr was a white slave of Turkish origin who became the concubine, and later wife, of Egypt's Ayubid ruler, al-Malek al-Saleh Najm al-Din Ayubi (r. 1240–1249). She was described by historians as beautiful and intelligent. Her rise to power was the result of palace intrigue and rivalries between members of the Ayubid dynasty, which was of Kurdish origin, and the class of Mamluks, who were of Turkish or Armenian origin and predominated around the palace. The Ayubid dynasty was founded by Saladin (Salah al-Din al-Ayubi) (r. 1138–1193), who was born in Takrit, Iraq, near the center of the Abbasid dynasty. When her husband died, Shajar managed to conceal this fact from the general public with the help of his military lieutenants in order to focus on threats to Egypt by the Seventh Crusade. She developed a military strategy with the help of her aides, leading the troops into battle and succeeding in imprisoning the Crusades' French leader, King Louis IX, in the town of Mansourah. In the meantime, word went out to her husband's son, Turan Shah, who was traveling, that he would be crowned as his father's successor. Turan Shah was proclaimed the Sultan of Egypt in February 1250, followed by the release of his father's death notice.

Before long, Turan Shah was opposed by the Mamluks, who considered him to be weak and inefficient. He was assassinated by Shajar's allies in May 1250, in the town of Farsikur, effectively ending Ayubid rule in Egypt. Shajar was installed as his successor, taking the name al-Malikah Ismat al-Din Umm Khalil Shajar al-Durr. As a sign of her total control over Egypt, prayers were called in her name during Friday services, and coins were minted in her name. But Syrian Ayubid princes rejected her authority, and those in charge of Iraq refused to pay tribute. The Abbasid Caliph al-Mustaqim also declined to support a female ruler. Rivalry between the two was exacerbated when she took the title "Queen of the Muslims." She ruled for barely three months before she lost the support of her military officers, who feared the wrath of the caliph. But Shajar was unwilling to give up power, so she married the newly installed sultan, Izz al-Din Aybak al-Turkumani, the former commander-in-chief favored by the Mamluks. She attempted to be a coruler but failed to dissuade her husband from taking another wife, who turned out to be the daughter of the Ayubid prince of Mosul, Badr al-din Lulu. After ruling together for seven years, she had him murdered by her servants while he was taking a bath. Her complicity in this crime was discovered by the sultan's widow upon obtaining confessions from Shajar's servants. Shajar was duly killed by being beaten with wooden clogs on 2 April 1257. Her naked body was thrown from a cliff in Cairo's citadel. Her supporters collected her body and buried it in the courtyard of a school that she had built. Shajar remains a significant figure in Egypt's history due to her two achievements: the defeat of the Seventh Crusade and the capture of Louis IX, as well as opening the way for the rise of the Bahri Mamluk line of rulers. She also occupies a significant position in the Egyptian folkloric imagination, expressed in many songs and poems celebrating her short but colorful rule over Egypt.

E

EBADI, SHIRIN (1947–). She was an Iranian lawyer and human rights activist who was born in Hamadan, where her father, Mohammad Ali Ebadi, was a professor of commercial law. She was raised in Tehran, where she studied law at Tehran University, graduating in 1969. She received a master's degree in law in 1971, and in 1975, she became the first woman to be appointed a judge during the regime of Shah Muhammad Reza Pahlavi (r.1941–1979). The Islamic regime of Iran dismissed her from this post, claiming that the **Sharia** banned women from such positions. She was demoted to an administrative position within the court, but she opted for early retirement instead. Because she was unable to practice law, she devoted her time to writing on the issue of violence toward women and children. She came to the attention of reforming President Mohammad Khatami (r. 1997–2005) through her articles in the feminist journal *Zenan*. He encouraged her activities, and her husband, Javad Tavassolian, worked as an adviser in his office.

Ebadi continued to work as a lawyer, handling high-profile cases of victims of human rights abuse such as Dariush Farouhar and his wife, Parvaneh Eskandari, two intellectuals whose death was blamed on the regime. Ebadi also worked on child abuse cases and fought against restrictions on freedom of the press and freedom of expression. She is credited with pushing for the passage of legislation outlawing physical abuse of children in 2002. In 2003, she was awarded the Nobel Peace Prize for her work in support of democracy, human rights, and the rights of women and children. She was the first Muslim woman to win this award, but the Islamist regime met this recognition with silence. Despite her criticism of some aspects of life under this regime, Ebadi never called for forcible regime change. She continues to consider herself an Iranian nationalist who opposed some of the shah's policies in the past but has always rejected the possibility of Western intervention in the interest of promoting a freer political climate. After winning the Nobel Prize she became a highly sought after lecturer outside of Iran, but was also harassed by the regime. She received several international awards in recognition of her work, from Human Rights Watch in 1996, the Norwegian

Rafto prize in 2001, the Légion d'honneur medal in 2006, and several honorary degrees from universities around the world. Her publications include coauthored works, *Democracy, Human Rights, and Islam in Modern Iran: Psychological, Social, and Cultural Perspectives* (2003) and *Iran Awakening: A Memoir of Revolution and Hope* (2006), with Azadeh Moaveni. Since 2009, Ebadi has been a political exile in Great Britain. *See also* FEMINIST MOVEMENT IN IRAN.

EBTEKAR, MAASUMEH (1960–). She is an Iranian female activist, born in Tehran, who is closely associated with President Mohammad Khatami. She spent part of her childhood in the United States. She received degrees in medical technology from Shahid Beheshti University in 1985 and a PhD in immunology from Tarbiat Modarres University in 1995, both in Tehran. She gained notoriety as a result of participating in the seizure of the American embassy building in Tehran in 1979, where she assumed the name "Mary" and was the militant students' liaison to the American media. She was a constant presence on U.S. television programs throughout the 444 days of the American hostage crisis. She wrote her own version of these events 21 years later, *Takeover in Tehran: The Inside Story of the 1979 Embassy Capture.*

Ebtekar also became an ardent supporter of women's rights and represented Iran at the 1985 Third World Conference on Women at Nairobi, Kenya. During the Fourth World Conference in 1995 at Beijing, she was the vice chair of the Iranian committee. Ebtekar was among the founders of the Center for Women's Studies and Research in 1986 and served on its board of directors. She wrote several articles on integrating women in society and the economy, serving since 1994 as the editorial director of the conservative publication *Farzaneh: Journal of Women's Studies.* Her editorship of the English-language daily *Kayhan International* paralleled Khatami's editorship of its Farsi counterpart, *Kayhan.* Her articles on immunology were limited in number and were never a match for her published works on women. Starting in 1994, she headed the Women's NGO Coordination Office. President Khatami appointed Ebtekar in 1997 as the first female vice president in the history of Iran, entrusting her with the portfolio of the department of the environment, an appointment that ended with his departure from public office.

EDIP, HALIDE (1883–1964). She is a Turkish political leader and feminist who was born in Istanbul, where she was tutored at home. Her father was the private secretary to Sultan Abd al-Hamid II. In 1901, she was the first Muslim Turkish student to complete her studies at the American College for Girls, which opened its doors in 1871. She began her long writing career in 1897 with a translation of *Mother* by Jacob Abbott. She married a famous astronomer, Salih Zeki Bey, who divorced her in 1910. She wrote extensively on women's **education** for *Tanin*, a Turkish daily. This led to her being hired by the Ministry of Education as a consultant on girls' education, later producing many tracts on curricular and pedagogical reform. Her services were abruptly terminated when she wrote about reforming girls' religious schools. She wrote many novels in which she called for an enhanced Turkish identity and adopting Western standards of government and education.

Edip became famous for her literary salon following her **divorce**. The salon was frequented by many famous figures of her day, who argued over new concepts of secular Turkish nationalism. She founded the Elevation of Women Organization (Taali-I Nisvan), and after her second marriage, to Dr. Adnan Adivar in 1917, she became fully involved with the country's national movement. She was the only woman to join the council of a nationwide organization known as Ojak, representing the nationalist movement behind the Young Turk Revolution of 1908. Edip came into her own as a nationalist organizer during World War I, at first as an inspector of girls' schools in other parts of the Ottoman Empire such as the Syrian Province. There, she reportedly quarreled with Jamal Pasha, the Ottoman governor, over forcing young Armenian orphaned girls to take Muslim names. When **Mustafa Kemal Ataturk** organized an army to defend his country against the British invasion during the latter part of World War I, she joined his forces. She and her husband fought in the war of liberation, during which she rose to the rank of sergeant. She was sentenced to death by the sultan's government, and in 1920, British forces attempted to exile her along with a number of Turkish leaders to the island of Malta. In 1926, she was among a group accused of treason, leading to her fleeing the country. She and her husband lived in Europe from 1926 until 1939, residing mainly in Great Britain and France. She lectured in several countries, including the United States and India. She returned to Turkey and taught English literature at Istanbul University's Faculty of Letters. In 1950, she was elected to parliament, where she served for four years before resigning.

Edip wrote many books, but her most famous novel was *The Clown and His Daughter*, which appeared first in English in 1935 and a year later in Turkish as *Sinekli Bakkal*. Her memoirs were published in English in 1926 as *The Memoirs of Halide Edip*. Another book, *Turkey Faces West*, appeared in 1930. She was the subject of a biographical work, *Halide's Gift*, published by Frances Kazan in 2001. Her character has been portrayed in several movie and television productions, such as *The Young Indiana Jones Chronicles*. Her life has also been made into a documentary for children, *The Greedy Heart of Halide Edip*.

EDUCATION: ARAB GULF STATES. One of the earliest Gulf States to emphasize the education of women was Kuwait. Although eventually enjoying membership in the six-state Gulf Cooperation Council (GCC), which included Saudi Arabia, Oman, United Arab Emirates, Qatar, and Bahrain, Kuwait was the first state to experience indirect British rule as a protectorate in the 1890s. Even before the discovery of oil in the 1930s, Kuwait, like other regional states, was an adherent of the Islamic religion, which calls for women's literacy to perform devotional services required of both genders. Most women received instruction as children in the village Islamic schools known as *kuttab*, which taught Arabic to facilitate the reading of the Quran as well as the basic elements of mathematics. Some women instructed girls in the reading of the Quran for a fee, such as Amina al-Omar, who taught girls in 1916. This instruction was conducted in private homes, where the teachers were known as *mutawaas*, or guides. The economy of Kuwait, as well as the rest of the Arab Gulf states, was based on pearl fishing, and its merchant class, which arose as a result of this trade, began to open private schools for boys in 1912. A decline in their income as a result of the development of Japan's cultured pearl industry in the 1930s prompted this same class to pressure Kuwait's rulers, the Sabah family, to provide a system of free public education.

In response, in 1936 Kuwait created the Council of Education, followed by a Department of Education in 1938. After the opening of boys' schools, which were financed by customs duties and the pearl diving tax, the first two public schools for girls were opened, in 1937 and 1938. These were staffed by Palestinian teachers recruited outside of the country. Although public schools for boys were free of charge, girls had to pay a fee to attend. The rise of cultural clubs in the late 1940s and 1950s took on the role of nationalist activity. The most prominent of these was the Teachers' Club which, though restricted to men, began to publish newspapers featuring modernizing activities and calling for the education of women. Much of the inspiration for this came from Egypt, where most of the male teachers were educated and witnessed the female emancipation movement firsthand. But for women, who could only aspire to complete their secondary education at home, the Teachers' Club and its paper *al-Raiid* (*The Pioneer*) proved to be invaluable allies. Beginning in 1953, Kuwaiti women began to question the value of their traditional outer **veil**, the *abaya*, in the pages of *al-Raiid.* The editors applauded the idea of doing away with this strict dress code, especially when some schoolgirls burned their *abayas* in 1956, resulting in the disruption of their education. It took about three years before the Council of Education succumbed to pressure and came up with a modern dress code for all schoolgirls, although the veil was maintained for all public employees, including non-Kuwaiti teachers, until 1961.

With Kuwaiti independence finally a reality in 1961, its constitution, under Article 40, guaranteed educational rights to all of its citizens. The 1965 Compulsory Education Act required school attendance for boys and girls between the ages of 6 and 14. With the proliferation of foreign schools serving children of expatriate workers, the Ministry of Education began to supervise the entire public and private school systems. After the establishment of Kuwait University in 1966, women were allowed to join the 400-strong student body, including its two colleges. Women qualified for government scholarships to study abroad, with the first group graduating from Cairo University. But women continued to outnumber men at Kuwait University due to family preference for keeping female students at their home institutions. By the late 1980s, almost 60 percent of all incoming students were women. However, female students at Kuwait University continue to be underrepresented in the fields of Islamic law and engineering.

Despite the fact that Kuwaiti women benefited from the earliest government-provided educational opportunities in the Arab Gulf region, they remained clustered around the ministries of health, education, social affairs, and labor. They also continued to face competition from non-Kuwaiti female professionals. The barriers were breached in 1962 when two women joined the Kuwaiti Broadcasting Service and another entered the Kuwaiti foreign office. Nouria al-Saadani gained access to a position with public radio after many years as a volunteer. Yet this educational revolution impacting daughters of the bourgeoisie did not alter the lives of poorer women. As the affluent upper classes began to hire foreign nannies, native women were reduced to performing domestic service and dress-making, which was the only available employment for the unskilled and uneducated. Two government policies worked to ameliorate the conditions of poor women: promoting the principle of favoring native workers over foreigners, or the policy of Kuwaitization, and encouraging women through the granting of government subsidies to marry and have large families to offset the diminutive size of the native population. The adult literacy rate for females in 2006–2007 was 93 percent, compared to 95 percent for males.

Neither of these policies tackled the issue of female illiteracy. This was left to private and voluntary associations such as al-Saadani's, which recommended through the 1971 Kuwaiti Women's Conference providing greater educational opportunities for women and the opening of **family planning** centers. Despite earning national esteem for their participation in the anti-Iraqi resistance movement during the invasion of 1990, women's employment opportunities remained limited and restricted to certain professions. Most women were employed by the educational sector, with more than one-third of them being teachers, social service employees, or clerical workers. Few wealthy women were visible in large commercial companies or as owners or workers in fashion houses catering to other women.

The education of women in Bahrain paralleled that of Kuwait in many ways. The first girls' public school on the primary level was established in 1928, about nine years after the founding of the first boys' school, the Khalifiya. A secondary school for girls was opened in 1951; the boys' secondary school had opened in 1939. By the 1960s and 1970s, girls' enrollment in all levels of education was greater than that of boys, by a ratio of two to one. Interest in educating girls was the result of nationalist ideas brought back by Bahraini males who studied in Egypt. Bahraini women quickly availed themselves of all available opportunities and were able to advance toward gaining enfranchisement sooner than other Arab Gulf women. Among the early organizations advocating voting rights for females was Nahdat Fatat al-Bahrain (The Renaissance of the Bahraini Woman), which sought to achieve women's rights by the 1970s. Bahraini males in general were very supportive of women's right to education, which they regarded as a necessary precondition for modernizing the country. By the 1980/1981 academic year, close to 45.8 percent of the total school population in Bahrain was made up of women. Women were also attending the American University of Beirut as early as the 1950s, which opened up many careers for them at home. This translated into diverse employment opportunities such as accounting, teaching school, nursing, and in higher education. The only occupation that did not appeal to Bahraini women was clerical work, which was dominated by non-Bahraini women. In 2002 two women, Shafiya Asaad and Bahiya al-Jalil, the latter the top female civil servant in the country, ran unsuccessfully for parliament. Most women, however, worked for a few years after marriage and completing secondary school and typically left the job market after the birth of their first child. Most working women were found in the educational or nursing fields. During the 1980s, almost 60 percent of female schoolteachers were Bahrainis, the rest being from other Arab countries. By the year 2006, the adult literacy rate for women in Bahrain was 86 percent, whereas for males it was 90 percent.

Women's education in Qatar dates back to the early part of the 20th century, when private religious schooling was opened to girls in some urban areas. Development in Qatar had to await the commercial production of oil in the 1940s. The first public school for boys was opened in 1952; it was followed by a girls' school in 1955. Directed by Amnah Mahmoud al-Gidah, this school had one teacher and an enrollment of 50 students, some of whom were married women. A Kuwaiti journalist, Hiddayat Sultan al-Salem, who visited Qatar in 1968, recorded her impressions of that country's commitment to women's education in her book *Papers of a Traveler in the Arabian Gulf*. She found that one Qatari woman was already enrolled at the University of Kuwait, and five other female students were slated to join her. Qatar produced its first female university professor, Johina al-Issa, in the mid-1960s; she taught sociology.

Following independence in 1971, Qatar pushed ahead with providing more educational opportunities for women. Figures for the total school population in 1981/1982 indicated that 26,802 students were enrolled in primary schools, and 15,346 were enrolled in secondary schools. The Qatari government provided students with free transportation, dormitory facilities, and school supplies. Figures for the same year indicated that there were 70 girls' schools with a total enrollment of 19,356 on the elementary and secondary levels. In order to decrease its reliance on foreign teachers, Qatar opened two teachers' colleges in 1973, with the girls' facility enrolling 103 students. Eventually, these colleges formed the nucleus of the University of Qatar, which opened its doors in 1977. During the 1980s, the university's student body consisted of 3,285 females and 1,530 males, a large number of males being educated abroad. Students were paid a monthly stipend, but in recent years this form of subsidy has been limited to students majoring in commerce, industrial sciences, religion, and education. Female graduate students continue to complain today of restricted study opportunities abroad because of the cultural requirement that they be accompanied by a male family member, or *mahram*. The Qatari government would only grant permission for this type of study if the girls' parents provided a male escort, whose travel expenses, as well as the equivalent of 60 percent of the student's grant, would be provided by the government. Despite these restrictions, figures for the 1980s show that Qatar had 500 female university graduates, 7 of whom held advanced college degrees. Figures for 1980 indicated that 50 percent of the female labor force held jobs in the educational sector. But for poorer and less-educated women, the most common form of employment was as office janitor or escort for female students on their daily bus travel to school. Figures also show that 1,614 women in 1980 were employed in senior civil service positions.

Qatari female students had the benefit of some unusual role models. Aisha al-Kawari, for instance, was the country's first pediatrician; she received her education at the University of Cairo while accompanied by her mother. She was familiar to all female students through her radio broadcasts, in which she encouraged them to emulate her career path. Al-Kawari later traveled to the United States to acquire more specialization. Another woman, Hissa al-Jabaar, studied engineering at the University of Kuwait but was unable to pursue a career in this field due to family restrictions. Another pioneer was Aisha Hassan, who entered the field of broadcasting by working for the national broadcasting service in 1968. The adult literacy rate for women in Qatar for 2006, which stood at 90 percent, was one of the highest in the Middle East. The adult literacy rate for males was 94 percent.

Women in the United Arab Emirates (UAE) lacked educational opportunities until the oil era. Due to the lack of funding, the level of illiteracy for both men and women when the Emirates were known as the Trucial States

(TS) was nearly 90 percent. With the exception of the traditional *kuttab*, the country lacked resources and qualified personnel to start a modern school system. The country's British rulers persuaded the state of Kuwait to come to the Trucial States' assistance, because the former had developed a regular educational system 20 years earlier. The first school for boys was opened in Sharjah, one of the seven city-states of the TS, in 1953. Great Britain provided the facilities and Kuwait the teachers. At the time, Sharjah constituted 12 percent of the total population of the UAE and was the first emirate to establish schools for girls, enrolling 70 students in 1958. But Abu Dhabi, the richest of the seven emirates and the earliest to develop its own oil fields, refused to accept Kuwaiti assistance. Under the tutelage of Abu Dhabi's ruler and the future UAE president, Sheikh Zayed Bin Sultan al-Nahyan, approximately $30 to $35 million was earmarked for the development of schools in the Abu Dhabi Development Plan adopted in 1968. At the time, there were only five elementary schools in the emirate, four for boys and one for girls. By the 1972/1973 school year, there were 30 schools, a student population of 13,916, and 200 students pursuing graduate studies abroad. There were 42,137 students enrolled in Abu Dhabi's schools in 1974, 30 percent of whom were females. By 1976, there were primary schools for girls in all seven emirates and one secondary school for girls in Sharjah. Most of the female teachers were Palestinian, Egyptian, and Lebanese. During that same year, 146 female teachers were assigned to 15 secondary schools for girls. Abu Dhabi took a giant step forward in the 1970s, when it welcomed its first private schools to educate children of expatriate families residing in the emirate. These schools, which were open to native students, offered British, American, French, Indian, and Iranian education.

By the time of the actual federation of the seven emirates in 1971, the authorities were rushing to make up for lost time. Until 1978, when half of the UAE's budget was allocated to defense, the second largest allocation was for education. By 1980, the UAE was operating 370 educational facilities for a total student body of 96,000. Almost 2,000 students were pursuing their education abroad on government scholarships, of whom one-quarter were studying in the United States. By 1979, only 361 teachers of a total of 5,500 were Emiratis. The remainder, including university teachers who contracted to teach at the University of Al-Ain in Abu Dhabi, came from Egypt. UAE authorities provided great incentives to promote school attendance by both genders. Almost all children between the ages of 6 and 11 attended public schools. After federation, students began to receive a monthly subsidy, school supplies, meals, medical care, uniforms, and shoes as incentives. Students who lived at a distance were provided free bus transportation and dormitory space if needed. Free literacy classes were provided for the adult population. Dubai, the most modernizing of the emirates, opened teacher-training colleges for both genders and welcomed foreign private schools. Women's literacy rate for 2006–2007 was 91 percent, whereas for men it was 89 percent.

Education in Oman has seen great advances due to the policies of the ruler, Sultan Qaboos. There was no interest in developing a modern educational infrastructure under his father, Sultan Said ibn Taymur, who was eased out of office in 1970. The Sultanate of Oman had to rely on a large contingent of foreign teachers as late as 1985. Up until that time, the Ministry of Education and Youth Affairs hired around 1,861 foreign teachers annually. The creation of the Education and Training Council in 1977, chaired by the sultan, took great steps toward increasing the number of students in elementary schools. Figures for the late 1970s indicate that 134,000 students were registered in primary schools, of which 40 percent were female. Around the same time, Oman operated 9 secondary schools, which increased to 29 in a matter of five years. Female students accounted for 30 percent of the total enrollment. Two teacher-training colleges for women were soon founded to reduce the state's dependence on foreign (other Arab) teachers. Sultan Qaboos University opened in 1986, and female students were not required to veil. The university's student enrollment by 1990 was 3,021, of which 47 percent were women registered in a number of colleges. The large female representation here, as in other Arab Gulf countries, was due to social disapproval of foreign study opportunities for women. The adult literacy rate for Omani women, which was 77 percent in 2006, is one of the lowest in the Arab Gulf region. The literacy rate for men in that same year was 89 percent.

Female education in Saudi Arabia lagged behind that of males due to the kingdom's conservative religious traditions and its *Wahhabi* sect of Islam, which legitimized the royal family's rule. Early boys' education was provided by the Arabian–American Oil Company (ARAMCO), the major oil concessionaire in the country in the early 1950s, but mainly for the children of its own employees. The company was the first to provide a limited version of modern education for its employees' dependents. Official attention to education by the Saudi state began in 1953, when the first formal cabinet emerged and a department of education was created. A huge expansion of boys' schools occurred under the tutelage of Prince Fahd ibn Abd al-Aziz (later King Fahd), who served as minister of education from 1953 to 1960. The first public school for girls was opened in 1961, but girls' education was accelerated when King Faysal took over the reins of government in 1964. The king's tenure, which lasted until 1974, increased educational opportunities for women on all levels. This was largely due to the efforts of his wife, **Queen Iffat**. The labor code of Saudi Arabia called for strict separation of the sexes in the workplace, which necessitated the importation of a large number of female teachers to staff the new girls' schools. Yet literacy remained a grave problem, especially for women, in a country with a vast territory and a large rural Bedouin population. By 1978, of the general population above 10 years old, 58 percent were fully illiterate. By 2006–2007, the adult literacy rate for women had risen to 79 percent, compared to 89 percent for men.

Starting in the 1960s, the government agency in charge of overseeing female education in the kingdom was called the Presidency for Girls' Education. Under King Fahd, the head of this agency was a prominent religious figure, Sheikh Abd al-Aziz Nasser al-Rashid, who was also known for his commitment to education and who made the idea of educating girls acceptable to the general public. Remarkably, and despite its late start in catching up with the rest of the Arab Gulf States, Saudi Arabia was able to expand its educational system greatly. It was reported that by 2001, there were one million school girls, many of whom aspired to careers other than teaching. Educational facilities were also expanded, covering rural as well as urban centers. During that same year, the country claimed to have founded 26,000 schools, 8 universities, and some institutes and colleges. Estimates indicate that at least five million Saudi citizens were enrolled in schools or institutes by the year 2000, which provided one teacher per 12.5 students. All levels of education were free, with the government providing educational material and health care to all students. Females were enrolled in 73 colleges designated specifically for them, and almost half of all enrollees in Saudi schools and universities were females.

The bureaucracy overseeing girls' education that was created by King Faysal suffered a great setback when a fire erupted in a Meccan girls' school in 2002, resulting in the death of 15 students and injuries to several others. It was reported that failure to summon firefighting equipment in time or to allow firefighters entry into the segregated school caused this significant loss of life. The Saudi government reacted to this incident by merging the Presidency for Girls' Education with the Department of Education, forcing the section's head, Ali al-Murshid, to resign. The practice of appointing religious scholars to head girls' education was discontinued, and an acclaimed expert with no religious credentials, Dr. Khidur Olayan al-Quraishi, was chosen as al-Murshid's replacement. This tragic incident also resulted in many influential Saudis calling for reform of the educational system. *See also* BEN BAZ, ABD AL-AZIZ (1912–1999); DASHTI, ROLA (1965–); FATWA; FAYSAL, HAIFA (1952–); KHAMIS, ZABYA (1958–); MISNAD, SHEIKHA MOUZA AL- (1959–); MUBARAK, SHEIKHA FATIMA BINT (ca. 1950–); OLAYAN, LUBNA (1955–).

EDUCATION: COLONIAL PERIOD. Many schools for girls sprang up during the 19th century throughout the Middle East and North Africa. Most were missionary schools encouraged by the colonial powers in order to disseminate Western social values. By the end of the 19th century, when the colonial powers firmly established themselves in control of these countries, a substantial network of missionary girls' schools was already in place. Most of these schools were founded in areas where Ottoman authority was weakening. European missionaries, motivated by a strong evangelizing impulse, found education to be the easiest means of reaching people's hearts, since Ottoman authorities banned direct missionary activities among the Muslim population. These schools began to proliferate in the Arab world due to the tolerant climate established by the Tanzimat, or Ottoman reforms, dating back to the first third of the 19th century. Organizations such as the Church Missionary Society (CMS), the Kaiserwerth Deaconesses, and Terra Sancta Custody sent scores of female European teachers to educate Arab girls.

The basic objective of these schools was to discourage girls from following in their mothers' footsteps and to help them embrace the new Christian values offered by these schools. Arab girls were also seen as crucial agents of change and a great potential influence over the Arab family. The curriculum of these schools emphasized the domestic arts, such as modern methods of raising children and homemaking as well as European languages and religions. The Europeans firmly believed in the superiority of their hygienic and health-care methods and sought to teach these to their native charges. Languages taught were English, French, and German, and to a lesser degree Italian, Russian, and Swedish. Arabic was sometimes offered. The same missionary organizations created "mothers' meetings," offering religious instruction along with the teaching of modern hygiene and the domestic arts. By the 20th century, these schools began to offer the study of mathematics and science. By the 1920s and 1930s, the most prominent schools began to prepare their students for university entrance exams for admission to European and Middle Eastern universities, especially in Lebanon. The American University of Beirut (AUB), founded in 1866, became coeducational in 1926. Until 1951, female students were required to attend Beirut College for Women for their first two years of study. Students who were encouraged to seek higher education usually ended up in typically gendered career tracks such as nursing and secretarial work. After independence, missionary schools for boys and girls were required to emphasize the study of Arabic and the Muslim religion. Among the most famous schools that catered to daughters of the affluent classes were the Sacre Coeur School in Cairo, Schmidt Girls School in Jerusalem, Rosary School in Nazareth, and CMS Girls School in Amman. Most of these schools survived into the postindependence period.

EDUCATION: EGYPT. Education for girls was part of the modernization project of most 19th-century Egyptian rulers. Some consider the **Egyptian School of Midwives**, established in 1832, to be the earliest school for girls in the country, but this claim is usually discounted due to the specialized nature of its curriculum. Among the earliest modern schools for girls were two established by Khedive Ismail (r. 1863–1873) in 1873. The first of these, al-Siyufiyya School, was opened by his wife, Tcheshme Hanum, in 1873; the second, the Qirabiyya School, was opened in 1874. The advancement of female education faced two obstacles: opposition by traditionalists, who saw no value in this education, and budgetary constraints, especially following the economic decline resulting from building the Suez Canal. Often British colonial authorities used the conservatives' opposition as an excuse to maintain their strict fiscal guidelines for operating in Egypt. When primary schools were made available, tuition fees were imposed, making education unaffordable.

Egypt's first constitution (1923) under the nationalist Wafd government made education compulsory for both genders between the ages of 6 and 12. However, the shortage of facilities and the expansion of the school-age population prevented the implementation of this law. Calls for providing universal education for men and women continued to be heard throughout the 20th century. It fell to the government of Jamal Abd al-Nasser after the 1952 revolution to fulfill this nationalist demand. Under his rule (1954–1970), secondary and university education for both genders became totally free, with university admission being based strictly on admission tests. Despite this commitment, universal primary education for girls has not been achieved, and a high female illiteracy rate lingers. In a 1994 official report, it was estimated that up to one million children, most of whom were females from the southern provinces, were still unable to receive primary education.

These figures, however, belie the sustained interest in girls' education from all levels of Egyptian society. During the 1840s, the greatest advocate of reform was Sheikh Rifaat Rifaa al-Tahtawi, who accompanied the first batch of Egyptian students to Paris on a government scholarship. Tahtawi called for educating girls and recommended a system similar to coeducational schools in France. Even after the decline of the two schools opened during Khedive Ismail's reign, their nuclei were combined together, resulting in 1889 in the creation of a successful teacher-training institute known as the Saniyya School. A system of state-supported primary schools for girls was created in 1895. Daughters of the elite, however, were not left behind due to lack of access to higher education. At first, they were taught Arabic and the basic elements of Islam by private tutors at home, and by the end of the 19th century, foreign tutors were available to teach them foreign languages. Women were admitted to the American University of Cairo (AUC) by 1929. When Cairo University (formerly King Fuad University) was opened in the 1920s, its rector, the famous educator, journalist, and liberal politician Ahmad Lutfi al-Sayyid (1872–1963), admitted the first class of women in the 1930s. This came after calls for women's education were sounded by **Qassem Amin** and **Sheikh Muhammad Abduh**, both of whom, with the support of the **Egyptian Feminist Union (EFU)**, called for the education of women as a way of achieving Egypt's political liberation. In the 1920s, journalist and feminist **Nabawiya Musa** (1886–1951) was named the first director of women's public education. She herself had been the first female admitted to a public secondary school by exam in 1907. Musa studied at home because there were no girls' public secondary schools at the time, but was able to train as a teacher at the Saniyya School.

Women in Egypt were able to excel in some branches of religious education, which constituted an important part of the general curriculum. Before the rise of the modern Islamic fundamentalist movement, some women attained a national reputation based on their expertise in a branch of religious study as well as their reputation as nationalist leaders. Among these were **Aisha al-Taymourieh**, **Malak Hafni Nasif**, and **Aisha Abd al-Rahman**. Another woman who studied religion, created the network of private Islamic schools, and became a feminist leader as a result of her association with the Muslim Brotherhood in the 1940s was **Zaynab al-Ghazzali**, who became a representative of a new school of Islamist feminism. The admission of women to Egypt's famed and ancient religious university, **al-Azhar**, had to await the integration of the school under President Jamal Abd al-Nasser in the late 1960s. Women remain clustered in the girls' Sharia college, however, which has always been headed by a female dean. Women have not been admitted to the Islamic Research Council, which is part of al-Azhar, specializing in issuing opinions on every innovation in the country.

The Egyptian constitution guarantees free and compulsory education to children through grade nine. Starting in the period of Jamal Abd al-Nasser (r. 1954–1970), education was made free through the university level, which opened public universities to rural and lower-income women for the first time in Egypt's history. However, this advantage has already disappeared due to Egypt's switch to capitalist economic policy under the regime of Anwar Sadat (r. 1970–1981). Disparities between educational opportunities for lower-income children and boys and girls of elite families usually begin early, as the government finds itself unable to enforce school attendance by those who drop out for economic reasons. As a result of constrained economic conditions, by 1990, one-fourth of Egyptian boys and one-third of Egyptian girls were not enrolled in schools at all. These figures were even larger among the rural population. As a result, figures for 2006–2007 show that the adult literacy rate among females was only 58 percent, whereas among males it was 75 percent.

Despite all this, educational enrollment increased dramatically between 1988 and 1998, largely due to expanded school construction projects in the provinces. Rural girls were the greatest beneficiaries of this growth, because they were the one group that lagged severely behind. In 1988, 62 percent of rural girls between the ages of 6 and 14 were enrolled in public schools, but the number jumped to 81 percent by 1998. These gains were offset by the high dropout rates of poorer girls, because boys were seen as a better invest-ment for the family's future. In addition, income disparity reduces the access-ibility of higher education among Egyptians, particularly when they prepare to enter universities. Due to the poor quality of secondary education, as evidenced by congested classrooms and unqualified teachers, parents are often forced to resort to paid tutoring services to improve the admission test scores of their children who are hoping to enter highly desired professions such as medicine and engineering. These economic considerations usually privilege boys over girls as potential supporters for their families.

EDUCATION: IRAN. The first schools to introduce modern education in Iran were started by Christian missionaries and were intended for boys, in-itially attracting non-Iranians. By the time of the Constitutional Revolution of 1906, the missionaries had established the first girls' school, which at-tempted to attract mostly Muslim students. But few elementary public schools preceded 1906, and only a handful were open in 1897–1898. The call to provide schools for girls and enhance female education was sounded by the **Bahai** movement in the middle of the 19th century. The topic of female education became part of the national modernizing discourse by the end of the same century, with most Iranians calling for nonmissionary institutions of learning. In addition, Iranian women were greatly mobilized as participants in the events of 1906–1911 and began to demand the opening of girls' schools. By the end of the Qajar dynasty in 1925, a number of girls' schools had been founded under the influence of the Supplementary Constitutional Law of 1907 and the Fundamental Law of Education of 1911. Both of these mandated the provision of universal public education for girls and boys. This process accelerated by 1918, with the creation of 10 primary schools for girls and a women's teachers' college.

With the rise of the Pahlavi dynasty in 1925, the state became committed to increasing educational facilities for both genders in the belief that educa-tion was the surest route to economic development. The new educational system was modeled after that of France, replicating its highly centralized structure, which administered a uniform curriculum in all schools. By 1943, primary education for both genders became compulsory. Shah **Reza Pahlavi** (r. 1925–1941) and Shah Muhammad Reza Pahlavi (r. 1941–1979) were also modernizers who admired Westernization, particularly in the area of educa-tion. Reza Shah provided literacy programs for boys and girls and allowed the admission of women to Tehran University a year after its inauguration in 1934. Muhammad Reza Shah followed in his father's footsteps and allocated a large portion of the country's oil wealth to educational programs. Under the White Revolution, a program of reform that he launched in 1963, a literacy corps was created, allowing young men to educate the rural population in lieu of military service. A women's literacy corps was established in 1968, and a large number of vocational schools, some for women, were opened. The emphasis on modernizing education entailed encouraging female teachers to shed their **veils** as well as providing coeducational institutions of various types. The White Revolution contributed to the enhancement of women's education when it finally enfranchised women, who became great advocates for female education from their newly won parliamentary seats. Among the first group of women elected to parliament was educator **Farroukhru Parsa**, who became the first woman to serve as minister of education, in 1968.

Female education changed course after the establishment of the Islamic Republic in 1979, whose leaders became hostile to Westernized systems of education, often viewing these as diminishing their control over religious schools. Despite this, women's desire to receive a formal education did not decrease. The Islamic regime showed a great interest in eliminating female illiteracy by creating the Literacy Movement of Iran, which targeted mainly women. Adult literacy rates for the year 2006–2007 are given as 77 percent for females and 87 percent for males. Compulsory education for girls was set until age 14, and by the year 2011 school enrollment rates for boys and girls became equal. However, sex segregation in schools was enforced, and females were denied admission to certain colleges deemed unsuited to their feminine nature. The Islamic Republic encouraged women to enroll in teachers' colleges and other training institutes leading to acceptable careers. All levels of the curriculum in these schools were infused with Islamic values. Gradually, women were allowed to specialize in all areas of study, with special encouragement for taking up vocational training. The bans on studying traditionally male-oriented subjects such as agriculture, geology, and accounting were lifted after **Ayatollah Ruhollah Khomeini**'s death in 1898. By 2011, one-third of medical students were females and few had even taken up the clerical vocation.

In 1979, the University of Tehran, which opened in 1934, was able to boast of creating an elaborate higher educational infrastructure consisting of 24 semiprivate and public universities throughout Iran's provinces. The total enrollment of these universities reached 104,400 in that same year, which was 10 percent less than the number of high school graduates. Fully one-third of university enrollees were women, in addition to the large number of females enrolled in private women's colleges.

EDUCATION: NORTH AFRICA. Prior to Algeria's occupation by France in 1830, education throughout North Africa was confined to the traditional primary school, known as *kuttab*, and to a limited enrollment in traditional Islamic universities. The Jewish minority in these countries enjoyed access to the *midrash* school, which was similar to *kuttab*. Few secondary schools served boys, while upper-class women were taught at home. The entire nature of this network of schools changed upon the arrival of the French, who took over the Islamic religious endowments (Arabic: *hubus*; French: *habous*), which had funded education in the past. Foreign missionaries, both Christian and Jewish, began to operate their own schools for native girls. The **Alliance Israélite Universelle (AIU)** opened its schools for girls precisely to forestall their conversion to Christianity.

In Algeria, French missionaries quickly arrived on the heels of the French military. Among the first groups interested in educating Algerian girls were the Sisters of Saint Joseph de l'Apparition, founded by Emilie de Vialar. The order opened a network of schools, as well as orphanages and hospitals, in Algiers, Bône, and Constantine. The order provided valuable service to women throughout the decade of the 1830s, filling a void created by the military authorities' lack of interest in providing humanitarian services. The French military eventually expelled all 40 members of this order in 1843, fearing its protective policies toward native communities and its deep intimacy with most layers of the Muslim population. The expulsion decision was made by the Bishop of Algiers, Antoine-Adolphe Dupuch. Another Christian order, the Sisters of Charity, was encouraged to educate and proselytize the Kabylia **Berber** population. The appointment of Charles Lavigerie (1825–1892) as the archbishop of Algiers in 1867 accelerated this effort; he secretly founded two new orders, the White Fathers and the sisters of Our Lady of African Missions. The two orders intensified the previous policy of converting the Berber population to the Christian faith, believing that their religious practices betrayed familiarity with ancient forms of Christianity. The conversion campaign, which focused mainly on orphaned girls, resulted in the opening of nine girls' schools in the Kabylia region alone.

Private efforts to teach Algerian girls in the 1850s were also supported by French officials. These projects, headed by women, such as Madame Allix-Luce and Madame Barriol, taught Algerian girls such skills as sewing and the French language. The French government followed these efforts by opening up a string of public elementary schools for girls in several cities, which came to be known as *écoles-ouvriers*, or school workshops, or vocational schools devoted to the teaching of domestic arts. Fearing the influence of Italian missionaries in Tunisia, where an Italian community had already established itself, the French attempted to duplicate these same schools in that country. Formal schools to educate Algerian Jewish girls were opened in Algeria in 1837, the first being a private effort by Helois Hartoch, who opened up a school in 1852 in Oran. The education of Muslim girls in Algeria continued to lag behind that of native males until World War I, when no more than 8 percent of Muslim girls were registered in the country's 16 French schools. But by the beginning of the 20th century, some of these schools began to alter their curriculum, introducing Islamic subjects and the study of Arabic. This, as well as approval by modernist Islamic scholars such as Algeria's Abd al-Hamid Ben Badis, founder of the Association of Algerian Ulema in 1931, gave a boost to girls' education. Ben Badis opened a modern girls' school in 1919, and by 1955, Algeria had at least 181 schools for boys and girls. By that time, the native population's fear of cultural and religious assimilation was beginning to subside.

Algeria emerged after its war of independence (1954–1962) with its educational system in shambles. Private schools were abolished as of 1970, and the government embarked on a large effort to build new schools and train natives to replace previous colonial teachers and switch the language of instruction from French to Arabic. Education was made free and compulsory for all children until age 16, but only one-half of all eligible students enrolled in secondary schools. Since secondary school students were able to choose one of three tracks, technical, vocational, and basic, only 6 percent of the population usually reached the university level. By 2005, 60 percent of secondary school graduates were females, but most chose nonuniversity vocations. Women have turned to driving buses and trains, though 70 percent of all lawyers in the country are women, and many are represented in the health-care sector. Security and police work has also been taken up by women, and 55 percent of all journalists are women. Algeria has opened eight universities since independence, and its adult literacy rate for 2006–2007 was 66 percent for females and 84 percent for males.

In Tunisia, the precolonial government of Ahmad Bey of the Husainid Dynasty (r. 1837–1855) offered to take in the Sisters of Saint Joseph after their expulsion from Algeria. This led to the expansion of the order's work into neighboring Mediterranean countries. When the influence of Italian missionary organizations began to manifest itself in Tunisia, an increasing effort was made to establish more schools for native girls. Among these projects was that of Charlotte Eigenschenk, who opened L'École Louise-Rénée-Millet in 1990 in the capital city of Tunis. But Muslim fears about these institutions persisted, and most of the missionaries ended up serving the educational and health needs of the European and Mediterranean communities. By the end of World War I, Muslim families began to shed their fear of assimilation and started sending their daughters to Catholic schools. Among the first Muslim girls to enroll in these schools was Nabiha Ben Miled (1919–), a future nationalist leader who was entrusted to a primary school operated by the Sisters of Saint Joseph. Among her later achievements was the creation of the Muslim Union of Tunisian Women in 1936. The direction of the colonial educational system changed course when the order of the White Fathers opened up a unique research institute devoted to the history and culture of North Africa, known as Institut des belles lettres arabes. Historians view this endeavor and the network of Catholic schools that pioneered the education of girls as the laboratory of nationalist ideas that led to independence.

Education became a major priority of the state following independence in 1956. Primary school enrollment was made free and compulsory for all students from the ages of 6 to 16. Since the educational reforms of 1991, the percentage of school-age enrollment has risen from 85.9 to 96.9 percent. By 2005, female students were 47.4 percent of the primary school population and 50.5 percent of all secondary school enrollees. By 2006, the adult literacy rate for females was 69 percent, compared to 86 percent for males. Tunisia had 13 public universities and more than 20 private institutions as of 2007. Women make up 59 percent of the total university enrollment in the country. Women also predominate in the ranks of the legal and health professions.

In Morocco, the history of foreign missionaries dates back to the 17th century, when a small number of Spanish Franciscans arrived in the city of Tangiers to minister to the needs of Spanish captives during the piracy wars. Since Morocco did not fall under the control of any European power until its division into two protectorates, one French and one Spanish, in 1912, no single missionary order dominated the educational landscape. Instead, the country welcomed the efforts of French, Italian, and Spanish Catholic schools anxious to reach native students, beginning in 1860 after Morocco was forced to trade with foreign powers. A French diplomat was the first to introduce French missionaries into the country when he brought six nuns to work in Tangiers European Hospital. The French were interested in combating the monopoly of Spanish missionaries over the educational and health facilities of this city.

Morocco began to feel the impact of Archbishop Lavigerie from his seat in Algiers; he extended his crusade to its borders in the late 1860s. Protestants soon followed; the North African Mission of the British Bible Society opened up a branch in Tangiers in 1881. Another group, the General Missionary Union of Kansas, established a mission in 1895. The first AIU School opened its doors to Tangiers' Jewish girls in 1866, with an initial enrollment of 60 students. It was reported that the majority of the Moroccan population displayed indifference, not enthusiasm, toward these efforts. Higher education, which was based on a religious curriculum, eluded Moroccan girls for several decades. The founder and endower of the oldest Muslim seminary in the world, al-Qarawiyin, which opened its doors in 857 in Fez, was a woman, Fatima al-Fihriya. However, women were not admitted to al-Qarawiyin until the 20th century.

Education became free and compulsory for all primary schoolchildren between the ages of 7 and 15, regardless of gender, as of independence in 1956. Students also had the choice of attending public or religious schools. There was a severe dropout rate affecting more girls than boys, however, particularly in poor rural communities. Some educational reforms impacted these schools by 2005, when enrollment for boys increased to 89 percent and for girls to 83 percent. There was a huge drop-off period after that, leading the government to declare the 2000–2009 decade the National Decade for Education and Training. Adult literacy rates for women, though improving, remain at 43 percent for females, which is among the lowest in the region, compared to 69 percent for males.

EDUCATION: PALESTINE. When Palestine was part of the Greater Syrian Province under Ottoman rule, girls had access to Islamic and Christian schools. The Ottoman Public Education Law of 1869 called for expanding public schools for boys and girls throughout the empire. By 1900, a number of secondary schools for girls, known as *rushdiyat*, were opened throughout the Syrian Province. Major urban centers such as Jerusalem, Beirut, and Damascus saw an increasing number of girls enroll in these schools. Native Christian minorities such as the Greek Arab Orthodox community and the Armenians ran their own girls' schools beginning in the 1840s in Syria and Palestine. Ottoman authorities allowed various religious communities to exercise autonomy in most of their affairs, education included. Major Western religious organizations began to set up schools for girls in Arab countries soon thereafter. Among these were the Christian Missionary Society (CMS), the Kaiserwerth Deaconesses, and the Catholic group known as Terra Sancta Custody. At the same time, Muslim foundations such as the Islamic Maqasid Society in Beirut and the Supreme Muslim Council in Jerusalem began to fund girls' schools beyond the traditional *kuttab* in an effort to counter Christian missionary education.

Christian missionary schools in Palestine predominated when the country was still under Ottoman rule. They were the Europeans' only recourse in a land where proselytization was prohibited by law. Women were especially targeted by these institutions as a way of influencing the Muslim family. Its being the holy land and the birthplace of Jesus attracted a variety of missionary organizations, particularly during the weakest period of Ottoman rule at the end of the 19th century. The earliest girls' school was the Friends Mission (Quaker) School in Ramallah, which opened in 1889. The boys' Friends Mission School was established in 1901, also in Ramallah, and both offered a secondary level education. When the British Mandate government succeeded Ottoman rule in Palestine after World War I, no resistance was offered to missionary groups arriving from France, Great Britain, Germany, and Italy. The British struggled to meet popular demand for public education on all levels, but their highest institution for women was a teachers' training center. Elementary schools for girls were set up by the Mandate government in every town and village by the end of British rule in 1948. Missionary schools for girls were particularly popular among Muslim elite families, such as the German Schmidt Girls' School in Jerusalem. These schools offered strict discipline, an all-female teaching staff, and compulsory church attendance.

During the period of Jordanian control over the West Bank and Egyptian rule in Gaza in 1948–1967, all foreign schools were required to offer instruction in Islamic subjects and the Arabic language. A private coeducational high school in the town of Beir Zeit, which was started by an Arab Christian family, the Nassers, became one of the first West Bank universities by the 1970s. Another private coeducational university, al-Najah, evolved from one of the oldest boys' schools in the country. It was founded in Nablus by a Muslim board of directors headed by the Touqan family. Islamic **nongovernmental organizations (NGOs)** built a number of colleges and training institutes for men and women after 1967. By 2003, it was estimated that 50 percent of the total student enrollment in universities and colleges was female. The size of the total student population in higher education for that year reached 80,500.

As of 1972, there were 10 universities in the West Bank and Gaza, most of which were coeducational. A parallel system of schools for girls, offering elementary, secondary, and teacher-training schools, was operated by the United Nations Relief and Works Agency (UNRWA) in the refugee camps of the West Bank and Gaza. These schools, which date back to 1950, follow the Jordanian system of education and its curriculum. The Gaza Strip gradually switched to the Jordanian system following the dismantling of its Egyptian administration in 1967 by Israel. The Palestine National Authority (PNA) took charge of the two systems in the West Bank and Gaza from 1996 until the separation of Gaza under **Hamas** in 2006. During that period, a Palestinian curriculum was developed that, though generally popular, has been widely criticized for depicting veiled girls in Islamic textbooks.

Despite the economic and security challenges the Palestinians face in the West Bank and Gaza, the adult literacy rate for women in 2006–2007 was 90 percent for females and 97 percent for males, placing it among the highest in the Middle Eastern region. The PNA is committed to enhancing the educational capabilities of its population and has made education compulsory for children from 6 to 15 years of age.

EDUCATION: SUDAN. Until the recent separation of the southern Sudan to form a republic independent from the Arab-dominated Republic of the Sudan in the north, two-thirds of the population lived in the north, while the remaining one-third lived in the south. These two areas, demarcated by an east–west line just south of the capital of Khartoum, were also dissimilar ethnically, linguistically, and religiously. The northern population was predominantly Arabic speaking and followed Sunni Islam, while the southern population spoke the languages of its various tribes, such as the Dinka, the Shilluk, and the Azande, and English remained the official administrative language. After years of European missionary activity, the majority of the southern population still adheres to indigenous religions, though some have converted to Christianity. The spread of education to the female population of these two regions follows different trajectories. In the north, young girls were taught to read the Quran in religious school, and in the south girls had limited access to missionary schools. The situation continued even after the creation of the Anglo–Egyptian Condominium (1898–1956). The British met native demand for education in the north by establishing a few British-style secondary schools for girls. Missionaries were secretly encouraged to operate their own schools in the 1920s, beginning with the Church Missionary Society (CMS) of Great Britain and the American Presbyterian Church, both of which could only serve the needs of the non-Muslim minority population. Fear of proselytization among the Muslim majority in the wake of the Mahdist revolt (1882–1898) limited the reach of these schools. The missionaries got around this barrier by enticing Muslim girls with a curriculum centered around "female arts."

A Sudanese merchant, Babikr Badri, became the father of girls' education in 1907, when he founded the first Sudanese Muslim girls' school in Rufaa. In order to reach a larger number from the same constituency, British and American missionaries began to open women's health centers after 1900. One unintended outcome resulting from this endeavor was coming face to face with the custom of female genital mutilation and its impact on girls' health. Missionary educators and health providers were the first to alert British authorities to the widespread nature of this custom. This generated a strong interest in promoting health education among native females, who were drawn by the missionaries to the study of midwifery and nursing. British authorities followed this with the expansion of their public school system on the elementary and secondary levels. They also opened a women's teachers' college and a school for the training of midwives in the 1920s. The missionaries provided a network of "needlework homes" as a type of finishing school for marriageable girls, which were very popular throughout the first half of the 20th century. British authorities also founded Gordon College (later Khartoum University), which offered higher education for males at first but was fully integrated after independence in 1956.

The first intermediate school for girls was opened in 1940 in Omdurman. By independence in 1956, only one secondary school served the needs of girls in the country. Vocational schools did not yet exist, and only one nursing school, the Nurses Training College, served the needs of girls. Education was made compulsory for boys and girls between the ages of 6 and 13. Schools were concentrated in the urban areas, but in the outlying provinces and desert areas, children had to walk great distances simply to reach their schools. During the 1960s and 1970s, the Sudanese authorities introduced many educational reforms that benefited women. Girls' education used up one-third of the total school resources of the country, as 1,086 primary schools were added and 268 intermediate schools were built for both genders. The Ahfad University College for Women was opened in 1966, offering an elite education and enrolling 1,800 students. Yet by 2006, 49 percent of all eligible girls were not attending primary schools due to the shortage of school space and qualified teachers.

The adult literacy rate in 2002 was 69 percent for males and 46 percent for females, showing a slow rise since the 1990s, when the total literacy rate was only 30 percent due to the expanding population and the continued civil war in the south. In addition, the Islamization policy of President Omar al-Bashir (r. 1989–) resulted in great pressure on female students and faculty, mandating the wearing of the strict Islamic *hijab*. Educational advances in the southern region were more limited, and public schools for girls did not become available until after 1956. However, the Sudanese civil war, which erupted soon thereafter, hampered access to education for members of both genders. During the 1960s, southern Sudanese girls accounted for 9 percent of the total primary school enrollment in the region and no more than 1 percent in secondary schools. According to a United Nations Educational, Scientific and Cultural Organization (UNESCO) report in 1990, female enrollment in southern primary schools rose to 40 percent and in secondary schools to 20 percent. Only 10 percent of southern females reached higher levels of education.

EDUCATION: TURKEY. Ottoman laws mandating the opening of girls' schools and compulsory attendance through the elementary level date back to 1824. Interest in advancing the education of women was the result of the affirmation of the right to education for both genders in the first Ottoman constitution of 1876. But even before primary education became compulsory, Islamic foundations supported religious education for boys before the 19th century in schools known as *sebyan mektepleri* (boys' schools) and for girls in similar schools. Boys had access to privately financed and public schools, but girls were excluded. The first government effort to create secondary schools for girls was in 1858, with the establishment of *rushdiyat* schools in major urban centers throughout the empire. By 1870, the first girls' teachers college was founded, and by 1911, a senior high school for girls, known as *idadi*, was opened. Women's medical education was permitted under Sultan Abd al-Hamid (r. 1876–1909); they were allowed to attend medical lectures at Istanbul University in 1893. By 1899, female students were able to obtain medical degrees. In 1914, a university for women grew out of the Girls' Teachers College. Women also benefited from a number of vocational training schools that taught domestic arts such as sewing, embroidery, and cooking. Most of these were located in Istanbul's outskirts, such as Uskudar and Yedikule. Sometimes the teaching staff in the high girls' institutes featured male teachers. Upper-class girls continued to be tutored at home, where they were taught European languages, modern housekeeping methods, piano, and painting.

Despite these advances, girls' education continued to lag behind that of males, especially in the rural areas. Government efforts to increase women's literacy rates continued for many years. With the advent of the Young Turk government after 1908 and **Mustafa Kemal Ataturk** in 1924, the education of girls became a priority of the state. Ataturk offered the model of the "new" Turkish woman as a pillar of the new society. This had to be a literate person, which spurred on a huge effort to expand girls' public schools. Once the Turkish Republic was established in 1923, the Ministry of Education assumed control of the existing school system in its various public, private, and religious forms, the latter being taken over as a result of abolishing religious foundations. A five-year period of compulsory education was mandated for boys and girls. Secondary education remained optional, offering two tracks of three-year periods of study, namely middle- and high-level schools. The tradition of government-supported vocational schools continued and remained gender-segregated. Women could join secondary schools to train as teachers. After 1940, a system of village institutes was put in place. The results could be seen as early as 1932, when girls' enrollment in primary schools doubled, rising to 9 percent at secondary schools. To overcome the problem of limited middle schools for girls, these became coeducational as of 1927. By the mid-1930s, high schools were also integrated. Universities were opened to both genders as of 1923. The only schools that were not eligible for government funding were preschools and kindergartens.

Female students were allowed into the traditionally all-male religious schools by the 1990s, despite limited career opportunities for females in this area. Religious education continued to attract female students due to the rise of Islamic political formations. In order to combat this tendency and to decrease the popularity of religious schools, the state increased compulsory education to eight years for both genders. This was achieved through the passage of the Basic Education Law (Law No. 4306) in 1997, which combined study at the primary and middle levels into an eight-year program culminating in a diploma. The government also undertook a program of constructing regional elementary boarding schools for the benefit of lower-income students. Girls' schools constructed under this program provided free school supplies, meals, and uniforms. Rural girls, however, did not flock to this program in large numbers. By 1999, there were still half as many girls as boys enrolled in high schools, and the number of girls' vocational schools remained limited. Girls were more likely to withdraw from these schools at a younger age than boys. Opportunities for rural girls were bleaker, especially due to the Kurdish emergency. Turkey continues to feel the pressure of the European Union (EU) to increase women's educational opportunities in order to qualify for accession. Thus, the Millennium Development Plan, adopted in 2000, made educational parity between the two genders a priority of the state. Government and private groups have committed themselves to persuade rural families to enroll and keep their daughters in school.

The fight against illiteracy in Turkey dates back to the early days of the Kemalist republican regime. Even today, "Open Schools" continue to provide distance education, a modification of the earlier innovation of "People's Houses," or *Halk Evi*. These schools provide adults with the means of completing eight years of study beyond the elementary stage and to receive a diploma. There are also Open Primary Schools for those who never received any kind of education. In 2001, almost 41.4 percent of adult students enrolled in these schools were women. Female enrollment in the Open High Schools during that same year was 32.6 percent, and in the Open Vocational and Technical High Schools it was 30 percent. Literacy rates in 2006–2007 reached 96 percent for adult males and 81 percent for adult females. *See also* EDIP, HALIDE (1883–1964).

EGYPTIAN FEMINIST UNION (EFU). Also known as the Egyptian Women's Union, this was the first self-declared feminist movement not only in Egypt, but also in the entire Arab world. Known in Arabic as *al-Ittihad al-nisai al-Masri*, its antecedents go back much further than its formal creation in Cairo on 19 March 1923. The founders of this organization were a small group of upper-class women headed by **Huda Shaarawi**, who had already made their mark on the Egyptian national consciousness during the 1919 Revolution. Christian and Muslim women marched side by side in demonstrations protesting British rule and the exiling of Egypt's male national leadership. During that revolution, women also led a successful economic boycott targeting British goods and services. Having aligned themselves with the leading nationalist formation of that period, the Wafd Party, women were shocked when their male national heroes denied them the right to vote in the 1923 constitution. There were two additional reasons for the decision to form a separate women's organization. One was a dispute between Shaarawi and **Safiyya Zaghloul**, wife of Wafdist hero and prime minister Saad Zaghloul (d. 1927), culminating in the creation of the Wafdist Women's Central Committee. The second reason was the need to organize formally in order to accept the invitation of the International Woman Suffrage Alliance (IWSA) to attend its meeting in Rome in May 1923.

The EFU had its own constitution, an elected board of directors, and an executive committee. It published two journals, *L'Égyptienne*, which appeared between 1925 and 1940, and *al-Misriyya*, which ran from 1937 until 1940. The organization was largely financed by Shaarawi's substantial personal fortune. Beginning in the 1920s, the EFU sent several female students to study abroad. Its membership during that same decade was given as 250.

Its headquarters as of 1932 were located at Qasr al-Ayni Street in Cairo. One of its first activities was to picket the Egyptian parliament building in 1924 when news of its failure to grant women suffrage was made public. Shaarawi and her colleagues pursued a diverse agenda, ranging from adopting specific positions on national issues, which irritated the male leadership of the Wafd, to demanding reforms of the **Sharia** and basic political rights for women, to creating philanthropic projects benefiting women.

The EFU's list of achievements fell short of its ambitious agenda. It included the passage of a law raising the **marriage** age for boys to 18 and for girls to 16, as well as making primary **education** for both genders compulsory. By 1928, the first group of women was admitted to the newly founded national university, King Fuad University (later University of Cairo), graduating in 1933. This opened the door for women to integrate higher institutes of learning; previously upper-class women had been tutored at home like Shaarawi or studied abroad at foreign universities. The EFU's philanthropic projects, on the other hand, were a carryover from Shaarawi's long years with institutions like **Mabarat Muhammad Ali**. A team of volunteers assisted in programs to help widows financially, to operate a vocational school for girls of modest means, and to staff a free clinic to serve needy families. The EFU reached the pinnacle of its prestige in the early 1940s, when the wife of Taha Hussein, Egypt's foremost man of letters, served on its board of directors. The only visible tilt in favor of the EFU was to allow women to observe parliamentary proceedings from a balcony, a small concession to an organization that was viewed by many as a quasi-political party. The union also did not limit itself to the Egyptian theater, convening an inter-Arab women's conference in Egypt to raise awareness of the Palestinian issue. Shaarawi's work with other Arab women led to the creation of the **Arab Feminist Union (AFU)**, with branches all over the Arab region. The EFU declined after Shaarawi's death in 1947. It was finally shut down in 1956, along with all of Egypt's independent organizations, by the government of President Jamal Abd al-Nasser (r. 1954–1970). *See also* MUSA, NABAWIYA (1886–1951); NON-GOVERNMENTAL ORGANIZATIONS (NGOs); SAID, AMINAH AL- (1914–1955); SHAFIQ, DURREA REGAI (1908–1975).

EGYPTIAN SCHOOL OF MIDWIVES. This was the earliest school for girls in Egypt, established by Muhammad Ali Pasha in 1832. The school was suggested by Dr. Antoine-Barthélemy Clot (Clot Bey), a French doctor brought over from Marseilles in 1825 to modernize Egypt's health system. Known also as the School for *Hakimas* (doctors), or the Midwifery School, it was intended to train female health professionals capable of accessing women at a time when venereal diseases, especially syphilis in women, were rampant due to the mobilization of a huge standing army. Clot Bey, who was credited with establishing Egypt's first modern hospital, Qasr al-Ayni, was greatly concerned with containing contagious diseases. The School of Midwives was founded as a follow-up to the opening of the first regular medical school in the country, which was attached to Qasr al-Ayni Hospital in 1827. The first director of the school, who served from 1832 until 1836, was Susan Voliquin, a French woman who was a feminist and a follower of Saint Simonian Utopian socialism. Women were taught the basics of modern medicine over a period of six years, devoting two of these to attaining literacy in Arabic. Other areas of study emphasized obstetrics, prenatal care, and vaccinations. Students were also trained to perform postmortem operations in order to report on the cause of death. The midwives who graduated from this school were issued a license to perform deliveries, administer vaccinations, and treat women and children free of charge. To encourage service in the provinces, the Egyptian government encouraged marriages between the midwives and male graduates of the medical school, assigning them to the same district and providing them with a free residence.

The government had always experienced difficulty meeting the target number of 100 enrollees. Many inducements were provided, such as free lodging and food, as well as a monthly stipend, to recruit students. The midwives were awarded military rank upon graduation in order to bring them up to the status of the male doctors. Some of the recruits to this school were freed slaves, and the directors were always French until the accession of Zarifa Umar to that position in the 1860s. One of the school's graduates who later served as an instructor was Jalilah Tamrahan (d. 1899), who became a prominent medical writer. Her contributions to the field appeared in one of Egypt's earliest medical journals, *Yaasub al-Tibb* (*Encyclopedia of Medicine*), established by Dr. Muhammad Ali al-Baqli in 1865. *See also* EDUCATION: EGYPT.

ERBIL, LEYLA (1931–). A Turkish novelist and poet who was a graduate of the Faculty of Literature at Istanbul University. She was born in Istanbul and completed her studies at Kadikoy Girls' School. After working as a translator and secretarial worker, she began to compose poetry in 1945. Her fame began with the publication of a number of short stories in the 1950s. Her focus changed over the years, moving from traditional themes to the struggle of individuals against society. Her published works include *The Wool Carder* (1960), *At Night* (1968), *A Strange Woman* (1971), *The Old Lover* (1977), and *The Day of Darkness* (1985).

ESTHER. A biblical character reputed to have been the daughter of Abihail, a Jewish exile in the Persian town of Sousa. Her life story is told in the Book of Esther in the Old Testament. According to this tale, she was raised by her cousin Mordechai after she lost her parents as a child. Her life took an unusual turn when she was presented as a gift to King Ahasuerus, after he dismissed his wife, Queen Vashti, for disobedience. The Persian king fell in love with Esther and made her a queen (her Jewish identity was concealed from him). She decided to reveal her identity when she pleaded with the king to save the Jewish population of Persia from the destructive plans of his chief minister, Haman. She persuaded the king that the minister was disloyal to his suzerain; the minister was executed. A shrine commemorating Esther's life is found in the Persian city of Hamadan.

ETESAMI, PARVIN (1906–1941). An Iranian poet and women's rights advocate whose poetry foreshadowed the works of Iran's great poet, **Forugh Farrokhazad**. Etsami was born in Tabriz, where she received a high school education before moving to Tehran, where she attended the American College for Women. Her father, Yussef Etesami (d. 1938), was a translator of Western literary works who encouraged her to write poetry and took her on many of his travels. She began to write poetry at age nine, producing work dealing with feminine feelings and touching upon philosophical and religious themes, which drew the attention of the public censor. She was buried in the holy city of Qom. *See also* FEMINIST MOVEMENT IN IRAN.

F

FADHIL, NAZLI (?–1914). An Egyptian princess who was the niece of Khedive Ismail (r. 1863–1879) and the daughter of Mustafa Fadhil. Her father was best remembered for donating his private library collection to Dar al-Kutub, Egypt's first national library. He was also the son of Ibrahim Pasha and a brother of Khedive Ismail. The princess was tutored by Arab and European tutors and completed her **education** in Great Britain and France. She lived in London while her husband served as the Ottoman ambassador to Great Britain. She hosted the first literacy salon in Cairo, which was attended by luminaries of her day, such as **Muhammad Abduh, Jamal al-Din Afghani**, Saad Zaghloul (1859–1927), Faris Nimir (1856–1951), Adib Ishaq (1856–1885), Dawad Barakat (1867–1933), and **Qassem Amin**. Her guests debated Egypt's social and political crisis, as well as holding discussions on the leading Arabic and European books of the day. Her input into these conversations influenced Qassem Amin's seminal work, *The Liberation of Women*, which began as a conservative reaction to attacks by duc d'Harcourt, but later emerged as a more liberal treatment. Her salon lasted for almost a quarter of a century, during which time she was able to promote the political careers of rising Egyptian nationalist leaders such as Zaghloul through her friendship with the British High Commissioner, Lord Cromer (1841–1917). She also introduced Zaghloul, who acted as her lawyer, to his future wife, **Safiyya Zaghloul** (1878–1946). Fadhil's lasting gift to Egypt was a large parcel of land that she donated for the national university, a project at the center of the reformist plans of Egyptian nationalists.

FAKHRO, MUNIRA (?–). A Bahraini feminist, educator, and political activist who received her MA from Bryn Mawr College and a PhD in social planning and administration from Columbia University, where she served at one time as a visiting professor. She was an associate professor at the University of Bahrain, where she conducted research on gender issues and on civil society in the Arab Persian Gulf region. She was forced to resign her teaching position in 1995 as a result of signing a petition with other women demanding an end to torture and the restoration of parliamentary life. When

117

King Hamad acceded to the throne, she was restored to her position through a general amnesty. Fakhro was later appointed to the Advisory Board of the Supreme Council for Women by Sheikha Sabeeka, the monarch's wife. In 2000, Fakhro ran in the general elections representing the leftist opposition party, *al-Waad*. In 2006, she was endorsed by the Islamist Shii party, *al-Wifaq*, the only female candidate to receive this endorsement. She has served as the head of the Welfare Section of the Ministry of Labor and Social Affairs and was a member of Bahrain's High Council for Culture and the Arts. She served on the advisory board of the United Nations Arab Human Development Report of 2004. She was also active in the Shii uprising of 2011, addressing crowds in al-Manama's LuLua Square. *See also* EDUCATION: ARAB GULF STATES.

FAMILY PLANNING IN EGYPT. Egyptian writers and statesmen began to assess the impact of uncontrolled rural migration to urban centers during the latter part of the 19th century. Census data that became available soon thereafter demonstrated the adverse effects of this population trend in terms of deteriorating hygienic conditions in the cities. The study of changing demographic trends received a boost when the Medical Association of Egypt met in 1937 to deal with the population problem. Spotlighting this issue led to the announcement of the first **fatwa**, or religious-legal opinion by the highest Muslim religious authority in Egypt, Mutfi Abd al-Majid Salim, approving the use of birth control methods. Socio-medical studies during the first half of the 20th century attempted to establish a link between runaway population growth and rampant poverty, but the role of women's status in society and its relevance to the problem of uncontrolled reproduction were absent from the debate.

A great leap forward was made when the revolutionary Free Officers seized power in 1952 and began to confront the challenge of feeding a large population while simultaneously undertaking the country's industrialization. President Jamal Abd al-Nasser (1954–1970) established the National Commission on Population Affairs in 1955 and invited several women's groups to operate eight family-planning clinics in major Egyptian cities, which expanded to 27 units in a matter of a few years. The clinics offered free contraceptives to married women who had a minimum of three children, but only with spousal approval. A national campaign involving the media, religious figures, and public personalities presented the state's population control policy as a grand national project designed to promote a nuclear family system based on autonomous men and women capable of determining their own future. Funding was made available to this project until the military reverses of the 1967 June War dramatically weakened the economy. Until that war, Egypt's official Muslim leadership partnered with the state in supporting family planning. One of the staunchest supporters was the rector of **al-Azhar University**, Sheikh Mahmoud Shaltout. He argued that a large population was a drain on the state and weakened the fabric of Muslim life.

Later, women's groups criticized Nasser's alliance with the clergy, which they felt was at the expense of **Sharia** reforms. Under President Anwar Sadat (r. 1970–1981), Egypt's demographic trends were mapped out with the assistance of international donor agencies, and a family planning program was instituted with great fanfare, billed as a giant step toward modernizing the country. The president's wife, **Jihan Sadat**, led a campaign to legislate curbs on **polygamous marriages** designed to improve the status of women, while at the same time placing controls on the country's expanding population. While much of the national discourse until that time had focused on the husband's necessary approval of limiting family size, newer trends began to stress the concept of women's reproductive rights and the relationship between family planning and women's health. Typical of this trend was the convening of the International Conference on Population Development (ICPD) in 1994, which arrived at a new definition of women's rights, especially in the area of reproduction, as human rights. On the other hand, Islamic groups in Egypt and throughout the Arab world viewed family planning as a Western construct intended to limit the size of Muslim populations. A more potent argument presented by Islamists and conservative Muslims claimed that family planning would inevitably produce moral decay and promiscuous behavior. The rest of the argument was that God will provide for all of his creation. Several sources, which had no faith in Western altruism, claimed that what was needed was not a national family-planning campaign but a revolution producing equitable income levels. *See also* HUSSEIN, AZIZA (1919–).

FAMILY PLANNING IN IRAN. Under **Shah Muhammad Reza Pahlavi** (r. 1941–1979), family planning was part of a wider modernizing policy spanning the 1960s and 1970s. The first official policy of family planning was launched in 1967, along with laws allowing female political participation and liberalized abortion laws. Initially, the Islamic Republic of Iran condemned these measures as un-Islamic. Until the death of **Ayatollah Ruhollah Khomeini** in 1989, the state followed a pro-natalist policy largely under the impact of the Iran–Iraq War (1980–1988). **Marriage** age for girls was lowered to nine years, and the shah's family protection laws were canceled. Divorced and widowed women were encouraged to remarry, while the ancient custom of **temporary marriage** was restored.

During the late 1980s, this trend was reversed as a result of several developments, such as rising fertility rates and economic pressures to feed and accommodate the country's expanding population. A new plan, dubbed "The Islamic Family Planning Program," was adopted by the republic, ostensibly to prevent unwanted pregnancies, to help those who wanted to have children, and to intervene in the issue of abortion by redefining it in terms of health rather than family planning. All media outlets were recruited as participants in this campaign by publicizing family planning as necessary for the survival of the nation. Islamic women's journals and organizations were in the forefront of this campaign, drawing attention to possible dependence on Western economies if the population of Iran was not trimmed in accordance with the country's resources. *See also* AFKHAMI, MAHNAZ (1941–); SHARIA.

FAMILY PLANNING IN ISLAM. Mainstream Muslim religious scholars have always approved the idea of family planning, with the exception of fundamentalists, who oppose it on ideological grounds. Ancient Islamic medical texts are replete with birth control techniques, including the use of magic. Modern readings of the Quran in the 20th century emphasize that although there is no direct mention of contraceptives, it is possible to deduce a divine call against the overburdening of God's creation with an expanding population. *Hadith* scholars, however, often cite statements by Prophet Muhammad, which may or may not be authenticated, permitting some forms of contraception. The great Islamic jurist Muhammad al-Ghazzali (1058–1111) endorsed the use of contraceptives as a form of family planning under the following conditions: a spouse with an infectious disease, the ill-effects of frequent pregnancy on a woman's health and physical attributes, and the husband's inability to support his progeny. At the same time, Ghazzali criticized the use of birth control for personal convenience or for sex selection of a child to avoid the birth of a daughter. During medieval times, contraceptives were favored as a means of protecting the health and welfare of nursing women and to avoid the likelihood of children being captured and enslaved in times of war. Operations to prevent pregnancy permanently on medical grounds were also approved by religious scholars. However, sterilization as a means of contraception was strongly disapproved of, because it contravened the divine will and the natural process of procreation. Today, most Muslim states regard family planning as consistent with Islamic teachings. Most Islamic governments fund contraceptives and allow women total access to family planning services, with the exception of such countries as Libya, Oman, the United Arab Emirates (UAE), and Turkmenistan. No such information is available for conservative countries like Saudi Arabia.

When it comes to abortion, the Quran and *Hadith* are silent. This void has been filled by the four Sunni schools and one single Shii school of Islamic jurisprudence. All schools legitimize abortion at any time to save the mother's life, but differ on the definition of ensoulment, which determines the timing of a permissible act of abortion. Most jurisprudential schools stipulate that ensoulment occurs around 120 days after the inception of pregnancy, while others place it as early as 40 days following conception. Some Islamic countries, such as Bahrain, Tajikistan, Tunisia, and Turkey, allow abortion on demand and with very few restrictions. In Turkey, for instance, abortion was legalized in 1983, stipulating that a medical reason to end a pregnancy must be provided for termination of a 10-week pregnancy. Countries that permit abortion only in order to save an endangered mother's life include Afghanistan, Chad, Egypt, Indonesia, Iran, Lebanon, Mali, and the UAE. In other countries, there is no official policy on abortion, but the practice prevails in secrecy. *See also* FEMINIST MOVEMENT IN EGYPT; FEMINIST MOVEMENT IN IRAN; SHARIA.

FAQIR, FADIA (?–). A Jordanian novelist and editor who is also a professor of Middle Eastern and Islamic studies. She received a BA degree in English literature from the University of Jordan and an MA and a PhD in creative writing from East Anglia University in Great Britain. Her first novel, *Nisanit*, was published in 1990. Another novel, *The Pillars of Salt*, was published by Quartet and was translated into several languages. She was appointed general editor of Garnet Publishing's series Arab Women Writers and was a lecturer for the Project of Middle Eastern Women's Studies at the Center of Middle Eastern Women's Studies at the University of Durham, Britain. Her work emphasizes the oppression of women by Islamic culture as well as the alienation and marginalization of women of color residing in Western countries.

FARAA, WAHEEBA (?–). She is the first woman appointed to the Yemeni cabinet since the unification of North and South Yemen in 1991. She was named minister of human rights in 2001. Before this appointment, she was a professor of education and deputy rector of the faculty of education at the University of Sanaa. In 1996, she was named the chancellor of Arwa University. Faraa also serves on Yemen's Higher Consultative Commission on Human Rights. Another of her interests is defending the rights of the child. Dr. Faraa presented a report on the Yemeni woman at the Beijing United Nations Conference on Women in 1995.

FARHA, WISAL (?–). Farha was the secretary general of the Syrian Communist Party from 1996 to 2010. She was elected to this office following the death of her husband, Khaled Bakdash (1912–1995), who served in this position from 1936 until 1995. The party suffered major splits following the demise of Bakdash, who had the distinction of being the first Arab communist leader to be elected to parliament. The Syrian Communist Party remains within the coalition group known as the National Front, headed by Syria's ruling Baath Party.

FARID, NAGWA KAMAL (ca. 1950–). A Sudanese legal pioneer and one of the first women to be appointed to the **Sharia** court system in all of Islamic Africa. Farid was appointed in 1970, shortly after her graduation from the University of Khartoum, by the chief justice of the Sudanese Sharia courts, Sheikh Muhammad al-Gizuli, who was her professor. Other women, such as Amal Muhammad Hassan, Rabab Muhammad Mustafa Abu Gusaysa, and Fatima Makki al-Sayyid Ali, quickly followed in Farid's footsteps. By steering away from political controversy, she was able to survive the legal instability generated during Jaafar Numeiry's presidency (1969–1985). In 1983, Sudan adopted Sharia as the law of the land and amalgamated the civil courts with Islamic courts, reducing judicial appointments drastically. In 1989, the Islamic government of the National Islamic Front (NIF) took over the reins of government and removed many liberal judges from their posts. Justice Farid, however, survived this turmoil and retained her office.

Prohibition against women's appointment to religious and legal institutions is attributed to tradition, which rejects women's authority over men as being contrary to Quranic teachings. Among conservative Muslims, it is believed that the Quran calls directly for men to be "responsible" (Arabic: *qawwamoun*) for women, hence their disqualification from professions where they will issue judgments against men. Popular opinion in general rejects the appointment of women to legal office, which is considered a rough and tumble profession, requiring interaction with unsavory males. Female judges have been appointed in Iraq, Jordan, Indonesia, and Tunisia, but not to the Sharia court system.

FARROUKHZAD, FORUGH (1935–1967). An Iranian modernist poet and film director who was the first in many years to express women's sentiments in Farsi verse. She was born in Tehran to Colonel Mohammad Bagher Farroukhzad and Touran Vaziri-Tabar. She stayed in school until the ninth grade before attending a manual crafts school where girls were taught painting and tailoring. Her husband, whom she married at age 16, was the satirical writer Parviz Shapour. She had a son, Kaymar, but was divorced by 1954. She began to lead a bohemian life and wrote poetry glorifying personal freedom and free love for both men and women. At the same time, she criticized the endorsement of Western values under the Pahlavis and rejected their gift to women, namely the right to vote, which she regarded as an empty right. Her poetry collections began to appear in the mid-1950s. She also fell under the influence of film producer Ebrahim Golestan, which led her to produce highly acclaimed documentaries. Her film *The House in Black*, which appeared in 1962, explored the lives of inmates in a leprosy center. Her poetry collections appeared under the titles of *The Captive*, *The Wall*, *The Rebellion*, and *Another Birth*. She wrote a total of 150 poems, the last collection being *Let Us Believe in the Beginning of the Cold Season*, published posthumously. She died of injuries suffered in a car accident. Today, her poetry is banned by Iran's Islamic regime. Her life has been the subject of three documentaries produced by Nasser Saffarian: *The Mirror of the Soul* (2000), *The Green Cold* (2003), and *Summit of the Wave* (2004). *See also* FEMINIST MOVEMENT IN IRAN.

FATEMEH ZAHRA RELIGIOUS SEMINARY. A religious school in Tehran that provides training for women as *mujtahids*, or interpreters of sacred texts and commentators on theological issues. Students are committed Shii women who are provided with financial assistance derived from religious foundations. The seminary was established in 1972 and named after **Fatima**, Prophet Muhammad's daughter. The founder of this school, Fatemeh Amini, declared at the time of its founding that the intention was to enhance the self-esteem of poor women by training them to provide this noble service. *Mujtahids* are highly regarded in the Shii community as men of learning, but this respect was never extended to women, although **Aisha**, the Prophet's wife, excelled in this profession. *See also* EDUCATION: IRAN.

FATIMA (ca. 604–632). The eldest daughter of Prophet Muhammad and his wife **Khadija**, considered the closest thing to a saint in Sunni and Shii Islam. Her birth date is uncertain, often given as the year of rebuilding the Kaaba by the pagan leaders of Mecca, or five years before Muhammad began his sacred career as the Messenger of God in 610 CE. Fatima died at the age of 28, around three months (some sources claim six months) after Muhammad's death in 632. She is the most venerated woman in Islam, honored by Sunnis as Muhammad's daughter, and by Shiis as the wife of the founder of their sect, Ali (d. 661) and the mother of the two Imams, Hassan and Hussein. Fatima was elevated to the rank of the five people of the mantle of the Prophet, and as such she enjoys the quality of immaculate nature. She shares this attribute with Muhammad, Ali, Hassan, and Hussein. She is regarded by Shiis as belonging to *"ahl al-bayt"* (the house of the Prophet), sharing with the other four the gift of infallibility (*isma*) and the power of intercession (*shafaa*). She approaches the status of a saint among the Shiis, who claim that she performed miracles during her lifetime. Both Sunnis and Shiis place her ahead of all women, based on one of Muhammad's authenticated traditions (as recorded in *Sahih al-Bukhari*), in which he said: "Fatime will be the first woman to enter paradise," adding "but only after Mary." Her name is always rendered by all Muslims as Fatima *al-Zahraa* (the resplendent one). She is often referred to as the virgin (Arabic: *al-batul*), bestowing on her the qualities of purity and piety, but not necessarily celibacy. Her life of suffering and her preordained marriage to Ali, as well as giving birth to Imam Hussein, the first martyr of Shii Islam, have elevated her to a status similar to that of Mary, mother of Jesus, in Christianity.

Very little information is found in early Islamic literature about Fatima. She was married to Ali, Muhammad's cousin, in whose household the orphaned Prophet spent his youthful years. Fatima was probably married at age 18 and lived her entire life in poverty. Ali did not take any other wife during Fatima's lifetime. She gave birth to two sons, who became the first Shii Imams, as well as two daughters, **Zaynab** and Umm Kulthum. She opposed the selection of Abu Bakr and Umar as the two caliphs to succeed her father and was an ardent supporter of her husband's candidacy for the top leadership position in the Muslim community. She also quarreled with Abu Bakr over her right to a portion of her father's estate, which eventually reverted to the public treasury. Abu Bakr repeatedly reminded her of Muhammad's statement that prophets had no heirs.

There are three contradictory views of Fatima, which shaped her legacy. The first was that of French historian Henri Lammens (d. 1937), who portrayed her as a plain-looking woman of limited intelligence and very little significance. He claimed that she was a weak and weepy woman who was denied any respect by her husband. Oriental scholar Louis Massignon (d. 1962), on the other hand, stressed her mystical attributes and her enormous religious impact on the Muslim community, likening her to Mary.

But Fatima's enduring legend casts her birth and **marriage** in mystical terms. which have taken over the historical narrative of her life. According to the Fatima legend, the Prophet received news of her impending birth from the archangel Gabriel, who assured him that the child would bring forth the line of Imams into the world. When Khadija was experiencing labor pains, four women descended from heaven to assist with Fatima's birth. When she was about to be born, the entire sky was flooded with light. The Prophet also refused to give her away in marriage to anyone other than Ali, since Gabriel had announced that the two were already married in heaven. The archangel was heard crying "God is great" when the actual wedding ceremony was performed. Her contemporaries reported that a veil of light always surrounded her face, hence the sobriquet *al-Zahraa*. Shiis refer to her as "her father's mother" (*ummu abiha*) for having cared for the Prophet as if she were his mother. They also continue to pray to her during religious festivals, and the only Shii dynasty to rule Egypt, the Fatimid, named the great university **al-Azhar** after her. Her memory is evoked annually during *ashura* celebrations commemorating the martyrdom of Imam Hussein at the Battle of Karbala in 680. Members of Shii communities in Iraq, Iran, and Lebanon beseech her for mercy for their children who have died in recent battles and wars.

Fatima's sainthood was firmly established by the Islamic Republic of Iran, which elevated her to the status of the highest representative of womanhood in Islam. Ali Shariati succeeded in recasting her legend in modern political terms as the counter model to the ideal of Western feminism. In his hands, she was made into the personification of the female Islamic qualities of service, sacrifice, and purity. The Islamic Republic of Iran celebrates Fatima's birthday as Women's Day, in lieu of International Women's Day. Fatima was buried in the Baqi cemetery in Medina. *See also* COUNCIL ON WOMEN'S AFFAIRS (CWA)—IRAN; MARY IN THE QURAN; SHARIA.

FATWA. The technical term for an authoritative opinion given by a *mufti*, or legal scholar, usually in response to an inquiry from a layperson or as a clarification of a matter of public interest. The authority of such an opinion rests on the status and qualifications of the *mufti*. Most jurists nowadays serve in a variety of positions, such as inspectors of markets, guardians of public morals, or advisers to rulers. *Fatwas* in the past carried a great deal of weight because the jurist was independent of the religious courts. During the height of the two latest Islamic empires, the Ottomans and the Mughals of India, only the top religious authority, or *Shaykh al-Islam*, was authorized to issue *fatwas*. In today's world, when secular laws have encroached on the **Sharia**, *fatwas* are not binding and are generally unenforceable. The rector of **al-Azhar** University is the only official whose explanatory opinions carry the weight of *fatwas*. The contemporary development of a state-appointed *mufti* who is charged with justifying and legitimizing government policy, such as Saudi Arabia's Sheikh **Abd al-Aziz Ben Baz**, is frowned upon by most religious scholars. Among the most famous *fatwas* in recent years was the opinion of al-Azhar's rector classifying fighting in the Arab–Israeli War of 1948 as jihad, and **Ayatollah Ruhollah Khomeini**'s *fatwa* in 1989 anathematizing Salman Rushdie for his book, *The Satanic Verses*. Most *fatwas* render quasi-legal opinions on matters pertaining to women. Nonprofessional Islamists like Osama Bin Laden have also been known to issue *fatwas*.

So far, *fatwas* have been issued only by men, although learned Muslim women were asked for their advice in past centuries. There have been no official female *muftis*, although some women are now aspiring to play that role. For example, the head of the department of jurisprudence at al-Azhar's faculty of Islamic and Arabic studies for girls, Dr. Suad Saleh, has appealed to the Grand Mufti of Egypt, Dr. Nasr Farid Wasil (r. 1996–2002), to appoint her as his assistant in charge of issuing *fatwas* confined to women's affairs. Despite reminding him of the absence of any clear text in the Quran or *hadith* barring women from playing this role, she never received an answer. Among the most famous *fatwas* issued in Egypt in recent years relating to women have been permitting **family planning** since the early 1930s; allowing women to pray in mosques since the 1940s; a 1952 opinion disqualifying women from enjoying suffrage by alleging that political rights were male prerogatives; and the opinion of Egypt's Grand Mufti Jad al-Haqq Ali Jad al-Haqq (r. 1978–1982) approving **Jihan Sadat**'s Law 44, which introduced reforms affecting the country's personal status law. One of the most controversial *fatwas* was that of Grand Mufti Sheikh Muhammad Tantawi (r. 1986–1996) in which he approved wearing the *hijab* (head covering for women) but disapproved of wearing the *niqab* (face covering). Secular feminists criticized him for bypassing the opportunity to discuss the disadvantages of wearing the *hijab*.

In Shii Islam, the clerical class enjoys greater autonomy than the clergy in the Sunni world, hence the Iranian clergy's strong vocal views on women's dress and behavior. Some Shii *fatwas* have been very progressive, such as the pronouncements of Ayatollah Yusef Saanei, who declared that the Quran mandates a state of equality among all peoples, Muslims and non-Muslims, men and women. He also stated that no religious barriers stand between women and political office, including that of Ayatollah. Saanei proved to be equally liberal on matters of reproductive rights and abortion, which he felt was permissible during the first trimester of pregnancy for a wide variety of reasons. Another high-ranking Shii cleric, Ayatollah Mustafa Muhaqeqdamad, called for outlawing summary **divorce** by reminding Muslims that marriage was based on the consent of both parties; hence it is illegal for one party only to end it. *See also* ABDUH, MUHAMMAD (1849–1905).

FAWWAZ, ZAYNAB (ca. 1850–1914). A Lebanese essayist, novelist, and poet who was born to a poor Shii family in Tibnin, in Jebel Amel, the southern Lebanese region. As a young woman, she worked in the household of Ali Bey al-Asaad, a leader of the Shii community, where she was taught reading and writing by al-Assad's wife. After her first marriage, she accompanied her master's family to Alexandria in 1870, where she studied rhetoric with some prominent teachers of Arabic. She began her writing career by producing essays on gender and nationalist issues for papers in Alexandria and Cairo. Her work appeared in the newspaper *al-Nil* during the 1890s and in women's journals shortly thereafter. In her widely read book *Zaynab's Letters*, she called for accepting women's rights to education and employment. All her novels were based on feminist themes, such as *Good Consequences, or Ghada the Radiant* (1899) and *King Kurush: First Sovereign of the Persians* (1905). Her most notable work was a biographical dictionary of women, *Scattered Pearls on the Generations of Mistresses of Seclusion* (1894), which covered the lives of Arab and European women. She was opposed to the custom of **veiling** at a time when the antiveiling campaign was still in its infancy. Her novel *Good Consequences*, which appeared in

1899, is now considered to be the first Arabic novel, preceding Muhammad Husayn Haikal's novel *Zaynab* (1914) by over a decade. She died in Egypt. *See also* SHAABAN, BOUTHAINA (1953–).

FAYROUZ (1934–). Famed Lebanese singer who, with the help of her husband and his brother, developed a new genre of music known as "The Rabbanic School." She was born Nuhad Haddad in Beirut and was given the name Fayrouz (turquoise) by musician Halim al-Rumi. Her parents were Wadii Haddad and Liza Bustani, both members of the middle class. Fayrouz was discovered while still attending public school by Muhammad Flayfal, a talent scout for the newly founded Lebanese Radio Station. She began to perform on Lebanese Public Radio in the early 1950s, where Rumi was the head station manager and while she was attending the National Conservatory of Music. Rumi introduced her to a rising composer, Aassi Rahbani (1923–1986), whom she eventually married. She formed an enduring musical partnership with Aassi and his brother Mansour Rahbani (1925–2009), both of whom were trained in Western music by French musicologists in Beirut. Her son, Ziyad Rahbani (1956–), also became a composer and influenced her musical style. The Rahbani brothers wrote music that suited her voice perfectly, largely by intertwining Oriental and Western musical elements and by rearranging the music of familiar folk songs from all over the Arab world.

Fayrouz sang old and beloved songs by Egyptian singer Sayyid Darwish (1892–1923), songs written in classical Arabic by Ahmad Shawqi (1869–1932), and folk tunes mostly in the Lebanese and Syrian dialects. She also recorded a few religious songs influenced by her Maronite Christian background. Most of her songs celebrated nature and the beautiful Lebanese countryside. Although she rarely delivered patriotic songs or succumbed to performing songs in praise of political leaders, she sang in support of Arab Palestine and the Palestinian refugees, particularly following the June War of 1967. These songs, which accompanied the rising popularity of Palestinian guerrillas in the 1970s, contributed greatly to her stature as the Arab world's foremost female singer, rivaling **Umm Kulthum** in Egypt. But her artistic reputation also grew as a result of performing at the Baalbek Festival in eastern Lebanon, which began in 1957 and continued to be held annually until the outbreak of the Lebanese Civil War in 1974. During the war, she maintained her residence in West Beirut, where she guarded her political neutrality until the very end.

Fayrouz performed at prestigious venues all over the world, such as Carnegie Hall in New York, the Masonic Auditorium in San Francisco, and the Olympia in Paris. When she performed in Las Vegas in 1999, an audience of about 13,000 from around the world came to hear her. Fayrouz was honored for her talent by the kings of Jordan and Morocco, and by Lebanese President Camille Chamoun, who in 1957 awarded her the Cavalier Medal, Lebanon's highest honor bestowed on members of the arts community. After she sang "Jerusalem, You Are the Flower of All Cities," she was given keys to the city in 1961 by Mayor Rouhi al-Khatib. In 1969, her image was imprinted on a Lebanese postage stamp. She returned to the annual Baalbeck Festival in 1998, where her star first became ascendant. Throughout the years, she remained a shy and conservative individual who shunned interviews and the glare of publicity. She also cultivated a performing style characterized by a rigid and serious demeanor, avoiding body movements and facial expressions typical of cabaret styles of entertainment. Fayrouz continues to enjoy the position of a consummate classical performer.

FAYSAL, HAIFA (1952–). A Saudi Arabian princess and philanthropist, the third child of King Faysal of Saudi Arabia (r. 1963–1974) and **Queen Iffat**. Both of her parents had a hand in developing her philanthropic interests. Her mother was educated in Jedda and Switzerland and was instrumental in promoting female education in the kingdom, where she single-handedly founded a school for girls in Khobar. Princess Haifa married Prince Bandar ibn Sultan in 1972, whom she accompanied to Washington when he was posted as ambassador to the United States from 1983 to 2005. One of her big projects was assembling a collection of 6,000 Saudi objects of art and material culture dating back to the year 1900. Her other well-publicized project was the creation of the Mosaic Foundation in 1998, which included other ambassadors' wives and focused on serving needy women and children. The foundation raised $500,000 for Saint Jude's Children's Research Hospital and at one time supported the Kosovo Red Cross Society and Save the Children Organization. Other beneficiaries of this foundation included the United Nations Foundation for Africa and public schools in the Washington, D.C., area.

After the attacks of September 11, 2001, the Mosaic Foundation changed course and began to plan various symposia dealing with popular misconceptions about Islam and Muslim women. Another innovation was the launching of a micro-credit organization, the Mosaic Fund for the Arab World, benefiting Arab women in various countries. Princess Haifa also created a philanthropic project to help the women and children of Iraq in 2003. She relocated with her husband back to Saudi Arabia in 2005. *See also* EDUCATION: ARAB GULF STATES.

FAYSAL, TOUJAN (1948–). The first woman elected to the Jordanian parliament, in 1993. She came from the Circassian ethnic minority, and as such was eligible to run for one of three seats reserved for her community. Jordanian women were enfranchised and granted the right to run for office in 1974, but had to await the reopening of parliament as part of a general liberalization program in 1989. Faysal graduated from the University of Jordan, earning an MA in English language and literature. She married a doctor, and by the time of the 1989 elections, she was a well-known television commentator with a considerable popular following. When she ran for office, she incurred the wrath of Islamists and conservative members of parliament with her demands for **Sharia** reforms and her refutation of their Quranic interpretations. She attacked laws permitting **polygamy**, calling for their elimination. The *mufti* (highest religious authority) of the Jordanian Army declared her an apostate in 1989, although there were no apostasy laws in Jordan. The courts rejected this case, and all charges against her were dropped upon intervention by King Hussein (r. 1953–1999). When she ran for a parliamentary seat again in 1993, she was opposed by the same forces who had opposed her in the past, but she won, serving until 1997. She was the only woman in the lower house, but lost her bid for another term in the 1997–2001 elections by a narrow margin. During that period, only two women were appointed to the upper house, **Layla Sharaf** and **Rima Khalaf**. In 2003, King Abdullah II issued a decree that reserved 6 out of a total of 110 seats in the lower house for women, but she was unable to take advantage of this opportunity.

Faysal had another confrontation with the authorities in 2002, when she was tried for publishing an open letter to the monarch on the website of the *Arab Times*, a newspaper based in Houston in the United States, in which she leveled charges of corruption against the prime minister, Ali Abu al-Ragheb. This resulted in an 18-month prison sentence for defamation and insulting religious authorities. She served only 29 days of her prison sentence and was granted a royal pardon after Amnesty International adopted her case as a prisoner of conscience. Since her conviction was not formally rescinded, she was legally barred from running for public office again. Faysal remained politically active and continued to call for investigating public corruption through appearances on the al-Jazeera television network.

FEMALE DRIVERS IN SAUDI ARABIA. Women staged a driving demonstration for the first time in November 1990. This took place in Riyadh, the Saudi capital, and women hoped to put an end to the official ban on female drivers. The direct impetus for this challenge to official authority was the presence of American troops and American female drivers of military vehicles in the Eastern Province during the first Gulf War in 1991. Also, unveiled Kuwaiti females who fled their country by driving family vehicles to Saudi Arabia during that time enhanced the Saudi women's disgruntlement with their own driving situation. They began to complain in the pages of Saudi newspapers, arguing that these conditions jeopardized their ability to drive children to a safe haven in case of a sudden attack.

The female letter writers also complained about the cost of retaining a full-time male driver and the inconvenience of total dependence on male family members for transportation. The demonstration that followed these complaints was well-planned and calibrated so as to avoid ruffling as many official feathers as possible. There were 47 demonstrators, driven by their male chauffeurs to al-Tammi Supermarket in downtown Riyadh. The women, who were fully **veiled**, quickly dismissed their male drivers and proceeded in a convoy, with some of the women riding in the passenger seats. They were only able to proceed for a few blocks before being stopped at an intersection by the vehicles of the moral police, *al-mutawieen*, representing the Committee for the Promotion of Virtue and the Prevention of Vice. The baton-wielding sheikhs of this committee ordered the women out of their vehicles and, before they were able to charge them with infringement of religious laws, Saudi regular police arrived and took control of the situation. The women were driven to a police station, with the sheikhs riding in the passenger seats.

Upon interrogating the women, it was discovered that they were educated professionals, some of whom belonged to families allied with the ruling al-Saud family and most of whom held international drivers' licenses. Others were academics and professionals, like Fatin al-Zamil, who was on the faculty of the women's branch of the University of Riyadh, and Aisha al-Mana, who held a doctoral degree in sociology from the University of Colorado and sat at the helm of a consortium of female-owned enterprises. These same women apparently sent a petition to Prince Salman ibn Abd al-Aziz, the governor of Riyadh, prior to the demonstration, in which they asked King Fahd to sympathize with their need to drive. Their main argument was that even during the period of Prophet Muhammad, women were allowed to drive camels on the battlefield. But as soon as the women were legally processed, Prince Salman sought the advice of a group of religious and legal scholars, who rendered a wide array of opinions and interpretations. The legal experts advised that the women had committed no civil violation because they possessed valid international driving licenses recognized under Saudi law. The religious experts added that the driving demonstration did not raise any issues, because the women were veiled and the Quran was silent on the question of driving.

The women were released to the custody of their male relatives, but the sheikhs continued their campaign. Some called for beheading the women involved, accusing them and their male relatives of committing the sin of apostasy. Religious leaflets flooded mosques and public spaces, listing the women's names and accusing them of communist leanings. Eventually, the Saudi government sided with the forces of religious extremism, ignoring the opinions issued by Prince Salman's committee and suspending the women from their government posts. By that time, pressure on female professors who had participated in the demonstration was being applied by their own conservative students, who boycotted their classes.

Similar attempts to challenge the ban on female driving took place in Jedda and Dhahran. These were also squelched, and the Saudi media refused to cover them. A Saudi journalist who leaked the story along with pictures to a British film crew was jailed. Instead of decreeing that the moral police and the sheikhs should have been lashed 80 times for smearing the women's reputations unjustly, as is called for in the Quran and **Sharia**, they were handed a victory in the form of a pronouncement by the government's chief *mufti* Abd al-Aziz Ben Baz. He issued a *fatwa* stating that the act of driving contradicted the Islamic traditions of the Kingdom's citizens. Analysts claimed, however, that the Ben Baz interpretation suited the royal family's intentions perfectly by diverting public attention from the more dangerous issue of permitting foreign troops to occupy the holy soil of Muhammad's birthplace.

Another attempt to force the revocation of the ban on female drivers was undertaken in the spring of 2011. Buoyed by stories of youthful rebellion by men and women in Tunisia, Egypt, Syria, Bahrain, Libya, and Yemen, Saudi women took to the wheels of their vehicles in several cities, this time accompanied by their husbands, but they were stopped by the police and detained. King Abdullah, however, pardoned all of them. *See also* EDUCATION: ARAB GULF STATES; WAHHABISM.

FEMALE INFANTICIDE. This practice existed in ancient times and was condoned by many societies. The practice was the result of a combination of factors that contributed to devaluing daughters. Among these were the scarcity of resources and frequent famines, a patriarchal social system that confined inheritance to the male line, and the need to provide girls with **dowries** to render them marriageable. Female infanticide increased in the Arabian Peninsula during the era preceding Muhammad's birth in 570 CE due to the intensification of intratribal warfare as Quraysh attempted to impose its sway over all the surrounding trade routes. The custom of enslaving young females of the defeated clans was viewed as a blow to the honor of their male relations. Increased warfare also created a surplus of women and increased the likelihood of their capture by the victorious side. In addition, the peninsula's weak ecological balance resulted in frequent periods of famine in which female, more than male, infants became an economic burden on their families. Evidence from the literature of that period describes the manner in which a young girl would be dressed in her finest and taken by her father on a pleasant journey, ending in her being buried alive in the sand. This was usually done with the mother's consent.

Prophet Muhammad strongly condemned this practice, while repeatedly glorifying the education and nurturing of daughters in *hadith*. When the Quran was revealed to Muslims, it included strong condemnation of this custom, reminding believers that the souls of innocent girls will be asked for what crime were they murdered just before the Day of Judgment. Muhammad outlawed this practice as soon as he established the first Medinian state in 622 CE. Consequently, all Islamic jurists have maintained the view that female infanticide was equivalent to murder. This practice and the emphasis placed on its suppression by Muhammad led to a lively debate in subsequent centuries over the permissibility and timing of abortion, as well as the morality of sex selection in abortion cases. *See also* FAMILY PLANNING IN ISLAM; SHARIA.

FEMINISM: THE TERM. Although the inception of feminist thought dates back to the period 1780–1860, the term "feminism" was not coined until the first quarter of the 19th century. Feminist ideas first developed in Great Britain, France, and the United States, but it was left to French utopian socialist philosopher Charles Fourier (1772–1837) to coin the term *féminisme*. Fourier first used the term in 1837, but he had argued as early as 1808, in his *Theory of the Four Movements*, that one of the main principles of social progress was the liberation of women. The English variant of the French term was first used in writing in 1894, according to the 1933 *Supplement to the Oxford English Dictionary*.

Because there is no equivalent to this term in Arabic, commentators on the Middle East had often assumed that feminism was a foreign idea. Arab and Muslim women continue to show discomfort when using the term. There have been efforts to use the Arabic terms *niswiyya* or *nisaiiyya* (from *nisaa*, or women), but neither of these became popular. In addition, there is no Arabic equivalent to the term "gender." Although Arab and Muslim women are the subject of unparalleled academic and popular curiosity around the world, any analysis of their lives and thought in native languages is often written without resorting to Western feminist terminology.

FEMINIST MOVEMENT IN EGYPT. Feminism in Egypt owes a great deal to the nationalist movement seeking independence from Great Britain and the male nationalist leaders who created the Arab renaissance. Nationalism provided an opportunity for women activists and bestowed legitimacy on their efforts to mobilize half of the nation to join the national liberation struggle. Women's participation in the 1919 revolution, which lasted until the writing of the 1923 constitution, showcased women as full partners in the battle for independence, and as such deserving of rights equal to those of the men. The leadership of this feminist campaign was made up of Christian and

Muslim elitist women who substituted for their exiled male relatives, the emerging leadership of Egypt. The new nationalist party, the Wafd, became a magnet for a wider base of emerging middle-class female elements. When the Wafd held its first public meeting in Cairo in 1920, a huge contingent of women showed up. A women's committee from within the Wafd was founded, leading in time to the creation of another women's organization, the **Egyptian Feminist Union**.

Women not only led the effort to boycott British goods, they also supplied the first martyrs. A young widow, Shafiqa bint Muhammad Ashmawi, was killed by British snipers as she led a demonstration on 10 April 1919, and four others followed her as the British intensified their efforts to quell the riots. **Huda Shaarawi**, who became Egypt's leading feminist, described in her memoirs how women pursued a general boycott and added an economic twist to their efforts. Since Muslim women had the legal right to control their wealth, she explained, many Egyptian women withdrew their assets from British banks and deposited them in the newly established Bank Misr, the national bank of Egypt. Women led by Shaarawi eventually broke off their relationships with the Wafd Women's Committee in 1924, becoming as much as possible an independent women's party. A vibrant women's press accompanied the rise of nationalist feminism. Egyptian women went on to experience different kinds of feminist ideologies, such as Nasser's state femi- nism, the neoliberal feminism of Sadat's era, and an Islamist feminism nur- tured by the Muslim Brotherhood.

Under the rule of Jamal Abd al-Nasser (r. 1954–1970), the state adopted a strategy of expanding women's participation in the workplace to advance the country's industrial goals. The official representative of the feminist sector became not the previous leadership of feminist organizations of the royalist period but the female head of the Ministry of Social Welfare. The thrust of the feminist movement shifted from the struggle to reform the Sharia to the enhancement of women's social and economic rights. The minister of social welfare became also the official face of Egyptian feminism in international conferences and meetings.

Under President Anwar Sadat (r. 1970–1981), feminist policy shifted again, moving in the direction of economic and political liberalization and modernization, known as the policy of *infitah*, or opening to the West. Dur- ing this era, the official leadership of the feminist movement was usurped by **Jihan Sadat**, the president's wife, who articulated and campaigned for the passage of legislative measures designed to force changes in **Sharia** but without the sponsorship of the religious institution. Dissident feminists of this period, like **Nawal Saadawi**, were sidelined and in some cases impris- oned because they did not espouse the goals of Sadat's neoliberal regime.

With the rise of Husni Mubarak to power (r. 1981–2011), the feminist movement was fragmented as younger women became active in the work of opposition groups and the labor movement such as the April 6 Movement (2011) and the Kifayeh Party. This was an expected outcome, because the hegemonic National Democratic Party co-opted the work of previous feminists by enrolling them in its ranks. At the same time, Egypt witnessed the rise of another type of feminism, exemplified by the leadership of **Zaynab Ghazzali**, who became the chief mobilizer of Islamic women and their recruitment for membership in the female wing of the Muslim Brotherhood. This fragmentation of the feminist front was evident in the absence of a clear feminist agenda during the initial period of democratization following the 2011 revolution. *See also* ABDUH, MUHAMMAD (1849–1905); FADHIL, NAZLI (?–1914); GHAZZALI, ZAYNAB (1917–2005); HARB, TALAAT (1867–1941); SHAFIQ, DURREA REGAI (1908–1975).

FEMINIST MOVEMENT IN IRAN. Iranian women played a significant role in the nationalist struggle beginning in the late 19th century. But even as early as the 1850s, women, like **Qurrat al-Ayn**, made their mark as the leaders of the Babi movement, leading to the breakaway **Bahai** faith. For the rest of the Muslim population, national events forced them to adopt activist roles and to demand their rights as a result. When senior members of the Iranian clergy and bazaar merchants began a boycott campaign against the tobacco concession granted by Shah Nasir al-Din to the British Imperial Tobacco Corporation of Persia in 1890, this inevitably involved women, who were also smokers of tobacco products. Resistance to British imperialism also reached the women's quarters of the shah's palace; the women reportedly threw away their water pipes (*hukkah*) on the clergy's orders. Women's role in the Constitutional Revolution of 1906 was on the side of national resistance, involving mostly women of the elite. They flocked to secret societies to organize activities such as mass demonstrations against the ruling Qajar dynasty. Not all men approved, and in many cases women were physically pushed out of public places. A famous incident involving women was reported by the American financial adviser to the shah, William Morgan Shuster, in his 1912 book *The Strangling of Persia*. He told the story of women storming the Majlis upon hearing rumors that the all-male chamber had decided to vote in a closed session in favor of Russian demands for ending economic reforms. The Tsarist government of Russia at the time had already forced the signing of the 1907 treaty that cut Iran into three spheres of influence. A force of 300 veiled women, some packing pistols under their garments, threatened to dispose of their husbands and male relatives if the deputies succumbed to Russian pressure. Armed women also participated in the Tabriz riots in defense of the same revolution. This played a role in persuading a wide segment of the male population to declare their support for women's right to **education** and full equality in the pages of the Persian press.

When **Reza Shah** came to power after the 1921 coup d'état, all independent groups were reined in, including famous women's organizations such as the Patriotic Women's League, which was shut down in 1932. A government-sponsored association known as Kanoon Banovan (Persian: Ladies Center) took its place, with emphasis on unveiling, which was favored by the shah. The association engaged in charity work benefiting women and children. The shah's reforms on behalf of women focused on the forcible removal of the veil, in which he emulated Turkey's bid for modernization and Westernization. Other items on the women's agenda, such as reforming the **Sharia**, were left untouched. **Marriage** and **divorce** customs and male guardianship over children in case of divorce were maintained, as well as the practice of temporary marriage. The shah himself had three wives. But laws did provide for greater education and employment opportunities for women, which privileged women of the elite.

Women were active within the ranks of the Tudeh Party and similar underground leftist groups even during the first half of the 20th century when Shah Reza's Westernizing program was at full strength. Iranian women also hoped to achieve their political rights by supporting the short-lived (1951–1953) government of Muhammad Mossadegh, but the Majlis at the time was involved in a life and death struggle with the forces of the shah's government. The shah's son, Muhammad Reza Shah (r. 1941–1979), made great strides toward reforming abuses of the Sharia, particularly in conjunction with his White Revolution and its set of new regulations. The trajectory of Iranian feminism, however, changed course dramatically with the rise of the Islamic Republic in 1979. The state took charge of the feminist movement, tolerating only a new breed of regime-friendly feminist movement with emphasis on Islamic dress and the valorization of Islamic family life and personal piety. An independent strain of Islamic feminism has arisen, developing its own Islamic feminist press and articulating the need to enact further reforms on behalf of women. Often Islamic women loyal to the regime oppose the prevailing male consensus on women's issues from within the Majlis. Secular women's organizations, including leftist groups associated with political parties, have become a thing of the past. *See also* AFKHAMI, MAHNAZ (1941–); EBTEKAR, MAASUMEH (1960–); GORJI, MUNIREH (?–); HABIBI, SHAHLA (?–); PAHLAVI, ASHRAF (1919–); RAHNAVARD, ZAHRA (1945–); *ZANAN* MAGAZINE.

FEMINIST MOVEMENT IN ISRAEL. The lives of Israeli women have been shaped largely by the ideology of political Zionism, the underlying ideology of the state, and by Jewish religious law. Before its establishment in

Palestine, European Zionism's attitude toward women was characterized by ambivalence. Women became heavily involved in agricultural projects in Palestine, particularly on kibbutzes, or collective farms, as early as the 1920s. They also served with men in underground militia forces that eventually became the Israeli Defense Forces (IDF). Israel's Declaration of Independence promised women full equality with men, but their access to positions of leadership and power remained restricted. The national draft, which applied to men and women, kept the latter largely confined to noncombat duties, although a few women have succeeded in achieving high military rank in recent years. Women predominated in the intelligence services and began to serve in the Knesset, as well as being appointed to the highest levels of the judicial institution in the 1950s.

The political careers of high-profile women such as **Golda Meir**, who served as prime minister or member of the cabinet from 1969 until 1974, and **Tzipi Livni**, who held the post of foreign minister from 2006 until 2008, were not typical of most Israeli women. The majority of women suffered from lack of a military experience in their backgrounds, which usually provided males with the surest and shortest route to political high office. Israeli women of non-European origin have also been held back by the Ashkenazi monopoly on power. Yet Israeli women are highly educated and contribute to the economy despite the state's pronounced pronatalist policies.

Several organizations, such as the Israeli Women's Network, founded by **Alice Shalvi** in 1984, have defended women's rights by supporting greater legislative efforts to open the door to women in various avenues of society. Since the June War of 1967, several women's groups have adopted political platforms calling for an end to the occupation of Palestinian territories. A group of pacifists known as Women in Black began to demonstrate against Israel's war with Lebanon in 1982. Another association, New Profile, calls for the adoption of a new system of education capable of inculcating children with peace values as a way of demilitarizing Israeli society from the bottom up. Women have figured prominently in another group, B'tselem, which defends the rights of Palestinians living under Israeli occupation.

Sexual harassment remains high on the agenda of women representatives in the Knesset, who gained everyone's attention following the conviction of former president Moshe Katsav in 2011 on sexual harassment charges. Israeli women have also complained about the supremacy of religious laws and the hegemony of Orthodox Judaic laws over Israeli personal status cases. A group of women continues to defy Orthodox control over such religious sites as the Western Wall in Jerusalem, attempting to hold prayer services in that vicinity despite a general ban on women because of antipollution laws. *See also* ALONI, SHULAMIT ADLER (1928–); BITTON, SIMONE (1955–);

DIVORCE IN JEWISH LAW; DOWRY IN JEWISH LAW; GOZANSKI, TAMAR (1940–); GROSSMAN, HAIKA (1919–1993); NAAMAT; NAMIR, ORA TOIB (1930–).

FRANCKE, REND AL-RAHIM (1949–). An Iraqi human rights activist and diplomat who was born in Baghdad to a Shii father and a Sunni mother. She attended boarding school in Great Britain and went on to earn an MA degree in English from Cambridge University. She also studied at the Sorbonne. Her first career was in banking, working mostly as a currency trader in Great Britain, Bahrain, and Lebanon. She moved with her family to Great Britain in 1978, and then to the United States in 1981, acquiring American citizenship in 1987. Francke's political career grew out of her concern for events in her mother country. She began lobbying for Iraqi democracy and regime change, establishing the Iraq Foundation in Washington, of which she became the executive director. This brought her before the U.S. Congress, offering testimony on conditions in Iraq, eventually becoming an adviser to the George Walker Bush administration. She joined the Committee for the Liberation of Iraq, which lobbied Congress in favor of mounting an invasion of that country, and she testified before the Senate Foreign Relations Committee advocating the pursuit of nation-building following the ouster of Saddam Hussein.

In 2003, she became the Iraqi ambassador to the United States despite her American citizenship, but was forced to resign a year later due to pressure from various quarters. Her removal from this position was attributed partially to her congressional testimony about the U.S. failure to rebuild Iraq and her relationship to her controversial cousin, Ahmad Chalabi, who established strong relations with Iran. Her organization, the Iraq Foundation, aided in the establishment of another controversial group, the Iraq–American Freedom Alliance, which tried to sell the American public on the positive aspects of the American occupation of Iraq. She continued to speak in favor of the American presence in Iraq as late as 2007, often through high-publicity television interviews. Her book, *The Arab Shi'a: The Forgotten Muslims*, coauthored with Graham E. Fuller, was published in 2000.

FRONT ISLAMIQUE DU SALUT (FIS). This is an Algerian political party with an Islamic agenda. which was founded in 1989. The party rose in opposition to the leftist ruling group, the FLN, which had ruled Algeria since independence in 1962. FIS calls for the establishment of a religious state based on the purist (Arabic: *salafi*) and strict compliance with ancient religious texts as they were applied in former centuries. The party's leadership was drawn from religious and university circles and was headed by Abbasi Madani, a university professor, and Ali Belhadj, an Islamic preacher. Due to their long imprisonment beginning in 1991, the leadership of the party has been held by Abdel Kader Hachani. Although the sources of its funding remain shrouded in secrecy, they are assumed to be local contributions and Saudi Arabian assistance. The party gained prominence among young and unemployed Algerians in urban centers and was able to score major electoral gains when President Chadhli Benjedid (r. 1979–1992) allowed local elections in the 1990s as a way of diffusing the country's economic crisis. When the FIS began to consolidate its power after winning in two consecutive municipal elections, the Algerian armed forces staged a coup d'état in 1992, arresting a large number of party followers. This led to a civil war that lasted until 2008, when President Abd al-Aziz Boutefliqa (1999–) was able to impose a cease-fire.

The FIS waged a violent war against secular women, including students and professional females. Its 1989 pamphlet, a sequel to *Projet de Programme du Front Islamique du Salut*, recommended that women be given a financial incentive to stay at home rather than working outside. This plan, the FIS argued, would preserve sexual segregation and eliminate the immorality of offices shared by men and women. At the same time, the FIS repeatedly called for increasing available jobs for men in order to ward off increasing unemployment. Belhadj emerged as the most dedicated enemy of women, gathering around him lower-class and uneducated youth who represented the extreme Salafi wing of the FIS. However, in the parliamentary elections of 2012, the FIS failed to achieve a majority and seemed destined to decline.

G

GENERAL DIRECTORATE ON THE STATUS AND PROBLEMS OF WOMEN. This is an office serving women's interests by interfacing with the Turkish government. It was established in accordance with the recommendations of the **Convention on the Elimination of Discrimination against Women (CEDAW)** in 1990. The directorate was made part of the office of the Turkish prime minister and was directed by the ministry responsible for women's and children's affairs. The work of the directorate falls under four departments, devoted to educational and social affairs; foreign affairs; economic affairs; and publications, statistics, and documentation. Much of its work takes the form of research projects resulting in policy recommendations, conducted with the support of women's associations. The directorate has also taken on the task of raising consciousness about women's concerns in the national media. *See also* NON-GOVERNMENTAL ORGANIZATIONS (NGOs).

GENERAL FEDERATION OF IRAQI WOMEN (GFIW). This is a major organization representing Iraqi women, which was founded soon after the 1968 Baathist coup d'état. The federation distinguished itself from other women's organizations in capitalist countries by dedicating itself to mobilizing women against Western imperialism. The GFIW was considered a semi-official affiliate of the Baath regime, its main goal being the improvement of the status of women so that they could contribute to the building of the Arab socialist state. Most gains made by Iraqi women starting in the 1970s were attributed to its efforts. The GFIW fought to attain many rights for working women, such as maternity leave, child-care services, literacy, and equality in wages. Due to its pressure, **Sharia** law was removed from the area of women's personal status regulations, **polygamy** was restricted, and women's **inheritance** rights were made equal to those of males. Fueled by economic gains from Iraq's recently nationalized oil industry, women were integrated in the economy and benefited from state policies on promotions and admission to most public sector positions. One of the greatest contributions of the GFIW to Iraqi women was in the area of literacy programs, which improved the literacy rates of Iraqi women perceptibly, only to decline again as a result of the first Gulf War of 1991. An arts committee was established, which was behind the erection of the Women's Museum in Baghdad, sponsored by the Baath government and the first of its kind in the Arab world.

The GFIW held its first general conference in 1969, revealing a well-organized structure that centralized all decisions in Baghdad, but spread its control to branches in the provinces. An elected president was at the apex of this structure, supported by a vice president and a general council, which had 33 members elected by the general conference. The bylaws of the organization called for an annual meeting of at least one month's duration and an annual election to choose all its officers. The general council was expected to direct the work of the executive bureau and the general secretariat. There was also a separate secretariat to manage the affairs of the autonomous Kurdish region. At its height, the federation had 18 branches representing Iraq's 18 governorates, each controlling its own sub-branches and centers. By the 1990s, membership was estimated at 1.5 million throughout the country. One of its unique projects was a large farm managed entirely by women, which had 2,000 acres. The farm provided work for unemployed rural women and had its own nursery school and literacy center. For many years, **Manal Younis Alusi** ran the GFIW as its president, assisted by Iftikhar Ahmad as vice president. Both were veteran members of the Baath Party. For all practical purposes, the federation functioned as a government ministry for women. It also published a magazine titled *Iraqi Woman*, but it disintegrated following the fall of Saddam Hussein in 2003. *See also* NON-GOVERNMENTAL ORGANIZATIONS (NGOs).

GENERAL FEDERATION OF SYRIAN WOMEN (GFSW). This is a semiofficial organization working on behalf of women in Syria. It was founded in 1967 by the merger of all women's welfare associations, volunteer committees, and literacy groups. The merger was called for by the Baath government, which also funds some of the federation's programs that assist children's development and women's education. The federation has 14 branches and centers in most villages that promote women's rights, and runs child-care centers, vocational training programs, and literacy classes. Due to the federation's emphasis on the rights of working women, the Syrian government adopted a law in 1989 that allowed the establishment of nurseries on the premises of public institutions and factories employing women throughout the country. By 1990, the Syrian government began enforcing equality in wages.

The federation serves as an official representative of the Baath government and sends delegates to general conferences on women throughout the Arab world. It also maintains links to UN groups and international **non-governmental organizations (NGOs)**. The leadership of the federation engages in public debates supporting the government's views on major foreign policy issues such as the Israeli occupation of the Golan Heights, Palestinian rights, and the threat of war in southern Lebanon. One of its unfulfilled demands is the question of the civil rights of Syrian women, especially in the matter of passing on citizenship rights to their offspring. *See also* ATTAR, NAJAH (1933–); SHAABAN, BOUTHAINA (1953–).

GENERAL UNION OF PALESTINIAN WOMEN (GUPW). This is the official cadre within the Palestine Liberation Organization (PLO) representing women. The GUPW was founded in 1965, a year after the creation of the first PLO in Jerusalem in 1964 under the chairmanship of Ahmad Shuqeiry. The union's membership extends to women in the Palestinian diaspora and has branches in many countries. The objective of this organization is to involve women in the economic, social, and political work of the PLO, serving the national cause and leading to their own development. Its main activities center on the creation of vocational training centers, **educational** programs, literacy centers, and nursery schools in Palestinian refugee camps, particularly in Lebanon. The GUPW Kuwait was charged with running schools for the expatriate Palestinian community until its expulsion from that country following the Iraqi invasion of 1990. The union was given a block of seats in the PLO's parliament in exile, the Palestine National Council (PNC).

There has always been debate over the wisdom of subordinating the women's agenda to the priorities of a national organization like the PLO. A large segment of the GUPW attempted to push for the adoption of a feminist agenda and feminist measures even before the creation of a Palestinian state. For instance, just prior to the convening of the PNC in Damascus, the GUPW prepared detailed proposals for extra funding for its own projects, as well as legal papers demanding reforms of the Islamic laws of **marriage, divorce,** and **inheritance.** This feminist thrust, however, was quickly withdrawn when military clashes between the PLO and Lebanese militias escalated in West Beirut.

Reticence to push for pro-feminist measures was most visible among pro-Fateh members of the union's executive committee, who constituted half of the membership. Other factions of the PLO and younger pro-Fateh affiliates were always underrepresented in the GUPW hierarchy. Occasionally, GUPW representatives in the PNC, both pro-Fateh and non-Fateh members, took a stand in defiance of the PLO's shift to a more centrist position choosing diplomacy over the armed struggle. At one time, Fateh suspended the membership of its allied women in the GUPW for six months as punishment for defying Yasser Arafat's decisions. The greatest defection from the PLO occurred when most of the GUPW withdrew their support after Arafat signed the Oslo Accords in 1993. Other women's groups were also critical of the women's loyalty to political factions rather than to a common pro-feminist agenda.

The GUPW played a significant role in gaining legitimacy for the PLO through participation in UN conferences on women and at other international meetings. Always claiming to be the second most popular cadre of the PLO, after the General Union of Palestinian Students (GUPS), in 1982, the women's groups spoke for a membership of 22,878 in Lebanon. The last general conference of the GUPW was in 1985, and it was not until 2009 that the organization was able to convene another conference, in Ramallah, Palestine, under the auspices of the Palestine National Authority (PNA). Voting was still on the basis of the PLO's factional system, and no effort was made to admit female representatives from Hamas or the Islamic Jihad. These two groups, which emerged in Gaza during the first *intifada* of 1987, continue to challenge Fateh groups and their monopoly on decision making. The GUPW emerged during this conference as a powerless organization, sharing the fate of the rest of the PLO's nonmilitary cadres, such as professional unions of writers and journalists. See also ABD AL-HADI, ISSAM (1928–); NON-GOVERNMENTAL ORGANIZATIONS (NGOs); SAYIGH, MAI (1940–).

GHANIM, AZZA (?–). A Tunisian feminist and organization builder whose activism began in 1978 when she and other feminists founded Club d'Etude de la Condition de La Femme as a section of the Club **Tahir Haddad**, named after Tunisia's first advocate for women's rights. The Club d'Etude became a forum for debating women's status in Tunisia and was restricted to women. Its main focus was the unrealized reforms sanctioned by the **Personal Status Code of Tunisia** of 1956. Ghanim participated in the establishment of another group in the 1980s, Femmes Démocrates, which supported the Palestinian cause during the Israeli invasion of Lebanon in 1982, leading to the massacres of Sabra and Shatila refugee camps. The Femmes Démocrates was a contributor to the Tunisian feminist journal *Nissa* (*Women*) and a strong advocate for women and children.

GHANNAM, LAYLA (1975–). She was the first woman to be appointed governor of Ramallah, the unofficial capital of the Palestine National Authority (PNA). The 2010 appointment was made by Mahmoud Abbas, the PNA's president. Ghannam was previously employed by the PNA's intelligence service and was selected for this post to alleviate the threat of a Hamas takeover of the West Bank. She is known for her tough decisions directed at dissidents of any variety and is rumored to have worked with international intelligence services such as Great Britain's MI6. She holds a PhD in psychology from an Egyptian university and is considered a loyal supporter of Fateh, the largest faction within the PLO. She wears a *hijab* (a head scarf) and hails from a religious family that draws a line between Islamic observance and Islamic militancy. She has made it clear that she will not tolerate any illegal activity by Hamas, which maintains a visible presence in the West Bank in addition to Gaza.

GHANNUSHI, RASHID (1941–). Tunisian Islamic ideologue and founder of al-Nahdha Party, who was born into a family of modest means in Hammah, Tunisia. He began his adult life as a student of agronomy at Cairo University and later at Damascus University, where teachings of the Baath Party were popular. He was also exposed to the thought of the Muslim Brotherhood while in Syria, but came under the influence of Western thought later when he studied philosophy at the Sorbonne, Paris. His experience as a schoolteacher in Tunisia and his exposure to poverty and other negative effects of colonialism made him espouse a philosophy of social justice and national revival. He created a political party called the Islamic Tendency Movement in 1979, which later became known as *al-Nahdha*, or Renaissance Party. He went into exile in Great Britain in 1988 after spending intermittent periods in jail in Bizerte since 1981. His rejection of Western secularism while embracing democratic ideals was widely known throughout the Arab world.

Ghannushi became known as an advocate of a moderate Islamic philosophy that sought the inclusion of women in political life through a quota system to ensure their representation in elected bodies. But he also criticized the **Personal Status Code of Tunisia**, which entailed abolishing **polygamy** and other traditional Islamic practices. In 1987, he revised his position, insisting that there were many ways of interpreting the Quranic verse legitimizing polygamy. He explained that the ruler of a Muslim nation, like former President **Habib Bourgiba**, who authored the personal status code, was fully qualified to formulate new ways of practicing Islam. Ghannushi suggested that a public referendum on the status of the Tunisian family be conducted. His position on the status code reforms became even more moderate as he began to speak on the legitimacy of *ijtihad*, or personal interpretation of the Quran, which is every individual's right.

However, Ghannushi cautioned women throughout his career against wholesale acceptance of Western values and capitalist economics, which reduced them to a commodity, substituting the enslavement of the market for that of the traditional household. He stated that women's liberation must be based on Islamic principles. He supported women's desire to break away from their domestic roles by claiming that Islam did not confine them to housework and rearing of children, and that husbands should compensate women financially for volunteering for these tasks. He reminded his followers that Muhammad himself performed household chores. He referred to claims made by the Egyptian modernist **Muhammad Abduh** that the Quranic statement regarding Adam does not necessarily imply that Adam was created first, unlike the Jewish claim that Eve was made from Adam's rib. This Islamic story of creation calls for gender equality and is confirmed not only by Abduh, but also by the Shii scholar Muhammad Hussein Tabatabai and **Sayyid Qutb**, Egypt's fundamentalist philosopher. Neither does the Quran make Eve responsible for the original sin and the fall from paradise, as is the case in traditional Judeo–Christian teachings.

He also clarified that several *imams*, or religious scholars, such as Abu-Hanifa, Ibn-Jarir al-Tabari, and Ibn-Hazm, approved of women's right to vote and be appointed to government and judicial positions. Women's participation in warfare was acceptable to the ancients, he added, citing the example of **Aisha**'s leadership of a 3,000-soldier-strong army in battle. He reinterpreted the principle of *qiwamah*, or men's leadership of all aspects of society, to be restricted only to the family in order to minimize domestic conflict. He disputed the contention of the Pakistani scholar Abu al-Aala Mawdudi (1903–1979) that Muhammad categorically condemned the idea of women rising to the headship of state, asserting that the Prophet was only referring to **Buran**'s succession to the Persian throne. Ghannushi returned from exile to his country in 2011 after the fall of President Zein al-Abidin Ben Ali. Ghannushi's party, al-Nahdha, eventuality won a majority of seats in the Tunisian parliament.

GHAZOUL, FIRYAL (?–). An Iraqi professor of English and comparative literature at the American University of Cairo (AUC). She was educated in Iraq, Europe, and the United States and is well known in Cairo's literary circles. She cofounded the trilingual publication *Alif: Journal of Comparative Poetics*, which appeared in Arabic, English, and French in Cairo. She published several works in these three languages, including two books: *The Arabian Nights: A Structural Analysis* (English, 1980) and *Sa'idi Yousef* (Arabic, 1989). She published two works in French on the poetry of the Syrian poet Adonis and the Egyptian poet Muhammad Afifi Mattar. She is the author of scholarly studies on the Brethren of Purity (Ikhwan al-safa), an Islamic philosophical group, and on Ibn Khaldoun (1332–1406), Arab theorist and philosopher. Other works in Arabic examined major literary figures, like the Palestinian American Edward Said (1935–2003), Edward Kharrat (1926–), Yousef Idris (1927–1991), Mahmoud Darwish (1941–2008), and Salwa Baker (1949–).

GHAZZALI, ZAYNAB (1917–2005). An Egyptian teacher of Quran and *hadith*, and a political organizer affiliated with the Muslim Brotherhood, whose full name was Zaynab al-Ghazzali al-Jabili. Born in Cairo, her father encouraged her to pursue higher Islamic studies, so she enrolled at the Law College of **al-Azhar** University. She became a regular lecturer to female crowds at Ibn Tulun's Mosque in Cairo. Her interest in feminist activism began when she joined **Huda Shaarawi's Egyptian Feminist Union**, only to leave this secularist organization in 1936. Ghazzali was credited with founding the Muslim Women's Association (Arabic: Jamaat al-sayyidat al-Muslimat) in 1936, which she declined to merge with the Muslim Brotherhood as an auxiliary upon the request of the founder, Hassan al-Banna. Under her leadership, the association became a lifeline for poor women, offering them financial assistance, religious classes, a women's magazine, and medical services.

When the Brotherhood was banned in 1945, she pledged allegiance to al-Banna, the supreme guide, and began to help the women whose male relatives suffered persecution and imprisonment by the authorities. She was effective in maintaining links to the imprisoned Brothers during Jamal Abd al-Nasser's anti-Islamic purges. Her own women's association was eventually banned in 1964 due to its underground activities. In that same year, she was imprisoned by the Nasserite regime, suffering torture as one of the main leaders of the Islamist movement. Ghazzali narrated her prison experiences after her release by the government of Anwar Sadat in a sensational book, *Days of My Life* (Arabic: *Ayyam min hayati*) (Cairo, Beirut, 1977). She married twice, divorcing her first husband because he interfered with her Islamic activities, and threatening her second husband with the same if he proved to be an obstacle to her activism. Since she was childless, she claimed that forsaking family duties in the service of Islam was perfectly justifiable. As she continued her lecturing and writing activities in the 1970s and 1980s, she came under criticism by secular feminists for leading a life that was quite dissimilar to that of the Muslim feminine ideal she held up to her followers. Although she never held any formal office, she was regarded as the true leader and representative of Islamic feminism in Egypt until her death. *See also* FEMINIST MOVEMENT IN EGYPT; SAADAWI, NAWAL (1931–); SADAT, JIHAN (1933–).

GHOSSOUB, MAI (?–). A Lebanese activist, publisher, and playwright who was born in Beirut. She moved to London in 1979, where she became the copublisher of al-Saqi, an elite publishing firm for Arab writers of fiction, memoirs, and sociological studies. Her work focuses on the impact of immigration on cultural identity. She also writes on the issue of transsexuality. She wrote several books, including *Leaving Beirut, Women and the Wars Within, Postmodernism, The Arab in a Video Chip, Male Identity*, and *Culture in the Middle East*. She also wrote several plays, mostly in English.

GHUNAIM, MAHA AL- (1960–). She is a Kuwaiti businesswoman and entrepreneur. She cofounded Global Investment House (GIH) in 1998 with another woman, Khamla Roomi, building on her long experience with state-owned investment firms. She served as the chairperson and managing director of GIH, after many years delegating this role to a male manager capable of participating in the deliberations of Kuwait's exclusively male salons, known as *diwaniya*. GIH had expanded to 16 countries and grew to a £514 billion portfolio under her management. Al-Roomi serves as senior vice president of the company. GIH was the first Kuwaiti firm to be traded on the London Stock Exchange. Al-Ghunaim, who has powerful family connections in the Kuwaiti business community, is considered one of the most successful female entrepreneurs in the Arab Gulf region.

GÖKALP, ZIYA (1876–1924). Turkish sociologist, nationalist leader, and modernist who was born in the predominantly Kurdish province of Diyarbekir. His original name was Mehmed Zia, but he adopted the name Gökalp, or "sky hero," as his pen name. This earned him erroneous identification as a Kurd. His father, Tevfik, was a prominent historian and head of the local archives, as well as the editor of the official gazette of the province. Ziya received a modern education but without forsaking his Islamic roots. During the twilight years of the Ottoman Empire, he was enrolled in Diyarbekir's military schools, later joining Istanbul's veterinary college, where the emphasis was on modern science. When his membership in the Committee for Union and Progress (CUP) was discovered, he was imprisoned and later exiled to Diyarbekir before completing his education. In his hometown he continued to pursue his own readings in the natural sciences and Sufi thought. He rose through the ranks of provincial government to become the assistant secretary-general of the Provincial Council of Diyarbekir in 1904. After the CUP seized power in 1908, he became the inspector of its affiliated offices in the region.

By 1910, he was a member of the CUP's Central Committee, which led to his appointment as a sociology professor at the party's college in Salonika. The CUP's eventual control of Constantinople under the name of the Young Turks led to his election to the second Grand National Assembly in 1923, representing Diyarbekir, where he participated in the writing of the constitution. By that time, he was a well-known theoretician of the CUP, having served as the first professor of sociology at Darulfunun, or college of social studies, in Istanbul. Gökalp's impact on his revolutionary colleagues was keenly felt when he taught a group of fellow political exiles while he was in Malta in 1919. He emerged after World War I as the major political theoretician of **Mustafa Kemal Ataturk**'s modernization program and was influential in developing the philosophy of Kemalism, or the leader's thoughts and subsequent reforms. He is considered the foremost philosopher of modern

Turkish nationalism as the country moved from its multi-ethnic imperial stage to being a secular, ethnically unified nation. His contribution was to reconcile the conflicting strands of emerging Turkish cultural nationalism based on language, or pan-Turanianism, and the ethical legacy of Islam. He was greatly influenced by Auguste Comte (1798–1857) and Emile Durkheim (1858–1917), advocating the separation of church and state, the importance of rationalization and science, as well as the necessity of advancing the status of women. Gökalp was credited with articulating the Young Turks' ideology, asserting that religion should be banished from society. This encouraged the general Kemalist trend of completely transforming the role and status of Muslim Turkish women.

GÖKÇEN, SABIHA (1913–2001). She was one of **Mustafa Kemal Ataturk**'s adopted daughters and the first female combat pilot in the world. She was born in Bursa to Mustafa Izzet and Hayriye, the latter being from a Bosnian background. Ataturk saw her on his visit to Bursa in 1925 when, as a 12-year-old, she told him of her desire to study at a boarding school. Ataturk adopted her, bestowing on her the surname Gökçen in 1934, meaning "belonging to the sky," and six months later she decided to study to be a pilot. She attended Cankaya primary school of the Turkish Aeronautical Association (TAA). She was later sent with several male pilots to the Crimean Peninsula, Russia, where she attained more training in glider and powered aircraft piloting. She became a military pilot in 1936 upon the completion of her studies at Eskipehir Military Aviation School. She became a flight instructor at TAA, where she taught until 1955, after which she joined its executive board. Gökçen flew bomber and fighter planes with the First Aircraft Regiment and participated in 1937 in military exercises over the Aegean Sea and Thrace. She played an important role in military operations to suppress the Dersim Rebellion, a Kurdish–Alavi uprising in southeastern Turkey. In 1938, she completed a five-day flight over the Balkan countries, and she continued to fly all over the world until 1964. The TAA published her book, *A Life along the Path of Ataturk*, in 1981 as part of the celebrations commemorating the centenary of the birth of the Turkish leader. She was the only woman who was admitted to the Turkish military before 1955. She died at age 88 in Ankara. Istanbul's second international airport, which was built on the Asian side of the city, was named after her. *See also* WOMEN IN THE TURKISH MILITARY.

GORJI, MUNIREH (?–). An Iranian schoolteacher who was the only woman elected in 1979 to the otherwise all-male, 73-member legislative body known as the Assembly of Experts. This was founded a few months after the establishment of the Islamic Republic of Iran, ostensibly to draft the country's first postrevolutionary constitution. She won support due to her membership in Khomeini's Islamic Republican Party. She appeared in the Majlis wrapped in her black **chador**, showing no sign of resistance to the new Islamic dress code for women. She was severely criticized by certain female sectors of Iranian society for failing to protect gains achieved under the family protection laws of the monarchic period and for her willingness to accept the imposition of the chador. She responded by stating that by wearing this cloak, she was restoring honor to her Iranian sisters, who had acquiesced in **Reza Shah Pahlavi**'s banning of the **veil** some 50 years before. She also declined to take up the secular feminist agenda in the Majlis, stating that she was ashamed to speak about women's rights since the assembly's male members had never spoken in defense of men's rights. She stressed that there were no separate and conflicting women's and men's rights in Islam, but only human rights. She often declared that the **Sharia** was her guide and defended many of its stipulations willingly. Even though opposed to **polygamy**, she blamed it on the readiness with which some women entered unions with married men with children. At the same time, she demanded elaboration of women's Islamic rights and the creation of a special court devoted to women's grievances and family issues. She expressed publicly the belief that women in general lacked the mental capacity to assume the position of prime minister or president. *See also* FEMINIST MOVEMENT IN IRAN.

GOZANSKI, TAMAR (1940–). She is a leading member of the Knesset and of the Israeli Communist Party who was born in the town of Petah Tikva. She earned a master's degree in economics from Leningrad University. She represented Rakah (the communist party previously known as Maki) in the Knesset in the 1980s and 1990s, where she sat on several committees such as labor, welfare, early childhood, women's, and foreign workers'. A member of the political bureau of the Communist Party, she was also the deputy chairperson of the Democratic Front for Peace and Equality (Hadash), which defended the rights of Israel's Arab minority. Her articles appear frequently in major Israeli dailies such as *Haaretz*, *Yedoit Aharanot*, and *Zu-Haderekh*, where she frequently calls for ending the Israeli occupation of Palestinian lands. She published two works: *Economic Independence: How?* (1969) and *The Development of Capitalism in Palestine* (1988). *See also* FEMINIST MOVEMENT IN ISRAEL.

GROSSMAN, HAIKA (1919–1993). She was a leading member of the Knesset and a heroine of the Jewish resistance in Poland during World War II. She was born in Bialstok, Poland, where she became a member of the central committee of the Zionist youth movement, ha-Shomer ha-Tzair. She arrived in Palestine in 1948, where she became involved in refugee assistance projects. She served in the Knesset for four terms representing the Labor Party and, later, Mapam, where she championed several social issues. She was a vocal critic of Israeli policies in the West Bank and Gaza and was a strong advocate of improving Jewish relations with Israel's Arab population. One of her enduring projects along these lines was a dialogue and educational center targeting Arab and Jewish youths, which she founded in the 1980s under the name Givat Haviva. She was also involved in international efforts to prosecute crimes committed during the Vietnam War. Her life in Poland's Jewish resistance was described fully in her book *The Underground Army: Fighters of the Bialstok Ghetto*, published in 1987 by the New York Holocaust Library. *See also* FEMINIST MOVEMENT IN ISRAEL.

H

HABASH, ASIA (1936–). A Palestinian educator and political activist who was born in Jerusalem and received a master's degree in educational psychology in 1954 from the American University of Beirut. She was a lecturer in psychology at the all-male Teacher Training Center. In 1975, she became the director of the Women's Training Center. Both centers were run by the United Nations Relief and Works Agency (UNRWA) at Ramallah. She was a cofounder of the Arab Studies Society, a research center focusing on Palestine and directed by Faysal Husseini (1940–2001). She was also a cofounder of the Arab Thought Forum in Jerusalem and the Early Childhood Resource center.

HABIBI, SHAHLA (?–). She was the first presidential adviser on women in the Islamic Republic of Iran. She cofounded the Iranian Council on Women's Affairs with **Marziyeh Seddiqi** in 1992. Habibi was appointed by president Ali Akbar Hashemi Rafsanjani (r. 1989–1997) as the director of this bureau and became his own adviser on women's affairs. Habibi tried to create a system by which cabinet ministers cooperated on women's issues. *See also* FEMINIST MOVEMENT IN IRAN.

HADASSAH. This is a Jewish public advocacy and social service group for women, founded in 1912 in New York. Its full name is Hadassah: The Women's Zionist Organization of America. It boasts a membership of 300,000 women. This claim makes Hadassah the largest Zionist organization in the United States. The name "Hadassah" is the Hebrew rendition of the name **Esther**, the Persian Jewish heroine of the biblical *Book of Esther*. The founder of Hadassah was Jewish American scholar and activist **Henrietta Szold**, who visited Palestine for the first time with her mother after joining Daughters of Zion, a study group based in New York. Szold witnessed much poverty among Palestine's early Jewish immigrants and asked her study group to undertake some relief projects in that country. Almost 30 women then regrouped as Daughters of Zion: Hadassah Chapter and chose Szold as its first president. Their first program of assistance targeted the health needs of women and children in a kibbutz in Palestine, and they later sent two nurses who opened up a health clinic in 1913 in Jerusalem. The work of Hadassah expanded following World War I, when a nurses' training college was opened in Jerusalem, along with a hygiene department serving school-children. Szold settled in Palestine in 1920 and devoted herself to improving the health conditions of women and children by eradicating some of the area's infectious diseases.

Hadassah was also influenced by Szold's commitment to Arab–Jewish peaceful coexistence and was interested in enlarging its humanitarian reach to cover both communities. The organization supported extending the right to vote to Jewish women, but its greatest achievement was in the field of health. By 1939, the organization succeeded in founding Palestine's first teaching and research medical facility in Jerusalem, namely the Rothschild-Hadassah University Hospital. Today, Hadassah operates medical centers in five countries but is still headquartered in New York City. A large office is maintained at Washington, D.C., and is devoted to lobbying efforts. Hadassah was nominated for a Nobel Peace Prize in 2005.

HADDAD, TAHIR (1899–1935). A Tunisian poet, author, labor activist, and defender of women's rights who was born in Tunis to a family of modest means. He was a modernist and an advocate of female emancipation before anyone in Tunisia supported this cause. He attended Tunisia's famed Islamic seminary, al-Zaytouna, between 1911 and 1920. He became involved with a Tunisian workers' organization in 1924 and wrote a book on trade unionism. Haddad's most famous book, however, was *Our Women in the Sharia and in Society*, which appeared in 1930. In it he argued that reforming the status of women and the family should take precedence over any other reforms. Haddad was an enemy of the custom of **veiling**, which he viewed as leading to seduction and symptomatic of society's mistrust of women. He based his reformist ideas on the Quran, which he considered to be open to modernizing ideas and reinterpretation. He wrote that Islam called for the education of men and women. By the time he died, his ideas had a powerful impact on all of North Africa. *See also* AMIN, QASSEM (1863–1908); PERSONAL STATUS CODE OF TUNISIA; SHARIA.

HADID, ZAHA (1950–). An Iraqi architect who was born in Baghdad, where her father was the minister of finance. She received a BA in mathematics from the American University of Beirut (AUB) and a degree in architecture from the prestigious Architectural Association School of Architecture in London. In 1977, she became a partner at the Office for Metropolitan Architecture, founded by her former teachers, Rem Koolhaas and Elia Zenghelis. She founded her own company, Zaha Hadid Architects, in 1980 while teaching at the Architectural Association, employing 300 people. She taught at prestigious schools all over the world, such as the Graduate School of Design at Harvard University, the University of Illinois–Chicago, the Hochschule für Bildende Kunste in Hamburg, Ohio State University, Columbia and Yale Universities, and the University of Applied Arts, Vienna. She was also an honorary fellow at the American Institute of Architects.

Hadid won several international competitions for design. Among her famous creations that were executed as major structures around the world are Singapore's one-north master plan and the casino at Basel, Switzerland. She is in the process of planning major building projects in Marseilles, Baku, Cairo, Singapore, and Istanbul. She will be designing the Central Bank building in Baghdad, the city of her ancestors, which she left in 1980. She was the first female to be awarded the Pritzker Architecture Prize, in 2004. She received two recognitions in 2006: one was an exhibit of her past work at the Guggenheim Museum in New York, and the other was an honorary degree from her alma mater, the AUB. *Forbes* magazine ranked her number 69 on its list of the world's most powerful women. In 2010, she was awarded the Stirling Prize for her Rome design, the Maxxi.

HAFIZ, THURAYA AL- (?–). In 1953, she was the first woman to run for a seat in the Syrian parliament. Although she lost her bid for election, other women followed in her footsteps, including Qamar Shora, president of the Syrian Red Crescent Society, who ran unsuccessfully for parliament in 1961. Al-Hafiz was a schoolteacher who campaigned for years against wearing the **veil**. She launched her own literary and political salon in Damascus, which was open to both genders. The salon was convened in her own house and was named after **Sukayna** bint al-Hussein, the great granddaughter of Prophet Muhammad, who presided over the first literary salon in Muslim history. *See also* ATTAR, NAJAH (1933–); SHAABAN, BOUTHAINA (1953–); ZAIM, HUSNI (1894–1949).

HAGAR. Biblical figure mentioned in the book of Genesis and in Arab legends. According to the biblical account (16:1–16), she was a handmaiden of Sarah (Serai), who was originally given to Abraham (Abram) as a concubine. When she became pregnant, she began to overstep her defined role and raise herself as an equal to the barren Sarah. When she was mistreated by her mistress, she fled into the desert, where an angel appeared to her, urging her to return to her home. The angel predicted that her child would be named Ishmael. In the second Genesis cycle (21:8–21), a rivalry developed between her and Sarah, especially after the older woman gave birth to a son, Isaac, who was seen playing with Ishmael. Abraham then exiled Hagar and Ishmael to the desert upon Sarah's urging. Hagar ended up wandering between the hills of Safa and Marwa, near Mecca, searching for water, and was saved after discovering the spring of Zamzam. These two sites later became sacred stations requiring Muslim pilgrims to wander between them as an enactment of Hagar's desperate search for water and God's intervention, which saved her and her child from dying of thirst.

The story of Hagar commands a central place in Arab legends and ancient genealogies. Muslim tradition regards Ishmael as the ancestor of the northern Arab tribes by virtue of his descent from Abraham, who is considered to be the founder of all the monotheistic faiths. It is said that Abraham visited Ishmael in Mecca and joined efforts in building the Kaaba on the site where a temple built by Adam once stood. The Kaaba became a major pagan temple, visited by all the Arabian tribes before Muhammad's return to Mecca and the destruction of all of its idols and pagan sites. Muhammad preserved the Kaaba as the foremost shrine marking the birthplace of the Arabs. Another Arab tradition claims that both Hagar and her son were buried next to the Kaaba in a place known as Ishmael's enclosure (Arabic: *hijr Ishmael*).

HAKIM, TAWFIQ AL- (1898–1987). A renowned Egyptian playwright, social critic, and iconoclast who was born in Alexandria to an Egyptian father who was a judge and a Turkish mother. After studying at Cairo, he proceeded to study law in France, but was distracted by his interest in the theater. He pioneered modern Egyptian drama, his most famous and widely read work being *People of the Cave* (Arabic: *Ahl al-kahf*), which he authored in 1933. He tackled many issues in his plays, but mainly two themes that concerned Egyptians most: British occupation and the liberation of women. The first theme was treated in *The Unwelcome Guest* (Arabic: *Al-Dhayf al-thakeel*), the second in *The New Woman* (Arabic: *Al-Maraa al-jadedeh*). A comical play, *The Honorable Female Deputy* (Arabic: *Al-Naibah al-muhtar-mah*), treated the **feminist** movement lightly. Other plays focused on feminist social issues, such as *Those of Blessed Marriages*, which dealt with problems confronting married couples, and *I Need This Solution*, concerning women's liberation. He also wrote a play titled **Shehrazad** (1934), about the iconic figure of Arabic literature by the same name. He was called *the enemy of women* (Arabic: *adow al-maraah*) throughout his literary career. *See also* FEMINIST MOVEMENT IN EGYPT.

HAMADEH, LEYLA SULH (1946–). A Lebanese politician and business leader who was born in Beirut. She was one of five daughters of Lebanon's first postindependence prime minister, Riyadh al-Sulh (r. 1943–1945, 1946–1951), and Faiza al-Jabri. Hamadeh majored in Oriental studies at Saint Joseph's University in Beirut and became the first female minister in Lebanon in 2004, when she was named minister of industry in the cabinet of

Prime Minister Omar Karami. She is the widow of a former minister, Majed Hamadeh. She was appointed vice president of al-Walid ibn Talal Humanitarian Foundation, created by her sister's son, Mona al-Sulh.

HAMAS. This is the Palestinian national liberation movement that adheres to Islamic principles. Hamas has established a separate Palestinian entity in Gaza following its victory in the elections of 2006 against the secular Fateh-dominated Palestine National Authority (PNA). Hamas became a participant in national politics for the first time during the first *intifada* of 1987, after operating in Gaza since the 1970s. Articles 17 and 18 of its charter when it was still a national movement emphasized the importance of providing young women with Islamic education to guide future generations and raise them as patriotic and Islamic citizens. Women's role in the battle for liberation is said to be as important as that of men, and women are called upon to resist Western cultural influences perpetrated through the media, the movies, and school curricula. Women must carry their share of the burden in families that suffer the loss of male members in the national struggle by raising their children in accordance with Islamic morals and values. Women must also be extra frugal in the disbursement of financial resources in order to maintain their flow to several generations of the family.

Hamas never imposed an Islamic government on Gaza, because its legitimacy derives from its electoral victory based on Palestinian civil law. This resulted in the absence of Iranian-style laws imposing a strict Islamic dress code on women and restricting them to certain professions. While most women and girls wear a head-scarf in public, some have publicly defied the custom of wearing long dark cloaks in favor of blue jeans. The Ministry of Education at one point sided with girls protesting efforts of school principals to enforce the wearing of long black cloaks. When a Supreme Court justice ordered female lawyers in 2011 to adhere to the scarf-cloak dress code rather than appear in his court dressed in pants, the women took their complaint to al-Arabiya television station. The order was rescinded by the minister of justice. A journalist named Asmaa al-Ghoul at one time defended her right to take a swim while clad in pants.

There are also Islamic female leaders who defend women from within the system, like Lama Hourani, who campaigns on behalf of female workers and protests against a pervasive conservative culture that threatens women's rights. During the 2006 elections for the Palestinian Legislative Council, six women were elected on Hamas's list. There are also two prominent women in the Hamas government, one of whom was listed as number three on the official party list and was easily elected. This was Mariam Farhat, known locally as "mother of martyrs" because she lost three boys in Gaza's ongoing military conflict with Israel. The other woman is Jamila al-Shanti, head of the Women's Ministry, which was opened in 2011. Her true relationship to

Hamas's leadership is uncertain, although some claim that she is the widow of Abd al-Aziz Rantisi, a prominent Hamas leader who was assassinated by the Israelis.

HAMDANI, RASHEEDA ALI HAMOOD AL- (?–). A Yemeni feminist and government official who serves as the director of the women's sector at the Prime Minister's Office and is the chairperson of the Women's National Committee (WNC). She is a psychologist by training who worked in the past at the Republican Hospital at Aden and at the Center Bank of Women. The WNC is a consultative body created by the government that prepares reports and maps out strategies for development concerning women. The committee maintains female liaisons at various government ministries and lobbies the government to introduce laws favorable to women.

HANBAL, IMAM AHMAD IBN (780–855). A Muslim theologian, jurist, and founder of a traditional and conservative school of jurisprudence who was born in Baghdad. He earned the reputation of a devout Islamic scholar early in life and spent his time teaching his students and studying the holy books of Islam. He became the most famous member of a group of scholars known as *ahl al-hadith* (followers of the Prophet's sayings), or the traditionalists who believe that abiding by the Prophet's *sunna* or the practices of Muhammad and the early Muslim community was only superseded in importance by the Quran. The traditionalists were opposed by the rationalists, represented by the Muatazilates, who practiced speculative thought about the contents of the Quran. The two schools quarreled about many things, but mainly about the divine nature of God. Caliph al-Maamoun (r. 813–833), who was a supporter of the Muatazilates, demanded that all high religious authorities publicly espouse this school's concept of the Quran as a created document. When Ibn Hanbal refused, he suffered a two-year period of imprisonment and torture. But he returned to teaching the doctrine of *ahl al-hadith* in 847 when a new caliph ascended the throne. Ibn Hanbal was buried in Baghdad, and his tomb continued to attract a stream of devout followers until it was washed away by floods in the 14th century.

The legal school of Hanbali interpretation evolved into the most conservative Islamic legal school of jurisprudence among the four schools of the **Sharia**. The Hanbali School eventually was taken up by the Wahhabi Muslim sect of the 19th century, which inspired all of Saudi Arabia's rigid rules of gender segregation and the exclusion of women from the public space.

HANOUNE, LOUISA (1954–). An Algerian human rights and workers' rights advocate who was the first female in her poor peasant family to receive a formal education. She completed a law degree at the University of Annaba in 1979. She joined the underground Socialist Workers Organization (Organisation Socialiste des Travailleurs, OST) and served a one-year jail sentence in 1983. Hanoune then became active on behalf of women's rights, serving as the first secretary-general of the Association for Equality before the Law of Men and Women. She also founded the Algerian Human Rights League. When the Algerian government canceled the results of local elections in 1991, the country was plunged in civil war between the Islamic movement and government forces. Hanoune was a signatory to the 1995 Rome Platform, which called for negotiations with the Islamic opposition to bring this war to an end. In 1997, she was elected to the Algerian parliament as one of four deputies representing the old OST, now renamed the Parti des Travailleurs (PT). Due to her efforts on behalf of pro-democracy forces, her party increased its parliamentary lead to 21 seats. She waged a strong campaign against the government of Abd al-Aziz Boutefliqa (r. 1999–) as the first woman to head a major political party in the country. In 1996, she published her major work, *Une autre voix pour l'Algérie* (*Another Voice for Algeria*).

HARB, TALAAT (1867–1941). He was the father of Egyptian economic independence and an opponent of women's rights who was born in Cairo. He founded Bank Misr (Bank of Egypt) in 1920. He developed a great dislike for **Qassem Amin**'s attacks on the **veil**, contending that the emancipation of women would lead to widespread immortality and would weaken the nation. He accused modernists and reformers of initiating Western customs that harmed the image of Egyptian women abroad. Harb also blamed these ideas on foreigners, an allusion to Amin's Turkish background. Part of Harb's disapproval of reformist ideas was his fear of women's competition with men in the workplace. One of Cairo's central public squares is named after him. *See also* FEMINIST MOVEMENT IN EGYPT; SHAARAWI, HUDA (1879–1947).

HAREB, SALMA (?–). She was a citizen of the United Arab Emirates (UAE) who became the first woman in the Middle East and North Africa to assume the position of head of an economic zone. Her full name is Salma Ali Saif Bin Hareb, and she became the chief executive of Jebel Ali Free Zone (Jafza) and of Economic Zones World in Dubai, one of the emirates. The free zone is an area where minimal tax, and sometimes no tax, is applied to stimulate development. Hareb graduated from al-Ain University in the UAE and enrolled as a postgraduate student majoring in medical laboratory sciences at the University of Cardiff, Wales. She became a board member of World Venture Forsa in Dubai, which provides investment opportunities for women. *See also* EDUCATION: ARAB GULF STATES.

HAREM. This is the practice of secluding women in a certain section of a royal or upper-class residence. The word "harem" (Arabic: *harim*) derives from the Arabic term *"haram,"* which connotes a sacred space unavailable to the general public. The harem was, thus, a place and an institution. The cultural antecedents of this practice extended to most of the ancient cultures of the Middle East, such as Mesopotamian, Greek, and Persian societies. Before this practice became closely identified with Islam, it was followed by members of Judaic and Christian persuasion. Pre-Islamic and early Islamic societies did not enforce this system, the first to adopt it being the Abbasid Empire (750–1258). Historians explain this by reference to several customs borrowed from neighboring Persia, the seclusion of royal women being just one among them. Orientalist scholars, however, described the institution of the harem as symptomatic of Islam's mistreatment of women. The most studied and thoroughly examined institution by Western scholars was the Ottoman Turkish harem, although similar practices paralleled it until after World War I.

The source from which women of royal harems originated changed over time. In the classical period, royal palaces acquired women as prisoners of war, and to a lesser degree, from slave markets, which were often based on war booty. An elaborate palace system of training and initiation assured a process of upward mobility and meticulous selection based on physical attributes and talent. During the Ottoman period, new arrivals, especially young girls, were moved from the rank of *cariye* (Turkish; female slave), to *sagira* (Turkish; student), to *gedikli* (Turkish; licensed), to *usta* (Turkish; master). *Usta* was the highest rank, the holder of which stood to be chosen by the *valide sultan* (Turkish; sultan's mother) as a consort of the reigning sultan. Under the Ottoman system, the harem was also the only pool from which royal wives were chosen. Other descriptions of the institution of the harem indicated that it was a pyramidal system divided into two classes of women: at the bottom, the large and undifferentiated strata known as *sagrideler* (Turkish; novices), and at the top, the strata of the most beautiful and talented women known collectively as *dikliler* (Turkish; privileged ones). The one who was finally chosen by the sultan to be his consort was often referred to as *gozde* (Turkish; favored). If the sultan became attached to one consort more than others, she was referred to as *ikbal* (Turkish; fortunate). The harem was managed by eunuchs attached to the royal palace and was headed by the *valide sultan*. Since most of the harem women were acquired at a young age, they spent their entire lives within the harem walls. When the Young Turk revolution removed Sultan Abd al-Hamid from power in 1909, confusion reigned, and the future of these women became uncertain. Eventually, the Turkish government issued a public call to Circassian villages in

Chechniya, the location of favored slave markets, to come to Istanbul to retrieve their female relatives. The royal harem of Ottoman sultans was finally dispersed.

HAREVEN, SHULAMIT (1931–). An Israeli novelist, poet, journalist, and peace activist who was born in Warsaw and moved to Palestine, where she and her family settled in Jerusalem in 1940. She took part in military operations around Jerusalem during the 1948 Arab–Israeli War, serving with the Haganah underground as a medic when Jordanian forces held the Old City of Jerusalem under siege. Hareven took part in the founding of the radio of the Israel Defense Forces (IDF) as soon as the Israeli state was established. During the 1950s, she helped with relief work when Israel was flooded with Jewish arrivals from Arab countries. She became a military correspondent, reporting from the front, until after the 1973 October War with Egypt. Her penchant for difficult assignments led her to file reports from Arab refugee camps in the West Bank and Gaza, which were the hotbed of Arab resistance during the first *intifada* (1987). She also became a member of the Israeli group known as Peace Now.

Hareven was the first female to be admitted to the Academy of the Hebrew Language. Her literary output amounted to 17 books of poetry and works of fiction. These included her first novel, *City of Many Days* (1972), which describes the life of Jerusalem's multi-ethnic communities during the British Mandate. Other works translated into English are *Thirst: The Desert Trilogy* (1996) and *The Vocabulary of Peace: Life, Culture, and Politics in the Middle East* (1995). Her autobiography, *Yamim Rabim* (*Many Days*), appeared in Hebrew in 2002.

HASHEM, MARYAM (1889–1948). A Palestinian patriot, philanthropist, and feminist who was born in Nablus to Abd al-Ghani Hashem, a descendant of Jaafar ibn Abi-Taleb, Muhammad's first cousin. Her family produced a large number of Islamic religious scholars who were well-known throughout Palestine and other parts of the Muslim world. Hashem played a significant and pioneering role in the rise of the modern **feminist** movement in Nablus and throughout Palestine. She was credited with the founding of the Arab Feminist Union of Palestine in 1922, which affiliated later with **Huda Shaarawi**'s pan-Arab organization by the same name. Hashem was an unmarried schoolteacher who mobilized Palestinian women to undertake charitable projects and to provide financial support to families of Palestinian fighters killed during the Arab Revolt of 1936. She enjoyed a high degree of respect among the Palestinian business community throughout her life, which led to the success of her "piaster project" (British currency = one penny) in support of her patriotic activities. She attended the Arab Feminist Union's 1944 conference at Cairo in support of Palestinian rights and the founding meeting of the League of Arab States in Alexandria in 1945.

HASHEM, SABRIYA (1899–1955). A notable Jordanian feminist and philanthropist who was born in Nablus, Palestine. She was the daughter of the Mufti of Palestine, Sheikh Munib Hashem. In 1912, she married Ibrahim Hashem, a future Jordanian prime minister, who is credited with the drafting of the country's first constitution and with negotiating with Great Britain over the treaty that granted Transjordan (Jordan's earlier name) independence in 1946. Sabriya Hashem was the founder of Jordan's Red Crescent Society in 1947 and became its long-serving director. Her daughter, Luli Hashem, served as the organization's secretary, and Queen Zein, mother of future King Hussein of Jordan, was the head of its board of directors. The first major crisis that faced the fledgling organization was the arrival of thousands of Palestinian refugees fleeing the turmoil of the 1948 Arab–Israeli War. These refugees were housed in temporary lodging in mosques, churches, and schools, while the Red Crescent Society labored to find food and clothing and provide schooling for young children. She also hosted a high-level Egyptian women's delegation in the 1940s, headed by **Huda Shaarawi**, in anticipation of the founding of the **Arab Feminist Union**.

HASHEMI, FAEZEH (1962–). She is the youngest daughter of former Iranian President Ali Akbar Hashemi Rafsanjani (r. 1989–1997). She served as a member of parliament but also became a sports advocate and journalist. She holds a BA in political science and in the physical sciences. She was a member of the Islamic Republic's High Council for Women's Sports as well as vice president of Iran's National Olympic Committee. She is best known for founding the **Islamic Countries' Women's Sports Solidarity Committee**, of which she is the president. A popular figure with young women due to her support for outdoor cycling, she was elected to the Majlis in 1996 with a wide margin of support. She was also actively involved in Mohammad Khatami's presidential bid in 1997. She began to publish a reform-oriented journal in 1998, called *Zan* in Persian (*Woman*), which was eventually closed by Iran's Revolutionary Court. *Zan*'s offense was the publication of a message on the Iranian New Year (*neiruz*) from former empress **Farah Pahlavi**. The paper also earned the traditionalists' wrath for publishing a cartoon mocking the custom of demanding half as much blood money for a female victim as for a male victim. Hashemi was always an outspoken member of the Majlis, calling for the employment of women and granting them more rights. *See also* FEMINIST MOVEMENT IN IRAN.

HASS, AMIRA (1956–). An Israeli journalist who is known for her independent reporting on the situation in the West Bank and Gaza. Born in Jerusalem to parents who were Holocaust survivors, she studied history at Hebrew and Tel Aviv Universities. She was distressed by the events of the first Palestinian *intifada* in 1987 and began working for the Israeli paper *Haaretz* as a staff editor in 1989. Her stories focused on the Palestinian territories beginning in 1991, producing a daily report on Gaza, where she took up residence for four years. It was there that she wrote her famous work, *Drinking the Sea at Gaza: Days and Nights in a Land under Siege* (translated in 1999). The book was critical of Israel's closure regime, in place since 1991, and of Israeli occupation policies in general. By 1997, she was living in Ramallah, the main city in the West Bank and the seat of the Palestinian Authority. Her second book, *Reporting from Ramallah: An Israeli Journalist in an Occupied Land* (2003), focused on the second *intifada* (2000) and was critical of Israel's repressive measures against the Palestinian civilian population and the violence unleashed by Yasser Arafat's militias in Nablus. The book won many awards, including the UNESCO/Guillermo Cano World Press Freedom Prize in 2003. Hass has won numerous awards for her work, such as Press Freedom Hero from the International Press Institute in 2002, Bruno Kreisky Human Rights Award in 2002, Hrant Dink Memorial Award in 2009, and Golden Dove of Peace Prize from Archivo Disarmo in Rome. Hass was arrested by Israel at the end of her four-year residency in Gaza for living in an enemy state, and again in December 2008 for traveling to Gaza with a peace flotilla to publicize the Israeli siege of that city. *See also* FEMINIST MOVEMENT IN ISRAEL.

HATSHEPSUT (1508–1458 BCE). She was the fifth pharaoh of the 18th Dynasty. She was the daughter of Thutmose I and married to her half-brother, Thutmose II. After her husband's death, she became a regent to the boy king Thutmose III. At first, she used the title of God's wife, but later she took up the title of King. Her legitimacy as a reigning king was based on fabricated textual proof of having been chosen by her father as his successor. She also strengthened this claim by recording her own divine birth on the walls of the mortuary funeral palace at the city of Thebes, where the sun king Amun Ra was depicted visiting her mother on the day Hatshepsut was born. There were a few queens before her, but her reign stood out as a period of political stability and prosperity. She reigned for a total of 22 years, during which she reestablished major trade routes that had been disrupted by the Hyksos conquest of Egypt. She sent military and trade expeditions to the land of Punt (either northern Somalia or in Arabia), Syria, and Nubia. Her reign was enriched by major building projects that raised Egyptian architecture to its highest level of perfection. Hatshepsut appeared on royal monuments in male garb, although this may not have been her manner of dress in real life. Historians are not sure whether her death was caused by a popular uprising or happened naturally. *See also* ANCIENT EGYPT, WOMEN IN.

HERZOG, SHIRA (1957–). An Israeli journalist who became a Middle East news analyst in Canada. Her father Yaacov Herzog was a rabbi who was born in Dublin, later serving as an Israeli diplomat. Her uncle, Chaim Herzog, became president of Israel (r. 1983–1993) after serving for many years as head of military intelligence. She completed a BA in history and English literature at Hebrew University, and an MA, also in English literature, at York University in Canada. After immigrating to Canada she was appointed in 1976 as the national director of the Canada Israel Committee, which works for the promotion of democratic ideals in Israel. As the vice president of Kahanoff Foundation, based in Calgary, she works for the development of community programs in Western Canada and Israel. Since 1994, she has been a feature writer for *Canadian Jewish News* and since 2002, Middle East analyst for the *Globe and Mail*. She also hosted a Canadian television program on Israel and has been named to the board of Tel Aviv's Israel Democracy Institute.

HIGH COUNCIL OF IRANIAN WOMEN'S ASSOCIATIONS. An umbrella organization of 17 women's groups, founded in 1959 by Muhammad Reza Shah (r. 1941–1979). The Shah's sister and the leading feminist in Iran, Princess **Ashraf Pahlavi**, became its honorary president. The council was renamed the Women's Organization of Iran (WOI) and became the only legally recognized group representing women in the country. Membership remained confined to professional women such as teachers, government employees, and nurses, and claimed around 70,000 members by the late 1970s. The High Council, however, failed to enlist the support of female intellectuals and members of the opposition. The WOI's affiliates represented groups that were supportive of the Pahlavi regime, such as the Association of Women's Lawyers, Parent–Teacher Association, the Zonta Club, International Women's Club, Society of Jewish Women, and Society of Zoroastrian Women. One of the WOI's main programs was the establishment of an urban network known as Family Welfare Centers. The organization split into two sections, one of which was anti-regime and quickly went underground. By the mid-1970s, civil society organizations such as Islamic cultural centers and other religious associations and clubs had spread all over the country, but particularly in Tehran, and were able to draw on a large pool of disaffected women. The WOI went out of existence upon the establishment of the Islamic regime in Iran. *See also* FEMINIST MOVEMENT IN IRAN; NON-GOVERNMENTAL ORGANIZATIONS (NGOs).

HIJJAWI, SULAFA (1934–). A Palestinian translator, political essayist, and poet who was born in Nablus, West Bank. She spent much of her life in Baghdad, where she married the Iraqi poet Kazim Jawad. She received a BA in English literature and an MA in political studies from the University of Baghdad, where she was a teacher for many years. Between 1974 and 1980, she worked as an editor of the *Review* of the Center for Palestine Studies, which was founded by the University of Baghdad. Her best known work was an English translation of a collection of Palestinian poetry, titled *Poetry of Resistance in Occupied Palestine* (1968). She published her own collection of poems, *Palestinian Songs*, in 1977, and authored many political articles in various publications throughout the Arab world. She lived in Tunis after the Palestine Liberation Organization (PLO) leadership moved there in 1982.

HONOR CRIMES. This is the practice of killing a woman by any one of her close male relatives, such as a husband, father, or brother, as punishment for engaging in unlawful sexual behavior. The practice is not limited to Arab and Islamic countries. Even though the Quran prescribes the punishment for adultery as 100 lashes for man and woman, it also makes proving such a crime very difficult. Punishment is applied to premarital and adulterous situations. Until recently, this crime has not been brought under the purview of the courts, but due to pressure by the new nationalist elites, the concept of sexual honor is being redefined. Increasingly, efforts are being made to limit or eliminate this practice by imposing penalties on the perpetrators of this type of killing. Up until now, most Arab legal codes that excuse this crime by defining it as an "honor crime" are based mostly on two not so dissimilar legal sources: the Ottoman Penal Code of 1858 and the French Penal Code of 1810. The French code added the concept of the female ascendants or descendants; if they are killed when caught in an adulterous situation, the perpetrator of the crime is not punished.

Until recently, many European penal codes contained similar categories of crimes that could be exempted from punishment. Spain, Portugal, and Italy abolished this exemption in 1979, and France in 1975. However, the French-inspired Lebanese legal code of 1943 is considered to be the legal antecedent of several Arab codes, such as the Jordanian Penal Code of 1960. Some Arab penal codes limit the application of the article absolving the murderer in cases of adultery, while the Egyptian, Tunisian, Libyan, and Kuwaiti penal codes allow the reduction of the sentence, not total exemption. The Iraqi Penal Code is distinctive in that it imposes the same sentence of three years on a either husband or wife who commits this crime as punishment for adultery. In the Moroccan case, a penal code amended since 2003 provides the same penalty for both genders in case of a crime committed in the heat of passion (flagrante delicto). In Syria and Lebanon, the penalty is no less than two years in prison for cases involving ascendants and descendants (meaning wife, mother, or sister), even if the perpetrators were the husbands, sons, fathers, or brothers. All are covered by this lenient sentence.

The Special Rapporteur of the United Nations Commission on Human Rights, in his 2002 report on crimes of honor, supplied information on the widespread practice of this act, as well as on its varying circumstances from country to country. He reported that in Brazil, punishment for these crimes has been contradictory, but in Peru, Argentina, Ecuador, Guatemala, Venezuela, Iran, Israel, the Palestine National Authority, and Jordan, legislative provisions could be found in the penal codes allowing for complete or partial exoneration of the murderers. There are some countries, like Turkey, where crimes of honor are not legal under any conditions but still occur in full view of the general public. The penalty for such crimes is a life prison sentence. One such case involved the prosecution of members of an entire Kurdish family by the Turkish courts for killing a young relative who was a victim of rape.

The legal codification of honor crimes in Jordan is often cited as an uncommon example of conflating crimes of honor with crimes of passion. Under Article 340 of the Jordanian Penal Code (1960), excuses for murder are defined as "he" who catches his wife or one of his female relatives in an act of adultery and kills or injures her or her partner. He is covered under this excuse if he kills female ascendants or descendants by Article 98 of the Penal Code, which allows the killer the benefit of a reduced penalty if the crime is committed in a "fit of fury" caused by a dangerous and unlawful act on the part of the victim. Yet Jordanian courts, as well as most Arab courts, have made great efforts to absolve crimes of honor. They have exempted the killing of a woman found not to be a virgin on her wedding night, and of a pregnant woman, from the category of honor crimes. The Jordanian government has tried in recent years to wage a public awareness campaign against crimes of honor through public demonstrations led by members of the royal family. The government also made two attempts to cancel Article 340, but was defeated in this effort by the lower house of parliament in 2003, which was dominated by tribal and Islamist representatives. The efforts of women's organizations, human rights groups, and others to end this legal exemption were motivated by seven crimes of honor committed during that one year.

The cultural explanation for honor crimes is tribal, rather than Islamic. The Jordanian constitution has often been cited as one of the few remaining legal documents in the Arab world in which customary law, or the law of tribal life, is fully enshrined. According to the ideal prototype of Arab gender relations, Arab women are expected to refrain from acts of premarital sex because virginity regulates gender. When a man kills his sister to defend his honor, he is considered to be rendering the highest performance of his gender. It is the male's duty according to this honor/shame social paradigm to engage in acts to ensure the premarital virginity of women in the entire immediate family. When a man declines to intervene in a situation involving a female relative's honor, he will suffer the diminution of his own gender in the eyes of society. In other words, he will no longer be regarded as a normal man.

A succinct critique of this honor/shame social system was provided by Lebanese lawyer **Laure Moghaizel**, who observed that the continued application of this honor code will result in reproducing the Arab tribal mode of thinking, which is detrimental to any semblance of social or intellectual change or development. Her argument also pointed to the violation of the principles of freedom of choice and gender equality embodied in the International Charter of Human Rights (ICHR) and the constitution of Lebanon. Her argument was often extended to most Arab constitutions, which call for gender equality but fall into the trap of upholding contradictory statements or concepts in their tribal or religious codes. In addition, some Islamic writers have observed that the tribal honor code severely contradicts **Sharia** rulings, which require rigorous presentation of evidence, such as testimony of four witnesses, before a judgment on an actual case of female infidelity can be made. Islamic reformers and modernists add that the Quranic sanctity of human life takes precedence over tribal customs that are pre-Islamic in nature. *See also* HUDUD; KHADER, ASMA (1952–).

HOUSE OF OBEDIENCE. This is a much criticized Islamic practice that was mainly limited to Egypt and known as *bayt al-taa* (Arabic). Because a passage in the Quran was interpreted by traditional Muslims as sanctioning men's role as the protectors of women, a custom developed over time of allowing the home confinement of a wife as a form of punishment. This practice was the subject of heated debate among Muslim reformers and traditionalist and Islamist writers during much of the 20th century. The traditionalists maintained that a wife owed her husband obedience if he fulfilled all of his obligations to the family. If a wife left her home without her husband's prior approval or manifested any other signs of disobedience, the husband had the right to discipline her. He could call on the police authorities to bring the wife back to her home and keep her locked up for any period of time. Most Egyptians, men and women, were deeply offended by this custom and repeatedly attempted to repeal it. In 1967, the government of Jamal Abd al-Nasser (r. 1954–1970) issued a ministerial decree that removed the possibility of the legal enforcement of the house of obedience by the authorities. When the minister of justice issued this law, he was severely criticized by members of the legislature, who considered the decree an attack on the **Sharia**. He replied that he did not repeal the law; he simply ended its legal enforcement. The speaker of the assembly then asked for a show of hands by those who favored the enforcement of the practice of the house of obedience, but no one came forward.

The practice came under direct attack again in 1979, when supporters of Law 44, the controversial reform decree pushed by the president's wife, **Jihan Sadat**, and her allies, called for its elimination. The law this time allowed a wife to resist being confined to the house of obedience by offering the court a counterargument justifying her refusal to obey her husband's court order. Under the new law, a woman lost her maintenance if she disobeyed her husband, but could not be imprisoned in her own home. Law 44 also called for mediation when the man and wife reached an impasse in their relationship, authorizing a **divorce**. Law 44, however, was overturned in 1985, when the High Constitutional Court determined that it was not promulgated according to acceptable procedures, violating article 147 of the constitution of 1971. The People's Assembly finally adopted Law 100 in its place, overturning key concessions made to women in the earlier law, but the "house of obedience" became a dead letter in word and deed, and was never restored. *See also* FEMINIST MOVEMENT IN EGYPT.

HOUT, BAYAN NUWAYHID AL- (1937–). A Palestinian historian, journalist, and university professor who is the daughter of renowned historian, orator, and translator Ajaj Nuwayhid (1896–1982). Born in Jerusalem, she studied at Schmidt Girls College and later received a PhD in political science in 1978 from the Lebanese University in Beirut. She worked as a journalist for the Lebanese publishing house, Dar al-Sayyad, from 1960 until 1965. Her appointment as head of the documentary section of the Palestine Research Center in Beirut (1977–1978) provided access to historical archives of the Palestinian national movement. She taught courses on the Palestine question and on the Middle East at the Lebanese University (1979–2001). All of her publications were in Arabic, focusing on major episodes in and figures of modern Palestinian history. Her titles include *Political Leadership and Institutions in Palestine, 1917–1948* and several studies on the life and times of Izz al-Din al-Qassam, Palestine's foremost exponent of guerrilla warfare. She also wrote about the 1982 massacres at the Palestinian refugee campus of Sabra and Shatila in Beirut. She married Shafiq al-Hout, who served for many years as the representative of the Palestine Liberation Organization (PLO) in Lebanon. She has been a member of the Arab National Conference since 1992 and was a founding member of the National Islamic Conference in 1996 and of al-Quds Institutes in 2000. She became a member of the World Arabic Translators' Association in 2004.

HUDUD. This is a system of severe punishments reserved for the most morally reprehensible crimes listed in the **Sharia.** The word *hudud* means "limits," or applying a severe separation between what is considered legal (*halal*) and what is considered forbidden (*haram*). Defined as such, these crimes were subject to fixed punishment. Originally they included the following: theft (punishable by amputating the right hand); illegitimate sexual relations (death by stoning or administering 100 lashes for both parties); apostasy (death or exile); and highway robbery (death). Evidentiary standards for reporting these crimes were set very high, such as providing eyewitness accounts of adultery, severely restricting the application of punishment. These laws are rarely witnessed in most Islamic countries today, with the exception of Saudi Arabia, which applies the Quran as a legal document. In most Muslim states, *hudud*, the penal code and financial code of the Sharia, were eliminated by the French and British colonial authorities during the latter part of the 19th century. The only remaining sets of Sharia laws that escaped any modification were family laws. Since the 1970s, Islamic fundamentalists in Sudan, Afghanistan, and Pakistan have called for the reinstatement of *hudud*. Under the Islamic Republic of Iran, modern legislation is applied as long as it does not contravene the Sharia, which put an end to *hudud* punishments.

HUSSEIN, AZIZA (1919–). An Egyptian diplomat and population expert who was born in the village of Zifta, in the Gharbiya Province. The eldest of five children, her family was of the elite, land-owning class, and her father was a doctor. She earned a degree from the American University of Cairo (AUC) in 1942. She married a prominent agricultural economist, Dr. Ahmed Hussein, who was interested in rural development and community assistance for much of his life. While on a development study tour in the Caribbean with her husband, he was called back to Egypt, and she went on a lecture tour throughout the United States arranged by the American Mid-East Educational and Training Service (AMIDEAST). She lectured on Egypt, the Palestine question, and women's issues. Her husband, who briefly served as the minister of social affairs before the 1952 revolution, was posted to the United States as his country's ambassador in 1953. She was named to the Egyptian delegation to the United Nations in 1954, the first Egyptian woman to serve in this capacity. In 1962, she was appointed Egypt's representative to the Commission on the Status of Women at the UN.

After years of studying the social and economic status of the Egyptian peasant and supporting her husband's Peasant Society, Hussein became an expert on fertility and population issues. Her work resulted in developing an official policy on population control in 1966, and the founding of the **Family Planning** Association in 1967. As head of this organization, she became one of **Jihan Sadat**'s advisers when the latter pushed for a major reform of the personal status law, known as Law 44. Hussein's influence in persuading the president's wife of the demographic danger of the country's unbridled multiple **marriages** and **divorces** was said to be the main inspiration behind this law. *See also* FEMINIST MOVEMENT IN EGYPT.

HUSSEINI, HIND (1916–1994). A Palestinian philanthropist and welfare provider who left her mark on the Arab community of Jerusalem. Her father was Tahir Shukri Husseini, who was a judge and a scion of the most recognized family among Jerusalem's Arab notables. She attended the Jerusalem Girls College, graduating in 1937, and developed an interest in social work through her studies with Victoria and Elizabeth Nasser of the founding family of Birzeit University. She taught at the Islamic Girls College in Jerusalem until the Arab–Israeli War of 1948. She is best known among Palestinians as the founder of The Home of the Arab Child (Arabic: Dar al-Tifl al-Arabi), an orphanage that she established in her family's home. She took this step to house the first batch of Palestinian orphans streaming into Jerusalem following the April 1948 massacre of the Arab village of Deir Yassin by the Haganah Jewish militia. Husseini became committed to saving and training young people for a better life, creating a nursery, a kindergarten, a school, a vocational training center, an experimental farm, a women's college affiliated with al-Quds University, and a Palestinian museum. At first, she financed this project from her family's assets, but she was eventually able to receive substantial funding from international donors. She received several awards in recognition of her humanitarian work, such as the Jordan Globe Medallion for Social Work in 1983 and the First Degree Medallion of the Federal Republic of Germany in 1989. Her life was featured in an American movie, *Miral*, in 2009.

HUSSEINI, JUMANA (1932–). A Palestinian painter who was born in Jerusalem. She studied art in Beirut and Paris and held her first exhibit in 1965 in Paris. Her work was exhibited in several Arab countries, as well as Japan, Italy, and the United States, where it was featured in 1994 at the Museum of Women in the Arts in Washington, D.C. In 1999, she was awarded the Palestine Award for the Visual Arts by the Palestine National Authority. She resides in Paris.

I

IBRAHIM, FATIMA AHMAD (1933–). A Sudanese veteran female activist, journalist, and socialist leader who was born in Khartoum to a middle-class, well-educated family. Her grandfather was the principal of the first boy's school in the country, and her father was a teacher who trained at Gordon Memorial College, later Khartoum University. She followed in their footsteps, becoming a teacher after graduating from Omdurman's Girls Secondary School. During the 1940s and early 1950s, she was heavily involved in anti-British activities until Sudan's independence in 1956. Her nationalist efforts resulted in collaboration with the Sudanese Communist Party (SCP), headed at the time by Abd al-Khaleq Mahjoub. She was one of the leaders of the women's section, known as the Sudanese Women's Union (SWU), in 1952, and became the editor of its publication, *al-Raida* (Arabic; *The Woman Pioneer*). She served prison terms due to her activities. She was the chief editor of *Sawt al-Maraa* (Arabic; *Women's Voice*), a magazine that in 1964 played a major role in the overthrow of General Ibrahim Abboud, the country's dictatorial president. Her husband, Al-Shafii Ahmad al-Sheikh, a union leader, was executed by the government of President Jaafar Nimeiry (r. 1969–1985).

In 1965, Ibrahim was elected to parliament, the first woman to reach this position in the Sudan, where she became the main voice calling for women's rights. When the Nimeiry government lost support, she was also in the forefront of the opposition calling for his overthrow. When the Islamic government of president Omar al-Bashir seized power in 1989, the SWU was banned. Ibrahim was imprisoned but chose to go into exile in Great Britain in the early 1990s. Her own political associates accused her of turning to political Islam and abandoning her leftist ideals for residing in that country, although she remained the head of the SWU. She also managed to retain her seat on the central committee of the SCP and to continue in her role as the editor of *al-Raida*. She was elected president of the Women's International Democratic Federation in 1991. She remained active among Sudanese opposition groups in exile, particularly within the umbrella known as the National Democratic Alliance. She is the recipient of several international honors,

169

including the 1993 United Nations Award for Outstanding Achievement in the Field of Human Rights and the Ibn Rushd Fund Prize. She returned to Sudan in 2005 and has been serving as a SCP representative in parliament.

IDELBI, ULFAT (1912–2007). A noted Syrian novelist and short-story writer who was born in Damascus to a traditional family, the only daughter among four brothers. Married at age 17, she managed to complete her high school education shortly thereafter. She furthered her intellectual development by reading books in the library of her uncle, author Kazem Daghestani. She struggled with her family, which hailed from the town of Idleb and was Circassian in origin, to participate in demonstrations. Just like the rest of her generation of Syrian men and women, she reacted strongly to the French occupation of her country. She won third prize in a short-story competition sponsored by the British Broadcasting Service–Arabic Section, which drew participants from all corners of the Arab world. She wrote four columns of short stories, the most famous being *Qisas Shamiyya* (Arabic; *Damascene Stories*) (1954), which received the recognition of an introduction by the Egyptian writer Mahmoud Taymour. *The Story of My Grandfather*, written for young adults (trans. 1991), and *The Thousand and One Nights* (1998) also proved to be a great success.

Her most admired novel, which was made into an Arabic language television series in Syria, was *Dimashq ya basmat al-huzn* (*Damascus, Smile of Sorrow*) (1980). This appeared in English under the title *Sabriyya Damascus Bittersweet* (1997). *Sabriyya* tells the story of coming-of-age in Damascus during the 1920s and 1930s, when young women like the protagonist fought for nationalist and feminist liberation and suffered the wrath of their oppressive families. Sabriyya is punished for marching in demonstrations and denied the right to continue her education or to meet with her lover, who is found dead later on. Yet Sabriyya's family expects her to perform filial duties to her parents and her brothers. She ends up forgoing **marriage** and devoting her life to serving the needs of her bedridden father. Critics lauded her novels for their honest portrayal of the ordeals of urban, middle-class women as they devise various coping mechanisms, including inhabiting a world of fantasy.

IFFAT, QUEEN (1910–2000). A Saudi queen who was the only royal consort to be given this title in recent years. Her full name was Iffat Bint Ahmad al-Thunayan al-Saud. She was the wife of King Faysal (r. 1964–1974). She grew up in Turkey and became an enthusiastic supporter of girls' education. She is credited with encouraging her husband to open the first girls' school in the country, in 1966. She also pushed for emphasizing science education and Western subjects in those schools. She often referred to the Quran in arguing that the fulfillment of religious duties was impossible without education. She founded the Taif Model School and The Girls College in Riyadh, which granted teaching certificates.

Additional light was shed on her personal background after she married the king. Her grandfather and father were taken prisoner by the Ottoman authorities following the collapse of the first Saudi state. Her father returned later as an adviser to the kingdom's founder, King Abd al-Aziz, during World War I. Her mother was either Hungarian or Circassian. Queen Iffat married Faysal in 1932 when he was still a prince and quickly became involved in the Saudi Renaissance Movement, becoming the honorary president of the Saudi Arabian Renaissance Society, which taught poor women arts and crafts in the capital of Riyadh. The same society branched off and sponsored literacy classes and free clinics for women. In the 1960s, she established the first social welfare agencies in the kingdom, such as the Women's Welfare Association in Jedda and a similar organization in Riyadh. In 1955, she opened Dar al-Hanan, a private women's school in Jedda. Queen Iffat was never photographed in public and was never seen on television. She was buried in Riyadh. *See also* EDUCATION: ARAB GULF STATES.

INDUSTRIAL LABOR, WOMEN IN. Industrial work is generally defined as participation in occupations such as mining, oil drilling, manufacturing, construction, and electricity, water, and gas utilities. There has always been a debate in the Muslim and Arab worlds over the suitability of this type of employment for women. The debate accompanied the earliest development of the industrial sector in Egypt, the first country in the Middle East to experience industrialization. Industry here developed toward the end of the 19th century, expanding slowly while attracting the rural population to urban centers. The first industries to attract wage laborers were manufacturing, particularly textiles, construction, and transportation. Women were slow to engage in this type of work and were initially concentrated in unskilled and low-paying jobs in the new industries. In the 1950s and 1960s, when Egypt experimented with socialist economies during the Nasserite regime, women were mobilized to join the expanding industrial sector as the country began to practice its own variation of import-substitution policies. Women's participation in the workforce rose only to 7 percent, but the era of industrialization was also characterized by the introduction of gender equalization measures such as an equal wage for both genders; free university education for all classes and groups, including women; and a generous package of maternity leave and special concessions to child-raising women. The public sector ballooned and opened up employment opportunities for men and women. Some jobs or trades became quickly feminized, such as textiles, absorbing 43 percent of women; food processing, which had 14 percent; and pharmaceuticals, which had 13 percent in the 1950s. As in all cases of early industrialization, textiles became the major industry employing large numbers of women. By the 1960s, women were 60 percent of workers employed by the Nasr Textile Company and 50 percent in the pharmaceutical industries.

When president Anwar Sadat (1970–1981) initiated the policy of *infitah* in the 1970s (open door to Western investments), Egypt was forced to implement the structural adjustment policies (SAPs) of the International Monetary Fund (IMF) and the World Bank (WB). This meant thinning the competitive sector and trimming the public sector. Privatization of public-sector companies, which were the main employers of female labor (besides agriculture), suffered greatly by reducing their excess labor, made up largely of women. Early retirement policies directed at women forced them to retire at age 45, while male workers retired at age 50. In addition, labor-intensive industries that employed large numbers of women, such as textiles and the garment industry, did not experience the same rate of growth seen in Tunisia and Morocco. Women's representation in trade unions also remained minimal, while the entire trade union movement acquired political overtones and was subjected to intensive government surveillance.

The industrial picture for Turkey, the other heavily industrial state in the region, is somewhat different. Due to the decline of the agricultural sector by the middle of the 20th century and large-scale rural–urban migration, women's participation in traditional agricultural occupations, mainly on family farms, greatly declined. Despite Ataturk's reforms affecting women's social and political rights, Turkish migrant women did not engage in urban employment and remained mainly housewives. Female labor participation in the mid-1950s was still 72 percent, but it was mainly found in agriculture. By 2005, this figure had fallen to 25. 5 percent due to the decline of agriculture. Women working in industry were reported to be only 14.8 percent in 2005, and 33.6 percent in the service sector. Of all the women engaged in manufacturing, 59.5 percent were employed in the textile and garment industries, while 14.4 percent were in the food industry. Only 12.2 percent of the female labor force was employed in metal production, such as machinery and other equipment. Women remain clustered in labor-intensive industries where wages are low and job security is minimal. *See also* ATATURK, MUSTAFA KEMAL (1881–1938).

INHERITANCE UNDER ISLAMIC LAW. In Islamic countries, inheritance is regulated by the **Sharia**. A specific and detailed formula governs this basic right, which granted Muslim women a firm economic status ahead of many other societies. For Sunnis, the Sharia calls for granting a daughter one-half of the share of her brother from a family estate, and the widow one-eighth of a husband's estate if he left any children, but one-fourth if he died childless. In a widow's case, the same formula applies whether her husband fathered children with her or with other wives. But if a widower survived his wife, he inherits twice the amount to which she is entitled as a widow. If a man dies without leaving any sons, his daughter is entitled to receive half of his estate, but if he had two or more daughters, they share two-thirds of the estate. If a man dies without leaving any sons, then a great portion of his estate devolves on his male agnates, or his paternal kinsmen. Preference for male children or male brothers and cousins in matters of inheritance has been the subject of bitter controversy between traditionalists and modernists in the Muslim world for years. Modernists claim that this formula has offset the significance of the Muslim claim to being the earliest to grant women economic rights.

There are differences between the Sunni law of inheritance, as stated here, and the Shii law. According to the latter, male agnates cannot inherit if an heir dies without any male issue. If a man leaves behind only one daughter, she is entitled to inherit the whole estate. Even a surviving paternal grandfather is excluded from the inheritance. Many Arab states have reformed Sunni practices to bring them in line with the Shii law. The government of Iraq since 1959 has adjusted the Sunni law in favor of granting daughters an equal share to the property like their brothers. These reforms began during the government of Iraqi President **Abd al-Karim Qassem** (r. 1958–1963). Egyptian women have fought against the preferential treatment of agnates in matters of inheritance for years. The **Personal Status Code of Tunisia** in 1956, however, introduced many reforms of the Sharia but left the law of inheritance unchanged.

INSTITUTE FOR WOMEN'S STUDIES IN THE ARAB WORLD (IWSAW). This is a center for research, study, and documentation on women in the Arab world. It was founded in 1972 by the recently established Beirut University College (BUC), which later became the Lebanese American University. One of the founders was Riyadh Nassar, the dean of BUC, who received a grant from the Ford Foundation to establish the center. A BUC faculty member, Juliana Abu Nasr, was a cofounder who served as the first director. The mandate of the institute was to conduct academic research on women in the Arab world, establish a database and a resource center on such issues as human rights policies, and network among various women's groups. Several projects were launched, such as producing publications on the educational, employment, social, and legal status of women. The institute sponsors annual conferences on women and publishes a journal titled *al-Raida* (*The Pioneer*). Some of the activities of the center reach out to rural women in an effort to teach them income-generating skills. The IWSAW cooperates with Lebanon's Ministry of Social Affairs and with a variety of international **non-governmental organizations (NGOs)**.

IRANIAN BUREAU OF WOMEN'S AFFAIRS (IBWA). The IBWA was founded in 1991 to identify and treat problems affecting Iranian women by coordinating the work of many agencies and government offices. The idea of this effort was first proposed by Marziyeh Seddiqi, who studied engineering in the United States and served in the Iranian Majlis from 1996 until 2000. The bureau was also the brainchild of President Ali Akbar Hashemi Rafsanjani's adviser on women's affairs, **Shahla Habibi**. Rafsanjani appointed Habibi as the head of this bureau, and Seddiqi became the head of planning and research. The IBWA was attached to the president's office and sought the cooperation of all government ministries to protect the rights of women. Projects initiated by the bureau targeted women's education and training, developing women's management abilities, reforming the Islamic law of **divorce**, encouraging women's studies abroad, and creating a center to assist in women's employment and another to provide women with legal expertise. The training and education program of the bureau was placed in 1997 under the direction of **Maasumeh Ebtekar**, editor of the journal *Farzaneh* and a university professor, who also became the vice president of the bureau. As a result of the work done by the IBWA, female members of parliament presented several motions to ameliorate the status of women, not all of them successful. After the election of Muhammad Khatami as the president of Iran in 1997, the bureau's name became the Center for Women's Participation, with Zohra Shojaie as its chair. *See also* FEMINIST MOVEMENT IN IRAN.

IRANIAN CONSTITUTION (1980). The constitution was ratified one year after the establishment of the Islamic Republic of Iran in 1979. Its ratification was achieved through a national referendum, with heavy female participation. The previous constitution, which was born out of the revolution of 1906–1907, lacked many of the Islamic principles present in the later document. By contrast, the 1980 constitution attempts to provide the framework for an Islamic state by stipulating that all future legislation covering every aspect of life must be based on Islamic principles as embodied in the Shii **Sharia**. A mechanism to ensure this outcome was provided by creating a committee of 12 jurists, 6 of whom must be members of the Muslim clergy, which was charged with vetting all legislative bills of the Majlis. Known as the Council of Guardians, the committee in effect had the power to reject any piece of legislation deemed in conflict with Islamic law.

Women's position in society, according to this constitution, was carefully described to reflect the mind-set of the new regime. There is reference to and acknowledgment of women's massive and visible contribution to all phases of the Islamic Revolution and a promise to improve their rights in order to end their oppression by the shah's regimes. This oppression is described as subjecting women to forces of consumerism and commercial exploitation.

The constitution calls on the state to secure the rights of all its citizens, both men and women. This commitment, which is stated in the preamble, is not an open-ended proposition but is subject to the specifications of Islamic criteria. The state is also called upon to adopt all measures that will protect mothers, especially during the periods of pregnancy and child raising. There are articles devoted to the protection of the family, with insurance for widows and needy women, and granting the guardianship of children to upright women when no male legal guardian is available. Finally, the constitution does not directly confirm women's suffrage, which was opposed by many clerical elements before the Revolution of 1979. Granting women their political rights has been achieved outside of the constitution. See also GORJI, MUNI-REH (?–); KHOMEINI, AYATOLLAH RUHOLLAH (ca. 1902–1989).

IRANIAN PEOPLE'S FIDAII GUERRILLAS (IPFG). This is an Iranian communist party that split from its parent group, the Organization of Iranian People's Fidaii Guerrillas (OIPFG), in 1979. The OIPFG first came into prominence when it attacked a military base near the Alburz Mountains, north of Tehran, in 1970. The split was directed by Ashraf Dehghani, the most famous female communist leader in Iran, who accused the parent organization of being willing to accommodate the shah's policies. She was born in 1948 to a poor Azerbaijani family and became a schoolteacher after completing high school. She was influenced by her brother Behrooz, who was killed while fighting for his group. Ashraf Dehghani was arrested by the shah's police and suffered torture while in prison from 1971 to 1973. After fleeing jail, she went abroad and launched coordinated attacks with other groups. She also wrote *Torture and Resistance in Iran* during her imprisonment, a widely read book about SAVAK, the secret intelligence organization during the reign of Muhammad Reza Shah (1941–1979). In her book, she stated that 39 women, including housewives, university students, and schoolteachers, were among the 341 casualties of police attacks.

When the Islamic Republic of Iran came into being, **Ayatollah Ruhollah Khomeini** strongly denounced the Fidaii organizations for being part of the communist parties. But the IPFG remained patriarchal in attitude, electing only Ashraf Dehghani to its central committee. The next highest female member was Rogheih Daneshgari, who became an adviser to the central committee. The only gesture of recognition made to women by the IPFG was to translate *The Origins of the Family* by Friedrich Engels (1820–1895) into Persian during the late 1970s. The IPFG was resentful of women's interest in studying **feminism**, which was viewed as an international capitalist movement. Neither was the IPFG alarmed at first at the Islamic attack on women and imposing the **veil** as part of the official dress code of the Islamic Republic. The Fidaii group continued to downgrade its members' feminist agenda, making it of secondary significance to the organization's strategic objectives. *See also* FEMINIST MOVEMENT IN IRAN.

IRAQI WOMEN'S UNION (IWU). A conglomerate of all legally approved women's groups and clubs, created in 1945 by elite women with a social agenda of their own. The objective of this union was to extend a system of support to needy women to help with their health, legal standing, and economic status within the family. The IWU resorted to civil, constitutional, and legal means to push for change. It also fostered close relations with women's groups in the Arab world and with international feminist organizations. The IWU attempted to force brothels to go out of business and trained women to volunteer their services in times of national emergency. On the legal front, the IWU pushed for expanding women's rights, such as getting priority in cases of child custody and overturning the much-criticized practice of giving male descendants twice the amount of **inheritance** as their sisters. A campaign of legal education for women was launched in 1954 by organizing a series of lectures by legal and political experts on women's rights.

The IWU was very effective on the Iraqi scene between 1951 and 1958. On the eve of the revolution that put an end to the monarchy, the IWU was in the midst of a campaign to introduce amendments to the Iraqi constitution to establish women's legal equality and grant women the right of political participation and running for public office. The revolutionary regime of **Abd al-Karim Qassem** adopted a different strategy to advance the status of women. The IWU was supplanted by other organizations, which adhered to the ideology of successive Baathist regimes in later years, such as the **General Federation of Iraqi Women (GFIW).** *See also* ALUSI, MANAL YOUNIS (1929–); NON-GOVERNMENTAL ORGANIZATIONS (NGOs); SHARIA.

IRYANI, RAMZIYA ABBAS (1954–). A Yemeni career diplomat and novelist who was also a short-story writer. She received her secondary education at the city of Taiz and studied philosophy at Cairo University, graduating in 1977. She also obtained an MA in Arabic literature a few years later. She began her career in the Yemeni Ministry of Foreign Affairs, where she became the first female career diplomat in 1979. She also wrote fiction, beginning with a novel in 1971, followed by four volumes of short stories, a historical novel, and some children's stories. Her novel, *Dhahiyat al-jashaa* (*The Victim of Greed*) appeared in 1971 and is considered to be the first novel by a Yemeni woman. Her first short-story collection, *Maybe He Will*

Return, was published in 1981 in Damascus. She published a book on Yemeni women in 1990, *Raidat Yemeniyat* (*Yemeni Women Pioneers*). She also served as the president of the Yemeni Women's Union.

ISIS. A major female deity of ancient Egypt. Her story was immortalized in countless stories and in temple paintings. Isis was the wife or royal consort of Osiris, god of the dead, as well as his sister. When he was killed by his brother Seth, Isis grieved for him and looked for his body throughout Egypt. After she found Osiris, she used her magic to bring him back to life. She bore him a son, Horus, who was hidden away in the Khemmis marsh in the Egyptian delta for fear of what might befall him if he were found by Seth. Isis became the great model of motherhood and magical spells, whose name was frequently invoked when children's lives were at risk. For the ancient Egyptians, she was often portrayed in the funerary paintings on the walls of tombs as a goddess who had the power of resurrecting the dead. *See also* ANCIENT EGYPT, WOMEN IN.

ISLAMIC CHARITABLE ENDOWMENTS. Muslim societies have established charitable endowments throughout history, some being family endowments, others organized as purely charitable foundations. An endowment is known as *waqf* (Arabic; plural *awqaf*), meaning an organization whose income is dedicated to a certain family and its offspring, or to a religious or charitable establishment. Endowments cannot be sold or change ownership. Historically, women were named as donors of property or administrators of endowments in 30 percent of surviving *waqf* documents in Islamic countries. Since Muslim women enjoyed economic rights and were always able to inherit and own property in their own names, they were never barred from running or endowing charitable foundations.

The highest percentage of women donors or administrators of foundations was in Mamluk Egypt (1250–1517), where male ownership of land was always unstable. Since Egypt's Mamluk rulers were a slave dynasty, the most common pattern of land ownership by males was the right of usufruct, or the right to use the land, rather than to own it permanently. Upon the user's death, usually his land reverted to the state. Another reason for vesting property rights in women more than in men was that the latter were a military caste. As such, they were vulnerable to assassination attempts due to palace intrigues and their own diminished legal authority. The Mamluks often appointed female relatives as administrators of endowments, especially in the case of family endowments. Women often became wealthy as a result and endowed charitable foundations on their own, benefiting hospitals, schools, and religious establishments. One such case in Cairo was that of a woman named al-Masuna Tarakhan, whose father appointed her as the administrator of a large estate composed of agricultural land and other property. A high-born Mamluk woman, Khatun Tughay, left much of her estate to her female slaves. In 15th-century Cairo, the grand cemetery known as the Qarafa Kubra contained houses specifically for the benefit of widows and unmarried women. Some of these houses, or *ribats*, were also built by Zaynab, wife of Sultan Ainad. Another instance from a previous age was that of Umm Musa, the wife of the Abbasid Caliph al-Mansour (r. 754–775), who endowed foundations supporting royal concubines whose progeny was limited to girls. Her sympathy for concubines stemmed from her disapproval of this institution, which victimized women. Another example of women's predominance as endowers or administrators was in 16th-century Ottoman Turkey, where elite women gave their female slaves large endowments as a form of old age insurance, because female slaves would normally be manumitted after their master's death. The most common type of *waqf* established by women was usually for the benefit of other women, most frequently their female slaves. In the modern period, the institution of family *waqf* has generally declined due to legislation by governments that viewed them as suffering from mismanagement and corruption. In countries where land reform programs have been introduced, such as Egypt, Syria, and Iraq, family endowments were also seen as a means of avoiding nationalization laws. *See also* ROXELANA (ca. 1504–1558).

ISLAMIC COUNTRIES' WOMEN'S SPORTS SOLIDARITY COUNCIL (ICWSSC). The ICWWSC was set up in 1991 by Iran's Islamic Women's Sports Solidarity Council. The moving spirit behind this effort was **Faezeh Hashemi** Rafsanjani, daughter of former Iranian president Ali Akbar Hashemi Rafsanjani. She won support for this initiative by recalling that Muhammad enjoined Muslims to teach their children, both male and female, swimming, horseback riding, and archery. She also stressed that these games were open to all people, whereas under the last shah, sports were reserved for the elite. She wrote that she was moved by the example of the Algerian gold-medal winner at the Barcelona Olympic games, runner Hassiba Boulmerka, who was denounced by Algerian Islamic groups, as well as Iranians, for wearing standard-issue shorts. The first countries to respond favorably to this idea were the Islamic republics of the former Union of Soviet Socialist Republics (USSR), who were eager to participate once Iran declared its willingness to finance the largest team in this group, that of Azerbaijan.

The first competition was held in Iran in 1991, with 11 countries participating. The number rose to 16 in 1997, and sports represented included archery, badminton, basketball, volleyball, swimming, and handball. Countries that won top honors were Kyrgyzstan in 1992 and Iran in 1997. The games were cosponsored by the International Olympic Committee. When the women's competition coincided with the Football World Cup qualifying game between Iran and Austria in Tehran in 1997, Iranian women defied the prohibition on attending male sports events, appearing in large numbers at the stadium. However, no male spectators were permitted at the women's games except at the shooting range. The games were intended to demonstrate the feasibility of athletic competition while retaining the Islamic dress code and to encourage friendly contacts with women from other Islamic countries.

ISRAEL, JEWISH WOMEN'S LEGAL STATUS. Although Israel's Declaration of Independence in 1948 promised equal rights to all of its citizens, regardless of religious, racial, or gender differences, the Orthodox Jewish rabbinate was granted exclusive control over all personal status matters, such as **marriage** and **divorce,** of all Israel's Jewish citizens. This was part of a grand bargain that David Ben Gurion, the first prime minister, struck with the Orthodox religious establishment to avoid the creation of a theocracy. This arrangement, in effect, entrenched Orthodox laws in the land and disadvantaged the reformed, conservative, and reconstructionist Jewish sects. Among the obvious disadvantages of this system is that the Halachah, which is the body of laws that supplanted scriptural edicts and became an important part of the Talmud, does not recognize the need for reform or the possibility of social change, thereby closing the door on such things as the ancient law of divorce. According to this body of laws, a woman is not permitted to seek a divorce without her husband's consent. Faced with this situation, a woman often finds herself unable to obtain a divorce without the payment of a substantial sum of money. In some cases, a man may refuse to grant such a divorce under any conditions, leaving his wife in legal limbo.

Jewish Israeli women began to organize themselves against this law by forming the International Coalition for Agunah (divorce) rights. But discriminatory practices against women appear in other areas, such as their slow integration in combat units of various military branches. Some women's groups, however, have been more diligent in pressing their case before the Knesset than others. In 2004, the Israel Women's Network, an advocacy group created by **Alice Shalvi** in 1984, prepared a report to the Knesset's Committee for the Advancement of the Status of Women, which concluded that Israel ranks number 66 among the world's 121 states that elect women to their legislatures. The report also made clear that only 15 percent of Israel's 120 Knesset members are women. These figures were surprising, given the fact that the official Authority for the Advancement of Women was created in 1998 in order to encourage local and governmental authorities to promote women's rights. Israeli universities also provide an uneven record of gender equality, where despite the fact that 57 percent of all academic degrees are granted to women, only 2 percent of senior faculty members are women. *See also* BEN PORAT, MIRIAM (1918–); ISRAEL'S WOMEN'S ARMY CORPS (CHEN); NAMIR, ORA TOIB (1930–).

ISRAELI PALESTINIAN WOMEN. A significant debate about Israel's Arab population, numbering over two million, presents them either as enjoying a high standard of living or living the life of a disaffected and unequal minority. The Arab Israelis are often depicted as living at the lower rung of the socioeconomic ladder, and statistics seem to confirm this view. For instance, the income of Arab households in urban areas is estimated to be 50 percent of the income of Jewish households. Twenty-two percent of Jewish children live in poor conditions, but the number jumps to 44 percent of Arab children. Arabs are mostly concentrated in rural areas. Cities like Haifa, where a substantial community of Arabs live, are an exception to this rule. Socially speaking, Arab society within Israel was always led by the clan. After the 1948 Arab–Israeli War, which gave birth to the State of Israel, most of the urban Arab population either fled or was driven out of the territory that became Israel. Arab lands were mostly confiscated by the Israeli military authorities. The loss of the urban Arab population resulted in the loss of the old women's organizations and their leadership. The steady proletarianization of the Arab population as a result affected the female population adversely. Israeli state policies, in addition, strengthened, rather than weakened, any prospect for a natural evolution of a native core of Palestinian leadership, including the feminine sector. Among the most impoverished areas in Israel are the Negev unincorporated villages, which are populated by Arab Bedouin families. Since the state does not extend development services to them or provide them with schools, the impact on girls' education has been drastic. Due to the expense of transportation to nearby villages where schools may be available, many girls forgo a high school education.

Whereas some maneuverability in matters of personal status has been granted to Jewish women, Palestinian, Muslim, Christian, and Druze women must resort to their own religious courts when fighting cases of child custody or gaining greater financial support in cases of **divorce**. Jewish women are given the option of appealing to civil courts in such matters, but the judgment of religious Arab courts is always applied to Arab women, who remain bound by tradition due to the Israeli decision to strengthen the authority of religious courts. Barring access to civil courts is also the natural outcome of a policy that treats the Arabs not as a national group but as different sectarian communities. For instance, the Druze population was officially designated a separate entity as of 1957, when it was accorded its own school system and distinct religious courts. This development was preceded by a 1955 law originating in the Israeli prime minister's office that divided the Arab population into four distinct entities: Muslim, Christian, Druze, and Bedouin. There are no separate state policies along such divisions in the Arab countries, which are not even sectarian because Druze and Bedouin women are also Muslim. Israel treats each group according to a different criterion. As a result, the Israeli government has empowered traditional elements among each of these communities, especially in matters of **honor crimes**, early and endogamous marriages privileging unions of cousins, general marriage practices, and divorce. For example, an Arab woman is not entitled to any property in the case of divorce, whereas a Jewish woman is entitled to receive half of any property accumulated during **marriage**. According to a 1993 study, almost 43 percent of all marriages in the Muslim community are endogamous, which in most cases occur without the woman's consent and are a reflection of the entrenched power of clan leadership. By comparison, similar marriages in Lebanon, Algeria, and Egypt do not exceed 20 to 28 percent, while in the traditional Persian Gulf societies and in Jordan, these marriages sometimes exceed 50 percent.

Since the creation of family courts in Israel to adjudicate personal status cases for the Muslim and Christian Arab populations, only one Arab woman has been appointed a judge since 2007. By comparison, 25 Jewish women have served as judges in similar Jewish courts. In matters of education, 93 percent of Jewish youths advance to the high school level, but among the Arab population, only 80 percent proceed to this level of education despite the fact that elementary school attendance is compulsory. Palestinian women lag behind Jewish women in university education. According to 1993 figures, 9.2 percent of Arab women and 28 percent of Jewish women advanced to the university level. According to statistics for the same year, the total number of Arab university graduates, both men and women, was only 5.2 percent of the total graduating. According to 2008 statistics, about one-half of all Israeli Arab women never finish high school, compared to 10 percent of Jewish women. By 2007, 33 Arab men reached the level of full professor at Israeli research universities. Only one Arab woman advanced to the position of full professor of education in Tel Aviv University by 2010. This was Fadia Nasser Abu Alhija from the Arab village of Tira.

The presence of Arab women in the Israeli political arena also lags behind that of Jewish women. The first Arab woman to be elected to the Knesset (parliament) was Hasniyya Jabara, who won a seat in 1999 on the Meretz list, one of Israel's leftist parties. The second Arab woman to be chosen to this national body was Nadia Helou, who was elected in 2000 on the Labor Party ticket. The presence of Arab women on local government councils is equally as limited. Most women acquired their early training in local government within the ranks of Democratic Women, the auxiliary of the Israeli Communist Party. The example of Violet Khouri (1929–1987) is a case in point. She was the first Arab woman to be elected as a mayor to a large Palestinian village, Kufur Yassif, in the Galilee region. She was one of the earliest women to receive a university education during the period of military rule imposed on Arab areas from 1948 until 1967. Her expertise and knowledge of municipal affairs was acquired from her husband, Fawzi Khouri, who headed Kufur Yassif's municipal council form 1962 until 1964. Her first entry into municipal politics was when she was elected indirectly to the municipal council by members who opposed continued control by the Arab Communist Party, the only party supportive of Arab rights at the time. In 1981, she became the mayor, a position she held until she died.

By 2009, the first Arab woman to run for legislative elections on an Arab Party list and win a seat in the Knesset was Hanin Zubi. She ran on the Balad Party list and became the third Arab woman to win a seat in the legislature since two women had won seats on Israeli party lists in the late 1990s. Born in Nazareth, she completed a degree in psychology and philosophy at Haifa University and went on to receive an MA in communications from Hebrew University, the first Arab to major in this field in an Israeli university. Arab women also continue to be underrepresented in municipal assemblies. In 2008, for example, 149 Arab women ran in municipal elections, but only 6 were elected.

ISRAELI WOMEN'S PEACE MOVEMENT (1983–2005). The first organized Israeli women's peace group was Women in Black, who protested Israel's invasion of Lebanon in 1983. These women opposed Israel's militarized culture, which did not augur well for normal gender interaction. The first Palestinian *intifada* (1987–1988) triggered another women's peace movement, taking on the same name. This movement came into being when the Israeli army stopped a group of 40 women from visiting Palestinian refugee camps in the West Bank to express solidarity with Palestinian women whose male relatives were involved in the hostilities. The Israeli women were also protesting exposing their husbands, sons, and brothers to the dangerous situation on the West Bank. Calling themselves Women in Black, they began to hold vigils in the streets of Jerusalem, Tel Aviv, and Haifa on Fridays, carrying signs demanding that the Israeli occupation of the West Bank be brought to an end and the Palestine Liberation Organization (PLO) be dealt with through diplomacy. The women often encountered a hostile reaction from the police and Israeli right-wing groups.

Another organization, called Shani, or Israeli Women's Alliance against Occupation, began to plan programs around lectures by Israeli and Palestinian women concerning the occupation. The issue of Palestinian political prisoners led to the rise of another group, Women's Organization for Women Political Prisoners, which assigned each member a Palestinian prisoner, whose case became her sole responsibility. This group made a point of releasing information about torture, especially the use of sexual harassment inside the jails. The group also cooperated with a leftist Arab women's organization within Israel, Tandi, or Movement of Democratic Women, which is an affiliate of the Communist Party known as the Democratic Front for Peace and Equality. It demanded, in addition to improved treatment of female prisoners, the reopening of schools that were shuttered during the *intifada* and the immediate release of female teachers from prison. Due to the increased violence of the second *intifada* (2000–20005), some of these groups lost membership and became less visible on the Israeli scene. *See also* CHAZAN, NAOMI (1946–); FEMINIST MOVEMENT IN ISRAEL; LANGER, FELICIA (1930–); SHALVI, ALICE HILDEGARD (1926–).

ISRAEL'S WOMEN'S ARMY CORPS (CHEN). Israeli women were no strangers to the Israeli Defense Forces (IDF), since they enrolled in its underground militias before statehood. But once Israel became a state, women were barred from military combat. Since that time, women have been expected to serve in the army for two years (currently only for 21 months), but only if they are single. The list of exemptions for women extends to those who are married, over 24 years of age, or who belong to Orthodox sects who harbor religious objections to serving in the military. The Women's Corps is autonomous and controls the terms and conditions of service. Generally speaking, members of CHEN are relegated to noncombat duties such as clerical work; driving vehicles; and employment as nurses, doctors, social workers, and teachers in various military schools. They also perform a variety of duties with the military intelligence services. Beginning in the mid-1990s, female soldiers were being integrated into some frontline units of the IDF, and on 1 August 2001, CHEN lost its independence and was absorbed into the general staff. The highest-ranking woman in CHEN, Brigadier General Suzy Yogev, became an adviser to the chief of staff on matters pertaining to women in the services. Her position was reduced to a lower rank later on, causing a major stir among feminist advocates who call for complete equality within the ranks.

In recent years, the military have been so liberal in granting exemptions to women that almost half of them escape the draft. But since 2000, and due to increasing reliance on technology, the number of women assigned for duty in the artillery corps, armored divisions, and infantry units has been increasing. Women have also been assigned to naval repair units. Latest figures for 2004 indicate that there were 450 women in combat units, and a year later, around one dozen women were combat pilots.

ITZIK, DAILA (1952–). An Israeli politician who served in many capacities and high governmental positions. She was born in Jerusalem to a family of Iraqi Jews and later became chairperson of the Jerusalem Teachers' Association. She earned a BA in literature and history from Hebrew University, a teacher's diploma from the Efrata Teachers Seminary in Jerusalem, and a law degree from the Interdisciplina Center in Herzliya. She was involved in municipal politics, serving as the deputy mayor of Jerusalem from 1989 to 1993. She became a member of the Knesset in 1992 and was reelected to that seat in 1976 and 1996. When Israeli Prime Minister Ehud Barak (r. 1999–2001) formed his first cabinet, she became the only female to join this group, as minister of the environment, in 1999. She was elected to the Knesset again in 2003 and served as minister of communications in 2005. Though she had always been elected on the Labor Party list in the past, she won a Knesset seat in 2006 on the Kadima Party list, becoming the first woman to serve as speaker of the house. She was also chosen to serve as the acting president of Israel from January to July 2007, when Israel's sitting president, Moshe Katsav, was given a leave of absence pending investigations of misconduct while he was in office. She was succeeded in that position by Shimon Peres, who was elected as the country's ninth president in 2007.

J

JABABDI, LATIFA (1955–). A Moroccan **feminist** activist and leftist who was born to a Berber family in Tiznit. She has a degree in sociology and feminist studies from Mohammad V University at Rabat and a PhD in sociology from the Université du Quebec at Montreal, Canada. She was an early student activist, joining the Party of Liberation and Socialism at a young age. She later became a member of the Party of Progress, landing in prison in 1977, where she shared quarters with feminist leaders such as Fatna al-Bouih, a member of the Marxist–Leninist group known as "March 23." Jababdi became the editor of the *8 Mars* newspaper, which commemorated International Women's Day. She was one of the founders of the Union d'Action Féminine (UAF) in 1987. This turned out to be one of Morocco's best-known organizations, with 17 branches throughout the country and 1 in Paris. The UAF provides literacy classes, organizes festivals celebrating women's achievements, and publishes works on women. Jababdi was in the forefront of an opposition group that demanded changes in al-**Mudawana**, the latest formulation of Morocco's personal status code. Many petitions were presented to King Hassan II (r. 1961–1999), asking for the abolition of polygamy and the placement of women under the tutelage of male family members as minors, as well as equality in **marriage** and **divorce**.

JAHILIYA. An Arabic term referring to the pre-Islamic age, used widely during the early Islamic era. Before Muhammad's call to Islam, which began in 610 CE, the social system of the Arab tribes in the Arabian Peninsula was characterized by fluidity and the absence of centralized controls. Several types of **marriage** were practiced, with some, like the matrilineal system, allowing a woman and her children to remain with her own tribe after marriage. In this case, the husband had the choice of paying occasional visits to his wife and children or remaining within her tribe permanently. There was also a widespread practice of polyandry, wherein a woman was allowed to take several husbands simultaneously. Around the time of Muhammad's birth in 570 CE, the system of marriage was gradually shifting to a patrilineal system. Muhammad accelerated this process in the interest of consolidating

185

these social trends and providing more stability. During the *jahiliya*, **divorce** and remarriage were also common, and the right to divorce could be initiated by either party. When Muhammad established rules for the Medinian state after the migration to that city in 622 CE, polygamous marriages became the norm, bringing Arab practice into line with those of Jewish and Zoroastrian societies. *See also* KHANSAA, AL- (ca. 575–645).

JAMAL, SAMIYA (1924–1994). An Egyptian stage and screen actress who was also a renowned Oriental dancer. Her real name was Zaynab Khalil Ibrahim Mahfouz, which she changed upon taking up her dancing career in order to escape family disapproval. Her first stage engagement was at the famous Cairo Casino of **Badiaa Masabni** in the late 1930s. She became a barefoot performer of the **belly dance**, rivaling such great performers of her day as **Tahiyya Cariyoca.** The two remained bitter rivals until Jamal's death. Jamal starred in 55 movies, becoming best known for her roles in musical films from 1947 until 1952. Her frequent romantic partner and costar in these movies was singer and actor Farid al-Atrash, who was also her lifelong paramour. Al-Atrash, who was a Druze prince and brother of the famous singer **Asmahan**, refused to marry her, believing that she was no match for his aristocratic pedigree. Jamal had contracted two brief marriages during her lifetime, one with a Texas millionaire, Sheppard W. King, the other with Egyptian actor and heartthrob Rushdie Abaza. Her dancing career ended in 1972, but she returned to the stage briefly in the 1990s. Although she was rumored to be illiterate, her dancing career defined the genre of Egyptian musical films.

JAYYUSI, SALMA AL-KHADRA (1928–). A Palestinian literary critic and anthologist who was born in the East Bank of Jordan to a Palestinian father and a Lebanese mother. She grew up in Acre and Jerusalem, where she attended Schmidt Girls College. She received a BA in Arabic literature from the American University of Beirut in 1945 and a PhD from the University of London. Her first book, *Return from the Dreamy Fountain*, a collection of poetry, was published in 1960. In 1977, she published a two-volume study based on her dissertation, *Trends and Movements in Modern Arabic Literature.* She taught at several universities in Baghdad, Khartoum, Jerusalem, Beirut, and the United States before devoting her energies completely to research. Beginning in 1980, she was engaged in a massive translation project of Arabic literature known as PORTA, or Project of Translation from Arabic Literature. She later founded another center, East–West Nexus, focusing on comparative cultural studies. Her latest work, a large collection of essays, *The Legacy of Muslim Spain*, was released in 1992, on the 500th anniversary of the termination of Muslim rule in al-Andalus.

JAZAIRLI, ADIL BAYHUM. A Syrian **feminist** and nationalist who was in the forefront of a reform movement made up of women. The movement sought better educational opportunities for women, reform of the personal status law, driving the French out of Syria, and support for the Arabs of Palestine. She founded the Syrian Women's Union in 1928 and supported the anti-French uprising of 1925–1928. When Syria achieved independence in 1946, the nationalist leadership rewarded women by granting them better access to education, but it was too weak to confront the Muslim Brotherhood over the issue of personal status legal reforms. Women were granted voting rights by Syria's first military leader, Husni al-Zaim (r. 1949) in 1949, upon the advice of Akram Hourani, who influenced al-Zaim to chart an Ataturk-like reform course. Syrian women were not granted the right to run for public office until 1953, when Adib Shishakly (r. 1953–1954) became president of Syria.

JEWISH ASCETICISM. This is a strict regimen of self-denial leading to an elevated spiritual consciousness. The Jewish faith, however, does not overemphasize ascetic practices for women. Limitations on women's asceticism are stated in the biblical book Numbers (30: 4–17), where it is stated that a woman cannot take vows of asceticism without the approval of a father, a guardian if a minor, or a husband. The only binding vows are those made by a **divorced** woman or a widow. The Talmud, on the other hand, reflects strong rabbinical disapproval of women undertaking extreme ascetic obligations. According to this source, women who observe excessive prayers and fasting are considered negligent of other basic duties toward their husbands and children as well as their religion. The rabbis base this disapproval on their strong endorsement of **marriage**, beginning in early adolescence. There were also instances of pushing women out of mystical centers. Today the scholarly consensus rejects the popular notion that many women became leaders of mystical groups under the East European Hasidic movement of the Middle Ages.

JIHAD FOR WOMEN. Several interpretations have defined the jihad obligation for women, ranging from describing it as a religious duty to something contrary to Islamic teachings. Muhammad defined jihad as two types of struggle, the lesser jihad and the greater jihad. The lesser jihad was the duty of self-defense, which falls to all the community in time of war. The greater jihad is the constant struggle against the self, bearing no semblance to military action. The five pillars of Islam consist of the following: profession of the faith, praying five times a day, fasting during the month of Ramadan, giving of alms, and performance of the pilgrimage once in a lifetime. The pillars, however, do not include the duty of jihad. Only Islamic fundamentalists have widened the definition of jihad, calling it the "lost obligation."

Women are known to have performed the lesser jihad during the earliest years of Islam. The first among these who fought in defense of the nascent Muslim community were **Khadija**, Muhammad's first wife **Aisha**, another of Muhammad's wives, **Zaynab**, Muhammad's granddaughter, and the daughter of Ali and Nusayba bint Kaab. The latter was one of the most famous early female warriors and was known by the titles al-Najariyya and al-Mazayniyya. She is credited with saving Muhammad's life during the battle of Uhud in 625 CE. The Kharijite sect of Islam in the seventh century made the jihad a religious obligation for women based on the early record of the Muslim era, producing one of the most famous female warriors themselves, Layla bint Tarif. Women who were present at battles but did not engage in fighting were also considered to have performed the lesser jihad. For example, the great elegiac poet al-**Khansaa** provided great support for men during battle through the recitation of her poetry in the 7th century. The role of women in battle diminished after Muhammad's death and final victory over the pagan Quraysh tribe of Mecca. Settled Islamic society was led by orthodox Muslim philosophers and jurists who increasingly promoted the idea of an exclusively male-dominated public space. Performance of the lesser jihad for women was a closed option after the Crusades.

The revival of the concept of jihad as an obligation for women grew out of the Islamic revival movement of the middle of the 20th century. Sayyid Qutb (1906–1966), Egypt's foremost ideologue of Islamist groups, resurrected the idea of jihad, making the concept of a military jihad in its defensive context a requirement of the *daawa*, or evangelization of the faith. Yet he only called for the participation of women in jihad when it was absolutely necessary. The most enthusiastic advocates of recruiting women for the jihad were the underground fundamentalist Egyptian groups in the 1970s and 1980s, who assassinated President Anwar Sadat in 1981. They argued in their writings that jihad was a requirement for men and women to establish the just Islamic society. This call to activism preached that a woman did not have to get the permission of a father or a husband to perform the jihad.

Since the launching of the second *intifada* in Palestine in 2000, incidents of suicide bombing by women have been attributed to the activation of al-Qaeda in Gaza and other parts of the West Bank. Similar and rare occurrences of suicide bombings by women in Iraq, Afghanistan, and other parts of the Muslim world have also been interpreted by the Western media as instances of jihad. In reality, several jihadist groups, like Hamas and Jihad Islami in Gaza, have distanced themselves and fully abandoned this practice in recent years. It has also become very clear that al-Qaeda and similar organizations lack the necessary religious legitimacy needed for declaring a jihad. Even al-**Azhar**'s announcements of jihads have been more and more infrequent in recent years as Muslims become more resistant to accepting such declarations at face value. *See also* WOMEN'S MILITARY ROLES IN ISLAM.

K

KAHINA, AL- (?–ca. 698). This is the title of a Berber leader, meaning "soothsayer" (Arabic; feminine form of *Kahin*). Her name could also mean "sorceress," but it is unlikely that it was the equivalent of "*cohen*" in Hebrew. Al-Kahina, as the Arabs called her, was a queen of the Aures Mountains in southeast Algeria. Her Jerawa tribe resisted the final push by Arab Muslim tribal armies across North Africa under her leadership. She succeeded at first in inflicting great losses on the armies of Hasan ibn al-Numan in 692, after he captured Carthage. Her armies drove the Arab forces of al-Numan all the way to the outskirts of Tripoli. She took prisoners in one of her battles, adopting one of them, Khaled ibn Yazid. She brought a huge territory across North Africa under her control but was finally killed in battle in either 698 or 702. Some legends surrounding her death claim that she was betrayed by her adopted son. Her defeat opened the way for the Arab invasion of Spain, which was accomplished with the help of Berber troops.

A major factor contributing to diffusing the theory of her Jewish origin was that her struggle against the Muslim Arabs was not religious in nature. She may have acquired the title of "the sorceress" because she performed divinations and made prophesies at the start of battle. Early Arab historians like al-Baladhuri and ibn abd al-Hakam, who wrote about a century after she died, briefly mention her military campaigns without any reference to her Jewishness. But by the time great historians like Ibn Khaldoun (1332–1406) and Ibn Idhari were writing their histories, 700 years later, her story had been greatly embellished. Ibn Khaldoun mentioned that the Berbers were converted to Judaism by Israelites from Syria, but offered no evidence of that. Modern French historians covering Algeria also cast doubt on her Jewish origin. Al-Kahina's background is still mired in controversy, with some historians today depicting her as a Christian. A play about her life was written in 1933 by Berthe Benichou-Aboulker. *See also* BERBER WOMEN.

KAMAL, ZAHIRA (1945–). A Palestinian political leader and women's rights advocate who was born in Jerusalem. Her father was a high school teacher of geography and other subjects at the Rashidiyah School. She re-

191

ceived a BA in 1968 from Ayn Shams University at Cairo, specializing in physics. She completed a teaching diploma in 1977 at the University of Jordan. Her involvement in Palestinian politics began before the first *infitada* (1987–1988), when she organized the **Women's Work Committee** in 1978. She was imprisoned in 1979 and placed under house arrest and administrative detention by the Israeli authorities in Jerusalem from 1979 to 1986. In 1988, when talk of creating a Palestinian state was in the air, she formed the Higher Council of Women to defend the future of women and their rights when the state became a reality. She became a member of the steering committee of the Palestinian delegation during the Madrid Peace Conference in 1991.

She also served as a member of the Democratic Front for the Liberation of Palestine (DFLP), a constituent member of the Palestine Liberation Organization (PLO). When the latter made its decision to proceed to the Oslo peace negotiations in 1991, the DFLP denounced this strategy. Kamal then left the party, following the lead of Yasser Abed-Rabbo, becoming a main figure in the new faction. This became known as the Palestine Democratic Union (FIDA), which persisted in supporting Arafat's Oslo peace strategy. As a result of her role in the splintering of the party, she was denounced by leading Palestinian female activist **Samiha Khalil**, another DFLP member. Kamal was strongly upbraided for embracing the principle of secret negotiations. Kamal went on to establish contacts with the Israeli peace community, especially women, cofounding the Link, an organization dedicated to the involvement of Palestinian women in the Israeli–Palestinian peace process. Upon the establishment of the Palestine National Authority (PNA) in 1993, she became the director of the Palestinian Women Research and Documentation Center, sponsored by United Nations Educational, Scientific and Cultural Organization (UNESCO). In 2003, she became the first head of the Women's Affairs Ministry. But the pinnacle of her political career had been reached two years before that, when she was elected the head of the central committee of FIDA, thereby becoming the first Palestinian woman to reach a leadership position in a political party.

KARAM, AFIFA (1883–1924). A Lebanese journalist and novelist who wrote in Arabic and English but increasingly in English after her immigration to the United States. Her first novel, *Badia and Fouad*, published in Arabic in 1906, tells the story of a love affair between a domestic maid and her employer's son. The story line follows Badia's cultural development as she moves between her Arab heritage and her Western identity. She eventually clings to her Arab identity, a theme frequently treated by later Arab novelists, such as Al-Tayyib Saleh in *Seasons of Migration to the North* (1987). *Badia and Fouad* is considered by many experts to have been among the earliest novels in the history of modern Arab letters. Karam published seven more novels in quick succession. She also left her mark on the literary output of the immigrant Syrian Lebanese community in New York by becoming the acting executive editor of *al-Huda*, the renowned journal of Arab poets and novelists in exile. In 1911, she began to publish a weekly supplement to this paper, under the title *Syrian Women in New York*. See also SHAABAN, BOUTHAINA (1953–).

KARMAN, TAWAKKUL (1979–). A Yemeni human rights activist and Nobel Prize winner whose father, Abd al-Salam Karman, was once the minister of legal affairs during the presidency of Ali Abdullah Saleh (r. 1990–2012). Originally from the southern city of Taiz, she is married to Muhammad al-Nahmi and is the mother of three children. She is a journalist who campaigned for freedom of expression and in defense of female journalists and organized a group known as Yemeni Journalists without Chains. Her activism began at the Girls College of Sanaa University, when she led demonstrations against the Saleh regime. Her efforts on behalf of democracy led to organizing additional demonstrations and sit-ins beginning in 2007. These actions earned her the title "the iron woman" by her devoted followers. She was also dubbed "the mother of the revolution." She was arrested for one day in 2011, but was released after thousands went out in the streets calling for her freedom.

Like most women in Yemen, Karman used to wear the *niqab* face covering, but changed to the *hijab*, or head covering, to deal with her compatriots "face to face." She is a member of the Islamist fundamentalist group the Islah Party (IP) (Arabic; reform party), some of whose members had once denounced her in mosque sermons. In 2009, she participated in a program sponsored by the National Peace Foundation, which arranged for visits to U.S. grassroots communities focused on peace and religion. She was awarded the Nobel Peace Prize in 2011 along with two Liberian women. The Nobel Prize committee said at the time that it wanted to send a message that the Arab Spring would not succeed without the participation of women. The award may have come as a surprise for other Arab and Muslim women, but for the Yemenis themselves, their history has been shaped by powerful women such as **Arwa, Sayyida Hurra**. *See also* VEILING IN ISLAM.

KARMI, GHADA (1939–). A Palestinian medical historian, physician, and political analyst who was born in Jerusalem in a mixed neighborhood of Arabs and Jews. She fled Palestine with her family as a result of the 1948 Arab–Israeli hostilities. The family settled in London, where her father, Hasan Said Karmi, landed a job with the Arabic Department of the British Broadcasting Corporation (BBC). She graduated from University of Bristol with a medical degree in 1964 and went on to complete a PhD in the history of Arab medicine at London University. She is a fellow and lecturer at the Institute of Arab and Islamic Studies at Exeter University. She is also an associate fellow at the Royal Institute of International Affairs and a visiting professor at London Metropolitan University. Karmi serves as the vice-chair of the Council for Arab–British Understanding (CABU).

Karmi has written several publications on political and medical issues, such as *Multicultural Health Care: Current Practice and Future Policy in Medical Education* (1995), *Proceedings of the First International Symposium for the History of Arabic Science* (with other editors; 1978), *Jerusalem Today: What Future for the Peace Process?* (1996), *The Palestinian Exodus, 1948–1998* (1999), *Married to Another Man: Israel's Dilemma in Palestine* (2007), and *In Search of Fatima: A Palestinian Story* (2002). Karmi writes on Palestinian issues for the *Guardian,* the *Nation,* and the *Journal of Palestine Studies.*

KAWWARI, WADAD AL- (1964–). A Qatari short-story writer and journalist who studied philosophy and psychology at Beirut University College (BUC). Since 1981, she has been working at Qatar's Ministry of Information. She has pursued research on the theater, television, and radio and is married to a journalist. She authored three short-story collections: *Sorrow Has Wings* (1985), *Good Morning, Love* (2004), and *This Is the Life* (2004). She also published two short novels: *Marriage and Tales* (1990) and *Behind Every Divorce Is a Story* (2002). *See also* EDUCATION: ARAB GULF STATES.

KAZIM-BOGHDADI, TAHIYA (1922–1990). The wife of President Jamal Abd al-Nasser of Egypt (r. 1954–1970), born in Cairo to a middle-class family made up of an Iranian-descended father and an Egyptian mother. Her father was a wholesale tea merchant. She was brought up as a proper young woman of that class, attending St. Joseph's School, where she was taught Arabic and French, and was given piano lessons at home. She was introduced to Nasser by her brother, Abd al-Hamid Kazim, and was married to the future leader by 1944. Nasser was the son of a postal clerk and shared many of the conservative values cherished by her family. She tried to avoid leading a public life for many years, raising four children while her husband was sent to various military posts, including the Palestine front. Neither did she appear in public on a regular basis after Nasser became the head of the Egyptian state and the most influential leader in the Arab world. She was only seen on rare occasions, such as when she escorted wives of foreign leaders like Nina Khrushchev or Yovanka Tito on a tour of Cairo. Tahiya Kazim accompanied her husband on a foreign trip only once, when she visited Yugoslavia. She lived all her life in the modest home where she began her married life, in one of Cairo's suburbs, Manshiyat al-Bakri. Her simple lifestyle contrasted sharply with the Europeanized styles of women of the royal family before the 1952 Revolution. *See also* ABD AL-NASSER, HODA (?–).

KEMAL, NAMIK (1840–1888). An Ottoman journalist, founder of the Young Ottoman Movement and passionate advocate of women's **education**, born in Tekirdag. His father was an Ottoman aristocrat who directed him to a career in the civil service at age 17. Namik worked with the reformer Ibrahim Sinasi as an editor of *Tasvir- i Efkar*, the journal of the Young Ottomans, which called for a constitutional system of government. He also published the first Ottoman journal for women, in which he advocated the adoption of a Muslim and Ottoman brand of modernization, although he was a great admirer of French philosophers. Kemal was also opposed to the Tanzimat, the Western-inspired and comprehensive reforms imposed on the sultan's government. He argued that aping Western mores and habits in the 19th century had weakened Ottoman women. He spent several periods of his life in Europe, beginning in 1867, to escape Ottoman authorities bent on sending him to jail. A widely read journalist, he was one of the framers of the 1876 Ottoman constitution inspired by Midhat Pasha (1822–1884). Kemal died while in exile on the island of Chios. In addition to editing the journal *Ibret*, he wrote a play, *Vatan*, in which he elaborated on the issue of the fatherland and what it means to be an Ottoman citizen. In 1867, he wrote a famous essay, "A Memorandum on the Education of Women." He wrote two novels critical of oppressive traditional **marriages** and their negative impact on families: *Intibah* (*The Awakening*) and *Zavalli Cocuk* (*Poor Child*). *See also* ATATURK, MUSTAFA KEMAL (1881–1938); GÖKALP, ZIYA (1876–1924).

KHADER, ASMA (1952–). A Palestinian Jordanian human rights lawyer and **feminist** leader who later became a government figure. In addition to spending over 23 years in private law practice, she headed several institutions and was deeply involved in defending and advocating women's human and civil rights. Born to a Palestinian Christian family in the Palestinian village of Zababida, she received a law degree from the University of Damascus in 1977. Prior to that, she was a high school teacher in Amman and a journalist for the *Jordanian News Journal*. She began her private legal practice in 1984 in Amman. She founded the Sisterhood Is Global Institute and Mizan: The Law Group for Human Rights in Jordan. She is also a founding member of the Arab Association for Human Rights (AAHR). Her associational affiliations include serving at one time as president of the Jordanian

Women's Union (JWU) and being a member of the Jordanian and Arab Lawyer's Unions. She was named to the executive committee of the International Commission of Jurists.

Khader was one of the people behind the creation of a legal literacy program for Jordanian women, as well as the Jordanian Children's Parliament. She founded the National Network for Poverty Alleviation, a project of the United Nations Development Programme (UNDP). In 1999, she was the legal counsel to the Jordanian National Campaign to Eliminate So-Called Crimes of Honor. She served as counsel to the Permanent Arab Court on Violence against Women in 1996. She also served as a judge in the court's open hearings held in Lebanon in 1997. Human Rights Watch named her to the advisory committee of its Women's Rights Division. Between 2003 and 2005, she was appointed minister without portfolio in the Jordanian cabinet, as well as the government's official spokesperson. She was the minister of culture from 2004 to 2005. *See also* HONOR CRIMES.

KHADIJA (ca. 565–ca. 619). She was Muhammad's first wife and the first convert to Islam. Her parents, Khuwailed bin Asad and Fatima bint Zaidah, were from the wealthy merchant tribe of Quraysh, which ruled Mecca at the time. Khadija was married twice before the Prophet, her husbands having preceded her in death. Her first husband was Abu Halah bin Zurarh, with whom she had two sons. Her second husband was Attiq bin Aaidh Makhzumi, with whom she had one daughter. Since the matrilineal system of **inheritance** prevailed in Arabia, she inherited much of her father's wealth in 585 and began to equip merchandising caravans to make the journey of summer to Damascus and the return journey of winter to Mecca. She met Muhammad when he was 22 years of age and asked him to lead her caravans due to his reputation for honesty and his sobriquet of *al-Amin* (the faithful one). She is reputed to have been 40 years of age when she proposed **marriage** to him, according to pagan customs of that period. Although her exact birth date is uncertain, the date of her marriage is usually given as 595. She was married to Muhammad for 15 years before he began to preach his new religion in 610. Her wealth provided the necessary stable and comfortable life for his devotions and meditations in the hills surrounding Mecca.

When Muhammad described his terrifying visions to her, she consulted one of her relatives, Waraqa ibn Nawfal, who is said to have been an uncle or a cousin and a recognized authority on Christianity and Judaism. Waraqa was the bishop of the Christian town of Najran, indicating that some of her relatives may have been of the Christian faith. He counseled her that Muhammad's visions resembled those of Moses when he received the books of law, which led her to comfort and support her husband. She was the only one of Muhammad's wives to bear him any children, four of whom, all females, survived into adulthood. These were Umm Kulthum, Ruqayyah, **Zaynab,** and **Fatima**. The latter, who was the youngest, went on to marry Ali ibn Abi Taleb, Muhammad's cousin and the founder of the Shii sect. Khadija also bore two boys, who died in infancy. While she lived, she was Muhammad's only wife and spent much of her fortune on Muhammad's religious endeavors. She died a few years before the *Hijra*, or migration to Medina in 622. *See also* AISHA (614–678).

KHALAF, RIMA (?–). A Jordanian international development expert and UN staffer who is also a policy maker. She holds a BA in economics from the American University of Beirut (AUB) (1976), an MA in economics, and a PhD in system science from Portland State University. She held many policymaking positions in Jordan, such as minister for industry and trade (1993–1995), minister for planning (1995–1998), and deputy prime minister (1999–2000). UN Secretary General Ban Ki-moon appointed her undersecretary general and executive secretary of the UN Economic and Social Commission for Western Asia (ESCWA). She also served as assistant secretary general and director of the Regional Bureau for Arab States at the UN Development Programme (UNDP) between 2000 and 2006. While holding this position, she prepared many projects to promote higher standards of governance, human rights, and human development. She is the author of the Arab Human Development Report of 2004. She serves on the board of trustees of AUB and has participated in a number of commissions, notable among them being the High Level Commission for the Modernization of the World Bank Group Governance (2008–2009). Khalaf is the recipient of several awards, including the Prince Claus Award and the King Hussein Leadership Prize.

KHALED, LAYLA (1944–). A Palestinian militant revolutionary who was born in Haifa and fled with her family to Lebanon due to the Arab–Israeli War of 1948. Her father remained behind to carry on with military resistance activities. At age 15, she joined the Arab National Movement (ANM) in Beirut, which split after the 6 June 1967 War, which resulted in several factions. The Palestinian branch became known as the Popular Front for the Liberation of Palestine (PFLP), headed by Palestinian revolutionary leader George Habash (1926–2008); it planned several of her future activities. She studied at the American University of Beirut (AUB) in the 1960s and the Soviet Union's Rostow University in the late 1970s. Her revolutionary activities catapulted her into the limelight as the first Arab female to participate in the hijacking of planes. She was involved in 1969 in the hijacking of a TWA flight, forcing it to land in Damascus, where it was detonated, but resulted in no loss of human life.

In 1970, and after undergoing several surgeries to alter her appearance, she joined Nicaraguan revolutionary Patrick Arguello in an attempt to hijack an Israeli El Al flight that originated in Amsterdam. Israeli security agents managed to foil this plan, killing Arguello in the process. Khaled was seized and handed over to British authorities after the plane was diverted to London, where she was imprisoned for one month and then released as part of a prisoner swap. She then moved to Syria, where she turned to politics, becoming a member of the central committee of the PFLP as well as secretary-general of the **General Union of Palestinian Women**. Her role as a hijacker ended when the Palestine Liberation Organization (PLO) phased out this tactic, but she continued to be an object of interest to Israel's secret intelligence service Mossad, which targeted her for assassination but ended up killing her sister instead.

Khaled returned to London on several occasions to deliver public lectures, until 2002. In 1994, she was allowed to attend a historic meeting of the Palestinian National Council (PNC), or parliament in exile, held in Gaza specifically to amend the PLO's charter. Since then, she has been living in Amman with her second husband, Fayez Rashid Hilal, a physician, and her two children. She authored a memoir, *My People Shall Live: The Autobiography of a Revolutionary* (1973). Her life became the subject of a film, *Leila Khaed, Hijacker,* which was shown at the 2005 International Documentary Film Festival at Amsterdam. *See also* JIHAD FOR WOMEN.

KHALIDI, WAHIDA (1900–?). A Palestinian nationalist and feminist who completed her education at a convent secondary school in Jerusalem, where she mastered several languages. Her husband was Dr. Hussein Fakhri Khalidi, a Palestinian national leader during the British Mandate (1920–1948), rising to the position of mayor of Jerusalem in 1934. Wahida became president of the oldest Palestinian women's organization, the **Arab Women's Executive Committee (AWEC)**, in the early 1930s. She called for allowing women into the political arena. She also participated in an organized women's effort to provide aid to the fighters of the Arab Revolt of 1936. She was chosen as a member of the Palestinian delegation to the Eastern Women's Conference on Palestine, convened by **Huda Shaarawi**'s **Egyptian Feminist Union (EFU)** in 1938. Her work with the AWEC ended around 1937, possibly due to her husband's banishment to the Seychelles Islands in that year.

KHALIFAH, SAHAR (1941–). A Palestinian novelist, educator, and feminist who was born in Nablus, where she attended al-Khansaa School. She completed her secondary education at the Rosary Sisters' School at Amman. After graduation, she accepted a traditional marriage at age 18. After 13 years, she divorced her husband and pursued higher education, graduating from Birzeit University, West Bank, with a BA in English and American literature. She became Bizreit University's director of cultural activities and public relations director (1976–1978). She also edited the university's principal journal, *Ghadeer* (1974–1977). Prior to that, she worked as a translator at the Nigerian Embassy, Libya (1972–1973).

Khalifah's literary career advanced quickly after she traveled to the United States, where she earned a PhD in American studies at the University of Iowa. Her first novel, *We Are No Longer Your Slaves*, projected strong demands for feminine freedoms. Her third and perhaps most famous novel, *Wild Thorns*, which appeared in Arabic in 1976, greatly enhanced her literary reputation and was translated into several languages, including Hebrew. The novel was among the first to deal with the 1967 Israeli occupation of the West Bank and Gaza, from the perspective of a variety of characters, male and female, Arab and Israeli. Her 1986 work, *Memories of an Unrealistic Woman*, described the life she endured as a member of an arranged and unhappy marriage. She established the Women's Affairs Center at Nablus, with branches in Gaza and Amman.

KHALIFAH, SHEIKHAH SABEEKA AL- (1948–). She is the wife of the ruler of Bahrain and an advocate of women's rights, born in the town of Muharraq. She was brought up largely by her maternal grandfather, Sheikh Salman bin Hamad al-Khalifah, when he was the ruler of that country. She received her education in Bahrain and Great Britain and married the future king of Bahrain, Sheikh Hamad bin Isa al-Khalifah, in 1968. Her activities as the consort of the ruler centered mainly on helping ordinary citizens increase their income by learning new trades as well as sponsoring the preservation of Bahrain's historic buildings. She is also interested in environmental protection and the expansion of green areas in her country.

After her husband became the ruler in 1999, she turned her attention to women's rights. Sheikhah Sabeeka's efforts in that regard built on strong foundations in a country that established girls' schools in the early 1940s. There was also a crop of women who had studied abroad. She became the chairperson of the Supreme Council for Women in 2001, an advisory body to the ruler. Bahraini women were given the right to vote in 2002, when the country held its first elections in 25 years. As a result of her encouragement, women voted in large numbers, though none were elected. The government appointed six women to the cabinet due to the strong feminine participation in the elections. Sheikha Sabeeka began to represent Bahrain in international meetings and joined the Arab Women's Organization. She invited the Arab Women's Summit conference to meet in Bahrain and led her country's delegation to the United Nations General Assembly's Extraordinary Session for the Child in 2002. Her work on behalf of women benefited **divorced** women with children, such as when she announced on Arab women's Day in 2004 that divorced women with children would be given free housing. She also called for a reevaluation of the amount of alimony given to divorced women. China's Women's University awarded her the title Honorary Professor of Social Science in 2002.

KHALIL, SAMIHA (1923–1999). A Palestinian nationalist leader, presidential candidate, institution builder, and charity provider for disadvantaged women and children, born in the village of Anabta, near the town of Toulkarm. She married Salamah Khalil at age 17. Following the hostilities of 1948, she fled with her husband to Gaza, where she raised five children. She completed her high school education in 1964, and a year later founded a charitable organization based on a 1950s institution known as the Arab Union Women's Society (AUWS). Her new institution, Inaash al-Usra (Rehabilitation of the Family), was founded in al-Bireh, Ramallah's twin town. Her previous organization engaged in visiting and assisting the wounded and their families who were injured as a result of Israeli retaliatory raids along the pre-1967 Israeli–Jordanian borders. Inaash al-Usra, however, was based on a novel concept of self-help through the training of disadvantaged refugee women so that they may become independent of the Israeli economic sector. She started with an annual budget of £500, which grew by 1986 to £42,000.

Inaash ran an orphanage for the children of those killed by the Israeli Defense Forces (IDF) on the West Bank, along with a bakery, a beautician training program, a dental clinic, a library, a folklore museum, a textile shop, and a food-processing plant. Her society offered literacy classes for women and a university scholarship program for 300 girls, and employed around 4,800 women in the production of Palestinian embroidery material, which they sewed in their own homes. The society employed a permanent staff of 152 full-time workers, offered vocational training to 200 women, recruited local financial sponsors for 1,500 needy families, and operated a special program for the assistance of families of political prisoners. Much of her budget came from marketing the products of her charitable society and from local donations, having resisted offers by various non-Palestinian donors who offered to help, such as American aid agencies, public and private. Inaash published a journal, described by one Israeli journalist as similar to the Kibbutz movement's publication, *Shdemot*.

Known to her friends and supporters as Umm Khalil (the mother of Khalil), her social welfare activities meshed perfectly with her political convictions, most of which were based on the Palestinian principle of *sumud* (resistance by staying on the land). She belonged to the Democratic Front for the Liberation of Palestine (DFLP), one of the radical groups within the Palestine Liberation Organization (PLO). Her two sons were expelled from the West Bank by the Israeli authorities, and her three other children were prevented from returning after the 1967 hostilities. During the 1970s, she was the only woman in a three-member shadowy group known as the National Guidance Committee, which coordinated national resistance efforts all the way down to the 1987 *intifada*. The Israeli occupation authorities imprisoned her six times, finally placing her under long stretches of town arrest. She was charged with influencing public opinion and threatening the public order. Later on she was charged with instigating women's participation in the activities of the *intifada*. Israelis came to know her through the publication of a letter in the Israeli papers *Davar* and *Hamishmar* titled "A Letter from a Palestinian Mother," addressed to Israeli mothers. Israeli military authorities prevented her from traveling abroad to participate in women's meetings such as the United Nations Nairobi Conference on Women (1985) or to visit her children in Jordan.

Samiha Khalil is also known as the first woman to run for president in Palestinian elections, when she opposed Yasser Arafat in his 1996 presidential bid, earning 11.5 percent of the vote. She held a seat in the Palestine National Council (PNC) starting in 1965. She was also the president of the Women's Federation Society at al-Bireh and the Union for Voluntary Women's Societies. Despite her leftist politics, Samiha Kahlil was identified as a conservative **feminist** who believed that motherhood was women's essential role and who supported a pro-natalist policy for Palestinian women. This often put her at odds with younger Palestinian feminists, who demanded more individual rights for women and reforming the **Sharia**.

KHAMIS, ZABYA (1958–). An Emirati poet, short-story writer, and translator, born in Abu Dhabi, the United Arab Emirates (UAE). She received a BA in philosophy and political science in 1980 from the University of Indiana in the United States, and in 1989 she completed a PhD at the University of London. She published several volumes of poetry and short-story collections, as well as two volumes of literary translations. She has been living in Cairo, where she holds a position with the League of Arab States. Some of her poetry landed her in jail in Abu Dhabi in 1987. *See also* EDUCATION: ARAB GULF STATES.

KHANIM, LAYLA (?–1847). A Turkish poet who lived during the first half of the 19th century, born in Istanbul. Her father was a judge, Morall-zade Hamid Effendi, who arranged for her to be tutored at home. She led an unusually free life after the dissolution of her **marriage**, leading others to view her as a lesbian. She became a well-known poet specializing in eulogies, and her collection of poetry, or *diwan*, was published in 1844. Her poetic style was simple and unadorned, contrasting sharply with the ornamental style of her literary contemporaries. She was also a practicing member of the Mewlewi Sufi order and was buried in the garden of its Galata Convent. *See also* SUFISM.

KHANSAA, AL- (ca. 575–645). A poet of the pre-Islamic and early Islamic age whose full name was Tumadir bint Amr ibn al-Sharid, of the tribe of Banu Sulaym. She was born in Najd, the Arabian Peninsula. Her sobriquet, al-Khansaa, meant gazelle. She is described by Arab literary historians as a *mukhadrama*, meaning someone who was born on the cusp of the Muslim era, straddling the pre-Islamic and the early Islamic periods. She was the only pagan female poet whose verses were collected in a *diwan* that survived through the ages. She specialized in composing dirges (Arabic: *marathi*) and remains the finest author of the funeral elegy and the greatest medieval Arab female poet of all times. Details of her life are sketchy, save for the fact that she was married and had six children. Her father was the head of al-Sharid clan, which engaged in constant warfare with neighboring tribes in a struggle over the scant resources of the arid desert. This type of life valorized horsemanship, eloquence, bravery, and generosity, attributes for which her two brothers were particularly known. Named Sakhr and Muaawiya, they were both famous raiders of neighboring lands, especially Sakhr, who was renowned for what the pagan Arabs admired most in a man. Muaawiya was killed in battle 10 years before the *hijra* (Arabic; migration to Medina) in 622, and Sakhr died of wounds sustained in battle five years later.

Al-Khansaa contracted more than one **marriage**, and all of her six children were poets. She came to Medina with members of her tribe around 629 to pledge allegiance to Islam. Four of her six sons were killed in the battle of al-Qadisiyyah (636) against the Persians, an indication of their having embraced Islam some time before that date.

Al-Khansaa participated in the Ukaz literary festival, which was held annually before the Islamic period, and established her reputation there through her poetry recitations. Her poetry provided a mixed portrayal of the violence of pagan warfare and her tender feelings toward her brothers, which were punctuated with inciting her tribe to avenge their death. Her recitation style was described as a swaying motion, as if she were in a trance due to the intensity of her poetic passion. She composed around 100 elegies about her two brothers alone. Her poetry was collected later in a single *diwan*, which experienced a revival during the Abbasid age (750–1258). Surprisingly, her pagan sentiments and celebration of pre-Islamic heroic values did not offend later generations of Muslim readers. As an example, in his poetic fantasy about heaven and hell, *Risalat al-Ghufran* (Arabic; *The Epistle of Forgiveness*), the celebrated Syrian poet Abu al-Alaa al-Maari (973–1058) depicts a scene in which he meets her in paradise in the company of other literary greats. *Risalat*, according to literary experts, inspired Dante's *Divine Come-*

dy. By the time she died during the term of the second caliph, Umar ibn al-Khattab (r. 634–644), al-Khansaa was blind and impoverished, having lived to an advanced age. *See also* JAHILIYA.

KHASHOGJI, SAMIRA (1940–1986). A Saudi Arabian novelist and journalist who was born in Mecca. She became a supporter of women's associations and charities, such as Young Women of the Arabian Peninsula Club. She received a BA from Alexandria University in economics. She is the editor of *al-Sharqiyah* (*Eastern Woman*). Her novels and short-story collections include *Farewell to My Dreams* (1958), *Teardrops* (1979), and *Life Journey* (1984). She also wrote *Rihlat al-Hayah* (*The Awakening of the Young Saudi Woman*). She wrote under the name Samira bint al-Jazira al-Arabiya (Daughter of the Arabian Peninsula). *See also* EDUCATION: ARAB GULF STATES.

KHATUN, NAFISA. She was the wife of Mamluk Egyptian ruler Ali Bey al-Kabir (r. 1760–1772) and later of another Mamluk leader, Murad Bey (ca. 1750–1801). Khatun was one of the most influential women in 18th-century Egypt. The clerical class (Arabic: *ulema*) praised her charitable projects in an age when high-born women controlled considerable wealth. Some of her female slaves were given in marriage to Mamluk leaders, who were the military caste of white slaves ruling the country from the 18th until the early 19th century. *See also* WAQF.

KHAYZURAN (?–789). She was the wife of an Abbasid caliph and mother of two caliphs. Khayzuran was the concubine of al-Mahdi (r. 775–785) before he made her his wife. She bore him two sons, one of whom, Musa al-Hadi, ruled from 785; the other was Harun al-Rashid, who ruled from 786 to 809.

Khayzuran was originally a Persian slave, and some accounts trace her lineage to the Persian rebel leader Ustadh Sis. Her name derives from the Arabic term for a branch of bamboo. Musa al-Hadi was resentful of her interference in matters of state and warned her to change her behavior. When he died after a brief period on the throne, his mother was accused of poisoning him. Harun, however, accepted his mother's influence when he became caliph. She became one of the wealthiest women of her time. She loved luxury and commissioned major public works projects, such as extending a canal to the Iraqi town of Anbar and purchasing Muhammad's birth place in Mecca and converting it into a mosque. *See also* WAQF.

KHIDHIR, ZAHRA (1895–1955). An Iraqi feminist who pioneered advocating women's rights and access to education. She was born in Baghdad to a family of religious scholars, her father being Mullah Khidhir al-Kutubchi (al-Kutubchi meaning a book seller) a teacher at the Abu Hanifa Mosque, which was a preeminent Sunni center of religion and learning. Al-Kutubchi opened the first bookstore in Baghdad, al-Zawra, in 1870, which specialized in publishing literary and political works. Zahra operated a private school for girls in 1918, one of the first to teach girls mathematics and other subjects beside Quranic studies. She joined nationalist groups that resisted British occupation of Iraq. She was appointed the principal of a girls' public school after the monarchy was established in the 1920s. She also founded the Young Women's Muslim Association (YWMA).

KHOMEINI, AYATOLLAH RUHOLLAH (ca. 1902–1989). The spiritual leader of the Islamic Republic of Iran (r. 1979–1989), who founded the Islamic regime in that country. He taught Islamic philosophy in the 1920s and graduated to teaching the religious sources of Islamic law in the 1940s. Khomeini's role as opposition leader began in 1963 when Shah Muhammad Reza Pahlavi introduced a package of reforms known as the White Revolution. These included women's suffrage, expanding women's rights under the **Sharia**, and land reform. Khomeini considered these reforms a threat to native Islamic culture and fled to Najaf, Iraq, where he began a period of exile that lasted 13 years. In 1978, and as a result of the signing of the Algiers Accords between Iran and Iraq, he was forced to seek exile in France.

While residing in Paris, and until his triumphant return to Iran in 1979, his views on gender issues were relatively moderate. He asserted that there was no barrier to having a female president in the Islamic state of the future. He declared that the Islamic family should remain an indigenous institution and not mimic the Western family. The issue of gender, he believed, was part of a new discourse emerging from the shah's reforms, which aimed at transforming women into consumers of Western goods and culture. Although he called for the elimination of the Family Protection Laws of 1967, he promised the restoration of male and female natural rights under the projected Islamic government of Iran. His appreciation of women was largely due to their participation in revolutionary activities, something he clearly admired. He would often recall women's heroic roles during the early years of Islam.

During the Paris period of exile, Khomeini was lenient on the question of women's Islamic dress. He said at one time that women could choose their dress freely as long as it met the standards of Islamic decency and that he would never impose **veiling** on women. However, no sooner he had seized the reins of government in Iran than most of his views were revised. Islamic standards of female dress were established, and women were barred from the judicial branch of government, because according to the **Sharia**, a man's testimony is equal to that of two women, and women were not allowed to testify in murder cases. Khomeini maintained the position that the **jihad** was not incumbent on women, but they were expected to defend the nation, allowing them to join the Revolutionary Guards (PASDARAN) and the army. Under the laws of the Islamic Republic, about which he had the final say, women were given the right to vote and be elected to public office. The **marriage** contract was redrawn, allowing women to stipulate certain conditions such as the right of divorce, with the husband's approval. He sanctioned polygamy, removing all restrictions imposed on it by the family protection laws. He returned to the Shii prohibition of bequeathing immovable property to women. On the question of work, he accepted the occasional need for women's employment to develop the country, but only with the husband's permission. A woman's first duty was to her husband and children. His teachings regarding questions of women are found in his book *Toziholmassel* (*Explanation of Problems*). *See also* INHERITANCE UNDER ISLAMIC LAW.

KHOMEINI, KHADIJA SAQAFI (1921–2009). She was the wife of **Ayatollah Ruhollah Khomeini**. The daughter of a prominent Shii cleric, also with the title of Ayatollah, she was married at age 15. She was Khomeini's only wife and maintained a low profile for much of her life. Although virtually unknown to most Iranians, she was greatly sought after by people seeking to contact her husband, over whom she exercised great influence. She bore Khomeini seven children, only five of whom survived into adulthood. She died in Tehran, surviving her husband by 10 years. *See also* MOSTAFAVI, ZOHRA KHOMEINI (1932–).

KHOURI, COLLETTE SUHAYL (1931–). A Syrian poet, novelist, and short-story writer who is the granddaughter of Syria's only Christian prime minister, Faris al-Khouri (r. 1944–1945, 1954–1955). Born in Damascus, she attended a French school in that city and received a BA in French literature from the University of Damascus. She has published twenty novels, four volumes of short stories, two volumes of poetry, and many political and literary articles. One of her novels, *Ayyam maahou* (*The Days with Him*, 1959), shocked conservative Arab readers with its frank discussion of her love affair with Syria's foremost poet, Nizar Qabbani (1923–1998). She became a literary adviser to President Bashar Assad (r. 2000–) in 2008 and is a regular contributor to the literary pages of Syria's official paper, *al-Baath*.

KHUBAR, SUMAYA BINT. She was the first female martyr in Islam, also known as Sumaya Umm Ammar. She converted to Islam before the migration of some early Muslims to Abyssinia in 615 to escape persecution by the pagan Quraysh tribe. There are several traditions describing the torture she and her husband Yasser suffered at the hands of the enemy of Islam, Abu Jahl, in Mecca. *See also* JIHAD FOR WOMEN.

KHULU. This is a newly sanctioned type of Islamic **divorce**. *Khulu* is a no-fault divorce in which the wife seeks to end the **marriage** by giving up her dowry and back alimony. This divorce was made acceptable following the passage of Law 44 in Egypt in 1978, when the legislature became involved in a heated debate over facilitating and speeding up divorce procedures. Under this divorce, a woman has a right to ask for a court divorce, irrespective of her husband's wishes. Legislation approving the procedure of *khulu* was passed early in the 21st century and became legal in many Arab countries. In Egypt, revisions were attached to the bill supporting this divorce by the grand sheikh of **al-Azhar** Seminary, Sheikh Muhammad Tantawi (r. 1996–2010), who then declared it in compliance with **Sharia**. The Islamic Research Academy, which is attached to al-Azhar and vets all new legislation, voted overwhelmingly in favor of the new law. The older form of divorce, wherein a woman can apply for a divorce while retaining her financial rights, is still valid and may be sought under the following conditions: if she suffered injury by the husband, lived periods of economic want and deprivation, or if the husband was mentally incompetent or was missing for a long period of time. Female judges, who may be expected to be more lenient in these cases, are only appointed to the bench in Jordan, Tunisia, and Sudan. *See also* SADAT, JIHAN (1933–).

KHUST, NADYA (1935–). A Syrian journalist, broadcaster, novelist, short-story writer, and literary critic who was born in Damascus. She studied at Moscow University, where she wrote her PhD dissertation in 1970 on Anton Chekhov's influence on modern Arabic literature. She has published five volumes of short stories and four novels, as well as works of literary criticism. She wrote *I Love Damascus* (1967), and a short-story collection. She waged a campaign against Syrian poet in exile Adonis (aka Ali Ahmad Said) in 1994 for calling for a dialogue between Arab and Israeli intellectuals. She is an urban activist who protested urban development in a traditional quarter of Damascus known as Suq Saruja. Among her well-known titles are *Departure from Paradise* (1989), *No Room for the Stranger* (1990), and *Damascus, Memory of People and Stone* (1993).

KIBBUTZ WOMEN. The kibbutz experience, or living within an economic and agricultural cooperative, was an important part of the life of most early Jewish immigrants to Palestine. The first wave of 19th-century immigration came from Russia following the pogroms of 1882. Known as the first *aliya* (rising up), it lasted until 1903 and was affiliated with the Hibbat Zion socialist movement. Some members of this early wave came from radical organizations in Russia, but the majority maintained patriarchal attitudes about gender relations. The early *moshavot* (settlements) were founded by members of the lower middle class and were financed by Baron de Rothschild, the French Jewish philanthropist. The oldest settlement was Ptah Tikva, where women were aggressively prevented from full participation in the activities of the kibbutz by the traditional male leadership on grounds of their biological differences and lack of political experience. Life at Ptah Tikva was typical of a pattern of gender marginalization and exclusion that occurred in most of the settlements. One incident that demonstrated resistance to women's inclusion was when the latter were prevented from attending a lecture on health by a Russian doctor. In another incident, a woman was prevented from taking part in a play celebrating a religious theme.

Women complained that decision making in these settlements was an exclusive male prerogative, while men enjoyed a fully democratic governing process. When women began to call for the right to vote on kibbutz matters, men objected, citing women's lack of education. Women eventually won this right by resorting to biblical quotations. Women were expected to stick to domestic roles and were prevented from taking on heavy farming duties. Many of these discriminatory practices ceased as the settlements faced resistance by the Palestinians. As the year 1948 approached and the Jewish Yishuv (commonwealth) faced hostile Arab armies, women's services were sought out. Women participated in guard duties and joined underground militias in large numbers. The Haganah, the Yishuv's largest militia, sprang from the kibbutz. The organized kibbutz movement has weakened in recent years due to economic developments. On the other hand, the illegal settlements that sprang up on the West Bank and Gaza following the 1967 June War were not inspired by the socialist movement, as the earlier agricultural settlements had been. The post-1967 settlements were mostly part of a religious movement that claimed rights based on a special reading of the Bible. Here, women were part of religious households and followed strictly domestic roles. *See also* COHEN, GEULAH (1925–); FEMINIST MOVEMENT IN ISRAEL.

KIRMANI, MIRZA AQA KHAN (1853–1896). A 19th-century Iranian intellectual who called for the elimination of the **veil** and integrating women in public life. A follower of the Babi movement, which led to the evolution of the Bahai faith, he authored several influential books. One of these, *Sad Khatabah* (Persian; *One Hundred Discourses*), elaborates on the main sources of everyone's ethics, such as the mother's womb, the mother herself, and the family. In another work, coauthored by Sheikh Ahmad Ruhi in 1892, *Hasht Bihisht* (Persian; *Eight Paradises*), he introduces and explains elements of the Bahai faith, expressing even more radical views on women and **marriage**. He rejects the idea of parental choice of marriage partners, arguing instead in favor of a long engagement so the couple can get to know one another. He also called for unveiling and the necessity of offering science education to girls. *See also* BAHAI WOMEN; QURRAT AL-AYN (1815–1851).

KURDISH WOMEN. These are women inhabiting an ancient land known as Kurdistan, which, since 1918, has been divided among Turkey, Iran, Iraq, and Syria. Some Kurds are also found in the Caucasus region, northeast of Turkey, and in parts of Central Asia. There are substantial Kurdish refugee communities in parts of Europe, Australia, New Zealand, Japan, and Lebanon. According to unofficial census reports, the total world Kurdish population varies between 25 and 35 million, making them one of the largest ethnic communities in the Middle East. Kurdistan has also been home to other ethnic populations, such as Armenians, Assyrians, and Jews. Mostly Sunni, Kurds also include smaller numbers of Shiis and minor strands of this sect, such as Yazidis. Kurdish society is divided among urbanized groups, tribal and nomadic communities, and farming populations.

There is scant information on Kurdish women in the earliest history of the Kurds, *Sharaf-Nami*, written in 1597. Its author, Prince Sharaf al-Din Bidlisi, describes only female members of the land-owning class, emphasizing their isolation and noninvolvement in public life. He described Kurdish practices as similar to other Islamic societies, such as accepting polygamy and maintaining slave women as concubines, but added that these were limited to the upper and religious classes. Only three women in the past had risen to power, in order to maintain claims of infant royal sons. A 17th-century traveler, Evliya Celebi, who was a Turk, painted a picture similar to that in *Sharaf-Nami*. He stayed at the palace of the ruling family of Bidlisi, a small state, reporting that all of the female palace residents, including royal women and female slaves, lived separately in a **harem**. But by the mid-19th century, a religious leader named Mela Muhammad Bayazidi provided a description of the life of nomadic and rural Kurdish women. His book, *Customs and Manners of the Kurds* (1859), referred to all **marriages** as being monogamous and claimed that women, who were unveiled, took part in farming and food production. Women engaged in defending their communities if they came under attack, especially nomadic women, who led a free existence and were punished only if they transgressed on the tribal code of sexual conduct. The rural Kurdish areas did not force **veiling** on women, and mixing freely by men and women was tolerated. Literacy was a male privilege, especially reserved for the clergy, merchant class, and scribes. Before World War I, few

Kurdish women followed any intellectual pursuits. A resident of the court of the Ardalan principality, Mah Sharaf Khanum, who also went by the name Mastura Kurdistani (1805–1847), was a poet, writer, and historian.

By the middle of the 19th century, the Kurdish independent principalities had been absorbed by the Ottoman and Persian Empires. After the end of World War I, the Kurdish part of the defeated Ottoman Empire was partitioned among the successor states of the Middle East, which continue to incorporate sizeable Kurdish populations today. The Caucasus Kurds fell under the control of the Soviet Union. By that time, Kurdish women had begun to be mobilized as nationalists, in the last quarter of the 19th century. The beginnings of a **feminist movement** accompanied this mobilization.

The call for creating a Kurdish state and uniting the Kurds in one nation was first heard in Istanbul among Kurdish journalists and intellectuals. The Badir Khan, rulers of the principality of Botan, found refuge in Egypt, where they launched the first Kurdish newspaper in Cairo in 1898, under the tolerant gaze of the British administration. A member of this clan, Haji Qadir Koyi (ca. 1817–1897), who was a religious figure, a poet, and a writer, became the greatest advocate of Kurdish nationalism, emphasizing education and women's rights. A debate on what constituted a Kurdish citizen developed on the eve of **Mustafa Kemal Ataturk**'s revolution, with many advancing the idea that women, especially in the rural areas, qualified for this privilege as the speakers of an unadulterated Kurdish language. They qualified for self-determination because they were touched by the "Turkification" process, which overcame the urban Kurdish population. Just as in Egypt, Kurdish national leaders in Istanbul called for women's emancipation, forming in 1919 the earliest advocacy groups, such as Kurd Kadinlari: Teali Cemiyetti (Society for the Advancement of Kurdish Women). These immigrant Kurdish groups at the center of the new Turkish Republic staged several revolts against Ataturk's rule after 1923, the most famous being the Dersim Revolt (1937–1938). **Sabiha Gökçen**, Ataturk's adopted daughter, flew fighter planes against Kurdish rebels during this revolt. The impact of this Turkish repression on Kurdish women was enormous, as they fought a losing battle against the enemy, often committing suicide to escape the threat of rape. Kurdish women's organizations were dismantled during Ataturk's period, the cause of women being upheld mostly by Marxist groups in the following years. These, however, did not encourage gender-based organizations, and the feminist cause was subsumed by their Marxist formations. The plight of female Kurdish victims of traditional rural mores was given an excellent treatment in the movie *Yul* (*Road*), produced by Marxist film director Yilmaz Güney. By the mid-1980s, the emergence of the Kurdistan Workers Party (PKK) attracted a large number of women as members of its guerrilla force; they suffered torture when captured by the Turkish army. Feminist journals, such as *Roza* and *Jujin,* were launched by Kurdish women in Istanbul in the 1990s to counteract the vilification of Kurdish women as terrorists on the pages of the Turkish press.

The story of Kurdish resistance and women's rights in Iraq is somewhat different. The fall of the Iraqi monarchy in 1958 opened the door for the underground Iraqi Communist Party to operate in public and its women's auxiliary to link up with the Union of Kurdish Women (UKW). Both groups began pushing for legal reforms to eliminate traditional marriage arrangements and bring them under the purview of the state. A big campaign was waged against **honor crimes,** which occurred frequently in the Kurdish tribal areas. The Kurdish Iraqi areas in the north suffered during the period of Baath rule (1968–1991); the majority of the male population of the Barzani tribe was slaughtered during the Anfal campaign. Women were left defenseless and suffered abuse under the control of Iraqi military troops.

A great opportunity for women occurred when the Kurdish areas were declared a no-fly zone and Iraqi control was eliminated in 1992 following the first Gulf War in 1991. Most Kurdish political groups united to form the Kurdistan Regional Government (KRG), which had its own parliament made up of 105 members. Despite segregating male and female voters during the elections, six women were elected. But the KRG resisted calls for repealing the personal status code, which operated during the Baath period, or Iraqi laws, which did not prosecute perpetrators of honor killings. Women also led a protest march in 1994 from the city of Sulaimaniyya to Arbil, the capital of the KRG, calling for a halt to the civil war raging among Kurdish parties. Kurdish women continue their struggle as nationalists and feminists and are still focused on the unfulfilled portion of their agenda.

L

LADIES CENTER OF IRAN. A semiofficial center dedicated to aiding poor mothers and orphans, founded in 1935. It maintained programs to teach women modern domestic management and provide charitable assistance to needy families. The center was under the control of **Reza Shah Pahlavi**'s two daughters, Princess **Ashraf Pahlavi** and Princess Shams Pahlavi, and was provided with government funding. The Ladies Center marked an important transition from the period of independent feminist and nationalist groups during the first quarter of the 20th century to the period of state-sponsored women's organizations. As early as 1906, a group of male and female intellectuals founded the Women's Freedom Society. In 1910, a group founded the National Ladies Society to encourage women's education and the patronizing of locally produced goods. In 1927, another group created the Association of Revolutionary Women in Shiraz specifically to eliminate the **veiling** of women. All of these were gradually phased out and were supplanted by the High Council of Iranian Women's Associations (HCIWA) in 1959, with Princess Ashraf at its helm. The Ladies Center was the first step on the way to state feminism, Iranian style. *See also* FEMINIST MOVEMENT IN IRAN; NON-GOVERNMENTAL ORGANIZATIONS (NGOs).

LAHIJI, SHAHLA (1942–). An Iranian publisher and women's rights activist who became a member of the Association of Women Writers and Journalists at a very young age. Her firm, Roshangaran Publishers, was founded in 1984. She also opened the Women's Studies Center to research women's issues. After attending a conference in Germany that focused on Iran's future direction, she was arrested by the Islamic government and was given a four-year sentence. She was released after only a few months but continued to agitate in favor of free speech and gender equality. She has written several books, which include *Portraits of Women in the Work of Bahram Beizaie, Filmmaker and Scriptwriter* (1989) and, with Mehrangiz Kar, *The Quest for Identity: The Image of Iranian Women in Pre-History and History* (1992). In 2000, she received the Women in Publishing Award. She resides in Iran. *See also* FEMINIST MOVEMENT IN IRAN.

LANGER, FELICIA (1930–). An Israeli lawyer and human rights activist who was born in Poland and immigrated to Israel in 1950. Her husband, Moshe (Meiciu) Langer, is a Holocaust survivor, and both were members of the Israeli Communist Party-Rakah. She received a law degree from Hebrew University in 1965. She began to represent Palestinians in cases accusing the Israeli authorities of disregarding provisions of the Fourth Geneva Convention (1947) on the rights of occupied people. She took on a mass of Palestinian cases during the first *intifada* (1987–1988), finally closing her office and leaving the country to register her personal protest against the Israeli government. She won very few cases in her career as a lawyer.

Langer moved to Tubingen, Germany, and turned to producing critical works targeting the Israeli authorities. Her support for Palestinian rights generated a lot of hostility against her within Israel, and she suffered from social ostracism and frequent death threats. She was president of the Israeli League for Human Rights and won many international awards, such as the Bruno Kreisky Award in 1991, the Federal Cross of Merit, First Class, from Germany in 2009, and the Erich Muhsam Prize in 2005. She is the author of several books on human rights, including *With My Own Eyes* (1975), *These Are My Brothers* (1979), *The Age of Stone* (1987), her autobiography, *Fury and Hope* (1993), *Appearance and Truth in Palestine* (1999), and *Quo Vadis Israel? The New Intifada and the Palestinians* (2001).

LAPIDOT, RUTH (1930–). An Israeli legal scholar, diplomat, and professor who was born in Germany and came to Palestine in 1938. She received a law degree from Hebrew University in 1953 and pursued further studies in France, where she received a PhD in law and a diploma from the Institut des Hautes Études Internationales in 1956. She has clerked at the Israeli High Court. Her teaching career was mostly at Hebrew University from 1956 until 2001, where she specialized in the law of the sea, the Arab–Israeli conflict, and international law. She taught and conducted research at various schools in several countries, such as the University of Paris, the Woodrow Wilson Center in Washington, D.C., the University of Geneva, the Bellagio Study and Conference Center, St. Anthony's College at Oxford University, the Ludwig-Maximillian University at Munich, and the University of Melbourne, Australia.

Lapidot served as a chairperson of the editorial board of the *Israel Law Review* (1984–1986) and as the director of the Institute for European Studies at Hebrew University (1994–1996). She enjoyed a long diplomatic career, beginning with membership in the Israeli delegation to the United Nations in 1976, as a delegate to the Humanitarian Law Conference in 1977, and as a participant in the 1981 conference of the International Red Cross. She joined the official Israeli team that negotiated with the Egyptians in 1979 over the Camp David Agreement. Between 1979 and 1981, she served as the legal adviser to the Israeli Ministry for Foreign Affairs. She was also the adviser to the High Commissioner on National Minorities of the Organization for Security and Cooperation in Europe. She participated in an arbitration panel dealing with Egyptian–Israeli boundary disputes, which included claims for sovereignty over the Taba resort area in Sinai, from 1986 to 1988. This stint led to her appointment as a member of the Permanent Court of Arbitration.

Lapidot has authored nine books on international law, dealing with such topics as the law of the sea, human rights issues, the Arab–Israeli conflict, and the question of Jerusalem. The American Society of International Law gave her the Prominent Woman in International Law Award in 2000, and she received the Gass Prize in 2001 for her research on the question of Jerusalem. The Israeli Bar Association gave her the Woman in Law Award in 2004, and she was given the Israel Prize in 2006.

LEBANESE WOMEN'S COUNCIL (LWC). This is an umbrella association of over 140 women's and human rights organizations dealing with religious, academic, and political issues. Founded in 1952 by veteran Lebanese feminists Ibtihaj Qaddura and **Laure Moghaizal**, it focused on achieving women's political rights. Eventually, the council broadened its mission to encompass advocating women's access to education and better health services and expanding their employment opportunities. The council encourages women to run for parliament, which included only three female representatives in 2003. One of its achievements was securing Lebanon's ratification of the **Convention on the Elimination of Discrimination against Women (CEDAW)** in 1996, adopted by the UN General Assembly in 1979. *See also* NON-GOVERNMENTAL ORGANIZATIONS (NGOs).

LEGAL REFORMS OF WOMEN'S STATUS IN ISLAM. With the exception of Tunisia and Turkey, all Islamic countries in the 56-member Organization of Islamic Cooperation (OIC) maintain a dual legal system. These are the civil code and personal status law, the latter being based on the **Sharia**. The term "personal status law" was coined by Muhammad Qadri, an Egyptian legal expert, in the 1880s to distinguish family law from the rest of the Sharia, which began to undergo massive modifications in the area of penal and commercial law. Turkey's switch to a totally secular body of laws based on the Swiss Civil Code in 1926 was a more radical approach than that of Tunisia, which adopted the Civil Code of 1956. The need to reform the Sharia was debated widely in Ottoman Turkey during the 19th century, but the reforms were not implemented until the creation of the republic in 1923, when the Sharia was totally abolished and all religious schools were closed. Tunisia's reforms followed quickly on the heels of the country's independence in 1956. These changes were presented to the Tunisian public as another form of *ijtihad*, or interpreting the sacred texts, and not as a total dismissal of the Sharia.

The call for reforming the Sharia and improving women's rights was first heard in Egypt in the middle of the 19th century, when educator, writer, and religious scholar Rifaa Rafei al-Tahtawi called for more educational opportunities for both genders. Later in the century, **Muhammad Abduh**, the *mufti* of Egypt, questioned the wisdom of maintaining **polygamous** practices and summary **divorce**, as well as the limited financial compensation offered to divorced women. He criticized basing Egypt's personal status laws exclusively on the Hanafi school of jurisprudence. His persistent criticism of the Sharia was backed by several noted feminists, such as **Huda Shaarawi**. Abduh achieved limited success in this area when Egypt adopted Law 25 in 1929, making it possible for a wife to seek divorce if she was able to prove to the court that her husband's second marriage to another woman made her life intolerable. Although Egyptian secularists hoped that President Jamal Abd al-Nasser would push for Sharia reforms, he never embraced this cause despite enjoying excellent relations with the Muslim clerical leadership. **Amina al-Said**, Egyptian university professor, journalist, and protégée of Shaarwai, attempted to place the issue of reforming personal status laws on the agenda of the Third Jurisprudential Islamic Conference, which met in Cairo in 1967. However, this conference had to adjourn due to the June War of 1967. The only successful bid to change Muslim **marriage** and divorce laws was **Jihan Sadat**'s Law 44 of 1979. "Jihan's Law," as it came to be known, introduced two radical changes to Law 25, making a husband's second marriage grounds for divorce by the first wife and granting the marital home to the first wife if she had small children. The law was rescinded in 1985 when the courts concluded that it was invalid because it was adopted when parliament was in recess.

In the case of Iraq, the personal status law was changed following the Revolution of 1958 when the Islamic law of **inheritance** was amended, allowing equal shares of a deceased father's estate to his sons and daughters. Polygamy was severely restricted in 1963, and again in 1978, allowing a second marriage by the husband only with a judge's approval. Reforms in Syria amended the 1953 personal status law in 1975, allowing greater financial support for a wife who was a victim of arbitrary divorce. *See also* FEMINIST MOVEMENT IN EGYPT.

LEMSINE, AICHA (1912–). An Algerian novelist and essayist whose real name is Aicha Laidi. She was born in Nemencha, Algeria, and began writing articles on Algeria's ethnic conditions and joining women's literary organizations at a young age. She wrote three novels, all in French, in which she describes the antipolygamy struggles of generations of Algerian women. Her first work, *La chrysalide* (*The Chrysalis*, 1976), describes the struggles of two generations of women, the eldest against polygamy and the youngest against conservative traditions. Her second novel, *Ciel de porphyre* (*Porphry Sky*, 1978), describes the experience of a young woman who joined the Algerian War of Independence. Her third work, *Ordalie des voix* (*Voices of Tribulations*, 1983), departs from her former pattern by presenting interviews with Arab women engaged in the battle for liberation and emancipation. In 2008, she published *Au Coeur du Hezbollah* (*In the Heart of Hizbollah*). Lemsine is a member of PEN Club's International Women's Committee and the vice president of WORLD, the Women's Organization for Rights, Literature, and Development. Her novels have been translated into Arabic and Spanish. She has written against the Islamist war on Algerian women during the Algerian Civil War, which began in 1991.

LIVNI, TALIA (?–). She has been the president of Naamat, the Israeli social welfare organization for women, since 2002. She is a member of the presidium of the World Zionist Organization and sits on the international board of governors of the Jewish Agency. Livni received a law degree from Tel Aviv University and completed a master's degree in political science from University of Haifa, in addition to receiving a graduate degree from the National Security College. She has also served as a legal adviser to the Israeli General Federation of Labor, the Israeli Ministry of Defense, and RAFAEL Israel Armament Development Authority, Ltd. She has fought against domestic violence for years.

LIVNI, TZIPI (1958–). An Israeli political leader and lawyer who was born in Tel Aviv to Eitan Livni, who immigrated from Poland, and Sara Rosenberg. Both parents were prominent members of the Irgun, the underground militia affiliated with the Revisionist Party before the creation of Israel. She received a law degree from Bar Ilan University and practiced constitutional and commercial law for 10 years before entering politics. She held the rank of lieutenant in the Israeli Defense Forces (IDF) and was also a member of Mossad, Israel's chief intelligence agency. She is married to Naftali Spitzer, an advertising executive, and is the mother of two children.

She was first elected to the Knesset on the Likud Party list in 1999, where she served on the Constitution, Law and Justice Committee as well as the Committee for the Advancement of Women. She held several ministerial posts in the cabinet of Prime Minister Ariel Sharon (r. 2001–2006). Later, she was acting prime minister before she was appointed foreign minister in 2006 in the cabinet of Ehud Olmert. She served in that position until 2009, becoming Israel's second female to hold this post, after **Golda Meir**. When a faction of the Likud Party split in 2008, calling itself Kadima, she emerged as its head, making her the first female to become the head of the opposition in Israel. However, she lost this position in 2012 when she was voted out by a former general, Shaul Mofaz. An arrest warrant was issued against her by a London court for her part in authorizing the Israeli attack on Gaza, known as "Operation Cast Lead," in 2008.

M

MABARAT MUHAMMAD ALI. An Egyptian women's organization, the title of which translates as Muhammad Ali's Benevolent Society. Named after the founder of modern Egypt, Muhammad Ali Pasha (r. 1805–1848), it was set up in 1908 by Princess Ayn al-Hayat Ahmad, the daughter of Khedive Ismail (r. 1863–1879). The princess was a noted philanthropist who began her work by opening a health clinic for women in a poor neighborhood of Cairo, which she funded with contributions from members of the royal family. The Mabarat is best known for launching the philanthropist and feminist career of **Huda Shaarawi**, who received her early training in volunteerism at this institution.

The society was directed by two aristocratic women, Hidaya Afifi Barakat (1899–1969), a Muslim, and Mary Khalil (1889–1979), a Christian, who raised funds by holding concerts and charitable bazaars. Eventually, they expanded the society's work to include establishing hospitals and outpatient health clinics for women in many cities. The society's work helped in alleviating some of the misery of the malaria and cholera epidemics of the 1940s. When the Free Officers' government closed most independent organizations, including charitable societies, after the 1952 Revolution, Mabarat Muhammad Ali was spared. Its two codirectors continued their work for several years, eventually receiving state honors for their volunteer activities. Hidaya Barakat was awarded the Order of Merit-First Class the day before she died in 1969, and Mary Khalil received hers in 1972. The society's hospitals were nationalized in 1964, having treated around 13 million women. *See also* FEMINIST MOVEMENT IN EGYPT; NON-GOVERNMENTAL ORGANIZATIONS (NGOs).

MAHD-E ULYA, MALAK JAHAN KHANUM (1805–1873). She was the wife of a Persian monarch and mother of another ruler. She was the wife of Muhammad Shah, the third ruler of the Qajar dynasty, as well as the mother of the fourth ruler, Naser al-Din Shah. The title of Mahd-e Ulya was bestowed upon her when her son ascended the throne in 1848. She was the daughter of Fath Ali Shah. She was married to Muhammad Shah in 1819, a

217

union that brought together two Qajar tribes. Her daughter, Malekzadeh Khanum, married Mirza Taqi Khan Amir Kabir, who rose to be the chief minister of Naser al-Din Shah, her brother.

Mahd-e Ulya was an accomplished queen who mastered Arabic, calligraphy, and literature and wrote poetry. When her husband's health waned, she was in charge of all state matters until the safe arrival of her son, the heir to the throne, from the city of Tabriz, where the crown prince usually resided. State officials presented their report to her from behind a curtain. She is said to have presided over palace religious ceremonies and brought all the palace women under her control. Her influence over her son did not cease, and she continued at the center of court intrigue, often feuding with the chief minister, her son-in-law. This led to the exile and eventual execution of Amir Kabir, who was engaged in introducing reforms that did not please Mahd-e Ulya. The dowager queen was blamed for her son's decision to kill Kabir.

MAHDIYYA, MUNIRA AL (ca. 1885–1930s). An Egyptian singer and stage entertainer who was born in the town of Zagazig and had a love for music at an early age. Her musical career began around the turn of the century, when she moved to Cairo and became an aspiring singer. She began performing at cafes along Imad al-Din Street, the center of night life at the time. One of her early patrons was the pioneer of Egypt's musical theater, Salameh Hijazi, who composed her songs. By the 1920s and 1930s, she had participated in at least 30 musical plays. She also sang Arabic versions of famous operas, such as *Carmen* and *Madame Butterfly*. She went on musical tours, where she performed in several Arab countries. She was reputed to be illiterate. *See also* UMM KULTHUM (ca. 1898–1975).

MALAIKA, NAZIK AL- (1923–2007). An Iraqi poet and a pioneer of the free verse movement who was born in Baghdad. Her mother, **Salwa Abdul Raziq**, was a poet, and her father, Sadiq al-Malaika, was also a poet and an Arabic language teacher. Nazik studied Arabic literature at Baghdad's Higher Teachers' Training College and later studied English literature at Princeton University. Her first poetry collection, *The Female Night's Lover*, was published in 1947. Her second collection, *Splinters and Ashes* (1949), was a new type of poetry that departed sharply from the strict meter and classic form of the ancient Arab poem known as *qasida*. Her experimentation with free verse emerged as part of a movement spearheaded by male poets such as Bader Shaker al-Sayyab. Other collections followed: *The Bottom of the Wave* (1957), *The Moon Tree* (1968), and *The Tragedy of Being and a Song to Man* (1970). Her most controversial book, *Issues in Contemporary Arabic Poetry*, published in Beirut in 1962, is still the subject of debate. Her poetry treated nationalist and feminist themes, such as the poetry collection *To Prayer and*

Revolution. A famous poem appeared under the title "Lament of a Worthless Woman," and yet another paid homage to the Algerian revolutionary icon **Djamila Bouhired.** She also delivered two lectures with a strong feminist message: "Women between Passivity and Positive Morality" (1953) and "Fragmentation in Arab Society" (1954).

Al-Malaika and her husband, Abd al-Hadi Mahbouba, were instrumental in the founding of the University of Basra in 1960. She was a formidable modern literary critic who contributed regularly to journals such as *al-Adab,* *Shiir,* and *Al-Adeeb,* all specializing in poetry and literature. She taught Arabic literature at University of Kuwait, where she and her husband and son, al-Buraq, lived for many years.

MAMDOUH, ALIA (1944–). An Iraqi novelist, short-story writer, and journalist who was born in Baghdad to an Iraqi father and a Syrian mother. She studied psychology at the University of Mustansiriya, Iraq, graduating in 1971. A collection of her short stories, *An Overture for Laughter,* was published in Beirut in 1973, followed by another collection, *Margins for Mrs. B.* In 1981, she published her first novel, *Layla and the Wolf.* She then wrote an English-language novel, *Mothballs,* followed by *The Passion,* which appeared in 1995. Currently residing in Paris, she was the editor in chief of *al-Rashid* magazine (1970–1982), serving in a similar capacity later at *al-Fikr al-Muaasir* (*Contemporary Thought*) magazine.

MANAA, SAMIRA (1935–). An Iraqi novelist and short-story writer who was born in Basra but chose self-exile in Great Britain, where she has been living since 1973. She holds a BA (Honors) in Arabic literature from the University of Baghdad. She taught at secondary schools in Baghdad before earning a diploma in library science in Britain, where she became employed as chief librarian at the Iraqi Cultural Center in London (1976–1980). A prolific writer, she published her first novel, *The Forerunners and the Newcomers,* in Beirut in 1972. A collection of short stories, *Singing,* followed in 1976. Another novel, *The Umbilical Cord,* appeared in 1990. A play written in English, *Only a Half,* was completed in 1984. Her latest novel, *Look at Me, Look at Me,* appeared in a literary magazine for writers, *Al-Ightirab al-Adabi* (*Literary Exile*), of which she was the assistant editor.

MANOUCHEHRIAN, MEHRANGIZ. An Iranian senator and lawyer who was a strong supporter of women's and children's rights. She was the first Iranian woman to be appointed to the Iranian Senate, in 1963. She leveled charges at the government in her first speech for not doing enough to provide legal recognition of women's and children's rights. She emphasized that granting women equal political rights would be ineffective as long as oppressive aspects of other laws, such as the criminal code, the citizenship law, and the personal status law, remained the same. She expressed strong objection to the **divorce** law, which robbed women of any semblance of stability in their married lives. She lamented the fact that women's custodianship of children in case of divorce or widowhood remained restricted, as well as their access to family wealth. She also criticized the passport laws, which required a written permission from a male relative before a woman could leave the country.

Manouchehrian was involved in the work of the National Council on Women, which was founded in the early 1950s. Her recommendations on reforming women's status were relayed to **Muhammad Reza Shah** (r. 1941–1979) through his wife, **Farah Diba Pahlavi**, who was an ally in the battle for women's rights. Manouchehrian is credited with providing the language for the Family Protection Laws of 1967. She also founded the Association for Women Lawyers, an early **non-governmental organization (NGO)**. Her work on behalf of women earned her the enmity of the Shii religious leadership at Qom, who declared her an infidel and called for her removal from the Senate. She was awarded the UN Human Rights Prize. *See also* FEMINIST MOVEMENT IN IRAN.

MARIAM THE COPT (?–637). She was the Ethiopian wife of Prophet Muhammad and mother of his only son, Ibrahim, who died before the age of two. She was born a Christian in Upper Egypt, where the population followed the rites of the Coptic church. She was sent as a gift to the Prophet by al-Muqawqas, the last Byzantine governor of Egypt, before the Arab conquest of 682. This was an indication of her slave status. Muhammad took her as his concubine, releasing her after the birth of her son, as was customary among Muslims. The community accorded her the status of a wife of the Prophet after his death in 632.

MARRASH, MARINNA (1849–1919). She was a Syrian poet, feminist, and mistress of one of the earliest literary salons in the Arab world. Only two famous literary salons preceded hers: **Sukayna** bint al-Hussein's (d. ca. 737) at Medina, and **Wallada bint al-Mustakfi**'s (d. ca. 1091) at Granada. Marrash was born in Aleppo, and her family was known for its literary interests. Her father owned a large library, and he and his sons tutored Marinna in Arabic literature. She was educated at the Coventry of Saint Joseph Missionary School in Aleppo and other missionary institutions in Beirut. She began to write poetry under the pseudonym *bint fikr* (Arabic; daughter of thought) and wrote extensively on the condition of Arab women. Her feminist ideas came to the fore upon her touring European countries and witnessing the rights enjoyed by women. She and her husband provided a literary salon for the rising and educated bourgeoisie of Aleppo and northern Syria as a forum for meetings and debating the necessary reforms to move the country forward, including improving the condition of women. Her salon was also frequented by the most celebrated writers of the day, including Arab nationalist writer Abd al-Rahman al-Kawakibi. Marrash was an accomplished musician who sang and played the *qanun* (zither) for her guests.

MARRIAGE IN ISLAM. There were several types of marriage practiced by the Arabs before Islam. The most common was matrilineal marriage, which was uxorilocal, wherein the wife remained with her own tribe and the husband had the option of residing with her permanently or paying frequent visits. In this type of marriage the children belonged to the woman's tribe. There were also polygamous marriages, in which the husband acquired numerous wives, and polyandrous marriages, in which the woman acquired several husbands. The Prophet Muhammad was familiar with the multifarious marriage types that existed in Mecca when he was growing up there. Anthropologists state that all these marriages were experiencing a gradual shift toward a patrilineal system, which Islam accelerated. The gradual erosion of the matrilineal system was the result of the growing urbanization and settled habits of the trading tribes of Arabia. A common distaste for this unstable social situation prevailed particularly when divorcing and contracting new marriages were common, with both men and women free to seek a **divorce**. Muhammad opted for a marriage resembling the Judaic and the Zoroastrian systems, which established an authoritarian role for men in marriage and eliminated matrilineal and polyandrous marriages. All of these changes were legislated during the Medinian period of divine revelation, beginning in 622. Under the second caliph, Umar ibn al-Khattab (ca. 586–590–644), **temporary marriage**, which was widely practiced by Zoroastrian Persians and some pre-Islamic Arabs, was abolished.

Since the establishment and spread of Islam, marriage has evolved as a written contract, not as a sacrament as in Christianity. For a marriage to be valid, it should be conducted by a judge and witnessed by two male witnesses. A marriage is also based on the role of the bride's representative, who signifies her consent to the agreement and who signs the marriage document on her behalf. Without the presence of the two male witnesses and the bride's representative, who cannot be her immediate relative, the marriage cannot be registered in the courts. The contract must specify the rights and obligations of each party, particularly the amount of dowry (Arabic: *maher*) to be paid to the woman and a larger amount to be paid to her as back dowry, or alimony, in the eventuality of divorce. It is also assumed in most contracts that the right of divorce belongs to the husband, although this privilege has devolved on women in some cases when the marriage document states that *haqq al-*

ismah (right to divorce) resides with the wife. The right to initiate divorce proceedings without showing cause is usually reserved to women who are socially empowered to demand such a privilege.

A definite shift away from the tradition of unrestrained **polygamy** has also taken place with the rise of Islam. Muhammad restricted this practice to marrying four wives only. The relevant passage in the Quran clearly states that a man may marry once, twice, three, and four times if he can be fair to all of his wives, adding "and you shall never be fair." This clear restriction was never addressed by the **Sharia**, which simply accepted the legality of polygamous marriages without stipulating the conditions under which such a marriage can be nullified. For most Muslims, however, polygamy can only be justified in extreme cases where the permanence of this institution is preferable to divorce, such as in the case of a childless or ailing wife. Indeed, polygamy was always viewed as the privilege of the rich and mighty and an institution of last resort.

Polygamous marriages have severely declined since the rise of modern **feminist movements** at the beginning of the 20th century and as a result of a mixture of female education and empowerment as well as changing economic conditions. Modernization and urbanization have also militated against polygamy. With the decline of the extended family and the acceptance of **family planning**, polygamy seems to be on its way to extinction despite infrequent calls for its reinstatement by emerging *salafi* and Islamist groups. Polygamy has been legislated out of existence in modern Turkey and Tunisia.

One challenge to the institution of monogamous marriage as it has been traditionally practiced is the spread of customary marriage in certain urbanized countries like Egypt. This type of union, which entails the signing of a private agreement by the two concerned parties but no involvement by parental or legal authorities, has emerged primarily among university students. It is usually attributed to the severe housing shortage that afflicts some countries and forces young people to postpone marriage pending the improvement of their economic status. Religious authorities and the courts have not accepted this custom and frequently preach against its informality and the possible damage it may cause, particularly to the woman. This marriage (known as *urf*), which is largely limited to Sunnis, is only matched by another form of unpopular and recently revived marital union among the Shiis, namely the custom of temporary marriage. *See also* JAHILIYA; ZOROASTRIAN WOMEN.

MARY IN THE QURAN. The Quran recognizes all of the prophets mentioned in the Old and New Testaments as precursors of Islam, which is presented as the highest stage of monotheism. Mary, mother of Jesus, whose name is rendered in Arabic as Maryam, receives the highest honors dedicated to a woman. She is referred to as "sister of Aaron" and is portrayed as a paragon of spiritual purity, and her deep faith in God is epitomized by being chosen to give birth to the Prophet Jesus, or *Issa*. Chapter 66, verse 12, in the Quran reads: "[S]o we breathed into her of our spirit and she testified to the truth of the words of her Lord and His Books, and she was one of the obedient ones." This verse indicates that Islam accepts the concept of the immaculate conception. Muslim writers compare Mary to **Fatima**, the Prophet's daughter, the wife of Caliph Ali, and the mother of Imam Hussein, the greatest martyr in Islam. Fatima's suffering, her faith in the message of Islam, and her marriage to Ali elevated her to the status of a near-saint and the most important woman in Islam, particularly in the Shii tradition. In one of his authenticated traditions, the Prophet reportedly said: "Fatima will be the first woman to enter paradise, but only after Maryam." Fatima is also described as *al-batool* (Arabic; the pure one), a reference to physical and spiritual purity and a title reserved to Mary. Maryam is a popular name for Muslim girls.

MASABNI, BADIAA (ca. 1892–?). A Lebanese dancer and comedian who achieved fame on the stage in Egypt. She arrived in Cairo in 1906 and began to perform with another Lebanese actor, playwright, and comedian, Naguib al-Rihani. Her star rose quickly after she received the sponsorship of several male entertainers, finally marrying Rihani in 1923. After three years, she left him to establish her own music hall in the center of Cairo's theater district, Imad al-Din Street. She became a formidable impresario on her own, sponsoring rising film and stage stars, such as singer **Layla Murad**, as well as new singing and dancing groups. Her theater, called "Badiaa's cabaret" and located at Giza, survived the tumultuous period of World War II, when Egyptian cities were flooded with British troops. German propaganda accused her of being a British secret agent. Her theater closed after she returned to Lebanon at the end of the war.

MEIR, GOLDA MYERSON (1898–1978). She was an Israeli political leader and the first woman to rise to the position of prime minister in that country. She was born Golda Mabovitch in Kiev, where her father, Moshe Mabovitch, was a carpenter. Her mother was Blume Naidtich. Golda migrated to Milwaukee, Wisconsin, with her family in 1906, where she began her studies at the Milwaukee Normal School for Teachers in 1916. She joined Poaali Zion, a youth socialist Zionist organization, in 1915. In 1917, she married Morris Myerson, and the two moved to British Palestine in 1921, where they settled in Kibbutz Merhavyah until 1924. Although she was known as Golda Myerson for some time, David Ben-Gurion, Israel's founder and prime minister, persuaded her to take a Hebrew name, as was customary among Palestine's early Zionist immigrants. She then became known as Golda Meir, her surname meaning "to burn brightly."

Beginning in the late 1920s, she became the executive secretary of the Women Workers' Council. In 1936, she was appointed to the executive committee of the Histadrut, serving as the head of the labor cooperative's political department. Her political ties with the centrist MAPAI, or Labor Party, resulted in her selection in 1946 to serve as the acting head of the Jewish Agency's political department, upon the arrest of Moshe Sharett by the British authorities. She served in that post, operating out of the Jerusalem office, until Israel was created in 1948. During the period of Arab–Jewish hostilities in 1947–1949, she became famous as a result of her secret meetings with King Abdullah of Transjordan.

She became Israel's first envoy to the Soviet Union, but returned to domestic politics, being elected on the MAPAI list to the first Knesset in 1949 and serving as minister of labor. Meir became internationally known when she became foreign minister (1956–1965), a period that witnessed the Suez War of 1956 between Great Britain, France, and Israel on one side and Egypt on the other. Following the election of 1965, Meir emerged as the secretary-general of MAPAI and managed to bring Ben Gurion's short-lived factional party, Rafi, as well as Ahdut ha-Avodah, into the MAPAI fold. When Levi Eshkol, Israel's prime minister during the June War of 1967, died in 1969, she was chosen as prime minister even though it was known that she had leukemia. In 1972, she was elected deputy chairperson of the Socialist International, representing most of Western Europe's democratic socialist parties, for a two-year term.

Meir's successful political career did not lack controversy. Despite her popularity at home, to the Arabs she was the Israeli official who denied the existence of the Palestinians. When Israel suffered the Egyptian surprise attack of October 1973, resulting in the October War (Yom Kippur War to the Israelis and Ramadan War to Egyptians), she was blamed by leftist critics for not doing enough to reach an accommodation with President Anwar Sadat of Egypt (r. 1970–1981). She came under withering attack for misreading all the signals leading up to the October War. Following the publication of the Interim Report of the Agranat Commission of Inquiry in 1974, which investigated the causes of this war, she submitted her resignation as prime minister. She was also criticized by the Black Panthers movement, or Oriental Jews, who complained of being neglected while she pressured the Soviet Union in the 1970s to allow the immigration of Soviet Jewry to Israel.

Meir was awarded the Israel Prize in 1975 for her special service to the state. She died in Jerusalem of lymphatic cancer. She stipulated in her will that no monuments or institutions be named after her, but a boulevard in Jerusalem and several streets and schools in Israel bear her name. The city of

New York dedicated a square to her on Broadway, and the University of Wisconsin–Milwaukee affixed her name to its library. The Center for Political Leadership at Metropolitan College in Denver was also named after her. Her autobiography, *My Life*, was published in 1974, and selections of her edited papers were published by H. Cristman. Another book, *My Father's House*, appeared in 1972. Her son, Menachem Meir, was born in 1924, and her daughter, Sara, in 1926.

MERNISSI, FATIMA (1940–). A Moroccan novelist, sociologist, and **feminist** who was born in Fez to a middle-class family and was brought up in a harem. Her semibiographical work, *Dreams of Trespass: Tales of Harem Girlhood*, published in English in 1994, describes her early years in Fez. She received a sound Islamic education, which enabled her later on to critique the traditional Islamic view of women. Her higher education was received at Muhammad V University at Rabat, after which she moved to Paris, where she worked as a journalist and studied political science at the Sorbonne. She received a PhD in sociology in 1973 from Brandeis University at Waltham, Massachusetts. Her dissertation, "Beyond the Veil: Male-Female Dynamics in Modern Muslim Society," was published in 1975. In it she disputes the common patriarchal view that Islamic jurisprudential texts promote the ideal of a silent and obedient Muslim woman. She has conducted research based on interviewing women for the United Nations Educational, Scientific and Cultural Organization (UNESCO) and the International Labour Organization (ILO). Her book, *The Veil and the Male Elite: A Feminist Interpretation of Islam*, which appeared in French in 1987, provides a fictional account of the lives of Muhammad's wives. Her other works include *Islam and Democracy: Fear of the Modern World* (1992), *Women's Rebellion and Islamic Memory* (1996), *Forgotten Queens of Islam* (1997), and *Scheherazade Goes West* (2001). Mernissi is currently a lecturer in sociology at Muhammad V University. She was awarded the Prince of Asturias Award with Susan Sontag. *See also* SAADAWI, NAWAL (1931–).

MISNAD, SHEIKHA MOUZA AL- (1959–). The wife of Sheikh Hamad bin Khalifa al-Thani, the ruler of Qatar, who is also a defender of women's rights and a formidable political force in that country. She was born in al-Khor, in the northern part of the Qatari Peninsula, where her father was an opponent of the ruler of Qatar, Sheikh Khalifa bin Hamad bin Abdallah al-Thani, her future father-in-law. Her family was exiled to Egypt and Kuwait, but returned later when she married the heir apparent in 1977. She is the second wife of the emir, or ruler, of Qatar, but is the most influential royal consort. She is also the mother of the crown prince, Sheikh Jassem bin Khalifa, and has played a prominent role in advancing women's rights.

Through her partnership with the ruler, she has pushed for the adoption of a constitution and granting the public freedoms of the press and of speech. She has succeeded in establishing women's rights to drive cars, run for public office, and choose whether or not to **veil** in public.

Sheikha Mouza accompanies her husband on most of his official travels abroad and sponsors frequent regional and international conferences on women's public roles in accordance with Islamic teachings. She has encouraged women's access to higher education and received a BA in sociology from the University of Qatar in 1986. She has been one of the most ardent supporters of American universities operating in Qatar and has worked toward the establishment of Education City, just outside the capital Doha, as a leading experiment for the promotion of university education in the Arab Gulf region.

Sheikha Mouza's involvement in Qatar's modernization and development plans has placed her at the center of Qatar's political life. Since 1999, she has served as chair of the Qatar Foundation for Education, Science, and Family Development, which was responsible for convening Qatar's first International Women's Conference on the rights of Arab working woman. Since 1989, she has been the president of Qatar's Ladies' Investment Company, which works to promote women's economic status in tandem with Qatar's National Bank. She created the Business Woman's Forum in 2000 to encourage women to play a role in development plans. The United Nations Educational, Scientific and Cultural Organization (UNESCO) has appointed her a Special Envoy for Education. Sheikha Mouza is viewed as a coruler of Qatar and often speaks authoritatively in public while her husband, sitting in the audience, remains silent.

Due to her influence, Qatari women make up around 40 percent of the country's workforce. Women were allowed to run for Qatar's municipal council in 1999, ahead of Kuwait, but none of the six who ran were elected. Around two-thirds of the University of Qatar's 9,000 students are females, as well as the dean of the university and several of its teaching staff. Despite her public role, Sheikha Mouza's picture was never published until recently due to the impact of Qatar's traditional Wahhabi culture. The taboo was broken when she appeared with her husband on a *Sixty Minutes* segment on the CBS television network. She is credited with establishing a ban on the use of young boys as jockeys in camel races, replacing them with robotic jockeys. *See also* EDUCATION: ARAB GULF STATES.

MOGHAIZEL, LAURE NASR (1929–1997). A Lebanese pioneer in the field of women's legal and human rights who was born in South Lebanon to a Christian Maronite middle-class family. She was an ardent member of the Kataib Youth Organization, established in 1936, which transformed itself into the Phalangist rightist political party after independence. Moghaizel pursued a law degree at Beirut's St. Joseph University while fully engaged in securing equal treatment for female members of the party. She and her husband, Joseph Moghaizel, broke away from the Kataib at the start of the Lebanese Civil War of 1958 due to its anti-Islamic ideology.

She founded *Bahithat* (Arabic; Researchers) with other female scholars opposed to the underlying sectarian tension of the second Lebanese Civil War (1974–1989). Her activities included joining efforts with like-minded Arab women in the region to form Arab Woman and Childhood Development and serving as the vice president of the International Council for Women. She was also a founding member of the Lebanese Association for Human Rights and of the Non-Violence Movement. In 1996, an organization named after her and her husband, the Moghaizel Foundation, was created to expand the principles they espoused.

Focusing on legal issues, she was successful in fighting for enfranchising women and granting them voting rights in 1953. One of her legal battles succeeded in 1959 in overturning laws that granted Christian women less than equal **inheritance** rights and required obtaining the husband's permission before a woman could travel outside the country. Moghaizel also published a great deal on women's and children's legal rights and on **honor crimes**. In recognition of her service, she was awarded the Order of the Cedar with the rank of Commander by the Lebanese government.

MOGHANNAM, MATIEL TOOMEH (ca. 1900–1992). A Palestinian **feminist** leader who played a noteworthy role in the history of Palestinian women beginning in the 1920s. She was born in Lebanon to parents who immigrated to the United States. She married a Jerusalem native, Moghannam Moghannam, while in the United States, where he was a lawyer and an officer of the Palestinian Defense Party. Upon returning to Palestine, she became one of the earliest general secretaries of the **Arab Women's Association (AWA)** of Palestine, in 1929. She gained notoriety after delivering a speech before Sir Edmund Allenby, the British commander who seized Jerusalem from the Ottomans, leading to the creation of the British Mandate Government over Palestine. Her speech was delivered when Allenby visited Jerusalem in 1933 to dedicate a Young Women's Christian Association (YWCA) building. She was chosen in 1933 to be the first Christian woman to address a large throng of people inside the Dome of the Rock Islamic shrine to emphasize the unity of the Palestinian national movement. During the same year, she gave a rousing speech from a balcony in Jaffa to demonstrators protesting the British Mandate and the Balfour Declaration, which opened the door to massive European Jewish immigration to Palestine. She left Jerusalem in 1938 and lived in Ramallah, finally returning to the United States when the Arab–Jewish War of 1948 began. Her book, *The Arab Wom-*

an and the Palestine Problem, appeared in 1937 and became a major reference work for the Palestinian feminist movement before the establishment of the state of Israel in 1948. *See also* ABD AL-HADI, TARAB (1910–1976).

MOSTAFAVI, ZOHRA KHOMEINI (1932–). She is the youngest of three daughters of **Ayatollah Ruhollah Khomeini**, born in the holy city of Qom. She grew up as one of five siblings and was tutored at home because her father mistrusted the secular educational system under the Pahlavis. She went on to complete a PhD in theology and Islamic studies at the University of Tehran, where she later taught philosophy to coeducational classes. She is said to be an admirer of the work of British philosopher Bertrand Russell (1872–1970) and German philosopher Emmanuel Kant (1724–1804). She chose a husband from a list of matrimonial candidates that her father preapproved. Her husband is an academic who runs a prestigious think-tank. She had always supported the right of Iranian women to study abroad, and her daughter studied law in Iran, then resided in London with her husband while he completed his medical training.

MOSTEGHANIMI AHLAM (1953–). An Algerian novelist and poet who was born in Tunisia and was the first female Algerian writer to use Arabic as a medium for her novels. She graduated from the Faculty of Letters at the University of Algeria and completed her PhD in 1980 at the Sorbonne in Paris. Her generation was the first postindependence group with some competence in the Arabic language, whereas previous generations of educated Algerians always wrote in French. Her professor at the Sorbonne was the renowned Arabist and sociologist Jacques Berque (1910–1995). He wrote the introduction to her dissertation, which appeared as a book in 1982 under the title *Algérie, Femmes et Écritures* (*Algeria, Women and Writing*). Another work that appeared in 1976 came out in Arabic: *Writing in a Moment of Nakedness*. Her most famous novel, which was read all over the Arab world, was *Memory of the Flesh* (*Dhikrayat al-jasad*), which appeared in Arabic in 1993. This novel is an imagined history of the **Algerian Revolution** (1954–1962) and the struggle of one woman, also named Ahlam, to reconstruct her Arab identity. *Memory of the Flesh* also elaborates on Algeria's postindependence problems. It is dedicated to Malek Haddad, a hero of the revolution, and to her own illiterate father. In 1998, she published *Chaos of the Senses* and in 2003, *Passing by a Bed*, both to critical acclaim.

Mosteghanimi received several literary awards, most notably for her novel *Memory of the Flesh*. This work received the Nur Award in 1996, for the best work by a woman written in Arabic. In 1998, she was awarded the Naguib Mahfouz Medal for Arabic Fiction for her novel *Chaos of the Senses*. She lives in Beirut.

MOYAL, ESTHER AZHARI (1873–1948). A Lebanese Jewish writer on women's issues and the publisher of a woman's magazine in Cairo, Egypt, who was born in Beirut. She graduated from the American University of Beirut (AUB), launching her career as a writer for several journals in the 1890s. Her husband, Simon Moyal, a physician, was also an author and shared her interest in women's issues. After immigrating to Cairo in 1899, she started publishing *al-Aila* (*The Family*) for a female readership. She also became a translator of novels and articles by European authors, such as the biography of Emile Zola (1840–1902), who wrote a series of essays condemning the trial of the Jewish French officer Emile Dreyfus. The Moyals left Cairo in the early part of the 20th century and settled in Jaffa. Simon died in Jaffa in 1915, and Esther died there in 1948 after spending a number of years in France.

MRABET, FADELA (1936–). An Algerian journalist and writer whose original name was Fatma Abda. A high school teacher at Constantine after Algeria achieved independence in 1962, she became a journalist, writing for *Alger-Républicain*, as well as a radio programmer. Her first book, *La femme algérienne*, published in 1964, criticizes the **Sharia** on the issue of women's rights, particularly the prohibition against a Muslim woman marrying a non-Muslim, whereas males are free to marry outside the faith. This was followed by *Les algériennes* (1967) and *L'Algérie des illusions* (1972), which was coauthored with her French husband, Mauric Tarek Maschino. Her fictional biography appeared in 2003 under the title *Une enfance singuliere* (*An Unusual Childhood*). In this book, she looks back with nostalgia on her early years in Algeria as well as describing instances of racism she experienced when she moved to France in 2004.

MUAWWAD, NAILAH AL-KHOURY (1940–). A member of the Lebanese parliament and the wife of a former Lebanese president, born in Beirut to Maronite Christian parents. She received her education at St. Joseph University in Beirut and started her career as a journalist for *L'Orient*. She married Rene Muawwad, who became the president of Lebanon in 1989, serving for only 17 days before he was assassinated. In 1992, she ran for election from her husband's district of Zgharta and won, becoming only the second female to serve in the Lebanese legislature, after **Myrna Bustani**. She was reelected in 1996, following in the footsteps of her father, uncle, and husband, all of whom had served in the same political body. She was related to Bechara al-Khoury, an independence-era president.

From the time she entered parliament, Muawwad was a strong advocate for increasing female representation in various government institutions through her work on the education committee. After the Lebanese Civil War ended in 1989, she became identified with the opposition, calling for Lebanon's independence from Syrian influence and control. She was successful in pushing for improved prison conditions for women and worked hard for the adoption of a new government policy allowing women to pass citizenship on to their children. She was nominated for president in 2004, in opposition to Emile Lahoud. She also established the Rene Muawwad Foundation (RMF) in 1990, which seeks to promote social justice and democracy through improved educational opportunities.

MUBARAK, SHEIKHA FATIMA BINT (ca. 1950–). She is the wife of Sheikh Zayed bin Sultan al-Nahyan (1918–2004), president of the United Arab Emirates (UAE). Sheikha Fatima is an award-winning leader who was recognized by the League of Arab States and the Egyptian government for her efforts on behalf of women. In 1972, she created the first women's organization, the Abu Dhabi Women's Society, with headquarters in the leading emirate of the UAE federation. Other branches developed in the rest of the emirates, leading to the creation of the UAE Women's Federation, which she headed. The Women's Federation has 31 affiliates, which provide services for needy women such as literacy classes, vocational training, child care lectures, and sport activities. The federation also has a semiofficial status and offers advice to the government on women's issues. The greatest challenge to this organization remains the difficulty in integrating Emirati women in the modern economy. Figures for 2003 indicate that women make up only 20 percent of the workforce. Yet Sheikha Fatima has succeeded in producing change in an unusual area, creating the first women's military academy in the Persian Gulf area. This allows Emirati women to join the army and the police force.

MUBARAK, SUZANNE SALEH THABET (1941–). She was Egypt's first lady from 1981 to 2011, the wife of Egyptian president Husni Mubarak, and was placed under house arrest with him at Sharm al-Sheikh in 2011. Suzanne Saleh Thabet was born in the town of al-Minya, south of Cairo, to an Egyptian father, Saleh Thabet, who was a pediatrician, and a British mother, Lily May Palmer, who was a nurse. Her father met her mother while he was a medical student at Cardiff University in Great Britain. Mubarak received her education at the elite St. Claire's School in Zeitoun, a Cairo suburb, where she met her future husband through her brother, a student of Mubarak, who was then an instructor in the Aviation Academy. They were married in 1958, and she spent the early years of her marriage raising her two sons, Alaa and Jamal. She enrolled at the American University of Cairo (AUC) in 1972, graduating in 1977 with a BA in political science. In 1982, she received an MA in the sociology of education from AUC.

Suzanne Mubarak at first avoided the limelight, preferring to remain in the background in reaction to the negative publicity resulting from **Jihan Sadat**'s public role during the previous presidency. But little by little, as Egypt's first lady, she began to play a visible role, particularly in the area of children's welfare and education. A noted exception was in 2008 when she served as a goodwill ambassador for the United Nations Food and Agriculture Organization (FAO). She was instrumental in the founding of the Child Museum at Cairo in 1985, in collaboration with the British Museum. She was the patron who introduced the Arabic version of *Sesame Street*, *Aalem Simsem*, to Egyptian television. She promoted this show to advance the reading skills of Egypt's children. She also convened the first Arab Women's Summit, in November 2000.

After the Egyptian uprising of 2011, she was accused of plotting the accession of her son Jamal to his father's position as president of Egypt. She was also accused of corruption, a charge that was largely leveled at her husband.

MUDAWANA, AL-. Also spelled Al-Moudawna, this is the set of laws governing family and **inheritance** matters in Morocco, or all matters of personal status. Its name in Arabic is *Mudawanat al-ahwal al-shakhsiyya*. The first Mudawana was issued in six books, as five *dhahirs* (or decrees), published between 22 November 1957 and 3 March 1958. Al-Mudawana is based on a significant text of Maliki law, which is the dominant jurisprudential school in North Africa, known as Sahnun ben Said's *Al-Mudawana al-kubra*, published in Kairouan, Tunisia, in the ninth century. Despite its Islamic genealogy, the Mudawana was codified in the manner of French laws, and was developed on the heels of Morocco's independence from France. When King Muhammad V first mentioned it in 1956 (r. 1957–1961), he presented it as an effort to reach back to Morocco's rich culture rather than rely on the legal codes of the colonial powers. The king also suggested that a new indigenous personal status law could emerge from the layers of outdated and traditional Islamic commentaries that overlaid the **Sharia**.

The reforms introduced in the Mudawana beginning in 1957 included raising the age of **marriage** for girls to 15 and for boys to 18. A woman's right to manage her own wealth, which was upheld by the Sharia, was now emphasized and written in the law. A woman's right to initiate **divorce** proceedings was made valid under certain circumstances clearly specified by the law. Yet the status of women in Morocco was still subject to conventions, traditions, and customary laws that never made their way into the Mudawana. In many ways, women's status remained minors under the law, but highly esteemed bearers of the national and cultural identity of Morocco. Often, women's social roles remained anchored within the patriarchal family even when civil constitutions, beginning in 1962, accorded all citizens, men and women, equality before the law. The Moroccan constitution, for instance, grants woman equal access to public employment, but women are denied the right to sign a marriage contract on their own without being represented by a male guardian. Nor were women able to voice objections to a husband taking additional wives or to get custody of their children after divorce.

There were additional efforts to reform the Moroccan personal status law over the years, beginning in 1972, when a royal commission of jurists drafted new laws. When these came to naught, two additional draft laws were prepared in 1979, but a group of clerical scholars was authorized by the Ministry of Justice to vet these proposals and managed to scuttle most of them. A severe financial crisis gripped Morocco in the mid-1980s, opening the way for additional popular demand for reforms when the country was forced to introduce structural adjustment changes to meet the demands of international lending agencies. These steps resulted in severe unemployment and the threat of popular uprisings, which led parliament to begin considering the possibility of writing a new constitution. Moroccan women seized this opportunity to hold meetings and engage in research to examine their Islamic rights according to the religious texts. A new group, the Union de l'Action Feminine, made up mostly of educated and upper-middle-class women, started a campaign to get a million signatures on a petition to rewrite the Mudawana. When the Union clashed with religious scholars, King Hassan II (r. 1961–1992) intervened by using his credentials as the Commander of the Faithful, which gives him jurisdiction over the clergy, to turn the union's reform suggestions over to a Council of Clergy in 1991. He named novelist **Leila Abuzeid** to another commission to evaluate and present recommendations for reform. Some of these measures were accepted, and the door to further reforms was opened. Among these were the need to obtain the wife's permission before seeking a divorce and permitting a widow who was at least 18 years of age to obtain custody of her children rather than turning them over to male relatives. A woman was no longer obligated to obey her husband, except where immoral conduct was involved.

After the death of King Hassan II, his modernizing son, King Muhammad VI (r. 1999–), was more willing to risk the displeasure of conservative religious elements in the interest of expanding the rights of women in the Mudawana. He introduced a set of sweeping reforms in parliament, which eventually passed in 2004 by using passages of the Quran as justification. These reforms made women's role within the family equal to that of men, reduced the dowry to a symbolic amount, equalized the marriage age of men and women, allowed women to stipulate monogamy as the basis of the marriage contract, restricted polygamy to two wives, recognized civil marriages contracted abroad, and allowed a divorced wife to keep the family home if she was awarded custody of minor children. Among the Islamic groups that opposed these changes was the Justice and the Spirituality Faction, led by a woman named Nadia Yassine (1958–), who maintained that the reforms were Western and did not adhere to native traditions.

MUFTI, INAAM QADDURA (1929–). A women's rights advocate and politician, she was born in Nazareth, Palestine. Her father was a judge and an Islamic scholar. She holds a BA in education and psychology, as well as a diploma in early education. She headed the Women's Teachers and Training College at Ramallah, the first educational institution created by the United Nations Relief and Works Agency (UNRWA) in the Middle East. She also produced radio programs for women at the Jordanian Broadcasting Service for many years.

Inaam Mufti was the first female member of a Jordanian cabinet, joining that of Prime Minister Abd al-Hamid Sharaf in 1979 as the minister of social development, a position she held for four years. In 2003, she was appointed to the Jordanian Upper House, where she is still serving. She also acted as a special development and international affairs adviser to Queen Noor of Jordan (r. 1978–1999). She is credited with establishing several institutions, such as the Noor al-Hussein Foundation, Women's Issues Organization, the Jubilee School of Amman, and the National Union for Jordanian Business Women. She has served on several United Nations Educational, Scientific and Cultural Organization (UNESCO) projects. She remains a firm believer in the education of women, which she feels is the surest road to social and political development.

MUHAMMAD, HARBIYYA (?–). An Iraqi novelist and **feminist** who held negative views of men. She condemned them because in her view, they lived like kings, disposing of women as they pleased. Her two novels, which elaborated on this theme, were *A Man's Crime* (1953) and *Who Is the Culprit?* (1954).

MURAD, LAYLA (1918–1995). An Egyptian singer and actress who appeared in numerous movies during the golden age of Egyptian musicals from the 1930s to the 1950s. She was born in Abbassiyya, a section of Cairo, to Ibrahim Zaki Murad, a well-known composer and singer from the 1920s to the 1940s. He was also the canter at one of Cairo's main synagogues.

Layla Murad's career took off under the tutelage of Togo Mizrahi (1901– ?), a prominent producer who featured her in most of his musical melodramas. One of these, which made her a star, was *Layla* (1942), based on Alexander Dumas's *La Dame aux Camilias*. Another musical in which she played a leading role was *Layla fi al-zalam* (*Layla in the Shadows*, 1944). She was also a protégée of Muhammad Abd al-Wahab, Egypt's best known singer, who starred in and composed for the early musical movies.

Murad gained great notoriety for converting to Islam in 1946 and her marriage to Anwar Wajdi, an actor and producer–director of films. Her two brothers, Ibrahim and Munir, were also involved in the movie industry. Munir, who established himself as a successful composer and actor, also converted to Islam. Before their divorce in 1953, Layla and Wajdi were leading actors in several musicals that captivated the Egyptian masses. She ended her film career suddenly in 1955, continuing to live in Cairo until her death in 1995. She had two additional failed marriages. Following rumors of a visit to Israel circulated on the pages of *Al-Ahram* daily, she was placed on the official Arab boycott list against Israel. President Jamal Abd al-Nasser, however, removed her name from that list, and an Egyptian commemorative stamp was issued in her name four years after her death.

MUSA, NABAWIYA (1886–1951). An Egyptian educator and advocate for women's rights to education and to work, she was born in the provincial town of Zagazig. Her father, who died before she was born, was an army captain named Musa Muhammad. Since there were no secondary schools for girls, she prepared for the state baccalaureate exam at home in 1907 and was the first woman to obtain this degree. She graduated from the Saniyya School, Egypt's first teacher-training school for women. She was the first woman to teach Arabic in government schools, which earned her the enmity of religious sheikhs, who monopolized this profession. She scored another first in 1909, being appointed as a school principal in Fayyoum, west of Cairo, from 1924 until 1926. She was later appointed by the Department of Education to be the chief inspector of women's education.

Musa was able to achieve most of her goals through dialogue and hard work. Having been denied admission to the newly opened Egyptian University in 1908, her reputation was such that she was invited the following year to lecture in Arabic to an extracurricular program for women. These lectures were created by **Huda Shaarawi** initially in French, but Musa was invited due to her reputation as an excellent Arabic teacher. She also founded two private schools for girls, Madrasat Banat al-Ashraf, in Cairo and Alexandria. Another of her organizations was the Association for the Progress of Women, which was founded in 1922, and a year later, she became one of the cofounders of the **Egyptian Feminist Union**. She attended the conference of International Woman Suffrage Alliance in 1923, which was held in Rome, where she delivered a speech in which she called for guaranteeing girls' right to education.

Musa was also a writer, beginning with her widely read biography, *My Story by My Own Pen*. In 1920, she published her influential book *Woman and Work*. She contributed pieces addressed to women in *Al-Balagh al-Usbuii* (*The Weekly Message*) and founded her own journal, *Al-Fatah* (*The Young Woman*), which ran between 1937 and 1943. She rejected **marriage** and was unveiled in the 1920s, dedicating her life to education. Her most famous work was *Woman and Work*, which argued that women had a right to work, dismissing all assertions of women's biological inferiority and weakness as unscientific. She maintained that women's work was the main guarantee of female emancipation, claiming that there were other occupations suitable for women besides midwife or teacher. She suffered a humiliating interruption to her otherwise illustrious career when she was sent to jail in 1942 for demonstrating against the government's pro-British policies. She died in 1951 after she retired from teaching and writing. A commemorative stamp was issued in her honor, and she remains a favorite of Egyptian feminists. *See also* FEMINIST MOVEMENT IN EGYPT.

MUSTAKFI, WALLADA BINT AL- (ca. 1001–1091). An Andalusian poet and princess during the Umayyid period in Spain (750–1031) who attained fame as the beloved of renowned Arab Spanish poet Abu al-Waleed Ahmad ibn Zaydun al-Makhzumi (1003–1071). She lived in Cordoba, the seat of the Umayyid rule in Spain, and was known for her blond mane and for being the daughter of one of the last caliphs in this dynasty. Wallada belonged to a large group of female poets who wrote verse during the Muslim period in Spain. Her fame derived from her literary salon, at which verses were read by male and female poets and where she followed the Arab custom of writing her verses on her elaborate sleeves. Ibn Zaydoun, a renowned poet in his own right, dedicated several poems to her. After a brief romance, Wallada rejected him and was the cause of his imprisonment by one of her lovers. Despite her literary prowess, only two of her love poems were preserved. She is said to have composed in a style for which the Abbassid poet Abu Nuwwas (747–815) was known. Her father, Caliph Muhammad al-Mustakfi III of Cordoba, was assassinated in 1024 after ruling for only two years.

MUZAHIM, ASIA BINT. She was one of the women mentioned in the Quran as deserving of paradise even if they were not Muslims. A wife of the pharaoh of Egypt, she declared her faith in the one God after witnessing the miracle of rescuing Prophet Yousef (Joseph) from the Nile River. Yousef became her adopted son, who grew up in the pharaoh's court. According to this story, which was based on the Quran, Asia believed in the one God and refused to follow the pharaoh's polytheistic system of belief. For this she was tortured until she died, and she will be among the first women to enter paradise. *See also* ANCIENT EGYPT, WOMEN IN.

N

NAAMAT. This was the first Jewish **feminist movement** in Palestine, originally known as Moetzet Hapoalot (Working Women's Council). It was founded in 1921 and sought equality for Jewish women in the workplace. Naamat sought to have women recognized as full partners in Israel's labor movement, which was among the major founders of the state when it became the Labor Party. Naamat affiliated with groups of American Jewish women, who helped with finances. The early programs established by this organization included vocational and agricultural schools and day-care services for working women. Special funds were dedicated to saving children in the early 1940s. As Naamat became a member of the World Jewish Congress, one of its activities after the establishment of the state was to encourage immigration to Palestine from other countries. It began to offer services to waves of Soviet and Ethiopian Jews who entered the country in the 1980s and the 1990s. But part of its agenda remained focused on women, creating special funds for women's higher education, legal aid departments, and centers for the prevention of domestic violence. Naamat partnered with the Tel Aviv municipality to found the Glickman Center for Battered Women.

Naamat is an international organization with 11 chapters in various countries. It is the largest women's organization in Israel, employing close to 5,000 individuals. Naamat enjoys a semiofficial status in Israel due to its close links with the Labor Party, the HISTADRUT, and the World Jewish Congress. The latest president, Talia Livni (2002–), is a member of the ruling committee of the World Zionist Organization and a graduate of Israel's National Security College. *See also* NON-GOVERNMENTAL ORGANIZATIONS (NGOs).

NAANAA, HAMIDA (1950–). A Syrian poet, novelist, journalist, and political activist who was born in Idlib, Syria. She received a BA in Arabic literature from the University of Damascus in 1971. She earned a postgraduate degree from the Sorbonne University in Islamic studies. She also worked for the United Nations Educational, Scientific and Cultural Organization (UNESCO) in Paris. Eventually, she headed the European and North African bureau of the Lebanese newspaper *Al-Safir*, which gave her an opportunity to interview major literary world figures such as Michel Foucault, Jean Paul Sartre, Simone de Beauvoir, and Aimé Césaire. Her interviews appeared in a book in 1990 titled *Debates with Western Thinkers*.

Naanaa's first foray into the world of literature was when she published her first poetry collection in 1970, *Anthems of a Woman Who Does Not Know Joy*. She wrote her first novel, *The Homeland in Our Eyes*, in 1979, which expressed the feelings of a restless generation of Arab women who participated in the Palestinian revolution. The heroine of this novel, Nadya, leads a life of fulfillment and adventure by taking part in Palestinian resistance operations, until she is expelled from her own political organization, to which she devoted several years of her life. Nadya's eventual immigration to Paris turns out to be a jarring experience and an adjustment challenge, during which she continues to advocate on behalf of the Palestinian cause. Naanaa's *Bloody Morning at Aden* (1989) dealt with the political split that destroyed the Yemen Socialist Party. She wrote two additional works of fiction: *Who Dares to Yearn?* (1992), which was translated into German, and *From the Notebook of a Woman* (1992), her political memoir. She lives in Paris with her French husband and is a senior correspondent for *Le Nouvel Afrique-Asie*.

NABRAWI, CEZA (1897–1985). An early Egyptian **feminist** and nationalist who was also a longtime protégée, and later associate, of **Huda Shaarawi**. Nabrawi's life story reads like fiction, with unexpected twists and turns. She was born outside of Cairo and taken to live in France by a distant and rich relative, Adila Nabrawi. She attended a convent school in Versailles and was enrolled later at the Saint Germaine des Près Institute in the French capital. Her foster mother sent her to a prestigious French school in Alexandria, Les Dames de Sion, where she studied until the suicide of Adila Nabrawi in Paris. Ceza Nabrawi refused to live with her birth parents and instead departed to Cairo to take up residence with another relative. It was then that Shaarawi, a friend of her late foster mother, took the young teen under her wing.

Nabrawi was already resistant to wearing the **veil** despite her grandparents' insistence. When she accompanied Shaarawi in 1923 to the meeting of the International Alliance for Women in Rome, she was more than willing to join her in a public act of unveiling at Cairo's train station upon their return. From that point on, she became Shaarawi's close assistant, joining in all of her projects. She was a cofounder of the **Egyptian Feminist Union (EFU)** and began her long tenure as the editor of *L'Égyptienne* when the famous magazine of the EFU first came out in 1925. The magazine enjoyed a long run but ceased publication in 1940, on the eve of World War II. The Arabic version of *L'Égyptienne*, *al-Masriyya*, which was started in 1937, quickly replaced the older publication under the editorship of Nimat Rashed. Nabrawi's involvement with the activities of the EFU developed on several levels. She represented the organization at various international conferences; lectured widely on the issue of female liberation, linking it always to national liberation; and was also an antiwar activist, campaigning for peace in Egypt and abroad. *See also* FEMINIST MOVEMENT IN EGYPT.

NAFZAWIYYA, ZAYNAB AL. A **Berber** queen who lived during the 11th century. She is mentioned by **Fatima Mernissi** in *The Forgotten Queens of Islam* (1997) as one of the major Berber queens of North Africa. She was married at first to Abu-Bakr ibn Umar, a leader of the Murabitun (Almoravids) federation, which swept through North Africa in the name of a purified brand of Islam. Abu-Bakr divorced her in 1071 when he proceeded to the Great Sahara region to conquer more territory, asking his cousin and military lieutenant, Yusef ibn Tashfin, to marry her. The latter was 63 years old at the time (ca. 1010 or 1020–1106) and a rising star as the leader of the Almoravid armies. Zaynab became a valued and powerful adviser and amassed more authority as ibn Tashfin swept through North Africa. He eventually conquered al-Andalus (Andalusia) in Spain, removing the quarrelsome Taifa kings from their seat of power. Ibn Tashfin consolidated his control over southern Spain and the Maghreb or all of North Africa, eventually building the then capital of Morocco, the city of Marrakech. He reigned from 1061 through 1106. Zaynab was a wealthy woman who let him use her fortune to build his army and equip it with modern weapons. Historians describe her as being in charge of his *"mulk"* (rule). He took her advice on all matters of state. *See also* KAHINA, AL- (?–ca. 698).

NAMIR, ORA TOIB (1930–). An Israeli politician, Knesset member, and social worker. She was born in Haderah, Palestine, and grew up on Hoglah, a moshav or cooperative farm. She was enrolled in the Jewish paramilitary units during the 1948 Arab–Israeli War, serving in the Upper Galilee region. She received her education at Lewinsky Seminary and Givat ha-Sheloshah Seminary, both in Israel. Between 1954 and 1957, she studied English literature at Hunter College, New York, while serving as a secretary with the Israeli delegation to the United Nations.

Namir worked as a secretary for the Tel Aviv architectural firm that designed the Knesset building, headed by Shimon Powsner. She married Mordechai Namir in 1959, who was elected Tel Aviv's first mayor on the Labor Party ticket that same year. She continued her work as a social worker, a career path that she followed from 1967 until 1979, serving on the secretariat of **Naamat**, the women's social service section of the HISTADRUT, Israeli's labor federation. Her service as a member of the Knesset began in 1973, but after her husband's death in 1975, Prime Minister Yitzhak Rabin appointed her as the chairperson of a committee of inquiry concerning the status of Israeli women. The committee's final report was presented to Prime Minister Menachem Begin in 1978, documenting great discrimination against women. Her service in the Knesset also included chairing the Labor and Welfare Committee. In 1989, she was considered a serious contender for the position of secretary-general of the Labor Party, opposite Michael Harish, but ended up withdrawing her name from the race. Prime Minister Rabin later appointed her as the first minister of the environment in Israel. In 1992, he named her as minister of labor and welfare. Her last public office was as ambassador to the People's Republic of China, 1996–2000. *See also* FEMINIST MOVEMENT IN ISRAEL.

NASER, NABIHA (1891–1951). A Palestinian educator who was born in Birzeit, Palestine, and received her high school education in Bethlehem. She left Birzeit as a young woman to join her sister Wadia in the Sudan, where the British administration had a great need for Arabic-speaking teachers. She is credited with founding a girls' school that became the nucleus for the future Birzeit University. She founded this school in 1924, with the help of her friend Ratibeh Shqeir. A boys' school developed next to it, and the two schools eventually merged and became first a junior college in the 1960s, under the direction of her brother, Musa Naser, and then a full-fledged university in 1974. Birzeit is the oldest university in Palestine, maintaining a tradition of coeducational and secular education. Nabiha Naser was also a feminist nationalist, like most Palestinian women of her generation. She was an advocate of pan-Arabism and addressed one of the **Egyptian Feminist Union**'s conferences in 1938 in Cairo. *See also* EDUCATION: PALESTINE.

NASIF, MALAK HAFNI (1886–1918). An Egyptian pioneering **feminist** and writer who was also known as Bahithat al-Badiya (Researcher of the Desert). She was born in Cairo to a father who studied at **Al-Azhar** with **Muhammad Abduh**. She was her father's eldest child and the object of his nurturing and encouragement. She attended the girls' section of Abbas Primary School in 1895 and was enrolled later at Saniyya School, Cairo's first teacher-training school for women, graduating in 1905. While at this school, she delivered lectures on Fridays at the Egyptian University's Women's program established by **Huda Shaarawi**. Her contributions to *al-Jarida*, a leading liberal paper, were published in 1910 under the title *al-Nisaiyat* (Feminist Pieces). In 1911, she presented a set of demands to a national meeting at Heliopolis, a Cairo suburb.

In 1907, Nasif married Abd al-Sattar al-Basil, a Bedouin chief of al-Ramah tribe, at the Fayyoum Oasis, west of Cairo. Although she left her teaching career after she went to live with him, she continued to write under the pseudonym Bahithat al-Badiya. She also continued to give public lectures, her feminist views being strengthened after discovering that her husband was already married and had a daughter. Her personal pain was expressed in letters to another feminist, **Mai Ziyadeh**, and in her letters to the government, calling for reforming the personal status code. Her other demands included allowing women to participate in congregational prayers on Fridays, opening all fields of study to women, condemning abuses in **divorce** cases, and addressing the injustices of polygamy. She wrote as an Islamic modernist following in Abduh's shoes and did not stress the need to end **veiling**, although she argued that the battle would be uneven until society recognized the un-Islamic origin of this custom. In response to the Italian invasion of Libya, which bordered on Egypt's western desert, she started a nursing training program for women. She died at age 32 after a bout of influenza and was publicly eulogized by Shaarawi and by many influential male figures. Nasif's brother, Majd al-Din Hafni Nasif, published her writings in 1962 under the title *Legacy of Bahithat al-Badiya*. See also FEMINIST MOVEMENT IN EGYPT.

NASIRI, BOUTHAINA (1947–). An Iraqi writer of short stories and a publisher, born in Baghdad, where she earned a BA in English literature in 1967 from the University of Baghdad. She began to publish her short stories in 1974, completing seven volumes of her collections. Among these, and the most well-known, is *Final Night*. She has been living in Cairo since 1970, where she is the director of Dar Ishtar Publishing House. In 1995, her collected essays appeared under the title *On the Borders of the Homeland*. She received a prize at the first Arab Women's Book Fair, held in 1995 in Cairo, for her story collection *Watan Akher (Another Homeland)*.

NASR, ZIYA ASHRAF. She was an Iranian defender of women's rights and descendant of two leading scholars of the constitutional period around the turn of the 19th century. On her father's side, she counted the most famous conservative scholar of his day, Sheikh Fazl Allah Nuri (1843–1909), and on her mother's side, she was descended from one of the backers of the constitutional movement, Sayyed Muhammad Tabatabai (1842–1920). She attended Madrassah I-Namus, Iran's first Muslim school for girls, which began to operate in 1907. Her friendship with Iran's leading feminist of that period, Siddiqeh Dawlatabadi, transformed her into a strong advocate for women's rights. See also FEMINIST MOVEMENT IN IRAN.

NASRALLAH, EMILY ABI-RASHED (1931–). One of Lebanon's most prolific writers and a famous novelist, born in the village of Kfeir in the southern part of the country. She attended a private boarding school in Shweifat. After graduation, she taught for a short period of time at the same school, then enrolled at Beirut University College, completing a BA in 1958 in education and literature. She taught at the Ahliya School and wrote for many years for *al-Sayyad*, one of Beirut's most popular magazines. In 1962, she became a well-known author after publishing her novel, *September Birds*, which was recognized as a major literary achievement and went into six printings. It also received three literary prizes. Her work became known as the finest writing on women's alienation during the time of the Lebanese Civil War (1974–1989) and women's relegation to an inferior corner by the attitudes and actions of educated men. She lived through the agony of seeing her husband, Philip Nasrallah, kidnapped by military troops. This incident inspired her novel, *Those Memories*, published in 1980. She refused to leave Beirut during the hostilities, and her house in West Beirut was burned during the Israeli invasion of 1982. Her other novels include *The Oleander Tree* (1968), *The Hostage* (1974), *Flight against Time* (1981), and *The Sleeping Amber* (1995). She also wrote short stories, children's stories, and three volumes of biographies of Oriental women. She continues to reside in Beirut.

NASSAR, SATHEJ (ca. 1900–ca. 1970). A Palestinian political activist, women's rights advocate, and journalist, of Iranian origin. She was the granddaughter of Bahaullah (aka Mirza Hussein Ali Nuri, 1817–1892), the founder of the Bahai faith, who left Iran to escape prosecution and settled near Haifa in British-ruled Palestine. Sathej was married to Najib Nassar (1865–1947), the Greek Orthodox editor of one of Palestine's oldest Arabic newspapers, *al-Karmel*, founded in 1908 in Haifa. Her husband was called the "Sheikh of Palestinian journalists" and was a leading anti-Zionist voice of his day. Her articles and translations from the foreign press began to appear on the pages of this paper in the 1920s. She wrote a special page for women, titled *Safhat al-nisaa*. This page and the rest of the paper became a vehicle for feminist advocacy and women's involvement in politics and national resistance to Zionism and British rule. As a founder of the Arabic Women's Union's Haifa branch, she called on Muslim and Christian women alike to resist foreign rule. This branch surpassed all others in its militancy and was often involved in violent demonstrations. She incurred the wrath of the British authorities, who came to view her as a dangerous agitator. She was incarcerated in Bethlehem's women's prison in 1939–1940 under the Emergency Regulations, but she continued her activities after her release. She managed to put out the paper herself between 1941 and 1944, despite being denied an official permit. Her husband was buried in Nazareth, but she continued to write for British and Syrian papers following her flight to Syria as a refugee. She is believed to have died in Damascus.

NATIONAL WOMEN'S COMMITTEE OF YEMEN (NWC). This is an official women's organization founded in 1993 by a ministerial decree. The committee changed its mission following the fulfillment of its official role as a coordinator of the Fourth World Conference on Women. By 2000, the NWC was attached to the Supreme Council for Women's Affairs, which was under the purview of the Prime Minister's Office. The NWC gathered together heads of women's departments in various ministries and government offices, as well as directors of women's bureaus within various political parties. The committee's role is purely advisory, consisting of following state policies on women and conducting surveys, such as the 1996 report *The Status of Women in Yemen*. Branches of the NWC offer seminars and special training programs for women, and it publishes a monthly newsletter, *Al-Yamaniyya* (*The Yemenite*). The NWC enjoyed the leadership of some well-known Yemeni women in the past, such as **Amat al-Alim al-Suswa**, Rashida al-Hamadani, and Huriya Mashhur. *See also* KARMAN, TAWAKKUL (1979–).

NEFERTITI, QUEEN (ca. 1370 BCE–ca. 1330 BCE). She was the principal wife of King Amenhotep IV (later known as King Akhenaten) of the Eighteenth Dynasty of Egypt, who became part of the religious revolution initiated by her husband. This revolution established the god Aten, or the Sun-God, as the god of the land, replacing Amun-Ra and other deities of previous dynasties. Nefertiti was depicted on temple walls more often than any other queen and was usually shown participating in the rituals of the new faith. One such example was when she was portrayed making an offering to Aten without the presence of Akhenaten, and as a queen receiving the submission of conquered populations. Although all principal wives and the mothers of pharaohs played ritual roles, she was shown to have been a major figure of the new faith, because she appeared on stelae from household alters seated with Akhenaten below the disk that depicted Aten. Her figure appears mostly in the Karnak temples, which her husband built after removing the capital from Thebes to Akhetaten, known today as Amarna, in an unsettled area in central Egypt. She had many titles, chief among them being Lady of the Two Lands, Mistress of Upper and Lower Egypt, Lady of All Women, and Great of Praises.

Changes in the insignia she wore illustrate the dimensions of the religious revolution begun by her husband. At first, she was depicted wearing the insignia typical of all Egyptian queens beginning in the Eighteenth Dynasty, which consisted of the double uraeus, or royal cobra. This represented Upper and Lower Egypt and was often decorated with horns and a sun-disk. She did not wear the vulture headdress common to all previous queens because it was inappropriate to the new faith, the vulture being a representative of Nekhbet, the goddess of Upper Egypt. Instead, Nefertiti wore a tall blue crown toward the end of her life, with which she is now identified due to her famous bust in Berlin's Neues Museum. This bust is thought to be the work of a famous sculptor, Thutmose, in whose workshop it was found. Due to her prominent role in the rituals of kingship, some historians assumed that she was co-regent rather than a principal wife of the pharaoh. Some have asserted that she did rule briefly after her husband's death and before the accession of Tutankhamun to the throne, identifying her with Neferneferuaten. Most historians, however, believe that she died around the 14th year of Akhenaten's reign, when she suddenly disappeared from the scene. There is no substantiated explanation of the manner of her death, but it is generally believed that she died as a result of a severe plague. She was not Akhenaten's sole wife, however, for he was known to have been married to Mitannian and to a Babylonian princess. Nefertiti achieved the greatest prominence of any queen in the monuments and ranks second only to Cleopatra as the most famous queen of Egypt. *See also* ANCIENT EGYPT, WOMEN IN.

NIATI, NOURIYA (1948–). A multifaceted Algerian artist: a painter, singer, poet, and performance artist. She was born in Algeria, where she received her early training, and studied art at the Camden and Croyden art schools in Great Britain in the 1970s. She is best known for her romantic portrayal of Arab women as they were depicted during the colonial period in postcards and orientalist paintings by famed artists like Eugéne Delacroix. Her most famous installation of paintings is titled No to Torture and Bringing Water from the Fountain Has Nothing Romantic about It, both produced in the 1990s. Her work exposes the complicity of French artists in the colonial violence inflicted on Algerian women by presenting sensual images of secluded Arab women. She also sings, performing in the Andalusian *shaabi* and *rai* styles. *See also* ALGERIAN REVOLUTION (1954–1962).

NON-GOVERNMENTAL ORGANIZATIONS (NGOs). Non-governmental organizations have had a great impact on women's lives in the Middle East and North Africa since the beginning of the 20th century. They are not necessarily political or civic in nature as in Western society, but are communal efforts that developed into an indigenous form of NGO. Most claim modest objectives focused on charity works and the immediate alleviation of poverty. Filling a space between government and society, these NGOs inevitably lead to a greater mobilization of their members and enhance their gender identity. Some of these early efforts evolved later into quasi-political activities that meshed seamlessly into other organized groups in society.

Egypt has featured one type of informed neighborhood organization exclusively for women, known as *jamiyyah*, for a very long time. This is a community-based association serving the needs of lower-income families. It is set up as a rotating credit or savings association and is usually led by an individual with a reputation for honesty and reliability. This leader is charged with vetting and approving new members, collecting the monthly contributions, and turning them over to the individual recipient of the monthly savings amount. Participants in this association are usually residents of the same neighborhood as their own friends and relatives. The success ratio of these associations is always high because the reputation of members rests on their compliance with the rules. Because no profit is made, and no interest on the investment is collected, the association is considered ethically sound and superior to banks in its adherence to Islamic principles, which oppose the payment of interest. The popularity of these organizations is also due to the unavailability of banking credit to poor families and the informality of the operation, which often results in awarding the monthly sum to the person who is most in need. In addition, these savings associations are outside of the purview of government agencies and are not subject to taxation. Egypt has had other NGOs that were women-directed and played a huge role in the emancipation of women, the most famous being **Mabarat Muhammad Ali** and the **Egyptian Feminist Movement.**

In the Arab Gulf countries, the NGO phenomenon is not as present as in other countries because of the general insularity of the family structure and women's limited mobility. Indigenous NGOs for women are found mostly in Kuwait and Bahrain and are restricted in the rest of the Gulf countries. Governments like those of the United Arab Emirates, Qatar, and Saudi Arabia tolerate only women's charitable organizations, which are usually sponsored by women of the ruling families.

In Syria, upper-middle-class women have organized themselves in NGOs in urban centers since the beginning of the 20th century. One of these is called The Light of Damascus. Most began as purely charitable endeavors, which later expanded into nationalist and feminist advocacy work. The rise of the Baath Party since the early 1970s brought about the demise of independent NGOs and the rise of quasi-governmental women's organizations. This is illustrated by the incorporation of the Syrian Women's Federation into the Baath Party. Much of its work centered on fighting illiteracy among women, which was a government priority. After 2000, when Bashar Assad assumed the presidency of Syria, his wife, **Asma Akhras**, devoted her energies to women's development projects in 2001, such as Firdos, or the Fund for Integrated Rural Development of Syria, the country's first rural development project for women.

In Jordan, NGOs began to appear under the sponsorship of the royal family and were centered largely on charitable work. Queen Zein (1916–1994), King Hussein's mother, along with **Sabriya Hashem**, sponsored the Jordanian Red Crescent Society for many years, culminating in building a hospital and other charitable projects benefiting women. A number of NGOs were also created by religious associations. The Jordanian Women's Union dates back to the 1940s. Some NGOs specialized in combating domestic violence and promoting health education and rural development. In the 1990s, a number of NGOs came together to form coalitions against **honor crimes**. These were led by **Queen Rania**, wife of King Abdullah II.

In Lebanon, several charitable organizations were formed by upper-class women at the beginning of the 20th century. These associations, however, reflected Lebanon's sectarian divisions. During the Civil War period (1974–1990), charitable associations multiplied to provide social services normally delivered by the government. The oldest NGO benefiting Shii women in southern Lebanon was El-Sadr Foundation, created by **Rabab al-Sadr**. Another group, the Women's Association of Deir al-Ahmar, is a rural development organization that advances micro-credit to women.

In Turkey, charitable foundations flourished during the Ottoman Empire, many being religious in nature. It is estimated that Turkey today has more than 90,000 civic associations and 5,000 foundations. Among the older organizations were the 1919 Anatolian Women's Protection of the Motherland and the Union of Turkish Women. The Union had a political background and was founded in 1924. Beginning in the 1970s, most women's NGOs became focused on women's rights and were increasingly affiliated with leftist parties. One such group, which operated between 1975 and 1980, was the Progressive Women's Association, which helped working women. Women's groups began to help Kurdish women by offering counseling and encouraging them to engage in politics. One such group was Jiyan (Life), which emerged in 1997. One of the most effective women's NGOs is Flying Broom, based in Ankara, which specializes in coordinating the activities of all women's organizations in the country through maintaining databases. Another NGO, Ka-Der, or the Organization to Educate and Support Women Political Candidates, assists in regional development programs and runs children's centers. The Women's Center in Diyarbaker, a predominantly Kurdish city, was founded in 1999 to provide shelters for victims of domestic abuse. Since the 1990s, Islamic NGOs have also begun to emerge, among which Women's Movement against Discrimination and the Association for Freedom of Thought and Educational Rights defend the right of Muslim women to wear the **veil** in the workplace and at universities. *See also* ARAB INTER-

NATIONAL WOMEN'S FORUM (AIWF); ARAB WOMEN'S ASSOCIA-
TION OF PALESTINE (AWAP); ARAB WOMEN'S DEVELOPMENT
SOCIETY (AWDS); ARAB WOMEN'S EXECUTIVE COMMITTEE
(AWEC); ARAB WOMEN'S SOLIDARITY ASSOCIATION (AWSA);
CAGDAS YASAMI DESTEKLEMI DERNEGI (CYDD); COUNCIL ON
WOMEN'S AFFAIRS (CWA)—IRAN; CULTURAL AND SOCIAL
COUNCIL ON WOMEN'S AFFAIRS—IRAN (CSCWAI); EGYPTIAN
FEMINIST UNION (EFU); GENERAL DIRECTORATE ON THE STAT-
US AND PROBLEMS OF WOMEN; GENERAL FEDERATION OF IRA-
QI WOMEN (GFIW); GENERAL FEDERATION OF SYRIAN WOMEN
(GFSW); GENERAL UNION OF PALESTINIAN WOMEN (GUPW);
HIGH COUNCIL OF IRANIAN WOMEN'S ASSOCIATIONS; LEBA-
NESE WOMEN'S COUNCIL (LWC); MABARAT MUHAMMAD ALI;
NAAMAT; ORGANIZATION FOR THE IMPROVEMENT OF THE
STATUS OF WOMEN; SUDANESE WOMEN'S UNION (SWU); UNION
OF FEMINIST ACTION; UNION OF TUNISIAN WOMEN; WAQF;
WOMEN AND FAMILY AFFAIRS CENTER—NABLUS; WOMEN'S
CENTER FOR LEGAL AID AND COUNSELING—JERUSALEM; WOM-
EN'S FORUM FOR RESEARCH AND TRAINING—YEMEN (WFRT);
WOMEN'S INTERNATIONAL ZIONIST ORGANIZATION (WIZO);
WOMEN'S LIBRARY AND INFORMATION CENTER—ISTANBUL.

NUUN MAGAZINE. This is a feminist quarterly publication of the **Arab Women's Solidarity Association** (AWSA) in Egypt. The title of this Arabic language magazine is derived from the letter "nuun" in the Arabic alphabet, which is added to all plural forms of feminine words. The magazine was first printed in 1989 and was read by AWSA's members only due to restrictions imposed on the recruitment activities of **non-governmental organizations (NGOs)**. Subjects covered on its pages ranged from gender issues to political questions, such as the quest for genuine democracy and independence in the Arab world. The magazine was shut down in 1991 by Egyptian authorities because of its criticism of the Egyptian–American alliance during the first Gulf War. *See also* SAADAWI, NAWAL (1931–).

OBEID, THORAYA (1945–). A Saudi United Nations official and social development and population expert, born in Baghdad to Saudi parents. She studied at the American College for Girls in Cairo and later at Mills College in California, where she was the first Saudi female recipient of a scholarship to study abroad. In 1974, she graduated from Wayne State University in Detroit with a PhD in cultural anthropology and English literature.

She was expected to take up the position of dean of the Women's College of King Abd al-Aziz University at Jedda, but instead became a social affairs officer for the Economic Commission for Western Asia (ECWA), where she directed women's programs. In 1984, she became involved with the League of Arab States, participating in the Arab States Working Groups for Formulating the Arab Strategy for Social Development.

Between 1991 and 1992, Obeid worked for al-Nahdha, a women's philanthropic organization in Saudi Arabia, transforming it into an institute offering a variety of training programs for women. In 1992, she returned to the UN as chief of the Social Development and Population Division. Her work with the UN involved convening conferences on women in the Arab world, such as the UN Inter Agency Task Force on Gender, which met in 1996 in Amman, Jordan. In 2001, she was promoted to the position of executive director of the UN Fund for Population Activities (UNFPA). By that time, the Population Fund had already come under the directorship of international female experts such as Dr. Nafis Sadik of Pakistan. This fund, the largest multinational resource for population assistance, which was founded in 1969, undertakes projects to assist developing countries in improving **family planning** and reproductive health, as well as preventing violence against women. In this position, Obeid has demonstrated great sensitivity to cultural and religious values, as called for by the 1994 Cairo International Conference on Population and Development. She has also supported programs to assist victims of sexual abuse during war.

OLAYAN, LUBNA (1955–). A Saudi financial chief who is also an invest-ment banker. She received a BA in agriculture from Cornell University in 1977 and an MBA from Indiana University. In 1983, she joined the family corporation, Olayan Financing Company (OFC), founded in 1947 by her father, Suleiman S. Olayan. The OFC is a holding company for more than 40 other companies, which owns major stakes in multinational banks, including Credit Suisse and JP Morgan. She rose to the position of chief executive officer, having joined the company in 1983. Her brother Khaled and her sisters Hutham and Hayat also sit on the board. In 2004, she was the first woman elected to the board of a Saudi-listed company, Saudi Hollandi Bank. She sits on boards of several international companies, such as Citigroup. As the most influential woman in Saudi Arabia, she has managed to break many barriers faced by women, such as when she addressed the Jedda Economic Conference in 2004, attended by then President Bill Clinton. She joined the international advisory board of Rolls Royce in 2006. She was a cochair of the World Economic Forum (WEF) at Davos in 2005.

Olayan has also participated in the work of nonbusiness groups, for exam-ple, joining the board of the Arab Thought Forum (ATF) in Beirut in 2002 and the board of King Abdullah University of Science and Technology. She is also on the advisory board of the U.S. Council on Foreign Relations. She was listed by *Time* magazine as one of the top 100 most influential people in the world for the year 2005. She was also ranked as the ninth wealthiest individual in the Arab world. She is married to an American attorney, John Xefos, and has three daughters.

ORGANIZATION FOR THE IMPROVEMENT OF THE STATUS OF WOMEN. This is the oldest women's organization in Turkey, which also translates as the Elevation of Women Organization (Tali-I Nisvan). It was founded in 1909 by pioneering Turkish feminist **Halide Edip** following the Committee of Union and Progress's seizure of power in 1908. It changed direction in 1913, when it was renamed the Organization for the Rights of Women, adopting a more radical agenda that called for granting women passports and allowing them to be employed in the postal service. The latter demand was granted when wartime conditions created a need for women's labor, recruiting them to replace males as clerical workers and even in street construction work. Women also volunteered for military duty during the Turkish–Greek War of 1920–1922. Both this organization and another more nationalist and pro-Islamic group known as the Islamic Association for the Employment of Ottoman Women were eclipsed after the establishment of the Republic of Turkey. **Mustafa Kemal Ataturk**'s reforms, particularly the new Turkish Personal Status Law, which changed women's status by decree, rendered these independent women's organizations redundant. *See also* NON-GOVERNMENTAL ORGANIZATIONS (NGOs).

OTHMAN, AMAL (1934–). An Egyptian cabinet minister who was also a member of parliament. She was a professor of law at Cairo University when she joined the Arab Socialist Union (ASU) in 1974. President Anwar Sadat (r. 1970–1981) appointed her in 1977 as minister of social affairs, a position she held until 1997, making her the longest serving cabinet member in the history of modern Egypt. After the creation of the National Democratic Party (NDP) in 1978 as Egypt's hegemonic political organization, Othman hitched her star to the party's fortunes. She became the first woman to occupy the position of deputy speaker of the People's Assembly, or parliament. She was elected as the NDP's secretary for women's affairs between 1979 and 1984. Under Husni Mubarack's presidency (1981–2011), she became even more important as a party loyalist, being appointed a member of the NDP's politburo. Since 2005, she has been the elected chair of the legislature and constitutional committees of the People's Assembly.

Othman's close alliance with the Sadat and Mubarak regimes exposed her to great criticism from the opposition. When she won a seat representing Cairo's Duqqi district at one point, the Muslim Brotherhood, then a quasi-party, claimed that her election was rigged in order to prevent its own supreme guide, Maamoun al-Hudhaybi, from being elected. She was also a close ally of **Jihan Sadat**, the president's wife, and may have participated in drafting Law 44, which introduced drastic reforms in Egypt's personal status law. Both Othman and Jihan Sadat were accused by independents of preselecting female loyalists to join the ranks of the NDP. After the assassination of President Sadat in 1981 and Jihan Sadat's departure from Egypt, Othman became the official representative of Egypt's women at international meetings and local conferences.

OUNISSI, ZHOR (1936–). An Algerian teacher, novelist, and politician who was born in Constantine and educated in Egypt. She was elected to the Algerian parliament, serving from 1977 until 1982 as only one of 10 women in the 260-member legislative body. She also became the first woman to be named to a cabinet post, when she became minister of social affairs and national guidance in 1982. She authored the following collections of short stories: *The Soft Pavement* (1967), *The Extending Shadows* (1982), *On the Other Shore* (1984), and *Old Women of the Moon* (1998). She also published two novels: *From the Diary of a Female Teacher* (1978) and *Lunja and the Monster* (1995).

P

PAHLAVI, ASHRAF (1919–). She is the twin sister of the last Shah of Iran, Muhammad Reza Pahlavi (r. 1941–1979). Her full name was Ashraf al-Mulki. She was the second daughter of **Shah Reza Pahlavi** (r. 1925–1941), the founder of the dynasty, and his wife, Taj al-Molouk. She and her older sister, Princess Shams, were among the earliest women in Iran to shed the **veil**. She became a close confidante of her brother the shah, carrying out several delicate negotiating missions on his behalf that produced landmark agreements such as the Algiers Accords of 1975 between Iran and Iraq. She is considered to have been the main influence behind her brother's decision to participate in 1953 in an American intelligence scheme, Operation Ajax, which toppled the nationalist premier, Muhammad Mossadegh (r. 1951–1953).

Princess Ashraf became the official face of the Iranian regime's reform program benefiting women. This was accomplished through her involvement with the United Nations and by creating and heading major organizations within Iran. She and her brother defined women's urgent needs as health, education, and food, but never supported the political rights of women of the opposition. She became a major force during the official campaign to combat illiteracy among women, joining the International Consultative Liaison Committee for Literacy. In 1965, she was chosen as chair of the United Nations Commission on the Status of Women. In 1967, she was made Iran's delegate to the UN Commission on Human Rights and to the UN Economic and Social Council (ECOSOC). She played a large role on the High Council for Women (later known as the **High Council of Iranian Women's Associations**), consisting of 17 organizations, serving as its honorary chair in 1959, with **Mahnaz Afkhami** as its secretary general. Female activists seeking to change such laws as requiring a male relative's permission for travel and handing down soft punishment for **honor crimes** found the Princess and **Empress Farah Diba Pahlavi** ready conduits of information to the shah. Her support for women's rights was instrumental in the adoption of the Family Protection Laws of 1967.

Forced into exile for the second time after the Islamic Revolution, she sought refuge in Paris with her third husband, Mehdi Bushehri. Her first period of exile was from 1951 to 1953, when Prime Minister Mossadegh nationalized Iran's oil industry. She also escaped an assassination attempt in 1976, but her son was killed in Paris by agents of the Islamic Republic of Iran. She has authored two memoirs: *Faces in a Mirror: Memories from Exile* (1980) and *Time for Truth* (1995). She wrote a book in French, *Jamais resignee* (1981). She is the only surviving child of Shah Reza Pahlavi. *See also* FEMINIST MOVEMENT IN IRAN; NON-GOVERNMENTAL OR-GANIZATIONS (NGOs).

PAHLAVI, FARAH DIBA (1938–). Iranian queen (1959–1979) and third wife of Shah Muhammad Reza Pahlavi. She was the daughter of Sohrab Diba and Farideh Ghotbi, born in Tehran and educated at Tehran's Jeanne d'Arc Lycee Razi and Tehran's Italian School, later majoring in architecture at the École d'Architecture in Paris. She was introduced to the shah while she was a student in Paris, becoming his third wife (after Princess Fawzia of Egypt and Soraya Esfendiary Bakhtiari) on 20 December 1959. She was the only one to produce a male heir, Cyrus Reza, born in 1960, later giving birth to two daughters, Farahanaz and Leila, and another son, Alireza. In 1967, she was made an empress and given the title Shahbanou, which allowed her to partici-pate in 1971 in the glittering celebration of 2,500 years of Iranian monarchic rule at the Persepolis ruins.

The greatest impact of the empress was on women's welfare and the improvement of the arts and architecture of Iran. During the 1970s, the monarchy's last decade before the Islamic revolution, she had some impact on the work of the Ministry of Culture and Art, opposing the construction of high-rise buildings. She supported women's organizations and children's welfare, and the shah claimed that she headed close to 40 organizations. The empress was elevated to the status of regent in the event of her husband's death before the heir attained his majority, a step undertaken in 1967 by amending the 1906 constitution. When her husband went into exile in 1979, she accompanied him on his quest for a final resting place, ending up in Cairo, where he died in 1980. She continues to live in the United States and France and maintains a strong interest in the internal affairs of Iran. She is the author of *An Enduring Love, My Life with the Shah: A Memoir*, published in 2004. *See also* PARSA, ESFAND FARROUKHRU (1922–1980).

PAHLAVI, REZA SHAH (1878–1944). The Iranian ruler and founder of the Pahlavi dynasty, originally an officer of the Cossack Regiment. He seized power in 1921 from the last Qajar shah with the help of his associate, Sayyid Zia Tabatabai. By the time, he declared himself the Shah of Iran in 1925, he had changed his name from Reza Khan (Khan being a military title) to Reza Pahlavi. He is considered the first major modernizing figure in modern Iran, who transformed the status of women considerably.

Some of his reforms entailed weakening and isolating the religious institution. Modern civil and penal codes replaced religious laws by 1928, and he staffed the judiciary with judges of secular background. But the stronghold of the Shii clergy, namely **Sharia** laws, which gave them powers over family law and the status of women, remained intact. Under Reza Shah, however, the state began to restrict certain practices by requiring the registration of marriage contracts in order to enforce the minimum age requirement for girls, keeping it at 15 years of age. Women were also granted the option of attaching a right to **divorce** clause to the marriage document. **Polygamy** was not outlawed, and the shah himself had three wives. He opened many secondary and vocational schools for girls, and by 1936, women were being admitted to the University of Tehran. The School of Nursing opened up under the patronage of one of his daughters.

Reza Shah waged his biggest battle against the **veil**, even though his wives continued to be veiled. The issue of unveiling was a central demand of women's organizations dating back to the turn of the century. He called his campaign "the opening of the veil" (*kashf-e hijab*), and it paralleled the campaign to encourage men to exchange their traditional garments and headwraps for Western outer garments and hats. The shah's government enforced the ban on veiling through various means. At first, female teachers were encouraged to shed the veil, then schoolgirls were required to do the same. Men whose family members continued to veil received a punishment, and shopkeepers were encouraged to refuse service to veiled women. Veiled women were also banned from buses, public baths, and government offices. Some women returned to veiling after the shah's exile in 1941, and at least some figures, like Ayatollah Kashani, began to speak publicly in favor of the veil during that period. But most elite women and government and professional workers continued with the unveiling custom, which they had begun before the shah's official backing of this measure, which lent their struggle great credibility. By the time he launched his reforms, women had already switched the color of the **chador** (the large body-covering veil) from black to brown in some regions, and by the late 1920s, some elite women had shed the chador altogether. Some organizations, like the Patriotic Women's League, made unveiling the centerpiece of their campaign and petitioned the shah for support.

The shah visited Turkey in 1935 and developed his ideas about modernizing women in that country. In 1936, the shah began his antiveiling policy in earnest, with police given the power to remove women's veils in public by force. The use of the police was bolder than the much-admired antiveiling measures instituted in **Mustafa Kemal Ataturk**'s Turkey. At one point, the use of the police to enforce unveiling led to a battle with members of the clergy at the mosque of Gowharshad at Mashhad. Conservative women who opposed this policy remained at home rather than face humiliation in the streets, but the shah rejected the suggestion that older women should not be subjected to the new regulation. The shah's policy received a boost when the queen of Afghanistan visited Iran unveiled with her husband. Women's organizations and journals, some predating the shah's regime, continued to support his policies until the mid-1930s. Resistance to the shah's efforts on behalf of women began to appear among the ranks of unionists, leftist groups, and others when his rule became increasingly repressive. When socialist men were jailed for conspiracy against the state, socialist women were not spared this fate. Most women's organizations were eliminated by the mid-1930s, as the shah tightened his authoritarian grip over all civil institutions. Prominent socialist women leaders like Roushanak Nowdoost and Jamileh Sedighi were jailed.

The shah continued his efforts to project a modern image to the outside world by sponsoring official women's activities. In 1932, Iran convened the **Second Congress of Women of the East** on its soil, inviting Middle Eastern and Asian women to participate. An effort was made to co-opt the women's movement by forming the Women's Center (Kanoon-e Banavan, literally Women's Center), a regime-friendly group that survived until his removal from office in 1941. The center was charged with improving women's **education**, with emphasis on housekeeping and child-rearing training. Women were also encouraged to devote their energies to charitable work by joining the Red Lion and Sun Society (the emblem of Iran's flag). By 1941, the center was headed by female activist **Siddiqeh Dowlatabadi**, who led women in focusing on charitable activities and eschewed open confrontation with the regime.

PARSA, ESFAND FARROUKHRU (1922–1980). An Iranian member of the Majlis and the first woman to be appointed to the cabinet, she was born in Qom, where her parents were forced to reside away from Tehran. Her mother, Fakhr-e Afaq Parsa, was a pioneering advocate of women's rights who published two **feminist** journals, *Zaban-I Zanan* (*Women's Tongue*) in 1919, and later *Jahan-e Zan* (*Women's World*).

Farroukhru Parsa studied biology and later obtained a medical degree. She taught at Jeanne d'Arc High School in Tehran, where she met the future empress, **Farah Diba Pahlavi**. Parsa maintained a long-lasting relationship with the empress, who became a conduit of women's demands to the shah. In 1963, Parsa was among the first six women to be elected to the parliament and was a member of the pro-shah Novin Party. She was the prime mover in the campaign leading to the adoption of Family Protection Laws. She was appointed minister of education in 1968 by Prime Minister Amir-Abbas Hoveyda (1919–1979).

Parsa was one of the most visible females to be tried and executed by the Islamic regime of Iran after a period of torture at Evin Prison. Charges brought against her consisted of aiding corrupt procedures at the Ministry of Education, embezzlement of general funds, collaborating with SAVAK (Iran's secret service), and prostitution. The Islamic regime accused her of belonging to the Bahai faith on the theory that members of this sect were ardent defenders of women's rights. Her relatives disputed this accusation. Hoveyda was executed in the same year. *See also* FEMINIST MOVEMENT IN IRAN.

PEOPLE'S MUJAHIDIN. This is an Iranian Islamic organization with Marxist overtones, founded initially in 1965 by university students opposed to the shah's regime. The student organization was first based on the principles of the Iranian Constitutional Revolution of 1906 and on Muhammad Mossadagh's resistance to Western influence dating to the early 1950s. It became known as a Marxist–Islamic movement in later years, and has done more for women than any other party in Iran. Known as Mujahidin-I-Khalq, it relocated to Baathist Iraq in 1986. The leadership of the movement was based in Paris, led by a husband and wife team, Masuud and Maryam Rajavi.

In 1993, the Mujahidin became affiliated with a coalition of other Iranian resistance groups in exile, under an umbrella organization known as the National Council of Resistance. Maryam Rajavi was elected the Council's president, the first woman to head such a political group in Iran. Born in 1953, she graduated from Ashraf University in Tehran with a degree in metallurgical engineering and was very effective in enlisting students in resistance activities. One of her sisters, Narges, was executed by the shah's government, and another sister, Massoumeh, was executed along with her husband by the Islamic Republic. The party advocates a classless society free from gender discrimination and believes in the *tawhidi* (unitarian doctrine) philosophy. Maryam has appointed many women to leading positions in the Mujahidin military, and more than half of the movement's military forces are women. Maryam Rajavi, who wears a head scarf in public, calls for the establishment of a secular society. The party's declarations, however, make no mention of polygamy or **temporary marriage**, despite women's long-standing opposition to these practices.

PERSONAL STATUS CODE OF TUNISIA. This code has resulted in the most progressive personal status reforms in the Arab world, and next to Turkish reforms, constitutes the greatest departure from **Sharia** law on family matters. It was legislated barely five months after Tunisia achieved its independence in 1956. Known also as CPS, it is considered a bold attempt, along with Turkey's 1926 adaptation of European codes, to eliminate gender inequality through a pioneering body of legislation. Unlike the case of Turkey, Tunisia's reformed personal status code was presented to the public by President **Habib Bourgiba** as a form of *ijtihad*, or reinterpretation of the Sharia. The other unusual aspect of these reforms was that they were introduced by the Neo-Destour Party under Bourgiba's leadership, before the emergence of grassroots feminist organizations. But Tunisia did not lack for women veterans of the nationalist struggle.

The CPS was issued in Arabic under the title *majalla*, the same name used by the Ottoman authorities during the 19th century for the publication that contained new Islamic codes. The Ottoman *majalla* published codes based on the Sharia, rather than imported European laws. Nevertheless, the CPS departed radically from Islamic laws. The *majalla*'s initial approach of gradual reform gave way in time to more radical overturning of Sharia, and it occurred periodically. The Tunisian *majalla*, likewise, constantly updated the laws. Islamists challenged Bourgiba once by sending a veiled woman, Hind Cheibi, to debate with him about the CPS. For instance, the code did not alter the law that granted women half the **inheritance** of their brothers. But female descendants who did not have male siblings were protected from the previous rule, which diverted their inheritance to male cousins. When polygamy was outlawed, the CPS imposed a punishment of one year in jail and a fine equal to one year's income on average for those who did not comply. Adoption of children was made legally valid, a huge change from the proscriptions of the Sharia.

In 1968, adultery laws were amended to make it punishable by the same prison sentence for both males and females. **Divorce** laws were made friendlier to women in 1981, when a divorced wife was granted the right to live in the family home and to maintain custody of her children. By 1993, the Sharia principle of *qiwameh*, or male headship of the family, requiring a wife to obey her husband, was changed in favor of imposing shared obligations on the husband and wife. Another long-standing grievance, that of prohibiting the transmittal of the mother's nationality to children born of a union with a non-Tunisian, was eliminated. The prohibition of a union between a Muslim Tunisian woman and a non-Muslim was also eliminated. No such daring overhaul of Sharia laws has been attempted elsewhere in the Arab world. Following the removal of President Zein al-Abidin Ben Ali from office in the popular uprising of 2011, Islamist forces have raised their voice in favor of restoring the Sharia as the basis of personal status laws.

PILGRIMAGE AND WOMEN. Performing the pilgrimage to Mecca and Medina once in a Muslim's lifetime is one of the five obligations of Islam required of both men and women. The equality of obligations, which does not recognize gender differences, however, does allow for some distinctions between the performance of males and females. Women must be accompanied by a male relative on the pilgrimage, but groups of women can travel to the site and perform the rituals together. Unlike the case of praying at other mosques, women are permitted to perform the communal prayers inside the grand mosque of Mecca (al-Masjid al-haram) while standing next to males, or even in front of them for safety considerations. Women perform the pilgrimage wearing white garments, but with their faces uncovered. Men may also substitute for women in the ritual of "stoning the devil," which involves throwing stones that may injure bystanders. Most of the rituals of the pilgrimage enhance the unity and classless basis of the Muslim community, as well as obliterating gender differences when performing the rituals of Islam. Rituals are the same for men and women, and there are no barriers to social mixing between them. There are regulations that ease the hardship of some rituals for women.

POLITICAL PARTICIPATION IN EGYPT. Political rights for women repeatedly eluded the organized **feminist movement** in Egypt from the 1920s until 1956. Even though the **Egyptian Feminist Union** struggled to achieve these rights, it only gained the privilege of attending parliamentary sessions from a balcony. Most of the gains of the women's movement were in the area of **education.**

Women were enfranchised in 1956 after a sensational and much-publicized women's hunger strike, led by **Durrea Shafiq** in 1954. Beginning with the era of Jamal Abd al-Nasser (1954–1970), however, the state took the initiative of introducing women in the political arena. Since that period, two females occupy cabinet posts on a regular basis, and some women have been elevated to ambassadorial posts. Yet women's willingness to register as voters did not match their numbers within the general population, hovering around 50 percent. The apathy may be traced to the regimental political participation decreed by the single-party system. The ruling party, the Arab Socialist Union (ASU), founded in 1962, included women in its popular committees, in the housing committee, and in committees assisting Cairo's governor in providing services for women. In addition, the ASU membership, which was based on occupational quotas, allocated 5 percent of its total membership to women. But many of these committees atrophied. The most visible effort made on behalf of women was the creation of a secretariat for women, similar to the youth secretariat within the ASU. But the number of women who stood for parliamentary elections was always disappointing.

Only two women were voted into the 1957 parliamentary session, six women in the 1960 session, and eight women in the 1964 session, out of a total number of 360 deputies.

By 1969, the number of women elected to parliament had dropped to three. The government, however, reserved two seats for women in every political section of the ASU, and the same was decreed for each provincial assembly. Voter registration numbers during that era also reflected cultural biases against women's participation, viewing them as lacking in the temperament and experience to enter the game of politics. The first election after the 1952 revolution took place in 1957, when 5,575,692 males registered to vote, but only 144,983 females did the same.

The period of Anwar Sadat (1970–1981) saw greater official backing for women's political participation despite the rise of Islamist trends that were absent during the Nasserite period. The women's secretariat within the ASU was reactivated in 1970 with the appointment of Suad Abu al-Suud as its head. The president's wife, **Jihan Sadat**, was elected as the head of the local council of the Minoufiyah governorate in 1975. Due to her encouragement, two women were elected in that same year to various local councils, with five women being seated in the Cairo Council alone. The ASU, which was renamed the People's Assembly in 1971, saw nine women join its membership. But the ratio of women to men in the People's Assembly remained small. In 1979, only 35 women were elected to the People's Assembly, compared to 357 men. Only 10 women were elected to the People's Assembly in 1992, while 444 males were chosen.

Under President Husni Mubarak (r. 1981–2011), an upper house, known as the Shura Council, was created, with a mixed appointed and elected membership. In 1992, when no women were elected to this council, Mubarak appointed 12 women, out of a total of 258 members. Women never reached the position of governor or mayor in any of Egypt's cities, towns, or villages. By 1979, the law that reserved 10 to 12 percent of parliamentary seats and representation in local councils to women resulted in a dramatic fall in the number of women in these councils. By 1992, only 1.2 percent of the total number of representatives were women. Generally speaking, rising Islamist trends were not the only cause of this decline. Other factors include the weakness of civil society, which has become increasingly elitist and limited in membership. Following the 2011 uprising, which allowed free elections, an Islamist-dominated People's Assembly emerged, with only four females as members.

POLITICAL PARTICIPATION IN TURKEY. Turkish women were the first to gain political rights in the Muslim and Arab worlds and entered the political arena ahead of several European countries. They received the right to vote in municipal elections in 1930 and in national elections in 1934. By

1994, however, female membership in the Turkish parliament was only 1.8 percent. The beginnings of the Islamic rise to power in the 1990s did have an impact on women's readiness to participate in local and national elections. After decades of secular cultural trends, the picture began to change. It was in 1995 that a woman, Serpil Ocalan, first appeared on Turkish television in a head scarf. Turkish women shattered many records by making it one of only five countries in the world to have a female prime minister (**Tansu Ciller**, r. 1993–1996). Turkey usually has one cabinet post filled by a woman. Yet the percentage of female members in parliament remains low, having risen to 4.4 percent in 2002 from 1.9 percent in 1990.

Only the Republican People's Party (RPP), which is the guardian of the Kemalist legacy in Turkey, supports the establishment of quotas for women in the legislature.

POLYGAMY. Several ancient religions allow the practice of polygamy in addition to Islam, particularly Judaism, which placed no limits on the number of wives belonging to one husband. Before Islam, the pagan Arab tribes practiced an unlimited form of polygamy, as well as polyandry, wherein one woman took several husbands.

There is only one passage in the Quran that discusses polygamy, placing specific limitations on this practice and allowing it under exceptional conditions. Islam does not mandate that men take several wives; it only permits them to do so in order to protect the rights of orphaned and fatherless children. A man may take up to four wives, but the Quranic passage attaches an ethical rider, that he can do so only if he can be fair to all of them, and this is a near impossibility. It is also stated that a man cannot take two sisters as wives simultaneously.

The polygamy passage is part of the Medinian verses, meaning that it was revealed to Muhammad when he began establishing an Islamic state in Medina in 622 and when he laid down the social foundations of the new Islamic community. By that time, following the severe battles fought against the pagan Qureish tribesmen in Mecca, many Muslim males had lost their lives, and many pagan wives left their husbands and converted to Islam. Confronted with this unexpected increase in the number of marriageable single women and fatherless children, Muslims searched for a way to support them. Thus, according to many theologians, sanctioning polygamy was not undertaken lightly but was an acute necessity. The Quran also allowed marrying a slave woman and provided several means of integrating her into the Muslim community, either by setting her free or by canceling her slave status upon the birth of a child. Modern experts on Islamic polygamy defend it as an alternative to **divorce** or forsaking a disabled or childless wife.

Since the beginning of the 20th century, the practice of polygamy has undergone severe changes. For economic reasons, as well as because of women's education and their insistence on exercising the right to accept or decline a marital match, polygamy has become a rarity. In addition, polygamy has been eliminated by reforming or discarding the **Sharia** in some Muslim countries, like Turkey and Tunisia. In several instances, permission by the first wife must be obtained before a husband can contract a second marriage, or he risks the dissolution of the first marriage. Granting women greater grounds for seeking divorce in some countries, and a new type of divorce, *khulu*, have also made polygamy less attractive for males. It is estimated that the incidence of polygamous marriages is no more than 3 to 4 percent in most parts of the Muslim world, with the exception of the Arab Gulf countries.

PUBLIC/PRIVATE SPACE. One of the confusions surrounding the issue of the veil is the erroneous assumption that Muslim women were barred from public spaces. The reality is that only elite women were secluded, particularly in the 19th century. This seclusion lasted until the middle decades of the 20th century in major urban centers. Not only Muslims, but women from various religious and ethnic backgrounds within this class were excluded from the public space.

Muslim and other Middle Eastern women, if they belonged to the urban lower classes, were a frequent presence in the streets on account of their participation in trading activities. Women also held urban properties, which necessitated their occasional presence in streets and alleys of various towns and cities. Alleys were of special significance here, since women who did not have domestic servants were often present in this space near their homes, observing small children at play. During the beginning of the modern colonial period of the early 20th century, major streets were being exclusively seen as male spaces, and even native males were not welcome in these modern additions to towns and cities.

In the 20th century, certain public spaces were prohibited to women by traditional male elements. Movie theaters, for instance, did not welcome women of various faiths in Syria and Lebanon down to the 1930s. Subsequent demonstrations by women forcibly integrated cinemas. The first cinema, which opened in Syria in 1916, did not receive women. Spaces frequented by foreigners or those that included centers of entertainment, like Marjeh Square in Damascus and Muhammad Ali Street in Cairo, did not welcome native women. In 1938, traditional groups demanded that the colonial government in Syria bar women from movie houses. A year later, female students in Damascus demonstrated to demand the right to visit movie theaters. Furthermore, the return of the **veiling** custom in the 1970s did not impose restrictions on women's movements or frequenting public spaces in their pursuit of **education** and **employment**.

Public spaces that are still unwelcoming to women are mosques, especially at the time of performing congregational prayers. But Muslim shrines dedicated to male and female holy individuals, by contrast, have always been open to women. Women pray, beseech the spirit of the deceased for help, and mostly ask for miracles in the case of infertility. Since shrines are not places of congregational prayers, there is no impediment to the presence of women in their confines. Some famous shrines, like the Hussein Shrine in Cairo, are barred to women after sundown. But the shrines most frequented by women are those of Shii holy personages in Iran and Iraq. Women who travel distances in order to visit the shrines of the martyred imams such as Ali and Hussein acquire a status similar to those who perform the **pilgrimage** to Mecca.

PURDAH. This is a head-to-toe **veil** worn by women in some Muslim Indian communities, but also by some Hindu women. The term means "screen" in Hindi (from the word *Parda*), which could also refer to the custom of seclusion of women. Indians generally attribute this custom to Muslim, or Mughal, rule in India from the 16th to the 19th centuries. Historical evidence, however, suggests that the purdah developed as a result of the caste system. There are marked differences between where Hindu and Muslim women don the purdah. Whereas Hindu women secluded themselves within the family to avoid contact with male family members, Muslim women wore the purdah garment as street attire. Muslim women did not seclude themselves from male family members, because Islam encouraged the marriage of cousins. Hindu women, by contrast, upheld the Hindu taboo on endogamous marriage by keeping the purdah while inside the family residence. Since Muslim influence was evident more in northern India than in the south, the custom of purdah was not as prevalent in southern India.

Indian reformers, particularly Muslim leaders, viewed purdah as a regressive custom limiting women's access to education and their political participation. An incident similar to **Huda Shaarawi**'s act of public unveiling took place in India to demonstrate the disadvantages of purdah. In 1929, during a meeting of the All India Women's Conference, the Begum of Phopal removed her purdah, publicly signifying rejection of the religious symbolism of this garment. The purdah has practically vanished from India and Pakistan since the middle of the 20th century, but a variation of this form of outer dress, namely the *burqa*, can be seen in Afghanistan.

QALAMAWI, SUHEIR (1911–1997). She was one of Egypt's earliest female graduates of the national university, a professor of Arabic and short-story writer, born in Cairo. She attended the American College for Girls in 1929 and received a PhD in Arabic literature from Cairo University in 1941. Her dissertation was a literary evaluation of the *Arabian Nights*, under the supervision of Egypt's famous man of letters, Taha Hussein. She was initially turned down by the School of Medicine at the same university. Throughout her life, she encouraged aspiring female writers to excel in their chosen vocations. While a professor of Arabic at Cairo University, a post she held until 1967, she headed several organizations, such as the **Arab Feminist Union** and the League of Arab Women University Graduates. She was also elected to the Egyptian Organization for Publishing and Distribution.

Qalamawi's own writing career began early. In 1935, she published *My Grandmother's Tales*, the first short-story collection by an Egyptian woman, which had an introduction by Taha Hussein. Another volume of short stories was published in 1964, *The Devils Are Dallying*. She has also produced 10 works of literary criticism and many Arabic translations of classical literary studies. In 1978, she was awarded the State Appreciation Prize for Literature. *See also* FEMINIST MOVEMENT IN EGYPT.

QASIMI, LUBNA (?–). She is the minister for the economy and planning in the United Arab Emirates (UAE) and a member of the ruling family of Sharjah, one of seven emirates of the UAE. She is the daughter of Khalid al-Qasimi and a niece of the ruling sheikh. She holds a bachelor of science degree in computer science from the University of California at Chico and an executive MBA from the American University at Sharjah. She was the first woman to be appointed to a cabinet post, in 2004. Before this appointment, she served as senior manager of the information systems department at the Dubai Ports Authority. She also serves as the chief executive officer of TEJARI, an electronic business-to-business marketplace.

She is the recipient of many awards, including Great Britain's House of Lords Entrepreneurship Award in 2004 and an Honorary Doctoral Degree from California State University at Chico.

QASSEM, ABD AL-KARIM (1914–1963). He was Iraq's first president, who came to power through a coup d'état with Abd al-Salam Aref on 14 July 1958 and greatly improved the status of Iraqi women. He and fellow military officers ended the Hashemite monarchy and ruled from 1958 until 1963. Qassem was descended from an Arab family and was born in Baghdad. His education was basically military in nature; he completed only one year of secondary school (he completed high school later) before being admitted to military school. He rose to the rank of officer in 1932, becoming one of the staff officers of the Iraqi army in 1933. Qassem earned meritorious recognition for his service against Kurdish rebels in the 1943–1945 uprising and later served as deputy commander of Iraqi forces in Palestine during the 1948 Arab–Israeli War. In 1950, he received further military training in Great Britain.

As a member of the Free Officers' secret organization, which toppled the monarchy, he became a prime minister and commander-in-chief, acceding to the presidency of Iraq in 1958. His interest in reforming Iraq's personal status law developed out of his concern for poor people in his country, his egalitarian sense, and his admiration for Baker Sidqi (1885–1937), the leader of Iraq's and the Arab world's first coup d'état in 1936. Qassem was also an admirer of **Mustafa Kemal Ataturk.**

Qassem introduced the 1959 Personal Status Code as an effort to reform the family and to grant women additional rights in recognition of their participation in Iraq's political struggles. The new law advanced the status of Iraqi women greatly, bringing it closer to the reforms enacted on behalf of women in Turkey and Tunisia. The new law allowed women to inherit a share equal to their brothers', the first such measure in the Arab world and surpassing Tunisian women in this regard. The law also made **polygamy** contingent on the consent of the first wife, thereby limiting it severely. A woman was appointed as a member of the cabinet, a step in the emulation of Jamal Abd al-Nasser's Egypt. She was **Naziha Jawdat al-Dulaimi**, the political activist and head of the League for the Defense of Women's Rights. Qassem was closely aligned with the Iraqi Communist Party, and he allowed women to join the party's military wing, the People's Resistance Force.

Women were encouraged to join both the Communist Party and its rival, the Baath Party. Women's formations, however, remained isolated form the male membership in both parties until the 1960s. The Baath Party, which followed the pan-Arabist ideology of Egypt's Nasser, created Women of the Republic as an organization rivaling the pro-communist and pro-Qassem group known as League for the Defense of Women's Rights. Due to the militarization of both of these women's groups, the Shawwaf Baathist uprising of 1963 took its toll on women. Iraqi communist women suffered imprisonment and execution in large numbers. The same uprising led to Qassem's execution by a firing squad. Many of his reforms on behalf of women were later canceled by those who drafted the Iraqi constitution following the American invasion of 2003.

QUEEN OF SHEBA. The legendary ruler of a Southern Arabian kingdom which, according to archeologists, was based in Yemen. The name Sheba refers to the Kingdom of Shebaa, or the Sabean Kingdom, with its capital at Mareb. Sheba's caravan trade with the Kingdom of Israel, Mesopotamia, and the classical world between the first and sixth centuries CE was dominated by the Himyarite state. Known to classical writers as Arabia Felix (Happy Arabia), the Sabean Kingdom was destroyed when the great Mareb dam, one of the seven wonders of the ancient world, ruptured, inundating terraced farmland below. The kingdom was best known for its frankincense products, which were highly valued as fumigating agents by the Greeks and Romans.

In the Jewish, Islamic, and Ethiopian versions of this legend, there are three prominent actors: the Queen of Sheba, King Solomon of the kingdom of Israel, and a mythical bird called hoopoe (Arabic: *hudhud*). The Jewish version appears in the Book of Kings and in Chronicles. Here, the story line states that the queen heard of the king's reputation and traveled to Jerusalem with precious gifts, seeking an alliance with him, after which she returned to her country. The *Aggadah*, which provides expositions of biblical stories, adds that the king's interest in the kingdom of Sheba was aroused by the hoopoe, who mentioned that the sun-worshipping queen was not yet a part of Solomon's kingdom. He sent an invitation to the queen attached to the hoopoe's wings, and she sent gifts and arrived after three years, although the journey was said to take seven years.

In the Islamic version, the story is similar to the biblical tale. The name Bilqis was attached to the queen by later Arab historians, such as Tabari, Zamakhshari, and Baydawi. The sun-worshipping queen arrives to visit King "Suleiman" and is deceived into uncovering her legs, reflecting her beauty, as she is made to step on palace floors built over running water. The Islamic version adds that she and Solomon eventually got married and became Muslims. Muslim commentators used this story to advance the claim that the Quran does not reject the idea of female queens. Instead, the Quran refers to Bilqis's magnificent throne and her conversion to Islam, bringing her people with her to submit to Allah.

In the Ethiopian version, the story is embellished with more details. It appears in the Amharic-language *Kabra Nagast* (*Story of the Kings*) book, which makes this legend the basis of the superior claims of the Amhara people. Here, Bilqis is referred to as Queen Makeda, and her affair with King

Solomon results in the birth of a son, known as Menelik I. He becomes the founder of the Ethiopian Solomonic dynasty. Henceforward, Ethiopian emperors all the way down to Haile Selassie, removed from office in 1974, took on the title of the Lion of Judah.

Modern archeologists have attempted to uncover traces of this queen in the southwestern Arab state of Yemen. A place of worship described as the Sabean Awwam Temple, known locally as Mahram (place of worship) Bilqis was uncovered. But no traces of the legendary queen herself have been excavated, and no inscriptions of her name were located. Some scholars deduced from this that the Queen of Sheba may have been a composite figure based on several queens. They also stress that there is no evidence that queens ever ruled in this remote corner of the Arabian Peninsula. The only ancient Arab queens came from the Nabatean Kingdom in southern Jordan, where the ancient town of Petra stood, and in Palmyra, in the Syrian desert, the home of Queen **Zenobia**.

QURRAT AL-AYN (1815–1851). She was the central figure in the Babi movement, which preceded the emergence of the Bahai faith, and a poet and literary figure in her own right. She was named Fatima Zarrin Taj Barangha-ni, but was given the titles of Tahira (the pure one), and Qurrat al-Ayn (the apple of the eye). Qurrat became a supreme role model for Bahai women in later years.

She was born into a well-known clerical family in Qazvin, Iran, to parents who were both *mujtahids*, or authorized to interpret the holy texts. Her father was Hajj Mullah Salik, known as "the sage of Qazvin." On her mother's side, she had followers of the Shaykhi sect of Shii Islam, but on her father's side, her relatives adhered to the more conservative Usuli school of Shiism. She and her sister were recipients of an excellent education at home by their father and other relatives, who instructed them in theological studies. Qurrat al-Ayn was married to a cousin on her paternal side but moved to the Iraqi holy city of Karbala to study, residing at a maternal relative's house, the leading Shaykhi philosopher Sayyid Qazim. She became a leader of the Shaykhis but later became a Babi.

The Shaykhi movement was founded by Shaykh Ahmad Ahsai (1753–1826), who began teaching at Karbala. His teachings were revolutionary and messianic, preaching that the time had arrived for a new prophetic cycle after Muhammad, meaning that the hidden imam would soon return. This was a central Shii doctrine, but predicting the timing of this appearance was always controversial. Ahsai also taught that if the imam did not appear, a figure heralding his imminent return, called the Bab, or doorway, would soon manifest himself. Shiis were receptive to this line of thinking because the year 1844, in which Ahsai preached this doctrine, marked the one-thousandth year since the disappearance of the twelfth Shii imam, Muhammad Mahdi, the central figure in Iran's Twelver Shii sect. In 1844, Sayyid Ali Muhammad pronounced himself to be the Bab to the long-awaited twelfth Shii Imam.

Qurrat al-Ayn became the most committed to this line of thought and courted controversy by claiming that the community was no longer obligated to obey Islamic law. She also alienated and provoked conservative Shiis who wore black during the Islamic month of Muharram to commemorate the martyrdom of Hussein, by wearing colorful clothes and appearing unveiled in celebration of the birth of the Babi movement. She was forced by the authorities to return to Qazvin, whereupon she divorced her husband, Mulla Muhammad, herself uttering the divorce vows. In support of her action, a member of the Babi movement took it upon himself to assassinate her husband. Qurrat al-Ayn became deeply involved with this movement, which called for reforms and a drastic change in the treatment of women. The act of uncovering her face in public was seen as a signal of her total rejection of Islam and its teachings, particularly on the subject of **polygamy**.

She also caused dissension among fellow Babis when they met in the town of Badasht in the province of Khurasan to discuss means of escaping the official wave of persecutions against them. Her position was that they should sever any ties with Islam and prepare to defend themselves militarily, while others were still willing to consider ways of reforming Islam. Shoghi Effendi, who later emerged as the guardian and head of the Bahai faith (r. 1921–1957), recorded in his work *God Passes By* (1944) how her fiery words inspired fear in the heart of listeners, promising to "put to flight the chiefs and nobles of the earth." When battles erupted between Babis and government forces in the province of Mazandaran and the cities of Zanjan and Nayriz, she went into hiding until her capture and transfer to Tehran, where she was placed under heavy guard. Despite her confinement to the house of the chief of police, she was allowed to preach to groups of women, including the Qajar princess, Shams-I Fitnih, a granddaughter of Fath Ali Shah, who became a Bahai. In 1852, Qurrat al-Ayn was implicated in a Babi plot to assassinate Nasir al-Din Shah (1848–1896) as his government was conducting a massacre of Babis. Males who were captured were executed publicly, but Qurrat al-Ayn was spared that humiliation, being strangled secretly in a garden. Shoghi Effedi quotes her as saying just before her death: "You can kill me as soon as you like, but you cannot stop the emancipation of women" (p. 75, *God Passes By*).

Qurrat al-Ayn was also a poet, who expressed her political and religious vision in verse. Her writings displayed enormous learning and familiarity with classical works. Iranian feminists today consider her an early and genuine feminist figure who never lacked for steadfastness or courage. *See also* BAHAI WOMEN.

QUT AL-QULUB (1898–1968). An Egyptian aristocratic novelist who was also known by her last name, al-Dimirdash. She was born in Cairo; her father was Ahmad Abd al-Rahman al-Dimirdash Pasha, who headed the Dimirdashiyya Sufi (mystical) order, which had roots in 16th-century Anatolia. Her mother was Zaynab Taudi, who gave her a strict upbringing at the al-Mahamadi Palace in Cairo and an education by private tutors. When Qut al-Qulub was 25 years old, an advanced age according to the **marriage** culture of the day, she was married off to a prominent and much older judge of the Mixed Court system, Mustafa Bey Mukhtar. After giving birth to five children during seven years of marriage, she left her husband. In a gesture of liberating herself, she kept the children and made sure they bore her name. She established her own palace residence, where she held a literary salon for Egyptian and visiting intellectuals and writers from abroad.

She began her own literary output in 1934, writing novels in French, a language she had mastered since childhood. Her novels depicted the disappearing **harem** life of the Egyptian aristocracy: *Au hasard de la pensee* (1934), *Harem* (1937), *Les trois contes de l'amour à la mort* (1939), *Zenoubia* (1946), *La nuit de la desinee* (1954), *Le coffret l'Hindou* (1952), *Ramza* (1958), and *Hifnawi le magnifique* (1962). Her most sensational work was *Ramza*, which told the story of a girl who fled with an army officer against her parents' wishes and later succeeded in annulling her own marriage.

QUTB, SAYYID (1906–1966). An Egyptian Islamic ideologue, educator, novelist, poet, and literary critic whose full name was Sayyid Qutb Ibrahim Hussein al-Shadhili. He is best known in the West for his intellectual impact on the Muslim Brotherhood movement in Egypt. His early life followed the trajectory of the native Islamic scholarly class. He was born in the provinces, in the village of Musha, in the province of Asyut, Upper Egypt. His family were landowners who made sure to send him to study at **al-Azhar**, the country's foremost Islamic seminary. He graduated from a famous British-style secondary college, Dar al-Ulum, and became a schoolteacher in the 1930s and 1940s. In 1939, he became an administrator in the Ministry of Education.

Qutb was deeply immersed in Islamic and linguistic sciences, becoming an authority on the aesthetics of the Quran. His exegesis of Quranic verses and his deliberations on the imagery of the Quran, which were influenced by the literary analysis of another expert on the language of the Quran, Amin al-Khuli (d. 1966), resulted in a 30-volume study titled *Fi zilal al-Quran* (*In the Shade of the Quran*) (first installment published in 1954) and an earlier work, *Artistic Imagery of the Quran* (1945). He also wrote a memoir reflecting on his early years, titled *Tifl min al-Qarya* (*A Child from the Village*, 1946), a secular work of a certain literary value. There is no discussion of religion in it, but it did depict the villagers' mystical approach to religion and the pervasive presence of superstition in their lives. In another literary work, *Book Critique: The Future of Culture in Egypt* (1939), he critiqued a seminal work by the eminent Egyptian man of letters Taha Hussein, for whom Qutb worked for a while. Up until the crystallization of his radical Islamic thought beginning in the early 1950s, Qutb's books were recommended reading in schools and universities. He published a total of 24 books. He also kept company with the best literary and intellectual minds of Egypt.

The definitive turning point in his life came as a result of his journey to the United States from 1948 until 1950, where he went for higher studies on scholarship. His experiences while he lived there had great relevance to the development of his views on gender relations. Qutb studied the U.S. system of education, spending several months at first at Colorado State College of Education (now the University of Northern Colorado) at Greeley. While in the United States, he published his book on social justice in Islam in 1949. He also worked and studied briefly at Wilson Teachers' College in Washington, D.C., and Stanford University, and traveled extensively throughout the country. He summarized his impressions in an article that he published as soon as he returned to Cairo, "The America That I Have Seen." His rejection of American life and customs was nearly total, as he severely condemned the emphasis on freedom, which came close to licentiousness; the economy, which led to severe class differences; racism, instances of which he personally experienced as a "brown" man; unstable friendships; unrestricted mixing of the sexes even in places of worship; and widespread pro-Zionist sentiment.

Just how much his American sojourn impacted his Islamic radicalism is a subject of constant debate. Other influences had to do with his imprisonment and severe torture from 1954 through 1964, as well as that of many Muslim Brothers, after being accused of participating in a conspiracy to assassinate President Jamal Abd al-Nasser. He was released in 1964 at the request of Iraqi Premier Abd al-Salam Aref, but was recaptured after eight months. He was executed by hanging after a controversial trial in which he was accused of plotting against the regime, based on his book *Maalim fi al-tariq* (*Signposts along the Road*, 1964). The book was a political manifesto detailing steps to bring about the ideal Islamic state through the creation of an Islamic generation, led by an Islamic revolutionary vanguard to fight the *jahiliya*, or the paganism and secularism of modern times.

His influence over the Muslim Brotherhood and another group, Jihad Islami, which was also the product of Nasser's jails, was undeniable. He resigned his civil service job with the Ministry of Education upon his return from the United States and joined the Muslim Brotherhood. He became the chief editor of the Brotherhood's weekly publication, *Al-Ikhwan al-Muslimin*, in effect being in charge of its propaganda activity. He also served as a member of the Guidance Council, the highest committee, which oversaw the

Brotherhood's activities under the direction of the Supreme Guide. The degree to which his thought influenced later Islamic militants is a matter of dispute and is largely based on speculation regarding contacts his brother, Muhammad Qutb, may have developed while in Saudi Arabia.

Sayyid Qutb's views on gender relations molded the perceptions of radical Islamists for many years to come. Just like the Pakistani ideologue Abu al-Aala Mawdudi, he argued that society normally regresses into paganism due to the granting of excessive sexual freedom to women. When women begin to feel that their primary role in life is seduction and self-adornment, they neglect their domestic duties and turn wholeheartedly to employment outside the home. Women's main role, as is specified by Islam, was giving children an Islamic upbringing and exercising moral guardianship over society. Qutb repeats what most Islamists stress, namely that Islam has elevated the position of women beyond any achievement of Western civilization. A virtuous woman has everything she needs, since Islam granted her property rights, the freedom to choose her own spouse, the freedom to seek employment and education, and freedom of movement as long as she is properly attired. He stressed that Islam views all human beings as equal, although the two genders inevitably differ according to their life experiences and physical ability. Here, Qutb repeated the often heard Islamic idea about woman's specific nature, which makes some types of work more suitable than others. He added that since women were protected by men, they were absolved from the performance of **jihad**, which he defined as being completely defensive in nature. He circumvented the participation of early Islamic women in jihad duties by explaining that these female warriors were the exception to the general rule. He went on to maintain that Islam gave women rights in the 14th century that were denied to French women in the 1960s, such as retaining their maiden names after **marriage** and the enjoyment of the their full civil identity. He also stated that women work outside the home in Western countries because men have ceased to support them.

Qutb's thought may still be relevant to the lives of radical Islamists, but scholars at **al-Azhar** seminary listed him as a heretic after his execution. He is still considered out of the mainstream of Islamic thought by a large segment of the Muslim population. He was accused by many conservative Islamic scholars of being a man of dubious scholarship who overused the freedom of *ijtihad*, or individual interpretation of the Quran. But to many Islamists both in Sunni and Shii circles, he still ranks among the greatest figures of revivalist Islam, such as **Ayatollah Ruhollah Khomeini**, Abu al-Aala Mawdudi, and Hassan al-Banna.

RAAB, ESTHER (1894–1981). An Israeli poet who was the first Palestine-born female poet to write in Hebrew, which became the official language of the land. Raab grew up in the kibbutz of Petah Tikva, which is also where she was buried. She began to publish her poetry in 1923 with "I Am underneath the Pramble Bush," a poem that appeared in a Hebrew literary journal titled *Hedim*. In 1930, she came out with her first collection of poetry, *Kimshonim* (*Thistles*), in which she adopted free verse, abandoning the traditional meter and stanza of earlier poetry. Her work was not received well, which led her to abandon the writing of poetry until the late 1950s. Among her other collections of poetry are *The Poetry of Esther Raab* (1963), *A Last Prayer* (1976), and *Root's Sound* (1976).

RAHHAL, AMINAH. An Iraqi communist leader who was the first female member of the Central Committee of the Iraqi Communist Party, serving between 1941 and 1943. Her brother was Hussein al-Rahhal, the first male feminist in Iraq. He was a Marxist, studied at Berlin after World War I, and then studied law in Iraq. He published *Al-Sahifa* (*The Journal*), which called for women's liberation in the 1920s. In the 1930s, Aminah was among a group of women, including university students, who publicly shed the *abaya*, the full-body outer black garment. At the time, al-Rahhal was a law student at the University of Baghdad. She was also among the earliest women whose families allowed them to drive a car. In 1938, she attended the Women of the East Conference in Damascus, which led to the founding of the Arab Women's Union. Communist women, who were mostly affiliated with the Iraqi Communist Party founded by Hussein Rahhal, created the Iraqi Women's Society against Fascism (IWSAF). The group included Aminah Rahhal and a number of Christian and Jewish Iraqi women who were the product of the same school system. This organization affiliated with the Women's International Democratic Federation. The women's activism led to jail sentences during the Iraqi royal regime, the first females imprisoned in Iraqi jails being three engineering students from the University of Baghdad. In 1952, the Iraqi Communist Party organized its own women's organization, the League for the Defense of Women's Rights (LDWR). After the 1958 Revolution, it became known as the Iraqi Women's League, which had a branch in the Kurdish area. *See also* QASSEM, ABD AL-KARIM (1914–1963).

RAHNAVARD, ZAHRA (1945–). An Iranian writer, artist, political activist, and **feminist** who was born in Barujerd to a religious family. She studied at Tehran's Teachers' College, earning a teaching degree. In 1969, she married Mir-Hussein Musavi, an opponent of the shah's regime who shared her Islamic political views. Musavi was the prime minister of Iran from 1981 to 1988; this office was abolished in 1989 in favor of transforming the top position of the country into an executive presidency. Rahnavard continued her education after marriage, earning a master's degree from the Department of Art at Tehran University and a PhD in political science from the Islamic Azad University. Her political activism became more pronounced after she joined the lecture circle of **Ali Shariati**, the so-called Husseiniyah Irshad, in the early 1970s, when she became one of the followers of the prominent ideologue of the Iranian Islamic Revolution. His arrest in 1976 by the shah's police prompted her to flee the country and settle in the United States. She became active with the Confederation of Iranian Students for a while, returning to Iran shortly before the revolution of 1979.

Rahnavard became a writer of seminal works, criticizing the Westernization of the shah's regime and defending women's right to follow a different path and to emulate early Islamic women like **Fatima** and **Zaynab**. She was appointed chancellor of al-Zahra Women's College from 1998 to 2006 and was an adviser to President Muhammad Khatami in 1999. She resigned this position when Islamic reformers fell out of favor after the end of Khatami's term of office. She founded a popular weekly magazine, *Rahe Zaynab*, which provided her with a forum from which to attack the policies of the shah's regime. She is the author of 15 books, which were translated into several languages, among them *The Uprising of Moses, The Beauty of the Veil and the Veil of Beauty*, and *Women, Islam and Feminism in Imam Khomeini's Thought*. In *The Colonial Motives for the Unveiling of Women*, she analyzed the reasons for **Shah Reza Pahlavi**'s adoption of a wholesale Westernization program. She was particularly critical of his 1936 decree banning wearing the **chador**. She took Marxists and other Westernizers to task, calling their influence marginal to Iran. Unveiling as a policy, according to Rahnavard, was meant to weaken and eventually erase Islam, because it was an attack on women's dignity, which in turn defined the Islamic nation's dignity. That is why women should follow the "path of Zaynab," the granddaughter of Muhammad and sister of Imam Hussein, who demonstrated great courage during the battle of Karbala. After Zaynab's capture by forces of the Umayyad state, she upbraided them with her fiery speeches, which inspired Shiis down the ages. Thus, following "the path of Zaynab" was a charge to Muslim women and men to speak truth to power, no matter what the consequences were.

Rahnavard was an outspoken champion of reform who addressed the Majlis on the issue of discrimination against women in employment. She also promoted women's education and their appointment to judicial careers. She became a member of the Green Path of Hope, the opposition movement that developed against the government of President Mahmoud Ahmadinejad. She was also an active participant in her husband's 2008 presidential campaign. Finally, her artistic talents are on public display in the form of a large sculpture, titled *Mother*, which sits in the middle of a Tehran square. *See also* VEILING IN ISLAM.

RATEB, AISHA (1928–). An Egyptian cabinet member, law professor, and diplomat who was born in Cairo. She graduated from Cairo University with a law degree in 1949. She also received a Diploma of Public Law in 1950, a Diploma of Private Law in 1951, and a PhD from the Faculty of Law at Cairo University in 1955. At age 21, she applied to be a judge in the State Council, Egypt's highest court, forcing its members to confront the issue of women's eligibility for the highest judicial office. She filed a lawsuit, but was not successful in her bid for this office. One of the judges confirmed in an opinion that neither Egypt's civil law nor Islamic schools of jurisprudence disqualify women from such service. He concluded that barring women from judicial duties was only a matter of social convention. This heated debate played itself out in the pages of the Egyptian media and was joined by the dean of Egyptian and Arab feminists, **Huda Shaarawi**.

Rateb became the first female professor of law at Cairo University and later headed the section on public international law. Her next major achievement was to be appointed as minister of social affairs in 1971, the second woman to hold such an appointment in the history of the Egyptian Republic. She held this position until 1977, as well as that of the minister of social insurance, simultaneously. She resigned her two positions in 1977 when she disagreed with the government's decision to crack down on hungry demonstrators protesting an increase in the prices of food items. In 1970, she was appointed Egypt's ambassador to Denmark, and in 1981, she became the ambassador to Germany. Due to her tireless efforts to open up the judicial institution to women, Egypt appointed its first female judge, Tahani al-Gebali, to the Supreme Constitutional Court in 2003. Rateb reminisced in public remarks that she was often called upon to give her legal opinion on matters of state to President Anwar Sadat. One of these occasions was prior to launching the surprise attack of the 1973 October War against Israel, a decision she supported. She also mentioned that she advised the Egyptian president to draw a clear line separating the position of the prime minister from that of the president.

Her many writings include *The Individual and International Law, Regional Organizations and Specialized Agencies, Diplomatic and Consular Organizations, The Contemporary Theory of Neutrality, The Revolution of July 23, 1952, International Relations, International and Arab Relations,* and *Demilitarized Zones.* She was granted the Social Sciences Award by the Egyptian Supreme Council of Culture in 1995. *See also* ABU ZEID, HIKMAT (?–); OTHMAN, AMAL (1934–).

RAUF EZZAT, HEBA (1965–). An Egyptian political scientist who is also an Islamist writer and activist. Her early education was at German Catholic schools, and she received a PhD in political science from Cairo University. She became an Islamic **feminist** advocate largely on the Internet, but she also wrote a weekly column, "Women's Voice," in the neo-Islamist paper *al-Shaab* (*The People*), the voice of the Labor Party.

She is a severe critic of Western feminists who critique the family institution only in the context of the development of bourgeois society and the patriarchal social system. She denies the relevance of this analysis to Islamic conditions and prefers to see changes instituted from within Muslim society. Although she considers herself the protégée of **Zaynab Ghazzali**, she grants gender greater prominence in her Islamist discourse. She affirms women's capability to assume political leadership roles as long as they comply with all Islamic rules mandated by the **Sharia**. But she does not accept the label "feminist," viewing feminism as a diversionary division of society providing a meaningless analysis for those focused on the problems of Muslim society. *See also* FEMINIST MOVEMENT IN EGYPT.

RAVIKOVITCH, DAHLIA (1936–). An Israeli poet, novelist, teacher, and journalist who was born near Tel Aviv. She lost her father in a car accident when she was a young girl, which she describes in her autobiographical book, *Death in the Family* (1976). She spent her early years on a kibbutz, as well as in Haifa. She completed her higher education at Hebrew University in Jerusalem and in Great Britain. She also worked as a teacher and a journalist. Her work includes short stories, children's literature, and translations of English poetry. Her political works include such collections as *A Dove and an Orange* (1959) and *The Third Book* (1969). Her opposition to Israel's invasion of Lebanon in the early 1980s inspired her to turn to the poetry of political protest. Her 1995 poetic collection, *The Complete Poems So Far,* has established her as Israel's leading female poet. She was awarded the Israel Prize for Literature in 1998.

REPUBLICAN BROTHERS OF SUDAN. This is an organization that calls for reforming the **Sharia** with emphasis on reexamining gender relations according to Islamic texts. The Republican Brothers were founded by Mahmoud Muhammad Taha (d. 1985), a Sudanese scholar who was originally involved in nationalist politics. After founding the Republican Party in 1945, calling for Sudanese independence, he underwent a religious experience in 1951, which caused him to transform this into a brotherhood of reformers. The Brothers called for a total reexamination of Islamic law and a second reading of the Quran to come up with a new vision of ideal gender relations, pluralism, and a society based on true Islam. Despite avoiding political involvement, Taha was executed by the regime of President Jaafar al-Nimeiry (r. 1969–1985) in 1985 when the latter began courting traditional Islamic elements in the Sudan and Saudi Arabia.

Taha's ideas found expression in a philosophy known as "The Second Message of Islam," which spread throughout the Muslim world. The message of the Republican Brothers has been passed on to Taha's student and successor, Abdillahi al-Naim, who is a professor of law at several U.S. universities. Al-Naim has succeeded in framing this view of reformist Islam in the context of modern human rights law and international law.

RIFAAT, ALIFA (1930–1996). An Egyptian short-story writer and novelist who was born in Cairo. She was married at an early age, putting an end to her secondary school education. Her husband was a policeman whose work took him all over Egypt. She accompanied him on his travels and transfers, living mostly in the provinces, leaving Egypt only once, to perform the **pilgrimage** to Mecca. Following her husband's death in 1974, she was able to publish freely and to visit London in 1984 to attend the International Feminist Book fair. She began to write short stories at age 17, only under a pseudonym. She continued to write in secret after her husband forbade this. Her first volume of short stories, *My Secret World*, gained some attention, and in 1975 she published another volume of short stories, *Eve Brings Adam Back*, in 1981. Her first novel, *Pharaoh's Jewel*, came out in 1991.

Most of her stories describe women's secret worlds and fantasies and the psychological scars caused by a social system that ignores their emotional needs. Her social critique, however, is religiously inspired, finding a great degree of support in the Quran. Her most famous story, "Distant View of a Minaret," published in 1983, was translated into English.

RIHANI, AMIN (1876–1940). A Lebanese American writer and one of the pillars of the Arab literary revival in the United States. He was born in the village of Freike, Lebanon, to a family of Maronite Christian silk weavers. He was sent to New York in 1888 ahead of his merchant father and attended school there before joining his family's business. He was sent back to Lebanon in 1897 to recover from a serious illness and taught English in high school. He returned to New York and began to write and translate major Arab poets into English. Most of his books dealing with Arab women appeared between 1910 and 1922, including *A Lily of Al-Ghor*, a novel about the oppression of Arab women; *Jihan*, about an Arab woman's life around World War I; and *Outside the Harem*, which dealt with the marginalization of Arab women.

RISHMAWI, MONA (1958–). A Palestinian human rights lawyer who received a law degree from Ayn Shams University at Cairo and an LLM from Columbia University in 1989. Her entire law career was spent as a lawyer before the Israeli military and civil courts in the occupied West Bank. She specialized in defending Palestinians in cases against the state, basing her defense on international instruments such as the Fourth Geneva Convention on the Rights of Occupied People. She was a member of the executive committee of the Palestinian law group al-Haqq, assuming the duties of director in 1989. She also worked with the International Commission of Jurists and is a legal adviser to the Office of the United Nations High Commission on Refugees.

ROSTAMEH, TOMIRIS. She was an Iranian heroine of the Babi movement, which preceded the Bahai revolution. She played a major role in the uprising against the Qajar dynasty in Zinjan when royalist troops laid siege to that town for a year. The resistance of Babi women during this siege made history, especially when Azari women called themselves "Tomiris' daughters" in the 1990s during the struggle against the Armenian attempt to seize Nagorno-Karabakh. *See also* BAHAI WOMEN; QURRAT AL-AYN (1815–1851).

ROXELANA (ca. 1504–1558). She was the wife of Ottoman Sultan Suleiman the Magnificent (r. 1520–1566) and the mother of Sultan Selim II (r. 1566–1574). She was known as Hurrem Sultan (Turkish; the laughing one), but was referred to as Roxelana in Western literature. She was the only legal wife of Sultan Suleiman; she came from a slave origin and was able to dominate the *seraglio* (Turkish; the Sultan's quarters) once she moved in with her servants. A great builder and philanthropist, she was the only royal woman to have her name inscribed on structures while her husband was alive.

Roxelana had mysterious origins, and no one seemed to know her real name. It was assumed by historical sources of this period that she was a Russian slave from the Ukraine, based on the title "Roxelana" or "Russalena," as it was sometimes rendered. What is known about her background was that she was a slave purchased by Suleiman's grand vizier and best friend, Ibrahim Pasha of Praga. She was also described as a beautiful woman who stood out in a crowd due to her flaming red hair. Once she gave birth to a son, the sultan married her and elevated her to the rank of third *kadin* (sultan's wife). This made her third, behind only the sultan's mother and his two senior wives.

Her elevation to this rank opened a period of great hostility between her and the first wife, Mahidevran, the mother of the heir to the throne, Mustafa. Roxelana was one of the most favored of the sultan's wives, and he shared a love for poetry with her. Her life was full of intrigue, giving rise to rumors regarding her boundless influence. First came the exiling of the sultan's son, Mustafa, by his father, who made him governor of distant Manisa in order to pave the way for the succession of Roxelana's son to the throne. This was followed by releasing all of the sultan's concubines from the palace as soon as she became his wife. Some of the concubines were married off to high-ranking officials. Rumors also claimed that she plotted the assassination of the sultan's closest friend, the Grand Vizier Ibrahim, in order to monopolize the sultan's favors. She was able to consolidate her influence over the **harem** following the death of the sultan's mother, Hafsa Sultan. Suleiman eventually killed his son Mustafa, presumably in order to satisfy Roxelana's wishes. She gave the sultan four sons; the eldest, Salim II, succeeded his father to the throne.

Roxelana is best remembered for her extensive and generous endowments on behalf of the poor. Her generosity in this regard, typical of powerful royal women, was designed to maximize her political influence and power. Her charitable works included mosques, religious schools, bath houses, and caravanserais, or travelers' resting places for pilgrims on their way to Mecca. She rebuilt some of the shrines of Mecca and Medina and ordered repairs to the bridges in the capital. She was behind the decision to commission Mimar Sinan (1492–1588), the greatest architect of his day, to construct Suleiman's Mosque in Istanbul. But her most famous charitable endowment was known as the Great Waqf of Jerusalem. This endeavor, completed in 1551, was often referred to as Khassiki Sultan Waqf. It entailed dedicating the revenues of villages and towns stretching from Tripoli in Lebanon all the way to Jerusalem for the support of the great soup kitchen of that holy city, as well as for the maintenance of al-Aqsa Mosque. *See also* ISLAMIC CHARITABLE ENDOWMENTS; WAQF.

RUSSELL, BERTRAND (1872–1970). A British philosopher who is often quoted by Iranian Shii religious scholars on the issue of **temporary marriage**. Russell provided an argument favoring different variations of marriage, including term (temporary) marriage, as alternatives to Christian marriage, particularly for young people. His book, *Marriages and Morals*, which gave expression to these ideas, was widely read in Iran.

S

SAADAWI, NAWAL (1931–). An Egyptian women's rights advocate, public health official, novelist, and social critic, born in the village of Kafr Tahla. She earned a medical degree in public health in 1955 from Cairo University, a degree in psychiatry from Ayn Shams University in 1974, and an MA in public health from Columbia University in 1966. She became Egypt's director of public health, but lost this position after the publication of her book *Woman and Sex* in 1969. All of her works were received with a great deal of alarm, as well as admiration, because she was the first female Arab writer to discuss sexual themes openly. Her nonfiction books, memoirs, and novels dealt with the issues of prostitution, female genital mutilation, incest, and other sexual abuses of women. In 1981, she was jailed by President Anwar Sadat and charged with being a threat to public morals. Her jail experience resulted in *Memoirs from the Women's Prison* (1984). As soon as she was released from jail by President Husni Mubarak, she attempted to form a women's party, a goal that was never realized by the previous generation of Egyptian **feminists**. Two of her journals, *Health*, founded in 1968, and *Nuun*, founded in 1989, were also closed on the government's orders, although she succeeded in founding the **Arab Women's Solidarity Association** in 1982. She was also the founder of Egyptian Women Writers Association, in 1971, and the African Association for Women on Research and Development at Dakar, Senegal, in 1977.

Saadawi published more than 24 books, most of which appeared in Lebanon in order to escape the censor's reach. Her books and novels have appeared in many languages, including English. They include *Memoirs of a Woman Doctor* (1969), *Man and Sex* (1975), *Woman at Point Zero* (1975), *The Hidden Face of Eve* (1980), *The Fall of the Imam* (1987), *Memoirs of a Child Called Suad* (1990), *Love in the Kingdom of Oil* (1993), *Ganat and the Devil* (1991), and *Zeina* (2009). *Awraq min Hayati* (*Leaves from My Life*), her memoir, appeared in 1995. She published *God Resides in the Summit Meeting* in 1996, which resulted in an unsuccessful attempt to try her as an apostate and strip her of her Egyptian citizenship.

She is the recipient of honorary doctorates from the University of Illinois–Chicago, Flemish University at Brussels, University of St. Andrews, Scotland, and several others. She was awarded a decoration of the first order by the government of Libya in 1989 and a literary award by the Supreme Council for Arts and Social Sciences at Cairo in 1974. In 2009, she delivered the Arthur Miller Lecture at the International Literary Festival of the PEN Writers' Association. Saadawi lives in Cairo and is married to prominent Marxist writer Sherif Hitata. Her daughter, Mona, is a writer, and her son, Atif, is a film director. *See also* FEMINIST MOVEMENT IN EGYPT; SADAT, JIHAN (1933–).

SABAH (1927–). A Lebanese singer and actress whose original name was Jeanette Faghali, born in Wadi Shahrur. She began singing early in life, acquiring the title Shahroura (song bird) later on. She became a movie star after relocating to Egypt and starred in more than 40 movies, mostly musicals. After 1964, she returned to Lebanon, where her singing career took off due to her participation in the annual Baalbek International Festival. She still performs in Egypt and Lebanon, where Arab musicians helped advance her career. She is also known for her six marriages, the last one to Fadi Lubnan. *See also* FAYROUZ (1934–).

SABAH, RASHA AL- (1950–). A Kuwaiti educator and advocate for women's rights who is also a member of Kuwait's ruling family. She completed her BA at the University of Birmingham in 1972 and received master's and doctoral degrees from Yale University in 1974 and 1977. She served as the head of the language center at the University of Kuwait, rising to the position of vice rector for community service and information in 1985. She then became the undersecretary for the Ministry of Higher Education and served as the Kuwaiti deputy-ambassador to the United Nations, 1990–1994.

As a close relative of the former ruling emir of Kuwait, Sheikh Jaber al-Ahmad al-Sabah, she played a crucial role in his attempt to push legislation through the Kuwaiti parliament in favor of women's political rights. The attempt failed twice in 1999, succeeding only several years later. She is also known as the first woman to hold mixed *diwaniyya* gatherings, or weekly meetings in a *diwan*, or salon. She has received several honors, including an honorary doctorate of law from Richmond University in London. *See also* EDUCATION: ARAB GULF STATES.

SABAH, SUAD MUHAMMAD AL- (1942–). A Kuwaiti poet, economist, children's and women's rights advocate, and publisher who is also a member of Kuwait's royal family. Her full name is Suad Muhammad al-Sabah. She received a degree in economics and political science from the University of

Cairo in 1973 and a doctoral degree in economics from Guilford University in Great Britain in 1981. She is best known in Kuwait for being the first woman to establish a publishing house, known as the Suad al-Sabah Publishing and Distribution House. She has published several poetry collections and many articles on economic and political issues, which appeared in Arabic and foreign-language publications.

During the Iraqi invasion of Kuwait in 1990, she launched a one-woman campaign to persuade Arab organizations to come to Kuwait's assistance. In one of her poetry collections, *Will You Let Me Leave My Country?* (1991), she expressed bitterness about events surrounding that war and gave vent to her traumatized state of mind as an intellectual facing the uncertainties of the new world order. In addition to her poetry, she published works in English on economic issues, such as *Development Planning in an Oil Economy and the Role of the Woman* (1983) and *Kuwait: Anatomy of a Crisis Economy* (1984).

She is a director of Kuwait's Stock Exchange, a member of the Higher Council of Education, and a founding member of the Arab Cultural Establishment. She is also a member of the executive committee of the Arab Intellect Forum, the Arab Human Rights Organization, and the Arab Council for Childhood and Development. She has also established an eponymous literary prize. *See also* EDUCATION: ARAB GULF STATES.

SABANCI, GULER (1955–). A Turkish businesswoman and a member of one of Turkey's most successful economic families. She is the chairperson of Sabanci Holdings, the second largest industrial conglomerate in the country. She was born in Adana, Turkey, to Ihsan and Yuksel Sabanci, and received her higher education at Bogazici University in Istanbul, where she obtained a degree in business administration. Her first employment with the family firm was as a director of tire production in Kocaeli Province. Her appointment as the chairperson of Sabanci Holdings followed the death of her uncle, Sakip Sabanci, in 2004, who had served in that capacity since the company's founding in 1967. She was named one of the world's 100 most powerful women by *Forbes* magazine in 2007. She speaks regularly at international conferences on Turkey's economic decline and has campaigned for Turkey's admission to the European Union. She was given an award by the Daughters of Ataturk in 2006 and received the Spanish Order of Civil Merit in 2009.

SADAT, JIHAN (1933–). Egypt's first lady from 1970 until 1981 and a women's rights advocate. She was born on Rawdha Island in Cairo's Nile River. Her father, Safwat Rauf, was a physician in Egypt's Ministry of Health, and her mother, Agnes, was a British citizen, formerly of Malta. Jihan met the future president of Egypt, Anwar Sadat, when he was a national hero and recently released from jail after being implicated in an anti-

British plot. At the time, she was only 16 years old, and he was 30 and already married to a relative of his. He and Jihan were married in 1949 after he divorced his first wife.

Sadat's awareness of **feminist** issues came to her through an aunt who informed her during the 1940s of **Huda Shaarawi**'s struggles. Sadat herself led the life of a busy spouse of a prominent Egyptian official while raising her four children, until her husband's rise to the position of first vice president of Egypt in 1969. She engaged in social welfare activities to benefit the women of Mit Abu al-Koam, her husband's ancestral village, as soon as she became aware of their plight and male-dominated lives. She also witnessed there the social and economic consequences of traditional preference for male children and its impact on Egypt's severe population problem. She organized a sewing cooperative and began to scout for marketing outlets outside the village. She also founded the Talla Society, named after a nearby village in the Minoufiah Governorate, which taught women carpentry and handicrafts. Her social welfare activities began on a large scale after the defeat of the June War of 1967. She filled a great need by organizing a brigade of female volunteers to support the work of military hospitals and aid to wounded soldiers. Her activities resulted in the founding of al-Wafa wa al-Amal (the Faith and Hope Society), which built a large hospital complex for disabled veterans. After her husband succeeded Jamal Abd al-Nasser as Egypt's president in 1970, she used his office to further her philanthropic activities, founding the Children's Villages International to provide opportunities for young orphans and leading a campaign to raise funds for renovating Egypt's oldest hospital, Qasr al-Ayni.

Her feminist activities became more pronounced after she became the "First Lady" of Egypt. President Sadat began to refer to her using this title in 1971, which many Egyptians criticized as a form of Western imitation. Attempting to encourage more women to run for seats in provincial councils, she herself ran for and was elected to a seat in the Minoufiah Council in 1974. She became president of this council in 1978. Her eagerness to run for office resulted from her displeasure with the state of women's representation in legislative bodies despite the absence of any legal bars to their election. At the time of her election, there were only eight women in the People's Assembly, Egypt's parliament, and none in provincial councils.

She also convinced her husband to let her accompany him at one time on a state visit to Saudi Arabia, descending from the plane with him rather than remaining in the cabin to be met by other women. She began to pursue a doctoral degree in Arabic literature at Cairo University when she was 41 years old. Firmly committed to the notion that women can benefit from public visibility, she took her oral exams on Egypt's public television. Her dissertation, which focused on the influence of romanticism on modern Egyptian literature, was completed after her husband's death. She summoned

Egypt's top scholars to tutor her in various subjects so that she could converse intelligently with world leaders and better represent the women of Egypt.

Once she became convinced that Egypt's population expansion was intimately linked to the personal status law, which permitted unrestricted **divorce** and **polygamy** in order to have male children, she began to organize a campaign for new legislation and reforms. She sought the advice of experts from the Ministry of Social Welfare and the Higher Council for **Family Planning** before she began working for a reform measure, eventually known as Law 44, or popularly, "Jihan's Law." Her public role, her high-profile higher degrees, her input into policy matters, and her political influence over many aspects of Egyptian life earned her the admiration of many, as well as the consternation of the country's emerging Islamist preachers. They feared her influence over women and her projection of a Western model of womanhood, and she was the target of many mosque preachers, particularly Sheikh Muhammad al-Mahilawi, a popular preacher in Alexandria.

Following President Sadat's assassination in 1981 by members of an underground Islamist movement, Jihan Sadat moved to the United States, where she became a professor of women's studies at such academic institutions as the University of South Carolina, Radford University, American University, and the University of Maryland. She was the moving force behind establishing the Anwar Sadat Chair for Population, Development, and International Peace, with Shibley Telhami as its inaugural professor. She continues to lecture on women's and peace issues at many campuses. She is the recipient of 18 honorary degrees and many awards.

Jihan Sadat's autobiography, *Sayyidah min Misr* (*A Woman from Egypt*), was published in Cairo in 1987 and was translated into several languages. *See also* HUSSEIN, AZIZA (1919–); OTHMAN, AMAL (1934–); SAID, AMINAH AL- (1914–1955); SHARIA.

SADR, RABAB AL- (1946–). A Lebanese leader of Shii women, philanthropist institution builder, and human rights activist whose full name is Rabab al-Sadr Sharaf al-Din. She is the sister of Lebanon's Imam Musa al-Sadr (1918–1978?). She was born in Iran, but moved to Lebanon with her family at age 15. A member of the leading Shii family, which is found in Lebanon, Iraq and Iran, her name is usually preceded by the title Sitt (Lady), an indication of her noble lineage. She earned a BA in art and an MA in philosophy from a Lebanese university.

Rabab al-Sadr became deeply involved in the humanitarian work of her brother, who is credited with transforming the lives and fortunes of members of Lebanon's poorest and most powerless sectarian community before his disappearance in 1978 while visiting Libya. He sought her involvement in 1960 in the work of the main humanitarian institution benefiting Shii women, the Imam al-Sadr Foundation, of which she assumed the presidency after his disappearance. The foundation expanded later to include six vocational schools and an orphanage. Intended as a showcase of Shii high regard for women's education and public roles, the foundation provides economic and social guidance in addition to education and vocational training for orphaned or economically deprived girls of various religious backgrounds. Money is raised for the foundation from expatriate Shii communities in West Africa and in the United States, particularly from the Detroit area. Rabab al-Sadr expanded the services provided by the foundation, opening two mobile medical clinics, which visit remote villages in the south of Lebanon, following Israel's 2001 withdrawal from that region.

Rabab al-Sadr participated in many regional and international women's conferences, where she repeatedly called for public commitment to gender equality to build better social relations between the sexes. Often mentioned as a potential candidate for a seat in Lebanon's parliament, al-Sadr has repeatedly expressed mistrust of politics and her preference for developing the social and family roles of women.

SAID, AMINAH AL- (1914–1955). An Egyptian **feminist**, journalist, and university professor, born in Asyut in southern Egypt. She attended Shubra Secondary School, the first public school to provide females with an education on a par with the best existing boys' school. She was one of the first women admitted to Cairo University in 1931, graduating in 1935 with a degree in English literature. An enemy of **veiling**, she took up the sport of tennis, which she played publicly while unveiled. She became a member of the **Egyptian Feminist Union (EFU)** and was mentored by veteran feminist **Huda Shaarawi**. She edited the Arabic version of the EFU's journal *al-Misriyyah*, and later became editor of the weekly magazine *Hawaa* (Eve), the organization's other journal.

Her journalistic career took off in the 1940s, when she became the first full-time female journalist on the staff of the publishing conglomerate Dar al-Hilal, and as such, the first professional female journalist in Egypt. She was elected vice president of the board of the Journalist's Syndicate, Egypt's second most powerful organization after that of lawyers. She also contributed articles to *al-Musawwar*, Egypt's first weekly pictorial magazine. In 1975, she became president of the administrative council of Dar al-Hilal, a position she held until her retirement in 1984.

Al-Said is noted for her unyielding opposition to the emerging veiling custom in the 1970s and to Egypt's personal status law. She petitioned the Conference of Islamic Jurists when it convened in Cairo on the eve of the 6 June 1967 War. She often spoke and wrote against President Jamal Abd al-Nasser's reluctance to confront the official Islamic institution on the question of **Sharia** reforms. But she continued to enjoy government support despite the demise and marginalization of most of her feminist colleagues from the royalist period. She was also openly critical of the first wave of veiled university women to appear in her journalism classes at Cairo University in the 1970s.

While a member of the Egyptian parliament, she became a key supporter of the group of female parliamentarians who pushed through Law 44, **Jihan Sadat**'s reform measure of 1978. During the early presidency of Husni Mubarak (1981–2011), she took a public stand against the government's efforts in 1984 to harness the power of the press. Her novel, *al-Jamihah* (*The Shrew, or the Defiant*), written in 1946, used the first-person singular to convey the traumas of its female antagonist. She published a second novel, *The End of the Road*, and an essay collection based on her weekly advice column for women, *Profiles in the Dark*. She translated several books from English, such as Rudyard Kipling's *Jungle Book* and Louisa May Alcott's *Little Women. See also* FEMINIST MOVEMENT IN EGYPT.

SAJAH. An Arab prophetess who belonged to the Tamim tribe of the Arabian Peninsula as well as to the Christian Banu Taghlib tribe of Iraq, on her mother's side. She was a contemporary of Prophet Muhammad and claimed prophethood after his death in 632 CE. She led an armed rebellion against the young Muslim state, creating a powerful tribal federation. Her career was reminiscent of the pre-Islamic phenomenon of female prophetesses, goddesses, and spiritual figures that dominated the lives of Arab tribes. She was a soothsayer before declaring her prophethood. Her full name was Sajah bint al-Harith ibn Suaeed, and she was originally a Christian. She declared herself a prophetess during the apostasy wars, which erupted soon after Muhammad's death when the news was disseminated of similar declarations being made by two male prophets, Musaylama (dubbed "the liar" by Arab chronicler al-Asadi) and Tulayha. She gathered an army of 4,000 people and prepared to march on Medina, but she called off the attack when she learned of Tulayha's defeat at the hands of the great Muslim warrior Khalid ibn al-Waleed. She later married Musaylama and merged her army with his, giving up the role of prophetess in favor of his prophethood. After Musaylama's death at the battle of al-Yamamah and the dispersal of his army, Sajah returned to the Muslim faith.

SAKAKINI, WIDAD (1913–1991). A Lebanese short-story writer who was also a novelist and scholar. She was born at Sidon and graduated from Beirut's Islamic College. After marrying a Syrian national, she moved to Cairo, where she became known for her superb literary style and advocacy of women's rights. Her best known work, a biography of the Lebanese expatriate and women's rights advocate **Mai Ziyadeh**, *Mai Ziyadeh: Her Life and Work* (1969), was carefully researched and based on interviews with Ziyadeh's friends and associates.

Sakakini wrote 20 books, including *The Saint-Lover Rabia al-Adawiyah*, which appeared in English under the title *First among Sufis: The Life and Thought of Rabia al-Adawiyya, the Woman Saint of Basra.* She also wrote Islamic biographies, such as *Mothers of the Faithful* (1945) and *The Prophet's Wives and Martyrs' Sisters* (1968). She wrote a book about the life of Egypt's greatest women's rights advocate, *Qassem Amin* (1965). A novel, *Arwa, the Daughter of Upheaval*, appeared in 1949. A book addressing men and women, *Doing Justice for Women*, was published in 1950.

Widad Sakakini was best remembered in Cairo for a public debate on the rights of women with Egyptian playwright **Tawfiq al-Hakim**. She died at Damascus. *See also* AMIN, QASSEM (1863–1908).

SALAM, ANBARA (1897–1986). A Lebanese female rights' advocate and nationalist who was also a pioneer of the Arab anti**veiling** movement. She was born in Beirut to a political family, which included her father, Salim Salam, a prominent nationalist leader, and her brother, Saeb Salam (1905–2000), a future Lebanese prime minister. She was tutored at home until age 10 and then sent to a Christian school to study French.

Salam resisted going out in public wearing the *abaya* (outer black garment) and settled for wearing only the face veil at an early age. Being veiled, however, did not deter her from becoming active with Arab nationalists in Greater Syria, who were fighting against Ottoman control on the eve of World War I. She published an article in 1913 calling for the participation of Arab women in the struggle for independence. In 1914, she was seen attending a public lecture at a club unaccompanied by a male relative. She continued to call on women to join the struggle against France in the 1920s and was greatly influenced by the writings of **Qassem Amin**.

In 1927, Salam addressed the Women's Renaissance Society in Beirut on her experience while living in Great Britain from 1924 to 1926. She gave this speech unveiled, replicating **Huda Shaarwai**'s act of public unveiling in 1924. This act also gained Salam notoriety and much scorn as the first woman in Greater Syria to unveil publicly, because she was descended from one of Lebanon's leading Sunni Muslim families. In 1929, she gained a measure of freedom when she married prominent Palestinian educator Ahmad Samih al-Khalidi (1896–1951) and moved to Jerusalem. Al-Khalidi was the principal of the elite boys' public school the Arab College and the deputy director of education in British Mandate Palestine. Together, they wrote works on history and educational theory. They were forced to flee their home and seek refuge in Beirut following the 1948 Arab–Israeli War. They both died in Beirut.

SAMMAN, GHADA (1942–). A Syrian novelist and short-story writer who was born in al-Shamiya, Syria. Her father was at one time the rector of the University of Damascus and later minister of education. She earned a BA in English literature from the American University of Beirut in 1964 and an MA in the literature of theater of the absurd from London University in 1966. She began a PhD program, also at London University, but left before receiving a degree. After returning to Beirut in 1969, she became a correspondent for the Lebanese magazine *al-Hawadeth*.

Al-Samman began to publish works of fiction, as well as doing investigative reporting, in the 1960s. Her first novel, *Your Eyes Are My Destiny*, appeared in 1962. All of her following novels and short stories express a strong Arab nationalist sentiment and criticize Zionism and imperialism, taking the side of the Palestinians. In some of her novels, like *Beirut '75* (1974), she exposes class divisions, gender conflict, and corruption in the Lebanese capital, almost predicting the descent into civil war that soon followed. *A Loaf of Bread Beats Like a Heart* (1975) deals with political corruption throughout the Arab world as well as the mistreatment of women. Another book, *The Incomplete Works* (1979), presents her recollections of various journeys to Arab and European countries. In another war-inspired novel, *Beirut Nightmares* (1976), she narrates stories based on her confinement to her hotel when hostilities broke out during the first year of Lebanon's Civil War. A short-story collection, *The Square Moon* (1999), is based on her experiences in Paris and the cultural conflict that she felt as a result of her life in French exile. Her other works include *The Body Is a Suitcase, There Is No Sea in Beirut, Swimming in the Devil's Lake, Sealing the Memory in Red Wax, A Female Citizen Accused of Reading, Love from the Vein to the Vein,* and *The Tribe Interrogates the Murdered Woman*. All of her works are about outworn traditions that force women to assume frozen and lifeless roles, and women's struggle to define identities of their own choosing. A famous article expressing her rebellion, "I Carry My Shame to London," generated a great deal of adverse reaction. Another controversial novel, *The Night of the Billion*, presents her view of the financial background of the Lebanese Civil War.

Since the 1980s, Al-Samman has been living in Paris with her husband, Dr. Bashir Daouq, who owns al-Taliaa Publishing house. Her latest controversial act was the publication of a series of love letters that she exchanged with Ghassan Kanafani, the most famous Palestinian fiction writer, who was assassinated by Israeli agents in 1972.

SAQQAF, KHAIRYA IBRAHIM AL- (1950–). A Saudi educator and journalist who was born at Mecca and later moved to Riyadh, where she received instruction at home before the opening of public schools for girls in 1960. She holds a BA from the University of Missouri at Columbia. She earned a PhD from the School of Social Sciences at Imam Muhammad ibn Saud University in 1988 in Arabic language and literature. She taught for a while at the Women's University College at Riyadh and became in 1981 the first female editor at a national newspaper in the Arab Gulf region, when *al-Riyadh* newspaper appointed her head of its newly established section for women journalists. Her husband, Dr. Yahya al-Saati, is chief editor of a literary periodical, *Alam al-Kateb* (*The Writer's World*). She writes short stories, as well as articles, and oversees a radio program devoted to literary topics. Her first collection of short stories, which appeared between 1978 and 1981, was *Sailing towards the Far Horizons*. She also wrote a collection of essays, *A Crisis in the Equation*. Her work often tackles the sensitive topic of arranged **marriage** and its negative impacts on the parties concerned. She is the mother of four children. *See also* EDUCATION: ARAB GULF STATES.

SAUD, NOURAH BINT ABD AL-RAHMAN IBN FAYSAL AL-(1875–1950). A Saudi princess who was the elder sister of the founder of the Kingdom of Saudi Arabia, King Abd al-Aziz al-Saud (r. 1932–1953). She was born in Riyadh and spent her early years traveling with her family as the Saud royal line continued its conquest of the Arabian Peninsula. Beginning in 1891, the family sought refuge in Kuwait as guests of the Sabah ruling house, where Nourah is known to have exercised great influence over her brother. She was said to be the main force behind the decision to recapture Riyadh from the Rashid family after an earlier failed attempt. She accepted a family-arranged match with the head of a recalcitrant al-Saud faction, Saud ibn Abd al-Aziz ibn Saud ibn Faysal ibn Turki, also known as Saud the Great. This **marriage** brought unity to her brother's faction and that of his al-Saud cousins, and is presumed to have taken place in 1904. The match also reconciled the al-Ajman tribe to her brother's line, since these were her mother-in-law's family. Her marriage, thus, continued the tradition of constructing tribal alliances through family-arranged matches, which her brother practiced to great advantage.

Nourah became, in time, the leader of royal women and settled family disputes, thereby shielding her brother from palace intrigues. She also took the role of "first lady" of the kingdom, receiving the wives of foreign dignitaries, whom she would permit to tour and have access to forbidden cities. Her assumption of this role to the exclusion of the king's wives was due to the difficulty of assigning precedence to any one of them over the others. King Abd al-Aziz's famed British adviser, Harry St. John Philby (1885–1960), was one of the first people to refer to her as "the First Lady in her country." It was said that the king paid her a visit every day seeking her advice on matters of state, because the political system was still informal and based on personal relationships. As evidence of the close relationship between the king and Nourah, royal anecdotes relate that when telephones were first introduced in the kingdom in the 1930s, the first line connected the royal palace to her residence. The king followed the custom of Najd, the central province where Riyadh is located, by proudly invoking her name, saying "I am the brother of Nourah."

SAUDI, MONA (1945–). A Jordanian artist, poet, children's advocate, and political activist who was born in Amman. She studied at the École Supérieure des Beaux Arts in Paris. The greatest influence on her sculptures was Romanian artist Constantine Brancusi (1876– 1957), but she was also sensitive to the Islamic and ancient Middle Eastern artistic and architectural heritage. One of the first women to produce works in stone in the Levant, she was preceded only by state-supported Iraqi female sculptors in the region.

She became a great advocate for the rights of Palestinian refugees and their children as a result of her residency in Beirut. This led her to become an engaged artist and poet with a political message. In 1970, she published a bilingual Arabic and English book in Beirut, *Shihadat al-Atfal fi Zaman al-Harb* (*The Testimony of Children in the Time of War*). She published a collection of poetry, *An Ocean of Dreams*, in 1999. She has been writing poetry since the 1960s, and her work appeared in such literary journals as *Shiir* and *Mawaqef*. She has produced notable examples of public art, which are located in Beirut, Amman, and the Institut du Monde Arabe in Paris.

SAYIGH, MAI (1940–). A Palestinian nationalist, leader, women's rights activist, and poet; she was born in Gaza and graduated from Cairo University in 1960 with a BA in sociology. She was active in women's organizations while living in the West Bank, her name often being mentioned in connection with the Baath Party's Palestinian branch. She resided in Beirut after the Israeli occupation of the West Bank in 1967, where she became president of the **General Union of Palestinian Women** in 1971. She became one of the main official female faces of the Palestine Liberation Organization (PLO), representing it at various international women's conferences.

Her publications include three poetry collections: *Garland of Thorns* (1968), *Love Poems for a Hunted Name* (1974), and *Of Tears and the Coming of Joy* (1975). Her long essay "The Siege" (1982) dealt with the Israeli invasion of Beirut in 1982. *See also* ABD AL-HADI, ISSAM (1928–).

SAYYAH, FATIMA (1902–1948). An Iranian professor and diplomat who was the first woman to become a full professor at the University of Tehran and the first to be named a member of the Iranian delegation to the United Nations. (Although Aminah Pakravan was the first female to be admitted to this university in 1936, rising to the position of lecturer, Sayyah was the first to climb to the highest academic rung.) Sayyah was also a prominent member of the Democratic Organization for Women (DOW), the auxiliary of the communist Tudeh Party. It is due to her efforts that Tudeh began to examine the working conditions of lower-class, unskilled women in the 1940s. Tudeh and the DOW were shut down by government orders in 1949, a year after her death, but did not end efforts to push for women's rights. Her comrades attempted to persuade the government of Muhammad Mossadegh (r. 1951–1953) to grant women suffrage, but a bill to that effect failed in the Majlis in 1952. *See also* FEMINIST MOVEMENT IN IRAN.

SEBBAR, LEÏLA (1941–). An Algerian novelist and social critic who was born in Aflou, Algeria, to a mixed Algerian–French family. She has lived in Paris most of her life and writes mostly in French. Her works attracted attention because of her emphasis on the dilemmas of the *beur,* the second-generation North African youths born in France. Her novels express the anger of this generation of North African youths, both males and females, who grow up to discover that the doors to integration are barred to them. She also describes the alienation of this generation from their families, whose language they do not share, in her novel *Parle mon fis, parle à la mere (Talk Son, Talk to Your Mother).* She also wrote three novels about **Shehrazad,** whom she calls Sherazade. These are titled *Shérazade, 17 ans, brune fisée, les yeux verts (Sherazad, 17, Brunette, Curly Hair and Green Eyes,* 1980) and *Le Fou de Shérazade (Crazy about Sherazad,* 1991). She exchanged correspondence with Canadian novelist Nancy Huston in 1986, which appeared under the title *Lettres Parisiennes, autopsie de l'exil (Parisian Letters, the Autopsy of Exile).*

SECOND CONGRESS OF WOMEN OF THE EAST. A meeting of female activists from Egypt, Lebanon, India, and Iraq, which took place in 1932 in Tehran. The meeting had the official backing of the government of **Shah Reza Pahlavi** to gain consensus for his reform plans. The organization elected Princess Shams, the shah's eldest daughter, as its president, and **Siddiqeh Dowlatabadi** as secretary. The agenda featured discussions of women's rights and their liberation in order to come up to Western standards. There was no discussion of the **veiling** issue.

SEMSEDDIN, SAMI FRASHERI (1850–1904). He was an Albanian advocate of women's rights. His book, *Kadinlar* (Turkish; *Women*), published in 1879, was one of the earliest defenses of women's rights to appear in the Ottoman Empire. Semseddin came to maturity at a time when the Ottoman Empire was riveted by a new discourse on women. He was born in the town of Fraser to a prominent Albanian family. He attended the local *tekke* (monastic school) of the Bektasi Sufi order, of which his family was the leader.

He was influenced by the Bektasi's support for gender equality and its early admission of women to its spiritual ranks. He was also an impressionable young man who imbibed his early views on gender relations from his brother Naim (1846–1900), whose writings and poetry condemned **polygamy**, summary **divorce**, and extreme **veiling**. Semseddin's books gained wide circulation because he wrote in Turkish, whereas his brother wrote in Albanian. He attended Zossimaia, a distinguished Greek gymnasium, where he was exposed to Western learning and modern ideas, especially French language and literature. He was also influenced by **Namik Kemal**, whom he had befriended after moving to Istanbul, and Ahmad Pasha (1844–1912), another pillar of the Tanzimat period of reform. Semseddin became an important figure who supported the Albanian national awakening.

After his Turkish wife, Emine Veliye, a high-born woman, died following nine years of marriage, he lamented her loss publicly, calling her his *refike* (Turkish; companion, friend). His work always stressed women's human dignity and worth as well as their claim to equality of mind and intellect. He published three major works in a period of 27 years, beginning by arguing against arranged **marriages** in the novel *The Romance of Talat and Fitnat* (1872), a Romeo and Juliet love story set in a poor neighborhood of Istanbul that ends in tragedy. His second work, *Kadlinar*, was the first book to speak for gender reforms. His final work was a six-volume encyclopedia, *Dictionary of Proper Names*, which was devoted to female contributors to Islamic and Western civilizations. He also suggested that reformed women's status depended on the creation of new and reformed males. He felt that all this could be achieved by reconciling Western and Islamic thought.

SHAABAN, BOUTHAINA (1953–). A Syrian Baathist government official who is also a women's rights advocate. She was born in Homs, Syria, and received a PhD in English literature from Warwick University in Great Britain. She became a professor of English literature at the University of Damascus, later serving as an official translator to President Hafiz Assad (r. 1973–2000). When Bashar Assad succeeded his father as president in 2000, she became, along with Dr. **Najah Attar**, one of the two most prominent female political figures in Syria. The young president appointed her minister for tourism and expatriate communities, after which she was attached to his staff as political adviser and official spokesperson for the regime.

Dr. Shaaban is a well-recognized authority on Arab and Syrian women and has authored several landmark studies in this area. In *Both Left and Right Handed* (1991), she criticizes the injustices inflicted on Syrian women because of the inadequacy of the personal status law. She also paints an admiring picture of the discipline, austerity, and independence of Lebanon's Shii women. In another work, *Voices Revealed: Arab Women Novelists, 1898–2000* (2009), she provides a revisionist history of Arab women and their achievements. She states that women writers, particularly in Lebanon and Syria, broached every topic, including war stories. She also challenges the established notion that men preceded women in producing the first Arabic novel. She attempts to dislodge Egyptian novelist Muhammad Hussein Haykal (1888–1956) from his position as the preeminent first novelist of modern Arabic literature, with his novel *Zaynab* in 1914, by citing at least 10 female novelists who preceded him. In her view, the development of the novel, a new Arabic literary genre, coincided with the development of Arab feminism at the end of the 19th century. She states that the first Arabic novel was *Good Consequences, or Ghada the Radiant*, written by **Zaynab Fawwaz** in 1899 and published in Cairo.

Shaaban emerged as the official spokesperson of the beleaguered regime of Bashar Asaad during the "Arab Spring" of 2011. She proved to be one of the most loyal Baathist figures in the country. Her life was the subject of a movie released in 2008, *Woman*, produced by Ziad Hamzeh. The movie was awarded the Golden Palm by the Beverly Hills Film Festival for that year. She is married to Khalil Jawad.

SHAARAWI, HUDA (1879–1947). Leading Egyptian feminist and the Arab world's first organizer and mobilizer of women. She was born in Cairo and is the daughter of Muhammad Sultan Pasha, president of Egypt's first national assembly, and his Turkish wife. Huda was tutored at her father's palace by Arab and French teachers. Her husband, Ali Shaarawi, who was her first cousin, was one of the three original rebels who sparked the 1919 Revolution and founded the Wafd Party, of which he later became the treasurer. He was one of the three men who proceeded to the residence of the British High Commissioner on 13 November 1919 to present Egypt's nationalist demands. When these men were exiled, their wives and female relatives were encouraged to take up the national burden by leading demonstrations and campaigns calling for the boycotting of British goods. The women's participation in the nationalist effort under Shaarawi's leadership included Coptic Christians as well as Muslim women, reflecting the secular orientation of the Wafd Party. Her husband's death in 1922 freed Shaarawi to devote all her energies and substantial financial assets to the **feminist** cause.

Shaarawi's initiation into the activities of civil society began when she joined **Mabarat Muhammad Ali** (founded in 1908) as a dedicated volunteer. During the 1919 Revolution, she was the informal leader of the Women's Wafd Committee (WWC), headed by **Safiyyah Zaghloul (1878–1946),** wife of Saad Zaghloul, Egypt's national hero and future prime minister. When this committee began to lose its effectiveness, Shaarawi formed the **Egyptian Feminist Union (EFU)** in 1923. She resigned from the WWC after she was excluded from the annual Wafd Party conference in 1922 for criticizing Zaghloul for overlooking the traditional role of the king as the ruler of Egypt and the Sudan. From that point on, she worked for a set of national goals, as well as for a purely feminist agenda. She said in one of her early lectures that she always knew that national upheaval inevitably leads to the advancement of women's rights.

But when the authors of the 1923 constitution ignored the WWC's demands for the franchise, the women's political agenda suffered a severe blow. Shaarawi came very close to transforming her creation, the EFU, into a women's political party, which would have happened had women been granted the franchise. Her eventual break from the Wafd Party and its foreign policy agenda also resulted from her disapproval of the Anglo–Egyptian Treaty of 1936, which stopped short of removing British military bases from Egyptian soil. This dispute with Prime Minister Mustafa al-Nahhas (1879–1965) caused her to switch allegiance to the Saadian Party. Her political allies proposed admitting women to the Egyptian senate in 1938, but again the measure failed. In 1946, Prime Minister Ali Aloubah submitted another resolution, calling for admitting women who had literacy qualifications to the senate, only to be turned down. A prominent Wafdist deputy, Ali Zaki al-Urabi, claimed in March 1947 that the Egyptian constitution did not specifically limit voting rights to males, but he was defeated by the decision of a senate constitutional committee specifically convened to study this matter. Only the demands of the feminist press forced parliament to reserve two balconies for women from which to observe its proceedings. By 1947, Egypt's and the Arab World's greatest feminist had died.

Shaarawi's achievements would eventually be measured by the success of her mobilization efforts on behalf of women and her unmatched contributions to the development of feminist consciousness throughout the Arab world. She gained publicity for the struggle of Egyptian women by linking up with the international feminist movement, represented by the International Alliance for Women (IAW), when the latter waged a campaign to achieve universal women's suffrage. But the EFU lost faith in the IAW's efforts when the latter became closely aligned with British imperialism and refused to take up the cause of Palestinian women against the Zionist movement. Her support for the rights of Palestine's Arabs began in 1936 when the EFU's Arabic journal, *al-Misriyah* (*The Egyptian*), began to cover news of the 1936 Arab Revolt in Palestine. In 1938, she convened the first Arab women's conference on Palestine at Cairo, calling it the Eastern Women's Conference. This was the first conference attended by women who traveled to Egypt without male escorts. Her commitment to pan-Arabism was strongly manifested through the convening of the Arab Feminist Conference, also at Cairo, in 1944, leading to the establishment of the **Arab Feminist Union (AFU)** the following year. Arab women in attendance not only called for the liberation of Arab lands, but also demanded reforms of personal status laws in their own countries.

Shaarawi's broad assault on traditional values began with her public unveiling at Cairo's train station when she returned with her assistant, **Ceza Nabrawi**, from Rome in 1924 after attending an IAW meeting. She and her generation of upper-class Egyptian women were greatly impacted by **Qassem Amin**'s criticism of the **veil** as unhygienic and un-Islamic attire. Shaarawi was preceded in this endeavor by Safiyyah Zaghloul, who met her husband, Saad Zaghloul, upon his return from exile in 1921 while unveiled, a step he had preapproved. Her lasting achievement turned out to be opening the field of higher education to women. Even though daughters of the bourgeoisie, both Christian and Muslim, had access to private Arabic and European schools as early as 1835, entry into higher academies and access to Egyptian universities remained blocked. Some of Egypt's male reformers encouraged women's admission to higher institutes of learning by allowing females to attend evening classes at the newly opened public university in 1908. In 1928, a total of five women were admitted to King Fuad University as full-time students, with the backing of liberal university president Ahmad Lutfi al-Sayyid. Yet conservative figures, such as a well-known sheikh of **al-Azhar** seminary, Muhammad Abu al-Uyoun, argued in the 1940s that if women were to be educated, they should receive instruction only in home economics and child care.

Women's right to work, another demand of Shaarawi and the EFU, fared much worse. Women's introduction to work in the industrial sector, in contrast to women's informal participation in farming, dates back only to the 1930s. Women were allowed to become textile workers at Mahillah al-Kubra factories, a project initially founded by Bank Misr (Bank of Egypt). But upper-class women were unable to join the professions or do anything other than teach school. Many voices rose in opposition, some, like novelist Muhammad al-Mazini, arguing that women's rightful place was in the home, and others, like Bank Misr's founder, economist **Talaat Harb** (1867–1941), claiming that women would take away men's jobs, The EFU, however, pushed for women's right to take up any occupation and called for special legislation to protect the rights of working women.

Shaarawi and her allied organizations, which numbered 15 by the time of her death, failed to force any meaningful changes in the personal status law, which followed the dictates of the **Sharia**. As early as 1924, the EFU and the WWC presented the Egyptian parliament with demands for opening higher education to women, the granting of political rights, the elimination of **polygamy**, and the restriction of **divorce**. The women's demands also included prohibiting legalized prostitution, raising the **marriage** age of females to 16 and males to 18, as well as reforming laws that favor husbands over wives in matters of child custodianship. Shaarawi's only success was on the educational front and in gaining changes in the marriage age of females and males.

Some of the limitations of Huda Shaarawi's feminist philosophy and the methods she chose to achieve her objectives must also be taken into consideration. She was always more in tune with the demands of upper-class women than those of other classes, which opened her to charges by Islamic critics of advocating a Western-style brand of feminism. It is noteworthy that the EFU's first journal, in 1925, was a French-language publication titled *L'Égyptienne*, edited by Cesar Nabrawi, because its membership was more fluent in French than in Arabic. By seeking her inspiration from the international feminist movement, Shaarawi aroused the ire of Islamic organizations such as the Muslim Sisterhood, founded in 1937 by Labibeh Ahmed. Shaarawi was also supported by some of the leading male secularists and thinkers of her day, such as Taha Hussein (1889–1973) and Muhammad Hussein Haykal. Both of them acted as legal advisers to the EFU, and Hussein's wife became a member of Shaarawi's union as early as the late 1920s.

Shaarawi wrote her memoir, *Asr al-Hareem*, which was translated by Margot Badran and published in 1986 as *Harem Years: The Memoirs of an Egyptian Feminist, 1879–1924*. Shaarawi was also decorated by the leaders of four Arab states. Her life became the subject of a parodic play by famed Egyptian poet Ahmad Shawqi (1869–1932), who was nicknamed "The Prince of Poets" (*Amir al-Shuaraa*). Titled *Al-Sitt Huda* (*Lady Hudda*), the play imagines Shaarawi as a rich lady living among Cairo's poor in the lower-class neighborhood of al-Sayyida Zaynab. Huda spends her days fielding marriage proposals by greedy suitors, eventually dying childless and bequeathing her wealth to the residents of another poor quarter and her land to a religious trust.

SHAFAQ, ELIF BILGIN (1971–). A Turkish novelist who resides in Istanbul and was born in Strasburg, France, where her father was a diplomat. She is the leading female novelist in her country; she became interested in writing when she was eight years old. She always believed that women carry within them a harem of female voices. An avid reader of Western literature, she was greatly inspired by the character of Jo March in *Little Women* (1868). She graduated from the Middle East Technical University in Turkey with a degree in international relations and a graduate degree in gender and women's studies. She is married to journalist Eyup Can and has two children, named after her favorite writers and works of fiction: a girl named Zelda Fitzgerald and a son named after a story by Jorge Luis Borges, "The Zahir."

Shafiq is interested in **Sufism**, which inspired most of her novels. In *The Forty Rules of Love: A Novel of Rumi* (2010), she describes a love affair between a Jewish American woman and a Sufi man living in Amsterdam. She writes both in Turkish and English and has published seven novels and two works of nonfiction. Among her publications are *The Mystic* (1997) and *The Flea Palace* (2002), both of which have been translated into many languages. She was awarded a prize by the Social Scientists Institute for her master's thesis on Islam, women, and mysticism. She also contributes regularly to journals in various countries. Among her awards are the Chevalier des Arts et Lettres from the French government; the International Journalism Prize of Maria Grazia Culti Award, Italy (2006); the Union of Turkish Writers Best Novel Prize for *Gaze* (2006); and the Great Rumi Award, Turkey, for *Pinhan* (1998). Her novel *The Bastard of Istanbul* (2006) was long-listed for the Orange Prize for Fiction, London, in 2008.

SHAFIQ, DURREA REGAI (1908–1975). An Egyptian women's rights activist and journalist who is also known as Doria Shafiq. She attended an Italian convent school as a child before being sent to the town of Tanta to live with her grandmother and attend a French mission school. When she was in secondary school, she wrote to **Huda Shaarawi**, offering to speak at the annual convention of the **Egyptian Feminist Union (EFU)** on the life of **Qassem Amin**. Shafiq later sought Shaarawi's assistance in obtaining a government scholarship to study at the Sorbonne, where she earned a doctorate in philosophy in 1940, writing a thesis titled "La Femme Égyptienne et L'Islam." Her French education, however, exposed her to charges of excessive Westernization.

Shafiq began to work as a journalist and teacher as soon as she returned to Egypt. She taught at Alexandria's College for Girls, serving a longer tenure at Saniyya School, the highly regarded public school for girls. She also served as an inspector of French at the Ministry of Education. In 1948, a year after Shaarawi's death, Shafiq founded Ittihad Bint al-Nil, an association modeled after the EFU, which she affiliated with the International Council of Women (ICW). The Ittihad, sometimes known as Rabitat bint al-Nil (Union of the Daughters of the Nile), had many branches in various cities and had a section devoted to women's political rights. She began to publish a monthly journal, *Majallat Bint al-Nil*, in 1945, which appeared without interruption until it was shut down in 1957. On the eve of the 1952 Egyptian Revolution, which swept away the monarchy, Shafiq led her organization in demonstrations that targeted the government and remaining vestiges of British colonial control. She led a demonstration of 1,000 women in 1951, calling on parliament to recognize women's political rights and disrupting parliament's proceedings for three hours. When the Egyptian political parties were mobilizing against British bases and interests, she led a women's parliamentary unit, which joined public demonstrations against King Farouq and Barclays Bank just before the great Cairo fire of January 1951.

After the Egyptian Revolution of 1952 swept the Free Officers into office, all the political organizations were outlawed by 1953, including Shafiq's Rabitat Bint al-Nil. When the officers' regime failed to appoint any women to the constitutional assembly charged with drafting a new constitution, Shafiq and her female followers decided to push for the franchise on their own. They staged a highly publicized hunger strike outside the Journalist's Syndicate offices at Cairo and Alexandria. Her 10-day strike came to an end when President Muhammad Naguib promised to take the women's request into consideration. The right to vote was granted in 1956, but it came with literacy qualifications, while men continued to enjoy the franchise with no qualifications except age.

Shafiq is best remembered for her much-publicized confrontation with President Jamal Abd al-Nasser. In 1957, she announced before members of the Egyptian and foreign press that she was going on a hunger strike to protest the Egyptian leader's dictatorship and his failure to remove Israeli troops from the Sinai in the wake of the Suez War. This was her greatest miscalculation, having ignored all signs of Nasser's immense popularity at this point in his political career. She also received no backing from any women's groups for her action, while her colleagues in Rabitat Bint al-Nil asked for her resignation. Other women called her a traitor. Nasser reacted to this public attack by closing her association and her journal and placed her under house arrest. But Shafiq continued to write, completing her unpublished memoirs and a French and English translation of the Quran. She remained in isolation for almost 18 years, eventually suffering a mental breakdown. She committed suicide in 1975 by jumping from a balcony.

Durrea Shafiq wrote numerous articles and her memoirs and was known to be an accomplished journalist. She published *The Egyptian Woman from the Pharaohs until Today* with Ibrahim Abduh, *The Development of Women's Renaissance in Egypt: 1798–1951*, and *The White Paper on the Rights of Egyptian Women. See also* FEMINIST MOVEMENT IN EGYPT.

SHALVI, ALICE HILDEGARD (1926–). A leading Israeli **feminist** who is also a peace activist, educator, and religious reformer. She was born at Essen, Germany, where her family practiced Orthodox Judaism and were active followers of the Zionist movement. After moving to London in 1934, she completed a BA in English literature at Cambridge University by 1944. Four years later, she received a graduate diploma in social work from the London School of Economics. In 1949, she and her family immigrated to Israel, where they settled in Jerusalem and she became a professor of English at Hebrew University. She received a PhD in English in 1962, also at Hebrew University. In 1950, she married an immigrant from New York, Moshe Shelkowitz, who later adopted the Hebrew version of his name, Shalvi. She headed the English Department at Hebrew University and at Ben Gurion University in the Negev.

Alice Shalvi founded several schools, institutions, and networks to ensure the survival of her projects and the perpetuation of her ideals. In 1975, she founded an unusual experiment, a Talmudic school for girls, called Pelech, which broke the ban on teaching Orthodox girls the Talmud. In 1973, she began the movement for neighborhood associations known as Ohalim. But she gained great notoriety through the founding of Israel's Women's Network in 1984, an organization that she also chaired until 2000. In 1990, she founded the International Coalition for Agunah Rights, which engaged Palestinian women in a serious debate on the possibility of achieving peace. In 1997, she became the first woman to integrate a prominent Orthodox center of learning by becoming the rector of the Schechter Institute for Jewish Studies in Jerusalem.

Shalvi is best known, however, for her critique of the training and staffing of women in the Israeli Defense Forces, (IDF). Although women are barred from combat duty, men remain in the reserves until age 55, performing military duties two months each year. This imbalance in the military experience of both sexes, in her opinion, is what fortifies the traditional role of women as mothers and housekeepers. She made the case that women used to fight in the Jewish underground in the most dangerous units, such as the elite Palmach militia, but were pushed out of these ranks during the 1948 Arab–Israeli War to shield them from viewing the mutilated bodies of war victims.

Shalvi is the recipient of several awards, including the Emil Grunzweig Human Rights Award (1989), the Israel Prize (2007), and the Liebowitz Prize, shared with Rabbi Arik Ascherman (2009). She is also a member of the board of the Israel/Palestine Center for Research and Information. *See also* FEMINIST MOVEMENT IN ISRAEL.

SHAMLAN, SHARIFA (?–). An Iraqi-born journalist, short-story writer, and government official. She was born in southern Iraq and earned a BA in journalism, then moved to Saudi Arabia, where she was appointed the director general of Women's Social Affairs in the Eastern Province at Dammam. Her three collections of short stories are *Eternal Tranquility* (1988), *Episodes of a Life* (1991), and *Tomorrow He Will Come*.

SHARAF, LAYLA (?–). A Jordanian cabinet minister and member of the senate who was born to a Druze family in Lebanon. She graduated from the American University of Beirut and married Abd al-Hamid Sharaf, a member of the Jordanian royal family. He became prime minister of Jordan in the 1970s until his untimely death in 1980.

Layla Sharaf was the second woman to be named to the Jordanian cabinet and was made minister of culture and information in 1984–1985. She was also appointed to the senate, serving in 1989, 1993–1994, and 2011.

SHARIA. The body of Islamic law, or jurisprudence, which dates back to the ninth century CE. Because Islam spread geographically to encompass various regions and cultures of the world, it became difficult to adjudicate the law by reference to the Quran and Hadith (the Prophet's statements) only. In time, four schools of jurisprudence developed, each named after its scholarly founder: Hanafi, Shafii, Maliki, and Hanbali. The Maliki school, which is found in North Africa, is the most liberal, and the Hanbali, which is found in Saudi Arabia and the Persian Gulf states, is the most conservative. A separate body of laws governing the Shii community is called the Jaafariyah. All schools of the Sharia are based on the scholar's interpretation of the Quran and Hadith as well as on customary law and comparative law. Most differences between these schools pertain to women and the family, such as **inheritance** rights, custodianship of children, compatibility in **marriage**, and qualifying for the judicial institution.

Colonial rule over much of the Islamic world resulted in the adulteration or total elimination of much of the body of commercial law and the penal code. Punishments imposed by the Sharia that were deemed "contrary to principles of natural justice" were eliminated. Islamic commercial law, which was considered inadequate by Western standards, was replaced by Belgian and Swiss laws. Only laws governing the lives of women and children remained unchanged, with the exception of those detailing the treatment of slave women and concubines. This led to the rise of dual systems of law, one relevant to civil relations and the other dedicated to the family. The latter system of law acquired the designation personal status law, a term first applied by an Egyptian jurist, Muhammad Qadri (1821–1888).

Reforming the Sharia proved to be a gradual and delicate task, first attempted by the Ottoman authorities in the 19th century. An official publication, known as *al majallet*, introduced new laws based on the Sharia but codified in the manner of European laws. The call for reforming the Sharia was taken up by figures of the Arab renaissance toward the end of the 19th century, including **Muhammad Abduh** and **Jamal al-Din Afghani**. The first Muslim ruler to confront upholders of the Sharia and its rigid laws was **Mustafa Kemal Ataturk** of Turkey, who dispensed with it altogether. President **Habib Bourgiba** rewrote much of the **Personal Status Code of Tunisia** in 1956, but insisted that he was merely reinterpreting the Sharia, a privilege reserved to the ruler. Today, few countries follow the Sharia without any adulteration, except for Saudi Arabia. The Islamic Republic of Iran officially follows the Sharia, but allows secular legislation to intrude on its domain if the new laws are deemed compatible with the Sharia. One of the most vigorous calls for reforming the Sharia in modern times was that of the **Republican Brothers**, a defunct movement in Sudan. Modern scholars view the Sharia as overly legislative in its approach to scriptures, particularly when compared to the intellectual richness of Islamic philosophy, *falsafa*, or the spirituality of Islamic mysticism, or Sufi thought. *See also* ALGERIAN FAMILY CODE (1984); AZHAR, AL-; BEN BAZ, ABD AL-AZIZ (1912–1999); FAMILY PLANNING IN ISLAM; FATWA; FEMINIST MOVEMENT IN EGYPT; FRONT ISLAMIQUE DU SALUT (FIS); GHAZZALI, ZAYNAB (1917–2005); HADDAD, TAHIR (1899–1935); HANBAL, IMAM AHMAD IBN (780–855); HUDUD; IRANIAN CONSTI-TUTION (1980); KHULU; MUDAWANA, AL-; PAHLAVI, REZA SHAH (1878–1944); POLYGAMY; QASSEM, ABD AL-KARIM (1914–1963); QUTB, SAYYID (1906–1966); SADAT, JIHAN (1933–); SHAARAWI, HUDA (1879–1947); SLAVERY; SUFISM; TURABI, HASSAN AL-(1932–); UMM AL-WALAD; URF MARRIAGE; WAQF.

SHARIATI, ALI (1933–1977). An important thinker of modern Iran who was the main ideologue of the Islamic Revolution during the 1970s. He also exercised great influence over Muslim Iranian women. He was born in the village of Mazinan, near the town of Sabzavar. His family produced several clergymen, but he attended public schools in Mashhad. During the early 1950s, he participated in public rallies by the National Front, the coalition that brought Muhammad Mossadegh to power in 1951. He graduated from the University of Mashhad in 1960 with a degree in French and Persian literature. Later on, he studied at the Sorbonne University, where he became acquainted with the works of major Third World intellectuals such as Aimé Césaire (1913–2008) and Franz Fanon (1925–1961). He maintained a long correspondence with the latter. He taught at Firdausi University at Mashhad before leaving for Tehran, where he and others established in 1965 a new type of learning institution known as Hussainieh Ershad. This school was a Shii establishment offering lectures to Iranian Shii youths, but it was closed by the authorities in 1973 due to its antiregime activity. Shariati was impris-oned as a result. He suffered many terms in prison throughout his adult years in Iran before finally departing for exile in London, where he died after a short illness. Many suspected that he was assassinated by the secret police (SAVAK) of **Shah Muhammad Reza Pahlavi**.

Shariati was a Muslim modernist who was more interested in formulating religion in sociological terms than in metaphysical terms. This distinguished him from **Ayatollah Ruhollah Khomeini** and his clerical followers. As an existentialist, he believed that the human will was capable of leading to salvation, rejecting the traditional belief in predestination. He reiterated throughout his career that every Muslim man and woman had a deep respon-sibility to study Islamic history and the Quran and assume his or her duties accordingly. He always emphasized the progressive values of Islam. Reject-ing Marxist elements in Fanon's philosophy, he was nevertheless greatly influenced by the latter's revolutionary thinking. As a result, Shariati was decidedly anti-Western, particularly on the subject of women. He emphasized one of the Prophet's *Hadiths* that called on believers to rely on him in matters of religion, but to rely on themselves in matters of this world. He began to acquire an international reputation during his final years in Iran. He was jailed in 1973, but was released as a result of the intercession of the Algerian government in 1975. By that time, the publication in Iran of his article, "Marxism and Other Western Fallacies: A Critique of Marxism from the Perspective of Islam," had made him famous. He was greatly interested in the life of an ancient Islamic figure, Abu Dhurr al-Ghifari (d. 657), who spent all of his life resisting injustice and was called in Persian "Abu-Dharr-iZaman" (the Abu-Dharr of Our Times).

Shariati strongly rejected Western culture because of its impact on Muslim women, arguing that it subjected women to capitalism and consumerism. Women's true emancipation would never be achieved by adhering to Western concepts, he often declared, claiming that their women were mere commodities dominated by conservative influences. He asked Muslim women to evaluate the true source of their freedom and reject Western forms of dress. It is said that due to his influence and his lectures, women willingly returned to wearing the **chador**. Shariati used the phrase, "the return to ourselves" as a motivator for women wishing to find their authentic culture. Many scholars credit him with being one of the first Muslims to advocate Islamic identity politics. He believed that only authentic and original Islam provided the true models of liberated women.

His groundbreaking book on this theme was *Fatema Fatema Ast* (1971), or *Fatima Is Fatima*. In it he argued that it is because of **Fatima** that the Prophet granted dignity and equality to women, for no one could belittle her devotion to the true faith and her readiness to sacrifice her life for Islamic ideals. She lived in poverty and hardship because her father's wealth reverted to the common treasury after his death. She was the mother of Imam Hussein, Islam's tragic martyr. Shariati held up the model of Fatima, not Western role models, as worthy of emulation. Shariati's writings had a great impact on some of Iran's renowned Islamic female reformers, such as **Zahra Rahnavard** and Fereshteh Hashemi. He was buried in Damascus near the tomb of **Zaynab**, the Prophet's granddaughter and Imam Hussein's sister, rather than in Tehran, because his wife opposed returning his body to his original homeland. Imam Musa al-Sadr (1928–1978?) of Lebanon officiated at his funeral.

SHAWWA, LAYLA (1940–). A Palestinian oil painter and silk screen artist who was born in Gaza. She studied at Cairo and at two art academies in Rome, the Italian Academia di Belle Arti and the Academia San Giacomo. She also studied with Oskar Kokoschka in Vienna. Returning to Gaza in 1965, she began to teach art to the poor children of her city as part of UN children's educational projects. But her most famous work remains a silk screen creation, *Walls of Gaza*, which she assembled from 1992 through 1995 to illustrate her people's political struggle against Israeli occupation. Another painting, representing breast cancer, was meant as a metaphor for the Gulf War of 1991. Her work also focuses on Middle Eastern women and is compared in style and color to the paintings of Henri Rousseau. It has been exhibited in most Arab countries and around the world. Her art is highly sought after by private collectors and art galleries, such as the National Gallery of Jordan and the British Museum in London. She has been living in Great Britain since 1979.

SHAWAA, RAWIYA (?–). A Palestinian legislator and businesswoman who was born in Gaza, where she completed her high school education. She lived in Saudi Arabia with her husband until 1974. After her return to Gaza, she became the first woman to own and operate a commercial business. A popular journalist, she was among a handful of women elected to the first Palestinian Legislative Council (PLC) from the Gaza district. She was also a member of the Council for Higher Education, representing all of the West Bank, as well as a member of the Arab Thought Forum. She served as president of the Gaza Cultural Group for many years. *See also* EDUCATION: PALESTINE.

SHEHRAZAD. This is the legendary heroine of the Arabic epic, *Thousand and One Nights*, who was known for her wisdom, courage, sacrifice, resistance to male oppression, and promotion of female solidarity. The genesis of her story and the spelling of her name are also claimed by Persian literature, which contributes to a great deal of confusion. Her stories revolve around saving women from death as she pacifies her husband, Shahriyar, by calling on him to wait another day to hear the conclusion of her tales. The story is structured as a "frame," the thousand and one nights, which describe the wiles of women and men's thirst for vengeance. The "frame" structure is not found among Arab letters and may have been borrowed from Indian literature. The basic story concerns King Shahriyar and his brother Shahzaman, both of whom discover that their wives have committed adultery in their absence. As a result, both depart to the wilderness, seeking solace, experiencing a wild adventure battling the *jinn* (spirits, muses), which convinces them that even these evil spirits are helpless before the wiles of women. Shahriyar returns to his kingdom, determined to marry and kill a new wife every day. Shehrazad, who was the daughter of the grand vizier, volunteers to marry the king in order to save the women of the kingdom. This becomes the "frame," which spins a new tale every night, until by the end of the thousand and one nights, the king has fallen in love with Shehrazad and cancels the order to kill all the women of his kingdom. His subjects celebrate this glorious ending, by which time Shehrazad has given him three sons.

Beginning in the 1930s, Shehrazad began to inspire major figures of modern Arabic literature. Egypt's greatest dramatist and playwright, **Tawfiq al-Hakim** (1898–1987), wrote a play titled *Shehrazad* in 1934, in which he portrayed the heroine as the eternal woman, or the goddess **Isis** of ancient Egypt, who brought her husband back from the dead. To al-Hakim, Shehrazad, like Isis, represents the mystical forces of birth and rebirth. Egypt's renowned literary giant Taha Hussein (1889–1973) wrote a novel, *Dreams of Shehrazad*, in 1943, in which he predicted the outbreak of a nuclear war. Another Egyptian novelist, Idwar Kharrat (1926–), who was born in Alexandria, gives the story of Shehrazad a modern Mediterranean rendition, making it an amalgam of various cultures and religions; in *Turrabaha Zaaffaran* (*City of Saffron*), he presents Alexandria, like Shehrazad, as an enigmatic force that helps define his identity. To modern feminists like **Fatima Mernissi** and others, Shehrazad and her story represent the force of creative subversion.

SHEIKH, HANAN AL- (1945–). A Lebanese novelist, short-story writer, playwright, and journalist who was born in Beirut to a poor Shii family originating in the south. She had an unhappy childhood due to her mother's travails, who was married at age 14, was not allowed to learn reading or writing, and abandoned her family and children altogether. This became the subject of al-Sheikh's short story "The Scratching of the Angels' Pens." Her father, though interested in pushing his children through school, attempted to place limitations on her freedom during her youth. She attended one of Beirut's prestigious institutions, the Ahliya School. In 1963, she felt compelled to leave Beirut and move to Cairo, where she enrolled at the American College for Girls. There, she wrote her first novel, *The Suicide of a Dead Man*, which describes the tyranny of the patriarchy and conflict between the sexes. Returning to Beirut, she became a journalist for *al-Nahar* newspaper, returning to fiction writing a few years later, coming out with another sensational novel, a semiautobiography titled *The Devil's Stallion* (1971). She moved to Saudi Arabia for one year only, eventually moving to London in 1982 during the civil war that racked Lebanon in the mid-1970s.

Hanan al-Sheikh's published novels treat some of the most scandalous taboos in Arab culture, such as prostitution and homosexuality. She also openly derides the influence of Islamic fundamentalism on women. Writing exclusively in Arabic, she attained international fame in 1980 due to the public uproar that resulted from the publication of her novel *The Story of Zahra*. Set in wartime Lebanon, the novel describes the tortuous search for individual freedom of a young woman named Zahra, who finally escapes the control of her family during the chaos of the civil war. Zahra engages in free sex, undergoes abortions, and eventually suffers a serious nervous breakdown. The novel was rejected by Lebanese publishers and was banned in much of the Arab world, eventually being self-published by the author, earning a certain niche for itself as one of Lebanon's novels of war and descent into madness. Another novel, *Women of Sand and Myrrh* (1989), was also banned because of its frank depiction of the struggle of four women against the traditional patriarchy and their suspension between traditional and Western values. Some of the main characters experiment with lesbianism as a way of escaping traditional life patterns of their culture. When it was translated into English, the novel proved to be immensely popular, being ranked among the 50 best books of 1992 by *Publishers Weekly*. This led to a promotional book tour in the United States, the first such success by an Arab fiction writer. Her two plays, *Dark Afternoon Tea* (1995) and *Paper Husband* (1997), were staged at the Hampton Theater in London. Her other published titles include *Praying Mantis* (1971), *The Musk of the Gazelle* (1988), *Beirut Blues* (1992), and *Only in London* (2000). A collection of short stories that she wrote in Saudi Arabia, *The Desert Rose*, was published in 1982.

SHEMER, NAOMI (1930–2004). An Israeli singer who was born near the Sea of Galilee. She studied music at Jerusalem's Rubin Academy, eventually settling in Tel Aviv. Like all Israeli women, she had a semimilitary affiliation in the 1950s, her experience being largely with the Nahal section of the Israeli Defense Forces (IDF), where recruits are trained in military and agricultural duties. Her songs exhibited patriotic characteristics, many Israelis reciting them as if they were military anthems. Her most famous song, "Yerushalayim shel Zahav" ("Jerusalem of Gold"), which she wrote during the June War of 1967, almost became Israel's official song. Another song, "O Captain, My Captain," which was based on a poem by Walt Whitman, treated the assassination of Prime Minister Yitzhak Rabin in 1995. She was awarded the Israel Prize in 1983 in recognition of her contribution to Israeli culture.

SHID, NAHID (1953–). An Iranian lawyer and social welfare expert who was instrumental in the passage of laws that expanded the benefits of Iranian women. She took up religious studies with a noted scholar, Ayatollah Maraashi-Najafi, and earned a law degree from Tehran University. Shid has been a practicing attorney since 1980, making a niche for herself in the field of women's legal rights. She served as a consultant to the High Council of the Cultural Revolution in Iran and was credited with initiating significant amendments to **divorce** laws. Among those that were adopted in 1993 was an amendment to *ojrat-ol misl* that changed the evaluation of the back **dowry**, payable upon divorce, to include compensation for housework performed during the marriage. Another amendment to the dowry regulation, passed in 1996, called for calculating the back dowry according to its current inflated value. Shid buttressed her demands by stating that all religious laws can be subject to change because they are based not on spiritual but on material principles rooted in the time and place of their adoption. She also attacked the pseudo-religious custom of demanding a lesser sum of money for a female victim in case of murder than for a male victim, pointing to the fact that women today occupy important positions in society. She also ran for a seat in parliament in 1996, but failed to win the necessary endorsement of the Council of Guardians. *See also* FEMINIST MOVEMENT IN IRAN.

SHIHABI, ZLEKHAH AL- (1903–1992). A Palestinian activist who pioneered the Palestinian feminist movement as early as 1929. She was born in Jerusalem, the daughter of Ishaq al-Shihabi, and was educated at the Sisters of Zion parochial school (Rahbat Sahyoun). She also received private instruction at home. She joined the Arab Women's Executive Committee in 1929 and was elected to the presidency of its successor organization, the Arab Women's Union (AWU), in Jerusalem in 1937. She held this office until her death and oversaw the creation of various programs, such as a sports club with its own tennis courts and a health clinic, which opened in 1946.

Shihabi played a large role during the Eastern Women's Conference on Palestine, held in Cairo at the behest of the **Egyptian Feminist Union** in 1938 and the Arab Women's Conference in 1944, representing Palestinian women. She was also a member of the preparatory committee that established the **General Union of Palestinian Women (GUPW)**, coinciding with the first Palestine Liberation Organization (PLO) meeting in Jordanian Jerusalem in 1964. The union was eventually banned by Jordan, as well as by Israel, but later became one of the official cadres of Yasser Arafat's second PLO, headquartered in Beirut. After the imposition of Israeli rule over the West Bank in 1967, Shihabi was expelled to neighboring Jordan because of her political activities. She did return to Jerusalem after only a few months and continued with her charitable work on behalf of Palestinian women until her death.

SHINNAWI, MONA AL- (1959–). An Egyptian banker who heads Islamic banks in the Persian Gulf area. She studied commerce in the Sudan and started her career at Cairo's Citibank, where she spent 13 years, eventually rising to the position of vice president. During that time she also married and raised three children. She moved to the United Arab Emirates (UAE) in 1998, where she worked at first for a number of local banks before joining the Sharjah Islamic Bank as a vice president in charge of financial analysis in an environment devoid of women bankers. She was drawn to this type of banking, believing that it was ideally suited for women's financial careers. She also founded a networking group for women employed by Islamic financial institutions in the UAE in 2007, known as *Durra* (Jewel), which now has 60 members.

SHOCHAT, MANYA (1879–1961). An Israeli Zionist pioneer and an activist on behalf of Russian Jews in Israel, who was also a **feminist** and an early founder of the kibbutz movement. She was born near Grodno in Belarus and was given the name Manya Wilbushevitz. She was originally involved in underground activities opposed to Tsarist rule but abandoned this movement, joining Jewish self-defense groups and nonrevolutionary socialist activities upon the outbreak of the 1903 Kishinev pogrom in Moldova (Romania). She was imprisoned for her involvement in the assassination of the Russian interior minister but managed to escape, arriving in Palestine in 1904. She was one of the group that founded Kibbutz Sejera, as well as Ha-Shomer, a Zionist militia. She became an emissary to Jewish communities overseas, seeking financial support for Russian Jewish immigrants and Jewish workers in Palestine. She became a gun-runner to local Jewish communities and served a jail sentence imposed by Ottoman authorities as a result.

Shochat channeled her energies into the support of the kibbutz movement during the British Mandate over Palestine, 1920–1948. She also supported the establishment of the Haganah, which was the largest underground militia of the Jewish community before statehood. Always interested in dialoging with Palestine's Arabs, she founded the small League of Arab-Jewish Rapprochement following the 1929 riots while still heavily involved in bolstering Jewish immigration and Jewish communal defense. She is considered the "mother" of the settlement movement in Israel.

SHUKUFAH. This is the second oldest women's journal in Iran. It was founded in 1914 and was intended to mold Iranian women, especially mothers, according to Western standards. Its first editor was Muzzayan al-Saltanah, who was an active builder of elementary schools. She also founded a girls' vocational school and served as an inspector of all other girls' schools in Tehran.

SIDAIRI, SULTANA AL- (?–). A Saudi Arabian short-story writer and poet who was born in the northern part of the country. She published her poetry in Beirut, using pseudonyms such as "Nida," "Uhud," and "**al-Khansaa.**" Her publications include political collections such as *The Fragrance of the Desert* (1956), *My Eyes Are Sacrificed for You* (1960), *A Cloud without*

Rain (1984), and *Subjugation* (1984). A short-story volume, *Images from Society*, appeared in 1975. She received a number of medals and honorable testimonials from Saudi Arabia and several foreign countries.

SIRRI, GAZBIYA (1925–). An influential Egyptian painter and teacher who was educated at Cairo University's faculty of fine arts. She also studied art with Marcel Gromaire in Paris and at the Slade School of Art in London. Her work was featured in 50 exhibits and was awarded many prizes in Egypt and abroad. She established a fund to support the education of young Egyptian artists.

Sirri's work blends personal perspectives with social and political issues. She often referred to her work as mainly a "sensual relationship with color," while at the same time describing it as an "obsession with the human condition." In the 1950s, she belonged to the Group of Modern Art, but she also dealt with nationalist themes such as portraying Egyptians who died battling the forces of British occupation and heroic figures of female Egyptian peasants. Her work was inspired by pharaonic art as well as European impressionist artists. During the waning days of the Nasserite era and following the military defeat of 1967, her paintings became more realistic, portraying prison, mourning for the fallen, and cases of racial discrimination. During the 1970s and 1980s, her work demonstrated a preoccupation with crowded cities, in contrast to the vistas of open desert and the sea that she had painted previously.

SITT AL-MULK (970–1023). A ruler of Fatimid Egypt who was the daughter of Caliph Al-Aziz (r. 975–996). She was also the eldest half-sister of the sixth Fatimid ruler, Al-Hakim bi-Amr Illah (r. 996–1021), who founded the Druze sect. Her own mother was a Christian follower of the Malachite Church. Upon her father's death, she made an attempt with the help of her cousin to usurp the throne from her brother, the legitimate heir, but was thwarted in her efforts by the eunuch Barjuwan, who was the chief vizier. She later became the regent for al-Hakim's son and successor, Ali al-Zahir. This allowed her to wield considerable influence as his adviser, which made her practically the ruler of Egypt even after he came of age. She managed to overturn many of al-Hakim's policies and corrected his deviation from mainstream Islam, such as preventing the **pilgrimage** to Mecca and decreeing a distinctive dress code for Christians and Jews. She also succeeded in stamping out the Druze sect in Egypt, forcing many to settle in the mountainous region of Lebanon. Her persecution of the Druze community resulted from its belief in al-Hakim's divinity. Her foreign policy was marked by conciliatory moves to ease tension with the Byzantine empire over the northern Syrian city of Aleppo. She died while still at the height of her power.

SLAVERY. Islam regards slavery as an inevitable institution arising mainly from war. But the Quran went a long way toward humanizing the condition of slaves, calling the act of the manumission of slaves the greatest thing a Muslim can do to gain God's favor. The number of female slaves in Islamic countries, particularly in north Africa, was usually higher than the number of male slaves. This was due to the absence or rarity of slave armies, with the exception of the mamluks, or white slave dynasties, which ruled Egypt from the 17th through early 19th centuries. Female slaves usually fetched higher prices than male slaves, with the exception of eunuchs. What was unique to the Muslim world was the legal status of female slaves who bore children for their masters. According to the **Sharia**, a female slave who bears a child cannot be resold, and she acquires the title of *umm al-walad* (mother of child), a more exalted sobriquet than a mere concubine. She is freed upon the death of her master. No child of a slave mother and a free master is born into slavery. Furthermore, the status of a royal concubine in the *seraglio* (quarters) of a sultan, known in Turkish as *odalisque*, easily changes to *umm al-walad*, a higher step on the wrung to full freedom.

Generally speaking, Muslim females were not enslaved, but this became law only with the rise of the Ottoman Empire (16th–20th centuries). Under this empire, all Ottoman subjects, irrespective of religion, race, or ethnicity, were immune to enslavement. Ottoman subjects were generally enslaved by others only as a result of war. In most cases, when a slave converted to Islam, his or her emancipation was hastened, but this was not a sure outcome comparable to what happened to a female slave who gave birth to a child. The only exception was the Janissaries, who were recruited at a young age from the empire's Christian territories for the sultan's army. They were automatically converted to Islam and lived on the grounds of the royal palace. Slaves under Ottoman rule enjoyed a legal status and were able to seek redress in an official court of law. They could also seek the payment of damages to compensate for injury or other forms of mistreatment by a master. Many complaints by female and male slaves are found among the records of Ottoman Sharia courts. These records mostly cover cases such as failure to grant manumission after promising to do so and clear and evident instances of deliberate physical harm.

Slaves mostly lived in urban settings and were rarely employed in agriculture. The most famous slaves were concubines of Ottoman sultans. Between the 16th and 17th centuries, the enormous power of concubines gave rise to the phrase "the sultane of the women." The homes of the Ottoman elite also boasted harem quarters for various concubines, in imitation of the design of Topkapi Palace. It was not unusual for some of these women to end up as legitimate wives of their masters. Having once been a slave did not usually reflect negatively on a woman. Although slavery was officially abolished in 1857, it lingered until its abolition by the Young Turks government at the start of the 20th century.

Slavery in the Persian Gulf area and Saudi Arabia persisted until the middle of the 20th century. Since these territories were not subjected to modern colonial rule, they did not experience the British ban on this trade. Slavery disappeared gradually, most of it being domestic slavery, leaving behind a generation of racially mixed Arabs. Under British pressure, Sultan Majid al-Bu Said of the Sultanate of Oman and Zanzibar declared a ban on the slave trade originating from his territories in 1864. Yet slave-carrying boats were often intercepted by the British navy until the early 20th century. African slaves continued to arrive in the Middle East much longer than those from the north, but Circassian female slaves were available in lesser numbers. Most slaves in the Persian Gulf area were engaged in domestic labor, but some female slaves were found in agriculture. More important, although Islam insists on compatibility in **marriage** and the equal status of bride and groom (*kafaah*), marriage between a free Muslim male and a slave female was permissible. *See also* HAREM; WAQF.

SOUEIF, AHDAF (1950–). An Egyptian novelist and political and cultural essayist who was born in Cairo. When she was four years old, her mother traveled to Great Britain to prepare for a doctoral degree, and Ahdaf acquired firsthand knowledge of the English language. Her mother, Fatma Mousa, was the chair of the English Department at Cairo University. Ahdaf was educated at the American University of Cairo and earned a PhD in linguistics (1973) from the University of Lancaster in Great Britain. Her first novel, *In the Eye of the Sun* (1993), tells the life story of an Egyptian woman who grew up in Egypt and England. Her most famous novel, however, was her second book, *The Map of Love* (1999), which was shortlisted for the Man Booker Prize. The novel tells the stories of love in the past and present between British officials and Egyptian nationalists and provides a sweeping view of Egypt's nationalist struggle. An epic historical romance that explores identities of men and women in the context of colonization, the book was an instant success. She is also the author of two collections of short stories, *Aisha* (1983) and *Sandpiper* (1996). Two other collections, *I Think of You* and *Stories of Ourselves*, appeared in 2007 and 2010, respectively. She is the translator of a novel, *I Saw Ramallah* (2003), by the Palestinian novelist Mourid Barghouthi. She writes mostly in English.

She wrote several essays about Palestinians and Palestine, such as "Under the Gun: A Palestinian Journey," which was originally published in the English newspaper *The Guardian*. The same story was included in her latest collection of essays, *Mezzaterra: Fragments from the Common Ground*

(2004). She was one of the founders of the Palestine Festival of Literature and was awarded the first Mahmoud Darwish Prize, named after Palestine's renowned poet.

SPORTS IN ARAB COUNTRIES. Segregation marked any group efforts to improve women's physical activities until the 19th century. Women's leisure activities consisted mostly of folk dancing. Unlike women, men's sports mostly took place in public events. A great variety of sports were played by males to demonstrate cherished values such as bravery, honor, and group solidarity. Among these sports were swimming, archery, stick fencing (in Egypt), wrestling (primarily in Turkey), shooting, and group dancing. Women, by contrast, had no need to demonstrate parallel values.

By the end of the 19th century, the European colonial powers were instrumental in introducing various sports to the Middle East, considered a controlled method of channeling violent instincts. At first, women engaged in some of these new sports in elitist sports clubs, but the majority were engaged in sports in modern public schools. Most of the activities here revolved around gymnastics, which, just as in boys' schools, were based on the notion that physical activity was the basis of sound mental activities. Local indigenous sports clubs were founded by Arab nationalists to strengthen the nation. Famous clubs, such as al-Ahli in Cairo, established in 1907, were the result of these efforts. Men and women's sports activities were also encouraged in Palestinian refugee camps in Jordan, Syria, Lebanon, and inside Israel, basically to instill a nationalist spirit and occupy idle hours. The Sports Association of Arab Women, established in 1997 to encourage intracountry sports competitions, was quickly eclipsed by the **Islamic Countries' Women's Sports Solidarity Games**, founded by **Faezeh Hashemi** Rafsanjani in Iran.

SUDAIRI, HASSAH BINT AHMAD (1900–1969). The wife of King Abd al-Aziz ibn Saud and the mother of several sons, all of whom succeeded to the throne; they were known as the "Sudairi Brothers." She was one of 300 women whom the king married at one point or another during his lifetime (1880–1953). She was a descendant of the Dawasir tribe, a Sharifian, or noble, tribe that settled near the Empty Quarter of the Arabian Peninsula starting in the 1400s. The Dawasirs became military and political allies of the Saud family during the 18th century. The town of al-Ghat in the Sudair region became the home of the Sudairi clan. Among the most famous members of this family was Ahmad al-Kabir (Ahmad the Great), who lived during the first two-thirds of the 19th century and served the Saud family as the governor of al-Hassa province. King Abd al-Aziz's mother, Sara, was the daughter of Ahmad al-Kabir, and his granddaughter Hassah became King Abd al-Aziz's wife. Abd al-Aziz was also married to Haya and Jawhara, two of Ahmad's nieces. Thus, 24 of Abd al-Aziz's sons and grandsons were descended from Sudairi mothers. Abd al-Aziz's son King Faysal (r. 1964–1975) was Sultana al-Sudairi's son, the younger sister of Hassah.

Hassah had several full siblings and half-siblings, male and female. She was married to King Abd al-Aziz in 1913 when she was 13 years old and decades before the Kingdom of Saudi Arabia emerged as a unified state in 1935. Her first son, Saad, died at age five as a result of the Spanish influenza epidemic of 1919. Hassah was divorced by Abd al-Aziz for a while, then married Muhammad, his brother, but she remarried the king in 1921. She bore Abd al-Aziz seven daughters and seven sons, including King Fahd, Prince Sultan (Crown Prince), and Princes Abd al-Rahman, Turki, Nayef, Salman, and Ahmad. For much of her life as the king's wife she was his favorite. Her influential children ate lunch in her quarters daily. She also arranged the **marriages** of some of her sons. Just like her husband, the reigning king, she kept her doors open to Saudi citizens, who came beseeching her for help and to intercede with the king. "The Sudairi Seven" was the title given in the West to King Fahd and his six full brothers. The term was not used in Saudi Arabia, where the Sudairi princes were known as the Fahd group. It is the largest group of full-blooded brothers among all the descendants of King Abd al-Aziz.

SUDANESE WOMEN'S UNION (SWU). This is a women's organization that evolved from the Educated Girls' Association and the Association of Sudanese Women. It was also affiliated with the Sudanese Communist Party. Founded in 1952, its first executive committee included some of Sudan's prominent female activists, such as **Fatima Ibrahim**, Fatima Talib, and Khalda Zuhair. The SWU's active years were from 1952 to 1956, when Sudan was on the verge of achieving its independence. By 1965, it had affiliates throughout the Sudan and boasted a widely read monthly journal, *Sawat al-Maraa* (*Women's Voice*). The SWU is credited with getting parliament to pass legislation on behalf of women's rights such as political rights, equal pay for equal work, and maternity leave for working women. The SWU president, Fatima Ibrahim, was the first Sudanese woman to be elected to parliament. She led the union to become the African continent's largest and most powerful women's organization, which at one time claimed a membership of 15,000. However, the SWU ran afoul of several dictatorial regimes, finally being forced to operate clandestinely following the Islamist coup d'état of 1989. Fatima Ibrahim went into exile in London, where she carried on her organizational work. Both Amnesty International and the United Nations gave the SWU awards in recognition of its work on behalf of women.

SUFISM. Mysticism in Islam was not restricted to men; neither was it dependent on education. Some rituals associated with Sufism, however, were not open to women. Among the earliest women to practice Sufism and to be accepted as such was the Iraqi mystic **Rabia al-Adawiyah** (ca. 717–801). Mysticism called for an independent approach to the divine, without mediation by the official class of Muslim clergy. Sufi leaders, mostly males who declared themselves Sufi shaykhs, often established their own *tariqas*, or monastic orders, and had their own followings. One such leader was a woman named Hagga (pilgrim) Zakiyya, an Egyptian, who was buried next to the shrine of Sidi Abu al-Hassan al-Shadhili (1196–1258), a Moroccan and founder of the Shadhiliyah *tariqa* who died in Egypt. The Iranian Sufi leader and psychiatrist Dr. Javad Nurbakh (1926–2008) has identified the biographies of 124 Sufi women in his book *Sufi Women* (London, 1983). Sufi women became prominent during the Mamluk dynasty in Egypt (1250–1517) and under the Ottoman Empire, where they were often freely admitted to various Sufi concerts (*dhikr*) when the names of God were recited.

Women generally were allowed to visit the shrines of various Sufi saints, whereas mosques sometimes constituted prohibited space. Religious shrines built around the tomb of a venerated Sufi shaykh were places of comfort for women, who would often pray for miracles (*barakat*), especially for children in an otherwise infertile marriage. Sometimes a Sufi attained the status of a saint (*wali*) within his lifetime, and his burial place became a shrine where miracles were performed. The Quran did not recognize sainthood, stating that only God was the *wali*. Sainthood was an informal status, attained by acclamation because no canonizing process existed within Islam. Shrines, however, were reserved for members of the Prophet's family (*ahl al-bayt*). Women, outside of the Prophet's family, rarely had their own shrines.

One of the greatest contributors to the legitimizing of the sainthood of women through the Sufi *tariqas* was the famed Ottoman Sufi poet Mevlana Celaleddin Rumi (1207–1273). Many women followed his path because of his pronounced tolerance of members of all religious backgrounds. Some women represented his order in the famous Sufi *dhikr* and whirling ceremony of the *dervishes*, which came to be known as *Mevlevi mukabele*. The women would be given the title of shaykha, were allowed to dress in traditional clothes, and whirl-danced with male Sufis. The Shaykhas also had their own *murids* (devotees) and were known as the female saints of Anatolia. Their tombs were regarded as shrines and places of miracles and holiness. The Mevlevi Order eventually became segregated, but the Bektasi and Alevi Sufi circles continued to allow female participation in their religious rituals.

In Mamluk Egypt, some women acquired the status of shaykhs, or Sufi leaders. One such figure was Zaynab Fatima bint al-Abbas (d. 1394), who headed a Sufi order in Cairo established by Princess Tadhkaray in 1285. The order was actually a hostel for widows and divorced women who had no independent means of support. The medieval Arab historian al-Maqrizi (1364–1442), who chronicled Mamluk Egypt, reported that some male Sufi retreats included female residents. The role of women changed again in the modern era, following the decline of the Sufi phenomenon and its disappearance from urban settings. The Sufi orders continue to operate in Turkey's provincial towns of eastern Anatolia, but the female relatives of shaykhs are only permitted to communicate with the female followers of these orders. Today, no women are allowed to hold formal office. There are currently two highly esteemed female chanters of Sufi music (*munshidat*) in Egypt: Aliyah al-Jaar and Sheikha Sabah. The idea of individual intercession with God has lost credence in today's technological culture. Scholars appreciative of the historical significance and philosophical and poetical heritage of Sufi Islam regard today's manifestation of the sect as no more than a degenerate form of folk Islam. *See also* WAQF.

SUKAYNA (671–737). She was the granddaughter of **Fatima**, daughter of Prophet Muhammad, whose full name was Umayma, or Amina bint al-Hussein. Her mother was al-Rabab bint Imri'i al-Qays al-Kalbiyya; she was the poet daughter of the military leader of the Kalb tribe. Sukayna lost both her father, Imam Hussein, and her husband, Abdullah ibn al-Hazan bin Abi-Talib, at the battle of Karbala in 680 CE. She was married either four or six times. Among her husbands was Musaab bin al-Zubayr, who was killed in 691 while fighting in the army of his brother, Abdullah ibn al-Zubayr. The latter was the caliph of Medina and Iraq, who defied the Umayyid dynasty in Damascus. After two **marriages** that ended in **divorce**, she married Zayd ibn Amr, a grandson of the third caliph, Othman ibn Affan, who was her husband at the time of her death.

Sukayna grew up in Damascus, but moved to Medina following the battle of Karbala. She enjoyed a vast personal fortune and was known for her intellectual pursuits. Insulated from public censure by her lineage and descent from *aal al-Bayt* (the house of the Prophet), she acquired the sobriquet of *barza*, or an unveiled woman who maintained a literary salon frequented by men. She expressed her independence by maintaining open opposition to the Umayyads at Damascus. She also committed her husbands to monogamy by adding a specific clause to the marriage contract. A trendsetter throughout her life, her name became associated with a particular hairstyle known as *al-turra al-Sakayniya*. She was also known for patronizing the arts by sponsoring and patronizing the two great poets of that era, Jarir (d. 728) and al-Farzadaq (d. 727). Among her protégés and the frequent performers at her salon was Ibn Surayj (d. 744), the greatest singer of the Hijazi school, who often performed her own poetical works.

SULH, ALYA (1935–2007). A Lebanese journalist and political activist who was born in Beirut. She was the eldest daughter of the first prime minister of independent Lebanon, Riyadh al-Sulh (r. 1943–1945, 1946–1951), and Faiza Jabri. Riad al-Sulh was assassinated while on a visit to Amman, Jordan, in 1951, by a member of the Syrian Social National Party (SSNP). Alya grew up in an intense political environment, and her career as a columnist was a natural path for someone living in these surroundings. Her columns expressed her strong criticism of Lebanon's oligarchic and sectarian politics, and she defended the Palestinian revolution and the actions of the Palestinian leadership in Lebanon. Writing in the 1960s, she became one of the prominent columnists of the Lebanese daily *al-Nahar*. Her views on Lebanon's corrupt politics were also aired on television. She was a supporter of Syria's pan-Arabist policies in the region under President Hafiz Assad (r. 1970-2000). But she changed direction during the 1980s, writing in support of Phalangist leader Bashir Gemayel, who was assassinated in 1983. She became a severe critic of Syria's dominance over Lebanon during the latter phase of the civil war. She died in Paris, where she had been in residence since the beginning of the civil war in 1974.

Alya was married at one time to Palestinian journalist and diplomat Nasser al-Din Nashashibi. Two of her sisters, Leyla and Mona, married Moroccan and Saudi princes, respectively. She was connected to various political families in the Middle East.

SURSUQ, YVONNE LADY COCHRANE (?–). A Lebanese patron of the arts who was born in Beirut. She was educated in Lebanon and in London, where she earned a degree in town planning. She became one of Lebanon's most prominent socialites and had a penchant for the arts. As a descendant of one of the richest families of that country, she was able to play a large role in the promotion of native art and the preservation of cultural sites. Her family were Greeks who had arrived in Lebanon via Turkey. She was appointed president of the Nicholas Sursuq Museum and was the founder and president of the Association for the Protection of Sites and Ancient Buildings. In the early 1970s, she presided over a new artistic endeavor, Les Jeunesses Musicales of Lebanon. Her most visible contribution to Lebanon's artistic life was as a founding member of the committee that ran the Baalbek International Festival. *See also* FAYROUZ (1934–).

SUSWA, AMAT AL-ALIM AL- (1958–). A Yemeni cabinet member who was the minister for human rights and only the second woman to serve in the cabinet, following **Waheeba Faraa,** who was also state minister for human rights. Suswa was trained in journalism and completed a BA in mass communication at Cairo University in 1980 and an MA in international communications at American University, Washington, D.C., in 1984. She enjoyed a long tenure as an announcer and program director at Yemeni public radio and television. She was a lecturer at Sanaa University in the Political Science Department and published several investigative reports on the condition of Yemeni women.

Before the unification of North and South Yemen in 1990, she joined the ruling People's General Congress Party, becoming in time a founding member of the National Women's Committee. She began her ascent to high public office in 1991 when she became assistant deputy minister of information, becoming a deputy minister six years later. She was also the Yemeni ambassador to the Netherlands (2001–2003). She became state minister for human rights in 2003. She continues to be an advocate for freedom of the press and freedom of opinion in Yemen. See also KARMAN, TAWAKKUL (1979–).

SZOLD, HENRIETTA (1860–1945). She was the founder of **Hadassah** Women's Organization in the United States and in Israel. Born in Baltimore, she was the oldest of eight daughters of Rabbi Benjamin Szold and became a teacher at Miss Adam's School and Oheb Shalom school, the educational arm of her father's temple by the same name. She pursued higher education at Johns Hopkins University and Peabody Institute, but did not receive a degree.

Szold was dedicated to serving the needs of Russian Jewish immigrants to Baltimore, establishing a night school for instruction in the English language and to provide vocational training. Her interest in Zionism was enhanced by her appointment to the Jewish Publication Society, where she worked for two decades. Upon journeying to Palestine in 1909, she became increasingly interested in furthering Jewish immigration to that country. In 1912, she founded a social welfare organization for women known as Hadassah, serving as its president, before finally settling in Palestine in 1933. She operated an organization called Youth *Aliyah,* which facilitated the arrival of 30,000 Jewish children from countries under Nazi control.

Szold's commitment to Zionism began as early as 1898, when she was the only woman elected to the executive committee of the Federation of American Zionists. Hadassah Hospital, with which her name became identified, started as the project of six other women who aimed at improving Jewish women's health care in Ottoman-controlled Palestine. Hadassah introduced innovative projects such as a visiting nurse program in Jerusalem as well as several hospitals, a medical school, dental clinics, infant care facilities, and soup kitchens, which were open to Arab as well as Jewish patients.

Szold is also remembered for her activities on behalf of Brit Shalom during the 1920s and 1930s. This organization counted Jewish philosopher Martin Buber among its members and advocated a binational Arab Jewish state.

In 1942, she joined others in founding the Ehud Party, the political arm of Brit Shalom. Szold died at the main Hadassah Hospital in Jerusalem and was buried on the slopes of the Mount of Olives, facing the Old City of Jerusalem. She died without leaving any offspring, but her life was commemorated in many ways. A kibbutz was named after her in the Upper Galilee region, Kibbutz Kfar Szold. A ship that ferried illegal immigrants to Palestine during the British Mandate period was named *Henrietta Szold*. The National Institute for Research and Behavioral Sciences in Jerusalem created a special institute, the Henrietta Szold Institute, in her name. A public school in Manhattan, New York, was named after her in 2007.

T

TAIMURIYA, AISHA AL- (1840–1902). An Egyptian advocate for equality between men and women as well as a distinguished poet and essayist. She was born in Cairo to a Turkish aristocratic family, consisting of a high government official, Ismail Pasha Taimur, and his Circassian concubine. She was tutored at home, receiving advanced training in Arabic and Islamic studies based on the literary merits of the Quran. She was competent in Arabic, Turkish, and Persian, learning to compose poetry in all three. Following the death of her father and her husband, Mahmoud Bey al-Islambuli, whom she married in 1854, she devoted all her time to her literary pursuits. In addition to poetical works, she published a novel, *Nataij al-Ahwal fi al-Aqwal wa al-Afaal* (*The Results of Circumstances in Words and Deeds*).

TAJ AL-SALTANEH (1884–1936). A Persian princess who was one of the younger daughters of Shah Nasir al-Din (1848–1896) of the Qajar dynasty. She was known to be an admirer of Western women, whom she described in her memoirs as enjoying equality with men, in contrast with the women of Iran. She described the latter as leading the lives of wild beasts, wrapped in black during their lives and in white during their funeral rites. She criticized the **veil** and the seclusion of women. She was also a nationalist, who, along with the majority of Iranian women of that period, criticized Iranian males for being overly eager to cede the nation's wealth to foreign companies. She was critical of rampant corruption at court and took part in several uprisings toward the end of the 19th century.

Later known as Tvus Khanum, she was tutored by the best teachers of her times, receiving instruction in French and music, among other subjects. She exercised freedom of choice when it came to **marriage**, choosing a man to her own liking whom she later **divorced**. She dressed in European clothes for much of her life and was often unveiled in public. As a result of her admiration for Western culture, a trait she shared with most educated Iranians of her day, she ceased to perform the Muslim prayers and was rumored to partake of alcoholic drinks. Her memoirs, titled *Khatirat* (English: *Taj al-Saltana: Crowning Anguish*) endeared her to later generations of Iranian feminists.

TAL, SUHAYR SALTI (?–). A Jordanian short-story writer and journalist who was born in the town of Irbid. She completed a degree in philosophy at Amman University and launched a career in journalism by becoming an editor of the daily *Sawt al-Shaab* (*The People's Voice*). She began publishing her work in the 1980s, producing a collection of short stories, *The Gallows*, in 1987. The title story in this volume was judged to be "offensive to public sensibilities" by the Jordanian authorities, resulting in a long trial and brief imprisonment. After her release, she continued to publish. In 1985, she published *Introduction to the Female Question and the Feminist Movement in Jordan*. She is also the author of a study of the Arab Nationalist Movement, *al-Qawmiyeen al-Arab*, which was published by the Center for Arab Unity Studies, Beirut.

TALAL, BASMA BINT (1951–). A Jordanian princess who is also a philanthropist and social activist. She is the only sister of King Hussein of Jordan (r. 1953–1999) and the youngest sibling in that family. She received her education in Jordan and attended the Benenden school in Great Britain. She also studied languages at Oxford University. In 2001, she completed a PhD in development studies at Oxford. In Jordan, she was known as an institution builder, her first project being the Queen Alya Fund for Social Development, which she founded in 1977. King Hussein suggested this name to commemorate his deceased wife, Queen Alya, after her untimely death that year. The fund's name was changed after his death to the Jordanian Hashemite Fund for Human Development.

Princess Basma was also interested in improving the status of Jordanian women. She founded the Jordanian National Commission for Women in 1992 and the Princess Basma Women's Resource Center in 1996, the latter being a branch of the Queen Zein al-Sharaf Institute for Development, named after King Hussein's mother. United Nations Secretary General Boutros Boutros Ghali appointed her in 1995 as special adviser on sustainable development. She also advised the United Nations Educational, Scientific and Cultural Organization (UNESCO) and the World Health Organization (WHO). Her book, *Rethinking an NGO: Development, Donors and Civil Society in Jordan*, was published in 2003.

TAWIL, RAYMONDA HAWWA AL- (1940–). A Palestinian journalist and political activist who was born in the city of Acre, Palestine, while under the British Mandate. She was separated from her mother and brothers after the 1948 Arab–Israeli War. Sent to a convent school in Nazareth, she moved later to Nablus, where she married Dawud al-Tawil, an Oxford-educated banker. Her activism began in that city, where she became a member of the Arab Women's Union (AWU). Having lived under Israeli rule as a youth, she came under the control of the Israeli occupation when the West Bank fell to the Israelis following the June War of 1967. In 1968, she organized a women's sit-in and a demonstration in front of the headquarters of the Israeli military governor of Nablus.

While living in Ramallah, she became increasingly active on behalf of the Palestine Liberation Organization (PLO). She founded the Palestine Press Service in East Jerusalem to provide a reliable and independent source of news for Palestinian nationalist papers in that city. Israeli authorities imprisoned her for short periods of time and placed her under house arrest in 1976. This resulted in a memoir, titled *My Home, My Prison* (1979), describing her confinement to the family residence by military order. She attended classes in French literature at Hebrew University in Jerusalem, but did not earn a degree. Throughout her life under Israeli occupation she maintained contact with Israeli peace activists, men and women. One such relationship was with Ruth Dayan, former wife of Israeli defense minister Moshe Dayan. The latter founded Brit Bnei Shem (Ibnaa Sam) or "the children of Sam," and she and Tawil planted a "peace forest" in Neve Shalom, a suburb of Jerusalem.

Raymonda Tawil became a close confidante of Yasser Arafat while he lived in exile, accompanying him at one time on an official visit to Austria at the invitation of the country's Jewish socialist president, Bruno Kreisky. She became internationally known after her daughter, Suha Tawil, married Arafat in a secret ceremony in Tunis in 1990. After her husband's death in 1995, Raymonda lived mostly in Europe, where her children maintained residences, returning to Ramallah intermittently.

TELEGHANI, AZAM (ca. 1945–). An Iranian advocate for women's rights whose father, Ayatollah Mahmoud Teleghani (d. 1980), was a liberal member of the Iranian clergy and also known for his support of women's rights. Azam Teleghani was born in Tehran and voluntarily chose to wear the traditional **chador** while still a young woman, years before it was imposed on females by the regime of **Ayatollah Ruhollah Khomeini**. She was a political activist who served a prison term for distributing anti-shah literature. After the Islamic revolution, her popularity won her a seat in the first Majlis elected in 1980, which had only 3 female representatives out of a total membership of 217. She was then chosen as the head of the Women's Society of the Islamic Revolution (WSIR), a popular organization that mobilized women to support the new regime. Her views on women frequently clashed with those of the Islamic government. She often protested against the imposition of **veiling** on women and condemned reviving the custom of stoning adulterers. She used the WSIR as a platform from which to call for legal reforms on behalf of women and for an end to all forms of gender discrimination.

In 1997, Teleghani announced her candidacy for presidential office, forcing a debate on women's qualifications for the highest position in the land. Her argument was based on linguistic analysis of the term used to specify that only males qualified for high office. She declared that the term *rejal*, used in the Iranian constitution for the presidency, means "men" only in Arabic; in Farsi, it becomes a generic appellation for all members of the male and female select group. When she sought the opinion of religious scholars in Tehran and the holy city of Qom, she was given a split opinion. Her campaign in favor of recognizing women as society's main culture bearers encouraged *Zanan*, the feminist journal, to run a series of articles on whether women's right to hold the great "imamate," or the top political office in a community defined by its faith, was a "natural" or an "Islamic" right. Despite all of this debate, her candidacy for the presidency was disqualified by the Council of Experts before she could actually run in the election. In the year 2000, her candidacy for the Majlis was scuttled by the Council of Guardians, which examines the credentials of all candidates.

After her exclusion from electoral office, Teleghani continued to work for women's rights in her own way. She established the Islamic Women's Institute of Iran, which helps women improve their wage-earning skills. She owns a small garment factory in Tehran, which doubles as a women's night school to compensate for women being denied entrance to the religious seminaries of Qom. In 2003, she staged a sit-in in front of the notorious Evin Prison, to draw attention to abuses against its male and female occupants. She continues to publish a widely read Islamic feminist journal, *Payam-e Hajar* (*Hajer's Message*), which provides a reinterpretation of Quranic texts amplifying women's rights. See also FEMINIST MOVEMENT IN IRAN; *ZANAN MAGAZINE*.

TEMPORARY MARRIAGE. This is a form of marriage sanctioned only in Shii Iran and reintroduced under the Islamic Republic of Iran, sometimes referred to as *sigheh*. Temporary marriage is not an Islamic form of union, but was an ancient custom practiced by many cultures. Some of the Arab tribes living in the Arabian Peninsula practiced this in the pre-Islamic phase. During that period, this form of marriage constituted a limited alliance, usually when a man sought the protection of a certain tribe and married its daughter. This union did not alienate the woman from her tribe, which continued to consider her one of their own. In this period before Islam, children from these marriages were ascribed to the mother's lineage, a practice not unknown in other forms of marriage. Neither spouse in these marriages was allowed to inherit from the other. The practice was pervasive enough that many converts to Islam claimed issuance from such unions. Temporary marriage was widely practiced in Zoroastrian Iran, when a man would seek a temporary marital alliance for his wife or daughter simply for the purpose of procreation. Any child from such a union was given to the woman's husband or father and raised as one of his own offspring. According to some historians, the Jews of Babylonia during the third century also practiced temporary marriage.

When Islam established its first official community, the Medinian state, it sanctioned only one form of marriage, which encompassed a **polygamous** union of one man and up to four wives. The custom of temporary marriage, however, persisted among Twelver Shiis of Iran, although it acquired new features. It became a marriage based on a contract between a man, who could be married at the time, and a woman who was unmarried, specifying how long they would be together and the amount of money to be paid to the woman. This gave rise to the term *sigheh* (Farsi; marriage), which literally means "legal contract." It is also known as a contract marriage, or *mutaa* (Arabic; pleasure) marriage. The second caliph during the early Islamic period, Umar ibn al-Khattab (ca. 586, 590–644) outlawed this type of marriage during the seventh century CE, and it disappeared from most Islamic lands. But Shiis in Iran never obeyed the ruling of Umar, whom they blamed for the Arab conquest of their country. Umar, a towering figure among Sunni Muslims, lacked authority in the eyes of the Shiis, who considered his opinions to be legally irrelevant and unbinding. They also argue that this form of marriage is allowed in the Quran (Chapter 4, verse 24) and that it was approved by Muhammad. In the ninth century CE, one of the Abbasid dynasty's most learned caliphs, al-Maamoun (786–833), legalized temporary marriage again, which was then referred to as *mutaa*. But under extreme pressure from the Sunni clergy, who threatened public denunciation of this form of marriage, al-Maamoun's edict was canceled.

In Iran, where the practice continued, it became increasingly confined to the cities and was associated with periods of long travel, such as during the **pilgrimage** to Mecca and Medina. In the 20th century, *sigheh* marriages were usually contracted near religious shrines. It has become a contract between a man, married or not, and a woman who is single but who can be widowed or divorced, in which the duration of the marriage and the amount of money paid to the woman are clearly designated. Many believe that the contract violates one of the main requirements of Sunni marriage, in which the role of witnessing the contract is central to its validity. In the *sigheh* marriage, no witnesses are required, and parents do not play a role. The adults need not be officially registered. In general, the duration of such a marriage can be anywhere from one hour to 99 years, according to the foremost authority on the subject, Shahla Haeri, an Iranian scholar, in *Law of Desire: Temporary Marriage in Shi'i Iran* (1989). The marriage ceases to be valid at the end of its specified period, and the two spouses separate without the necessity of **divorce** proceedings. A Shii male is allowed to enter into as many temporary marriages as he wishes, although there is no agreement on this among Shii clergy, in addition to maintaining up to four legal wives, as is permitted in Islam. A Shii woman, however, can only marry one man at a time. She is required to undergo a period of abstinence (*uddah*) extending to four months, normally required by all sects, to determine the presence of pregnancy before she can marry again. Any child born of such contract marriages is considered legitimate and treated equally with all of the man's other offspring. Supporters of temporary marriage argue that legitimizing the paternity of children in such marriages is what distinguishes this practice from prostitution.

The practice of temporary marriage gained popularity only among religious circles in Iran before the Islamic Revolution of 1979. Most secular Muslims viewed the custom with disdain and considered it of ambiguous legal status. Religiously inclined individuals, on the other hand, praised temporary marriage as a safeguard against immorality, sexual relations outside of marriage, and producing children out of wedlock. The popularity of this form of marriage was always influenced by the relationship of the ruling regime to the religious establishment. It was not surprising, therefore, that the two Pahlavi periods of **Shah Reza Pahlavi** and Muhammad Reza Shah (1925–1979) were marked by disdain for this practice. While temporary marriage was not outlawed, its practice was shrouded in secrecy and limited to those adhering to a strict Islamic culture. By contrast, temporary marriage was practiced in the open under the Islamic government beginning in 1979, and the clergy in particular took a proactive stand by educating the public about its merits. Temporary marriage was openly endorsed in religious sermons and advertised in high schools and in the media.

Much of the clerical enthusiasm for temporary marriage was the result of the Iran–Iraq War (1980–1989), which decimated the Iranian male population. Khomeini called on men to emulate the example of Muhammad, who, when confronted with a rising surplus of war widows, set an example for others by entering into permanent unions with such women and encouraged others to contract temporary marriages. Ali Akbar Hashemi Rafsanjani reinforced this message after he rose to the presidency in 1989, lecturing women on the advantages of temporary marriage. Despite this official endorsement, most Iranian women remained hostile to this practice, arguing publicly and in the pages of the Islamic feminist press that it demeans women, offering them only unstable unions. Some of the *sigheh* marriages today may last for an entire lifetime, but they are not as widespread as the authorities wish them to be. Although some religious figures continue to praise temporary marriage, citing the husband's privilege of ending it without formal divorce proceedings, others, such as Ayatollah Sayyid M. Shariatmadari (1905–1986), cautioned that it was only intended for wartime or for men engaged in long-distance trade away from their legitimate wives. Islamic figures in Iran also cite the work of British philosopher **Bertrand Russell** and American anthropologist Margaret Meade (1901–1978) as additional justification for entering into these marriages to suit the needs of modern times.

TEQLA, LAYLA (?–). An Egyptian member of parliament and prominent leader of a socialist party who holds a PhD from an American university. She is descended from a prominent Coptic family and was allied with President Anwar Sadat for a while, serving as the chairperson of the Foreign Affairs Committee of the People's Assembly during the early and mid-1970s. She broke ranks with Sadat over the Camp David Agreement in 1978, but found it difficult to secure reelection to parliament without the support of the country's semiofficial National Democratic Party. She assumed the position of deputy-chair of the Socialist Party in 1979, serving in this office for five years.

TIKELI, SIRIN. A Turkish activist and author who is considered the foremost feminist writer of Turkey' second generation of **feminists**. Both of her parents were philosophy teachers and very keen on giving her, their only child, the best educational opportunities available. After completing her high school education at Ankara, she studied political science at a college in Lausanne, Switzerland. She later specialized in the work of political scientist David Easton for her doctoral studies at Istanbul University. In her PhD thesis, which was published under the title *Kedinlar ve Siysal-Toplumsal Hayat* (*Women and Political-Social Life*), she lamented the increased marginalization of women in social and public life. The book provided a Marxist analysis of the feminist question and had a great impact beyond the confines of the academy.

In 1981, Tikeli left her position as an associate professor at Istanbul University to devote her time entirely to the feminist cause. She was one of the founders of Kadin Eserleri Kutuphanesi ve Bilgi Merkezi (**Women's Library and Information Center**) and Cati Kadin Siginagi (Purple Roof Women's Shelter), both in 1990. When women prisoners, who were mostly Marxist and Kurdish, staged a hunger strike in 1997, Tikeli decided to focus on increasing women's representation in parliament. She became the president of a new organization, Association to Support and Educate Women Candidates, between 1997 and 1999. In recognition of her work, in 1996, the French government awarded her the *Officier de l'Ordre des Palmes Académiques*.

TOUBIA, NAHID (1951–). A Sudanese physician and pediatric surgeon who was a consultant at Khartoum Teaching Hospital. When she completed her medical education at Cairo University and in Great Britain in 1981, she became Sudan's first female surgeon. She is very active on behalf of the rights of Sudanese women and is in the forefront of the native movement against female genital mutilation. She is the head of the Female Circumcision Information and Resource Center at the Traditional Medicine Research Institute of the Sudan Research Council. She is also on the editorial board of *Sudan Medical Journal*. See also ARAB WOMEN'S SOLIDARITY ASSOCIATION (AWSA); SAADAWI, NAWAL (1931–).

TOUMI, KHALIDA (1958–). An Algerian feminist and a former minister of culture and communications, born in Sidi Ali Mossa, a small village in the Kabylia area. She was known as Khalida Massodi before reverting to her original name, Khalida Toumi. She attended the University of Algiers in 1977, majoring in mathematics. She eventually graduated from the prestigious École Normale Supérieure in Paris and taught mathematics until 1993. She became active in the feminist movement, establishing in 1981 the Collectif Féminin, primarily to oppose the restriction on women's travel in Algeria that required them to be accompanied by a male guardian, but also to mobilize women against the 1984 Family Code. After the National Assembly of Algeria adopted the Family Code, Toumi became the president of a Trotskyite organization called the Association for Equality between Men and Women. A year later, she became a member of the executive committee of the Algerian League of Human Rights, which she helped found. She severed her ties with the Algerian Trotskyites in 1990 and established the Independent Association for the Triumph of Women's Rights.

Toumi became a strong and vocal opponent of the rising Islamist ideology sweeping over Algeria in the early 1990s. When President Chadli Boujadid canceled the 1992 elections to prevent the assured victory of the Islamic Salvation Front (FIS), she was among those who supported this move. She claimed that the Islamists were poised to impose a totalitarian regime on Algeria. When the Islamists waged a violent campaign against the government and the civilian population, she left the country, living mostly in Western countries. She later became a member of the Rassemblement pour la Culture et la Démocratie (RCD) (Rally for Culture and Democracy), serving as its national vice president for human rights and women's issues. After disagreeing with the policies of the RCD's president, Said Sadi, she was expelled in 2002. Toumi moved closer to the government, and was appointed in 2002 as the minister of culture and communication, which made her a spokesperson for the government and the first woman to serve in that capacity in Algeria. Her close association with President Abdul-Aziz Boutefliqa (r. 1999–present) diminished her credibility as an independent activist on behalf of human rights, as he adopted authoritarian measures and established an alliance of convenience with the Islamist movement.

TOUQAN, FADWA (1917–2003). A Palestinian poet who was born in Nablus to a distinguished family of literary figures and political leaders. Her older brother, Ibrahim Touqan (1905–1941), who taught her traditional Arabic poetry, was the acknowledged leading poet of Palestinian Arabs. She lived a secluded and traditional life and had to establish her identity and pursue her literary ambitions on her own. Her poems began to be published in the mid-1950s and were at first characterized by romanticism and feminist yearnings. After the June War of 1967 and the imposition of Israeli occupation over the West Bank, including Nablus, her poetry became decidedly more nationalistic and political in nature. Her first collection of poetry, *Wahdi maa al-ayyam* (*Alone with the Days*), appeared in 1955. Another collection of poetry, *Nightmare in Daylight*, appeared in 1974. Her autobiographical work, *Rihla saaba* (*A Mountainous Journey*), was published in 1985. She wrote two additional collections of poetry with strong political themes: *Before the Closed Door* (1967) and *The Freedom Fighters and the Land* (1968). Both were published in Beirut.

Touqan wrote to illustrate her uphill struggle against traditions and the patriarchy. Her poetry eventually won her great acclaim in various Arab countries, and she exchanged poetical works with the distinguished poet of Palestinian nationalism, Mahmoud Darwish (1941–2008). She was touched by controversy when she was approached by Israeli Defense Minister Moshe Dayan, who sought to establish contact with leading Arab intellectuals. He first met her in 1968, a year into the occupation, and succeeded in convincing her to pass a secret message to President Jamal Abd al-Nasser of Egypt. Touqan was granted the Jerusalem Award for Culture and the Arts in 1990, as well as the Honorary Palestine Prize for Poetry in 1996, both by the Palestine Liberation Organization (PLO). She was buried in Nablus, her birthplace and hometown for much of her life.

TSEMEL, LEA (1945–). An Israeli lawyer and human rights activist who was born in Haifa to Russian and Polish parents who were both Holocaust survivors. In 1968, she completed a degree in criminal law at Hebrew University in Jerusalem. While still a university student, she became affiliated with Matzpen, a radical movement that opposed the Israeli occupation of Palestinian lands. She was opposed to Zionism and developed a commitment to Palestinian human rights, declaring her support for an independent Palestinian state within the 1967 borders and with Jerusalem as a shared capital between Palestinians and Israelis. She called for accepting the Palestinian right of return, the concept of the return of Palestinian refugees from the 1948 Arab–Israeli War to their original homes within Israel.

In the 1970s, Tsemel began to represent Palestinians in Jerusalem seeking legal redress for cases of identity card confiscation, family reunification, house demolition, expulsion of political prisoners to neighboring countries, and land confiscation. She also defended Palestinians accused of attempting suicide bombings. She carried her battle against the use of torture in Israeli jails to international legal circles. One of her major triumphs, in 1999, was forcing the Israeli Supreme Court to disallow the use of torture by the Israeli security services to obtain confessions. She was variously recognized by international groups for her work on behalf of human rights. In 1996, the French government awarded her the Human Rights Award of the French Republic as the representative of the Israeli Public Action Committee against Torture. She left Israel to live in Europe, fearing mounting Israeli hostility to her work.

TUDEH PARTY. This was Iran's Marxist party, which originated as the Iranian Communist Party. Tudeh, meaning "The Masses," was created in 1941, but its parent organization was founded in 1920. Tudeh was headed by Soleiman Mohsen Eskandari for many years and played a large role in supporting Mohammad Mossadegh's government of 1951–1953.

Tudeh was supportive of women's rights until the takeover of Iran by the Islamist forces of **Ayatollah Ruhollah Khomeini** in 1979. The party's paper, *Mardom*, published articles on injustices such as barring women from admission to the judiciary, the **marriage** of underage girls, and the inadequacies of the Family Protection Law, which the shah pushed through using imperialist pressure. The paper also called for abolishing **polygamy**, doing away with the custom of traditional marriage, and ending the practice of executing women who were charged with corruption or engaging in prostitution. Tudeh, however, did not antagonize the new Islamic regime, preferring to join those who regarded Khomeini as a genuine savior who had toppled the shah from the throne. Tudeh firmly believed that the Islamic regime would push through reforms on a broad front. When severe measures were taken against prominent women from the royalist era, the rest of Iranian women were expected to maintain their silence in the interest of national unity. Tudeh itself was eventually banned and suffered mass arrests in 1982 and the execution of its leaders in 1988. It continues to exist mostly in exile but as a shadow of its former self.

TURABI, HASSAN AL- (1932–). A Sudanese Islamist reformer and ideologue who was born in Kassala in the eastern Sudan. His father was among the first to be trained as an Islamic judge under the aegis of the British colonial administration. Al-Turabi was given a traditional Islamic education by his father, later graduating from the faculty of law at Khartoum University (formerly Gordon College) in 1955. He earned an MA in law from the University of London in 1957 and a PhD from the Sorbonne in 1964. He became an influential member of the Sudanese Muslim Brotherhood, which, after its establishment in the early 1950s, became increasingly opposed to the rule of President Jaafar Numeiri (r. 1969–1985). But when the latter switched gears in the 1970s and adopted a pro-Islamist policy, Turabi supported him and expressed enthusiasm for his regime, including the September Laws of 1983, which imposed the Islamic **Sharia** on the largely pagan and Christian south.

When Numeiri was ousted in 1985, Turabi emerged as a power broker and transformed the Muslim Brotherhood into the National Islamic Front of Sudan. When another military strongman, Umar al-Bashir, took over the reins of government in 1989, Turabi became the regime's chief theoretician and the leading influence behind the campaign to re-Islamize the Sudan. Among the measures inspired by Turabi was a 1991 decree requiring women to dress in long black dresses and veils, contrary to the traditional *thoab* worn by all Sudanese women. Those who did not conform to the new dress code were to be whipped. Turabi's followers called him a "renewer of the faith" and the first to create a true Sunni state in the 20th century.

Turabi also exercised his own brand of *ijtihad*, taking upon himself the privilege of reinterpreting the sacred Islamic texts to suit modern times and assuming the role of *mujadid*, or renewer of the faith, which was denied to ordinary Muslims by the religious establishment but was the privilege of Islamic experts and scholars. Among Turabi's new interpretations was one claiming that nowhere in the Quran does it say that a Muslim woman cannot marry a non-Muslim. His first publication, a pamphlet titled *Women's Islamic Teachings* (1959), was a best seller and a testament to the general Muslim public's interest in this kind of reinterpretation. He insisted that the oppression of Muslim women was not the result of applying Islamic teachings but a natural outcome of the age of decline and the degradation of Islamic scholarship. The kind of liberated Muslim woman that he called for was one whose traditional fetters were removed but who also resisted the lure of Western exploitation and economic enslavement. He declared that his reading of the Quran convinced him that **veiling** was required of women in the Prophet's immediate family only, adding that a veiled woman nevertheless is demanding to be treated as a human being, not as a sex object in the Western sense. These views widened Turabi's popularity in the Muslim world, especially his advocacy for establishing democratic Islamic regimes. President al-Bashir eventually felt threatened by Turabi's popularity and rising stature in the Muslim world and forced him to relinquish his position. Turabi was jailed in 1999, and was released only in 2010. *See also* TURABI, WISAL AL-MAHDI (?–).

TURABI, WISAL AL-MAHDI (?–). A Sudanese Islamist supporter of women's rights, also the wife of Islamist ideologue **Hassan al-Turabi**. She is the sister of Sadiq al-Mahdi (b. 1935) a former prime minister of the Sudan and influential leader of the Ummah party. Despite the rivalry between her husband's party, the National Islamic Front (NIF), and that of her brother, she encouraged both to move in the direction of supporting women's rights. She became a spokesperson for the NIF after it began to mobilize women and encourage their political activism. Her position reflected her husband's views on mandating **veiling** for women and freeing them from inappropriate employment, such as tending tables or working in gas stations. Instead, she called for admitting women to prestigious positions, such as the judiciary or the cabinet. She never strayed from the ideology of the NIF, calling for basing state laws on the **Sharia**. A trained lawyer, Wisal Turabi never practiced in her field and prides herself on maintaining a conservative Islamic home.

TUWAIJRI, HUSSA AL- (?–). A Saudi director of social work and women's rights advocate, born in Riyadh. She received her higher education in the kingdom before earning a master's degree in social services from the University of St. Louis, Missouri. Upon her return to her country, she assumed the position of director general of the care and guidance department of the Ministry of Labor and Social Affairs. She was also a founding member of the Wafaa Charitable Society for Women in Riyadh. Al-Tuwaijri has produced a number of literary works.

U

UMM AL-WALAD. This title was bestowed on a concubine upon giving birth to the child of her master. This status, which means "mother of child" (Arabic), granted a semi-free status to the mother and ended her status as a slave. The child of such a union was always born free and considered a legitimate child, though he or she might not enjoy the same social standing as other children born of a free mother. The concubine mother normally was freed upon the death of her master. This aspect of **slavery** in the Muslim world led some scholars to consider the institution limited to the first generation of slaves. *See also* HAREM; SHARIA.

UMM KULTHUM (ca. 1898–1975). An Egyptian iconic singer and towering figure of the Arab entertainment industry, born in the hamlet of Tamay al-Zahiriyya in the Governorate of Dakahaliya. Her father, Sheikh Ibrahim al-Sayyid al-Baltaji (d. 1932), was a religious teacher and chanter of the Quran, and her mother, Fatima al-Maliji (d. 1947), was a homemaker. Umm Kulthum was born Fatima Ibrahim al-Sayyid al-Biltaji, but it is not known who named her after one of the granddaughters of the Prophet Muhammad and a daughter of Ali and Fatima. She attended the village religious school and was taught recitation of the Quran and religious chanting by her father. When she proved at age 12 to have more talents in this area than her sister and brother, she was taken on singing tours of nearby villages in the eastern Delta region by her father. She was always dressed as a boy, because female singers often had unsavory reputations.

In 1923, she and her family moved to Cairo, where she gained a foothold in the world of commercial entertainment. The first master to discover her talents and train her was Abu al-Ula Muhammad, a composer who had also trained another famous singer, Sayyid Darwish (1892–1923). Her singing career continued to be directed by her father until she rose to the pinnacle of the singing ladder in 1928. Her voice was readily recognized as the greatest natural singing instrument in the Arab world by the 1930s and 1940s. She was assisted by Cairo's best musicians and lyricists, such as Muhammad al-Qasabji, Riyadh al-Sunbati, the poet Ahmad Rami, and Zakaria Ahmad, the latter being one of the greatest composers of his age.

The only competition she faced was from her contemporary during the 1940s, the Syrian Druze singer **Asmahan**. Unlike Asmahan, whose career was punctuated by scandal, Umm Kulthum maintained a cultivated and well-guarded image. She projected the figure of a consummate artist, totally dedicated to her art. She was truly deserving of the title bestowed upon her by the media, *Kawkab al-Sharq* (The Star of the East), presenting an image that contrasted sharply with the typical cabaret performer in Egypt's disreputable nightclubs.

Umm Kulthum helped develop Cairo's reputation as the artistic center of the Arab world. Her voice was chosen to inaugurate Radio Cairo's broadcasts when it began transmitting in 1934, and her image was the first to adorn the Egyptian television screen when it began its programming in 1960. She began her first singing tour of Arab capitals in 1931 at Damascus and launched her movie musical career when the Egyptian movie industry was still in its infancy. Eventually, she shifted away from singing Arabic classical poetry to performing love poems of some of her great contemporaries, like the poet Ahmad Shawqi, dubbed "the Prince of the Poets." It was said that her singing taught poetry to the masses, who became familiar with their classical poetical heritage. Her weekly radio concerts were virtuoso performances, sometimes lasting up to three or four hours, in which she would sing two to four songs. Her longest concert took place in Paris in 1967, when she sang for seven hours. Although she discontinued delivering primarily religious songs, a more sophisticated brand of religious poetry continued to appear in her musical repertoire even after she switched to romantic songs. She was always admired for her unrivaled performing technique, her impeccable diction, and her physical stamina.

Umm Kulthum's musical career, however, was not free of political controversy. She was decorated by King Farouq of Egypt (r. 1936–1952) with the Order of al-Kamal (Perfection) in 1944, while at the same time the palace and the government were opposed to her marriage to the king's uncle, Sharif Sabri Pasha. Her association with the monarchy cost her the friendship of the musicians' syndicate, which froze her membership after the Free Officers revolution of 1952. But her songs in support of the Egyptian war effort on the Palestine front in 1948 earned her the undying admiration of Jamal Abd al-Nasser, the future president of Egypt. She demonstrated her patriotism and deep love for Egypt by singing patriotic songs during several wars and raising funds for the country's military charities. She was also decorated by Nasser and the heads of several Arab countries. She financed many projects in her ancestral village and was considered a source of pride for the beleaguered Arab nation through several military defeats on the Arab–Israeli front. Her last concert was performed in 1973. Her last recorded song was "*Hakam alayna al-hawa*" ("Love Has Commanded Us").

Umm Kulthum married a much younger man, an Egyptian physician, Dr. Hassan al-Hifnawi, in 1954, with nary a negative or lascivious comment from the watchful media. It was a testament to her stature as a consummate artist and universally acknowledged national treasure that her private life was never exposed to the public eye. When she died of a heart attack four years after the passing of Nasser, Egypt's and the Arab world's national hero, her funeral eclipsed his and was attended by a frenzied crowd of more than four million people. The stricken mourners passed her coffin from one group to another, until the religious sheikhs pleaded that all Muslims should be laid to rest as quickly as possible. Radio Cairo followed her death announcement with the chanting of the Quran, a treatment usually accorded only to heads of state. There have been scores of Umm Kulthum imitators since her passing, but none could rival her winning combination of powerful voice, strong musical instincts, and dedicated and admiring musical directors. Her residence has become part of a modern hotel in Cairo's upper-class neighborhood of Zamalek, with her statue standing erect by the entrance. A small exhibit of her outfits and recording artifacts was placed in a pavilion near Cairo's Monasterly Palace, overlooking the Nile.

UMM SALAMA (ca. 580–680). She was one of the wives of Prophet Muhammad. Her full name was Umm Salama Hind bint Abi Umayya. She and her first husband, Abdullah ibn Abd al-Assad, were early converts to Islam and suffered persecution by the Quraysh tribe. They were, thus, among a select group of early converts that included **Khadija**, Ali ibn abi-Taleb, and Abu Bakr al-Siddiq. Her husband was killed in the battle of Uhud (625), leaving her a widow with four children. She accepted Muhammad as her husband after rejecting marital offers from two future caliphs, Abu Bakr and Umar. She was 29 years old when she married the Prophet. She lived to be his last surviving wife, titled "Mother of the Believers." She died at an advanced age at Medina and was buried at the Baqi Cemetery, where most of the Prophet's family members and companions were interred.

Her union with the Prophet began the custom of marrying war widows, and many followed in Muhammad's footsteps. But Umm Salama was exceedingly beautiful, which stirred some jealousy in the heart of **Aisha**, the Prophet's younger wife. Umm Salama also advised Muhammad during the crisis of Hudaybia in 628, leading to the Muslim conquest of Mecca. *See also* MARRIAGE IN ISLAM.

UMM WARAQA. She was a contemporary of Prophet Muhammad who was appointed as an *imam* (religious judge). Her full name was Umm Waraqa bint Abdullah, and she was a companion of the Prophet, the only woman in addition to **Aisha** to enjoy that status. She was well versed in the Quran, receiving much of her religious knowledge from the Prophet directly. She pleaded with him to allow her to participate in the battle of Badr in 624 in order to tend to the wounded. After she survived this battle, the Prophet granted her the title "the female martyr."

Umm Waraqa is at the center of a great controversy and dispute surrounding women's right to lead prayers or act as an *imam*. According to some historical sources and testimony by a few companions (*al-Sahaba*), the Prophet allowed her to lead the prayers of mixed groups of women and men, but it is not clear whether these were informal groups, a family, or a regular community. Apparently, she was also permitted to be the *imam* over her own clan, which was of a substantial size that warranted its having its own *muezzin*, or caller to the prayers. These facts are disputed by some scholars and interpretive schools of Islam, which categorically deny women's eligibility to lead the prayers. Umm Waraqa is also said to have been appointed by Caliph Umar (586, 590–644) to act as the head of the market committees of Mecca and Medina, but some sources ascribe that role to another woman. What is agreed upon, however, is that Umm Waraqa met her death at the hands of two slaves who, when questioned by Caliph Umar, admitted to having been instigated by others to commit this deed.

UNION OF FEMINIST ACTION. Also known as L'Union de d'Action Féminine, it is an organization founded specifically to wage a campaign for reforming Moroccan family law. It was founded just before King Hassan II accepted the recommendations of special committees in 1992 to adopt **al-Mudawana**. The union mobilized large segments of the population, gathering one million signatures in a petition drive supported by men and women calling for major reforms. The king accepted these signatures and formed a special committee of men and women to make formal recommendations before writing the final version of the Mudawana. *See also* SHARIA.

UNION OF TUNISIAN WOMEN. The official name of this organization is L'Union Nationale des Femmes Tunisiennes (UNFT). It was created in 1956, the year of Tunisian independence, as an auxiliary to the main party the Neo-Destour. Most of the time it implemented programs approved by the parent party, such as stamping out illiteracy among women and creating awareness of the government-initiated **Personal Status Code of Tunisia** of 1956. Its membership reached 135,000 by 2000 and became a prominent Destour-supporting voting bloc. The union has regional representation throughout the country and in each of its 23 governorates. It works with all women's advocacy groups and NGOs. For many years it was headed by **Wasilah Bourgiba**, wife of President **Habib Bourgiba**. The union faced strong pressures by Islamist forces seeking to overturn the Personal Status Code of Tunisia following the uprising of 2010–2011.

URF MARRIAGE. This is a new type of Islamic **marriage** that emerged largely in Egypt during the last decades of the 20th century. It is often described as a marriage based on customary law (*urf* in Arabic), which derives its inspiration from the pagan, pre-Islamic customs of Arabia. The marriage entails two consenting adults signing a paper in which they commit themselves to each other without the benefit of witnesses. The personal contract is never registered in a court of law. It is now commonly agreed that this type of irregular marriage has spread due to socioeconomic pressures confronting young people, especially in Egypt. In a culture that looks askance at sexual relations outside of marriage, and at a time when adequate housing in urban centers is not readily available, young people find themselves forced to endure many years of being single before they can enter into a traditional form of marriage. Parental demands for excessive **dowry** are also forcing young males to seek special arrangements that don't comply with traditional customs.

Urf marriages were also rumored to be the preferred form of matrimony among Islamic fundamentalist groups who formed their own secret communities in the hills outside of Cairo during the early 1980s. After most of these groups were disbanded, this type of marriage became popular among secular university students. A strong backlash against urf marriage was generated, mostly by religious scholars. They argued that the contracts were invalid in **Sharia** courts and could not be applied to **inheritance** claims, alimony, or disputes over child support. According to this view, not only were these marriage unregistered, but they also lacked some of the essential foundations of Islamic marriage, like witnessing by adults, announcing it to the public, and complying with the Islamic requirement of compatibility. The representation of the bride by a male relative was also eliminated and made this contract totally unbinding. Urf marriage became particularly risky for women, even though some continued to resort to it as a way of pressuring parents to accept marriages based on individual choice, rather than negotiated by families. *See also* TEMPORARY MARRIAGE.

USAYRAN, LAYLA (1936–). A Lebanese novelist and erstwhile supporter of the activities of the Palestine Liberation Organization (PLO) in Lebanon during the 1960s and 1970s. She was born in Baghdad to a Lebanese Shii family. She studied in Cairo and Beirut, earning a degree in political science from the American University in Beirut (AUB) in 1954. As a student activist, she espoused leftist causes, proclaiming her support for the "armed struggle," which meant support for Palestinian military activities in southern Lebanon. She was a columnist for the PLO's paper, *Fatih*, and later for *Filastin al-Muhtalla* (*Occupied Palestine*), which ran during the Lebanese Civil War (1974–1989). She is the author of several novels, including *Asafir al-Fajr* (*Birds of the Dawn*, 1968), *Khatt al-Afaa* (*The Snake's Script*, 1970), *Qalaat al-Usta* (*The Master's Fortress*, 1979), and *Jisr al-Hajar* (*The Stone Bridge*, 1982). She also wrote *Lan Namut Ghaddan* (*We Shall Not Die Tomorrow*), *al-Hiwar al-Akhras* (*The Mute Dialogue*), and *Al-Madinah al-Farighah* (*The Empty City*, 1996), the novel that catapulted her to national prominence. Most writers compare her style of writing to that of another Lebanese novelist, **Layla Baalbaki**. Usayran left her political attachments behind her when the civil war ended, declaring her preference for an isolationist and independent Lebanon, free from any outside intervention.

UZZA, AL- . One of three major female goddesses who were worshipped by the Arab pagan population of Mecca. The two others were al-Lat and Manat. All three were considered daughters of a great deity named Allah. These were the favorites of Mecca's commercial elite before the advent of Islam, and each was enshrined in her own temple. Al-Uzza had a temple dedicated to her at Nakhla, east of Mecca. The Quraysh tribe, which ruled Mecca and warred against Prophet Muhammad and his followers, considered the greatest deity to be the God Hubal, a male representation who dominated al-Kaaba. According to **Fatima Mernissi** in *Islam and Democracy: Fear of the Modern World* (1992), all these gods and goddesses were associated with human sacrifice, and the prophet's own father, Abdullah, barely escaped the fate of being sacrificed to Hubal. Mernissi theorizes that these goddesses in particular were loved and feared at the same time and may have alienated the early figures of Islam against women. Ul-Uzza, however, though also placated with offers of human sacrifice like the rest of the deities, was regarded as the goddess of beauty, or the nearest thing to the Greek Aphrodite, by the Nabatean Arabs of the city of Petra. As soon as Muhammad's armies entered Mecca in 630, he and others, but mainly the future caliph Umar, went from temple to temple, destroying the figurines of these goddesses with great enthusiasm. Once the Kaaba was cleansed of these pagan relics, it was rededicated as a Muslim shrine. Anger at these stone images and the practice of idol worshipping proved to be a strong motivation against artistic representation of the human form under Islam. *See also* JAHILIYA.

V

VAZIRI, QAMAR AL-MULUK (1905–1959). She was one of the earliest female professional singing performers in Iran, born in Qashan to a middle-class family. She was raised by her maternal grandmother, who performed religious dirges at women's gatherings during the *Ashura* festival. Qamar, who learned these dirges from her grandmother, also received instruction in classical Persian music and singing from the great musical masters of her day. Her grandmother, Molla Khayr al-Nissa, was given the title *Eftekhar al-Dakerin* (The Glory of Narrators) by Nasir al-Din Shah in recognition of her considerable musical talent. Qamar al-Muluk may have taken the name Vazirizada, her full original name, in honor of a famous music teacher, Ali-Naqi Yaziri. She began performing in 1924 at Tehran's Grand Hotel, where she was the first female to sing while unveiled. She also performed in the Iranian capital's Sepal and Palace movie theaters before performing in Radio Tehran's musical broadcasts in 1940. She died in dire straits, because Radio Tehran paid her a meager salary. She was buried at the capital's Dhahir al-Dowlah cemetery.

VEILING IN ISLAM. This is the custom of women covering their faces when in public places. The covering material itself is called the *hijab* (Arabic), meaning a screen or a curtain concealing the face and/or the hair. It could mean also covering of the entire body, except for the hands, face, and feet.

Veiling was not originally an Arab or Muslim custom, but has a long history among women of other civilizations. The Assyrians of Mesopotamia made an elaborate legal distinction between those who were to be veiled and those whom law mandated were not to be veiled. The Assyrian law givers tied these distinctions to their class system. The following categories of women were expected to cover their heads in public: noble women by birth, respectable married women, free women, widows, and women who were Assyrian by birth. Law 40 of the Middle Assyrian Laws also required the following type of women not to veil themselves in public: concubines, servants (except when accompanying a veiled noble woman), harlots, and

337

slaves. Those who violated this code by illegally veiling in public were subject to flogging or having pitch poured over their heads. Their ears might also be cropped. These distinctions stemmed from the fact that the aristocracy, especially women, was marked by their distinctive manner of dressing. The veil was the most significant and visible marker of the aristocracy, denoting exclusivity and high status. This law dated back to the second millennium before the Christian era.

The *hijab*'s ancient roots also extend to the Hellenic period, when Aristotle emphasized women's social, biological, physical, and mental- inferiority to men. These differences, in his view, justified subordinating women's needs to men's, because nature intended their position to be subservient. These ideas influenced the Byzantine Empire, which favored the seclusion of women and called for the donning of special clothing to hide them from the casual glances of strangers. During this period, women were valued for their submissiveness, silence, and obscurity.

Although ancient Egyptian women enjoyed almost total equality with men, the imposition of Greek and Roman rule in Egypt led to the erosion of most of their rights. Only the Ptolemaic period in Egypt ameliorated the status of women, allowing them to sign contracts and terminate their own **marriages**, while **polygamy** went out of existence. But Byzantine rule after that led to the decline of women's status and the seclusion of women centuries before the advent of Islam. Evidence of the veiling of women during the Christian period is found in the Arabian Peninsula, where the Christian women of the city of Najran, located south of Mecca, wore the veil during the sixth century CE. When Islam spread over Arabia, the first women to wear the veil and lead secluded lives were those of the Prophet's family. Indeed, those who argue that the *hijab* is not religiously mandated stress that relevant verses in the Quran refer only to the seclusion of women in the Prophet's household, adding that they were unlike other women. Yet **Aisha** and Asma, daughters of Caliph Abu-Bakr, were both unveiled. **Sukayna**, the great granddaughter of Prophet Muhammad, maintained a literary salon for mixed gender groups.

Historians stress that the first time Muslim armies encountered veiled women in large numbers was when they conquered the Christian Byzantine territories of Syria and the Sassanid Empire of Persia. Arab rulers, such as the Caliph al-Mutawwakil of the Abbasid dynasty (r. 847–861), began to emulate these customs. He earned the title "Nero of the Arabs" when he began to imitate the Byzantine system of segregating men and women during public festivals. Until the eighth century CE and the end of the Umayyid dynasty, men and women attended mixed public events. Despite the Abbasid Empire's (750–1258) cultural borrowings from the Persians, only elitist Arab women were veiled.

Beginning in the age of *Nahdha* (renaissance) at the turn of the 19th century, Muslim male reformers began to question the religious and scriptural validity of the veil. By that time, the veil amounted to the total seclusion of women, particularly upper-class women. Modernists such as author and judge **Qassem Amin** in Egypt began to attack the custom of veiling, linking it directly to the declining status of women. The **Egyptian Feminist Union (EFU)** began to make its antiveiling campaign the centerpiece of its agenda in the late 1920s. The veil was derided by Egyptian feminists like **Huda Shaarawi, Ceza Nabrawi, Aminah al-Said**, and **Durrea Shafiq** as a detriment to women's educational and employment potential and an obstacle to modernization. They all disputed the religious rationalization of the veil. Secular male reformers anxious to see their countries catch up with the West, like **Mustafa Kemal Ataturk** and **Reza Shah Pahlavi**, strongly discouraged veiling and used the power of the state to abolish this form of dress in Turkey and Iran during the first decades of the 20th century. For these rulers, discarding the veil was also necessary for the integration of women into the national economy. The veil became a symbol of cultural degradation and the low status of women, particularly when colonial apologists used this custom to justify their continued political control of countries like Algeria and Egypt. The French in Algeria in particular described the veil as a woman's movable prison. The veil was an important element justifying the "civilizing mission" concept underlying the colonial ideology of such powers as the French in North Africa.

The veil, however, made a remarkable comeback in Egypt during the 1970s and spread from there to other Arab countries. The emphasis here was on covering a woman's hair and much of her body, resulting in a new style of dress rarely seen before. The first to convert to this custom in Egypt were female students of public universities, but the **Azhar** institution, which normally issues opinions on such behavioral matters, did not mandate wearing of the veil. Many scholars explain the new veiling phenomenon by referring to the spread of Wahhabi Islam and Saudi Arabian influences throughout the Muslim world. Yet Iran's role in popularizing this type of covering cannot be ignored. It was the ideologue of the Islamic revolution of Iran, **Ali Shariati**, who called for the return to veiling as a means of discarding Western cultural hegemony. The Iranian Republic decreed the wearing of *hijab* for female workers in public institutions in 1983 and has since enforced this custom on city streets. The rise of Islamic parties in Turkey, such as the Refah and the AKP toward the end of the 20th century, was accompanied by increasing popularity of the *hijab* as normal street wear for women.

The wearing of the *hijab*, in essence, became a movement to recapture the civilization of the earlier centuries of Islam, which according to this view, symbolized community, a purified Islam, and political activism. Its most visible feature was a rejection of Western consumerist habits, including

Western dress, in favor of outer modesty and an emphasis on Islamic identity. The *hijab* that was born out of this movement, commentators quickly noted, had nothing to do with traditional forms of Islamic dress such as the *safsari* in Tunisia, the *thoub* in the Sudan, or the *abaya* in Iraq. The *hijab* did not interfere with women's employment, since those who chose this form of dress have taken up various occupations and quickly became part of the general scene in almost all Middle Eastern street settings. The *niqab*, the latest metamorphosis of the *hijab* phenomenon, which involves covering the hair and the entire face, leaving only the eyes uncovered, has been seen in modest numbers in urban centers recently. Unlike the *hijab*, however, the *niqab*'s supporters have been unable to prove an Islamic or Arab genealogy and quickly earned the scorn of many religious circles, including that of al-Azhar. Wearing of the *niqab* outside of the Arab Gulf region has only been championed by the *salafis*, or extreme Islamists. Arab nationalists and secularists, both men and women, continue to oppose all manifestations of the *hijab*, both as a symbol of Islamic political identification and of rising Saudi influence. Secular feminists like **Fatima Mernissi** and **Nawal Saadawi** have been in the forefront of this antiveiling movement. *See also* ANCIENT EGYPT, WOMEN IN; GHAZZALI, ZAYNAB (1917–2005); KHOMEINI, AYATOLLAH RUHOLLAH (ca. 1902–1989).

VEILING IN JUDAISM. Veiling or covering the face by women is not required by Jewish law. Married women, however, were obligated to cover their hair, at the penalty of being **divorced** and forfeiting their **dowry**. Jewish communities living within Islamic empires during the Middle Ages generally imitated the cultural variants of the dominant Arab and Muslim communities. As long as these customs did not contradict the Halacha, they were easily assimilated. There was a safety rationale at work here, because veiled women on the street could not be distinguished from Muslim women. Some exceptions to this general rule prevailed in Iran during the Qajar dynasty (1785–1925), when Jewish women and other *dhimis* (protected communities of the Bible) were required to uncover their faces in public.

The veiling of Jewish women in the Middle East was determined by the space they inhabited at any given time. Women were expected to cover their heads only when inside their private residences. When in the Jewish quarter, outside of their homes, they were expected to lower their head veils and cover part of their faces. But when they moved outside of the Jewish quarter and among the non-Jewish population, they were expected to be veiled fully and blend in with the general female population. These strictures survived into the 20th century and were progressively eliminated, beginning with the residents of urban centers. Jewish women who lived in distant and isolated villages in the Middle East retained the custom of covering the face until they migrated to Israel, with young women quicker to unveil than older women.

Jewish and Christian women who continued to live among Muslim neighbors in major Middle Eastern cities, such as Cairo and Baghdad during the early decades of the 20th century, were quicker to discard the face veil than their Muslim compatriots, largely due to the impact of Western education provided by the **Alliance Israéalite Universelle**. For members of Iraq's Jewish community during the Hashemite monarchy (1932–1958), the unveiling of women was largely the project of the Iraqi Communist Party, in whose ranks they predominated. Both Muslim and Jewish women who came from leftist families in Iraq were quick to discard the veil during the first half of the 20th century.

Jewish women arriving in Palestine beginning in the latter part of the 19th century were thoroughly Europeanized. For these women, veiling was a cultural habit associated with Mizrahi Sephardi Jews with which they were thoroughly unfamiliar. Within Palestine, the veil was a marker of Arab and Muslim culture from which they separated themselves.

W

WAFDIST WOMEN'S CENTRAL COMMITTEE (WWCC). This was an early Egyptian committee that mobilized women in the national struggle against British rule. The committee dated back to 1920 and emerged as an unofficial adjunct of the Wafd Party, Egypt's nationalist group, which struggled to achieve Egyptian independence. Pressure on nationalists to allow the participation of women in political activities predated the 1919 Revolution by about nine years. Even before the emergence of the Wafd Party of Saad Zaghloul (1859–1927) after World War I, an appeal for independence by a woman named Inshirah Shawqi was read by a male before the 1910 Brussels congress of the Nationalist Party (Hizb al-Watani). The Wafd Party came under pressure by an Indian nationalist leader, Bhikaji Cama, to include women in its ranks. When the 1919 Revolution began, female relatives of Wafd leaders were encouraged to launch demonstrations and lead a boycott against British goods.

The Wafdist Women's Central Committee came into being officially in 1920 as a result of public meeting at Cairo's St. Mark's Cathedral. Women leaders exemplified the nonsectarian spirit of the Wafd Party by recruiting Muslim and Coptic Christian women alike. The committee was most successful in managing the finances of the entire nationalist effort. Its first elected president was feminist and nationalist leader **Huda Shaarawi**. The WWCC's founding members included daughters of Egypt's Muslim and Christian elite, such as Ulfat Rateb, Regina Habib Khayyat, Wissa Wasef, Sharifa Riyadh, Ester Fahmi Wissa, Louise Majorelle Wasif Ghali, Ihsan al-Qusi, and Fikriyya Husni. The committee established links to other women's organizations such as the New Women Society, the Society for the Renaissance of the Egyptian Woman, and the Society of Mothers of the Future.

One year after its founding, when Egypt was not yet fully independent, the WWCC experienced the first sting of exclusion when Zaghloul and the rest of the Wafd leadership made no effort to consult it on the emerging blueprint for independence. The majority of the membership followed Shaarawi when she left the WWCC to form her own **Egyptian Feminist Union**, after publishing a scathing rebuke of Zaghloul. The remaining loyalist members of the

WWCC renamed their rump organization the "Committee of Saadist Women," under the leadership of Zaghloul's wife, **Safiyya Zaghloul** who was called "The Mother of the Egyptians" (*Umm al-Misriyoun*). The Wafd Party's commitment to women's emancipation weakened, as women were expected to devote their total energies to the national question.

WAHHABISM. This is an Islamic reform movement that emerged in Arabia in the 1740s. Ostensibly a puritanical movement, it was given its name by its ideological foes, who referred to it by the name of its founder, Muhammad ibn Abd al-Wahhab (1702–1792). A religious scholar of notable reputation, ibn Abd al-Wahhab hailed from a small town in eastern Arabia, near the modern capital of Saudi Arabia, Riyadh. He gained notoriety upon publishing a theological tract in 1740 in which he condemned many current Islamic practices, calling them *bidaa* (innovations). According to this view, innovations or adaptations to conform to modernity were simply deviations from the true faith; hence Wahhabism was the only pure sect. All other sects were declared to be heathen, which justified subjecting them to a **jihad**. Common practices such as erecting shrines to honor saints were compared to idolatry, as was the custom of visiting shrines to seek the intercession of saints. Ibn Abd al-Wahhab was a strict unitarian, preaching that no one should be worshipped but God. This led to attacks on Iraq's famed Shii shrines by Wahhabi tribesmen and became a convenient justification for warring against other communities, especially after the Saud family hitched its star to the Wahhabi doctrine. Zealot tribesmen of the Sauds and their allies became known as *ikhwan* (Brothers); they marched across Arabia, proceeding to the Red Sea coast over a period of a century. Eventually, the Sauds consolidated their rule over all of Arabia, minus a few eastern sheikhdoms and the Yemen in the south, creating the kingdom of Saudi Arabia in 1932 under the dynasty's founder, King Abd al-Aziz (1876–1953).

The alliance between the Sauds and Ibn Abd al-Wahhab surprised many Islamic scholars, because the extreme rejection of the possibility of change was usually aroused under the impact of colonial domination. Eastern Arabia in the early 19th century lacked this history and followed strict interpretations of Islam. But the most significant outcome of this alliance was the durable Wahhabi influence within the kingdom, which still determines cultural practices and the treatment of women today. The *ikhwan* make up the bulk of the Saudi National Guard, and Wahhabi religious scholars maintain a monopoly over educational policy, religious worship, and the pace of modernization within the kingdom. Some of their puritanical practices, such as burying the dead in unmarked graves, persist. But their most controversial aspect is their continued harassment of women. This is achieved through their monopolization of the ranks of the moral police (*mutawiin*), which enforce **veiling** in public places, the ban on women driving, and strict gender segregation in education and the workplace. Wahhabi doctrinal influence has recently spread to other countries, primarily Egypt, where its followers sometimes are too willing to resort to violence to enforce their views. *See also* FEMALE DRIVERS IN SAUDI ARABIA; HANBAL, IMAM AHMAD IBN (780–855).

WAKIL, ZAYNAB AL (?–1967). She was the wife of Egyptian Prime Minister Mustafa al-Nahhas, who was also the leader of the Wafd Party. Al-Wakil was famous for her extravagant tastes and using her husband's office for nepotistic and financial manipulation. Her personal lifestyle reflected negatively on her husband, who was her senior by many years. But she is also known for having enjoyed the title "she who controls her **divorce**" (*sahibat al-isma*), meaning one of the few Muslim women of that era who could demand a divorce irrespective of the husband's wishes. She married al-Nahhas in 1934 when she was in her twenties and he was 55 years old. Her family's corruption and scandalous commercial dealings were exposed by Nahhas's Coptic colleague and rival for the Wafd leadership, Makram Obeid, causing a split in the Wafd Party. When the Free Officers took over the reins of office in 1952, al-Nahhas was brought to trial, and he and al-Wakil were placed under house arrest. She was also stripped of much of her wealth, palaces, and landed estates. Egypt's first President, Muhammad Najib (r. 1952–1954), was placed under house arrest in one of her villas. Nahhas died in 1965, receiving a tumultuous send-off by his followers, who shouted "no leader after Nahhas," and Al-Wakil followed him in death two years later.

WAQF. The Islamic system of creating charitable endowments for religious or family purposes. Muslim women played a major role in establishing these *awqaf* (plural of *waqf*), which were known as *hubus* (isolated property) in North Africa. Since Islamic law granted women the right to own and dispose of property, wealthy women often partook of this activity as a sign of piety. As an institution of Islamic law, the *waqf* entails the irrevocable allocation of wealth, usually derived from immovable and income-producing property, to enterprises of a religious or charitable nature. The income from such property cannot be diverted to uses other than those stipulated by the founder. Endowments in Islam cannot support secular foundations in the modern sense and are inalienable. The endowers, whether men or women, must be free (not slaves) and of sound mind since they are, in effect, disinheriting their own descendants. In some cases, primarily in North Africa where the Maliki school of Islamic law is followed, temporary endowments are also allowed, although in the majority of cases, this would subvert the original intent of the law. These foundations normally support religious projects such as schools, mosques, public water fountains (*sabeel*), soup kitchens, students and scholars, hostels for **divorced** and widowed women, Sufi hostels, clinics, hospitals, and public baths. **Sharia** law allows women to act as supervisors (*nazirat*) over a *waqf* belonging to someone other than themselves. A woman is also eligible for the role of agent (*wakil*), designated by the endowers to conduct transactions on their behalf. The right to establish endowments is allowed to women of all classes and was not restricted to the rich and powerful.

Creating endowments was more common in certain periods of Islamic history than in others. Historians, however, are discovering that the apparent presence or absence of women's endowments was often just a function of the availability of records. Therefore, Egypt and Ottoman Turkey, which boast extensive historical archives, provide more information on these activities than other countries. Among the earliest endowments by women was an extensive network of waterworks near **Zubayda**'s well, which irrigated the plain of Arafat near Mecca. These were endowed in 808 by the Foundation of Amat al-Aziz, the wife of Harun al-Rashid, the Abbasid caliph. Amat al-Aziz was the nickname of Zubayda, who wanted to ease the hardship of the pilgrimage for Muslims by endowing this costly project from her own *waqf*. Notable among the early women who endowed *waqf* projects out of their personal wealth was Fatima al-Fihriyya, who inherited great wealth from her husband and her maternal family in Morocco during the 10th century. She established a great mosque, which became the University of al-Qarawiyin, known for Islamic studies, similar to **al-Azhar** mosque/university in Cairo. Ibn Batuta, the famed traveler, reported coming across charitable foundations in Damascus that provided wedding garments to disadvantaged young women during the 14th century. Women frequently resorted to the law of endowments during the Mamluk and Ottoman periods, especially in Egypt, in order to bypass **inheritance** formulas and specify their own female relatives as endowed beneficiaries. Some scholars claim that the available data show fewer women than men as endowment creators or supervisors.

The history of establishing endowments dates back mainly to the Fatimid period and continues into the 11th and 12th centuries in Egypt and North Africa. Foundations primarily supported mosques, such as al-Azhar, which functioned as religious schools. Fatimid women of the aristocracy, who often had the title of *sharifa*, or descendant from the Prophet's family, contributed part of the wealth to these state-supported mosques, which were the centers of Shii education in a predominantly Sunni country. Fatimid women also established foundations for the benefit of widowed and aging women and public water fountains, which were of tremendous help to the poor. When the Sunni Ayubid dynasty succeeded the Fatimids in Egypt, endowed centers of Sunni learning began to replace and eradicate the teaching of Shii doctrine, and royal and aristocratic women played a similar role as under the Fatimids. One of the hallmarks of the Ayubid period was Sufi-endowed hostels, which were often supported by women.

During the Mamluk period (13th to 19th centuries), many types of foundations supporting schools and Sufi lodges proliferated. Historians explain this phenomenon as a clear attempt by the Mamluk elite families, an aristocracy of white slaves of east European extraction, to win the favor of Egyptian society. What was at stake was gaining political legitimacy by appealing to the mass of the Egyptian population. Many of the Mamluk endowers were princesses who were eager to establish schools. The habit of engaging in these acts of public charity also extended to concubines of men of state. The only project that seemed to be beyond the reach of women was endowing hospitals, which were mostly endowed by the Mamluk rulers. For example, a Mamluk concubine in Egypt who became the wife of Murad Beik (Bey) (late 18th century), Nafisa al-Bayda, devoted the revenue of her extensive commercial enterprise (*wikalah*) to the support of an Islamic school for children and its attached fountain. Al-Bayda was also known for interacting with invading officers of the French Expedition (1798–1801) to maintain the privileges of her family.

During the Ottoman Empire, many pious foundations by mothers and wives of sultans focused largely on the capital. The Misir Carsisi (Egyptian Market) in Istanbul was founded as a *waqf* by Safiye Sultan, mother of Mehmed III (r. 1595–1603), to provide revenue for her charities. Kocem Sultan, mother of Sultan Murad IV (r. 1623–1640) and Sultan Ibrahim I (r. 1640–1648), endowed the Cinili Mosque and its school out of her substantial properties, which included public baths, markets, and hostels for travelers. The Cinili Mosque school was a large complex that operated several Islamic cultural programs in the suburb of Uskudar. **Roxelana** had a *waqf* specifically devoted to providing disadvantaged girls with **dowries**. A recent study of the reign of Suleiman I in the mid-16th century discovered that about one-third of the endowments in Istanbul were founded by women. Roxelana also provided for the maintenance of mosques, schools, three Sufi lodges, and a center of higher studies (Kulliye) near the women's market. The beloved wife of Suleiman the Magnificent (r. 1520–1566) also founded the Haseki *waqf*, which endowed projects in the three holy cities of Islam, Mecca, Medina, and Jerusalem, while bolstering her own legitimacy and political influence. She used the revenue of villages and extensive farmlands to endow mosques, soup kitchens, hospitals, and hostels for pilgrims in Jerusalem, as well as Sufi lodges with attached drinking fountains in Mecca and Medina. Other *awqaf* established by women supported rehabilitation programs for wayward females and buying the freedom of enslaved women. Some of the wealthy royal women endowed properties in order to support their freed slaves after their own deaths.

The Ottoman period in Egypt and Anatolia saw further changes in the system of endowments, especially during the 18th and 19th centuries. Charitable foundations were brought into line with the government's modernizing plans by being managed centrally and eliminating the freer and multiple operations of the past. Female members of royal households, however, continued to dedicate large farms and urban properties for charitable projects, which were mostly mosques. When Egypt's national struggle was launched against the British during the latter part of the 19th century, revenue from endowments was used by women to offset British efforts to limit public expenditures on schools, orphanages, and modern schools for girls. Revenue from some endowments was also spent on scholarships for women to study abroad, such as **Huda Shaarawi**'s scholarships bestowed on promising young women to study in Europe and dedicate their lives to the cause of women's emancipation upon their return.

In Iran, women appear as endowers beginning in the 11th century, when royal figures of the Seljuk period contributed greatly to the expansion of religious schools. This process was visible throughout the 12th and 13th centuries, when Terken Khatun (d. 1264), who ruled over the province of Fars, endowed a college with a very generous source of revenue. Her granddaughter, Princess Koradujin (d. 1338), also endowed charitable enterprises such as schools and hospitals. Zahida Khatun, wife of another ruler of Fars, endowed her agricultural properties to set up perpetual revenue for a new school in the city of Shiraz.

A great expansion in the number of foundations established by women of the Iranian elite occurred during the Safavid dynasty, 16th to 18th centuries. Thus, Shahzada Sultanum, sister of Shah Tahmasp (1524–1576), created *awqaf* for pious institutions named after the so-called Fourteen Immaculates, or the Prophet Muhammad, Fatima, and the 12 Shii imams, including Ali, the founder of the sect. Safavid women mostly established foundations to support religious schools, which were expected to provide seminarians with free lodging and food. Among the famous founders of such schools were Dilaram Khanum, grandmother of Shah Abbas II (1642–1666); Maryam Begum, daughter of Shah Suleiman (1666–1694), who built a school in 1703; and Shah Banu, sister of Shah Sultan Hussein (1694–1722). The latter endowed the revenue of a commercial public bath to support a religious school. Occasionally, a nonroyal woman, such as Zinat Begum, the wife of an Isfahani physician, also during the Safavid period, supported a school from some of her endowed property.

When Iran's last dynasty before the Pahlavis, the Qajars, ruled the country (1792–1925), endowments established by women became smaller and focused on local events such as supporting public ceremonies to commemorate the martyrdom of imam Hussein ibn Ali. Some of these endowments also by Qajar royal women, such as Hajiya Khatun Khanum and her daughter, Sara

Sultan Khanum, created a shopping complex (*wikalah*) and endowed its income for the ritual sermons (*rawza khani*) commemorating the Shii immaculate imams.

With the advent of the Pahlavi state, the government began to play a larger regulatory role in the management of the endowments through the Civil Code of 1928. This eventually led to the near absence of women from endowment management and the latter's full secularization. In 1934, the Department of Endowments was established to exercise oversight of the financial aspects of the religious foundations. The White Revolution of 1963 nationalized most of the large landholdings and established further control over the freewheeling *waqf* institution. Individuals lost access to large landed estates, and women lost the religious incentive to create state-managed pious foundations. The Pahlavi regime also succeeded in controlling the clergy's basis of power, always claiming that the management of *waqf* was riddled with corruption. The Islamic regime further accelerated the process of centralizing these foundations when it came to power in the revolution of 1979. Middle-class women, who are among the major supporters of the Islamic state, were given a direct role in managing the foundations. These became public charities, and women were useful in bolstering the image of a pious and charitable community.

Increasingly during the 19th and 20th centuries, foundations were manipulated to disinherit women and bypass the rigid rules of Islamic inheritance. Sometimes women played a similar role, setting up foundations to deprive male relatives of their rightful share of the inheritance. Governments of newly independent states in the middle of the 20th century made sure to establish ministries of *awqaf* in order to bring the vast properties under state control. Centralization, however, did not mean complete takeover of these tax-free properties. Governments began to look seriously into the transactions of the endowments and the rationale behind setting them up, often penalizing family endowments that were clearly set up to avoid land reform legislation. The ministries also intervened to stop the ouster of female *waqf* managers by their own male relatives. Thus, Syria and Egypt disbanded family endowments that hid landed property from the purview of land reform laws, and Lebanon protected women from exclusionary activities of male inheritors of family property and endowments.

WAZIR, INTISAR (1941–). A Palestinian nationalist leader and women's rights activist whose revolutionary name is Umm Jihad, just like the name of her husband, Abu Jihad, aka Khalil al-Wazir. She was born in Gaza and married her husband in 1962. Khalil al-Wazir was a cofounder of the revolutionary organization Fateh and second in command to Yasser Arafat. He was assassinated in Tunis in 1988, reputedly at the hands of Israel's secret intelligence service Mossad. Intisar al-Wazir graduated from al-Zahraa secondary school in 1960, receiving a BA in history from the University of Damascus in 1978.

Intisar al-Wazir's affiliation with Fateh, the major political faction of the Palestine Liberation Organization (PLO), began in 1959 when she became its first female member. After marrying Abu-Jihad, who was a political exile for much of his life, she lived with him in various Arab capitals from Algiers to Damascus, Beirut, and Tunis. In 1965, she was one of the founders of the **General Union of Palestinian Women (GUPW)**, serving as its secretary-general (1980–1985). She held powerful positions within the PLO hierarchy and is remembered best for being the secret acting chairperson of the PLO when the entire leadership, including Arafat, was briefly jailed by the Syrian government in the 1970s. She was elected as a member of the Palestine National Council (PNC) in 1974, which acted as the Palestinian parliament in exile, and became a member of Fateh's Central Committee beginning in 1987. In 1983, she was the deputy secretary-general of Fateh's Revolutionary Council. One of her most powerful positions was as the PLO's head of the Martyrs' Organization in Lebanon, where she oversaw a large network of social welfare projects benefiting the widows of PLO soldiers and their families.

After the signing of the Oslo Peace Agreement between the PLO and Israel, she returned to Gaza from her exile in Tunis in 1995 and was elected to the first Palestine Legislative Council (PLC) in 1996. She also became the first female member of the Palestinian cabinet when she was chosen to be the minister of social affairs in the Palestine National Authority's government, 1996–2000. Intisar al-Wazir has five children, the eldest being Jihad al-Wazir, who holds a PhD in economics from Marquette University, Milwaukee. He served for many years as the governor of the Palestine Monetary Authority.

WEINSTEIN, CARMEN (1931–). A Jewish Egyptian community leader who was born in Cairo. Her mother was Esther Weinstein, president of the Cairo Jewish Community Council. Carmen followed in her mother's footsteps, leading this council since 2004. Cairo's Jewish community dwindled drastically by the 1960s as a result of Arab anger at the State of Israel. She was focused on preserving as many monuments and artifacts of Egyptian Jewish life as possible, especially the Bassatine Cemetery, considered the second oldest Jewish cemetery in the world after that of the Mount of Olives in Jerusalem. Carmen found herself at the center of a legal battle when she was accused of pocketing money from the sale of an old synagogue and its land to an Egyptian developer, but she refused to surrender the deed. An Egyptian court issued a warrant for her arrest in 2010, but she was in Switzerland at the time, leading to rumors that she was spirited out of Cairo with the help of the Mossad. The judgment against her was eventually reversed, and she was allowed to return to Egypt.

Carmen Weinstein worked hard to distance herself from Israel and its policies. She was dedicated to the task of registering ancient Jewish buildings and artifacts with the Egyptian Supreme Council of Antiquities. This earned her the scorn of the American Jewish community and Israel, both of which feared that this would make removing any of these artifacts to Israel impossible. But she distanced herself from Zionist circles and maintained a strong allegiance to Egypt.

WEINSTEIN, ESTHER (1910–2004). She was a Jewish Egyptian community leader, born Esther Chaki to a Greek Jewish father and an Egyptian Jewish mother. She was among the minuscule Jewish community that remained in Egypt when most left due to a breakdown in Arab–Jewish harmony. She rose to prominence in 1996 when members of the Jewish community, most of whom at the time were aging females, decided to oust the predominantly male board of the Cairo Jewish Community Council, headed by Emile Rousseau, and put her in his place. This maneuver was executed by her daughter, **Carmen Weinstein**, who succeeded her as the chief leader of this council. The community, led by Carmen as its spokesperson, was infuriated by the selling of some ancient synagogues and the land on which they stood. Esther Weinstein was also involved in non-Jewish charities, receiving a decoration from the Vatican in 2002 because of her service with the Catholic charity Caritas Egypt.

WOMEN AND FAMILY AFFAIRS CENTER—NABLUS. This is a Palestinian **non-governmental organization (NGO)** dedicated to the advancement of women's rights and gender equality. The center was founded during the first *intifada* (1987–1990) in the West Bank's major city by one of Nablus's prominent feminists, novelist **Sahar Khalifah**. It became a template for other women's centers wishing to remain outside of official reach. Similar organizations were founded by Birzeit feminist university professors such as Rita Giacaman, Rima Hammami, and Islah Jad. In 1991, the center opened a branch in Gaza under a similar name, but the two were separated by a decision of the steering committee in 1994, leaving the Gaza branch under the name Women's Affairs Center. Iitimad Muhanna assumed the leadership of the Gaza branch, and despite severe financial constraints, managed to train some women in research and work with the media. Both organizations retained their independence from the Palestine National Authority (PNA), the **Hamas** government in Gaza, and the Israeli administration of the West Bank. A third branch was opened in Amman, Jordan, but did not survive. The

Nablus parent organization produced a journal, *Women's Affairs*, which also had a short lifespan. Heavily dependent on outside sources of funding, the center coordinates its activities with other women's NGOs.

WOMEN IN THE TURKISH MILITARY. The first woman to be formally inducted into the Turkish army in modern times was **Mustafa Kemal Ataturk**'s adopted daughter, **Sabiha Gökçen**. She entered the air academy in 1936, the only woman allowed to enroll in such an institution until 1955. In that year, several women won a court judgment allowing them to be admitted to the War College. The court accepted their argument that official regulations defining the qualifications of candidates did not specify gender limitations. Thus, the door opened wide for women to enter military colleges of all three branches of army, air force, and navy. In the early 1960s, the regulations were amended to specify that only males qualified for admission, and only after 1992 were women again legally allowed into military academies. Women's representation was still very slim; figures for 2001 show that out of a total of 800,000 male officers, only 918 were women. The limited presence of women in Turkish military branches represents the lowest ratio of women to men in NATO's forces, along with Italy and Poland, despite the fact that Turkey supports the largest military contingent in NATO after that of the United States. Even this limited presence is the result of pressure by NATO's Committee on Women. Advocates of women's rights also complain of very little information on women's experience in the military and insist that the claim of Turkey's military being open to women has no factual basis.

WOMEN'S CENTER FOR LEGAL AID AND COUNSELING—JERUSALEM. This is a Palestinian **non-governmental organization (NGO)** that was founded as a branch of one of the Palestine Liberation Organization's major affiliates, the Popular Democratic Front for the Liberation of Palestine (PDFLP). It was founded by the feminist leader **Zahira Kamal** when she was still a member of this organization in 1991 and included on its board several female activists such as Lamees Alami, Siham Barghouti, Rawdha al-Basir, Arham al-Dhamen, Samar Hawwash, Rana Nashashibi, Mukarram Qasstawi, and Lamia Quttaineh. The center separated from the PDFLP in a matter of years under the strains of the Oslo Peace Agreement and has branched off, with a new center in Hebron. It is now totally preoccupied with persuading the Palestine National Authority (PNA) to apply the **Convention on the Elimination of Discrimination against Women (CEDAW)**. The center maintains extensive contacts with local, international, and Israeli organizations, as well as the PNA.

WOMEN'S CULTURAL AND SOCIAL SOCIETY—KUWAIT (WCSS). This is one of the oldest and most exclusive women's societies in Kuwait, which was founded in the early 1970s. It was headed by Luulua al-Qatami as its salaried president after she ended a long career as president of a girls' college. The society's members are descendants of Kuwait's prominent merchant families, who rival the royal family of al-Sabah for influence and authority. Al-Qatami resigned from this position in 1993 after serving for 20 years and was succeeded by an elected president, Adela al-Sayer.

The society's work is divided among four committees: the *zakat* (alms giving) committee, adult literacy committee, cancer committee, and social committee. Connections between the WCSS and the Kuwaiti government are a matter of public knowledge, which enables its members to serve as their country's official representatives at international and regional women's gatherings and congresses. The WCSS had always represented Kuwaiti women where official delegations were seated per country, such as the United Nations conferences on women. In 1975, the first Regional Conference on Women in the Arabian Gulf was convened by the society. In the absence of a royal dynastic government, WCSS acts as Kuwait's public face whenever visiting foreign delegations of women visit the country. But the main function of the society has always been to provide social services wherever possible. One of its spectacular projects was the building of an ideal village for disadvantaged people in the Sudan in 1978. Built outside the capital of Khartoum, the village was provided with schools for both genders, a training center for women, a mosque, and a clinic. This achievement was carried out by the WCSS but with the help of the Kuwaiti ministry of religious foundations, which designated it as the agent for the massive project. The WCSS raised funds through some of its own charitable projects for the expenses of the village. The society also operates literacy classes for Kuwaiti women and supports orphanages in Palestine and Lebanon. Leaders of the WCSS also expressed vocal support for granting women the right to vote when the Kuwaiti parliament approved this measure in 2010. *See also* NON-GOVERNMENTAL ORGANIZATIONS (NGOs).

WOMEN'S FORUM FOR RESEARCH AND TRAINING—YEMEN (WFRT). This organization is the major human rights organization for women in Yemen. Founded in 2000, it seeks to coordinate the work of all women's and human rights groups. The founder and manager of the WFRT is Saud al-Qadasr, a prominent Yemeni human rights advocate and a former chairperson of the Yemeni Women's Union of the city of Taiz. The WFRT, which is managed by young Yemeni women, has always been located at Taiz, rather than in the capital city of Sanaa. The organization promotes change through the rule of law by seeking a consensus on women's human rights among all segments of society and encourages development policies to incorporate a gender perspective whenever possible. The WFRT works toward acquainting women with their rights under the law and the best means of attaining them. Workshops are often provided for the benefit of state officials to introduce them to the issue of women's human rights. The organization has its own publication program and has produced the following titles: the pamphlet "Street Children Phenomenon in Yemen, a 2003 Survey: Questions and Answers" and *Multaqa* (*Forum*), a periodical. *See also* NON-GOVERNMENTAL ORGANIZATIONS (NGOs).

WOMEN'S INTERNATIONAL ZIONIST ORGANIZATION (WIZO). This organization was founded in London in 1920 by the Federation of Women Zionists of Great Britain and quickly directed its efforts toward providing agricultural training for Jewish female immigrants to Palestine. Part of these services included training women to be education providers for children and to be good citizens. Among the founders of the WIZO were Vera Weizmann, Edith Eder, Romana Goodman, Henrietta Irwell, and Rebecca Sieff, the organization's first president. She held that position until her death in 1966. The WIZO did not confine itself to Britain, but established branches and federations wherever Jewish immigrants and supporters were to be found, except in the United States and the Union of Soviet Socialist Republics. The WIZO eventually moved its headquarters to Israel in 1949 and became affiliated with the World Zionist Organization and the World Jewish Congress. The WIZO's activities in Israel have proliferated into services for children's homes, organizing youth clubs, summer camps, and kindergartens for newly arrived children. The organization became a supporter of agricultural schools and community centers that serve the immigrant population of new settlements along the turbulent Arab borders of Israel, adjacent to the Jordanian and Syrian borders, and the so-called development towns in the same areas. The WIZO seeks to strengthen the Jewish diaspora's links to Israel. *See also* NON-GOVERNMENTAL ORGANIZATIONS (NGOs).

WOMEN'S LIBRARY AND INFORMATION CENTER—ISTANBUL. The library was formally known as Kadin Eserli Kutuphanesi ve Bilgi Merkezi, and was established in Istanbul in 1990 as a foundation. Its founders, who housed it in a building donated by the Istanbul municipality, included activists and writers such as Asli Davaz Mardin, **Sirin Tikeli**, Jale Baysal, Fusun Akatli, and Fusun Ertug-Yaras. The purpose of the foundation was to preserve women's history and records for the benefit of future generations. The library has a general board and an executive board, both of which are elected annually. There are more than 8,500 books in the collection, in Ottoman and modern Turkish as well as in several foreign languages. There are also journals and special collections of manuscripts and archival material. Personal documents were presented to the library by several famous women, such as Hasene Ilgaz, who is a teacher and writer; Mufide Ilhan, the first female mayor in Turkey; and Sureyya Agaoglu, a writer and jurist. The library also houses an oral history collection and boasts a sizeable budget that is supported by private donations and the sale of its own publications.

The Women's Library has maintained friendly relations with various political parties that dominated the mayoralty's administration of Istanbul, including the Islamist Party, which ran the city under Recep Tayyib Erdogan (1994–1997). The library is supported by the Global Fund for Women and the Turkish government, which frequently assigns it projects concerning women.

WOMEN'S MILITARY ROLES IN ISLAM. Women have always played military roles in pre-Islamic Arabia. They also participated in some of the early military confrontations between the believers, or early converts to Islam, and Mecca's merchant community, which rose to defend its deities and its way of life. Muslim teachings and the Quran did not forbid females from joining men on the battlefield, and many female warriors defended the Prophet as well as their own male kin in times of war. Among the well-known female fighters were Safiyya, Muhammad's aunt, and Asma bint Yazid, who was credited with killing nine fighters in the battle of Yarmouk. A famous warrior, Khawla bint al-Azwar, took part in some of these military engagements with her face covered. The most renowned female Muslim warrior, however, was Nusaybah bint Kaab, who acted quickly and saved the Prophet's life in the battle of Uhud. Nusaybah and 10 other fighters managed to protect Muhammad during that battle after most of the soldiers took flight, receiving several wounds in the process.

Muhammad's death in 632 did not remove women from the battlefield. When a Muslim army faced the Persians in battle in the Persian Gulf region, Azzdah bint Harith organized an all-female group to protect the fighters' phalanx.

Several women engaged in battles waged against Muhammad and his followers before the establishment of the Medinian state. Among the most notorious in this category was Hind bint Utbah, the wife of a Meccan grandee. Her primary role during the battle was reciting heroic poetry to encourage the fighters to show their prowess. Hind was rumored to have chewed the liver of Hamza, Muhammad's uncle, after he fell during the battle of Uhud.

Some modern states provided military training for women, invoking the memory of these fabled female fighters. The United Arab Emirates (UAE) provided military training for any woman wishing to join the armed services. An American officer, Major Janis Karpinski, provided the required training. The UAE's first female municipal engineer, Hassa al-Khalidi, was charged with organizing and leading the country's first all-female military unit. Libya during the rule of Muammar Qhaddafi's (r. 1969–2011) recruited females to serve as the president's personal bodyguards. But female service in most units of the military was only practiced widely in the modern Turkish republic. See also WOMEN IN THE TURKISH MILITARY.

WOMEN'S PEOPLE'S PARTY—TURKEY. This was the first women's political party to be founded in Turkey and became known as Kadinlar Halk Firkasi. It was founded in Istanbul in 1923 by some of the leading women's rights activists of that era, such as Nezihe Muhittin, who served as president; Nimet Remide, who was the first vice president; Sukufe Nihal, who was the general-secretary; and Latife Bekir, who served as spokesperson. The party failed to obtain permission to register from the Istanbul Provincial Administration, which argued that since women were not enfranchised, they could not form a political party. The women involved in this effort felt that the rejection of their bid for recognition was due to the ongoing preparations for the creation of the Republican People's Party (RPP), which became the ruling party until the mid-1940s. The organizers of the women's party were not perturbed by this obstacle and proceeded in 1924 to organize a new party, Kadinlar Birlgi (Women's Federation), which sought to obtain suffrage and to improve the conditions of rural Turkish women. Women's suffrage was not granted until the convening of the 12th Congress of the International Women's Union, which was held in 1935 in Istanbul. The Kemalist government, ever wary of public pressure by the women's lobby, convinced the Kainlar Birlgi to disband 10 days after the congress ended. The RPP's argument was that the main agenda of the women's party had been fulfilled. See also CILLER, TANSU PENBE (1946–).

WOMEN'S PRESS IN EGYPT. Women's magazines and publications began to emerge in Egypt during the latter part of the 19th century, although some faded away quickly. Most of these were written from a feminine perspective and addressed an overwhelmingly female readership. Women sought to establish their presence in this institution as soon as they began to enter society and played notable public roles. Much of this revolution took place in Egypt, where the press was among the most developed in the Arab world. Among the earliest women's publications to appear was Hind Nowfal's The Young Woman, which debuted in 1892. Another early journal was al-Rihana (The Fragrant Plant), which came out in 1907 under the direction of Turkish journalist Jamila Hafez. Her magazine carried the logo of the Egyptian nationalists, "Egypt for the Egyptians." Another publication, Women's Return Magazine, founded by Fatma Rashid, became the voice of working women who were mostly on the lower wrung of the economic ladder.

The majority of these papers, however, ranged over a wide spectrum concerning women's domestic roles and their emerging public careers. By the first half of the 20th century, there were 33 women's magazines in Egypt, some quickly disappearing for financial reasons.

Among the first of the pioneering journalists to broach the subjects of **marriage, divorce,** and **veiling** was **Malak Hafni Nasif.** Another early journalist, whose weekly newspaper was titled *al-Amal* (*Hope*), was Muna Thabit, nicknamed "The Rebel." Her inflammatory rhetoric on behalf of women's political rights gained her the enmity of the conservative Muslim clergy. **Huda Shaarawi,** the famous women's rights advocate, started publishing a landmark journal, *L'Égyptienne,* in 1925. It targeted the French-speaking Egyptian elite and international feminist circles. The monthly's logo was a drawing of a woman in the process of removing her veil. **Durrea Shafiq,** a feminist and a journalist, brought out *Bint al-Nil* (*Daughter of the Nile*) in 1945, which remained devoted to women's political rights until its closure in 1957. The women's press met the needs of an increasingly literate female readership, but the cost of this press and later pressures placed on it by the state in the 1950s eventually reduced its reach and led to its decline. Few journals survived the restructuring of the press institution under Jamal Abd al-Nasser's presidency. Instead of the independent women's press of past decades, national newspapers like *al-Ahram* (*The Pyramids*) gave two columns to discussion of women's affairs on its back page. In time, new journals devoted to the woman question, like *Hawaa* (*Eve*), which appeared in 1954, attempted to reach a mixed gender readership but eventually declined. Having monopolized the field as the only journal treating women's issues, it ceased publication in 1964.

By that time, another national paper, affiliated with Egypt's military regime, *al-Akhbar* (*The News*), began producing its own women's magazine, *Hiya* (*She*), which targeted women of the elite. It proved to be very short-lived, producing only 21 issues, but it inspired a similar venture by *Al-Ahram.* Focusing on the concerns of working women, in 1989 *al-Ahram* published a woman's magazine called *Nisf al-Dunya* (*Half of the Universe*). This journal, unlike its immediate predecessor, filled a gap, acknowledging in its stories the latest legal, political, and social concerns of Egypt's expanding sector of women professionals and workers. But the phenomenon of journals wholly directed and published by women appears to have disappeared altogether. Women remain conspicuously absent from editorial boards despite the presence of a sizeable number of active female journalists in the field. Almost one-quarter of the total membership of the press syndicate is women, and some are prominent political journalists, like Farida and Aminah al-Naqqash of *al-Ahali* (*People*) newspaper. The memory of prominent female journalists who did not own their papers, like **Aminah al-Said** and **Suheir Qalamawi**, still lingers. One journalist and publisher who did not emphasize women's issues was Fatima al-Yousef of *Rose al-Yousef* magazine. *See also* FEMINIST MOVEMENT IN EGYPT.

WOMEN'S SOCIETY OF THE ISLAMIC REVOLUTION (WISR). This is an Iranian reformist organization founded after the establishment of the Islamic republic, boasting the largest membership among similar associations. At first, the state was neutral toward it, neither encouraging it nor forcing it to close its doors. The society was spared despite its harsh line against the regime because it provided a useful entrée to a large circle of Islamic women ready to engage in the mass demonstrations and public activities of the regime. Yet financial support from the Islamic government was withheld, leading the WSIR's membership to complain about the lack of official support for its efforts to raise the Islamic and cultural consciousness of women. The authorities' attitude toward the WSIR has deteriorated since the revolution, with the society complaining bitterly against having its offices attacked and sometimes burned down by mobs.

One of the reasons for the regime's hostility was the society's main publication, *Payam-e Hajer* (*Hagar's Message*), which presented innovative and unorthodox interpretations of key segments of Islamic dogma pertaining to women. Claiming to follow the spirit of **Ayatollah Ruhollah Khomeini**'s teachings on women, WSIR nevertheless came out with its own independent ideas. *Payam* has discussed many sensitive issues, such as **veiling** and whether or not it was the only marker of women's identity, the exclusion of women from the judiciary, and the need for appointing a female cabinet minister. The paper concludes that the veil should be a matter of personal choice and called for limiting **polygamy**, eliminating the practice of **temporary marriage**, and doing away with similar practices that are no longer justifiable. The WSIR has harbored two contradictory tendencies ever since its founding, one a trenchant conservative inclination and the other a reforming and progressive tendency. The first trend was represented by **Munireh Gorji**, the female representative in the Assembly of Experts, which drafted the constitution of the Islamic Republic, the second by **Azam Teleghani**, the daughter of the liberal Ayatollah Mahmoud Teleghani. *See also* FEMINIST MOVEMENT IN IRAN.

WOMEN'S WORK COMMITTEES (WWC). These are Palestinian women's organizations created in the West Bank in 1978 to serve the social and economic needs of women living under Israeli occupation. These committees also espoused a political agenda to mobilize disadvantaged and rural women and harness their energies to the Palestine Liberation Organization's (PLO) national liberation program while pursuing gender-based objectives.

Several women from a variety of ideological backgrounds claim to have founded the committees, but experts credit **Zahira Kamal** of the Democratic Front for the Liberation of Palestine (DFLP) with being the original organizer. The committees attracted the support of many leading feminist figures who were professional career women and moderately allied with the PLO, such as Rita Giacaman and **Mona Rishmawi**. Although they remained independent of the committees, they shared the movement's goals of providing services such as child care and training programs designed to provide women with independent means of support. The child-care centers encouraged women to join political parties and devote time to the national effort. By 1985, the committees were promoting gender-consciousness programs, an effort that was interrupted by the first *intifada* of 1987.

During this uprising, the women's committee networks became extremely useful to the Palestinian national leadership, as women applied their newly acquired food-processing skills to enforcing the boycotting of Israeli-made food products. The Israeli military authorities' school closing effort was defeated by the committee's encouragement of alternative, home-based education. As the *intifada's* twin objectives of national and gender liberation became clearer, the women's committees mobilized larger numbers of women for acts of resistance, such as stone-throwing, food production, and neighborhood protection against attacks by the Israeli military. Women's involvement in resistance efforts led to a relaxation of the conservative social code, prompting women's groups to limit financial expenditures on weddings and the payment of a large dowry. Younger women began to insist on choosing their own mates, disregarding parental wishes. All of these changes were eroded by a conservative backlash toward the end of the *intifada* in 1989. The rise of **Hamas** in the West Bank and Gaza led to new pressures in favor of **veiling** and early **marriages** in order to protect young women against the hazards of life under the occupation.

The end of the *intifada*, however, was not the only cause of the demise of these committees. The WWCs began to splinter as early as 1981, three years after their founding. The first group to go its separate way was the Union of Palestinian Working Women's Committee (UPWWC), which was associated with the Palestine Communist Party. During the same year, the Popular Front for the Liberation of Palestine (PFLP) founded another group, the Palestine Women's Committee (PWC). This contingent was interested in providing income-generating programs, such as opening up sewing workshops and small food-processing industries for women. In 1983, the Women's Social Work Committee, later referred to as the Union of Women's Committees for Social Work (UNCSW), was founded by the PLO's largest constituent party, Fateh. This faction sponsored vocational training programs for women, but also involved women in large strikes and in political prisoner support campaigns. The original core group, the WWC led by Kamal, moved closer to its ideological sponsor, the DFLP, and became known for its vocational and first-aid training and prisoner-assistance efforts. *See also* BARBARI, YUS-RA (1923–); NON-GOVERNMENTAL ORGANIZATIONS (NGOs).

Y

YACQUBI, RACHIDA (1946–). A Moroccan novelist and feminist who was the first female to address women's issues in her country. Until the publication of her first novel, *Ma vie, mon cri* (*My Life, My Scream*), in 1995, Moroccan novelists writing about women, such as Tahar Ben-Jelloun, Driss Chraibi, and Abdelhak Serhane, were all males. Women writers who discussed female concerns were mostly academic researchers, not novelists. What her first novel achieved was to give women a voice, describing their poverty and suffering as seen through her own experiences. It was a story of a woman's suffering and eventual survival following her marriage to an alcoholic husband. The protagonist never rises above the rampant and entrenched poverty that affects most women, but manages to leave the marital home with her young children in tow. Yacqubi received many accolades as a result of the positive reception given this novel. In 2002, however, her activism resulted in a jail sentence, where she experienced not only humiliation but unequal treatment from that given male inmates. Her prison story appeared under the title *Je denounce* (*I Denounce*).

YAMANI, MAI (?–). She is an anthropologist, law professor, and researcher who was born in Saudi Arabia. She received a BA from Bryn Mawr College in the United States and a PhD in social anthropology from Oxford University. An expert on Middle East women, she became a lecturer at King Abd al-Aziz University in Riyadh and served as an adviser for the Center for Contemporary Arab Studies at Georgetown University. She was also a research associate at the Center for Islamic and Middle Eastern Law (CIMEL) at London University's School for Oriental and African Studies. She writes regularly for *al-Hayat* and *al-Rajul*, Arabic newspapers in London.

YAZIJI, WARDAH (1838–1924). A Lebanese poet and essayist who was the daughter of renowned poet and scholar Sheikh Nasif al-Yaziji (1800–1871). She and her two brothers were taught Arabic grammar and the writing of poetry by their father. She was born in Kafr Shima, Lebanon, and moved to Beirut, where she received her education. She began to compose poetry at age 13, but was always accused of being assisted by her father and siblings, her talent never accepted at its face value. She married Francis Samun in 1860, but continued to teach school while raising five children. She moved to Alexandria in 1899 following her husband's death, where she continued her education and embarked on a new writing career. She contributed articles on women for a magazine, *al-Dhiyaa* (*Light*), which was founded in Cairo in 1898 by her brother, Ibrahim al-Yaziji.

YEMENI WOMEN'S UNION (YWU). Known as Ittihad Nisaa al-Yaman, this was the oldest women's organization in the country, dating back to the period before independence. The organization today is the result of unifying its northern and southern branches following the unification of Yemen in 1990. The northern branch, the Yemeni Women's Association, was established in 1965 and spread to various towns. It operated as an independent effort by women determined to contribute to the elevation of poorer women by offering them literacy programs and vocational training. The southern branch, known as the General Union of Yemeni Women, was created in 1968 as a continuation of the activities of two women's associations that were prominent during the British colonial period: the Arab Women's Club and the Aden Women's Association.

Unification of the northern and southern branches in 1990, however, failed to bring about a unified agenda. The southern branch remained Marxist in orientation, whereas the northern branch, in the capital of Sanaa, was under the control of women affiliated with the Islah (Reform) Party. The YWU's combined membership was estimated to be around 4,000, and it constantly strove to achieve women's social and political equality, with special emphasis on bringing about women's greater participation in national elections. The organization's branches in different towns operate microcredit projects, offer health-care services, and hold literacy and vocational training programs for women, all financed by foreign donors and governments. All the branches share an interest in bringing violence against women to an end.

Z

ZAGHLOUL, SAFIYYA (1878–1946). An Egyptian feminist leader and wife of Saad Zaghloul (1859–1927), also known as *Umm al-Masriyyin* (The mother of all Egyptians). It was believed that her husband, the leader of the 1919 Revolution, told her that even though they might not be able to have any children, all Egyptians were her sons and daughters. She was the only child of Mustafa Fahmi, who served as Egypt's prime minister for 15 years. Her marriage to Zaghloul, who was a rising star in Egyptian national politics, was arranged by Princess **Nazli Fadhil**. Benefiting greatly from his wife's connections, Zaghloul was devoted to her all of his life. When he was sent into exile by the British authorities along with the leadership of the Wafd political party, she and the rest of the female relatives of this leadership began to direct women's demonstrations and boycott activities against the British authorities and their products. They organized the **Wafdist Women's Central Committee (WWCC)**, which at first included all the prominent feminist leadership of that era, including **Huda Shaarawi**. Shaarawi broke off from the WWCC when it refused to take a stand against some of the Wafd's policies, establishing the **Egyptian Feminist Union**, which carried on its struggle against British colonial control and the forces opposed to female emancipation. Safiyya remained a strong feminist and a political power after her husband's death in 1926. Their house, which was the center of the activities of Egypt's nationalist movement, was known as *Bayt al-Masriyyin* (The House of the Nation). It faced her husband's impressive pharaonic-style mausoleum, and she continued to live in it for the rest of her life. Following her death, the house became a museum. *See also* FEMINIST MOVEMENT IN EGYPT.

ZAHAWI, JAMIL SIDQI (1863–1936). An Iraqi poet who was among the first in Ottoman-controlled Iraq to call publicly for women's education and unveiling. His views were first aired in 1904, and in 1923, he supported his sister Asma Zahawi in her attempt to publish a magazine. This became the first women's publication in the country, *Layla*. He was also a secularist who took great interest in studying science and philosophy, although he did not attribute women's lack of rights to Islam. He did stir a lot of emotions by attacking the veil and calling it a perpetrator of women's backwardness. In some of his poems, he referred to veils as "dark shrouds." He was joined in these attacks on the **veiling** custom by another descendant of a prominent religious family, fellow Iraqi poet Maarouf al-Rasafi (1875–1945). Although the Iraqi government during the monarchy accused the latter of being a communist, they both persisted in advocating women's liberation as a necessary component of the larger task of liberating Iraq from British and royalist controls.

ZAIM, HUSNI (1894–1949). He was a former Syrian president and the first military officer to stage a coup d'état in that country. Born in Aleppo to a Kurdish-descended business family, he served a stint in the Ottoman army before joining the French colonial force known as Troupes Spéciales. He had already reached the rank of lieutenant colonel in 1941 when he was charged with embezzlement by the Vichy government in Syria. When the Free French forces took over the country, they detained him for a period of time, which earned him the reputation of being a patriot. In 1948, he became chief of staff of the Syrian armed forces under the new independent government, but he ran into trouble with Syria's president, Shukri al-Quwatli, when he defied orders to arrest Colonel Antoine Bustani for involvement in a minor scandal. In 1949, Zaim succeeded in overthrowing the government of Khaled al-Azm and arrested him along with the president. He then established the first military government in Syria since independence in 1943.

Zaim's coup was encouraged by the representative of the Central Intelligence Service in Damascus, and he quickly began to explore the possibility of reaching a peace agreement with Israel. But one aspect of his erratic foreign policy and repressive rule deserves special mention. He was impatient with traditional customs that stood in the way of his progressive program. Secretly advised by Akram Hourani (1912–1996), who later emerged as one of the leaders of the Baath Party, he was persuaded to introduce drastic and unprecedented reforms. Among these was granting women the right to vote, in imitation of the reforms of **Mustafa Kemal Ataturk**, whom he greatly admired. This made Syria the first Arab country to enfranchise women. The right to vote was granted by a presidential decree in 1949 and was never rescinded by any subsequent government. Zaim's regime was overthrown in August 1949 by another military figure, Sami Hinnawi. Zaim, who was executed, unwittingly began the cycle of short-lived military governments that plagued Syria until the rise of President Hafiz Assad's authoritarian civilian government in 1971.

ZAIN AL-DIN, NAZIRAH (ca. 1908–1976). She was an early Druze Lebanese feminist and essayist, born in Baaqlin. Her father was Said Zain al-Din, an Islamic scholar and the first president of Lebanon's High Court of Appeals. He encouraged his daughter's education and interest in religious studies, permitting her to meet the greatest learned men of the day. His house became a meeting place for these luminaries, where the latest ideas and theories were debated.

In 1927, Nazirah wrote a book, *Unveiling and Veiling: Lectures and Views on the Liberation of the Woman and Social Renewal in the Arab World*, which attacked the patriarchal system and its association with Islam. She contended that **veiling** was not Islamic but was inherited from pagan societies preceding Islam. She expressed little respect for traditional commentators and interpreters of the Quran. She called for an immediate abandonment of the veil, in contrast to **Qassem Amin**'s approach. The book polarized public opinion about Islam, women, and their liberation while earning praise from the Mufti of Lebanon, the country's highest Sunni authority, as well as the Syrian head of the Arabic Language Academy in Damascus. The greatest opponent of her ideas was another Islamic figure, Sheikh Mustafa al-Ghalaini. In his book *Al-Islam ruh al-madaniya* (*Islam Is the Essence of Civilization*), he agreed that the veil was not mandated by Islam, but accused Nazirah of falsely presenting the book as her own. In reality, he wrote, it was authored by Christian missionaries. Zain al-Din's response to these attacks appeared in *The Young Woman and the Sheikhs: An Outline and Discussion of Unveiling and the Veil* (1929).

ZANA, LAYLA (1961–). She is a Kurdish legislator who sat in Turkey's parliament but was accused of sedition and jailed. She was born in a village near the town of Silvan, eastern Turkey, where she lived a traditional Kurdish life. She was married to her father's cousin, Mehdi Zana, at age 14 and moved with him to the city of Diyarbakir, a predominantly Kurdish city in eastern Turkey. There, her husband was elected mayor, but he was sentenced to a 30-year prison term when the 1980 military coup d'état clamped down on Kurdish activists. Zana organized other women to help defend her husband's rights as a political activist. She also continued her education at home, earning a high school degree and actively engaging in political journalism. This led to her arrest in 1988, but in 1991 she became the first Kurdish woman to win a seat in the Turkish parliament and to debate issues in the Kurdish language. Her speeches always called for improved relations between the Turkish and Kurdish people despite being called a traitor by the Turkish media. In 1994, Zana was accused of belonging to an illegal party and sentenced to 15 years in jail. But her activism won her several awards, including the European Parliament's Sakharov Prize for Freedom of Thought. She was also nominated for the Nobel Peace Prize. She was given an additional two-year sentence in 1998 for publishing an article about New-roz, the Kurdish new year. She was retried in 2003 as a result of pressure from the European Union, but this did not result in her release. *See also* KURDISH WOMEN.

***ZANAN* MAGAZINE.** This is an Iranian magazine that began publishing independently in 1992, unaffiliated with the government and espousing a feminist line. *Zanan* (*Women*) appeared at first under the editorship of Shahla Sherkat, who came to this endeavor after serving a 10-year membership on the board of directors of another Iranian women's magazine, the modernist *Zan-e Ruz*. The magazine expanded with the help of two journalists, acquiring a 30-member staff. Dogged by financial problems and political opposition, it survived against all odds and became the voice of a reformist Islamic **feminism** seeking to move away from the conservative feminism of the Islamic Republic and its patriarchal values. The magazine received the support of liberal theologians like Sayyed Mohsen Saidzadeh and secularist lawyers such as Mehrangiz Kar and was able to challenge many conservative interpretations of women's rights in Islam. It insisted that everyone has an obligation to resort to *ijtihad*, or individual reinterpretations of the Islamic texts. This was a direct challenge to the Islamic clergy in Iran, who have monopolized the definition of women's rights.

The paper attracted younger writers such as Parastu Dokoohaki and Shadi Sadrand Royan Karimi, who offer a feminist perspective on movies and literature while focusing on specific problems of women such as poverty, drug addiction, and domestic abuse. The paper's readership consists of urban middle-class women who in the past have been mobilized to vote for liberal presidential candidates such as Mohammad Khatami and for moderate members of the Majlis. Its editorials are written in spiritual, nonviolent, Sufi style, which emphasizes personal choice as a way of ensuring freedom and democratic rule. It also provides translations of the work of Western feminists, suggesting that much can be learned from an exchange of ideas and that there is nothing to fear in reading such works. *See also* FEMINIST MOVEMENT IN IRAN.

ZANGANA, HAIFA (1950–). She is a Kurdish Iraqi novelist, artist, and feminist who was born in Baghdad to a Kurdish father and an Arab mother. She graduated from the school of pharmacy of Baghdad University in 1974. She joined the Palestine Liberation Organization (PLO) in Syria and served in its pharmaceutical unit before being imprisoned in the early 1970s at Abu-Ghraib jail under orders of the Iraqi Baathist regime. She suffered torture at this notorious prison and was released in a deal between the regime of Saddam Hussein and her political organization, the Iraqi Communist Party.

Zangana immigrated to London in 1976, where she began writing for the *Guardian*, *Red Pepper*, *Al-Ahram Weekly*, and *al-Quds*. She also authored several books, the most famous being *Women on a Journey between Baghdad and London* (2001), which deals with exile, identity, and alienation affecting Iraqi women. Her other works include *Through the Vast Halls of Memory* (1991), *Beyond What the Eye Sees* (1997), *The Presence of Others* (1999), *Keys to a City* (2000), *Not One More Death* (2006), and *War with No End* (2007). Her latest book, coauthored with Maysoon Pachachi and Nadje Ali, is *Behind the Numbers—Beyond Sanctions: Women's Voices on Iraq*. She was opposed to the American invasion of Iraq as much as she was opposed to the dictatorship of Saddam Hussein. She is a founding member of the International Association of Contemporary Iraqi Studies and a member of the Advisory Board of the Brussels Tribunal on Iraq. *See also* KURDISH WOMEN.

ZAYNAB (ca. 625–?). She was the granddaughter of the Prophet, daughter of **Fatima** and Ali, and one of two sisters of Imams Hussein and Hassan, who was born in Medina a few years after the *Hijra*. She was the third child in her family and suffered the loss of her mother when only three years old. It was said that this brought her closer to her brother, Hussein, a relationship that lasted until his death. She was married to her first cousin, Abdullah ibn Jaafar, a man of great generosity who dedicated his wealth to the nascent Muslim community. Zaynab is revered by all Muslims, but especially by Shii Muslims because of her stand in defense of her brother and the suffering and humiliation she experienced at the hands of the Umayyids. She followed Hussein to the battlefield at Karbala in 680, along with all members of his family. After he and his 72 companions were killed, Yazid, Muawiyah's son and future Umayyid caliph, ordered that all women and children be taken prisoners. They were marched to Damascus, with the women of the Prophet's family stripped of their **veils**. Zaynab emerged as the leader of this group, defending women and children and condemning those who did not support her brother in a powerful oration. She displayed sheer courage at the court of the Umayyids while still their captive.

Zaynab became an instant heroine after her release, especially for her role as the keeper of her brother's memory. She is credited with initiating the commemoration ceremonies of Ashura and the tradition of *taaziyah*, or wakes held by women in their homes, in which they eulogize Hussein with tearful poetry and prayers. Sayyida Zaynab, or Our Lady Zaynab, became a model of ideal Islamic womanhood, especially for Shii women, who celebrate her resistance to oppression and her courage when she confronted Yezid at his court. She is especially revered by Shii women in southern Lebanon, who refer to her as "the heroine of heroes" of Karbala. Since the establishment of the Islamic regime in Iran, her birthday has been celebrated as

Nurse's Day, just as her mother's birthday is celebrated as Women's Day. There are two shrines claiming to house her remains: one is at the Mosque of Sayyida Zaynab in Damascus and the other bears a similar name but is located in Cairo. Each supplies a different version of the story of her death and burial, although both agree that she was sent to Mecca after being freed by the Umayyids.

ZAYYAT, LATIFA (1923–1996). An Egyptian novelist, professor of English literature, political activist, and literary critic, born in Dimyat (Damietta). She was enrolled at Cairo University when it was still called King Fuad University. Secret British embassy reports identified her as a communist as a result of her election to the student communist organization. In 1957, she completed her doctoral studies at Cairo University, where she had pursued a teaching career since 1952. She became the chair of the English Department at Ayn Shams University. She also served briefly as the director of the Arts Academy (Kulliyat al-Funun) in Cairo in the 1970s. She gained additional national prominence beginning in 1979, when she chaired the Committee for the Defense of National Culture to counter President Anwar Sadat's project of normalization of relations with Israel following the signing of the 1978 Camp David Agreement. In 1981, she was jailed along with many intellectuals and activists because of her opposition to Sadat's program of economic liberalization.

Zayyat gained literary prominence after publishing in 1960 a stunning literary work, a novel titled *Al-Bab al-Maftouh* (*The Open Door*). The story elaborated on the social, physical, and political maturation of a young girl belonging to the middle class. The novel was unusual in that all political awakening and rites of passage stories in the past had focused on young men, not women. Al-Zayyat's strength was her ability to use her recollections of her own political activities in her youth to provide the background for this story. She also used colloquial Egyptian Arabic in her dialogue, the better to link with the political experiences of the Egyptian middle-class family. The novel presents the struggles of various people who lived through the tumultuous years between 1946 and 1956 and their attempts to achieve national liberation from British control and social liberation from the hypocrisy of traditional culture, including securing women's freedom and equality. The story concludes with the triumph of personal choice over family diktat as the young heroine persuades her family of the merits of abandoning a successful suitor in favor of the poor man of her dreams, whom she intends to accompany to the Suez front. *The Open Door* has had a long successful run, never going out of print since its first publication in 1960.

Al-Zayyat produced original literature with themes never approached previously by female writers. An example is *Al-Shaykhukha wa qisas ukhra* (*Old Age and Other Stories*, 1986), which examines the question of aging from several perspectives. She was also a literary critic, producing works such as *Images of Women in Arabic Novels and Short Stories* (1989), in which she demonstrates how novelists often portray women as strictly home-makers and mothers, never venturing beyond the typical stereotypes of women's societal roles. Within this genre of writing, she also produced *Najib Mahfouz: The Image and the Ideal* (1986). In 1995, she wrote *The Man Who Did Not Know of What He Was Accused.* She also wrote a play, *Selling and Buying* (1993), and a year later she produced an anthology of short stories by women writers, *All Those Beautiful Voices.* Her autobiography, *Hamlet taftish: awraq shakhsiyya* (*Arrest Search Campaign: Personal Papers*), appeared in 1992.

Zayyat's 70th birthday was celebrated as a major national event. She was awarded Egypt's State Prize for Literature in 1996, shortly before her death.

ZELDA (1914–1984). An Israeli poet whose original name was Zelda Shneurson, who occasionally went by the name Zelda Mishkovsky. Her poems were written under her first name. She arrived in Palestine from the Ukraine in 1926. She was one of the few literary women who were competent in memorizing and analyzing the ancient Jewish religious texts. Although a devout Hassidic woman, her poetry was appreciated by secular readers because it was suffused with mystical qualities and transcendental ideas. She projects a great appreciation of nature's beauty and the sacredness of human creation. Her first volume of poetry, *Leisure*, was published in 1968. This was followed by six other volumes: *The Invisible Carmel, Be Not Far, Neither Mountain nor Fire, Tiny Poems, The Spectacular Difference,* and *Beyond All Distance.*

ZENOBIA (ca. 240–271). An Arab queen of the kingdom of Palmyra in the Syrian Desert, which was a great caravan center controlling trade routes to Mesopotamia and Arabia. She was the wife of Odenathus (Little Ear) Septimius, who ruled from 258 to 267 CE as a vassal of the Roman Empire. Her full name was Zenobia Julia Aurelia Septimia. She succeeded her husband as regent for their son Vaballathus (r. 267–272) and led a tumultuous life, oscillating between Roman vassalage and independence. The desire to free her state from the Romans dated back to her husband's rule; he occasionally demonstrated his loyalty to the Romans by fighting the Persians on the eastern periphery of Roman-dominated Syria. His loyalty was recognized by the Emperor Gallienus (r. 253–268), who gave him the title Corrector Totius Orientis, as the viceroy of Rome over the east. At the time of his assassination, Palmyra was at the peak of its power.

Zenobia was known for her beauty and political skills and was able to extend her control to all of Syria, Egypt, and Palestine. In 271, she declared herself Augusta, thereby signifying her independence from the Romans. She expelled the roman prefect of her territory, Tanagino Arobus, and killed him when he attempted to reclaim Palmyra. The Emperor Aurelian (r. 270–275) was able to defeat her and reestablish Rome's control over her territory, taking her prisoner. There are conflicting stories about her death in Roman sources. One such source, *Zosimus Historiae*, claims that she died while crossing the Bosphorous Straits. Most other historians reject this version and adhere to the story of Flavius Vopiscus and Trebellius Pollio, who claim that she was marched to Rome as a caged exhibit but survived the victory march and ended her life after living peacefully on an estate at Tibur (Tivoli).

Zenobia's life became the stuff of legends in the hands of later Arab historians. Arab Islamic sources identify her as the daughter of the ruler of al-Jazira (the area between Syria and Mesopotamia), Amr ibn al-Zarib. In this version of events, Zenobia rose to prominence as a result of the military defeat and death of her brother by the king of al-Hira in Mesopotamia. She in turn proposed to marry the king in order to unite their two kingdoms and invited him to come to Palmyra, where he was killed. When besieged by avenging Roman troops, she is said to have escaped and killed herself by sucking poison from her ring. In Arab sources, she is portrayed as a builder of two castles on the Euphrates, from which she launched many of her campaigns. The remains of her city, Palmyra (Tadmur in Arabic), survive today as a magnificent Roman center with columned streets, a huge amphitheater, and impressive tombs. It is the main tourist attraction of present-day Syria. Many statues and artifacts belonging to her reign are at the Louvre Museum in Paris. She remains a major figure in an Arab tradition of pre-Islamic queens who ruled magnificent kingdoms outside Arabia.

ZIYADEH, MAI (1886–1941). A Lebanese and Palestinian poet, fiction writer, and essayist who presided over the most prestigious literary salon in the 20th century. She was born in Nazareth to a Lebanese father and a Palestinian mother, her original name being Mary until it was changed by her mother. She was educated in missionary schools in Nazareth and at boarding schools in Lebanon, later attending a French school in Beirut. She immigrated to Cairo in 1908 with her family. Her father bought the newspaper, *al-Mahrouseh* (another name for Cairo) in 1909 and turned it into a literary publication, for which Mai began to write under a pseudonym. She also furthered her studies, eventually mastering several languages. She became a translator, literary critic, and poet, whose early work was characterized by romanticism. She connected with Egyptian women's groups and became interested in sociopolitical writing, producing essays on women's rights,

British colonialism, and socialism. She was a great admirer of two female French luminaries, Madame de Sévigné (1626–1696) and Madame de Staël (1776–1817), and their role in the world of French letters.

Mai formed her own literary salon in 1913, which lasted until 1932. She took over her father's paper following his death in 1929. Her salon became a major feature of Cairo's intellectual life, attracting local and international visitors, women as well as men. A select group of writers met at her salon every Tuesday to read their own poetry, listen to musical performances, and debate major literary and political issues of the day. Among the regular visitors to her salon were major Egyptian figures such as the poet Ahmad Shawqi, editor of *al-Ahram* Dawud Barakat, president of the Egyptian University Ahmad Lufti al-Sayyid, essayist Mahmoud Abbas al-Aqqdad, and literary writer and leftist critic Salameh Musa. Among the female participants in her salon were **Huda Shaarawi** and **Malak Hafni Nasif**. Taha Hussein, the future literary giant of Egyptian life and head of Cairo University, was invited to attend by Mai, who recognized his talents early on. She also received many prominent visitors from other parts of the Arab world and abroad, including Henry James. Her liberalism alienated many sections of Egyptian society, which circulated unfounded rumors about her romantic adventures with leading men of her day.

Mai maintained a long-lasting correspondence with American Lebanese writer, poet, and artist Kahlil Gibran (also Jubran Khalil Jubran) (1883–1931). Their correspondence was reputed to be of an intimate nature, although the two never met in person. Acting as his muse, she also wrote many articles about the genius of the Arab Mahjar (exile) literary renaissance, making him famous in the Arab world. Her publications include *Fleurs de rêve* (Cairo, 1911), which she wrote under the pseudonym Isis Copia. When she met Ahmad Lufti al-Sayyid (d. 1965), he encouraged her to write in Arabic. Her mother and the Lebanese writer Shibli al-Shemayyil pushed her to do the same. She wrote three biographies, of **Wardah al-Yaziji**, **Aisha Taimuriya**, and Malak Hafni Nasif. Her essays, which were collected in 10 volumes, were published in her lifetime. Her work appeared in the press of Cairo and Beirut and always defended women's right to education and seeking employment outside the home. She was one of the first writers to take women's literary output seriously and to eulogize them formally. A popular public speaker as well as a writer, she dispersed her salon shortly after her mother's death. She suffered a deep depression in 1936 and was persuaded by her relatives to seek professional care in Beirut, where she was placed in a mental institution. After gaining her release, she returned to Cairo, where she died in 1941. She was never married, and she lived much of her life in Cairo.

ZOROASTRIAN WOMEN. Zoroastrianism, or "the good religion," is an ancient monotheistic belief system of Iraq and Iran prior to the advent of Islam. The religion was founded by Zarathushtra, otherwise known as Zoroaster, between 1400 and 1200 BCE. It reached Iran from central Asia by the ninth century BCE and remained Iran's main religion until the fall of the Sassanid dynasty in 651 CE, during the reign of Yezdegird III. In the *Gihan*, which is the oldest core of the *Avista* or the central sacred document of this faith, men and women are said to be equal adherents, who are called upon to perform the same religious duties. The *Avista* and other texts, however, discuss only the religious obligations of the male members of the community. In addition, the middle Persian, or Pahlavi, texts may provide a different description of women's role in the new faith. The tablets that recorded the history of the Sassanid dynasty (224–651) provide numerous names of queens and female founders of the dynasty, as well as goddesses. These records also indicate that upper-class women controlled their own wealth and enjoyed the services of male assistants. **Veiling** and seclusion of females were reserved for the aristocracy, and royal males were also hidden from the public's gaze.

The Sassanids were the first to establish Zoroastrianism as Iran's state religion, when King Ardashir I defeated the Parthian monarch Ardaban V in 224 CE. Zoroastrianism remained a predominantly patriarchal religion, with an all-male priesthood and a patriarchal descent system, which left women completely out of official and family genealogies. Women were expected to tend to domestic duties and to submit to male guardians all of their lives. Some religious texts make no distinction between the status of aristocratic women and slaves. A woman could be divorced if she disobeyed her husband. Her main duty was to produce children.

A strict class system mandated that a woman should always marry within her class. Two types of **marriages** prevailed under Zoroastrianism, the *padikhshay* marriage and the *cagar* marriage, which followed either **polygamy** or monogamy. Although polygamy was rampant among members of the upper classes, the poor elements in society were generally monogamous. The main or first wife was titled *zan-I padikhshay* (wife with authority) and exercised control over the internal management of the family unit. If she excelled in this role, she was rewarded with the use of half of her husband's wealth, a privilege subject to withdrawal if she disobeyed him. The *cagar* type of marriage designated the second wife or the remarried widow (still considered part of her husband's family) as the *cagar-zan*. In the second type of marriage, a wife could be given to someone else for the sake of producing children, but she remained part of her husband's household, and her children belonged to him. A *padikhshay* wife could also enter another marriage as a *cagar-zan*, where she would be allowed to produce children for a brother who died childless and would be called *stur* or guardian. The *cagar* wife enjoyed a marital gift and rights similar to those of other members of the household, even while remaining under the authority of the *padikhshay*, and lacked any **inheritance** rights. The *cagar* wife, if she had children, could be raised to the status of *padikhshay* wife upon the death of the senior wife.

Fathers normally arranged marriages for their daughters at age 15, but these matches could be rejected, and love matches were not uncommon. The husband was expected to give his bride a **dowry**. **Divorce** was generally by agreement between the two parties, but the husband could ask for a divorce on specific grounds such as sorcery, disobedience, and moral misconduct. A man could also take concubines from among his female slaves. Children from such unions were raised as family members, although legally they were still **slaves**. If a free woman had a child with a slave father, the head of the household considered him a slave. Despite these male advantages, women did enjoy certain rights, especially if they belonged to the upper class. A woman had recourse to the courts to act as a witness and sometimes as a judge.

The Zoroastrians recognized a special cult of a goddess by the name of Ardwisur Anahid, who dominated a temple at the old capital of the province of Pars, Estakhr. The temple was the site where Sassanid kings were crowned, despite the fact that Ctesiphon was their official capital. Reverence for Anahid by the royal line was due to the pedigree of this goddess, who was also worshipped by Sasan, a priest and founder of the dynasty. Anahid was recognized mostly as the protector of women and was portrayed as a strong female wearing beaver skin garments. The senior wife of the king (Shahanshah, or "King of Kings") was also crowned the "Queen of Queens," in reference to the Asian subroyalties controlled by the Sassanian emperor. Her major role was to preside over the women's section in the palace. The Sassanids had a great ruling queen, **Buran**, who ruled briefly on the eve of the Arab invasion of Iran. Most Zoroastrians migrated to India after the Islamization of Iran.

The modern Zoroastrian family is monogamous, with a patrilineal system of descent. Laws pertaining to inheritance have improved in favor of women. Nowadays a daughter inherits a share of the estate equal to her brother's. The 1936 Iranian laws against veiling led to abandonment of their traditional clothes and moving closer to the condition of Muslim women. Living conditions among the Iranian Zoroastrians improved perceptibly after an emissary of the Indian community, the Parsis (also Parsees) of Mumbai, succeeded in 1854 in getting the Qajar dynasty to lift the poll tax imposed upon them by the first Muslim rulers. The two Pahlavi shahs acknowledged members of this faith as belonging to the ancient heritage of Iran, while the Islamic Republic still regards them with suspicion.

ZUBAYDA (?–832). She was a queen of the Abbasid dynasty (750–1258) of Iraq and the wife of Harun al-Rashid, who ruled as caliph from 786 until 809. She was the daughter of Caliph al-Mansour and married Harun, her cousin on her mother's side, in 781. Her name at birth was Amat al-Aziz. Zubayda was famous for sponsoring major water projects, such as the building of reservoirs and pools for the benefit of Muslim pilgrims on their way from Kufa in Iraq to the Arabian Peninsula. The route covered by these projects was known as *darb Zubayda* (Zubayda's route). Her name was associated with luxury because she lived when the Abbasid Empire was at its zenith. Even today, to be described as "sitt Zubayda" (lady Zubayday) conjures up images of extreme opulence and glamor. Tales of her extravagant lifestyle describe her wearing jewel-encrusted footwear and eating using silver and gold tableware. Zubayda also appears in the *Tales of the Arabian Nights*, which take place during Harun al-Rashid's reign. *See also* WAQF.

Bibliography

CONTENTS

INTRODUCTION

The field of studying Middle Eastern and North African women is both young and old. It is an old field in the sense that women have always been part of the ancient societies of this region, which can claim many centuries and multiple civilizations. It is a young field in the sense that its historiography and scholarship are as new as the Western interest in this area; hence the problem of identifying Western-language literature without overlooking indigenous reference works in native languages. There is, in addition, the issue of locating gender studies related specifically to women in this region. Anyone who has written on this topic must appreciate this difficulty. Not only are women's studies a new development and a young branch of social studies curriculum in Western academies, the focus on Middle Eastern women in particular had to await the uncovering of the necessary research data and information. Access to this information was always contingent upon familiarity with the area's multiplicity of languages, which until today has not been achieved by many. There was also the question of examining Middle

Eastern women through the prism of Western feminist theory, which often did not do justice to the complexity of the historical development of Middle Eastern feminism.

Another problem confronting Middle East scholars is that of historical periodization. This is simply, one discovers in due time, the result of the overlapping of regimes over different parts of the region. The Ottoman Empire in Turkey, for example, coincided with the Mamluk period and the rule of Muhammad Ali's dynasty in Egypt as well as the minor ruling families of North Africa, all nominally vassals of the Ottomans. This presents a problem for bibliographic classification, because it makes distinguishing between various historic epochs rather problematic.

The study of Middle Eastern women also suffers from the rise and weakening of certain ideologies and the concomitant popularity and decline of scholarly interest in these developments. Any recent bibliographic survey of this topic will inevitably reflect this tendency, such as the current overemphasis on Islamic feminism and Islamist trends. Segregating these works from the more general bibliographic lists on the modern history of women in this area can also be very challenging. This bibliography has attempted to deal with all of these issues by creating a rational system of categorization that does not ignore the specificity of certain periods and themes, while maintaining an overall historical system of classification.

The "General Studies" section ranges over a variety of periods, but with emphasis on theoretical analysis of such topics as gender in Islam, social protest within certain sects and their impact on women, as well as Muslim juridical opinions on the family system. Some works within this group examine Islamic feminism, but a huge lacuna exists here simply due to the problematic nature of the feminist question in Islamic, and even secular, Arab feminist writings. Most studies, not surprisingly, focus on the impact of modernization on Muslim women, rather than dealing with their changing lives from the perspective of gender consciousness in a Western sense. Women's human rights receive some attention as authors struggle to present women's access to education and work as a normal prerequisite for emancipation. More important, the connection between women's liberation and nationalism receives a great deal of coverage.

This is followed by the section "Reference Works," which encompasses a large number of country-specific historical dictionaries to provide the context for women's history and social movements. By themselves, these are quite inadequate as reference works on women. But the section also includes well-known encyclopedias of the modern Islamic world that contextualize women's roles within this rich geographic area, such as the works of John L. Esposito, Suad Joseph, Richard Martin, and others. Skolnik's *Encyclopedia Judaica* complements previous works on Islamic civilization and its treatment of Islamic women. But this section also offers bibliographic guides to the study of women writers and Islamic women in general, such as Kimball and von Schlegell's *Women in the Muslim World: A Bibliography.*

The section "Pre-Islamic Period" reflects the paucity of research on one epoch in particular, namely the Arab pre-Islamic terrain, which actually presents a startling picture of women's empowerment during the pagan tribal period of the Arabian Peninsula. Much of this work can only be accessed by examining ancient Arabic texts and 19th-century works in European languages, such as German, which are based on archeological evidence. Yet, one subtopic within this category, namely ancient Egypt, is abundantly researched. There are excellent treatments of ancient Egyptian women, specifically Gay Robbins's *Women in Ancient Egypt*, which are essential guides to most studies of this subject. But here again, studies in English that appeared in German-language journals predominate. This section covers ancient Egyptian women's literacy, clerical roles, polygamy and adultery, property-ownership rights, and royal titles.

The section on "Classic Islamic Period" provides many titles on women's literary and social achievements during the classic Islamic dynastic periods. Several studies highlighting the lives of women of the Prophet's family and the early Islamic period, which are hugely popular today, are represented here by such works as Shariati's *Fatima Is Fatima*, Stowasser's "The Mothers of the Believers in the Hadith," and Stern's "The First Women Converts in Early Islam." The first centuries of Islam, the Umayyad, Abassid, and Fatimid dynasties, are covered by such works as Roded's *Women in Islamic Biographical Dictionaries: From Ibn Sa'd to Who's Who*, Beeston's *Arabic Literature to the End of the Umayyad Period*, and Cortese and Calderini's *Women and the Fatimids in the World of Islam.*

The "Medieval Period" group covers general titles such as Hamby's *Women in the Medieval Islamic World* and Mernissi's *The Forgotten Queens of Islam*, as well as treatments of specific periods such as Sayyid's *Women and Men in Late Eighteenth-Century Egypt*. Topics encompassed in this category include women's manners and customs, mystical orders, economic roles, and family chronicles in Egypt and Turkey. Shahrazad, the mythical central figure in the *Thousand and One Nights* literary cycle, has evolved as a subject of fascination during the modern period, and several titles reflect that.

A wide range of topics and countries are covered under the heading "19th and 20th Centuries," which mirror recent scholarly interest in specific periods and topics concerning Middle Eastern women. Works on women's roles in certain critical nationalist uprisings, such as the Constitutional Revolution of Iran and the 1919 Revolution in Egypt, abound. One need only mention under this category Afary's definitive study *The Iranian Constitutional Revolution: Grassroots Democracy, Social Democracy and the Origins of Feminism* and Badran's authoritative *Feminism, Islam and Nation: Gender and the Making of Egypt*. Several studies concentrate on the impact of modern colonial regimes on women, particularly in North Africa, such as Lazreg's comprehensive, thoughtful, and authentic analysis of French colonialism, *Algerian Revolution: The Eloquence of Silence*. The section also includes studies on the harem, based mostly on the Turkish experience, reflecting Western fascination with this topic but also misconceptions about this institution's significance as a ladder of social mobility for enslaved women. Secor's "Orientalism, Gender and Class in Lady Mary Wortley Montagu's Turkish Embassy Letters" and Mernissi's *Dreams of Trespass: Tales of a Harem Childhood* should be read in conjunction with Nerval's exaggerated account of the degradation of 19th-century Egyptian women, *Women of Cairo*. There are also a number of works on Palestinian gender consciousness dating back to the early decades of the 20th century and the later phase of female mobilization during the period preceding the 1948 Arab–Israeli War.

The section "Postindependence Period" includes coverage of recent history since the 1950s and ranges over most countries of the Middle East. One begins to see here a clear outline of the rise of feminist consciousness as expressed in literature and social activism of practically all countries in the Middle East. There are studies on the roles of women in the first Palestinian *intifada*, in Iran's Islamic Revolution, and in Egypt's post-1952 revolutionary phase, as the organized feminism of the liberal phase was forced to accept the strictures of state feminism. There are also several titles on Kuwait and other Arab Gulf States as these began to express their concerns through organized activity or literary works. Among these are Fakhro's *Women at Work in the Gulf: A Case Study of Bahrain*, Arebi's *Women and Words in Saudi Arabia*, Azri's *Social and Gender Inequality in Oman*, and Tijani's *Male Domination, Female Revolt: Race, Class and Gender in Kuwaiti Women*. This section also provides titles on Arab and Jewish Israeli, Berber, Turkish, and Yemeni women.

Due to the visible rise in studies on the impact of the Islamic revival on women in this region, it was felt best to segregate titles dealing with this topic into one section, "Islamic Feminism." One glance over this section should convince the reader of what is easily recognized by scholars of this region, namely the ability of politics to influence scholarship and its written output and direction. Here we encounter a great interest in studying the fate of Iranian feminism under the Islamic Republic and as a result of Ayatollah Ruhollah Khomeini's intense interest in remolding the social roles of Iranian women. There is also an unusual interest in veiling and the debate over its authenticity, historical roots in non-Arab cultures, and religious authorization and meaning. A number of studies focus on the reinvention of women's ideal Islamic roles, such as Lamia Shehadeh's *The Ideal of Women under Fundamentalist Islam*, which provides a comprehensive survey of the thought of modern major Islamist figures concerning women.

A special section titled "Works in Arabic" covers a variety of topics. These may not be readily available to the Western researcher, but could easily be located by searching the author's name. Themes treated in this section include theoretical issues such as the classic Islamic view of women, women and the law, and the Islamic family system. Some of these works tend to be polemical in nature, but they do shed some light on the intellectual orientation of defenders of the traditional roles of women. Some, however, like Kamal and Hind's *Women and Decision-Making in Palestine* and Khalidi and Farrukh's *The Missionary Movements and Colonialism*, are more secular in nature.

GENERAL STUDIES

Abdulhadi, Rabab, Evelyn Alsultany, and Nadine Naber, eds. *Arab and Arab-American Feminisms: Gender, Violence and Belonging*. Syracuse, N.Y.: Syracuse University Press, 2011.

Abu Ali, Khadija. *Introduction to Women's Reality and their Experience*. (Arabic). Beirut: General Union of Palestinian Women, 1975.

Abu el-Fadl, Khaled M. *Conference of Books: The Search for Beauty in Islam*. New York: University Press of America, 2001.

Abu-Khalil, As'ad. "Towards the Study of Women and Politics in the Arab World: The Debate and Reality." *Gender Issues* 13, 1 (1993): 3–22.

Abu-Lughod, Leila. *Remaking Women, Feminism and Modernity in the Middle East*. Princeton, N.J.: Princeton University Press, 1998.

Ahmed, Leila. *Women and Gender in Islam: Historical Roots of a Modern Debate*. New Haven, Conn.: Yale University Press, 1992.

Arkoun, Muhammad. *Rethinking Islam: Common Questions, Uncommon Answers*. Translated and edited by Robert D. Lee. Boulder, Colo.: Westview, 1994.

Badran, Margot. *Feminism in Islam: Secular and Religious Convergence*. Oxford: Oneworld, 2009.

Bayat, Asef. *Making Islam Democratic: Social Movements and the Post-Islamist Turn*. Stanford, Calif.: Stanford University Press, 2009.

Beck, Lois, and Nikki Keddie, eds. *Women in the Muslim World*. Cambridge, Mass.: Harvard University Press, 1980.

Boudjedra, Rachid. *La répudiation*. Paris: Denoël, 1969.

Boullata, Kamal, ed. *Women of the Fertile Crescent: An Anthology of the Fertile Crescent*. Washington, D.C.: Three Continents, 1978.

Bourqia, Rahma, M. M. Charrad, and N. Gallagher, eds. *Femmes, Culture et Société au Maghreb*. Casablanca: Afrique Orient, 1996.

Bowen, Donna Lee. "Muslim Juridical Opinions Concerning the Status of Women as Demonstrated in the Case of *Azl*." *Journal of Near Eastern Studies* 40 (1981): 323–38.

Bugeja, Marie. *Nos soeurs Musulmanes.* Alger: Éditions de France, 1931.

Bullock, Katherine, ed. *Muslim Women Activists in North America: Speaking for Ourselves.* Austin: University of Texas Press, 2005.

Center for Studies, Documentation and Information on Women (CRÉDIF). *Femmes de Tunisie: Situation et perspectives.* Tunis: CRÉDIF, 1995.

Chabaud, Jacqueline. *The Education and Advancement of Women.* Paris: UNESCO, 1970.

Chanine, M. *Women of the World: The Near East and North Africa.* Washington, D.C.: USAID, 1985.

Chase, Anthony Tirado. *Human Rights, Revolution and Reform in the Muslim World.* Boulder, Colo.: Lynne Rienner, 2012.

Chesler, Phyllis. "Worldwide Trends in Honor Killings." *Middle East Quarterly* (Spring 2010): 3–11.

Cohen-Mohr, Dayla. *Arab Women Writers: An Anthology of Short Stories.* Albany: State University of New York Press, 2005.

Cole, Juan R., and Nikki Keddie, eds. *Shi'ism and Social Protest.* New Haven, Conn.: Yale University Press, 1986.

Combs-Schilling, M. E. *Sacred Performances: Islam, Sexuality and Sacrifice.* New York: Columbia University Press, 1989.

Cooke, Miriam. *Women and the War Story.* Berkeley: University of California Press, 1996.

Corbin, Henri. *Histoire de la philosophie Islamique.* Paris: Gallimard, 1986.

Coulson, Noel. *A History of Islamic Law.* Edinburgh: Edinburgh University Press, 1964.

Dris-Ait-Hamadouche, Louisa. "Women in the Maghreb: Civil Society's Actors or Political Instruments?" *Middle East Policy* 14, 4 (2007): 115–32.

Eickelman, Dale. "Mass Higher Education and the Religious Imagination in Contemporary Arab Societies." *American Ethnologist* 19, 4 (1992): 643–854.

Engineer, Asghar Ali. *Justice, Women and Communal Harmony in Islam.* New Delhi: Indian Council of Social Science Research, 1989.

Ennaji, Moha, and Fatima Sadiqi. *Gender and Violence in the Middle East.* London: Routledge, 2011.

Ennaji, Moha, *Women in the Middle East and North Africa: Agents of Change.* London: Routledge, 2010.

Esposito, John L., chief ed. *The Islamic World: Past and Present.* With Tamara Sonn and John Voll. Vols. 1–3. Oxford: Oxford University Press, 2004.

Esposito, John L. *Women in Muslim Family Law.* Syracuse, N.Y.: Syracuse University Press, 1982.

Faqir, Nadia, ed. *In the House of Silence: Autobiographical Essays by Arab Women Writers.* Reading, UK: Garnet, 1998.

Farag, T. I., and A. S. Toughan. "1001 Nights in Old and Modern Yemen." *The Ambassadors Online Magazine* 5, 1 (2002): 1–11. http://ambassa dors.net/archives/issue11/Profile Yemen 2htm.

Fernea, Elizabeth W., ed. *Remembering Childhood in the Middle East.* Austin: University of Texas Press, 2002.

Fernea, Elizabeth W. *Women and the Family in the Middle East: New Forces of Change.* Austin:University of Texas Press, 1985.

Ghassoub, Mai. "Feminism—or the Eternal Masculine—in the Arab World." *New Left Review* 16 (1987): 11.

Giddens, Anthony. *The Consequences of Modernity.* Stanford, Calif.: Stanford University Press, 1990.

Gocek, Fatma Muge, and Shira Balaghi, eds. *Reconstructing Gender in the Middle East: Tradition, Identity and Power.* New York: Columbia University Press, 1994.

Golley, Nawar al-Hassan. "Is Feminism Relevant to Arab Women?" *Third World Quarterly* 25, 3 (2004): 521–36.

Guindy, Fadwa. *Veil: Modesty, Privacy and Resistance.* Oxford: Berg Press, 2003.

Haddad, Yvonne, and Allison B. Findley, eds. *Women, Religion and Social Change.* Albany: State University of New York Press, 1985.

Hallaq, Wael. *An Introduction to Islamic Law.* Cambridge: Cambridge University Press, 2009.

Harbi, Dalal Mukhlid. *Prominent Women from Central Arabia.* Reading, UK: Ithaca Press, 2008.

Hazimi, Mansour, Salma Jayyusi, and Izzat Khattab, eds. *Beyond the Dunes: Modern Saudi Literature.* London: I. B. Tauris, 2006.

Hijab, Nadia. *Womanpower: The Arab Debate on Women at Work.* New York: Cambridge University Press, 1988.

Hodgson, Marshall. *The Venture of Islam: Conscience and History in a World Civilization.* Chicago: University of Chicago Press, 1974.

Hoffman-Ladd, Valerie. "Polemics on the Modesty and Segregation of Women in Contemporary Egypt." *International Journal of Middle East Studies* 19 (1987): 23–50.

Ismael, Jacqueline, Shereen Ismael, and Chris Langille. "Post-Conflict Restructuring and Women in the Muslim World." *Arab Studies Quarterly* 32, 1 (2011): 21–43.

Jad, Islah. "The NGO-ization of Arab Women's Movements." In *Feminisms in Development: Contradictions, Contestations and Challenges*, edited by A. Cornwall, E. Harrison, and A. Whitehead, 177–90. London: Zed Books, 2007.

Jawzi, Abd al-Rahman ibn Ali. *Women's Roles.* Edited by Ali ibn Muhammad Yusuf al-Mahdi. Arabic. Beirut: Al-Manshurat al-Arabiyah, 1981.

Jayawardena, Kumari. *Feminism and Nationalism in the Third World.* London: Zed Books, 1986.

Jayyusi, Salma Khadra, ed. *Anthology of Modern Palestinian Literature.* New York: Columbia University Press, 1992.

Joseph, Suad, and Susan Slymovics, eds. *Women and Power in the Middle East.* Philadelphia: University of Pennsylvania Press, 2001.

Katouzian, Homa. *The Persians: Ancient, Medieval and Modern Iran.* New Haven, Conn.: Yale University Press, 2009.

Khadduri, Majid. *The Islamic Conception of Justice.* Baltimore, Md.: Johns Hopkins University Press, 1984.

Khuri, Fuad. "Parallel Cousin Marriage Reconsidered: A Middle Eastern Practice that Nullifies the Effects of Marriage on the Intensity of Family Relationships ." *Man* 5 (1970): 597.

Lerner, Gerda. *The Creation of Patriarchy.* Oxford: Oxford University Press, 1986.

Levy, Reuben. *The Social Structure of Islam.* London: Cambridge University Press, 1965.

Lobban, Richard A. *Middle Eastern Women and the Invisible Economy.* Gainesville: University of Florida Press, 1998.

Mayer, Ann Elizabeth. *Islam and Human Rights: Tradition and Politics.* Boulder, Colo.: Westview, 2006.

Mernissi, Fatima. "Virginity and Patriarchy." *Women's Studies International Forum* 5, 2 (1982): 183–91.

Minai, Naila. *Women in Islam: Tradition and Transition in the Middle East.* New York: Seaview Books, 1981.

Minces, Juliette. *The House of Obedience: Women in the Arab World.* London: Zed Press, 1980.

Moghadem, Valentine, ed. *Democratic Reform and the Position of Women in the Transnational Economies.* Oxford: Clarendon, Press, 1993.

Mussawi, Muhsin Jasim. *The Post-Colonial Arabic Novel: Debating Ambivalence.* Leiden: A. J. Brill, 2003.

Naim, Abdullahi An-. "The Rights of Women and International Law in the Muslim Context." *Whittier Law Review* 9 (1987): 491–516.

Norton, Augustus Richard, ed. *Civil Society in the Middle East.* Leiden: A. J. Brill, 1995.

Obermeyer, Carla, ed. *Family, Gender and Population in the Middle East: Policies in Contest.* Cairo: American University of Cairo Press, 1995.

Qazzaz, Ayad. *Women in the Middle East and North Africa: An Annotated Bibliography.* Austin: University of Texas Press, 1977.

Rahman, Fazlur. *The Role of Muslim Women in Society.* London: Seerah Foundation, 1986.

Rendall, Jane. *The Origins of Modern Feminism: Women in Britain, France and the United States, 1780–1860.* Chicago: Lyceum Books, 1985.

Roded, Ruth, ed. *Women in Islam and the Middle East: A Reader.* London: I. B. Tauris, 1999.

Rowbotham, Sheila. *Women, Resistance and Revolution.* New York: Vintage, 1974.

Sakr, N., ed. *Women and Media in the Middle East: Power Through Self-Expression.* London: Longman, 2004.

Seif-Amirhosseini, Zahra. "Underlying Reasons for Women's Oppression." *Islam* 21, 22 (2000): 12–13.

"Sexual Harassment at the United Nations." *Mahjubeh: The Islamic Magazine for Women* 4 (1994): 5.

Shaaban, Bouthaina. "Arab Women Writers: Are There Any? " *Washington Report on Middle East Affairs* (February 1993): 364.

Shaaban, Bouthaina. *Voices Revealed: Arab Women Novelists, 1898–2000.* Boulder, Colo.: Lynne Rienner, 2009.

Sharabi, Hisham. *Neopatriarchy: A Theory of Distorted Change in Arab Society.* New York: Oxford University Press, 1988.

Shazli, Heba, ed. "Arab Women in Civil Society." *Al-Raida,* 19, 97–98 (2002): special issue.

Starkey, Paul. *Modern Arabic Literature.* Washington, D.C.: Georgetown University Press, 2007.

Stowasser, Barbara. *Women in the Quran, Traditions, and Interpretation.* New York: Oxford University Press, 1994.

Stromquist, Nelly P., ed. *Women in the Third World: An Encyclopedia of Contemporary Issues.* London: Garland, 1998.

Talidi, Maliki. *Women and the Issue of Democracy.* (Arabic). Casablanca: Afriqiyah al-Sharq, 1991.

Toubia, Nahid, ed. *Women of the Arab World: The Coming Challenge.* London: Zed, 1988.

United Nations. Economic and Social Commission for Western Asia. *Women in Arab Society: Work Patterns and Gender Relations in Egypt, Jordan and the Sudan.* New York: United Nations Economic and Social Commission for Western Asia, 1990.

"Violence against Women." *Mahjubeh: The Islamic Magazine for Women* 5 (May 1994): 23–24.

Waddy, Charis. *Women in Muslim History.* London: Longman, 1980.

Walther, Wiebke. *Women in Islam.* Translated by C. S. V. Salt. Montclair, N.J.: Abner Schram, 1981.

REFERENCE WORKS

Ashur, Radwa, Ferial Ghazoul, and Reda Mekdashi, eds. *Arab Women Writers: A Critical Guide, 1873–1990.* Translated by Mandy McClure. Cairo: American University of Cairo Press, 2008.

Burrows, Robert D. *Historical Dictionary of Yemen.* 2nd ed. Lanham, Md.: Scarecrow Press, Inc., 2010.

Commins, David. *Historical Dictionary of Syria.* Lanham, Md.: Scarecrow Press, Inc., 2004.

Esposito, John L. *The Oxford Encyclopedia of the Modern Islamic World.* Oxford: Oxford University Press, 1995.

Ghareeb, Edmund, and Beth Dougherty. *Historical Dictionary of Iraq.* Lanham, Md.: Scarecrow Press, Inc., 2004.

Gibb, H. A. R., et al., eds. *Encyclopedia of Islam.* New ed. Leiden: A. J. Brill, 1960.

Glass, Cyril. *The New Encyclopedia of Islam.* 3rd ed. Lanham, Md.: Rowman and Littlefield, 2008.

Goldschmidt, Arthur. *Biographical Dictionary of Modern Egypt.* Boulder, Colo.: Lynne Rienner, 2000.

Hillauer, Rebecca. *Encyclopedia of Arab Women Film Makers.* Cairo: The American University in Cairo Press, 2005.

Institute for Women's Policy Research. *The Status of Women in the Middle East and North Africa.* www.iwpr.org/initiatives/swmena.

Kimball, Michelle, and Barbara R. von Schlegell. *Women in the Muslim World: A Bibliography with Selected Annotations.* Boulder, Colo.: Lynne Rienner, 1997.

Krikos, Linda, and Cindy Ingold. *Women's Studies: A Recommended Bibliography.* 3rd ed. Westport, Conn.: Libraries Unlimited, 2004.

Lobban, Richard A., Robert S. Kramer, and Carolyn Fluehr-Lobban. *Historical Dictionary of Sudan.* 3rd ed. Lanham, Md.: Scarecrow Press, Inc., 2002.

Lorentz, John H. *Historical Dictionary of Iran.* 2nd ed. Lanham, Md.: Scarecrow Press, Inc., 2007.

Martin, Richard, ed. in chief. *Encyclopedia of Islam and the Muslim World.* Farmington Hills, Mich.: Macmillan-Thomson, Gale, 2004.

Matter, Philip, ed. in chief. *Encyclopedia of the Modern Middle East and North Africa.* Farmington Hills, Mich.: Macmillan Reference, USA, 2004.

Motzafi-Haller, Pnina. *Women in Agriculture in the Middle East.* Burlington, Vt.: Ashgate, 2005.

Naylor, Philip. *Historical Dictionary of Algeria.* 3rd ed. Lanham, Md.: Scarecrow Press, Inc., 2006.

Nazzal, Nafez Y., and Laila A. Nazzal. *Historical Dictionary of Palestine.* Lanham, Md.: Scarecrow Press, Inc., 1997.

Park, Thomas K., and Aomar Boum. *Historical Dictionary of Morocco.* 2nd ed. Lanham, Md.: Scarecrow Press, Inc., 2006.

Peck, Malcolm C. *Historical Dictionary of Gulf Arab States.* 2nd ed. Lanham, Md.: Scarecrow Press, Inc., 2008.

Perkins, Kenneth J. *Historical Dictionary of Tunisia.* 2nd ed. Lanham, Md.: Scarecrow Press, Inc., 1997.

Peterson, J. E. *Historical Dictionary of Saudi Arabia.* 2nd ed. Lanham, Md.: Scarecrow Press, Inc., 2003.

Reich, Bernard, and David H. Goldberg. *Historical Dictionary of Israel.* 2nd ed. Lanham, Md.: Scarecrow Press, Inc., 2008.

Skolnik, Fred, ed. in chief. *Encyclopedia of Judaica.* 2nd ed. Farmington Hills, Mich.: Macmillan Thomson Gale, 2007.

Somel, Selcuk Aksam. *Historical Dictionary of the Ottoman Empire.* Lanham, Md.: Scarecrow Press, Inc., 2003.

St. John, Leonard Bruce. *Historical Dictionary of Libya.* 4th ed. Lanham, Md.: Scarecrow Press, Inc., 2006.

Stillman, Norman A., executive ed. *Encyclopedia of Jews in the Islamic World.* Leiden: A. J. Brill, 2010.

Tucker, Spencer C., and Priscilla Mary Roberts, eds. *Encyclopedia of Arab-Israeli Conflict.* Santa Barbara, Calif.: AB-CLIO, Inc., 2008.

WORKS ON SPECIFIC PERIODS

Pre-Islamic Period

Allam, Schafik. "Quelques aspects du marriage dans l'Égypte ancienne." *Journal of Egyptian Archeology* 67 (1981): 116–35.

Bakir, Abd El-Mohsen. *Slavery in Pharaonic Egypt.* Cairo: Department of Antiquities, 1952.

Bryan, B. M. "Evidence for Female Literacy from Theban Tombs of the New Kingdom." *Bulletin of the Egyptological Seminar* 6 (1984): 17–32.

Bunson, Margaret. *A Dictionary of Ancient Egypt.* New York: Oxford University Press, 1995.

Cerny, J., and T. E. Peet. "A Marriage Settlement of the Twentieth Dynasty." *Journal of Egyptian Archeology* 13 (1927): 30–39.

Eyre, C. J. "Crime and Adultery in Ancient Egypt." *Journal of Egyptian Archeology* 70 (1984): 92–105.

Gay, Robbins. *Women in Ancient Egypt.* Cambridge, Mass.: Harvard University Press, 1993.

Gitton, M. "Le rôle des femmes dans le clergé d'Amon à la 18c dynastie." *Bulletin de la Sociétié Française d'Égyptologie* 75 (1976): 31–46.

Glover, Elizabeth R. F. *Great Queens, Famous Rulers of the East.* London: Hutchinson, 1928.

Goldman, Shalom. *The Wiles of Women/The Wiles of Men: Joseph and Potiphar's Wife in Ancient Near Eastern, Jewish and Islamic Folklore.* Albany: State University of New York Press, 1995.

Groom, Nigel. *Frankincense and Myrrh: A Study of the Arabian Spice Trade.* London: Longman, 1981.

Kanawati, N. "Polygamy in the Old Kingdom." *Studien zur Altagyptischen Kultur* 4 (1976): 149–60.

Kemb, B. J. "The Harim-Palace at Medinet el-Ghurab." *Zeitschrift für Agyptische Sprache und Altertumskunde* 105 (1978): 122–33.

Lesko, B., ed. *Women's Earliest Records from Ancient Egypt and Western Asia. Brown University's Judaic Studies* 16 (1989).

Newberry, P. E. "Queen Nitocris of the Sixth Dynasty." *Journal of Egyptian Archeology* 29 (1943): 51–54.

Nims, C. "The Date of the Dishonoring of Hatshepsut." *Zeitschrift fur Egyptische Sprache und Altertumskunde* 93 (1966): 70–100.

Pestman, P. W. *Marriage and Matrimonial Property in Ancient Egypt.* Leiden: A. J. Brill, 1961.

Schulman, A. "Diplomatic Marriage in the Egyptian New Kingdom." *Journal of Near Eastern Studies* 38 (1979): 177–93.

Simpson, W. K. "Polygamy in Egypt in the Middle Kingdom." *Journal of Egyptian Archeology* 60 (1974): 100–105.

Smith, William Robertson. *Kinship and Marriage in Early Arabia.* London: A. & C. Black, 1907.

Troy, L. "Good and Bad Women." *Gottinger Miszellen* 80 (1984): 77–82.

Troy, L. "Patterns of Queenship in Ancient Egypt: Myth and History." In *Boreds 14.* Uppsala: Acta Universitatis, 1986.

Ward, William A. *Essays on Feminine Titles of the Middle Kingdom and Related Subjects.* A Supplement to his Index of 1985. Beirut, 1986.

Whale, S. *The Family in the Eighteenth Dynasty of Egypt.* Sydney: Australian Center for Egyptology, 1989.

Classic Islamic Period

Abu-Bakr, Omaima. "Articulating Gender: Muslim Women Intellectuals in the Pre-Modern Period." *Arab Studies Quarterly* 32, 3 (2010): 127–44.

Beeston, A. F. L., et al., eds. *Arabic Literature to the End of the Umayyad Period.* Cambridge: Cambridge University Press, 1983.

Cortese, Della, and Simonetta Calderini. *Women and the Fatimids in the World of Islam.* Edinburgh: Edinburgh University Press, 2006.

Croutier, Alev Lytle. *Harem: The World behind the Veil.* New York: Abbeville Press, 1989.

Darwish, Linda. "Images of Muslim Women: 'Aisha, Fatima and Zaynab Bint Ali in Contemporary Gender Discourse'." *McGill Journal of Middle Eastern Studies (Revue d'études du Moyen-Orient de McGill)* 4 (1996): 93–132.

De Long-Bas, Natana. *Notable Muslims: Muslim Builders of World Civilization and Culture.* Oxford: Oneworld, 2006.

Hermansen, Marcia K. "Fatimeh as a Role Model in the Works of Ali Shari'ati." In *Women and Revolution in Iran,* edited by Guity Nashat, 87–96. Boulder, Colo.: Westview, 1983.

Hermansen, Marcia K. "The Female Hero in the Islamic Religious Tradition." *Annual Review of Women in World Religions* 2 (1992): 111–43.

Hussein, Fida. *Wives of the Prophet.* Lahore, Pakistan: Ashraf Printing Presses, 1952.

Irwin, Robert, ed. *Night and Horses and the Desert: Anthology of Classical Arabic Literature.* Woodstock, N.Y.: The Overlook Press, 1999.

Kadra-Hadjaji, Houria. "La Kahina, personage littéraire." In *Présences de femmes.* Alger: Office des Publications Universitaires, 1984.

Kahf, Mohja. "Braiding the Stories: Women's Eloquence in the Early Islamic Era." In *Windows of Faith,* edited by Gisela Webb, 147–71. Syracuse, N.Y.: Syracuse University Press, 2000.

Majid, Anouar. "The Politics of Feminism in Islam." *Signs* 23, 2 (1998): 321–61.

Mernissi, Fatima. *Scheherazade Goes West.* New York: Washington Square Press, 2001.

Roded, Ruth. *Women in Islamic Biographical Dictionaries: From Ibn Sa'd to Who's Who.* Boulder, Colo.: Lynne Rienner, 1994.

Shariati, Ali. *Fatima Is Fatima.* Translated by Laleh Bakhtiar. Tehran: Shari'ati Foundation, 1981.

Smith, Jane I. "Women in the Afterlife: View as Seen from the Qur'an and Traditions." *Journal of the American Academy of Religion* 43 (1975): 39–50.

Smith, Margaret. *Rabi'a the Mystic and her Fellow-Saints in Islam.* Cambridge: Cambridge University Press, 1928.

Specktorsky, Susan A. *Chapters on Marriage and Divorce: Responses of Ibn Hanbal and Ibn Rahwayh.* Austin: University of Texas Press, 1993.

Spellberg, D. A. *Politics, Gender and the Islamic Past: The Legacy of Aisha bint Abu Bakr.* New York: Columbia University Press, 1994.

Stern, G. H. "The First Women Converts in Early Islam." *Islamic Culture* 13 (1939): 290–305.

Stowasser, Barbara. "The Mothers of the Believers in the Hadith." *The Muslim World* 82 (1992): 1–36.

Stowasser, Barbara. "The Status of Women in Early Islam." In *Muslim Women,* edited by Freda Hussain, 11–43. New York: St. Martin's, 1984.

Watt, Montgomery. *Muhammad at Medina.* Oxford: Clarendon Press, 1956.

Medieval Period

Awad-Geissler, Johanna. *Die Schattenkalifin.* Munich: Droemer, 2007.

Ayalon, David. *Islam and the Abode of War: Military Slaves and Islamic Adversaries.* Aldershot, UK: Variorum, 1994.

Ayalon, David. *Studies on the Mamluks of Egypt.* London: Variorum Reprints, 1977.

Behrens-Abouseif, Doris. *Egypt's Adjustment to Ottoman Rule: Institutions, Waqfs, and Architecture in Cairo.* Leiden: E. J. Brill, 1994.

Daftary, Farhad. "Sayyida Hurra: The Isma'ili Sulayhid Queen of Yemen." In *Women in the Medieval Islamic World,* edited by Gavin R. Hamby, 117–30. New York: St. Martin's, 1998.

Fariq, K. A. *History of Arabic Literature.* New Delhi: Vikas Publications, 1972.

Gauch, Suzanne. *Liberating Shahrazad: Feminism and Islam.* Minneapolis: University of Minnesota Press, 2007.

Hamby, Gavin G., ed. *Women in the Medieval Islamic World.* New York: St. Martin's, 1998.

Holt, P. M. *The Age of the Crusades.* London: Longman, 1986.

Ilias, Jamal. "Female and Feminine in Islamic Mysticism." *The Muslim World* 78 (1988): 209–24.

Imad, Leila S. *The Fatimid Vizirate, 969–1172.* Berlin: Klaus Schwartz, 1990.

Jennings, Ronald C. "Women in Early 17th Century Ottoman Judicial Records of the Shari'a Court of Anatolian Kayseri." *Journal of the Economic and Social History of the Orient* 18 (1978): 53–114.

Lutfi, Huda. "Manners and Customs of Fourteenth-Century Cairene Women: Female Anarchy Versus Male Shar'i Order in Muslim Prescriptive Treatises." In *Women in Middle Eastern History,* edited by Nikki Keddie and Beth Baron, 99–121. New Haven, Conn.: Yale University Press, 1991.

Meri, Joseph W., ed. *Medieval Islamic Civilization.* London: Routledge, 2006.

Mernissi, Fatima. *The Forgotten Queens of Islam.* Minneapolis: University of Minnesota Press, 1997.

Petry, Carl F. "Class Solidarity versus Gender Gain: Women as Custodians of Property in Latter Medieval Egypt." In *Women in Middle Eastern History*, edited by Nikki Keddie and Beth Baron, 122–42. New Haven, Conn.: Yale University Press, 1991.

Petry, Carl F. *Protectors or Praetorians? The Late Mamluk Sultans and Egypt's Waning as a Great Power.* Albany: State University of New York Press, 1994.

Sayyid, Afaf Lutfi, ed. *Society and the Sexes in Medieval Islam.* Malibu, Calif.: Indena Publications, 1979.

Sayyid, Afaf Lutfi. *Women and Men in Late Eighteenth-Century Egypt.* Austin: University of Texas Press, 1995.

Schimmel, Anne-marie. *My Soul Is a Woman.* Cairo: American University of Cairo Press, 1998.

Shatzmiller, Maya. "Aspects of Women's Participation in the Economic Life of Later Medieval Islam." *Arabica* 35 (1988): 36–58.

Shatzmiller, Maya. "Women and Wage Labour in the Medieval Islamic West." *Journal of Economic and Social History of the Orient* 39, 4 (1997): 1–33.

Shoshan, Boaz. *Popular Culture in Medieval Cairo.* Cambridge: Cambridge University Press, 1993.

Stillman, Yodidak. "Cover the Face: Jewish Women and Veiling in Islamic Civilization." *Israel and Ishmael: Studies in Muslim-Jewish Relations* (2000): 13–31.

Tugay, Emine Foat. *Three Centuries: Family Chronicles of Turkey and Egypt.* London: Oxford University Press, 1963.

Zilfi, Madeline. *Women in the Ottoman Empire: Middle Eastern Women in the Early Modern Era.* Leiden: A. J. Brill, 1997.

19th and 20th Centuries

Abadan-Unat, Nermin, ed. *Women in Turkish Society.* Leiden: A. J. Brill, 1981.

Abaza, Mona. *The Changing Image of Women in Rural Egypt.* Cairo: American University of Cairo Press, 1987.

Afary, Janet. *The Iranian Constitutional Revolution: Grassroots Democracy, Social Democracy and the Origins of Feminism.* New York: Columbia University Press, 1996.

Antonious, Soraya. *Miss Alice and the Palestinians: The Lord.* New York: Henry Holt, 1986.

Antonious, Soraya. *Where the Jinn Consult.* London: Hamish Hamilton, 1988.

Agayev, S. L., and V. N. Plastun. "The Communist and National Liberation Movement in Iran in the 1920s." In *The Cominturn and the East: A Critique of the Critique*, edited by R. A. Ulyanovsky. Moscow: Progress Publishers, 1978.

Agmon, Iris. *Family and Court: Legal Culture and Modernity in the Late Ottoman Palestine.* Syracuse, N.Y.: Suracuse University Press, 2006.

Ahmed, Leila. "Between Two Worlds: The Formation of a Turn-of-the-Century Egyptian Feminist." In *Life/Lines: Theorizing Women's Autobiography*, edited by Bella Brodzki and Celeste Schenck. Ithaca, N.Y.: Cornell University Press, 1988.

Alloula, Malek. *The Colonial Harem.* Minneapolis: University of Minnesota Press, 1986.

Auclert, Hubertine. *Les femmes arabes en Algérie.* Paris: Société d'Éditions Littéraires, 1900.

Badran, Margot. *Feminism in Islam: Secular and Religious Convergence.* Oxford: Oneworld, 2009.

Badran, Margot. *Feminism, Islam and Nation: Gender and the Making of Egypt.* Princeton, N.J.: Princeton University Press, 1995.

Badran, Margot. "What's in a Name? " *Al-Ahram Weekly*, 17–23 January 2002. http://www.weekly. ahram.org.eg/2002/569.

Badran, Margot, and Miriam Cooke, eds. *Opening the Gates: A Century of Arab Feminist Writing.* Bloomington: Indiana University Press, 1990.

Baron, Beth. *Egypt as a Woman: Nationalism, Gender and Politics.* Berkeley: University of California Press, 2005.

Baron, Beth. *The Women's Awakening in Egypt: Culture, Society and the Press.* New Haven, Conn.: Yale University Press, 1994.

Beck, Lois, and Guity Nashat, eds. *Women in Iran: From 1800 to the Islamic Republic.* Chicago: University of Illinois Press, 2004.

Booth, Marylin. *May Her Likes Be Multiplied: Biography and Gender Politics in Egypt.* Berkeley: University of California Press, 2001.

Brand, Laurie A. *Women, the State and Political Liberalization: The Moroccan, Jordanian and Tunisian Cases.* New York: Columbia University Press, 1998.

Chatiba, Khalid. *Le mariage chez les musulmans en Syrie.* Paris: Libraire Orientaliste, 1934.

Cheneviere, Alain. *L'Oman et les Emirates du Golfe.* Paris: Hachette, 1990.

Christelow, Allan. *Muslim Law Courts and the French Colonial State in Algeria.* Princeton, N.J.: Princeton University Press, 1985.

Danielson, Virginia. *The Voice of Egypt: Umm Kulthum, Arabic Song and Egyptian Society in the Twentieth Century.* Chicago: University of Chicago Press, 1997.

Di-Capua, Yoav. "Sports, Society and Revolution: Egypt in the Early 1950s." In *Rethinking Nasserism*, edited by E. Podeh et al., 144–62. Gainesville: University Press of Florida, 2004.

Djebar, Assia. *Femmes d'Alger dans leur appartement*. Paris: Édition des Femmes, 1981.

Doumato, Eleanor Abdella. "Women and Political Stability in Saudi Arabia." *Middle East Report* 171 (1991): 34–37.

Fischer, Michael. *Iran: From Religious Dispute to Revolution*. Cambridge, Mass.: Harvard University Press, 1980.

Gaudry, Mathéa. *La femme Chaouia de L'Aurès. Étude de sociologie Berbère*. Paris: Libraire Orientaliste Paul Geuthner, 1929.

Gawrych, George W. "Semseddin Sami, Women and Social Conscience in the Late Ottoman Period." *Middle Eastern Studies* 46, 1 (2010): 97–115.

Gordon, D. C. *Women of Algeria*. Cambridge, Mass.: Harvard University Press, 1968.

Graham-Brown, Sarah. *Images of Women: The Portrayal of Women in Photography of the Middle East, 1860–1950*. New York: Columbia University Press, 1988.

Granqvist, Hilma. *Marriage Conditions in a Palestinian Village*. Helsingfors: Commentationes Humanarum Litterarum, 1931.

Haddad, Taher. "Notre femme dans la loi et la société." *Revue Islamique* (1935): 201–30.

Haeri, Shahla. *Law of Desire: Temporary Marriage in Shi'i Iran*. Syracuse, N.Y.: Syracuse University Press, 1989.

Hart, Ursula Kingsmill. *Two Ladies of Algeria: The Lives and Times of Aurelie Picard and Isabelle Eberhardt*. Athens: Ohio University Center for International Studies, 1987.

Hassan, Ihsan M. *The Effects of Industrialization on the Social Status of Iraqi Women*. Baghdad: General Federation of Iraqi Women, 1980.

Hillman, Michael C. *A Lonely Woman: Forugh Forrokhzad and Her Poetry*. Washington, D.C.: Three Continents Press, 1987.

Horne, Alistair. *A Savage War of Peace, Algeria 1954–1962*. New York: Viking Press, 1977.

Ingrams, Doreen. *The Awakening: Women in Iraq*. London: Third World Center, 1983.

Jad, Islah. "From Salons to Popular Committees: Palestinian Women, 1919–1989." In *Intifada: Palestine at the Crossroads*, edited by Jamal Nassar and Roger Heacock, 125–42. New York: Praeger, 1989.

Kateb, Yacine. *Nedjma*. Paris: Editions du Seuil, 1956.

Katz, Sheila H. *Women and Gender in Early Jewish and Palestinian Nationalism*. Gainesville: University Press of Florida, 2003.

Keddie, Nikki. *Religion and Rebellion in Iran: The Iranian Tobacco Protest of 1891–1892*. London: Frank Cass, 1966.

Kerr, Malcolm. *Islamic Reforms: The Political and Legal Theories of Muhammad Abduh and Rashid Rida.* Berkeley: University of California Press, 1966.

Khater, Akram Fouad. "House to Goddess of the House: Gender, Class and Silk in 19th Century Mount Lebanon." *International Journal of Middle Eastern Studies* 28, 3 (1996): 325–48.

Lazreg, Marnia. *Algerian Revolution: The Eloquence of Silence.* London: Routledge, 1994.

Lazreg, Marnia. "Feminism and Difference: The Perils of Writing as a Woman on Women in Algeria." *Feminist Studies* 14, 1 (1988): 81–107.

Longva, Ahn Nga. *Walls Built on Sand: Migration, Exclusion and Society in Kuwait.* Boulder, Colo.: Westview, 1996.

Mahnaz Afkhami. http://www.learningpartnership.org/viewProfiles.php?profile1D=389.

Makhlouf, Carla. *Changing Veils: Women and Modernization in North Yemen.* London: Croom Helm, 1972.

Mernissi, Fatima. *Dreams of Trespass: Tales of a Harem Childhood.* Cambridge, Mass.: Persus Books, 1995.

Messaadi, Sakina. *Les femmes romancières coloniales et la femme colonisée.* Contribution à une etude de la litérature coloniale en Algérie. Alger: Enterprise Nationale du Livre, 1990.

Mikail, Mona N. *Seen and Heard: A Century of Arab Women in Literature and Culture.* Northhampton, Mass.: Olive Branch Press, 2004.

Moghannam, Matiel. *The Arab Woman and the Palestine Problem.* London: Herbert Joseph, 1937.

Moors, A., ed. *Discourse and Palestine: Power, Text and Context.* Amsterdam: Het Spinhuis, 1995.

Moubayid, Sami. *Steel and Silk: Men and Women Who Have Shaped Syria.* Seattle, Wash.: Cune Press, 2005.

Mughni, Haya. *Women in Kuwait: The Politics of Gender.* London: Saqi Books, 2001.

Naghibi, Nima. *Rethinking Global Sisterhood: Western Feminism and Iran.* Minneapolis: University of Minnesota Press, 2007.

Naguib, Nefissa. *Women, Water and Memory: Recasting Lives in Palestine.* Leiden: A. J. Brill, 2009.

Najjar, Urayb. *Portraits of Palestinian Women.* Salt Lake City: University of Utah Press, 1992.

Nazzal, Rima. *Palestinian Women between Military Siege and Social Rights.* (Arabic). Ramallah, West Bank: Ramallah Center for the Study of Human Rights, 2002.

Nerval, Gerard de. *Women of Cairo.* 2 vols. New York: Harcourt Brace, 1930.

Paider, Parvin. *Women and Political Careers in Twentieth-Century Iran.* Cambridge: Cambridge University Press, 1995.

Ruete, Emily. *Memoirs of an Arabian Princess from Zanzibar.* New York: Markus Weiner, 1989.

Saadawi, Nawal. "Dissidence and Creativity." *Women: A Cultural Review* 6, 1 (1995): 1–17.

Saadawi, Nawal. *The Hidden Face of Eve.* London: Zed Books, 1980.

Sabbagh, Suha, ed. *Arab Women between Defiance and Restraint.* New York: Olive Branch Press, 1996.

Sanea, Rajaa. *Girls of Riyadh.* New York: The Penguin Press, 2007.

Secor, A. "Orientalism, Gender and Class in Lady Mary Wortley Montagu's Turkish Embassy Letters." *Cultural Geographies* 6, 4 (1999): 375–98.

Shaaban, Bouthaina. *Both Right and Left-Handed: Arab Women Talk about Their Lives.* Bloomingon: Indiana University Press, 1991.

Shaaban, Bouthaina. *Voices Revealed: Arab Women Novelists, 1898–2000.* Boulder, Colo.: Lynne Rienner, 2009.

Shalaq, Ali, et al. *Women and their Role in the Arab National Movement.* (Arabic). Beirut: Markaz Dirasat al-Wihdah al-Arabiyah, 1982.

Smith, Peter. *The Babi and Baha'i Religions: From Messianic Shi'ism to a World Religion.* New York: Cambridge University Press, 1987.

Stockdale, Nancy L. *Encounters among English and Palestinian Women 1800–1947.* Gainesville: University Press of Florida, 2007.

Talhami, Ghada. *Women, Education and Development in the Arab Gulf Countries.* Emirates Occasional Papers. Abu Dhabi, UAE: Emirates Center for Strategic Studies and Research, 2003.

Thomson, Maria Elizabeth Bowen. *Daughters of Syria.* London: Seeley, Jackson & Halliday, 1872.

Tillion, Germaine. *My Cousin, My Husband: Class and Kinship in Mediterranean Societies.* Berkeley, Calif.: Saqi Books, 2007.

Tucker, Judith, ed. *Arab Women: Old Boundaries and New Frontiers.* Bloomington: Indiana University Press, 1993.

Van Nieuwkerk, Karin. *"A Trade Like Any Other": Female Singers and Dancers in Egypt.* Austin: University of Texas Press, 1995.

Vinogradov, Amal. "French Colonialism as Reflected in the Male-Female Interaction in Morocco." *Transactions of the New York Academy of Sciences* 36 (1974): 192–99.

Woodsmall, Ruth F. *Moslem Women Enter a New World.* New York: Roundtable Press, 1936.

Woodsmall, Ruth F. *Study of the Role of Women in the Near East.* New York: International Federation of Business and Professional Women, 1956.

Zuhur, Sharifa, ed. *Colors of Enchantment: Theatre, Dance, Music and the Visual Arts in the Middle East.* Cairo: American University of Cairo Press, 2001.

Postindependence Period

Abdo, Nahla. "Nationalism and Feminism: Palestinian Women and the Intifada." In *Gender and National Identity,* edited by Valentin Moghadam, 149–52. London: Zed Books, 1994.

Abu-Lughod, Leila. *Veiled Sentiments: Honor and Poetry in a Bedouin Society.* Berkeley: University of California Press, 1986.

Abu-Saud, Abeer. *Qatari Women: Past and Present.* London: Longman, 1984.

Abu-Zu'bi, Nahla. *Women and Social Change in the Middle East: The Palestinian Case.* Toronto: Scholar's Press, 1987.

Afary, Janet, and Kevin Anderson. *Foucault and the Iranian Revolution: Gender and the Seductions of Islamism.* Chicago: University of Chicago Press, 2005.

Afkhami, Mahnaz, ed. *Faith and Freedom.* London: T. B. Tauris, 1995.

Afkhami, Mahnaz, and Erika Friedl, eds. *In the Eye of the Storm.* Syracuse, N.Y.: Syracuse University Press, 1994.

Ahmed, Leila. "Feminism and Feminist Movements in the Middle East, a Preliminary Exploration: Turkey, Egypt, Algeria, People's Democratic Republic of Yemen." *Women's Studies International Forum* 5, 2 (1982): 153–68.

Akhavi, Sharough. "Islam, Politics and Society in the Thought of Ayatollah Khomeini, Ayatollah Taliqani and Ali Shariati." *Middle Eastern Studies* 24, 4 (1988): 404–31.

Al-Ali, Nadje Sadiq. *Iraqi Women: Untold Stories from 1948 to the Present.* New York: Palgrave Macmillan, 2007.

Al-Ali, Nadje Sadiq, and Nicole Pratt. *What Kind of Liberation? Women and the Occupation of Iraq.* Berkeley: University of California Press, 2009.

Alamuddin, Nora S., and Paul D. Starr. *Crucial Bonds: Marriage among the Lebanese Druze.* Delmar, N.Y.: Caravan Books, 1980.

Alya, Chérif Chamari. *Femmes et loi en Tunisie.* Casablanca: Éditions le Fennec, 1991.

Amnesty International. *Tunisia: Rhetoric versus Reality—The Failure of a Human Rights Bureaucracy.* New York: Amnesty International, 1994.

Amowitz, L. I. "Human Rights Abuses and Concerns about Women's Health and Human Rights in Southern Iraq." *Journal of American Medical Association* 291, 12 (2004): 1471–79.

Arebi, Saddeka. *Women and Words in Saudi Arabia.* New York: Columbia University Press, 1994.

Ashman, Anastasia M., and Jennifer Eaton Gokmen, eds. *Tales from the Expat Harem: Foreign Women in Modern Turkey.* Emeryville, N.Y.: Perseus Books, 2006.

Atakav, Eylem. *Women and Turkish Cinema.* London: Routledge, 2012.

Attir, Mustafa O. *Modernization and Development: Results of an Empirical Study in Libya.* Tripoli: The Arab Development Institute and University of Garyunis, 1980.

Azri, Khalid. *Social and Gender Inequality in Oman.* London: Routledge, 2012.

Bagader, Abubaker, et al., eds. *Voices of Change: Short Stories by Saudi Arabian Women Writers.* Boulder, Colo.: Lynne Rienner, 1998.

Bendt, Ingela, and James Downing. *We Shall Return: Women of Palestine.* London: Zed Books, 1980.

Bennoune, Karima. "Between Betrayal and Betrayal: Fundamentalism, Family Law and Feminist Struggle in Algeria." *Arab Studies Quarterly* 17, 1 & 2 (1995): 51–76.

Berik, G. *Women Carpet Weavers in Rural Turkey.* Geneva: International Labour Office, 1987.

Buti, Muhammad Sa'id Ramadan al-. *Women between the Tyranny of the Western System and the Mercy of the Islamic Law.* Translated by Nancy Roberts. Damascus: Dar al-Fikr, 2006.

Colman, Isobel. "Women, Islam and the New Iraq." *Foreign Affairs* 85, 1 (2006): 24–38.

Cooke, Miriam. *War's Other Voices: Women Writers on the Lebanese Civil War.* Cambridge: Cambridge University Press, 1988.

Dajani, Souad. "The Struggle of Palestinian Women in the Occupied Territories: Between National and Social Liberation." *Arab Studies Quarterly* 16, 2 (1994): 13–26.

Daoud, Suheir Abu-Oksa. *Palestinian Women and Politics in Israel.* Gainesville: University of Florida Press, 2009.

Efrati, N. "Negotiating Rights in Iraq: Women and the Personal Status Law." *Middle East Journal* 59, 4 (2005): 577–95.

Eickelman, Christine. *Woman and Community in Oman.* New York: New York University Press, 1984.

"Elif Shafak." *Financial Times,* 19 February 2011, 17.

Fakhro, Munira. *Women at Work in the Gulf: A Case Study of Bahrain.* London: Keegan Paul International, 1990.

Falbel, Rit, et al., eds. *Jewish Women's Call for Peace: A Handbook for Jewish Women on the Israeli/Palestinian Conflict.* Ithaca, N.Y.: Firebrand Books, 1999.

Fathi, Asghar, ed. *Women and the Family in Iran.* Leiden: A. J. Brill, 1985.

Fleishman, Ellen. "The Emergence of the Palestinian Women's Movement, 1929–1939." *Journal of Palestine Studies* 29, 3 (2000): 17–31.

Ghabra, Shafiq. *Palestinians in Kuwait: The Family and the Politics of Survival.* Boulder, Colo.: Westview, 1987.

Ghabra, Taghreed al-Qudsi. "Women in Kuwait: Educated, Modern and Middle Eastern." *The Washington Report on Middle East Affairs* (July 1991): 29.

Gorkin, Michael, and Rafiqa Othman. *Three Mothers, Three Daughters: Palestinian Women's Stories.* Berkeley: University of California Press, 1996.

Guindi, Fadwa. "The Status of Women in Bahrain: Social and Cultural Considerations." In *Bahrain and the Gulf: Past Perspectives and Alternative Futures*, edited by Jeffrey Nugent and Theodore H. Thomas, 78–86. New York: St. Martin's Press, 1985.

Habash, George. *On the Liberation of Women.* Arabic. Beirut: Information Center of the Popular Front for the Liberation of Palestine, n.d.

Hammami, Rima. "Women's Political Participation in the Intifada: A Critical Overview." In *The Intifada and Some Women's Social Issues*, edited by Women's Studies Committee, 73–84. Jerusalem: Beisan Center, 1991.

Hatem, Mervat. "Egypt's Middle Class in Crisis: The Sexual Division of Labor." *The Middle East Journal* 42, 3 (1988): 407–22.

Hatem, Mervat. "Privatization and the Demise of State Feminism in Egypt." In *Mortgaging Women's Lives: Feminist Critiques of Structural Adjustment*, edited by Pamela Sparr, 40–60. London: Zed Books, 1994.

Hendousa, Heba, ed. *Arab Women and Economic Development.* Cairo: Arab Fund for Economic and Social Development, 2005.

Hiltermann, Joost. *Behind the Intifada: Labor and Women's Movements in the Occupied Territories.* Princeton, N.J.: Princeton University Press, 1991.

Hoodfar, Homa. *Between Marriage and the Market: Intimate Politics and Survival in Cairo.* Berkeley: University of California Press, 1997.

Hopwood, Derek. *Bourgiba, Habib of Tunisia: The Tragedy of Longevity.* London: Macmillan, 1992.

Howard-Merriam, Kathleen. "Women, Education and the Professions in Egypt." *Comparative Education Review* 23 (1979): 262.

"Iraqi-American Freedom Alliance." http://www.untoldiraq.org./story/index .cfm.

Ismael, Jacqueline, and Shereen Ismael. "Iraqi Women under Occupation: From Tribalism to Neo-Feudalism." *Journal of Contemporary Iraqi Studies* 1, 2 (2007): 247–268.

"Israel and the Occupied Territories: Conflict, Occupation and Patriarchy." *Amnesty International Report* (March 2005).

Jawahiri, Yasmin Husein. *Women in Iraq: The Gender Impact of International Sanctions.* Boulder, Colo.: Lynne Rienner, 2008.

Karim, Persis M., ed. *Let Me Tell You Where I've Been: New Writing by Women of the Iranian Diaspora.* Fayetteville: University of Arkansas Press, 2006.

Kawar, Amal. *Daughters of Palestine: Leading Women of the Palestinian National Movement.* Albany: State University of New York Press, 1996.

Khadi, Ann Bragdon. "Schools as Mediators in Female Role Formation: An Ethnography of a Girls' School in Baghdad." Ph. D. dissertation, State University of New York at Buffalo, 1978.

Khalaf, Roseanne Saad. *Hikayat: Short Stories by Lebanese Women.* London: Telegram, 2006.

Khalili, Ghazi. *The Palestinian Woman and the Revolution.* (Arabic). Beirut: PLO Research Center, 1977.

Khayyat, Sana. *Honor and Shame: Women in Modern Iraq.* London: Saqi Books, 1990.

King, Mary Elizabeth. *A Quiet Revolution: The First Palestinian Intifada an Non-Violent Resistance.* New York: Nation Books, 2007.

Kocturk, Tahire. *A Matter of Honor: Experiences of Turkish Women Immigrants.* London: Zed Books, 1992.

Kuehnast, Kathleen, Manal Omar, Steven E. Steiner, and Hodei Sultan. *Lessons from Women's Programs in Afghanistan and Iraq.* Washington, D.C.: United States Institute of Peace, 2012.

Larson, Barbara K. "The Status of Women in a Tunisian Village: Limits to Autonomy, Influence And Power." *Signs* 9, 3 (1984): 417–33.

Layish, Aharon. *Women and Islamic Law in a Non-Islamic State: A Study Based on Decisions of Sharia Courts in Israel.* New Brunswick, N.J.: Transaction, 2006.

"Leading Businesswomen in the Arab World." *Financial Times,* 23 June 2008, 4.

League of Arab States. *Women's Associations and Committees in the West Bank and Gaza Strip.* (Arabic). Tunis: League of Arab States, 1984.

"Leila Shawa." http://www.leilashawa.com.

Levy, Gideon. "Samiha Khalil: First Lady." *New Outlook* (June–July 1989): 38–39.

Longva, Anh Nga. "Kuwaiti Women at a Crossroad: Privileged Development and the Constraint of Ethnic Stratification." *International Journal of Middle East Studies* 25 (1993): 443–56.

Looney, R. "The Economics of Coping: The Plight of Women in Iraq's Informal Economy." *Journal of Social, Political and Economic Studies* 30, 3 (2005): 285–304.

Malki, Amal al-, David Kaufer, and Suguru Ishizaki. *Arab Women in Arab News: Old Stereotypes and New Media.* London: Bloomsbury, 2012.

Malti-Douglas, Fadwa. *Men, Women and God(s): Nawal El Saadawi and Arab Feminist Poetics.* Berkeley: University of California Press, 1995.

Mavini, Azadeh. *Lipstick Jihad: A Memoir of Growing Up Iranian in America and American in Iran.* New York: Public Affairs, 2006.

Medimegh, Aziza Darghouth. *Droits et vécu de la femmes en Tunisie.* Lyon, France: Hermes-Edilis, 1992.

Meleis, Afaf, et al. "Women, Modernization and Education in Kuwait." *Comparative Education Review* 23, 1 (1979): 115–24.

Moghissi, Haideh. *Populism and Feminism in Iran: Women's Struggle in a Male-Dominated Revolutionary Movement.* London: Macmillan, 1994

Mojab, Shahrazad. *Women of a Non-State Nation: The Kurds.* Costa Mesa, Calif.: Mazda Publishers, 2001.

Moubayed, Sami. "The Face That Launched a Thousand Ships." http://wwwmideastviews.Php?art=64.

Nashat, Guity. *Women and Revolution in Iran.* Boulder, Colo.: Westview, 1983.

Odeh, Rasmiyeh, and Soraya Antonious. "Prisoners for Palestine: A List of Women Female Political Prisoners." *Journal of Palestine Studies* 9, 35 (1980): 29–80.

Othman, Ziad. *Gender Participation in Palestine.* Ramallah, West Bank: Center for Human Rights Studies, 2003.

Peteet, Julie M. *Gender in Crisis: Women and the Palestinian Resistance Movement.* New York: Columbia University Press, 1991.

Powers, Janet M. *Blossoms on the Olive Tree: Israeli and Palestinian Women Working for Peace.* Westport, Conn.: Praeger, 2006.

Rachid, Abderrazak Moulay. *Femmes et loi au Maroc.* Casablanca: Editions le Fennec, 1991.

Rauch, Margaret. *Women and the Spirit Possession: Moroccan Women and the Revision of Tradition.* Bielefeld, Germany: Transcript, Verlag, 2000.

Richter-Devroe, Sophie. "Gender, Culture and Conflict Resolution in Palestine." *Journal of Middle Eastern Women's Studies* 4, 2 (2008): 30–59.

Saadie, Nouredine. *Femmes et loi en Algérie.* Casablanca: Éditions le Fennec, 1991.

Sabbagh, Suha. "Interview: Yasser Arafat on the Role of Palestinian Women." *The Return* 3 (1990): 9–13.

Sabbagh, Suha, and Ghada Talhami, eds. *Palestinian Women under Occupation and in the Diaspora.* Washington, D.C.: Institute for Arab Women's Studies, 1999.

Salloom, Hamad, ed. *Education in Saudi Arabia.* Rev. ed. Beltsville, Md.: Amana, 1995.

Sayigh, Rosemary. "Palestinian Women: Triple Burden, Single Struggle." In *Palestine: Profile of an Occupation,* edited by Rosemary Sayigh. London: Zed Books, 1989.

Seikaly, May. "Women and Social Change in Bahrain." *International Journal of Middle Eastern Studies* 26 (1994): 415–26.

Shehadeh, Lamia, ed. *Women and War in Lebanon.* Gainesville: University of Florida Press, 1999.

Shironi, Simona. *Gender and the Israeli-Palestinian Conflict.* Syracuse, N.Y.: Syracuse University Press, 1995.

Siddiq, Muhammad. "The Fiction of Sahar Khalifah: Between Defiance and Deliverance." *Arab Studies Quarterly* 8, 2 (1986): 143–60.

Soffan, Linda Usra. *The Women of the United Arab Emirates.* London: Croom Helm, 1980.

Strum, Phillippa. *The Women Are Marching: The Second Sex and Palestinian Revolution.* Chicago: Lawrence Hill, 1992.

Suleiman, Michael. "Socialization to Politics in Morocco: Sex and Regional Factors." *International Journal of Middle East Studies* 17, 3 (1985): 313–27.

Talhami, Ghada, guest ed. "The Impact of War and Revolution on Women in the Arab World." *Arab Studies Quarterly (Special Issue)* 15, 2 (1993).

Tawil, Raymonda Hawa. *My Home, My Prison.* London: Zed Books, 1983.

Tetreault, Mary Ann, and Haya Mughni. "Gender, Citizenship and Nationalism in Kuwait." *British Journal of Middle Eastern Studies* 22, 1 & 2 (1995): 64–80.

Tetreault, Mary Ann, and Haya Mughni. "Women's Rights in Kuwait: Bring in the Last Bedouins? " *Current History* 99 (2000): 27–32.

Tijani, Ishaq. *Male Domination, Female Revolt: Race, Class and Gender in Kuwaiti Women.* Leiden: A. J. Brill, 2009.

Toth, James. "Pride, Purdah or Paychecks: What Maintains the Gender Division of Labor in Rural Egypt?" *International Journal of Middle East Studies* 23 (1991): 213–36.

Waller, Margaruite, and Jennifer Rycenga, eds. *Frontline Feminisms: Women, War and Resistance.* New York: Garland, 2000.

Wikan, Unni. *Behind the Veil in Arabia: Women in Oman.* Baltimore, Md.: Johns Hopkins University Press, 1982.

Wing, Adrien Katherine. "Palestinian Women: Their Future Legal Rights." *Arab Studies Quarterly* 16, 1 (1994): 55–73.

"Women in the Middle East: Progress or Regress?" *Middle East Review of International Affairs* 10, 2 (June 2006). meria.idc.ac.il/journal/2006/issue 2/ jv10no2a2.html.

Young, Elise G. *Keepers of the History: Women and the Israeli-Palestinian Conflict.* New York: Teachers College Press, 1992.

Zangana, Haifa. *City of Widows: An Iraqi Woman's Account of War and Resistance.* New York: Seven Stories Press, 2007.

Zartman, I. W., ed. *Tunisia: The Political Economy of Reform.* Boulder, Colo.: Lynne Rienner, 1991.

ISLAMIC FEMINISM

Afary, Janet. *Sexual Politics in Modern Iran.* Cambridge: Cambridge University Press, 2009.

Afshar, Haleh. "Khomeini's Teachings and their Implications for Women." *Feminist Review* 12 (1982): 59–72.

Afzal-Khan, Fawzia, ed. *Shattering the Stereotypes: Muslim Women Speak Out.* Northampton, Mass.: Olive Branch Press, 2005.

Aghaie, Kamran Scot. *The Women of Karbala: Ritual Performances and Symbolic Discourses in Modern Shi'i Islam.* Austin: University of Texas Press, 2005.

Azari, Farah, ed. *Women of Iran: The Conflict with Fundamentalist Islam.* Reading, UK: Ithaca Press, 1983.

Azhary, Amira Sonbol. *Women of Jordan: Islam, Labor and the Law.* Syracuse. N.Y.: Syracuse University Press, 2003.

Bakhash, Shaul. "Veils of Fears: Khomeini's Strange Way of Wooing Iranian Women." *New Republic*, 28 October 1985, 15–16.

Burgat, François, and William Dowell. *The Islamic Movement in North Africa.* Austin: University of Texas Press, 1993.

Cooke, Miriam. "Ayyam min hayati": The Prison Memoirs of a Muslim Sister." *Journal of ArabicLiterature* 26 (1995): 147–63.

Cooke, Miriam. "Prisons: Egyptian Women Writers on Islam." *Religion and Literature* 20, 1 (1988): 139–53.

Deeb, Lara. *An Enchanted Modern: Gender and Public Piety in Shi'i Lebanon.* Princeton, N.J.: Princeton University Press, 2006.

Doumato, Eleanor Abdella. *Getting God's Ear: Women, Islam, and Healing in Saudi Arabia.* New York: Columbia University Press, 2000.

Faust, Kimberly, et al. "Young Women Members of the Islamic Revival Movement in Egypt." *The Muslim World* 82 (1992): 55–65.

Ferdows, Adele K. "Women in Shi'i Islam and Iran." *Oriente Moderno* 62 NS 1–12 (1982): 71–81.

Ferdows, Adele K. "Women and the Islamic Revolution." *International Journal of Middle East Studies* 15 (1983): 283–98.

Gruenbaum, Ellen. "The Islamist State and Sudanese Women." *Middle East Report* 22, 6 (1992):29–32.

Guindi, Fadwa. "Is There an Islamic Alternative? The Case of Egypt's Contemporary Islamic Movement." *International Insight* 1, 6 (1981): 19–24.

Guindi, Fadwa. "Veiled Activism: Egyptian Women in the Contemporary Islamic Movement." *Peuples Méditerranéens* 22–23 (1983): 79–89.

Haeri, Shahla. "Ambivalence towards Women in Islamic Law and Ideology." *Middle East Annual* 5 (1985): 45–67.

Haider, Khalil. *Islamic Awakening and Women.* Kuwait: al-Tanwir, 1989.

Hatem, Mervat. "Towards the Development of Post-Islamist and Post-Nationalist Feminist Discourse in the Middle East." In *Arab Women: Old Boundaries, New Frontiers*, edited by Judith Tucker, 29–58. Bloomington: University of Indiana Press, 1993.

Heath, Jennifer, ed. *The Veil: Women Writers on its History, Lore and Politics.* Berkeley: University of California Press, 2008.

Hibri, Azizah. *Women and Islam.* New York: Pergamon, 1982.

Hoffman-Ladd, Valerie. "Women's Religious Observances." In *The Oxford Encyclopedia of the Modern Muslim World*, 4th ed., edited by John Esposito, 327–31. New York: Oxford University Press, 1995.

Hussein, Aziza. *Religion and Politics.* Boulder, Colo.: Westview, 1981.

Kian, Azadeh. "Gendered Occupations and Women's Status in Post-Revolutionary Iran." *Middle Eastern Studies* 31 (1995): 407–21.

Kok, Peter Nyot. "Hasan Abdallah al-Turabi." *Orient* 33 (1992): 185–92.

Lawrence, Bruce B. "Woman as Subject/Woman as Symbol: Islamic Fundamentalism and the Status of Women." *Journal of Religious Ethics* 22, 1 (1994): 163–85.

Mabro, Judy. *Veiled Half-Truths.* London: I. B. Tauris, 1996.

Mahdavi, Shireen. "Women and Shii Ulama in Iran." *Middle Eastern Studies* 19, 1 (1983): 17–27.

Mahmoud, Saba. "Feminist Theory, Embodiment and the Docile Agent: Some Reflections on the Egyptian Islamic Revival." *Cultural Anthropology* 16, 2 (2001): 202–36.

Majid, Anouar, "The Politics of Feminism in Islam." *Signs* 23, 2 (1998): 321–61.

Mernissi, Fatima. *Beyond the Veil.* New York: Schenkman, 1975.

Mernissi, Fatima. *The Veil and the Male Elite: A Feminist Interpretation of Women's Rights in Islam.* Reading, Mass.: Addison-Wesley, 1991.

Milani, Farzaneh. *Veils and Words: The Emerging Voices of Iranian Women Writers.* Syracuse, N.Y.: Syracuse University Press, 1992.

Mir-Husseini, Ziba. "Divorce in Islamic Law and Practice: The Case of Iran." *Cambridge Anthology* 11, 1 (1986): 41–69.

Mir-Husseini, Ziba. "Muslim Women's Quest for Equality: Between Islamic Law and Feminism." *Critical Inquiry* 32 (2006): 629–69.

Moghissi, Heideh. *Feminism and Islamic Fundamentalism: The Limits of Postmodern Analysis.* London: Zed, 1999.

Moussalli, Ahmad. *Moderate and Radical Islamic Fundamentalism: The Quest for Modernity, Legitimacy and the Islamic State.* Gainesville: University of Florida Press, 1999.

Najafabadi, Dari. "The Veil and Women's Rights in Islam." *Ittila'at*, 3 March 1986, 13.

Osman, Dina Sheikh el-Din. "The Legal Status of Muslim Women in the Sudan." *Journal of Eastern African Research and Development* 15 (1985): 124–42.

Ozcetin, Hilal. "Breaking the Silence: The Religious Muslim Women's Movement in Turkey." *Journal of International Women's Studies* 11, 1 (2009): 106–19.

Ramazani, Nesta. "Islamic Fundamentalism and the Women of Kuwait." *Middle East Insight* (January–February 1988): 21–26.

Reeves, Minou. *Female Warriors of Allah: Women and the Islamic Revolution.* New York: E. P. Dutton, 1989.

Rizzo, Mary Helen. *Islam, Democracy and the Status of Women.* London: Routledge, 2005.

Ruedy, John, ed. *Islamism and Secularism in North Africa.* Paris: Editions du Centre National de la Recherche Scientifique, 1987.

Saadawi, Nawal. "Women and Islam." *Women's Studies International Forum* 5, 2 (1982): 193–206.

Sabah, Fatna A. *Women in the Muslim Unconscious.* New York: Pergamon Press, 1984.

Scott, Joan Wallach. *The Politics of the Veil.* Princeton, N.J.: Princeton University Press, 2007.

Seline, Z. *Between Feminism and Islam: Human Rights and Sharia Law in Morocco.* Minneapolis: University of Minnesota Press, 2011.

Shariati, Ali. *Fatima Is Fatima.* Translated by Laleh Bakhtiar. Tehran: Shariati Foundation, 1981.

Shehadeh, Lamia R. *The Idea of Women under Fundamentalist Islam.* Gainesville: University of Florida Press, 2003.

Shoaee, Rokhsareh. "The Mujahid Women of Iran: Reconciling Culture and Gender." *Middle East Journal* 41, 4 (1987): 519–37.

Solh, Camilia Fawzi, and Judy Mabro, eds. *Muslim Women's Choices.* Oxford: Berg Publishers, 1994.

Stowasser, Barbara F., ed. *The Islamic Impulse.* Washington, D.C.: Georgetown University Press, 1989.

Tabari, Azar, and Nahid Yeganeh, eds. *In the Shadow of Islam: The Women's Movement in Iran.* London: Zed Books, 1984.

Talhami, Ghada. "The Legitimacy of the Reformer: The Neo-Cons and Arab and Muslim Women." *The Muslim World* 101, 3 (July 2011): 441–63.

Talhami, Ghada. *The Mobilization of Muslim Women in Egypt.* Gainesville: University of Florida Press, 1996.

Talhami, Ghada, ed. *Women in the Islamic Maelstrom. Muslim World* 86, 2 (April 1996): special issue.

Tessler, Mark. "Arab and Muslim Attitudes: Stereotypes and Evidence from Survey Research." *Contemporary Conflicts.* http://www.conflicts.ssrc.org/archives/mideast/tessler.

Tessler, Mark, and Jolene Jesse. "Gender and Support for Islamist Movements: Evidence from Egypt, Kuwait and Palestine." *The Muslim World* 86, 2 (1996): 200–28.

Wadud, Amina. *Inside the Gender Jihad.* Oxford: OneWorld Publishers, 2006.

Yamani, Mai, ed. *Feminism and Islam: Legal and Literary Perspectives.* New York: University of New York Press, 1996.

Zebiri, Kate. *Mahmoud Shaltout and Islamic Modernism.* Oxford: Clarendon Press, 1993.

Zuhur, Sharifa. *Revealing Reveiling: Islamist Gender Ideology in Contemporary Egypt.* New York: University of New York Press, 1992.

WORKS IN ARABIC

Arkoun, Muhammad. "Women in Islam." *Al-Safir*, 21 October 1994.

Attar, Abd al-Nasir Tawfiq. *Polygamy.* Cairo: Silsilat al-Buhuth al-Islamiyah, 1972.

Banna, Hassan. *The Muslim Woman.* Beirut: Dar al-Jil, 1988.

Barakat, Halim. "The Social System and Its Relation to the Problems of the Arab Woman." *Al-Mustaqbal al-Arabi* 34 (1981): 51–63.

Bassiouni, Amir Abdul Mun'im. *The Egyptian Family.* Cairo: Dar al-Katib al-Arabi, 1954.

Dibi, Zuhair. *An Introduction to the Personalities of Nablus in the 20th Century: A Preliminary Study.* Nablus, West Bank: Haj Nimer Tamimi, Publisher, 2000.

Fadlallah, Muhammad Husayn. *A New Reading of Women's Legal Rights.* Beirut: Publications of the Center of Women's Affairs, 1996.

Fadlallah, Muhammad Husayn. *The World of Women.* Beirut: Dar al-Malak, 1997.

Hufi, Ahmad Muhammad. *Women in Pre-Islamic Poetry.* Cairo: Dar al-Fikr al-Arabi, 1963.

Ibrahim, Ahmad Muhammad. "The Family System in Islam." *Majallat al-Fikr al-Islami* 6, 5 (1975): 43–48.

Kahallah, Umar Rida. *Women in the Arab and Islamic Worlds.* Beirut: Mu'assassat al-Risala, 1977.

Kahallah, Umar Rida. *Women in Old and Recent Times.* Beirut: Mu'assassat al-Risala, 1979.

Kamal, Zahira, and Soumaya Hind. *Women and Decision-Making in Palestine.* Ramallah, West Bank: The Publishing Center, 1997.

Khalafallah, Muhammad Ahmad. "Women's Rights and the Personal Status Code." *Al-Yaqzah al-Arabiyah* 1, 4 (1985): 48–56.

Khalidi, Mustafa, and Umar Farrukh. *The Missionary Movements and Colonialism.* Beirut: Islamic Bookshop, 1953.

Khatib, Umm Kulthum Yahya Mustafa. *The Question of Birth Control in the Islamic Sharia.* Jedda: al-Dar al-Saudiyah lil-Nashr wa al-Tawzii, 1982.

Khattab, Abd al-Mu'izz. *Twenty Women in the Quran.* Cairo: Dar al-Hammami li al-Tiba'ah, 1970.

Mallas, Mustafa. "The Muslim Woman and the Judiciary: A Contemporary Vision." *Al-Nahar Daily,* 8 August 1998, 15.

Mawdudi, Abu al-A'la. *The Family Planning Movement.* Cairo: Mu'assassat al-Risala, 1975.

Moussa, Salama. *A Woman Is Not a Man's Toy.* Cairo: Salama Moussa lilnashr wa al-tawzee, 1953.

Saadani, Nouriya. *The Book of Historical Documents of Women's Political Rights in Kuwait.* Kuwait: Mahfudha Press, 1994.

Saadani, Nouriya. *The History of Kuwaiti Women.* 2 vols. Kuwait: Matba'at Dar al-Siyaseh, 1972–1980.

Samman, Ghada. *There Is No Sea in Beirut.* Beirut: Ghada al-Samman, Publisher, 1985.

Shaaban, Muhammad Abd al-Sami. *The Family System in Christianity and Islam.* Cairo: Dar al-Ulum, 1983.

Shalabi, Ahmad. "Inheritance and Wills." *Majallat al-Fikr al-Islami* 6, 5 (1975): 24–25.

Shaltout, Mahmoud. *The Quran and Women.* Cairo: Matba'at al-Nahdha, 1963.

Tal, Suhayr Salti. *An Introduction to the Women's Question and the Women's Movement in Jordan.* Beirut: al-Mu'assassah al-Arabiyah lil-Dirasat wa al-Nashr, 1985.

Uthman, Ziyad. *A Critical Reading in the Political Participation of Palestinian Women.* Ramallah, West Bank: Ramallah Center for the Study of Human Rights, 2003.

Weidy, Maysoon. *Palestinian Women and the Israeli Occupation.* Jerusalem: Arab Studies Society, 1986.

Yahya, Yahya Bashir Haj. *Women and Life's Questions in the Modern Islamic World.* Kuwait: Dar Hawa.

OTHER SOURCES

Middle East Women's Journals

Ahfad Joournal: Women and Change (Ahfad University for Women—Sudan)

Bridges —Jewish feminist journal

Farzaneh—Iranian Islamist journal
Hawwa —Journal of women in the Middle East and the Islamic world
Journal of Middle East Women's Studies
Mahjubah—The Islamic Magazine for Women
Nashim—Journal of Jewish women's studies
Nida' —Iranian Islamist journal
Nissa—Tunisian journal
Nunn —Egyptian secularist journal
Payam-I Hajir —Iranian Islamist journal
Al-Raida —Institute for Women's Studies in the Arab World
Shahrazad —Limmasol, Cyprus
Women in Judaism —A multidisciplinary journal
Al-Yamaniyya
Zanan—Iranian Islamist journal
Zan-I Ruz—Iranian Islamist journal

Journals Frequently Carrying Middle East Women's Topics

Arab Studies Quarterly
Contemporary Arab Affairs
International Journal of Middle East Studies
Journal of Islamic Law and Culture
Majallat al-Fikr al-Islami
Middle East Journal
The Muslim World

Films on Middle Eastern Women and Related Topics

The Andalusian Epic: Islamic Spain
Dishonorable Killing: Punishing the Innocent
Full Cover Girl: How Fundamentalism and Democracy Are Eroding Women's Rights in Iraq
Golda
Leila Khaled: Hijacker
The Messenger
The Noble Struggle of Amina Wadud
Once upon a Time: Baghdad during the Abbasid Dynasty
The Ottoman Empire
Renaissance of Glory: The Rise and Fall of Sassanid Iran
The Thousand and One Nights: A Historical Perspective

About the Author

Ghada Hashem Talhami is D. K. Pearsons Professor of Politics, emerita, at Lake Forest College in Lake Forest, Illinois. She was born in Amman, Jordan, and received her education in Palestine, Jordan, Great Britain, and the United States. She was a Senior Fulbright Scholar in Syria in 1997. In 2009, she was the inaugural Susan B. Currier Chair in Women's Studies at California State University at San Luis Obispo. She is the past editor of *Arab Studies Quarterly* and currently serves on the board of editors of the same journal as well as *Muslim World*. She is the author of several books, including *The Mobilization of Muslim Women in Egypt* (1996) and *Palestine in the Egyptian Press* (2007). She is also the editor of *Children in the Middle East and North Africa*, which is part of a series titled Children in the World, published by Greenwood (2007).